Microsoft®

Microsoft® Exchange Server 2003 Administrator's Companion

Walter J. Glenn and Bill English

PUBLISHED BY
Microsoft Press
A Division of Microsoft Corporation
One Microsoft Way
Redmond, Washington 98052-6399

Library of Congress Cataloging-in-Publication Data
Glenn, Walter J.
Microsoft Exchange Server 2003 Administrator's Companion / Walter J. Glenn, Bill English.
p. cm.
Includes index.
ISBN 0-7356-1979-4
1. Microsoft Exchange Server. 2. Client/server computing. I. English, Bill, 1961- II. Title.

QA76.9.C55G62 2003
005.7'1376--dc22 2003061595

Printed and bound in the United States of America.

1 2 3 4 5 6 7 8 9 QWT 8 7 6 5 4 3

Distributed in Canada by H.B. Fenn and Company Ltd.

A CIP catalogue record for this book is available from the British Library.

Microsoft Press books are available through booksellers and distributors worldwide. For further information about international editions, contact your local Microsoft Corporation office or contact Microsoft Press International directly at fax (425) 936-7329. Visit our Web site at www.microsoft.com/mspress. Send comments to *mspinput@microsoft.com.*

Acquisitions Editors: Jeff Koch, Martin DelRe
Project Editor: Maureen Williams Zimmerman
Technical Editor: Nick Cavalancia

Body Part No. X10-08356

I'd like to dedicate this book to my father, Bill English. (No, not my coauthor—just a curious coincidence.)

Walter

I'd like to dedicate this book to my wife, Kathy English. Your love and support are unending.

Bill

Contents at a Glance

Part V
Clients

Part VI
Functionality

Part VII
Security

Part VIII
Maintenance

Part IX
Appendixes

Table of Contents

Part II
Planning

Part III
Deployment

Part V
Clients

Part VII
Security

Acknowledgments

As usual, a lot of people did a lot of work to put this book into your hands. Foremost, I'd like to thank my co-author, Bill English, for all his work. He signed on to the previous edition of this book at the last moment when another author dropped out. Bill took up the challenge and did a great job, and he's done that same great job this time around. I'd also like to thank Nick Cavalancia for a great technical review.

I'd also like to thank the folks at Microsoft Press for guiding this book through its various stages. Jeff Koch, our acquisitions editor, showed his faith in the project and in us. Maureen Zimmerman and Karen Szall, our project managers, helped to make sure that this book is of the best quality and that it was published on schedule.

Finally, as always, I'd like to thank Neil Salkind and everyone else at StudioB for helping put this project together.

Walter J. Glenn
Hunstville, Alabama
September 17, 2003

It seems like just last week that Walter and I were working on the *Microsoft Exchange 2000 Server Administrator's Companion*, and here we are, putting out this book on Microsoft Exchange Server 2003. The time sure has gone by fast. But maybe it just seems that way because I'm a bit older than I was in 2000.

I'd first like to thank Walter Glenn, my co-author. Walter is a great co-author, one on whom I can count to write great chapters. Thanks, Walter, for doing this project again and for being an easy person to work with. I'd also like to thank Jeff Koch, Karen Szall, and Maureen Zimmerman at Microsoft Press for keeping this project on track, as well as Nick Cavalancia for doing a great job of performing the technical edit this book. Nick added real value with his comments and insights, and I'm very grateful for his assistance.

I'd also like to thank Neil Salkind and the StudioB folks for helping to guide this project through every stage. Neil, you did your usual great job!

I'd also like to thank my wife, Kathy, for her support, encouragement, and love as I continue to keep weird and (sometimes) insane hours to get these books out the door. Your understanding, Kathy, is really amazing.

Finally, I'd like to thank Jesus Christ, who gave me the opportunity to write this book and without whom I'd be lost forever.

Bill English
Nowthen, Minnesota
September 24, 2003

Introduction

Welcome to Microsoft Exchange Server 2003! Whether you are an experienced Exchange administrator or just learning this product, you are going to be impressed with its new features, increased flexibility, and expanded information management capabilities. The development team at Microsoft has done an outstanding job of continuing the Exchange tradition of offering superior messaging services—Exchange Server 2003 really is the best ever!

Microsoft Exchange Server 2003 is designed to meet the messaging and collaboration needs of businesses of all sizes. *Microsoft Exchange Server 2003 Administrator's Companion* is designed to not only bring you up to speed in setting up the various features of Exchange Server 2003, but also to show you how these features work and why you might want to use them. We also offer advice from first-hand experience in the real world of Exchange networks.

It's impossible to cover every element of Exchange Server 2003 in detail in one book. However, this Administrator's Companion is a great place to start as you consider implementing Exchange Server 2003 in your Windows organization. This book can be used in several different ways. You can read it as a

- Guide to planning and deployment
- Ready reference for day-to-day questions
- Source of information needed to make decisions about the network
- Thorough introduction to the particulars of Exchange Server 2003

We assume that the reader has a fundamental understanding of networking concepts and of Microsoft Windows Server 2003. We have attempted to provide background at appropriate points as well as references to additional resources.

Overview of Contents

The *Microsoft Exchange Server 2003 Administrator's Companion* is divided into multiple parts, each roughly corresponding to a stage in the implementation of an Exchange organization or covering a particular functionality.

Part I: Introduction

We begin by outlining the new features of Exchange Server 2003. Then we dive in for a closer look at the program's storage and routing architecture. Chapter 1, "Introducing Exchange Server 2003," is designed to get you up to speed quickly on what Exchange Server is and some of the features it offers. This first chapter also serves as a roadmap for the rest of the book. Chapter 2, "Understanding Exchange Server Storage Architecture," and Chapter 3, "Understanding Exchange Server Routing Architecture," detail the storage and routing architecture of Exchange Server 2003. They illustrate how the databases and transaction logs provide you with a high level of recoverability and discuss the new link state protocol. Chapter 4, "Understanding Windows 2003 Integration," explains the tight integration between Exchange Server 2003 and Active Directory, Microsoft Internet Information Services 6.0, and Windows 2003 DNS.

Part II: Planning

Every successful implementation of a messaging system requires good planning, and Exchange Server 2003 is no exception. Two chapters are devoted to planning issues. Chapter 5, "Assessing Needs," looks at methods for taking stock of a current network and assessing the needs of users on that network prior to an Exchange Server 2003 deployment. Chapter 6, "Planning for Development," examines ways to create an actual deployment plan, based on the needs assessment methods outlined in Chapter 5.

Part III: Deployment

After learning about the architecture of Exchange Server 2003 and how to plan for its deployment, you're ready to get your hands dirty. In this part (the longest), we outline how to install Exchange Server 2003 and how to implement its various features in the way that best suits your organization. Chapter 7, "Installing Exchange Server 2003," details the various methods of installing Exchange Server 2003, including installing a new organization and installing into an existing organization. This chapter also shows how to make sure a server is ready for Exchange Server 2003 installation. Chapter 8, "Managing Exchange Server 2003," introduces you to Microsoft Management Console (MMC)—the management interface included with Windows Server 2003. This chapter also provides a tour of the management resources in the Exchange System snap-in for MMC.

The next group of chapters—Chapter 9, "Creating and Managing Recipients," through Chapter 13, "Connecting Routing Groups"—covers a whole host of other topics: creation and management of recipients (users, contacts, groups, and public folders), storage groups, routing and administrative groups, and routing group connectors, such as the SMTP and X.400 Connectors.

Part IV: Upgrading and Migrating

Since many of you will be performing migrations from previous versions of Exchange Server, Part IV, "Upgrading and Migrating," covers this very important topic. Chapter 14, "Planning a Migration to Exchange Server 2003," covers the important topic of planning an upgrade or migration. Chapter 15, "Migrating to Exchange Server 2003," details migrating from previous versions, including the use of the Active Directory Connector and Site Replication services. Chapter 16, "Coexisting with Previous Versions of Exchange," explains methods for enabling a peaceful coexistence between Exchange Server 2003 and previous versions on the same network.

Part V: Clients

The best implementation of Exchange Server 2003 won't do your organization much good if there aren't any clients to connect to it and use it; in this section, we provide an overview of the clients for Exchange Server 2003. The topics presented here could easily be expanded into their own book, so we cover the more important topics and reference other materials where appropriate. Chapter 17, "Overview of Exchange Clients," gives a general introduction to the various types of clients that can be used to connect to an Exchange server. Chapter 18, "Deploying Outlook 2003," focuses on Microsoft Outlook 2003 and examines the issues surrounding its deployment. Chapter 19, "Supporting Outlook Web Access," covers the use of Outlook Web Access. Chapter 20, "Supporting Internet Protocols and SMTP," details the configuration of basic Internet protocols: NNTP, SMTP, POP3, and IMAP4. We go over the basic commands of each and discuss how to use the logging features for troubleshooting purposes.

Part VI: Functionality

Exchange Server 2003 ships with support for many extra features. Chapter 21, "Connecting to Other Messaging Systems with X.400," looks at the procedures for connecting Exchange Server 2003 organizations to foreign messaging systems, such as Microsoft Mail for PC Networks and X.400 systems. Chapter 22, "Mobile Services in Exchange Server 2003," focuses on new wireless access functions that increase mobility options in Exchange Server 2003.

Part VII: Security

Security is a primary concern of any network administrator, and Exchange 2003 in collaboration with Windows Server 2003 offers enhanced options for protecting your organization. Although this is another topic that could easily fill a book of its own, in this part, we offer as comprehensive a look at security as this space permits. Chapter 23, "Security Policies and Exchange Server 2003," looks at planning Exchange security policies. Chapter 24, "Exchange Server Security," covers the basics of Exchange Server security; and Chapter 25, "Securing Exchange Server 2003 Messages," looks at methods for securing messaging in an Exchange organization.

Part VIII: Maintenance

Every system—even Exchange Server 2003—needs maintenance. We address the most important maintenance tasks in this section. In Chapter 26, "Monitoring Exchange Server 2003," we outline how to monitor your Exchange 2003 servers. Chapter 27, "Disaster Recovery of an Exchange 2003 Server Database," covers the critical topic of backup and restoration of your databases. Chapter 28, "Troubleshooting Exchange Server 2003," looks at how to perform basic troubleshooting for a server; and Chapter 29, "Tuning Exchange Server 2003 Performance," examines how to tune your Exchange servers for maximum performance.

Overview of Conventions

Within the chapters we've tried to make the material accessible and readable. You'll find descriptive passages, theoretical explanations, and step-by-step examples. We've also included a generous number of graphics that make it easy to follow the written instructions. The following reader's aids are common to all books in the Administrator's Companion series.

Note Notes generally represent some information that needs to be highlighted or alternate ways to perform a task.

Tip Methods of performing tasks more quickly or in a not-so-obvious manner will show up as Tips.

More Info References to other books and sources of information are offered throughout the book.

Caution Don't skip over these boxes because they contain important warnings about the subject at hand—often critical information about the safety of your system.

Planning As we stress throughout the book, proper planning is fundamental to the smooth operation of any network. These boxes contain specific and useful hints to make that process go smoothly.

Real World **Real World**

Everyone benefits from the experiences of others. Real World sidebars contain elaboration on a particular theme or provide background based on the adventures of IT professionals just like you.

Talk to Us

We've done our best to make this book as accurate and complete as a single-volume reference can be. However, because Exchange Server 2003 is a large and complex product, we're sure that alert readers will find omissions and possibly some errors—though we really hope that there aren't too many of those! If you have suggestions, corrections, or comments, you can write to the co-authors using the following e-mail addresses:

- Bill English, at benglish@networknowledge.com
- Walter Glenn, at books@walterglenn.com

We genuinely appreciate hearing from you and sincerely hope you will find the *Microsoft Exchange Server 2003 Administrator's Companion* to be enjoyable and helpful.

Part I

Introduction

Chapter 1

Introducing Exchange Server 2003

Microsoft Exchange Server has been a leading collaborative product since its introduction in April 1996. Exchange Server is one of the best-selling server applications in Microsoft's history. With each new release, Microsoft has added functionality to enhance Exchange Server's capabilities. The latest version, Microsoft Exchange Server 2003, builds on the superior performance and features that Exchange users have come to expect.

This chapter provides an overview of the capabilities and structure of Exchange Server, discussing the components of Exchange Server architecture—in particular, how those components are organized and how they interact to provide a comprehensive messaging system. It also offers a look at the powerful new features of Exchange Server 2003. Exchange Server is a complex program, but with a little dissection you will see how its complexity can benefit any enterprise.

What Is Exchange Server?

So, what is Exchange Server? Ask three different administrators and you're liable to get three different answers. Is it a messaging system? Is it a groupware product? Is it a development platform? The answer is all three.

As a messaging system, Exchange Server 2003 represents the state of the art in reliability, scalability, and performance. Over the past couple of decades, electronic messaging has become one of the dominant methods of business communication, and Exchange Server is one of the most popular messaging systems in the world.

The term *groupware* was coined in the 1980s to describe products that could be used to create collaborative applications in which people share access to a collection of centralized documents and resources. These days, we just call it *collaborative software*. Exchange Server 2003 lets you store and share virtually any type of document within the Exchange system. Exchange Server can also automatically send copies of documents to different physical information stores, making the use of shared documents across an organization much more efficient.

Microsoft Outlook 2003 is the newest version of Microsoft's premier messaging and collaboration client for use with Exchange Server 2003. It allows users to send and receive messages that include many different types of data, to share scheduling and contact information, to participate in public folder discussions, and even to access both network and local file systems.

Exchange Server is also increasingly being used as a development platform—that is, as a basis for creating applications and systems to address the specific needs of organizations. For example, you can use it to create forms that extend the capabilities of a simple message. You can even attach application logic to those forms and then configure Exchange Server to route the forms to specific users or destinations, where they can undergo further modification. Additional tools allow you to access and manipulate the information stored in Exchange Server or to take advantage of Exchange Server's delivery services.

As you can see, Exchange Server is a multifaceted and complex product. By the time you complete this book, you will fully understand how to use Exchange Server to implement and administer all these features, and you will be equipped to exploit Exchange Server to its fullest.

Versions of Exchange Server 2003

Microsoft provides two distinct editions of Exchange Server 2003. Each is basically identical in function but includes a slightly different set of features. The two editions are Exchange Server 2003 Standard Edition and Exchange Server 2003 Enterprise Edition.

Exchange Server 2003 Standard

The standard edition is designed to meet the basic messaging needs of small to medium-sized companies. Exchange Server 2003 Standard Edition has the following limitations:

- It offers support for only one storage group per server; each storage group can contain only two databases.
- Databases are limited to 16 GB.
- Clustering is not supported.
- The X.400 connector is not included.

Exchange Server 2003 Enterprise

The enterprise edition is designed to meet enterprise-level messaging and collaboration needs. Exchange Server 2003 Enterprise Edition includes all the features in Exchange Server 2003 plus the following:

- It offers support for up to four storage groups per server. Each storage group can contain up to five databases.
- Databases are limited to 16 terabytes.
- Clustering is supported through the Microsoft Cluster Server service.
- The X.400 connector is included.

Note Throughout this book, we refer to Exchange Server in different ways, and each has a different meaning. Typically, we refer to the software product as "Exchange Server." If you see this term, you can take it to mean Microsoft Exchange Server 2003 Enterprise. When necessary, we use "Exchange Server 2003" to draw attention to the fact that we are discussing a feature that is new or has changed in the most recent version of the product. Each of these terms means essentially the same thing. If we refer to a previous version of Exchange Server, we always do so specifically, such as "Exchange 2000 Server" or "Exchange Server 5.5." Finally, we often use the term "Exchange server" (note the lowercase s in "server") to refer to an actual server computer, as in "There are eight Exchange servers in this routing group."

Basic Concepts

The next few chapters give you an in-depth look at the architecture of Exchange Server 2003. Before learning the specifics of Exchange Server, however, you need to understand some of the concepts that form its foundation. This section describes the basics of messaging systems, how an Exchange Server environment is organized, how Exchange Server stores information, and the key services that make up Exchange Server.

Messaging Systems

When most people think of electronic messages, they first think of e-mail, but an electronic messaging system can do more than just deliver e-mail. The term *electronic messaging* describes a more generalized process that can be used to deliver many different types of information to many different locations. A messaging system has several specific characteristics. First, it involves the participation of at least two parties: the sender and one or more recipients. Second, when a sender dispatches a message, the sender can count on the message being delivered. If the messaging system cannot deliver a message to a recipient immediately, it keeps trying. If, after repeated tries, the messaging system fails to deliver the message, the least it should do is inform the sender of this failure.

Although a standard messaging system can guarantee the reliable delivery of messages, it cannot guarantee exactly how long it will take to deliver a particular message. This uncertainty is due to the asynchronous nature of a messaging system. In an *asynchronous system*, two related events are not dependent on each other; in a messaging system, for example, the sending of a message and the receipt of the message are not tied together in any fixed span of time.

There are two basic types of messaging systems: shared-filed systems and client/server systems. Although client/server systems have almost entirely replaced shared-file systems in modern messaging products, administrators need to have a good understanding of both.

Shared-File Systems

Many older messaging products, such as Microsoft Mail, are shared-file systems. A *shared-file* e-mail system, as shown in Figure 1-1, works fairly simply. A messaging server contains a shared folder (a mailbox) for each user of the system. When a user sends a message, that user's e-mail client places a copy of the message into the shared folders of any designated recipients. Clients are generally configured to check their shared folders at set intervals. If the recipient client finds a new message in the folder, it alerts the user. Shared-file systems are generally referred to as *passive* systems, in that it is up to the messaging software running on the client to carry out the operations of the e-mail transaction. The messaging server itself plays no active role (other than housing the e-mail system's shared folders) in passing the message from sender to recipient.

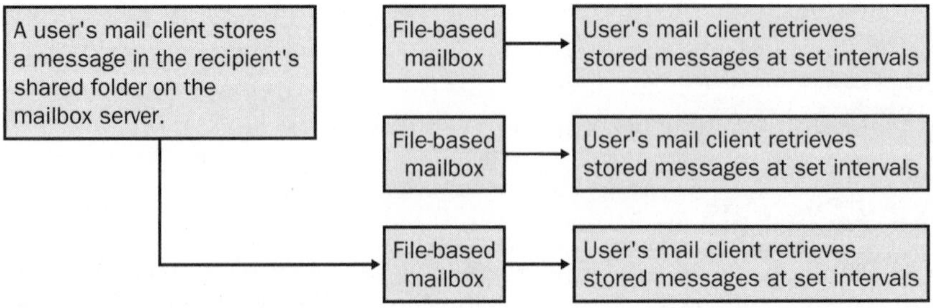

Figure 1-1. *A shared-file e-mail system.*

Client/Server Systems

An Exchange-based system is a form of *client/server* system (Figure 1-2). This type of system is referred to as an *active* system because the server takes a much more active role than it does in a shared-file system. In an Exchange-based messaging system, client software delivers outbound messages to a service on an Exchange server. That service places the messages in the recipient's mailbox or in a queue destined for another Exchange server or for a foreign messaging system. Exchange Server itself is then responsible for alerting users that new messages await them. In addition, Exchange Server takes on many other responsibilities. For example, each Exchange server does the following:

- Manages the messaging database
- Manages the connections to other Exchange servers and messaging systems
- Indexes the messaging database for better performance
- Receives new messages and transfers them to their destinations

To provide these services, Exchange Server is typically installed on more powerful server machines than those used for shared-file messaging systems, which means that a client/server system such as Exchange Server is inherently more scalable than a shared-file system. The server-based agents that implement Exchange Server can also provide a higher level of security, reliability, and scalability than a simple shared-file messaging system can. All these features allow Exchange Server to support many more users than simple file-based systems.

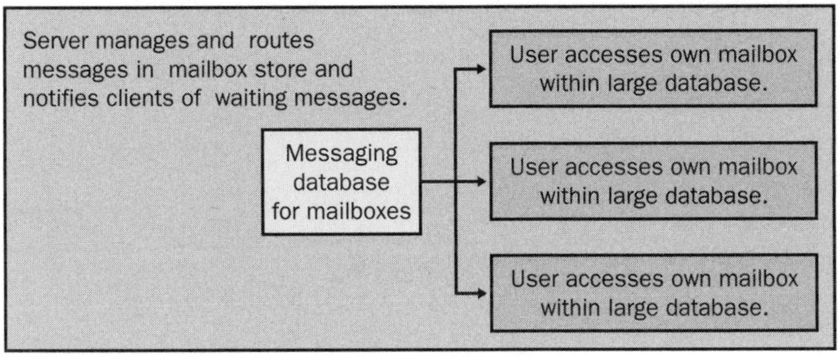

Figure 1-2. *The Exchange client/server system.*

As the name implies, a client/server system has two distinct components: a client and a server. The client and the server use a specific interface to cooperate. The fact that Exchange Server distributes functions between the client and the server means that more processing power is available systemwide for messaging in general. In comparison, a shared-file system depends on the client to constantly check and pull mail, a process that can result in poorer performance as well as increased network traffic on a workstation client. (Exchange Server is the server component of an Exchange system, but the server does not exist in a vacuum. You will also learn about the clients that participate in an Exchange system.)

Multiple clients can access a server at the same time. As a result, a server must be designed to handle many types of requests from many sources simultaneously. The need to service many clients is one of the primary factors that led to the architecture used to implement Exchange Server, in which several separate processes in the server cooperate to handle client requests. (These server processes and the way they interact are described later in this chapter.) Each Exchange Server process handles one type of task. This structure means that Exchange Server can execute different functions simultaneously rather than sequentially, as a monolithic, single-process messaging architecture would do. The overall result is that Exchange Server is a robust system that improves upon legacy messaging architectures.

The Organization of an Exchange Environment

In versions of Exchange Server prior to Exchange 2000 Server, each group of Exchange servers was known as a *site*, and each site defined the group's boundaries for both administration and routing. Exchange 2000 Server did away with sites and instead separated the boundaries by allowing Exchange servers to be grouped into administrative groups and routing groups. Exchange Server 2003 continues to use this architecture. This split allows administrators to deploy their organizations along boundaries that are more closely aligned with the real world than was previously possible. In addition, the integration of Exchange Server 2003 with the Microsoft Windows Server 2003 Active Directory service has brought about changes in the way the various recipients are managed. This section outlines the basic organizational features of Exchange Server 2003.

Administrative Groups

An *administrative group* is a collection of Exchange servers and administrative objects that are logically grouped together for common administrative purposes. For example, your organization might have two system administrators, one responsible for administering collaborative services and the other responsible for administering servers and connectors. You could use administrative groups as a way of assigning permissions and policies to each administrator. An administrative group can contain policies, routing groups, public folder trees, servers, and more.

Routing Groups

A *routing group* is a collection of Exchange servers that are all physically connected by a permanent, reliable, high-speed network. A server is contained within one—and only one—routing group. The routing group is the closest thing to a site in previous versions of Exchange Server. Messages sent between servers in a routing group are delivered directly from source to destination. Messages sent between servers in different routing groups must be routed through *bridgehead servers*, which are specifically designated to route messages from one routing group to another over specialized connectors.

Policies

Policies are collections of configuration settings that are applied to one or more Exchange configuration objects. For example, an administrator could configure a set of parameters to govern a certain aspect of server behavior and then assign those parameters, as a policy, across tens or even hundreds of servers. Once policies are implemented, changes to the policies affect all objects to which the policies are assigned, making it easy to change the configuration of entire groups of objects at a stroke. Exchange Server 2003 uses two basic types of policies: system policies and recipient policies.

System policies are used to configure servers and the message store databases on those servers. Three classes of system policies are defined: mailbox store policies, public folder store policies, and server policies. A system policy defines configuration settings for a class of objects (such as public folders). Once you define a policy, you can apply it to existing objects or create new objects using that policy. You can then change the configuration for all those objects with one stroke. For example, you might create a system policy that limits the size of messages that can be posted to a group of public folders. Once that policy has been applied to those folders, you could change the limits at any time for all the folders simply by changing the policy.

Recipient policies are used to configure objects such as users, mailboxes, groups, and contacts—objects typically associated with the user side of the system. Because much of this directory information resides in Active Directory, recipient policies actually apply settings to Windows domain containers. Recipient policies work in much the same way that system policies do. You can use them to apply and modify configuration settings to groups of recipients all at once. For example, you might configure a recipient policy that defines how an SMTP address is created for certain recipients or another policy that defines the storage space allowed to mailboxes. Once that policy has been applied, you can change the addressing scheme for all of the recipients by changing the policy.

Servers

Server is the term used in the Microsoft Exchange topology to refer to an individual computer that has the Microsoft Exchange Server messaging application installed and running on it. The name of the server is the same as the name of the Windows computer that hosts the Exchange Server application.

There are no hard-and-fast rules as to how many servers you should have within a particular routing group. The size of the machine acting as the server will have some bearing on how many users and how large a store the machine can support. In addition, you should put some thought into which servers to place users on. When individual users on the same server communicate through Exchange Server, they do not add to network bandwidth because the message does not need to move across the network between separate physical machines. By grouping users according to how they interact with one another, you can improve the Exchange server's performance and even the performance of the entire messaging system.

Recipients

Although the recipient is the lowest level of the Exchange hierarchy, it is a critical component of the Exchange organization. As the name implies, a *recipient* is an entity that can receive an Exchange message. Most recipients are associated with a single, discrete mailbox, although this mailbox can be represented by several addresses, depending on the addressing types implemented within Exchange.

In versions of Exchange Server prior to Exchange Server 2000, a separate tool—the Exchange Administrator—was used to create recipients and to associate them with Microsoft Windows NT user accounts. With the introduction and integration of Microsoft Windows 2000 Server and Exchange 2000 Server (and now Microsoft Windows Server 2003 and Exchange Server 2003), that changed. Installing Exchange Server 2003 adds Exchange-related functionality to the user objects in Active Directory and to the interface in the Active Directory Users and Computers snap-in. This tie to Active Directory means that, in addition to mailboxes, Exchange Server 2003 supports other types of recipients, including groups and contacts.

Mailboxes A *mailbox* is an area of an Exchange Server's mailbox store database in which a particular user's private messages are stored. An Active Directory user object that has been given a mailbox is referred to as *mailbox-enabled*. Only user objects can be mailbox-enabled.

> **Note** You can make other objects participate in Exchange Server 2003 routing simply by giving them an e-mail address. Such objects are referred to as *mail-enabled* and are not associated with an actual mailbox.

Distribution Groups A *distribution group* is a collection of users, contacts, and even other groups that is able to receive messages. When a distribution group receives a message, Exchange Server sends a copy of the message to each of the recipients within the group. The term *group* also refers to an Active Directory security object that is a collection of users and other groups. An Exchange group is always based upon an Active Directory group. A group is the functional equivalent of a distribution list in previous versions of Exchange Server.

Contacts A *contact* is an Active Directory object that is not an actual user and thus cannot log on to the network. Contacts can receive e-mail from Exchange users, just as standard Exchange recipients can, after their addresses are defined in the Exchange system's Global Address List. Through the use of contacts, you can integrate external recipients, such as Internet e-mail addresses, into the address list of your Exchange system. Contacts are the functional equivalent of custom recipients in previous versions of Exchange Server.

Address Lists

An *address list* is simply a list of recipients. The Global Address List is the list of all Exchange Server recipients in the entire Exchange organization. Exchange Server uses address lists to hold and organize the names of the recipients associated with the system.

An Exchange system can have hundreds of thousands of recipients, making it difficult for a user to locate an individual recipient's name. In addition, e-mail addresses can be somewhat cryptic. Various legacy messaging systems have restrictions on the length of the user's mailbox name, and some administrators assign puzzling mailbox names. All in all, it can be difficult to guess a user's e-mail address. The primary purpose of an address list, from a user's point of view, is to provide a way to locate an e-mail address for a recipient. When the administrator of an Exchange environment creates a recipient, the person's name—not a cryptic e-mail address—shows up in the Global Address List, making it easier for Exchange users to locate and send e-mail to recipients.

In addition to the Global Address List maintained by Exchange Server, individual users can create their own personal address lists, called *address books*. Personal address books can contain a portion of the Global Address List, as well as other custom addresses added by the user, to make it easier to access the addresses he uses most frequently.

Connectors

You should understand one more piece of the Exchange Server topology before moving on: connectors. A *connector* is a piece of software that acts as a gateway between Exchange Server routing groups or from an Exchange environment to a non-Exchange e-mail system (such as foreign X.400 messaging systems). A connector enables the Exchange system to interact directly with a foreign e-mail system, as though its users were part of your Exchange system.

Connectors can integrate foreign address lists into the Global Address List, enable message exchange, provide access to shared messaging folders, and make other functions available. Some connectors simply enable a consistent mail-forwarding and receipt operation. In addition to providing a link between Exchange Server and other messaging systems, a connector can be extremely useful if you are in the process of migrating to Exchange Server or connecting to non-messaging systems such as fax or voice mail.

Exchange Server Storage

Exchange Server uses several types of *message stores*, or storage databases, to hold the messages that make up its information environment. Within these stores, Exchange Server organizes the messages and other material in folders. A folder has the same relationship to its messages that a directory in a file system has to its files. Because Exchange Server manages the storage of its own data, there is not a strict one-to-one relationship between a folder in an Exchange Server store and a directory in the operating system. Exchange Server uses two types of stores: a mailbox store and a public folder store.

When you install an Exchange server, you have to specify locations for the public folder store and the mailbox store. Each store acts as a database for all the objects that it contains: mailboxes for the mailbox store and public folders for the public folder store.

Mailbox Store

The *mailbox store* is a database on an Exchange server that contains all the mailboxes of Exchange users associated with that Exchange server. The mailbox store manages the data within the mailboxes, tracking deleted messages and mailbox sizes and assisting in message transfers. A *private folder* is a secured folder component within a mailbox for an Exchange Server recipient. Each private folder holds information that is available only to a single Exchange user and to others to whom that user has granted access permissions.

Exchange maintains private folders and the mailboxes that contain them within the mailbox store of the associated Exchange server. Although the folders are "secured" in the sense that an Exchange user must have an account and a password to access each mailbox, Exchange Server does manage the contents of mailboxes. For example, the mailbox store is included in standard Exchange Server backup and recovery operations.

Exchange users are not limited to using the Outlook or Exchange client to access their mailboxes. They can also access private stores through various Internet mail protocols and even through a standard Web browser, if the Exchange environment is configured to allow those types of access.

Note Many companies using Exchange also make use of *personal stores*, which are databases of messages controlled by a messaging client rather than by Exchange Server. Typically, personal stores reside on a user's local machine or on a shared network volume. After materials are placed in a personal folder, they are the exclusive responsibility of the user. Other users cannot access the materials in a personal folder. If users create or modify any of the documents in the personal folder and want others to access these documents, they have to explicitly place these documents in a private or public folder in order to put them back under the care of an Exchange server.

Public Folder Store

The *public folder store* is a database that stores public folders, indexes their contents, and assists in the replication of the folders with other Exchange servers. As the name implies, a public folder is accessible to more than one user. Administrators can define the specific security restrictions on a public folder to limit the types of users who have access to it. Public folders are the basis of a great deal of Exchange Server's functionality. They are ideal places to keep information that is accessed by large numbers of people. If, for example, your organization has marketing materials or human resources policies that you want to make available to everyone as soon as they are created, you can put them in a public folder.

The reason for the separation between the public folder store and the mailbox store lies in the way Exchange Server treats the information in the public folder store. Because everyone in what could be a widely dispersed organization can access public folders, Exchange Server allows you to set up automatic replication of the contents of public folders. Exchange Server handles the replication of documents in a public folder with no intervention on the part of an administrator after the replication is defined. Users who request a document in a public folder retrieve it from the closest copy of the public folder rather than from a single location. In this way, public folders help expand the scalability of Exchange Server by reducing the bandwidth requirements for the access of common documents.

Exchange Server Services

From the outside, Exchange Server looks like a single, monolithic software system. Internally, Exchange Server uses three key services to perform its tasks: the Information Store service, the Routing Engine service, and the System Attendant service. A *service* is a piece of software that runs in the background on Windows, performing its tasks without requiring any specific administrative intervention.

The following sections describe the three basic Exchange Server services. Note that some optional features of Exchange Server create their own services, and so additional Exchange Server services might also be running on your system.

Information Store

As you know, Exchange Server information stores are kept as database files that are managed by the Exchange server. The Information Store service is responsible for storing and retrieving information from those stores. It is involved in sending messages and also handles certain automatic functions of Exchange, such as replication.

Routing Engine

The most active part of an Exchange server is the Routing Engine. If this service shuts down, the Exchange server can no longer move e-mail through the system. The Routing Engine service is responsible for coordinating the transfer of messages between Exchange servers. It acts as a traffic cop and a crossing guard combined, directing messages to their destinations as well as ensuring that the messages arrive safely.

System Attendant

The System Attendant (SA) is the background manager for the Exchange system. The SA maintains the link state tables used for message delivery, monitors the connections between servers, and collects feedback that is used by other monitoring tools. These unseen activities are vital to the continuing successful operation of your Exchange environment.

> **More Info** You can learn more about the services used by Exchange Server 2003, as well as how these services depend on one another and on other Windows services, by searching the Microsoft Knowledge Base. Go to *http://support.microsoft.com*, choose the Search The Knowledge Base link, choose Exchange Server 2003 as the product, and use the keyword "services."

New Features in Exchange Server 2003

Exchange Server 2003 provides a number of new features and enhancements to existing features in the areas of reliability, management, and security. This section takes a look at the important enhancements to Exchange Server 2003.

Deployment Tools

The new Deployment Tools feature consists of a help-based document and a group of utilities (including the Exchange setup program) designed to make installation, migration, and upgrading easier. The document walks you through the planning, preparation, and deployment of an Exchange environment. You can even perform actions such as launching the forestprep and domainprep tools, installing the Active Directory Connector, and launching the installation of Exchange right from the document. Deployment tools are covered in Chapter 7, "Installing Exchange Server 2003."

Active Directory Connector Tools

The Active Directory Connector (ADC) is a tool designed to allow Exchange Server 2003 and Microsoft Exchange Server 5.5 to exist within the same organization. The ADC lets administrators replicate directory information between the Exchange Server 5.5 directory and Active Directory. It allows for multiple-master, bidirectional replication. New enhancements improve deployment and migration by analyzing an existing Exchange 5.5 configuration, automatically preparing the Exchange 5.5 directory, and automatically creating connection agreements. Active Directory Connector tools are covered in Part IV, "Upgrading and Migrating."

Security

Most modern network operating systems and services emphasize security as a major concern, and Exchange Server 2003 is no exception. Exchange Server 2003 is more tightly integrated with Windows Server security than its predecessors. The Key Management feature in prior versions of Exchange has been removed; instead, Exchange Server 2003 takes advantage of the Windows Server 2003 Public Key Infrastructure (PKI) to create a secure messaging environment. You can learn more about Exchange Server and messaging security in Part VII, "Security."

A number of other security enhancements are also featured in Exchange Server 2003, such as the ability to filter connections based on external real-time blacklists of known senders of unsolicited e-mail. You can also filter incoming e-mail so that messages to invalid recipients are blocked. Another feature enables you to restrict the relaying of SMTP mail based on membership in Windows security groups (in addition to the existing ability to restrict based on IP address, domain, or subnet).

Cross-Forest Authentication

If Exchange Server 2003 is running on a Windows Server 2003 network, cross-forest authentication allows users to access services in a trusted forest. This means that Exchange users do not have to be in the same forest to access and take advantage of Exchange servers.

Outlook 2003

Although the introduction of the latest version of the Outlook mail client, Outlook 2003, is not strictly considered part of Exchange Server 2003, numerous enhancements to both products make them work very well together. For example, Outlook 2003 supports a new cached mode (enabled by default) in which Outlook downloads a local copy of the user's Exchange mailbox. Users work primarily from this cached copy, reducing the network traffic between client and server and allowing the users to continue working during periods when the Exchange server is unavailable.

Exchange Server 2003 now allows Outlook (and Outlook Web Access) clients to authenticate with an Exchange server using Kerberos authentication. Outlook 2003 can also connect to an Exchange server using remote procedure call (RPC) over HTTP. This allows the connection of clients to the Exchange server over the Internet without having to use Virtual Private Network (VPN) access. You can learn more about Outlook 2003 in Chapter 18, "Deploying Outlook 2003."

Outlook Web Access

Outlook Web Access (OWA) has been significantly enhanced in Exchange Server 2003. OWA now comes in two versions: Rich Experience Outlook Web Access and Basic Outlook Web Access. Rich Experience Outlook Web Access takes advantage of features in Microsoft Internet Explorer 5 (or later) to provide features such as secure messaging, rules, spell-checking, and reminders. Basic Outlook Web Access can be used with any Web browser but does not support all the features of the Rich Experience Outlook Web Access. You'll learn more about Outlook Web Access in Chapter 19, "Supporting Outlook Web Access."

Wireless Access

Wireless access to network services is growing more popular, providing a unique opportunity for knowledge workers and IT personnel to have instant access to company information no matter where they are. Exchange Server 2003 supports wireless access through the introduction of two new features: Wireless Synchronization Access and Outlook Mobile Access.

Wireless Synchronization Access lets users of Pocket PC and Smartphone devices synchronize information directly with an Exchange server using the Microsoft ActiveSync application. Users can access and manipulate information while disconnected from the Exchange server and use a wireless carrier or a network connection to synchronize data.

Outlook Mobile Access provides real-time access to Exchange data for users with mobile devices such as Pocket PCs and Smartphones. Outlook Mobile Access allows access only while connected.

Mailbox Recovery Center

The new Mailbox Recovery Center allows you to recover multiple disconnected mailboxes (i.e., mailboxes no longer associated with a user) simultaneously. This improves on the Exchange 2000 Server requirement that each mailbox had to be recovered one at a time.

New Mail-Enabled Objects

Mail-enabled objects are Active Directory objects that are given an e-mail address but are not associated with an Exchange mailbox. Users, contacts, groups, and public folders can be mail-enabled. In addition, Exchange Server 2003 adds two new mail-enabled objects: InetOrgPerson and query-based distribution groups.

The *InetOrgPerson* object is a general-purpose object class that defines attributes for people. InetOrgPerson is used in LDAP and X.500 directories other than Active Directory. It is now featured as a mail-enabled object in Exchange Server 2003, mainly for the purpose of migrating users from other LDAP directory services to Active Directory.

Query-based distribution lists function like regular distribution lists, except that their membership changes based on queries. Regular distribution lists have a static membership. An example of a query-based distribution list would be one that includes all members of a particular department, based on the properties defined for the user object. Query-based distribution lists can include users, groups, contacts, and public folders.

Volume Shadow Copy Backup

Exchange Server 2003 supports the new Windows Server 2003 shadow copy backup technology, which creates a snapshot of a drive just before the backup process. The backup then uses the snapshot instead of the original information. This allows normal operation of the original drive to proceed so that users won't be interrupted by the backup process and files currently in use can be backed up while open.

Recovery Storage Group

A *recovery storage group* is an additional storage group (i.e., one that can be created in addition to the maximum number of storage groups allowed by the server) that is used as an intermediary storage group for recovering data. You can recover data to the recovery storage group and then use the Merge Mailbox tool to transfer that data from the recovery storage group to the original storage group. You can find more information on recovery storage groups in Chapter 27, "Disaster Recovery of an Exchange Server 2003 Database."

Internet Mail Wizard

The Internet Mail Wizard walks you through the process of setting up basic Internet e-mail connectivity for users. The wizard creates an SMTP connector for outgoing messages and an SMTP virtual server for incoming messages. You'll learn more about using the Internet Mail Wizard in Chapter 20, "Supporting Internet Protocols and SMTP."

Summary

This chapter introduced you to Exchange Server 2003, giving you the background you need to delve into the Exchange Server architecture in detail. It described basic concepts, including how an Exchange environment is organized, how different types of information are stored, and how services work behind the scenes to accomplish the many tasks that Exchange Server performs. In addition, the chapter gave an overview of the new features in Exchange Server 2003. The next three chapters take a deeper look into the Exchange Server architecture, beginning with its storage architecture.

Chapter 2
Understanding Exchange Server Storage Architecture

This chapter describes the storage architecture in Microsoft Exchange Server 2003. We'll cover the database file structure, the Extensible Storage Engine (ESE), the change made to the Installable File System (IFS), and the way Exchange Server 2003 handles public folders. Finally, we'll look at indexing and how clients access Exchange Server 2003 stores, as well as the front-end/back-end server architecture.

Storage Design Goals in Exchange Server 2003

The storage architecture of Exchange Server 2003 has three goals. The first is to minimize loss of productivity when a database goes offline. Exchange Server 2003 achieves this goal by spreading users across multiple databases that can each be mounted (started) or dismounted (stopped) individually. If one database in a storage group goes offline for some reason, the other databases continue to run, minimizing the number of users who are affected by the downtime.

The second goal is to allow a single server to host more users than is pragmatically possible in Microsoft Exchange 5.5. Spreading the users across multiple databases on a single server accomplishes this goal as well. Since the databases are smaller, creating more databases on each server allows each server to host more users. For instance, it is easier to manage six databases with 1000 users per database than it is to manage one database of 6000 users. Not only can backup and restore times be scheduled individually and run faster, but if one database becomes corrupted, only 1000 users are affected instead of 6000 users. In addition, Exchange Server 2003 can group multiple databases into a single storage group and host multiple storage groups on a single server.

The third goal, better recoverability in the event of a disaster, was a major concern of the design team and is also achieved by spreading users across databases, allowing individual databases to be restored while other databases are running. The result is shorter downtimes and greater productivity for users because only a subset of the organization's users is affected when a database goes offline.

Database File Structure

Each Exchange 2003 database consists of two files: the rich text file (ending in .EDB), which holds e-mail messages and Message Application Programming Interface (MAPI) content; and the native content "streaming" file (ending in .STM), which holds all non-MAPI information. Hence, a mailbox store (formerly known as a private information store in Exchange 5.5 and earlier) now consists of an .EDB and an .STM file pair. The default name for the first mailbox store is Priv1.edb and Priv1.stm (Figure 2-1). Similarly, a public folder store (formerly known as a public information store in Exchange 5.5) now comprises the files (named by default) Pub1.edb and Pub1.stm (Figure 2-2). Each database incorporates both files, and Exchange Server 2003 treats the files as one unit. When Exchange reports the size of the store, it gives the combined size of the rich text file, the native content file, and the transaction logs. Both types of data are stored in an Extensible Storage Engine (ESE) database format. (ESE is discussed later in this chapter.)

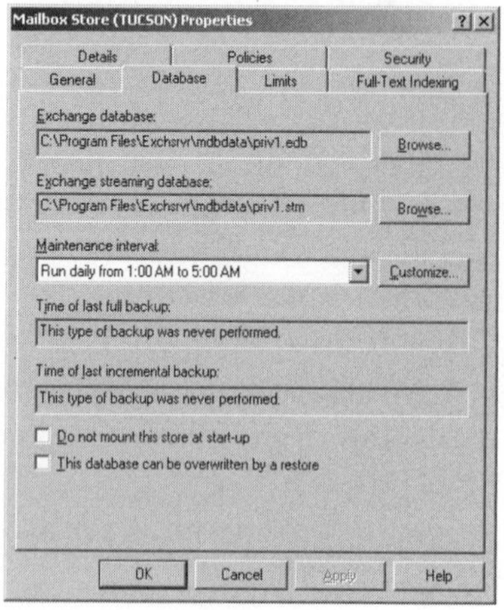

Figure 2-1. *The Database tab for a mailbox store property sheet.*

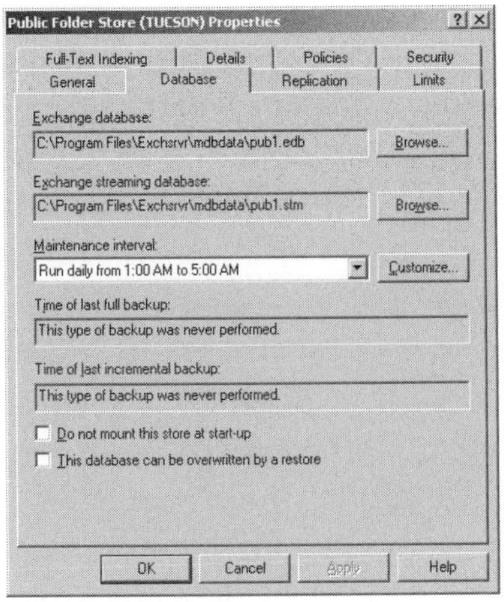

Figure 2-2. *The Database tab for a Public folder store property sheet.*

Rich Text File

The rich text file holds messages from MAPI clients such as Microsoft Outlook. MAPI clients access these messages without a conversion process running on the server. The rich text file is the same as the Exchange 5.5 information store. It is an .EDB file that uses transaction logging just as it did in Exchange 5.5.

On-Demand Content Conversion

When a MAPI client attempts to read a message from the rich text file, no conversion is necessary when the message format was originally rich text or plain text, since the message is in the client's native format. However, if another type of client, such as an HTTP client, attempts to read a rich text or plain text message from the rich text file, Exchange converts the message to the requested format. This process, in which messages are converted for dissimilar clients, is known as *on-demand conversion*.

When a MAPI client attempts to read a message that was originally formatted as an HTML message, portions of that message might reside in the .STM file. If they do, this message will also need to be converted in the memory space of the Exchange server.

Exchange Server 2003 does not automatically convert data when it writes the data to the database. Instead, client actions, such as a dissimilar client requesting data from the rich text file, cause the data to be converted. This is known as *deferred content conversion*. For example, suppose that a Web-based client posts a message to an Exchange server. That message is stored in the native content file. If another client requests this message over TCP port 80, Exchange streams it out of the native content file without converting it. However, if an Outlook client requests that message, that client is attempting to read information from a database that is not in its native format. In this case, Exchange converts the message in the memory of the server and then passes it to the client. The message is not moved from the native content file to the rich text file before being sent to the Outlook client.

If the Outlook client makes a change to the message and then saves it, the message is copied from the native content file to the rich text file and then deleted from the native content file. During the copy process, the updated message is converted from its native content to rich text before being written to the rich text file.

Native Content File

In Exchange 5.5, messages are always written to the database in Microsoft Database Encapsulated Format (MDBEF). If a message in non-MDBEF format needs to be written to the database, the Imail process converts it to MDBEF format so that it can be written to the information store.

In Exchange Server 2003, the native content file holds all non-MAPI messages in their native format, including HTTP and IMAP4. Native content files can include audio, video, voice, HTML-formatted messages and other multimedia formats. This file simply holds the raw data with no overhead, such as compression or B-tree overhead. In addition, the page checksums and space-usage information (information that tells ESE which pages in the database are used and which ones are free) are stored in the .EDB file.

Messages delivered from the native content file are streamed to the client. The streaming is fast due to the presence of the Win32 kernel mode component ExIFS, the Exchange Installable File System. (See the next section, "How Streaming Works," for more about this component.)

Any Win32-based client is able to access the data in the native content file over server message block (SMB) architecture. This capability means that any kind of data can be placed in the native content file, and it will be accessible to your LAN-based clients as regular file shares as well as being available over standard Internet protocols such as HTTP.

How Streaming Works

Figure 2-3 illustrates how streaming works in Exchange Server 2003. Let's assume that a Post Office Protocol 3 (POP3) client requests a message from the native content file. The POP3 client connects to the POP3 server in Internet Information Services (IIS), and the server asks the Store process (Store.exe) to manifest a handle to the message inside the native content file. The Store process negotiates a handle for the message with the kernel mode Exchange Installable File System (ExIFS) driver. The ExIFS driver locks the message, creates the handle, and presents the handle back to the Store process. It is also worth noting that page checksums are not verified during outbound transmission. Once manifested, the handle is handed back to the POP3 virtual server across the epoxy layer in user mode. (The "Front-End/Back-End Servers" section, later in this chapter, discusses the epoxy layer.) The POP3 virtual server then issues a TRANSMITFILE command, which is a high-performance API that uses both the handle and sockets to transmit the file. The TRANSMITFILE command is issued to the Auxiliary Function Driver (AFD), which essentially acts on behalf of Winsock, streaming the file out of the NT Cache Manager by talking to the ExIFS driver. It is important to note that at no time does the streaming data enter user mode, which makes this architecture very fast and very reliable. The handle contains the list of database pages that hold the information being requested. During the locking phase, ESE reserves the pages that hold the information and gives them to ExIFS.

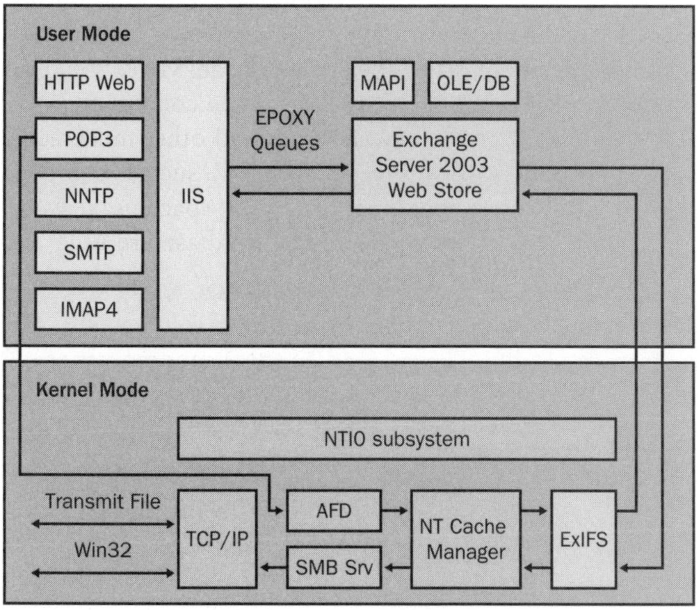

Figure 2-3. *Streaming architecture of the native content file.*

IIS can write to the native content file as well. ExIFS will make the native content file appear to IIS as multiple, yet virtual, files. When IIS wants to write to the native content file—as would be the case, for example, when an inbound message has a graphics attachment—ExIFS creates virtual files to which IIS can write. Then ExIFS streams this data into the native content file and passes the list of pages to the Store process. ESE then commits the pages by logging the information in the transaction logs. Page checksums are stored in the rich text file so that only data is held in the native content file.

ExIFS requests database space from ESE when necessary and allocates space for new messages from its reserved space. This allocation makes the write operation faster than if the space was not previously allocated.

Single-Instance Message Store

Exchange 2003 databases continue to support the Single-Instance Message Store (SIS) feature, meaning that a message sent to multiple recipients is stored only once as long as all the recipients are located in the same database. SIS is not maintained when a mailbox is moved to a different database, even if it still resides in the same storage group. Moreover, SIS does not span multiple databases in a single storage group.

Here is an example of how SIS works. John, the Exchange administrator at (a fictional) company named Trains by Dave, Inc., has deployed two storage groups consisting of four databases each. Each group contains two mailbox stores and two public folder stores. Mary, a user in John's network, sends a 1-MB message to a distribution group of 40 recipients, all of them residing in the first storage group, with 30 of them on mailbox store 1 and the other 10 on mailbox store 2.

Without SIS, the message would be copied 42 times (40 copies for 40 users plus 1 copy for the transaction log plus 1 copy in the Sent Items folder of the sender), requiring a whopping 42 MB of total disk space to store the message. However, as Figure 2-4 shows, with SIS only three copies of the message are held: one in the database of mailbox store 1, one in the database of mailbox store 2, and one temporarily in the transaction log. Hence, sending this message to these 40 recipients requires only 3 MB of total disk space, saving 38 MB.

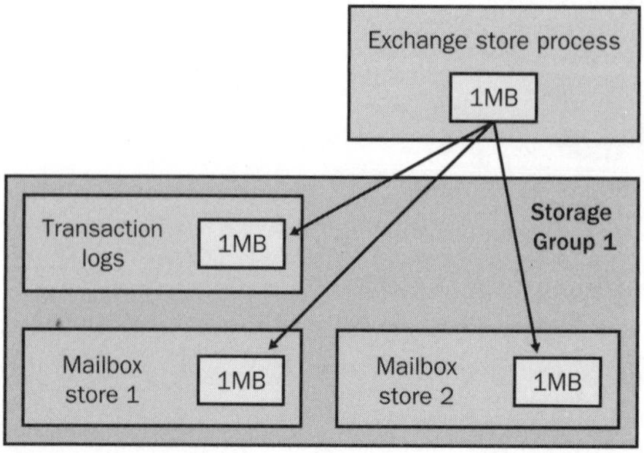

Figure 2-4. *How the Single-Instance Message Store feature works.*

Storage Groups and Multiple Databases

A storage group consists of an instance in memory of the Extensible Storage Engine (ESE) transaction logging system (described later in this chapter), the set of transaction logs, and their corresponding databases in the group. The ESE instance is managed by the Store.exe process, which runs as a single process. Each storage group can hold up to 5 databases. There can be up to 4 storage groups per server, and each group can hold up to 5 databases, so the limit is 20 databases per server. Each database can be either mounted (started) or dismounted (stopped). Although a corrupt database cannot be mounted, it also cannot stop the Store.exe process from running or stop other stores in the storage group from being mounted or dismounted. (Exchange Server 2003 introduces a new Recovery Storage Group disaster recovery function. This feature will be discussed in Chapter 28, "Troubleshooting Exchange Server 2003.")

Having multiple databases in multiple storage groups gives you great flexibility regarding how you manage your users and databases. For instance, you can group your users together by department or location and create their accounts in a common database. You can also control your user-to-database ratio, so as your company grows, you can keep your databases at a predetermined size and simply create another database for new users when necessary.

Also, the databases are very scalable, meaning that a single database can have from one mailbox up to (theoretically) an unlimited number of mailboxes. Neither extreme is recommended, however, and the actual limit to the number of mailboxes in a database will depend on factors such as hardware capacity or the amount of time necessary to back up or restore your databases. In addition, databases can be scheduled individually for backup, and you can perform multiple backups on multiple databases to multiple tape drives simultaneously. This feature helps reduce the window of time necessary to back up your databases.

Data Recovery and Transaction Logs

Three of the top 10 questions that Microsoft's technical support receives are related to the ESE and data recovery. This section discusses the role of transaction logs and describes how they are used in the recovery of your databases in the event of a catastrophe. It also covers why databases fail and looks at some of the common error messages that accompany a database failure. See Chapter 28 for a step-by-step description of how to restore a database.

The Extensible Storage Engine

The Extensible Storage Engine is a transaction logging system that ensures data integrity and consistency in the event of a system crash or media failure. The design of the ESE was guided by four criteria. The first was a question: "What happens if there's a crash?" Every development was guided by the notion that it should improve recoverability in the event of a disaster. The second criterion was to reduce the number of I/O operations that ESE would perform, and every effort was made to do so. Three I/O operations are better (faster) than four, and four are better than five. Even if it means expanding an I/O operation to include additional calculations, eliminating one I/O operation greatly improves performance. The third criterion was for the database engine to be as self-tuning as possible. Finally, ESE is designed to provide an uptime as close to 24 hours a day, 7 days a week as possible. Achieving the online maintenance level will enhance the success of this last goal.

How ESE Works

The main function of ESE is to manage transactions. ESE applies four tests to the databases to ensure their integrity. They are sometimes referred to as the ACID tests:

- **Atomic** Either all the operations performed in a transaction must be completed or none will be completed.
- **Consistent** A transaction must start with a database in a consistent state and leave the database in a consistent state when finished.
- **Isolated** Changes are not visible until all operations within the transaction are completed. When all operations are completed and the database is in a consistent state, the transaction is said to have been *committed.*
- **Durable** Committed transactions are preserved even if the system experiences significant stress such as a system crash.

Note Durability can be seen when the system crashes during the performance of the operations. If some of the operations were completed before a system crash (for example, if the e-mail was deleted from the Inbox and copied to the Private folder but the item count on each folder was not updated), when the Store.exe process starts on reboot, it will detect that the database is in an inconsistent state and will roll back the operations. This precaution means that the e-mail message cannot be lost while it is being moved, nor will there be two copies of the message upon reboot. ESE ensures that, when restarted, the database is in the same state it was in immediately before the operations began.

Real World What Happens When a Change Is Made to a Page in the Database?

Let's say that you move an important e-mail message from your Inbox to a private folder named Private. The following operations occur to complete this transaction:

- Inserting the e-mail message into the Private folder.
- Deleting the e-mail message from the Inbox folder.
- Updating the information about each folder to correctly display the number of items in each folder.
- Committing the transaction in the temporary transaction log file.

Because these operations are performed in a single transaction, Exchange either performs all of them or none of them. This is the Atomic test. The commit operation cannot be carried out until all the operations have been performed successfully. Once the transaction is committed, the Isolated test is passed. And since the database is left in a consistent state, the Consistent test is passed. Finally, after the transaction is committed to the database, the changes will be preserved even if there is a crash. This meets the Durable test.

How Data Is Stored Inside an ESE database file, data is organized in 4-KB sections called *pages*. Information is read from an ESE database file and loaded into memory in the form of a page. Each page contains data definitions, data, indexes, checksums, flags, timestamps, and other B-tree information. The pages are numbered sequentially within the database file to maximize performance. Pages contain either the actual data or pointers to other pages that contain the data. These pointers form a B-tree structure, and rarely is the tree more than three or four levels deep. Hence, the B-tree structure is wide but shallow.

More Info If you'd like to learn more about the B-tree database structures, you can find plenty of information on the Internet. You can start by going to *http://www.bluerwhite.org/btree*. For a short definition of a B-Tree structure, go to *http://searchdatabase.techtarget.com/sDefinition/0,,sid13_gci508442,00.html*. And, as always, a Google search on "B-tree" will yield other sites with more information than you'll be able to read in a single sitting.

A *transaction* is a series of modifications to a page in a database. Each modification is called an *operation*. When a complete series of operations has been performed on an object in a database, a transaction is said to have occurred.

Note An ESE database can contain up to 2^{32} or 4,292,967,296 pages. At 4 KB per page, an ESE database can hold 16 terabytes (4,292,967,296 × 4096 = 17,583,994,044,416 bytes). Practically speaking, your database size will be limited by hardware space or backup and restore considerations rather than by ESE design.

When a page is first read from disk and stored in memory, it is considered *clean*. Once an operation has modified the page, the page is marked as *dirty*. Dirty pages are available for further modifications if necessary, and multiple modifications can be made to a dirty page before it is written back to disk. The number of modifications to a page has no bearing on when the page will be written back to disk. This action is determined by other measures, which we will discuss later in this chapter.

While the operations are being performed, they are being recorded in the version store. The version store keeps a list of all of the changes that have been made to a page but have not yet been committed. If your server loses power before the series of operations can be committed, the version store will be referenced when ESE starts again to roll back, or undo, the unfinished operations. The version store is a virtual store—you won't find a Version Store database on the hard disk. The version store is held in RAM and really constitutes versioned pages of a single page that was read from the disk to memory. Figure 2-5 illustrates this process.

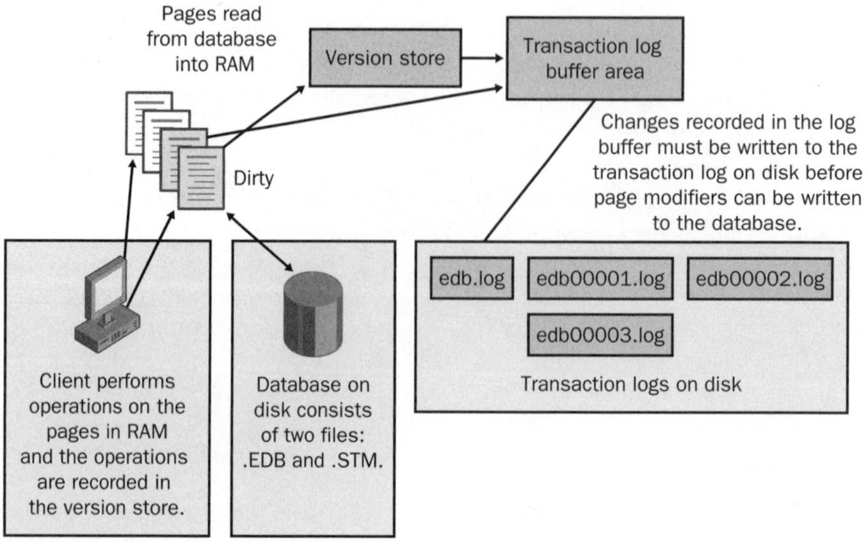

Figure 2-5. *How ESE handles transactions.*

To actually commit a transaction, the operations must be written to the transaction log buffer before being written to the transaction logs on disk. ESE uses "write-ahead" logging, which means that before ESE makes a change to the database, it notes what it's going to do in the log file. Data is written to a cached version of the log in the log buffer area, the page in memory is modified, and a link is created between these two entries. Before the modifications of the page can be written to disk, the change recorded in the log buffer must first be written to the log file on disk.

Tip One operation can hang or be so large that the version store takes up hundreds of megabytes. This situation could occur if your operation is indexing a large table or writing a very large file to the database. Because the version store keeps track of all changes that have occurred to the database since the oldest transaction began, you might get the following error: "-1069 error (JET_errVersionStoreOutOfMemory)." If this happens, consider moving your databases and stores to another disk with more free disk space, and also consider increasing the RAM on your system.

Often, the cached version of the changes to the pages is not written to disk immediately. This does not present a problem, since the information is recorded in the log files. Should the modifications in memory be lost, when ESE starts, the log files will be replayed (a process discussed in more detail in the section "How Log Files Are Replayed During Recovery," later in this chapter), and the transactions will be recorded to the disk. Moreover, not writing cached information to the database right away can improve performance. Consider the situation in which a page is loaded from memory and then modified. If it needs to be modified again soon thereafter, it does not need to be reread from the disk because it is already in memory. Thus, the modifications to the database can be batched to increase performance.

Database Files The database itself is a combination of the .EDB and .STM files stored on the hard disk. Eventually, all transactions are written to one of these files. Before a page is written to disk, however, a checksum is calculated for that page, and the checksum is then written to the page along with the data. When the page is read from disk, the checksum is recalculated and the page number is verified to be sure that it matches the requested page number. If the checksum fails or if there is a mismatch on the page number, a -1018 error is generated. This error means that what was written to disk is not what was read by ESE from the disk into memory.

Note Beginning with Service Pack 2 (SP2) in Exchange Server 5.5 and continuing in Exchange Server 2003, ESE attempts to read the data 16 times before generating a -1018 error, reducing the chance that a transient event might cause a problem. Hence, if you receive a -1018 error, you know that ESE attempted to read the data repeatedly before warning you.

ESE and Memory Management Before it can load a page into memory, ESE must reserve an area in memory for its own use. *Dynamic buffer allocation* (DBA) is the process of increasing the size of the database buffer cache before the memory is needed. More than a few Exchange administrators have complained that Exchange eats up all the memory on their servers. This situation is by design, although the design doesn't necessarily call for using all the memory, nor is the memory allocated to Exchange unavailable for other system processes. If other processes need more memory, Exchange will release the memory to that process so that it can run efficiently. This happens on the fly, and the methods used by ESE are not configurable.

In Exchange 4 and 5.0, the size of the cache was set by the Performance Optimizer. In Exchange 5.5, the process was changed to be dynamic: ESE observes the system and adjusts the size of the database cache as necessary. To observe how much of your RAM is being reserved by the Store process, use the Cache Size performance counter.

At this point, it might be helpful to take a look at the overall design goals of the DBA process. Understanding these will answer any questions you might have about memory management in Exchange Server 2003. The two design goals of DBA are as follows:

- **Maximize system performance** The Store process uses the amount of overall paging and I/O activity, among other factors, to determine how much RAM to allocate for the database buffer. Overall system performance really is the focus of this goal. It does no good to have Exchange running quickly if the operating system is constantly paging.
- **Maximize memory utilization** Unused system memory is wasted dollars. ESE will allocate to itself as much memory as it can without negatively impacting other applications. If a new application starts that needs additional memory, ESE will release memory so that the other application can run efficiently.

As you can see, you don't need to be alarmed if you go into Task Manager and see that, for example, out of the 1 GB of RAM on your system, only 200 MB is left and the Store.exe process is using 800 MB of RAM. You're not running out of memory and the Store.exe process does not have a memory leak. All it means is that the DBA feature of ESE has allocated additional RAM to increase your system performance. Figures 2-6 and 2-7 illustrate what this looks like in Task Manager. In Figure 2-6, you can see both the Store.exe and Mad.exe processes using more memory than most of the other processes. This figure was shot on a server that was not busy and still the Store.exe process was at the top of the memory usage list. Figure 2-7 shows that only 49,176 KB is available in physical memory. Look under the Physical Memory (K) box for the Available value.

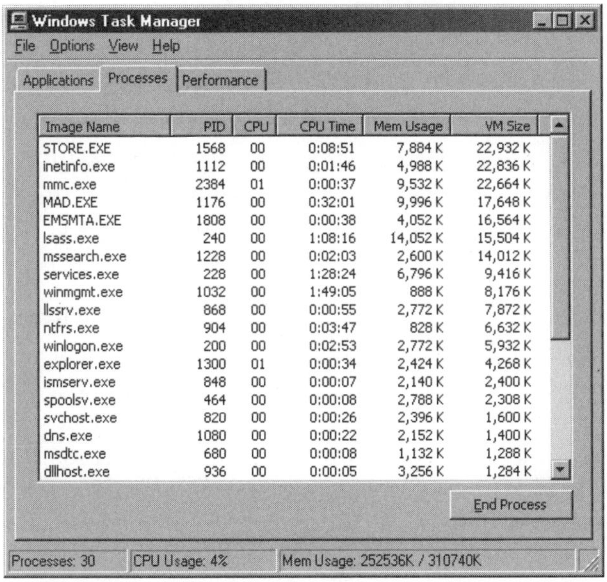

Figure 2-6. *The Processes tab in Windows Task Manager, showing the memory allocated to Store.exe and Mad.exe.*

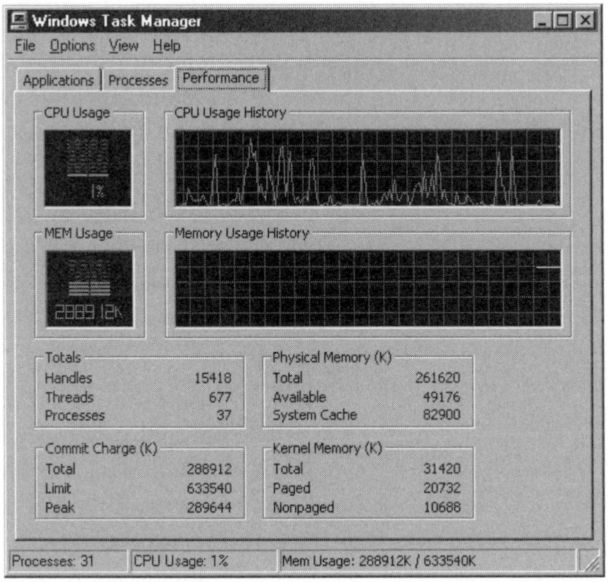

Figure 2-7. *The Performance tab in Windows Task Manager, showing memory usage and availability.*

Transaction Log Files In theory, the transaction log file could be one ever-expanding file. But it would grow so big that it would consume large amounts of disk space, thus becoming unmanageable. Hence, the log is broken down into *generations*—that is, into multiple files, each 5 MB in size and each representing a generation. The generations are named Edb*XXXXX*.log, where the *XXXXX* is incremented sequentially, using hexadecimal numbering.

The Edb.log file is the highest generation. When it becomes full, it is renamed with the next hexadecimal number in sequence. As this happens, a temporary log file, Edbtemp.log, is created to hold transactions until the new Edb.log can be created.

Each log file consists of two sections: the header and the data. The header contains hard-coded paths to the databases that it references. In Exchange Server 2003, multiple databases can use the same log file, since the log files service the entire storage group. From an administrative perspective, this arrangement simplifies recovery. No matter which database in a storage group you're restoring, you will reference the same log files for that group. The header also contains a signature matched to the database signature. This keeps the log file from being matched to a wrong but identically named database.

You can dump the header information of a log file with the command ESEUTIL /ML (Figure 2-8). The dump displays the generation number, the hard-coded database paths, and the signatures. The data portion of the log file contains the transactional information, such as BeginTransaction, Commit, or Rollback information. The majority of it contains low-level, physical modifications to the database. In other words, it contains the records that say, "This information was inserted on this page at this location."

When a database is modified, several steps occur. First, the page is read into the database cache, and then the timestamp on the page is updated. This timestamp is incremented on a per-database basis. Next, the log record is created, stating what is about to be done to the database. This occurs in the log cache buffer. Then the page is modified and a connection is created between these two entries so that the page cannot be written to disk without the log file entry being written to disk first. This step guarantees that a modification to the database will first be written to the log file on disk before the database on disk is updated.

Hence, there is legitimate concern over the write-back caching that can be enabled on a log file disk controller. Essentially, *write-back caching* means that the hardware reports back to ESE a successful disk write even though the information is held in the disk buffer of the controller to be written to disk at a later time. Write-back caching, while improving performance, can also ruin the ESE process of writing changes to the log file before they are written to the database. If a controller or disk malfunction of some sort occurs, you could experience a situation in which the page has been written to disk but not recorded in the log file—which will lead to a corrupted database.

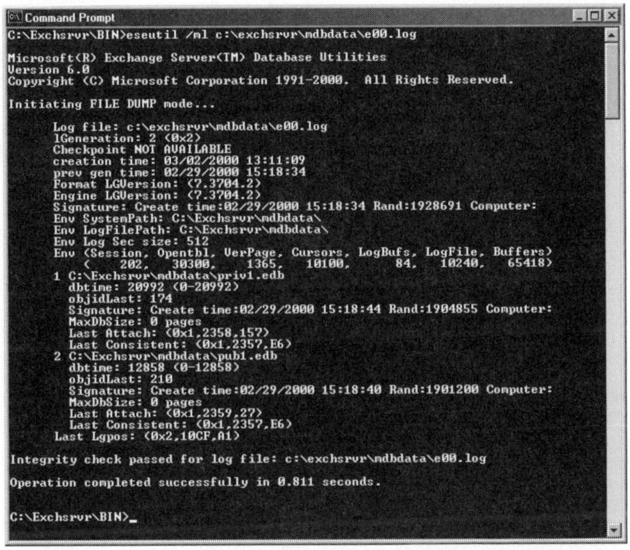

Command Prompt
C:\Exchsrvr\BIN>eseutil /ml c:\exchsrvr\mdbdata\e00.log
Microsoft(R) Exchange Server(TM) Database Utilities
Version 6.0
Copyright (C) Microsoft Corporation 1991-2000. All Rights Reserved.
Initiating FILE DUMP mode...
Log file: c:\exchsrvr\mdbdata\e00.log
lGeneration: 2 (0x2)
Checkpoint NOT AVAILABLE
creation time: 03/02/2000 13:11:09
prev gen time: 02/29/2000 15:18:34
Format LGVersion: (7.3704.2)
Engine LGVersion: (7.3704.2)
Signature: Create time:02/29/2000 15:18:34 Rand:1928691 Computer:
Env SystemPath: C:\Exchsrvr\mdbdata\
Env LogFilePath: C:\Exchsrvr\mdbdata\
Env Log Sec size: 512
Env (Session, Opentbl, VerPage, Cursors, LogBufs, LogFile, Buffers)
(202, 30300, 1365, 10100, 84, 10240, 65418)
1 C:\Exchsrvr\mdbdata\priv1.edb
dbtime: 20992 (0-20992)
objidLast: 174
Signature: Create time:02/29/2000 15:18:44 Rand:1904855 Computer:
MaxDbSize: 0 pages
Last Attach: (0x1,2358,157)
Last Consistent: (0x1,2357,E6)
2 C:\Exchsrvr\mdbdata\pub1.edb
dbtime: 12858 (0-12858)
objidLast: 210
Signature: Create time:02/29/2000 15:18:40 Rand:1901200 Computer:
MaxDbSize: 0 pages
Last Attach: (0x1,2359,27)
Last Consistent: (0x1,2357,E6)
Last Lgpos: (0x2,10CF,A1)
Integrity check passed for log file: c:\exchsrvr\mdbdata\e00.log
Operation completed successfully in 0.811 seconds.
C:\Exchsrvr\BIN>_

Figure 2-8. *A header dump produced using ESEUTIL /ML.*

How Log Files Are Replayed During Recovery After you have restored your database, the logs will be replayed when you start the Store.exe process. Replaying the logs and then rolling back operations constitute the "starting" of the Store process; this is often referred to as the recovery process. Replaying the transaction logs is the first part of the recovery process, and it consumes most of the time necessary to start the Store.exe process.

Replaying the transaction log files means that for each log record, the page is read out of the database that the record references, and the timestamp on the page read from the database is compared to the timestamp of the log entry that references that page. If, for example, the log entry has a timestamp of 12 and the page read from the database has a timestamp of 11, ESE knows that the modification in the log file has not been written to disk, and so it writes the log entry to the database. However, if the timestamp on the page on disk is equal to or greater than the timestamp on the log entry, ESE does not write that particular log entry to disk and continues with the next log entry in the log file.

In the second and last phase of the recovery process, any uncommitted operations are rolled back: If a piece of e-mail was transferred, it is untransferred. If a message was deleted, it is restored. This is called *physical redo, logical undo*. Recovery runs every time the Store.exe process is started. If you stop and then start the Store process five times, the recovery process runs five times.

Even though the recovery process is run on the log files and not on the databases, if you've moved your databases, recovery won't work because the hard-coded path to the database in the header of the log file will no longer point to the database. At the end of recovery, the process will appear to have been successful, but when you attempt to use that database, you'll get an error with an event ID of 9519 from MSExchangeIS in the application log, indicating an error in starting your database (Figure 2-9).

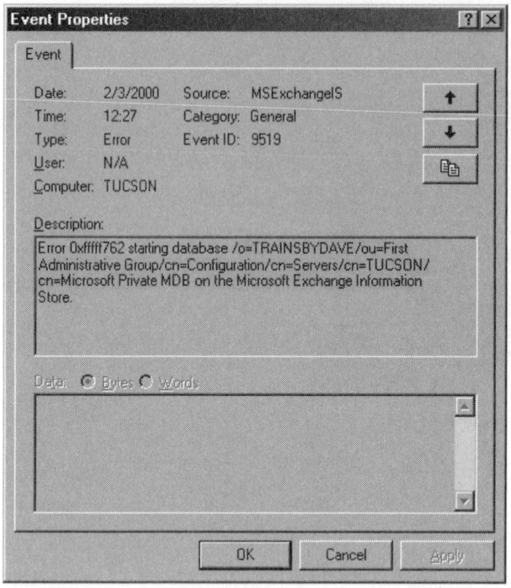

Figure 2-9. *Message indicating that an error occurred when starting the database.*

If you move the database back to the location where the log file is expecting to find it and then start the Store process, you should find that recovery brings your database to a consistent and usable state.

Checkpoint File The *checkpoint file* is an optimization of the recovery process. It records which entries in the log files have already been written to disk. If all the entries in the log files have been written to disk, the log files don't need to be replayed during recovery. The checkpoint file can speed up recovery time by telling ESE which log file entries need to be replayed and which do not.

Faster recovery of a database is sometimes why circular logging is enabled. *Circular logging* deletes log files older than the current checkpoint location. The problem with circular logging is that you lose the ability to roll forward from a backup tape. If some of your log files since the last full backup have been deleted by circular logging, you'll be able to recover only to the last full backup. However, if you have all your old log files, restoring the last full backup of your database from tape will allow for a full restore up to the point of your disaster, because all the log files can be replayed into the restored database. Remember that in order for a full restore to work, the database must be in the same physical condition as it was when the log files were written. A physically corrupt database cannot service a restore process.

> **Caution** Never, never, never delete your log files! Here's why: Assume that log file 9 contains a command to insert a new page at a particular place in the database. Log file 10 contains a command to delete this page. Now suppose that an administrator deletes log file 9, perhaps thinking that the file's timestamp is too old, and also deletes the checkpoint file. The administrator then needs to reboot the system for unrelated reasons. When the Store.exe process is started, ESE automatically enters recovery mode. Finding no checkpoint file, ESE has no choice but to replay all the log files. When log file 10 is replayed, the delete command will be carried out on that page, and its contents will be destroyed. ESE won't know that there was an earlier command to insert a new page in that location in the database because log file 9 was deleted. Your database will be corrupted. Whatever you do, *do not delete your log files*. Furthermore, be aware that *write-back caching can have the effect of deleting log files*. The best practice is to disable write-back caching and never delete your log files or checkpoint file.

How Log Entries Are Written to the Database As we mentioned earlier, modified pages in memory and committed transactions in the log buffer area are not written immediately to disk. Committed transactions in the transaction log file are copied to the database when one of the following occurs:

- The checkpoint falls too far behind in a previous log file. If the number of committed transactions in the log files reaches a certain threshold, ESE will flush these changes to disk.
- The number of free pages in memory becomes too low, possibly affecting system performance. In this case, committed transactions in memory are flushed to disk to free up pages in memory for system use.
- Another service is requesting additional memory and ESE needs to free up some of the memory it is currently using. ESE flushes pages from memory to the database and then updates the checkpoint file.
- The database service is shutting down. In this case, all updated pages in memory are copied to the database file.

Bear in mind that pages are not copied from memory in any particular order and might not all be copied at the same time. The random order in which the pages are copied back to disk means that if there is a system crash while pages are being written to disk, the database file might have only portions of a committed transaction updated in the actual file. In this event, when the Store.exe process is started, the transaction will be replayed from the transaction log files and the database will be updated completely.

Installable File System

In Exchange 2000 Server, the ExIFS was mounted by default and was a recommended method of managing users' data. As you might recall, the Installable File System allowed users to place any kind of document in the native content file (the streaming file) and then access it from almost any client, regardless of whether that client was a browser, a MAPI client, or Microsoft Internet Explorer.

However, Microsoft has backed off from using the IFS for data and file management. In Exchange Server 2003, the IFS is not mounted by default. If you want to mount the IFS to expose the databases as a virtual file system, you must re-enable the M: drive through the following registry parameter:

```
HKEY_LOCAL_MACHINE\SYSTEM\CurrentControlSet\Services\EXIFS\parameters
Parameter:  DriveLetter
Type: String
Value: M
```

You should use the M: drive only for gaining access to non-MAPI file data. You should not share out portions of the M: drive for server message block (SMB) user access. The preferred method is to use the Web Folder client to access data in the stores for applications such as Microsoft Word, rather than use the M: drive and SMB access.

More Info If you'd like to learn more about SMBs, go to *http://probing.csx.cam.ac.uk/about/smb.html* or *http://wwwacs.gantep.edu.tr/foldoc/foldoc.cgi?Server+Message+Block*. Essentially, SMBs are commands sent from a client to a server to request file-type actions, such as Copy, Create Directory, and Delete. Much like SMTP (Simple Mail Transport Protocol), which uses a request-response architecture, SMB commands are a series of requests from the client and responses from the server. The number and type of commands used between client and server are determined during the direct negotiation while the TCP three-way handshake is occurring, when the session is being established between the client and the server. To better understand the TCP three-way handshake, take a look at the *Microsoft Windows Server 2003 TCP/IP Protocols and Services Technical Reference* (Microsoft Press).

The Web Folder Client

As we mentioned earlier, information that is held in the native content file can be accessed over the Web using HTTP. You accomplish this by giving each object in the file a unique URL that lets the object be accessed from the browser, which allows a customized application to call directly into the Exchange store to retrieve data from both mailboxes and public folders.

WebDAV (Web Development Authoring and Versioning) is an extension of the HTTP protocol and represents a standards-based layer that is built on top of HTTP 1.1. Specifically, it supports a more complex command structure, adding commands such as COPY or MOVE that manipulate individual objects on a Web server. In addition, this new protocol allows read/write access to the information store over HTTP using the browser as your client. It supports relational database structures, semistructured databases (such as Exchange databases), and standard file systems. Furthermore, WebDAV clients can be synchronized to server-side stores over the Internet through replication, allowing efficient online access and offline usage of data. This feature enables you to, for example, publish an hourly update of current inventory to a nationwide sales force. Each salesperson would be able to view this information over the Internet, enter orders and comments, and have current information at a client site as long as Internet access was available.

WebDAV can accommodate all types of content, which means users can use WebDAV to work collaboratively on a word processing document, a spreadsheet, or an image file. Potentially, anything you can put in a file can be authored using WebDAV. WebDAV makes the Web, from the point of view of the client, a writable medium. Microsoft Internet Explorer 5 and Microsoft Office 2000 (and later) are compatible with WebDAV. Here are some features of WebDAV:

- **Overwrite protection (file locking)** Users can write, edit, and save shared documents without overwriting another person's work, regardless of which software program or Internet service they are using. This is a key collaborative support feature.
- **Namespace management** Users can conveniently manage Internet files and directories, including moving and coping files. This process is similar to file management in Explorer.
- **Property (metadata) access** Users can index and search metadata information about a document, such as the author's name, copyright, publication date, or keywords, to find and retrieve relevant documents. (For more information about this, see the "Indexing" section later in this chapter.)

Web folders are designed to let clients access a Web server in the same way they access a file server. Exchange Server 2003 allows a client to access directories and items in the information store just as it would access them on a file server, and to manage the data in the Web folder as if it were a file server. Public folders are also exposed as Web folders in Exchange Server 2003. The Web Folder client ships with Microsoft Windows 2000 Professional and Microsoft Windows XP.

To create a Web Folder to a resource in the Exchange store, use the Add Network Place Wizard in My Network Places and enter one of the following:

- The server share location using a Universal Naming Convention (UNC), such as *servername**sharename*
- A Uniform Resource Locator, such as *http://www.microsoft.com*
- An FTP site using this syntax: *ftp://ftp.microsoft.com*

Once created, the Web Folder client can be used to access information by an application, Windows Explorer, or other client-side utilities.

This shift from using the IFS to using the Web Folder client is indicative of a much larger shift that moves us away from using SMBs to using Web-based technologies for managing and manipulating information, data files in particular. Moreover, if you get a chance to take a look at the Windows SharePoint Services service from Microsoft, you'll find that file management is moving away from a file server–based architecture to a database architecture. This shift is part of an overall strategy to move away from what we would traditionally think of as LAN-based technologies to Web services–based technologies. This shift is well underway and is represented in nearly every new platform that Microsoft is introducing.

What if you've been using Exchange 2000 Server and you've dumped a truckload of documents into public folders that users are accessing via the IFS? Well, in Exchange Server 2003, you can continue to leave those documents in public folders and, if you really want to, you can mount the IFS and use SMBs to get at those documents. However, bear in mind that at some point in the future, all data will be held in a SQL-like database. The Web Storage System as we know it will give way to the next big database engine, which will be SQL-based. You might want to consider planning for this impending change now.

Public Folders

In Exchange Server 2003, public folders are managed similarly to the way they are managed in Exchange 2000 Server. This approach includes the following features:

- Administration of public folders is accomplished through the Exchange Folders Microsoft Management Console (MMC) snap-in.

- Public folder trees are far more scalable and flexible. You can now create public folder trees by geography, department, or function. The next section, "Multiple Public Folder Trees," discusses this feature in more detail.
- Public folders are integrated with Active Directory, which means that e-mail entries enable you to send messages to a public folder instead of posting them directly to the public folder.
- Public folders use the users and groups in the Active Directory directory service for security.
- Accessing a public folder over the Web is more direct and much easier. With a standard URL, it's possible in Exchange 2003 to open up the contents of a public folder.
- Full-text indexing is built in with public folders. Outlook clients automatically use this new index when performing a Find or Advanced Find search.
- Referrals are enabled by default. Public folder referrals enable clients to gain access to any folder in the organization because referrals between routing groups are now enabled by default.
- Public folders can be created with the Exchange Folders snap-in. You are no longer required to use Outlook to create a public folder, though this capability still exists.

Multiple Public Folder Trees

In Exchange Server 2003, you can create multiple public folder trees for a variety of purposes. For instance, suppose that you have a project team composed of three internal LAN clients, two users in your company at remote locations, and three consultants outside your organization. You can create a public folder tree for these users that is separate from the default public folder tree (Figure 2-10).

Each public folder tree stores its data in a single public folder store on a per-server basis. You can replicate specific folders in the tree to every server in your company that has a public folder store associated with that public folder tree. The default public folder tree is available via MAPI, IMAP4, Network News Transfer Protocol (NNTP), and HTTP. Additional public folder trees are available to only HTTP and NNTP clients.

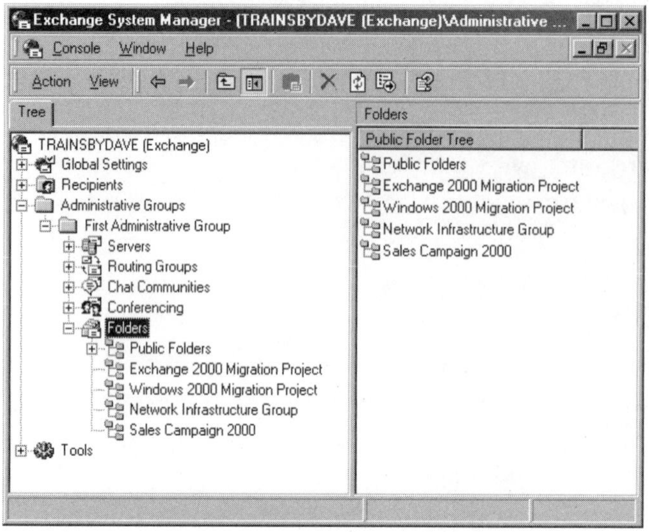

Figure 2-10. *Multiple public folder trees.*

Client Access to Exchange 2003 Stores

An Exchange 2003 client can access the Exchange store in multiple ways. Clients can access the information store through POP3, NNTP, IMAP4, HTTP, Simple Mail Transport Protocol (SMTP), property promotion, standard URLs, and WebDAV.

The information store specifically supports MAPI so that users can send and receive e-mail. The store also provides a URL to each item in the store. As each message or file is created in the store, Exchange creates a unique URL for that object. For example, a user's Inbox can be accessed via the URL *File://./BackOfficeStorage/server_name.domain_name.com/mbx/user_name/inbox/document_name*.

Indexing

The information store process creates and manages indexes for common key fields to enable faster lookups and searches of documents that reside in a store. An index allows Outlook users to search for items more easily. With *full-text indexing*, the index is built prior to the client search, thus enabling faster searches. Text attachments can be included in the full-text indexing. Each information store can be indexed individually for flexibility.

Property promotion allows for advanced searches on any document property, such as Author, Lines, or Document Subject (Figure 2-11). When Exchange stores a document in a supported file type, the document's properties are automatically parsed and promoted to the information store. Hence, the properties become a part of the document's record in the database. Searches can then be performed on these properties.

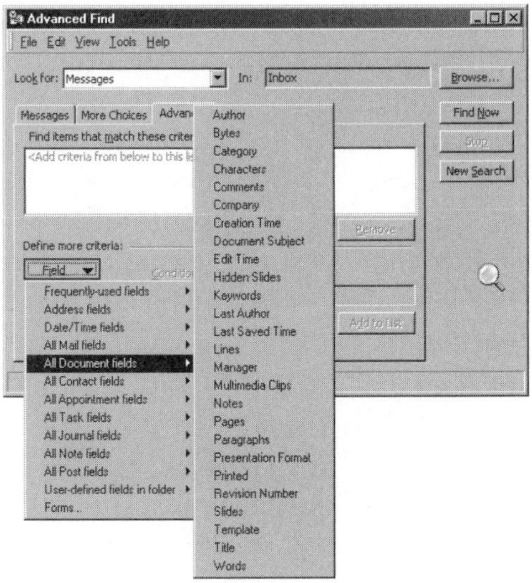

Figure 2-11. *Advanced search for document properties that have been promoted to the information store.*

The index is word-based, not character-based. This characteristic means that if a user performs a search for the word "admin," only those documents that have the word "admin" will be returned. The word "administrator" will not be identified as a match. Both the message and attachments can be indexed. Binary attachments and document properties are not indexed. Not all file types are indexed either; the following documents are the only types that are indexed by default:

- Word documents (*.doc)
- Excel documents (*.xls)
- PowerPoint documents (*.ppt)
- HTML documents (*.html, *.htm, *.asp)
- Text files (*.txt)
- Embedded MIME messages (*.eml)

Indexing is provided by the Microsoft Search service. Both the information store service and the search service must be running for the index to be created, updated, or deleted. Depending on the size of your store, completing a full index could take hours. Therefore, it's best to have this activity occur at a time when your server will be underutilized. Remember that indexing consumes about 20 percent of the disk space of your database. Also, individual indexes cannot be backed up; they must be backed up at the server level. Finally, even though multiple instances of a message might be held in the database, the message is indexed only once. This single-instance message indexing results in smaller indexes that can be created more quickly.

The Indexing Process

Microsoft Search builds the initial index by processing the entire store one folder at a time. The Search process identifies and logs searchable text. During the indexing process, you will see heavy CPU utilization; depending on the size of the store, this process could take hours.

After the index is created, any change to a folder within the store causes a synchronization event to notify the Microsoft Search service of the change. Depending on how you have configured the Search service to run, the service will either wait for the scheduled time to regenerate the index so that the new change is included or update the index shortly after the change is made.

Updating the Index

The time delay for an immediate (automatic) update of the index will vary based on the current server load. You can optimize this setting on the Full-Text Indexing tab of the Information Store's property sheet (Figure 2-12).

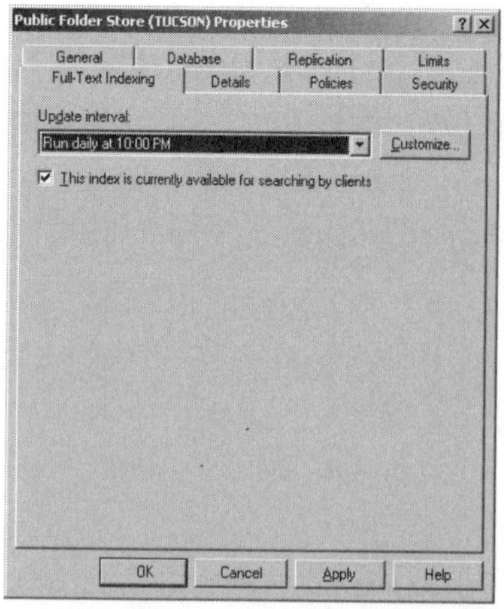

Figure 2-12. *The Full-Text Indexing tab of the property sheet for a public folder store.*

Scheduled updates allow granular control over when the index is updated. The advantage of scheduling the index update is that it can be planned for off-peak hours when the server is not heavily accessed by users. The disadvantage is that the index can become out-of-date over the course of a day. However, this might not be a big problem, since most users search for documents that were received and indexed more than 24 hours before the search. Try to schedule your updates to occur at least once each day.

Search Architecture

If you want to implement full-text searching widely in your organization, you'll need to consider which messaging clients to deploy. Only online MAPI and IMAP4 clients are able to perform full-text searches on the server. POP3 and WebDAV clients do not have search capability.

Exchange Server 2003 can perform two types of searches. The first is a full-text query of the index that has been built using Microsoft Search service. The second type is a query based on the properties of the documents that are not available in the full-text index.

When a user performs a search in the Outlook client by choosing Advanced Find from the Tools menu, several options are available (Figure 2-13). Once the user enters the desired variables, the query is sent to the Query Processor, which determines how the search should be conducted. If the search is based on both a string of text characters and a desired property variable, the Query Processor splits the query request into two parts. For instance, suppose that the request is for all documents that are larger than 5 MB *and* that have the phrase "building plan" in the subject line. The Query Processor splits this request and has the Microsoft Search service generate a list of documents that have "building plan" in the subject line. It then evaluates the size of each document that the Search service returned to find all those larger than 5 MB and generates a new list of documents that meet both criteria.

Finally, Exchange Server 2003 applies security restrictions to the remaining documents to ensure that the client does not receive a document that the client is not supposed to see. After this security enforcement, the matching results are returned to the client.

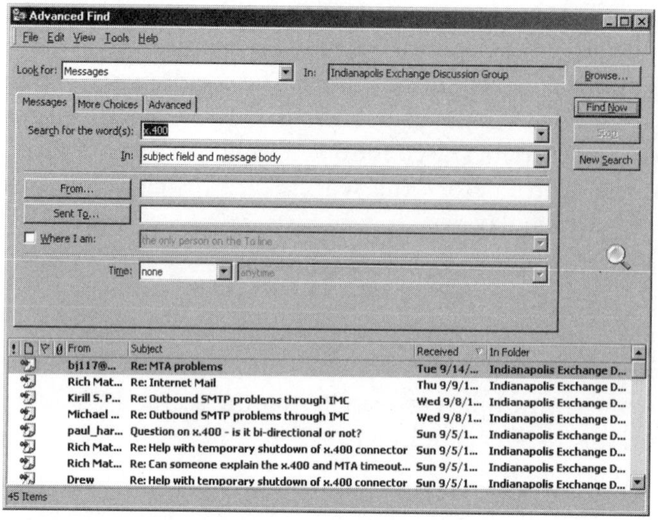

Figure 2-13. *The Advanced Find dialog box in Outlook 2003.*

Gather Files

Gather files are created during each index process. They are located by default in the ExchangeServer_<*servername*>\Gatherlogs directory and end with the extension .GTHR. You can use these text files to identify every document and message that was not successfully indexed. For example, if a document is named with an extension indicating a supported file type, but it is not actually that type, the indexing component halts, fails the index, records the URL of the document in the gather file (Figure 2-14), and then continues with the next message or document.

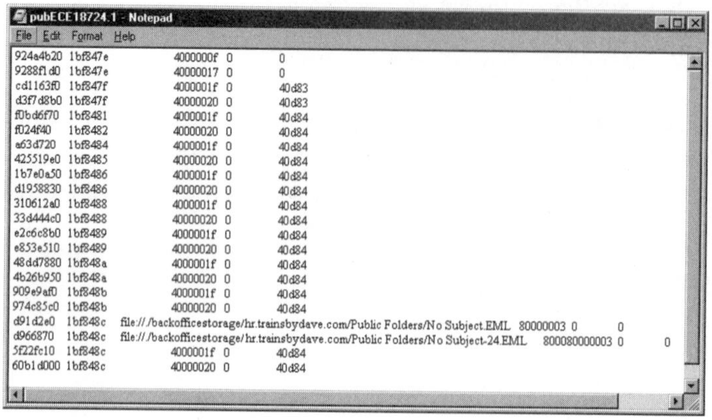

Figure 2-14. *A URL in a gather file.*

In addition to the URL, the subject or filename and the error code are also recorded in the gather file. To decode the error number, use the Gthrlog.vbs utility in the \Program Files\Common Files\System\MsSearch\Bin directory. The syntax for this utility is as follows:

Gthrlog <filename>

The name of the gather file is *<filename>*. You will be prompted with a series of dialog boxes that contain the data found in each line of the gather file, as shown in Figure 2-15.

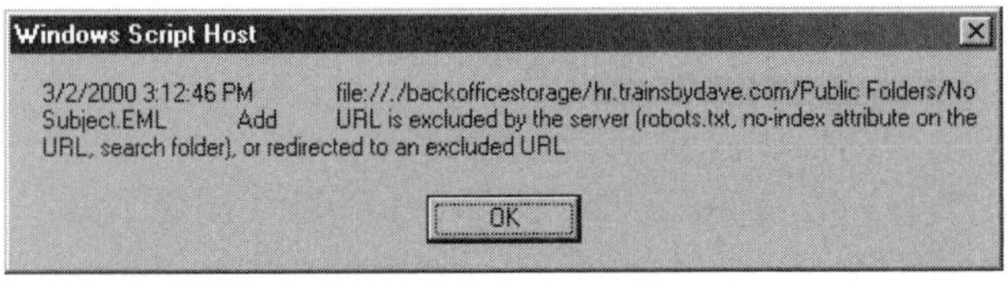

Figure 2-15. *A dialog box containing a line from the gather file.*

Moving the Index When It Gets Too Big

If your catalogs become so large that you're running out of disk space, you might want to move the index to another server. To do this, stop the Search service and use the Catutil.exe utility located in the Program Files\Common Files\System\MSSearch\Bin directory. For help in using this utility, type *Catutil Movecat /?* at the command prompt.

Front-End/Back-End Servers

Between the Exchange store architecture and the Internet access protocols lies a layer called the Exchange Interprocess Communication Layer (EXIPC), now known as the *epoxy* layer, which is an efficient, asynchronous shared area in memory to which both the Store.exe process and the IIS protocols can read and write. This queuing layer permits information to be exchanged very quickly between the IIS protocols that run inside the Inetinfo.exe process and the Store.exe process. The epoxy layer uses shared memory to communicate between these processes and is optimized for small packet communication.

To keep track of the binding, connection to, and use of the epoxy layer's queues, Exchange Server 2003 uses the Central Queue Manager. This manager is also responsible for unbinding and queue cleanup in the event of a catastrophic failure in the other process. Because the transport protocols are decoupled from the information store, we can implement a front-end/back-end architecture, which makes it possible to run some of the Internet protocols on different servers than the servers on which the store and the databases are running. The major advantage to this feature is the ability to scale Exchange for any installed base that is desired. To enable Exchange Server 2003 to act as a front-end server, you simply select a single check box on the General tab of the Exchange server's property sheet in the Exchange System snap-in (Figure 2-16).

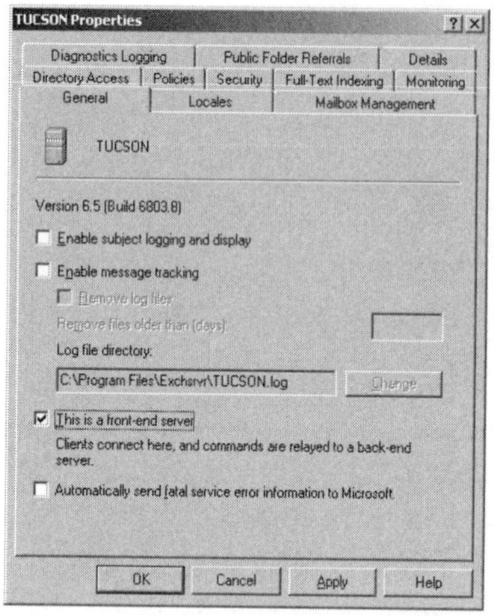

Figure 2-16. *Enabling a server to act as a front-end server.*

When this check box is *not* selected, the protocol DLLs, such as Pop3be.dll, Imap4be.dll, and Httpbe.dll, are loaded into memory. When the server is marked as a front-end server, these protocols are unloaded and front-end-specific DLLs are loaded into memory, such as Pop3fe.dll, Imap4fe.dll, and Httpfe.dll. To fully balance the load between client requests on front-end servers, you will need to use a DNS round-robin scheme (in which multiple IP addresses are assigned to one host name), Network Load Balancing (NLB), or third-party software.

Summary

This chapter has brought you up to speed on the storage architecture used in Exchange Server 2003. You learned, for example, that the Store.exe process can manage many databases on a single server and that databases are divided into stores, each of which can hold up to five databases, either private or public. You have also seen some of the new architecture for public folders, WebDAV, indexing, ExIFS, and front-end/back-end servers. The next chapter takes a look at the message routing architecture in Exchange Server 2003 and describes how messages are passed between servers.

Chapter 3

Understanding Exchange Server Routing Architecture

One of the most significant differences between Microsoft Exchange Server 5.5 and Microsoft Exchange Server 2003 lies in the basic architecture of an Exchange system. The message routing topology in Exchange Server 5.5 is based on sites. As you'll recall, a site is a logical grouping of servers that enjoy permanent, high-bandwidth connectivity. Architecturally, each site defines three distinct boundaries: the boundary for single-hop routing, the administrative unit, and a namespace hierarchy in the directory structure.

In Microsoft Exchange 2000 and later, these three boundaries have been separated into individual elements. Single-hop routing is defined by a routing group, the unit of administration is defined by the administrative group, and the namespace hierarchy exists in the Active Directory directory service in the form of a domain. This architecture gives administrators much more flexibility in determining how Exchange Server 2003 is administered because administrative assignments can be divided along functions and activities rather than by geography.

This chapter focuses on the routing architecture used in Exchange Server 2003. It describes what routing groups are, how to plan and name them, how they connect, and how link state information works to provide better message routing than Exchange 5.5 Server. We'll also look at the transport architecture and discuss some of the transport architectural features.

Routing Groups

Each routing group in an Exchange organization consists of a collection of well-connected Exchange servers for which full-time, full-mesh connectivity is guaranteed. Most often, routing groups will closely map to the physical topology of your network. Connectivity among servers in a routing group is based entirely on Simple Mail Transfer Protocol (SMTP).

Using SMTP as the native protocol provides several advantages over the remote procedure call (RPC)–based communications in Exchange 5.5. First, it allows for a more flexible routing and administrative scheme because SMTP is more tolerant of low-bandwidth and high-latency topologies than RPC-based communications. This tolerance allows you to group servers into a single routing group in Exchange Server 2003 that you could not place into a single site in Exchange 5.5. Second, the use of SMTP allows a division between the routing architecture and the grouping of servers for administrative purposes. In Exchange 5.5, both of these elements were dictated by the site, forcing many companies to map their administrative boundaries to their site boundaries. Third, SMTP requires less overhead and bandwidth than RPC-based communications.

In addition, Exchange Server 2003 features a new routing calculation engine that eliminates the problems associated with the Gateway Address Routing Table (GWART), replacing it with link state information (discussed in the "Link State Information" section, later in this chapter).

> **Note** SMTP doesn't replace the Message Transfer Agent (MTA) in Exchange Server 2003. Instead, the MTA has been improved and works in both Exchange 5.5 and Exchange 2000 systems. However, it is now used mainly for connectivity to external X.400 systems.

In the object hierarchy of Exchange Server 2003, routing groups are located beneath administrative groups (Figure 3-1). Within an administrative group (which is a logical collection of Exchange-related objects such as servers, connectors, and policies that you administer as one group), you can configure the servers so that some of them route messages directly to one another while others forward their messages to a bridgehead server. (Bridgehead servers are discussed more fully in the "Message Routing to Other Routing Groups" section later in this chapter.)

Exchange Server 2003 stores its routing information in the configuration naming partition of Active Directory. Even though this information will be made available through replication to your entire Exchange organization, you still need to define the connectors between servers because these connectors help form the routing topology in the configuration naming partition. Using connectors, you can create customized routing topologies for maximum flexibility.

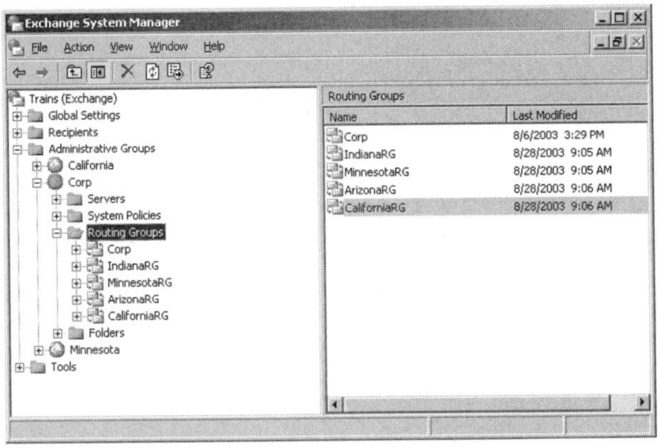

Figure 3-1. *Object hierarchy showing routing groups located beneath administrative groups.*

Routing Groups and Public Folders

An Exchange 2003 client uses the routing information in the configuration naming partition in Active Directory to locate a public folder server. By default, users will attempt to connect to a public folder replica on their home server and then on another server in the local routing group. If a client attempts to connect to a replica of a public folder that resides on a server in a remote routing group, the connector costs determine the order of the routing groups to which the client is directed. You can also set a flag on a messaging connector to prevent public folder referrals across the link (Figure 3-2), which was not possible with site affinities in Exchange Server 5.5.

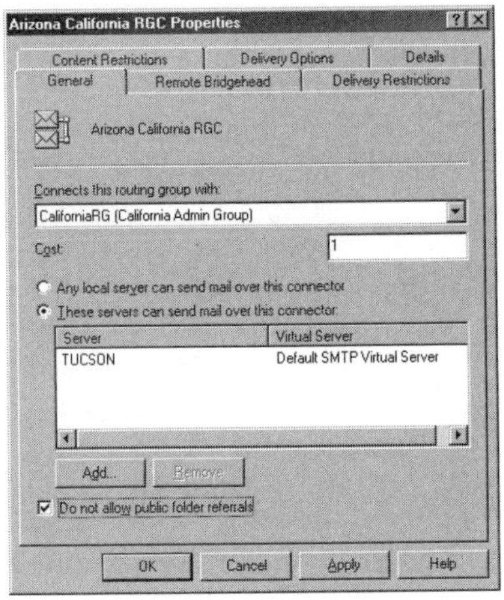

Figure 3-2. *The property sheet for a messaging connector, showing the Do Not Allow Public Folder Referrals option.*

Note Connector costs are arbitrary "costs" that you assign to the Routing Group Connector (RGC) to reflect the bandwidth associated with the connector and the amount of messaging you want the connector to receive. For instance, if you have an RGC configured over a T1 link and an SMTP connector over a satellite link, you would assign the RGC a cost of 1 and the SMTP connector a cost of 100. Message routing will attempt to use the lower-cost connector first.

Let's look at an example of how this routing works. Suppose that you have three routing groups, each with two servers named Server1 and Server2. In each routing group, Server1 is the e-mail server and Server2 is the public folder server. Sally is a member of routing group A.

Let's say that Sally attempts to connect to a public folder called Memos in her home routing group. Unfortunately, Server2 in routing group A is down for maintenance. In this instance, Sally is directed across the RGC to the public folders in routing group B and routing group C to access a replica of the Memos folder. If the connector cost on the RGC between routing group A and routing group B is 10, and the connector cost between routing group A and routing group C is 30, Sally will first be sent to routing group B because it has a lower connector cost.

Now let's say that the physical connection between routing group A and routing group B is severed by a construction crew. The administrator in routing group A could select the Do Not Allow Public Folder Referrals check box on the connector to routing group B, thereby taking that connector out of consideration the next time Sally needs to access the Memos folder. When the line is repaired, the administrator could clear the check box, permitting public folder referrals to once again flow across that connector.

Tip Another situation in which it is a good idea to enable the Do Not Allow Public Folder Referrals option is when you know that a public folder server in a remote site is down and will be for a sustained period of time. Selecting this option will eliminate public folder requests across that connector. You might also want to use this option if all instances of public folders are housed in one routing group and you want to focus client traffic on that routing group. In this scenario, all the RGCs that connect to the routing group containing the public folders will have this check box cleared, while all other RGCs will have this check box selected.

Overview of the Transport Architecture

Before we discuss how messages are routed within the same group or between groups, it might be useful to have a basic understanding of how messages are transferred internally within an Exchange 2000 server. Knowing how messages arrive in an outbound SMTP queue, for example, will help complete the overall routing picture that will be presented in the next several pages.

Messages can flow into an Exchange Server 2003 in one of three ways. The first is through the SMTP service. An example of this type of message is Internet e-mail. The second is through a store submission, such as a message created by a Microsoft Outlook (MAPI) client or an Outlook Web Access (OWA) client. The third way is for the message to come in via the Message Transfer Agent (MTA). Messages arrive in this way via an X.400 connector from a foreign e-mail system or via any Exchange Development Kit (EDK)–based connector.

As Figure 3-3 shows, SMTP messages are first sent to the NTFS queue because not all messages coming in from SMTP are destined for the local Exchange store. Thereafter, SMTP messages are sent to the precategorization queue for further processing.

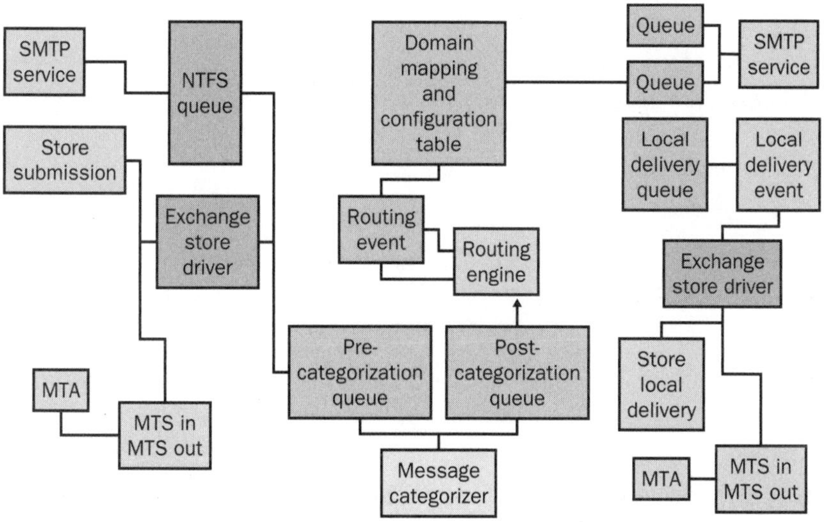

Figure 3-3. *Internal transport architecture for Exchange Server 2003.*

Messages submitted via either a store submission or the MTA are dropped into the Exchange store driver. The Exchange store driver picks up these messages and passes them to the precategorization queue. The precategorization queue is the first opportunity you have to fire your event sinks. *Event sinks* are scripts that can be run against the message to perform certain functions, such as adding a disclaimer or running an antivirus program.

The message is then passed to the message categorizer, which is essentially a collection of event sinks that perform address resolution on both the originator and recipient of the message. In addition, the message categorizer retrieves from Active Directory attributes that apply to the message, such as the originator's or recipient's size limits for outgoing and incoming messages, delivery restrictions, forwarding specifications, and other settings that might restrict the message in some way. Any restrictions that do exist are applied to the message. Once these tasks have been accomplished, the message is placed into a postcategorization queue, which allows more event sinks to fire on the message, if you choose to set them up.

After the message is processed in the postcategorization queue, it is given to the routing engine, which parses the destination address against its domain mapping and domain configuration table. The routing engine then decides whether the message is destined for the local store, or if a temporary outbound queue (referred to as a destination message queue) should be created to pass the message to another SMTP server.

Destination message queues are created based on the destination domain name. The advanced queuing engine is able to create as many destination message queues as needed. From these queues, the SMTP service reads the message out of the queue and then passes the message to the next SMTP server. If the message is destined for the local store, it is placed in the local delivery queue. The Store.exe process then reads the message out of the queue and writes it to the local database. Thereafter, the message is associated with the destination mailbox, and the recipient is notified that new mail has arrived.

Note The SMTP service comprises two components: the protocol stack and the advanced queuing engine (AQE). The AQE makes up the majority of the SMTP service and manages the passing of messages through the queues from the time they enter the transport core until the time they are placed in an outbound queue or delivered to the Exchange store driver. Thus, even though the AQE isn't depicted in Figure 3-3, it is the managing component that works behind the scenes to move messages through the transport core.

Message Routing Within the Same Server

When Exchange Server 2003 determines that the recipient of a message is on the same server as the sender, it delivers the message to the recipient's Inbox. The steps involved, shown in Figure 3-4, are as follows:

1. The client sends the message.
2. The message is passed to the categorizer, parsed against the domain mapping table, and then placed in the local delivery queue.

3. The information store associates the message with the recipient's mailbox.

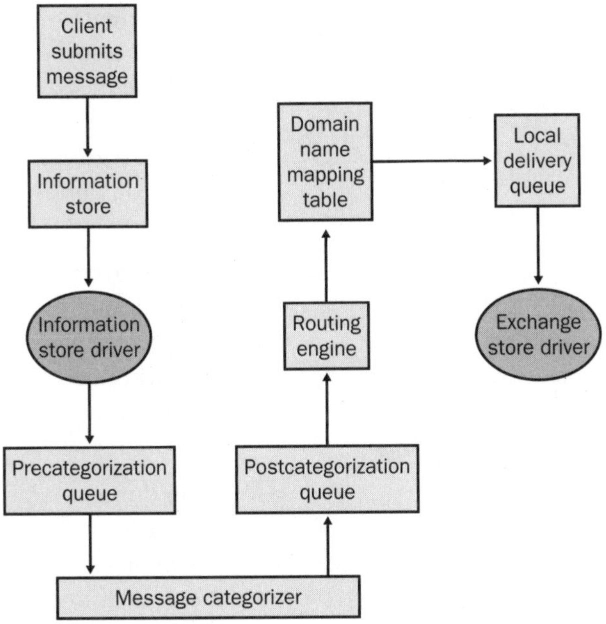

Figure 3-4. *How Exchange Server 2003 routes a message to a recipient from a sender housed on the same server.*

Message Routing Within the Same Routing Group

Messages sent between servers in the same routing group use SMTP as their transport. The steps involved in routing a message between two servers in the same routing group, shown in Figure 3-5, are as follows:

1. The client sends the message.
2. The message is passed to the categorizer, which applies any restrictions found in Active Directory. It is then passed through the postcategorization queue and on to the routing engine.
3. The routing engine parses the message against the domain name mapping table and then places it in the outgoing SMTP queue for the destination server. This queue is dynamically created for the message based on the destination domain name, which becomes the name of the queue—in this case, hr.trainsbydave.com (Local Delivery).

4. The sending server looks up the recipient's mailbox directory in Active Directory, conducts a DNS lookup for the mail exchanger (MX) record associated with the destination server on which the recipient's mailbox is stored, and then creates a TCP connection to that server over port 25.
5. The message is transmitted to the destination server.
6. The destination server accepts the message from the SMTP service and places it in the NTFS queue. The AQE reads the message out of the queue and takes the message through the transport core.

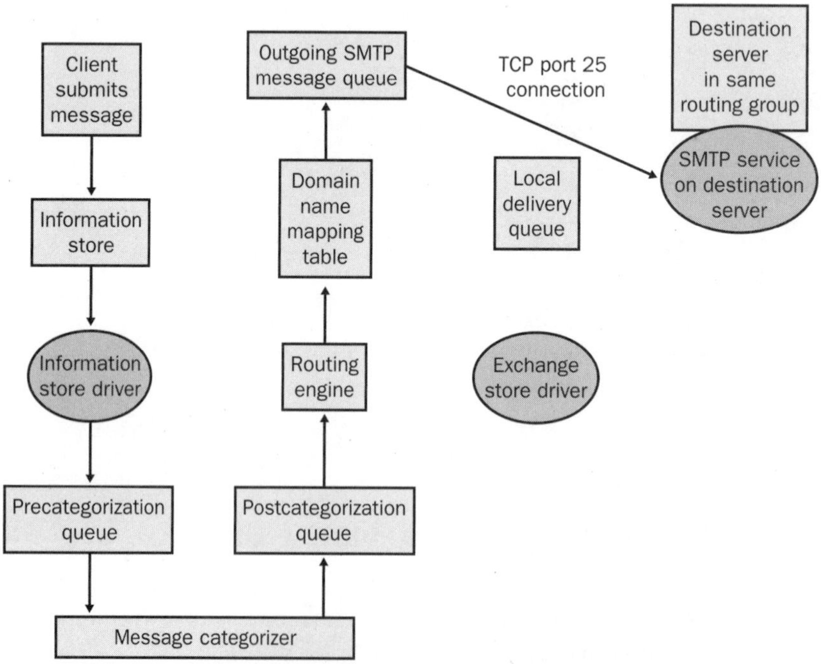

Figure 3-5. *How Exchange Server 2003 routes a message to a recipient on another server.*

Message Routing to Other Routing Groups

Messages routed to servers in other routing groups pass through a bridgehead server (BHS) at each end of the connector if one is explicitly configured in the connector. With an RGC, the destination server can be configured to be any server in the target routing group. The steps involved in routing messages to servers in different routing groups, shown in Figure 3-6, are as follows:

1. The client sends the message.
2. The message is passed through the transport core and then placed in an outgoing SMTP message queue.

3. The routing group information is gathered from the configuration naming partition of Active Directory.
4. The link state information is consulted to determine the best routing path. (For more information, see the section "Link State Information" later in this chapter.)
5. The message is passed to the BHS over TCP port 25.
6. The BHS passes the message over TCP port 25 to the BHS in the destination routing group.
7. The receiving BHS passes the message to the destination server in its group over TCP port 25.
8. The message is brought into the destination server via the SMTP service and is placed in the NTFS queue.
9. The message is taken out of the queue by the AQE and associated with the recipient's Inbox.

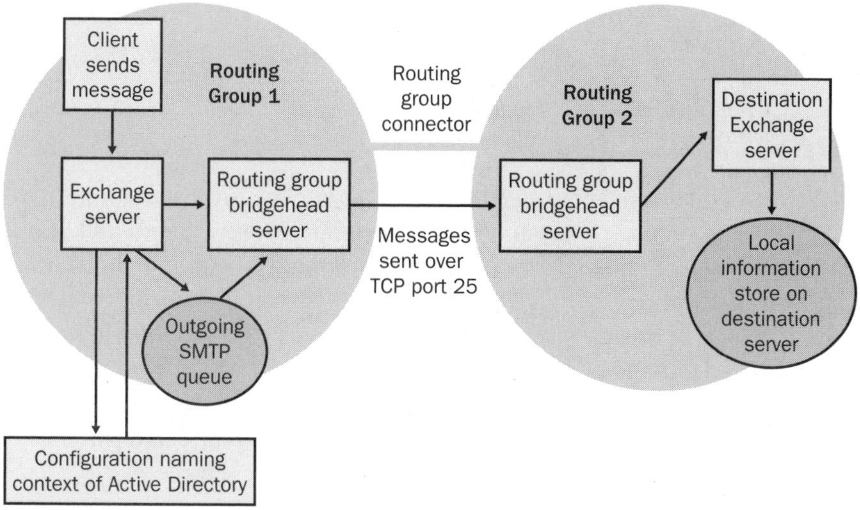

Figure 3-6. *How Exchange Server 2003 routes a message to a recipient in another routing group.*

Message Routing to Foreign E-Mail Systems

Messages are routed to foreign e-mail systems over the X.400 connector if it is a direct, continuous connection. Otherwise, they are routed over the Internet via SMTP. Here are the steps involved in routing messages to another e-mail system when using SMTP. These are illustrated in Figure 3-7.

1. The client sends the message.
2. The message is placed in the outgoing SMTP message queue.
3. The SMTP service reads the message out of this queue and sends it over TCP port 25 to the destination SMTP server.

If the message is being routed to a foreign e-mail system over an X.400 connector, these steps are essentially the same as routing over SMTP, except that an X.400 connector is used and no port number is involved.

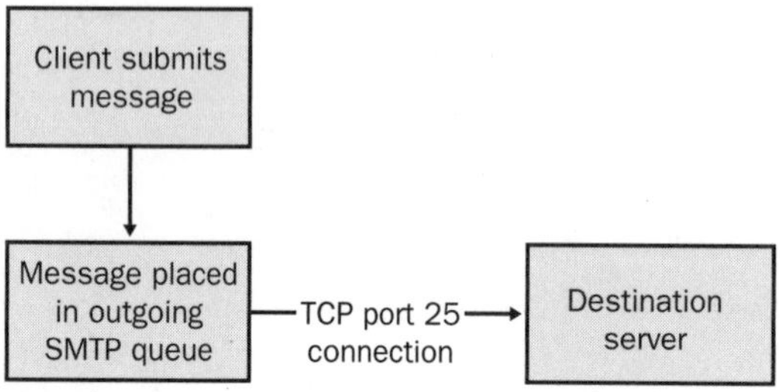

Figure 3-7. *How Exchange Server 2003 routes a message to a recipient in a foreign e-mail system over SMTP.*

Routing Group Topologies

You can connect your routing groups in several ways. The most common topologies are the hub-and-spoke and the modified mesh topology. A hub-and-spoke topology, as the name indicates, has a central routing group to which all other routing groups are connected (Figure 3-8). Administration is easier in a hub-and-spoke topology because there aren't as many RGCs to create and maintain. The one huge disadvantage of this topology is that there is a single point of failure. If either the Exchange Server 2003s or the physical connections into and out of the hub become unavailable for any reason, messaging between routing groups is effectively terminated until the problem can be resolved.

In a mesh topology, each routing group has an RGC configured to every other routing group in the organization. This topology provides redundancy in the event of a link or server failure at any given point; the link state information will reroute the message via another path. However, administration is more difficult since there are more RGCs to create and maintain. Figure 3-9 illustrates a mesh topology.

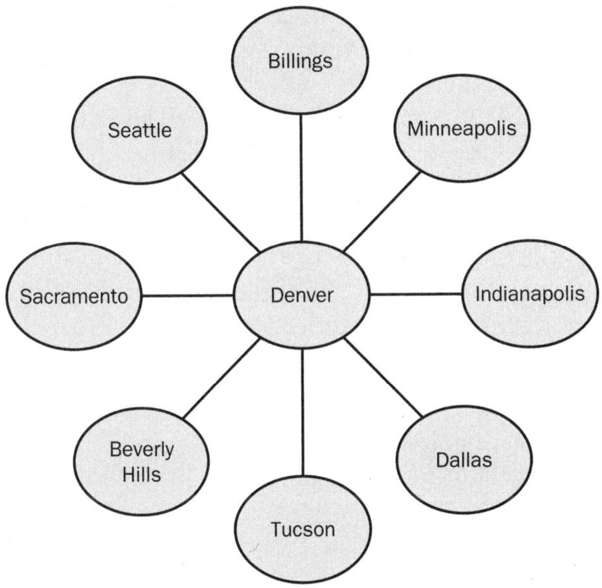

Figure 3-8. *Hub-and-spoke topology.*

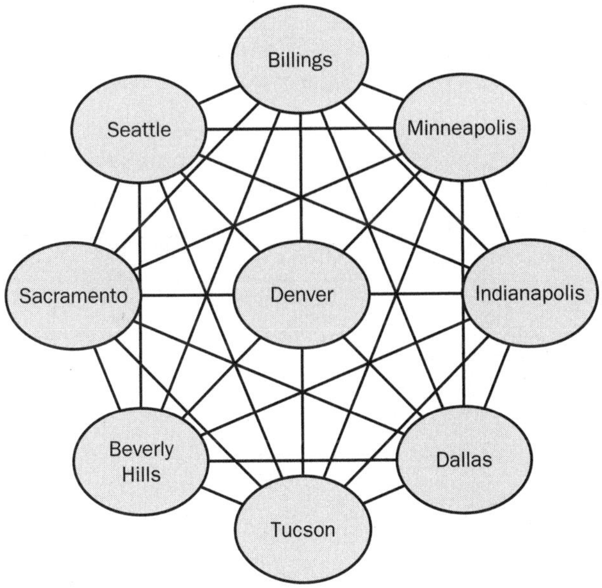

Figure 3-9. *Mesh topology.*

A less common method of connecting routing groups together is the linear topology (Figure 3-10). In this topology, all routing groups are connected by placing them in logical order in a straight line. Although this topology might be the easiest to set up due to the limited number of RGCs needed, it is fraught with potential problems. For instance, there is no redundant routing; therefore, the loss of a link between any two routing groups means that messaging will be hindered across the entire organization. Second, messaging from one end to the other can take longer than is pragmatically good for the organization. In the absence of alternate routes, messaging latency could become a real problem. This topology is the least desirable, and best practice would favor either the hub-and-spoke topology or the modified mesh topology, described next.

The modified mesh topology (Figure 3-11) has multiple routes to each routing group but does not concern itself with making sure that each routing group is connected to every other routing group in the organization. In most cases, a modified mesh topology is the best choice.

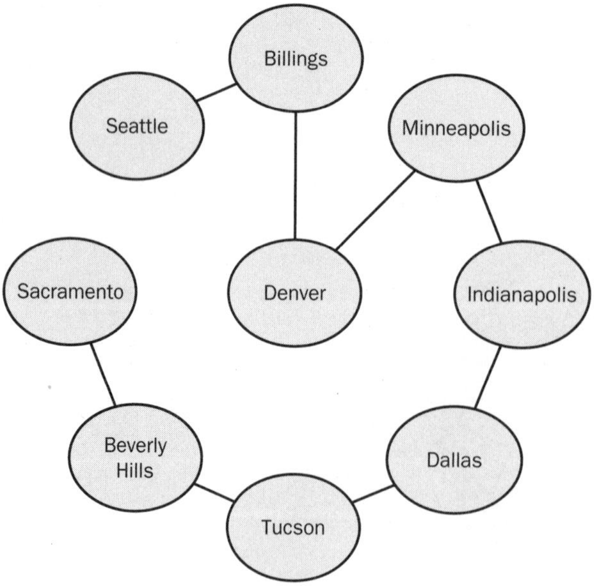

Figure 3-10. *Linear topology.*

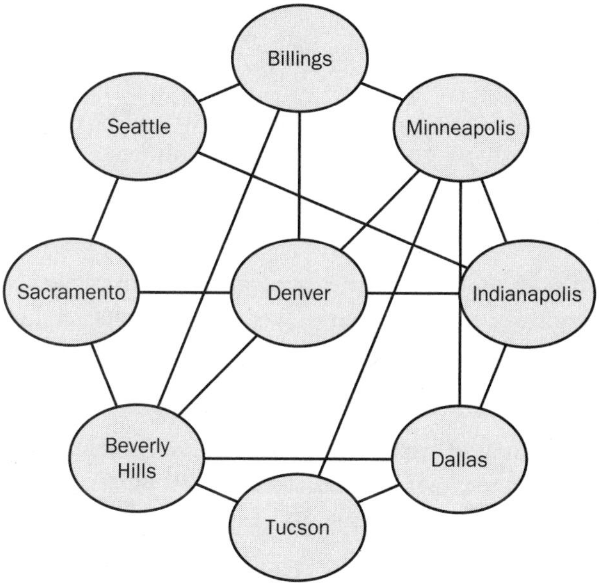

Figure 3-11. *Modified mesh topology.*

Link State Information

The link state protocol is a binary protocol that greatly improves message routing in Exchange 2003 over Exchange 5.5. Message routing in Exchange 5.5 is based on the GWART, which is a table that keeps track of each available connector in the Exchange 5.5 organization, along with the cumulative cost of using those connectors. The GWART is limited in that it contains only next-hop information. It doesn't monitor whether the link is actually up or down. The GWART is located in the Site Addressing object and is referenced by the MTA when determining messaging paths to a destination server.

The link state protocol operates over TCP port 691 within the routing group. In each routing group, one server is configured as the *routing group master* (RGM). The RGM receives link state information and propagates this information to the other servers in the routing group, including the BHS. When one BHS connects to another BHS in a different routing group, the exchange of link state information occurs over TCP port 25, using SMTP. The RGM keeps track of which servers are up and which are down and propagates that information to the RGM in every other routing group.

Link State Algorithm

The *link state algorithm* is new to Exchange Server 2003, although it has been around for many years. First developed by Edsger Dijkstra in 1959, it forms the foundation of the Open Shortest Path First (OSPF) protocol, used extensively by routers today. Although Exchange Server 2003 incorporates routes and costs, it also relies heavily on link state information to route messages between routing groups.

The link state algorithm propagates the state of the messaging system almost in real time to all servers in the organization. There are several advantages to this:

- Each Exchange server can make the best routing decision before sending a message downstream where a link might be down.
- Message "ping-pong" is eliminated because alternate route information is propagated to each Exchange Server 2003.
- Message looping is eliminated.

Given the extensibility of this protocol, it is possible that future versions will be able to interact with network routers to achieve even greater routing capabilities. Networks that collaborate in this way are known as directory-enabled networks.

Link State Concepts

Link state information is rather important when an organization has multiple routing groups with multiple paths between the groups. The RGM maintains the link state information, sending it to and receiving it from the RGMs in other routing groups. The RGM is not necessarily the same server as the BHS, which is the server that you designate to send and receive messages across a given connector to another BHS. The RGM, by default, is the first server installed into the routing group. You can change this in the ESM by right-clicking a server that is not the RGM and selecting Set As Master. You can also manually configure one server to perform both roles.

The RGM ensures that all the servers in its routing group have correct link state information about the availability of the messaging connectors and servers in other groups. In addition, it ensures that other groups have correct information about its servers.

Link state information is propagated among the servers within a group over SMTP. Between groups, however, link state information is replicated from RGM to RGM over TCP port 25. There are only two states for any given link: up or down. The link state information does not include any connection information, such as whether a link is in a retry state. This information is known only to the server involved in the message transfer.

Note Connectors such as the Lotus cc:Mail Connector, the Microsoft Mail Connector, and other EDK-based connectors will always display their link state information in Exchange System as up, even if the link is unavailable.

Link state information is held in memory, not on disk. If the RGM goes down or needs to be rebooted, it will need to replicate in all current link state information from other RGMs in the organization. Since the routing group information is held in the naming partition of Active Directory, the definitions of connectors and costs are also held in Active Directory. The link state protocol references each connector by its globally unique identifier (GUID).

Note When a BHS determines that a link is unavailable, it marks the link as down. It then sends this information to all the servers in its own routing group (over TCP port 691) and to the bridgehead servers in the other routing groups (over TCP port 25). If you are performing a trace for link state data, look for the X-Link2state command verb, which denotes this type of data. The information is sent in chunks labeled "first chunk," "second chunk," and so on, up to "last chunk."

Figures 3-12 and 3-13 illustrate what you'll see in Network Monitor. Figure 3-12 shows the link between Folsom and Minneapolis as DOWN. After you restore the link, you can see that Figure 3-13 shows the link as being UP. However, the X-Link2state command doesn't appear in the description of the packet. You'll need to read the data in each packet to find the X-Link2state command packets.

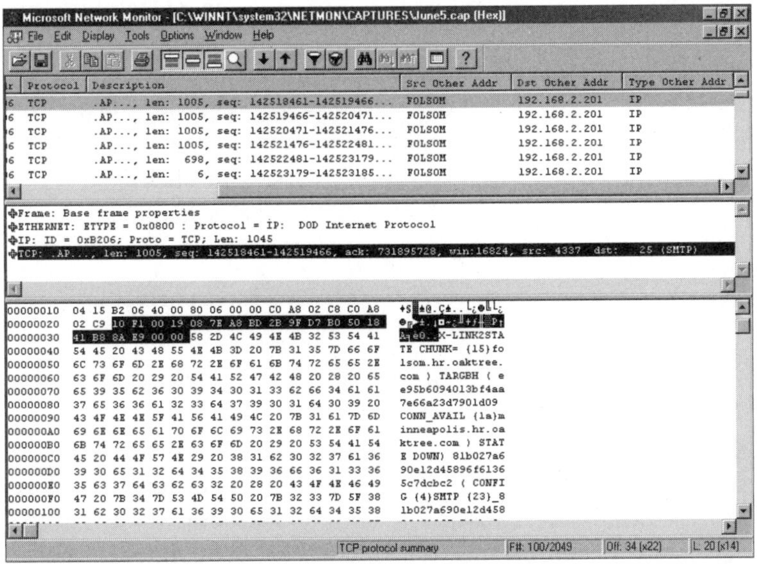

Figure 3-12. *Trace showing link state as DOWN.*

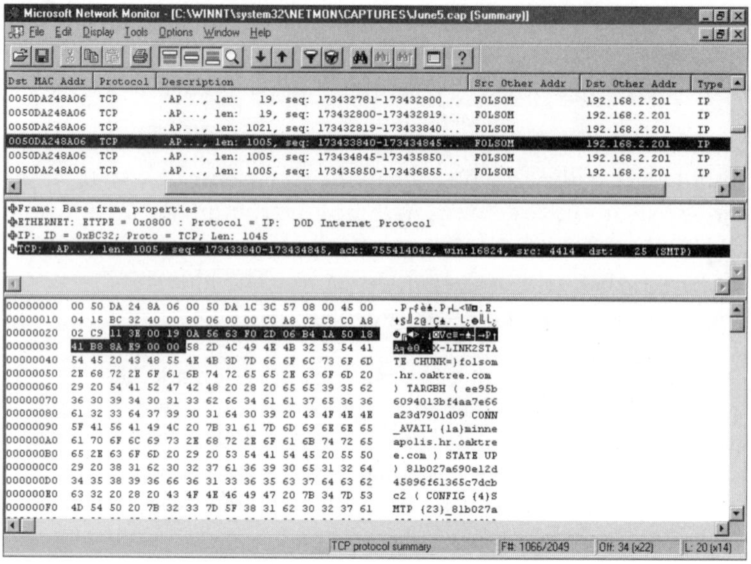

Figure 3-13. *Trace showing link state as UP.*

How Link State Information Works

Let's look at how link state information works and what happens to messages in the event of a failure. Figure 3-14 shows the topology for a network consisting of five routing groups and indicates the connector cost for each connector. We will assume that all connectors are RGCs.

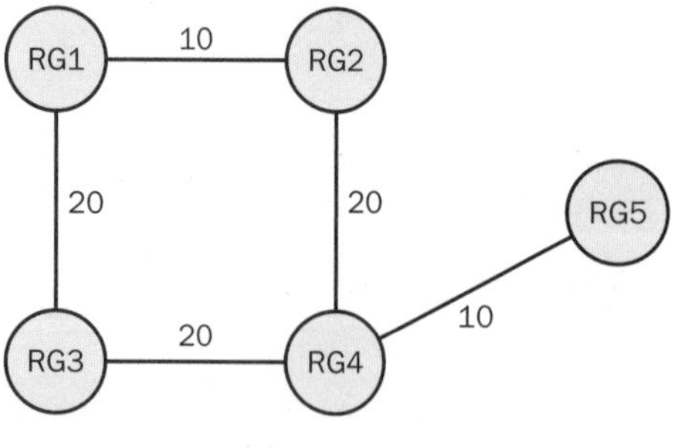

Figure 3-14. *Routing topology for link state example.*

Failure of a Single Link

Normally, a message sent from a server in RG1 to a server in RG5 will pass through RG2 and RG4 because it is the route with the least cost. Let's assume, however, that there is a link failure between RG2 and RG4. In this type of single-line failure, the link state protocol causes the routing processes to carry on as follows:

1. The BHS in RG1 sends the message to the BHS in RG2.
2. The BHS in RG2 attempts to open an SMTP connection to the BHS in RG4. If RG4 contains more than one BHS, the BHS in RG2 attempts to open a connection to each BHS in sequential order.
3. The BHS in RG2 is unable to contact any of the BHSs in RG4 because the physical link is down. Therefore, the BHS in RG2 places the connection into a glitch-retry state. The BHS waits for 60 seconds and then attempts to retransfer the message to the BHS in RG4.
4. After three unsuccessful attempts to connect to RG4, the BHS in RG2 marks the link as down, updates the link state information on the RGM in RG2 over TCP port 691, and makes a call to reroute the message that is sitting in the SMTP out queue.
5. The RGM, upon receiving the notification that the link is down, immediately floods this data to all other Exchange Server 2003s in the routing group.
6. The BHS in RG2 recalculates an alternate route to RG5 via RG1, RG3, and RG4.
7. Before rerouting the message back to RG1, the BHS in RG2 sends the information about the down link to the BHS in RG1. This communication occurs on TCP port 25 and consists of an EHLO command and a X-Link2state command. (For more information about these and other SMTP commands, see Chapter 20.)
8. The BHS in RG1 immediately connects to the RGM in RG1 over TCP port 691 and transfers the information about the down link.
9. The RGM in RG1 immediately floods this data to all other Exchange Server 2003s in the routing group.
10. Using the new link state information, the BHS in RG1 calculates the best route to RG5, through RG3 and RG4.
11. Before routing the message to RG3, the BHS in RG1 propagates the link state information to the BHS in RG3. This process continues until all the routing groups know of the down link between RG2 and RG4.

It is highly likely that subsequent messages will be sent to RG5 from RG1. When this happens, the messages will be routed through the alternate route (RG1-RG3-RG4-RG5) because each server in the organization knows that the primary route is down.

The BHS in RG2 will continue to try to contact the BHS in RG4 every 60 seconds, even if no messages are awaiting transfer. This value is not configurable. When a link becomes operational again, the new link status is replicated to all the other Exchange servers in the organization. The BHS transmits the "up" status to the local RGM, which in turn floods the Exchange Server 2003 servers in the local routing group. Then, similar to the way in which the "down" message was propagated, the "up" message is sent to the rest of the Exchange organization.

Tip As Figure 3-15 shows, by default the SMTP virtual server will check the status of the link after 10 minutes for the first retry interval, after 10 minutes for the second retry interval, after 10 minutes for the third retry interval, and then every 15 minutes for each subsequent check. Reduce these intervals if the link is passing mission-critical information between two routing groups. Each retry interval can be as short as 1 minute.

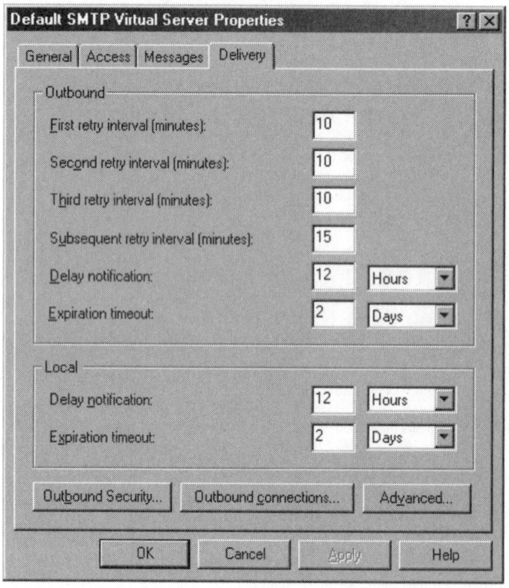

Figure 3-15. *Default retry intervals for SMTP virtual server.*

Note In both this example and the next example on multiple link failures, link state information might appear to be transmitted only immediately ahead of a user-initiated message. This is not the case. Link state information is always transmitted immediately, independently of whether other messages need to be transmitted. We mention that the link state information is transmitted ahead of a user's message to indicate the importance that Exchange Server 2003 places on replicating link state information to all its servers. There is no necessary connection or correlation between the transfer of a user-initiated message and the sending of a link state message to another routing group master.

Failure of Multiple Links

If more than one link fails at any given time, the link state protocol ensures that the message doesn't bounce back and forth between routing groups in a continual attempt to find an open message path. Let's look again at the example of a server in RG1 attempting to send a message to a server in RG5. This time, however, let's assume that both the link between RG2 and RG4 and the one between RG3 and RG 4 is unavailable. RG1 sends a message to RG2, and RG2 returns the message to RG1, as it did in our single-link-failure scenario. Here are the steps that the link state protocol will then perform:

1. The BHS in RG1 opens a connection to the BHS in RG3. Before sending the message, however, it propagates the down status of the link between RG2 and RG4 to the BHS in RG3. The BHS in RG3 forwards this information to the RGM, which floods the other servers in the routing group with this information.
2. Then the BHS in RG1 sends the message to the BHS in RG3. The BHS in RG3 sees that the message is intended for RG5, attempts to open a connection to the BHS server in RG4, and fails. The BHS server marks the link as being in the glitch-retry state and retries three times at 60-second intervals.
3. If it cannot establish a connection, it marks the link as down and notifies the RGM, which in turn floods the other servers in the routing group with this new information.
4. The BHS in RG3 attempts to calculate a new route for the message, given the new information. With both the link between RG2 and RG4 and the link between RG3 and RG4 in the down state, the cost of routing a message to RG5 becomes Infinite.
5. Once the cost has been calculated as Infinite, the message remains in the queue of the BHS in RG3, which makes calls to routing, based on the schedule you have configured on the Delivery tab in the property sheet for the SMTP virtual server, to see whether either link has become available.
6. When a link becomes available, the message is rerouted as appropriate. If the message stays in the queue for more than 48 hours, it is returned to the sender in RG1 as a non-delivery report (NDR).

If additional messages are sent to RG5 from RG1 while both links are down, the messages remain queued at the BHS in RG1 until one of the links becomes available and a fully functioning route can be established. This is the best place for the messages to remain queued.

Note The 48-hour time period is the default length of time for messages to sit in a queue before an NDR is generated and sent back to the user in Exchange Server 2003. You can configure this value on the Delivery tab of the property sheet for the SMTP virtual server.

Unchanging Link State

If no alternate path exists for a link to another routing group and the physical link goes down, Exchange 2003 will not change the link's state to DOWN. This functionality is a change from Exchange 2000 and was implemented to enhance performance by reducing unnecessary link state propagation traffic on your network.

Hence, if you have two routing groups connected by a single physical link and that link goes down, the link state table will continue to show the link as UP and will allow e-mail to be queued for that link. Once the link becomes available, mail will flow normally between the two sites.

Oscillating Link State Information

Sometimes, a physical link can go up and down during maintenance or repair operations. In Exchange 2000, each change in the physical link triggered a change in the link state information, which led to the flooding of link state information multiple times in the Exchange environment.

This tendency to flood has been resolved in Exchange 2003. If a link is oscillating between up and down, Exchange 2003 will leave the link in the UP state. Microsoft feels that leaving an oscillating connector up is better than continually changing the link state, which floods the network with link state packets at each change. This reduces the amount of link state traffic that is replicated between the servers.

Failure of a Routing Group Master

If the RGM goes offline, a new master is not automatically nominated. Therefore, the link state information held by other servers in the routing group could, over time, become increasingly antiquated. If the RGM will be down for a period of time, it is very important that a new RGM be manually configured. This action will ensure that other servers in the routing group have up-to-date link state information.

To manually configure a server to become the RGM, navigate to the routing group in which the server resides, highlight the Members folder for the server, right-click the server in the details pane, and choose Set As Master. Figure 3-16 illustrates this process.

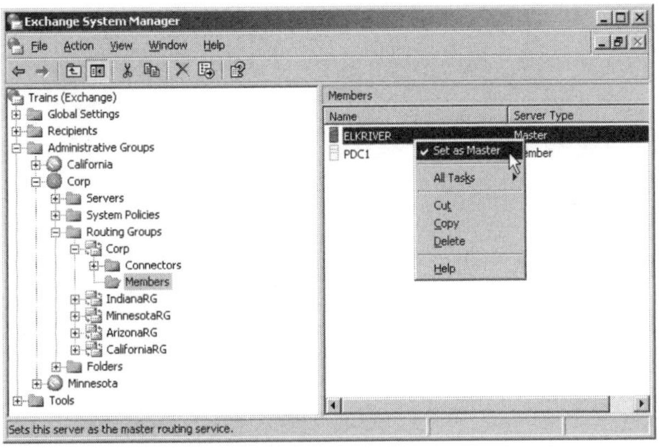

Figure 3-16. *Selecting a routing group master in Exchange System Manager.*

Summary

In this chapter, you learned that Exchange Server 2003 improves upon the site concept in Exchange Server 5.5 by introducing routing groups and link state information. SMTP, which is now the default protocol for message transfer, is more tolerant of higher latency and lower bandwidths than an RPC connection, and hence has several advantages, which were outlined in this chapter. You also saw how link state information works after certain kinds of failures. The next chapter introduces you to the Active Directory Connector and provides an overview of how Exchange Server 2003 integrates with Microsoft Windows 2000 and Microsoft Internet Information Services.

Chapter 4

Understanding Windows Server 2003 Integration

In the last two chapters, you learned about the storage and routing architectures in Microsoft Exchange Server 2003. This chapter builds on that knowledge by describing how Exchange Server 2003 integrates with Microsoft Windows Server 2003 and how it uses the services in Windows Server 2003 to its advantage. We'll begin with a brief overview of the Windows Server 2003 Active Directory directory service and then finish the chapter by describing how Exchange Server 2003 uses Active Directory and discussing some of the more important Internet information protocols.

Note In various parts of this chapter, we will compare Exchange 2003 Server with Exchange 5.5 Server because at the time of this writing, a large Exchange 5.5 install base remains, and many users will be upgrading directly to Exchange 2003 Server, bypassing Exchange Server 2000. If you've been running Exchange 2000 Server, you can skip those parts that discuss Exchange 5.5.

Brief Overview of Active Directory

A full explanation of Active Directory is outside the scope of this book but a brief overview is warranted. Because Exchange Server 2003 is heavily dependent on the underlying network operating system, it is important to have a basic understanding of Windows Server 2003 Active Directory.

More Info For a more thorough discussion of Active Directory and the other concepts discussed in this chapter, see *Microsoft Windows Server 2003 Administrator's Companion*, by Charlie Russel, Sharon Crawford, and Jason Gerend (Microsoft Press).

Directory Structure in Active Directory

Before we discuss what Active Directory is, you should first understand what a directory is. As an analogy, think of a generic file system. Perhaps in this file system, you have a C: drive, and on that drive, you have a root folder named Memos. Under C:\Memos, you have a folder for each of the 12 months of the year, so you would find a folder in the structure named July. Under C:\Memos\July, you have a folder named Departments; the full pathname to Departments is C:\Memos\July\Departments. This is a hierarchy of folders in a file system.

A directory is no different from a folder list, except that the hierarchy consists not of folders but of objects. An *object* is an entity that is described by a distinct, named set of attributes. Instead of using Windows Explorer to search through this hierarchy of objects, we'll be using a protocol designed to search a directory, called the Lightweight Directory Access Protocol (LDAP).

> **Note** The original protocol for accessing a directory was called Directory Access Protocol (DAP), but it had a high overhead and tended to be slow. Lightweight Directory Access Protocol (LDAP) is an improved version that is faster and requires less overhead. For more information about the LDAP protocol, see Chapter 20, "Supporting Internet Protocols and SMTP."

With Active Directory, Microsoft has made significant improvements to the directory concept, such as dynamic DNS. The "Active" in Active Directory describes the flexibility and extensibility that has been built into Microsoft's directory service.

Logical Structure of Active Directory

The components that form the logical structure of Active Directory include domains, organizational units, trees, and forests.

Domains

A *domain* is the core unit in Active Directory and is made up of a collection of computers that share a common directory database. The computers that share this common directory database are called domain controllers. A domain controller is a Windows Server 2003 server that has Active Directory installed. It is able to authenticate users for its own domain. Each domain controller holds a complete replica of the domain naming partition for the domain to which it belongs and a complete replica of the configuration and schema naming partitions for the forest. Dcpromo.exe is the utility used to promote a Windows Server 2003 server to a domain controller. We'll discuss these partitions later in this chapter.

All Active Directory domain names are identified by a DNS name as well as by a NetBIOS name. The following is an example of the two types of names:

DNS-style domain name: sample.microsoft.com
NetBIOS name: SAMPLE

Generally, the NetBIOS name is the same as the first naming component in the DNS name. However, a NetBIOS name can be only 15 characters in length, whereas each name in the DNS naming convention can have up to 64 characters. During installation, both names can be configured to meet your needs. In the initial release of Windows Server 2003, Active Directory names cannot be changed.

The domain is also a security boundary in Active Directory. Administrators in a domain have the permissions and rights to perform administrative functions in that domain. However, since each domain has its own security, administrators must be given explicit permissions to perform administrative tasks in other domains. Members of the Enterprise Admins group have rights to perform administrative tasks in all domains across the forest. Hence, you can have domain administrators and a higher level of administration from the Enterprise administrators.

A Windows Server 2003 Active Directory domain can be in either mixed mode or native mode. The default installation is mixed mode. In mixed mode, a Windows Server 2003 domain controller acts like a Microsoft Windows NT 4 domain controller. Active Directory domains in mixed mode have the same limitations on the security accounts database as Windows NT 4 domain controllers. For example, in mixed mode, the size of the directory is limited to 40,000 objects, the same restriction imposed by Windows NT 4. These limitations allow Windows NT 4 backup domain controllers to exist on the network and connect to and synchronize with the Windows Server 2003 domain controllers.

The PDC Emulator is one of the five Flexible Single Master Operation (FSMO) roles that makes the Windows Server 2003 look like a Windows NT 4 PDC. Only one Windows Server 2003 domain controller can act as the PDC Emulator. By default, the PDC Emulator role, like all other FSMO roles, is installed on one domain controller in each domain, by default, on the first domain controller of each domain. (We will discuss the FSMO roles in just a moment.) To run Windows Server 2003 in native mode, you must not have any reason or desire to connect to a Windows NT 4 backup domain controller. In other words, when you decide to run Windows Server 2003 in native mode, you won't be able to use a Windows NT backup domain controller again on your network, and no applications running on your network will be able to use Windows NT to operate. The switch to native mode is a one-time, one-way switch and is irreversible. Native mode allows your Windows Server 2003 domain controllers to have millions of objects per domain. In addition, native mode allows the nesting of groups, something that is advantageous if you anticipate large distribution groups in Exchange Server 2003.

A Windows Server 2003 network running in native mode can accommodate Windows NT 4 stand-alone and member servers. Windows NT 4 workstations must be upgraded to Windows Server 2003 Professional to participate in Active Directory, or you must install the Directory Service Client. Windows Server 2003 implements Active Directory in a multimaster model because objects in Active Directory can be modified on any domain controller, which accounts for the emphasis on directory replication between domain controllers. However, some roles are either too sensitive to security issues or too impractical to perform in a multimaster model because of potential conflicts that could arise from the replication traffic. An understanding of these roles is important; if a domain controller that is performing a particular role becomes unavailable, the function it performed will not be available in Active Directory. These roles are schema master, domain naming master, relative identifier master, PDC emulator, and infrastructure master.

Schema Master The *schema* is the set of object classes (such as users and groups) and their attributes (such as full name and phone number) that form Active Directory. The schema master controls all aspects of updates and modifications to the schema. To update the schema, you must have access to the schema master. There can be only one schema master in the forest at any given time.

Domain Naming Master The domain naming master controls the addition and removal of domains in the forest. This is the only domain controller from which you can create or delete a domain. There can be only one domain naming master in the forest at any given time.

Relative Identifier Master The relative identifier (RID) master allocates sequences of RIDs to each of the domain controllers in its domain. Whereas the schema master and domain naming master perform forestwide functions, one RID master is assigned per domain. Since each domain controller can create objects in Active Directory, the RID master allocates to each domain controller a pool of 500 RIDs from which to draw when creating the object. When a domain controller has used more than 400 RIDs, the RID master gives it another batch of 500 RIDs.

Whenever a new user, group, or computer object is created, the object inherits the security identifier (SID) of the domain. Appended to the end of the domain SID is the RID, which makes up the unique SID for the object. In addition, when an object is moved from one domain to another, its SID changes, because it receives a new SID (made up of both the domain SID and the RID) in the destination domain. By allowing only the RID master to move objects between domains, Windows Server 2003 ensures SID uniqueness, even across domains. Objects maintain a SID history for security access to resources.

PDC Emulator Each domain in the forest must have one domain controller that acts as the PDC emulator. If Active Directory is running in mixed mode with Windows NT 4 domain controllers on the same network, the PDC emulator is responsible for synchronizing password changes and security account updates between the Windows NT 4 servers and the Windows Server 2003 servers. Moreover, the PDC emulator appears to downlevel clients, such as Windows 95, Windows 98, and Windows NT 4, as the PDC of the domain. It functions as the domain master browser, is responsible for replication services to the BDCs, and performs directory writes to the Windows NT 4 domain security database.

In native mode, the PDC emulator receives the urgent updates to the Active Directory security accounts database, such as password changes and account lockout modifications. These urgent changes to user accounts are immediately replicated to the PDC emulator, no matter where they are changed in the domain. If a logon authentication fails at a domain controller, the credentials are first passed to the PDC emulator for authentication before the logon request is rejected.

Infrastructure Master The infrastructure master is responsible for tracking group-to-user references whenever the user and the group are not members of the same domain. The object that resides in the remote domain is referenced by its GUID and SID. If an object is moved from one domain to another, it receives a new SID, and the infrastructure master replicates these changes to other infrastructure masters in other domains.

Organizational Units

An *organizational unit* (OU) is a container object that is used to organize other objects within a domain. An OU can contain user accounts, printers, groups, computers, and other OUs.

> **More Info** The design of Active Directory is based on the X.500 standard, which can be procured from *www.itu.org*. The standard is rather short—around 9 pages—but reading it will give you a great background for understanding Active Directory and, for that matter, Novell Directory Services.

OUs are strictly for administrative purposes and convenience. They are transparent to the user and have no bearing on the user's ability to access network resources. OUs can be used to create departmental or geographical boundaries. They can also be used to delegate administrative authority to users for particular tasks. For instance, you can create an OU for all of your printers and then assign full control over the printers to your printer administrator.

OUs can also be used to limit administrative control. For instance, you can give your help desk support personnel the permission to change the password on all user objects in an OU without giving them permissions to modify any other attributes of the user object, such as group membership or names.

Because an Active Directory domain can hold millions of objects, upgrading to Windows Server 2003 allows companies to convert from a multiple-domain model to a single-domain model and then use organizational units to delegate administrative control over resources.

Trees and Forests

The first Windows Server 2003 domain that you create is the root domain, which contains the configuration and schema for the forest. You add additional domains to the root domain to form the tree. As Figure 4-1 illustrates, a *tree* is a hierarchical grouping of Windows Server 2003 domains that share a contiguous namespace. A contiguous namespace is one that uses the same root name when naming additional domains in the tree.

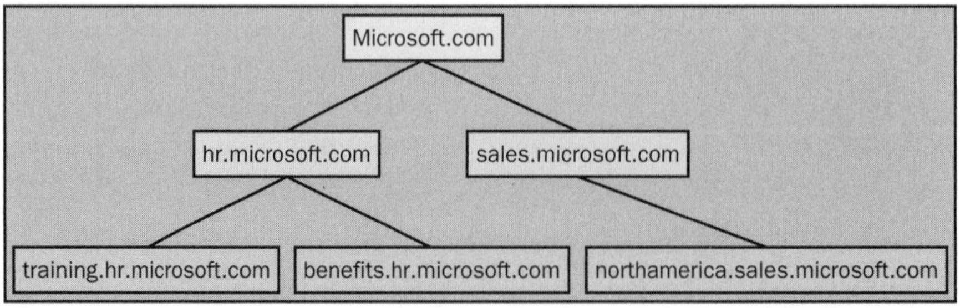

Figure 4-1. *Fictitious tree of Microsoft.com.*

A collection of trees that do not share a contiguous namespace can be placed in the same forest. They then share a common configuration, schema, and Global Catalog (GC). By default, the name of the root domain becomes the name of the forest, even though other trees will not share the same name as the root domain.

Even though they don't share the same name, transitive trust relationships are automatically established between the root domain servers in each tree, as long as they are members of the same forest. Figure 4-2 shows two trees, Microsoft.com and trainsbydave.com, in the same forest.

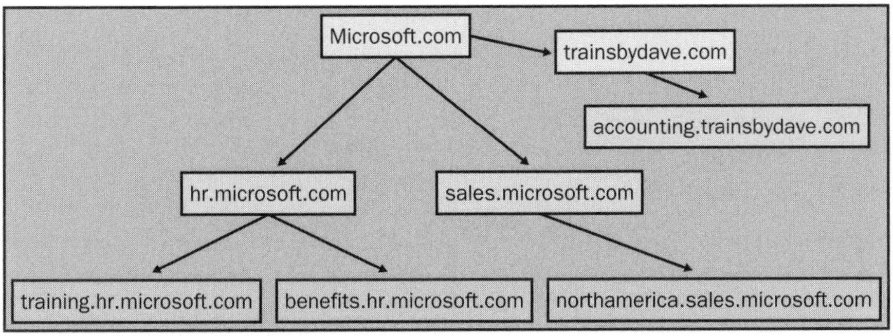

Figure 4-2. *Forest consisting of Microsoft.com and trainsbydave.com.*

The schema and configuration partitions for Active Directory are replicated to all domain controllers in each domain. Whereas a domain represents a boundary for security and the logical grouping of objects, a forest represents the boundary for Active Directory and the Exchange 2000 organization.

In addition, other domain names cannot be represented above the first domain name. For instance, if your root domain name is hr.trainsbydave.com, you can never install a domain named trainsbydave.com in the same forest. You can join other domain names to the forest, such as microsoft.com, as long as they are in a different namespace.

Groups

Windows Server 2003 enhances the group structure of Windows NT 4. Groups are used to reduce administrative effort and to enable the management of many user accounts simultaneously. Windows Server 2003 uses groups to reduce the number of objects that require direct administration.

There are basically two kinds of groups in Windows Server 2003. Each has its own advantages and restrictions that you must take into account when using them. Exchange Server 2003 uses both kinds of groups from Windows Server 2003:

- **Security groups** Security groups host security principles within Active Directory. They are used to group users or computers for the purpose of reducing the points of administration and providing permissions to network resources.
- **Distribution groups** Distribution groups are meant to perform distribution functions. In cooperation with Exchange Server 2003, these groups are the replacement for distribution lists in Exchange 5.5. You cannot use them to assign permissions to network resources.

Global Groups Global groups, in mixed mode, can contain users only from the domain in which they are hosted. In native mode, they can contain users and global groups from the local domain in which they were created. However, they can be used to assign permissions to resources in any domain. Global groups can contain users, computers, and global groups from the local domain. They can be members of any other type of group.

Typically, you'll use global groups for administering user membership that has permissions to a network resource. The group itself is replicated as part of the Global Catalog, but its membership is not. This restriction means that adding user accounts to or removing user accounts from a global group will not trigger a new replication of the Global Catalog. Global groups can be converted to universal groups (discussed shortly) as long as the global groups do not contain other global groups and the domain is in native mode.

Domain Local Groups Domain local groups in native mode can contain other domain local groups, users, global groups, and universal groups from any domain in the forest, but they can be granted permissions only in the domain in which they reside. In mixed mode, they can contain only user and global group accounts.

You'll grant permissions to domain local groups only for objects in the local domain. The existence of the domain local group is replicated to the Global Catalog server, but its membership is not replicated. Domain local groups are flexible in that you can use any other security principle inside the domain local group (when running in native mode) to reduce administrative effort. You can convert a domain local group to a universal group in native mode as long as it does not contain other domain local groups.

Universal Groups Universal groups can contain users, global groups, and other universal groups from any Windows Server 2003 domain in the forest. The domain must be operating in native mode to create security groups with universal scope. You can grant permissions to resources anywhere in the forest to a universal group.

Universal group membership must be determined at the time of logon. Because the scope of the universal group is universal, this group is propagated through the Global Catalog. Hence, not only is the group itself propagated in the Global Catalog, but its membership is propagated as well. A universal group with a large membership will generate additional replication overhead if the membership changes. Universal groups as security groups are available only in native mode. Table 4-1 summarizes group membership rules.

Table 4-1. Comparison of various types of groups

Group Scope	In Mixed Mode Can Contain	In Native Mode Can Contain	Can Be a Member Of	Can Be Granted Permissions For
Domain local	User accounts and global groups from any domain	User accounts, global groups, and universal groups from any domain in the forest, and domain local groups from the same domain	Domain local groups in the same domain	The domain in which the domain local group exists
Global	User accounts	User accounts and global groups from the same domain	Universal and domain local groups in any domain and global groups in the same domain	All domains in the forest
Universal	Not applicable	User accounts, global groups, and other universal groups from any domain in the forest	Domain local and universal groups in any domain	All domains in the forest

Other Active Directory Components

Active Directory is a complex system that includes far more than the basic logical structure just described. This section highlights several other components that play a critical role within Active Directory.

Naming Partitions

You can think of Active Directory as being divided into three distinct directories, or partitions: the domain partition, the configuration partition, and the schema partition. Each partition is a self-contained section of Active Directory that can have its own properties, such as replication configuration and permissions structure. A Windows Server 2003 domain controller will always hold three naming partitions in its database file (Ntds.dit). These are the default LDAP paths for these partitions:

- Configuration: cn=configuration,dc=sales,dc=microsoft,dc=com
- Schema: cn=schema,cn=configuration,dc=sales,dc=microsoft,dc=com
- Domain: dc=sales,dc=microsoft,dc=com

In a multidomain structure, domain controllers belong to different domains. These servers share a common configuration and schema naming partition but have a unique domain naming partition. Exchange Server 2003 stores most of its information in the configuration naming partition. Because this partition is replicated throughout the forest, global administration is easier than in Exchange 5.5.

Sites

A *site* within Active Directory is a collection of Internet protocol (IP) subnets that enjoy permanent, high-bandwidth connectivity. Active Directory assumes that all computers in the same site have permanent, high-speed connectivity with one another. Sites tend to map to the physical structure of your network: slow WAN links will be considered outside your sites, and high-speed links will form your sites.

Site and domain topologies are not dependent upon each other; a single domain can span multiple sites, or multiple domains can be located in a single site. Since the bandwidth between sites is assumed to be slow or unreliable, it stands to reason that some type of connector is needed to connect the sites. That connector is called a site link.

Site links are built manually by the administrator and form the physical topology of the network. To create replication paths between domain controllers across the site links (as well as between domain controllers within the same site), Windows Server 2003 employs the knowledge consistency checker (KCC), which runs automatically but can be configured manually, if necessary. The KCC creates *connection objects* on each domain controller in the configuration naming partition; these connection objects form the overall replication topology over which Active Directory information can be replicated. The KCC is a service that runs on each domain controller to create the connection objects for that domain controller.

Location Service Providers

In Windows NT 4, to find a service such as the server service on a domain controller, the client needs to contact the Windows Internet Name Service (WINS) to obtain the IP address of the server offering that service. (WINS offers dynamic mapping of NetBIOS names to IP addresses.) In Windows Server 2003, DNS takes on this role and helps the client find the services it needs on the network. Dynamic DNS is supplied with Windows Server 2003 and is a standard part of the Active Directory installation. With dynamic DNS, clients query DNS service (SRV) records to locate services on the network.

Global Catalog Servers

In a multidomain environment, it is reasonable to assume that some users will need access to objects outside of their own domains. For instance, a user in domain A might need access to a color printer located in domain B. Since domain controllers maintain only a replica of objects in their own domain, a special service is needed in the forest to gain access to objects located in remote domains. The Global Catalog server performs this function. This server holds a replica of all objects in the forest, with a limited set of attributes for those objects. The schema defines which attributes are listed for each object in the Global Catalog. The Global Catalog is not a separate file; it is instead held inside the NTDS.DIT file. The GC will be roughly 40 percent of the size of your active directory, or the size of the your NTDS.DIT file on a non-GC domain controller.

> **Tip** By default, there is only one Global Catalog server in the entire forest, and that is the first domain controller installed in the first domain of the first tree. All other Global Catalog servers need to be configured manually. You can do this by opening the Active Directory Sites And Services snap-in, navigating to the NTDS settings on the server you want to install this service on, right-clicking NTDS Settings, choosing Properties, and selecting the Global Catalog Server check box.

In addition to users needing access to services outside their domain, some applications need access to a forestwide listing of objects. Exchange Server 2003 is one of those applications. For instance, a user might want to browse the Global Address List, which is generated by the Global Catalog server. The Global Catalog server gathers each mail-enabled object into a list and returns this list to the user inside the address book interface.

Even in a single-domain environment, Exchange clients are referred to the Global Catalog server for address book lookups. In this scenario, the default is to refer all those lookups to the root domain controller. The best practice is to create two or more Global Catalog servers for redundancy and scalability.

A Global Catalog server is represented as an SRV record in the DNS database. There are two ways to locate the Global Catalog server: by service and by both service and site name. To find a domain controller without specifying the site name, you would specify a node path of ._tcp._gc._msdcs.*domain*. The entry name would be _LDAP, and the entry data would be [0][100][3268] *servername.domain*. Figure 4-3 illustrates what this entry looks like in the DNS snap-in.

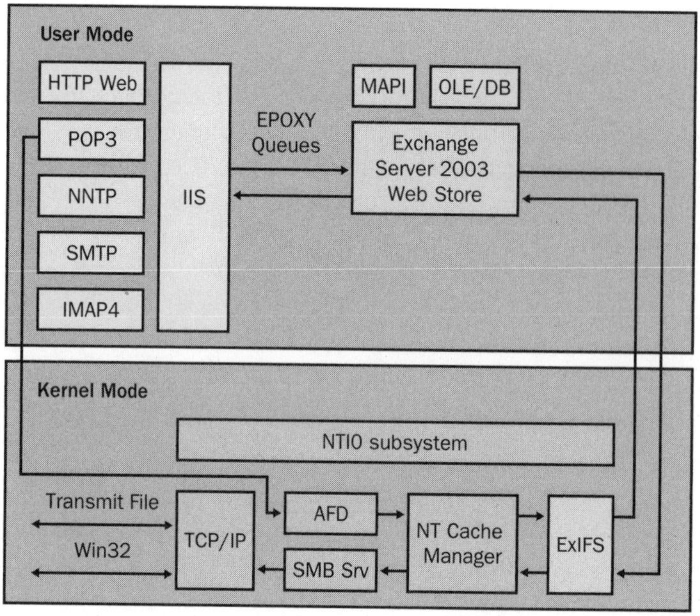

Figure 4-3. *DNS entry for Global Catalog services on indianapolis.trainsbydave.com.*

It is helpful to note that a Global Catalog server will pass back different attributes depending on the TCP port used for the query. For instance, a query to port 389 (the default LDAP port) allows a client to search for objects only within the home domain, with the full set of attributes for the object being returned. In contrast, a query over port 3268 allows a client to search for domain objects from all domains in the forest, including the home domain of the Global Catalog server. However, a query over this port returns only a subset of the attributes available, even if the object is in the home domain of the Global Catalog server.

Client Authentication

When a client attempts to log on to the domain, it queries DNS SRV records to locate a domain controller. DNS attempts to match the client's IP address to an Active Directory site and then returns a list of domain controllers that can authenticate the client. The client chooses a domain controller at random from the list and then pings it before sending the logon request. In native mode, the authenticating domain controller passes the client's credentials to the local Global Catalog server so that the Global Catalog can enumerate universal security group access.

Active Directory Names

Both users and applications are affected by the naming conventions that a directory uses. To locate a network resource, you'll need to know its name or one of its properties. Active Directory supports many naming schemes for the different formats that can access Active Directory.

Distinguished Name

Each object in the directory has a *distinguished name* (DN) that identifies where the object resides in the overall object hierarchy. For example,

cn=benglish,cn=users,dc=microsoft,dc=com

would indicate that the user object Benglish is in the Users container that is located in the microsoft.com domain. If the Benglish object is moved to another container, its DN will change to reflect its new position in the hierarchy. Distinguished names are guaranteed to be unique in the forest. You cannot have two objects with the same distinguished name.

Relative Distinguished Name

The *relative distinguished name* of an object is the part of the distinguished name that is an attribute of the object. In the former example, the relative distinguished name of the Benglish object is Benglish. The relative distinguished name of the parent organizational unit is Users. Active Directory will not allow two objects with the same relative distinguished name under the same parent container.

User Principal Name

The *user principal name* that is generated for each object is in the form username@DNSdomainname. Users can log on with their user principal name, and an administrator can define suffixes for user principal names if desired. User principal names are required to be unique, but Active Directory does not enforce this requirement. It's best, however, to formulate a naming convention that avoids duplicate user principal names.

Globally Unique Identifier

Some applications require that an object be referred to by an identifier that remains constant. This is achieved by adding an attribute called the *globally unique identifier* (GUID), a 128-bit number that is guaranteed to be unique. A GUID is assigned to an object when it is created, and it will never change, even if the object is moved between containers in the same domain.

Exchange Server 2003 and Active Directory

Exchange 5.5 Server employed a dedicated directory that provided a central location for the organization's objects, such as addresses, mailboxes, distribution lists, and public folders. This directory service also managed object replication among the Exchange 5.5 servers.

Exchange Server 2003 no longer uses a dedicated directory. Instead, it integrates with the Windows Server 2003 Active Directory service. Integration with Windows Server 2003 provides several benefits, including the following:

- **Centralized object management** Administration is unified for Exchange Server 2003 and Windows Server 2003. Directory objects can be managed from one location, with one management tool, and by one team.
- **Simplified security management** Exchange Server 2003 uses the security features of Windows Server 2003, such as the discretionary access control list (DACL). Changes to security principles (such as user or group accounts) apply to data stored in both Exchange 2003 and Windows Server 2003 file shares.
- **Simplified creation of distribution lists** Exchange Server 2003 automatically uses Windows Server 2003 security groups as distribution lists, eliminating the need to create a security group for each department and a corresponding distribution group for the same department. Distribution groups can be created in those instances when e-mail distribution is the only desired function of the group.
- **Easier access to directory information** LDAP is now the native access protocol for directory information. In earlier versions of Exchange, lookups in the directory were conducted over the Named Service Provider Interface (NSPI).

Storing Exchange 2003 Data in Active Directory

Earlier we mentioned that Active Directory is divided into three naming partitions: configuration, schema, and domain. In this section, we'll discuss how Exchange Server 2003 uses each of these partitions and which kind of data is stored in them.

Domain Naming Partition

In the domain naming partition, all domain objects for Exchange 2003 are stored and replicated to every domain controller in the domain. Recipient objects, including users, contacts, and groups, are stored in this partition.

Exchange Server 2003 exploits Active Directory by adding attributes to user, group and contact objects for messaging purposes. Because Exchange Server 2003 uses the same database as Windows Server 2003, some terminology has changed from Exchange 5.5 Server. Table 4-2 lists directory objects in Exchange 5.5 Server and their Active Directory equivalents, and Figure 4-4 shows the dialog box used to mail-enable a user object.

Table 4-2. Comparison of Exchange 5.5 and Exchange 2003 directory terminology

Exchange 5.5 Directory Object	Equivalent Active Directory Object	Comments
Mailbox	Mailbox-enabled user	Mailbox-enabled users are security principles in Active Directory that can send and receive messages.
No direct correlation with a 5.5 object	Mail-enabled user	Mail-enabled users are those who can logon to your domain with a user account in your domain, but whose e-mail is sent to an external address. This type of user is best suited for long-term contractors who need access to resources on your network but who need to send and receive e-mail through their employer's e-mail system.
Custom recipient	Mail-enabled contact	All mail-enabled contacts have an SMTP address. These are always users outside your Exchange organization.
Distribution list	Mail-enabled group	Domain local, global, and universal groups can be mail enabled.
Public folder	Public folder	Mail-enabled public folders can be created only in the Exchange System snap-in or the Active Directory Connector.

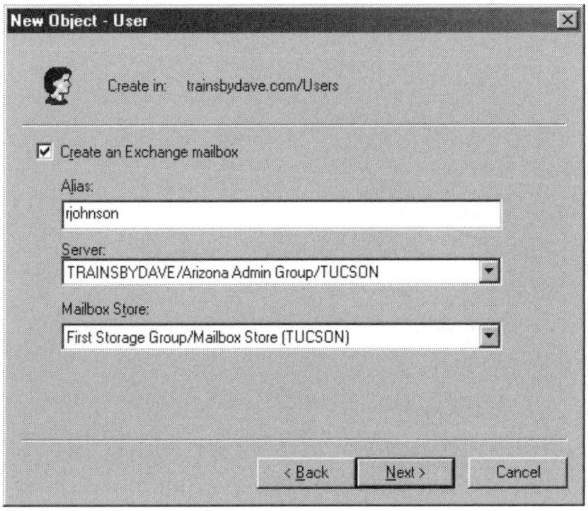

Figure 4-4. *Mail-enabling a user object.*

Designing a Group Implementation Strategy Previous versions of Exchange use a distribution list to send the same message to a large number of recipients. Exchange 2003 uses groups for this function. Any user accounts that are placed inside the group will receive the message. In Windows Server 2003 native mode, groups can be nested inside of groups, effectively creating a multitiered distribution list. The two types of groups you will use most often for large distribution of a message are global and universal.

If you want to optimize the universal security groups that have been set up in Active Directory, you can mail-enable the groups (Figure 4-5) and then add an SMTP e-mail alias (Figure 4-6). Once completed, the group will be visible in the Global Address List (Figure 4-7). To mail-enable a group, right-click the group, choose Exchange Tasks, and then follow the prompts in the Exchange Task Wizard.

The largest downside to universal groups is that membership is fully replicated to each Global Catalog server, which means that replication traffic occurs whenever a Universal Group's membership changes. Therefore, it is best to populate a universal group with other global groups so that when membership changes in the global group, the universal group is not changed and traffic is not replicated.

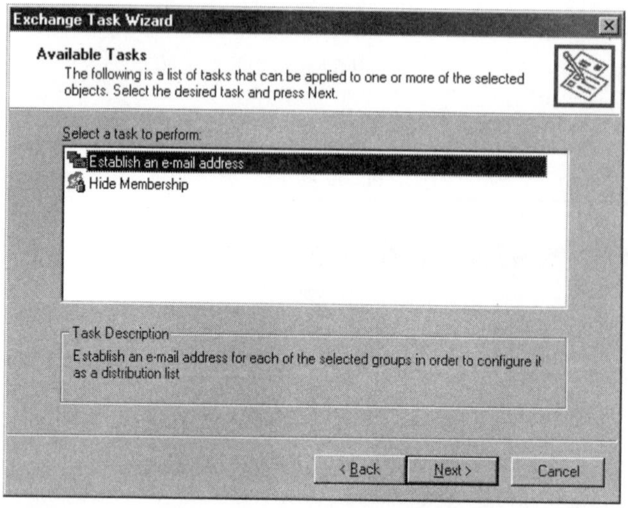

Figure 4-5. *Mail-enabling a group using the Exchange Task Wizard.*

Global groups can also be mail-enabled for message distribution. If you choose not to use universal groups, you can mail-enable global groups. Membership for a global group is not promoted to the Global Catalog server, which presents some issues to consider when working in a multidomain environment.

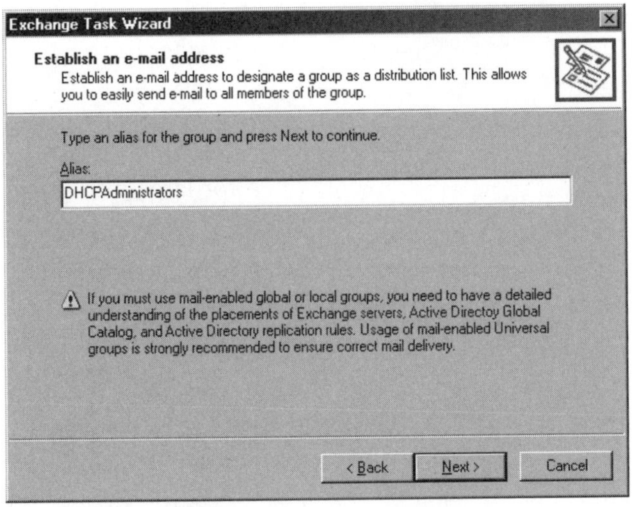

Figure 4-6. *Creating an SMTP alias in the Exchange Task Wizard.*

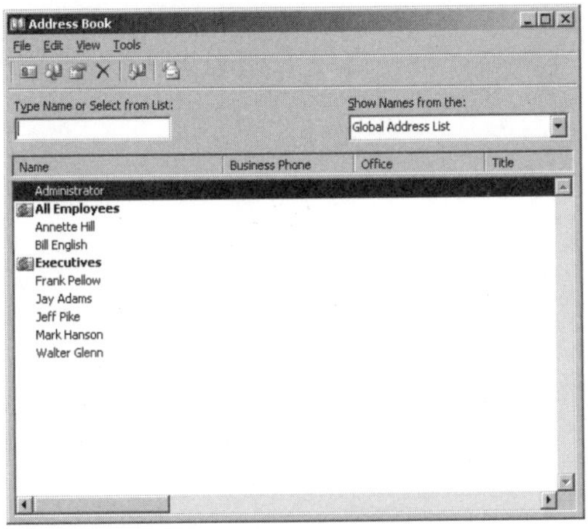

Figure 4-7. *Viewing the mail-enabled group in the Global Address List.*

When a message is sent to a global group in a remote domain, the expansion server must connect to a domain controller in the group's home domain and retrieve the membership list. In addition, the expansion server must have IP connectivity to a domain controller in the group's home domain. If bandwith between the two domains is slow or unreliable, retrieving membership from a remote domain might take time and slow down message delivery, which will affect overall performance. It is best if Exchange Server 2003 is in the remote domain. Then you can set the expansion server to be the remote Exchange 2003 server instead of retrieving the membership remotely and expanding the group membership locally.

When deciding which group type to select, consider the following implications:

- **Whether you have a single-domain or multiple-domain environment** If you have a single domain, you don't need to use universal groups, because all of the domain objects are local. When you have multiple domains, use universal groups if the membership is fairly static (that is, global groups as opposed to individual users), and remember that users might not have access to all object attributes from other domains in universal groups.
- **Whether direct IP connectivity is possible between all domains** If you have IP connectivity, use global groups when membership changes frequently or you have Exchange servers in each domain that can act as expansion servers. Otherwise, use universal groups, since membership is static and the local expansion server can expand the list.
- **Whether membership changes frequently** If membership changes often, use global groups. If membership changes infrequently, use universal groups.

Microsoft Outlook users will not be able to view the user memberships of a group that has been created in a remote domain. They can view membership only in global groups and domain local groups that have been created in their home domain.

An Expansion server, which has been mentioned several times, requires some explanation. When a message is sent to a mail-enabled group, the message needs to be expanded and individually addressed to each member of the group. By default, the local SMTP server performs the expansion and uses LDAP to contact the Global Catalog server to deliver the message to each member of the group. If the message is intended for a local group in the domain, the local Global Catalog server is contacted.

By default, an SMTP message can be routed to only 100 recipients. This is a limitation of the SMTP protocol, not of Exchange Server 2003. You can adjust this limit as required in one of three places:

- On the Message Delivery object properties sheet under Global Settings, where the default for the entire organization is 5000 recipients per message
- On the properties sheet for each SMTP virtual server in the Exchange System snap-in (Figure 4-8)
- On the individual user's account properties sheet in AD Users and Computers (Figure 4-9), where you can enter the value needed for that user. You access the Delivery Options screen by clicking the Delivery Options button on the Exchange General tab.

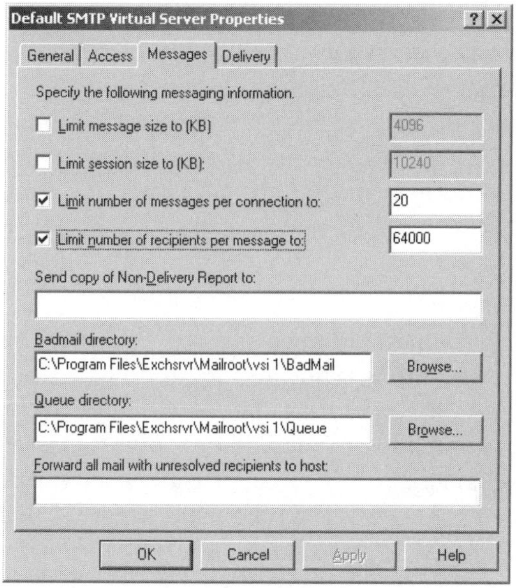

Figure 4-8. *Adjusting the SMTP recipient limit in the Exchange System snap-in.*

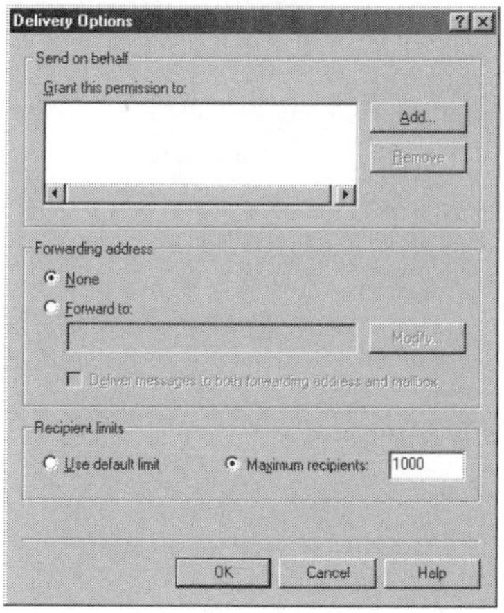

Figure 4-9. *Adjusting the SMTP recipient limit in AD Users and Computers.*

Note SMTP messages with more than 100 recipients are divided into multiple messages before being expanded, each with 100 recipients or less. If the number of recipients exceeds the limit specified in the global SMTP settings, the message will not be processed. Limits are imposed by the transport core categorizer, which is discussed more fully in Chapter 3, "Understanding Exchange Server Routing Architecture."

Configuration Naming Partition

The configuration partition of Active Directory stores information regarding how your Exchange 2003 system is organized. Because this information is replicated to all domain controllers in the forest, the Exchange 2003 configuration is also replicated throughout the forest. The configuration information includes the Exchange 2003 topology (such as routing group information), connectors, protocols, and service settings.

Schema Naming Partition

The schema partition contains all object types and their attributes that can be created in Active Directory. This information is replicated to all domain controllers in the forest. During the first installation of Exchange Server 2003 in the forest, the Active Directory schema is extended to include new object classes and attributes that are specific to Exchange 2003. These new classes start with "ms-Exch" and are derived from the LDAP Data Interchange Format (LDIF) files on the Exchange Server 2003 CD-ROM.

Given that these extensions represent more than 1000 changes to the schema and that these changes will be replicated to all the domain controllers in your forest, you should run ForestPrep for Exchange Server 2003 at the beginning of a period of time when you anticipate that network activity will be relatively light—for instance, on a Friday night. This schedule will give the domain controllers time to replicate all the schema changes into their own databases.

> **Tip** You can install Exchange Server 2003 using the */forestprep* switch, which will write the new Exchange object classes and attributes to the schema but will not install Exchange itself. Plan on this activity taking anywhere from 30 to 90 minutes, depending on the speed and capacity of your hardware. Also, generally, the earlier in an AD deployment that you extend schema, the better, because as domain controllers are added to the forest, they inherit the extended schema, thus reducing replication traffic when */forestprep* is run. For more information on installing Exchange Server 2003, consult Chapter 7, "Installing Exchange Server 2003."

Generating E-Mail Addresses

Exchange Server 2003 gives you flexibility regarding how your e-mail addresses are generated. As Figure 4-10 shows, e-mail address generation is controlled by the recipient policies in the organization. The user's e-mail address will likely be different from the user's principal name. Since the e-mail address is just another attribute of the user object, you can set it up so that the user's logon name and e-mail address are simplified, thus hiding the complexity of the underlying domain infrastructure.

Note In Figure 4-10, an X.400 address is associated with the user account. This X.400 address is required by Exchange Server 2003 and cannot be removed. Under the hood, Exchange is really an X.400-compliant message handling system. So is Novell's GroupWise, IBM's Lotus Notes, and other similar systems. Learning the X.400 standard will help you immensely in understanding the architecture of most e-mail systems that are in use today. You can purchase this standard from the folks at *www.itu.org*.

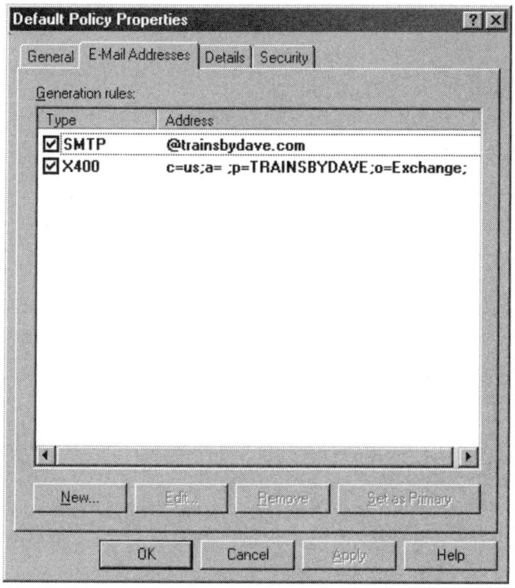

Figure 4-10. *Recipient policy properties.*

Exchange Server 2003 and Forest Boundaries

Since Exchange Server 2003 stores much of its information in the configuration naming partition, an Exchange 2003 organization cannot be extended past the boundaries of the forest. This is one area in which your Active Directory structure will directly influence your Exchange topology. Having multiple forests in a company incurs the following limitations:

- You have separate Exchange organizations to administer.
- You have separate Global Address Lists, with no automatic directory replication between them.
- You need to use SMTP and/or X.400 Connectors to connect the multiple organizations.
- No link state data will be transferred because Routing Group Connectors (RGCs) cannot be used.

Cross-Forest authentication is available, however. See Chapter 25, "Securing Exchange Server 2003 Messages," for a discussion about this topic.

If you want to synchronize directory information among multiple forests, you can use Microsoft MetaDirectory Services (MMS). Public folders can be synchronized with the Public Folder Inter-organization Replication tool. This tool will also replicate Free/Busy system folders as well. Even with this functionality, users cannot open calendars across forest boundaries. In addition, bear in mind the additional administrative overhead of synchronizing public folders in this manner compared to performing this function in a single organization. If possible, the best practice is to create additional domains rather than forests to eliminate the need for multiple Exchange organizations in your company.

Integration with Global Catalog Servers

Exchange Server 2003 needs regular access to the Global Catalog server for activities such as producing a Global Address List for mail-enabled users as well as for use by DSAccess and DSProxy. (These two Exchange services are discussed in the sections that follow.) Unless your network is small, with fewer than 20 light users, consider implementing at least two Global Catalog servers per Windows Server 2003 site for scalability and redundancy. In a multidomain environment, be sure to place a Global Catalog server in each domain as well. Large installations can require more Global Catalog servers.

DSProxy

To determine how many Global Catalog servers you need for your site and domain structure, you need to understand how a Microsoft Outlook user and an Exchange Server 2003 access Active Directory. In Exchange 5.5, every server has a complete copy of the directory, which enables Outlook clients to refer to the directory on their home server. The Message Transfer Agent (MTA) uses the local directory to route messages. Now that Exchange Server 2003 uses the directory in Windows Server 2003, directory calls need to be referred to Active Directory.

DSProxy acts as a facilitator to allow Outlook clients to access the data within Active Directory. It performs two important functions. The first is to proxy directory requests on behalf of clients to Active Directory through the Named Service Provider Interface (NSPI). Older Messaging Application Programming Interface (MAPI) clients, such as the older Exchange client or Microsoft Outlook 97/98, make MAPI Directory Service (MAPI DS) requests to an Exchange server over a remote procedure call (RPC) connection.

When an older MAPI client makes a directory request, the request is made to the Exchange Server 2003, as shown in Figure 4-11. The DSProxy NSPI then blindly forwards the MAPI DS directory call to a Global Catalog server. It does not open and evaluate the RPC packet because doing so would incur too much system overhead for the Exchange Server 2003 as well as complicating the security structure. It also does not change the request into an LDAP call over port 389. Active Directory can be accessed over a number of protocols, including LDAP and MAPI DS, so the forwarding of the packet has no effect on its ability to access Active Directory.

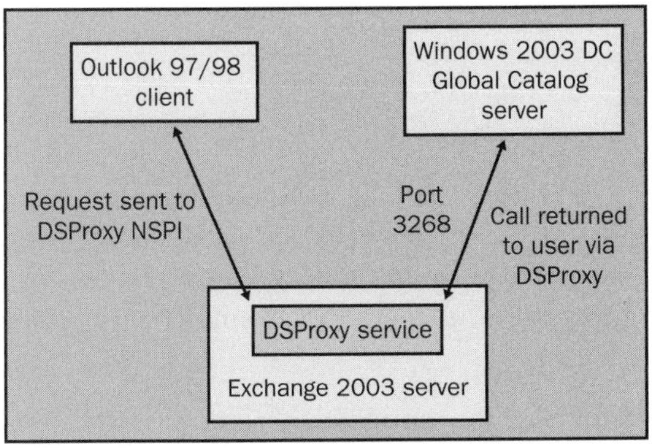

Figure 4-11. *How older MAPI clients access the Global Catalog via DSProxy.*

The Global Catalog server returns the results of the request to the Exchange 2000 DSProxy service, which in turn passes the results to the client. This entire process is transparent to the user.

> **Tip** If you need to specify the server that DSProxy uses manually, you can do so with the following registry entry:
>
> HKEY_LOCAL_MACHINE\System\CurrentControlSet\Services
> \MSExchangeSA\Parameters
> Value name: NSPI Target Server
> Value Type: STRING
> Value data: GC-Server-name
> HKEY_LOCAL_MACHINE\System\CurrentControlSet\Services
> \MSExchangeSA\Parameters
> Value name: RFR Target Server
> Value type: STRINGValue data: GC-Server-name

The second function performed by DSProxy is to request that more recent versions of Outlook, such as Outlook 2000 or 2002, send all future directory calls directly to a specified Global Catalog server. Outlook 2002 clients first go through the DSProxy process for the initial directory lookup. DSProxy then passes back to the Outlook 2002 client a referral to send all future directory calls to a specified Global Catalog server, thus reducing the load on the Exchange Server 2003 and minimizing any possible latency issues for directory calls. If the Global Catalog server fails, the Outlook 2000 client will need to be restarted to obtain a new referral from DSProxy.

The Outlook 2002 client writes the referral in its registry under the following key:

HKEY_CURRENT_USER\Software\Microsoft\WindowsNT\CurrentVersion \Windows MessagingSubsystem\Profiles\profilename\cda7392...2fe19873
Value name: 001e6602
Value type: STRING
Value data: \\Directoryserver.domain
Example: \\indianapolis.trainsbydave.com

If your clients need to access Active Directory through a firewall, you can open up the firewall to allow the Exchange Server 2003 to access Active Directory and turn off the DSProxy referral process to your Outlook 2000 clients. You can instruct the Exchange Server 2003 not to give out referrals in the following registry key:

HKEY_LOCAL_MACHINE\System\CurrentControlSet\Services\MSExchange SA\Parameters
Value name: No RFR Service
Value type: DWORD
Value data: 0x1

If the Global Catalog server being used by DSProxy fails, DSProxy issues a call-back to the System Attendant service (Mad.exe), which, in turn, issues to DSProxy a new server name to use. This process is known as *retargeting*. The System Attendant will not retarget unless it receives a request from SProxy to do so. When the Exchange System Attendant service starts, it finds the most appropriate Active Directory server by referencing DNS, and then it passes the server's name to the DSProxy process (Dsproxy.dll).

You can also determine which Active Directory domain controller a given Exchange server is using by viewing the properties of the Exchange computer in the Exchange System snap-in. In Figure 4-12, since Tucson is both an Exchange server and a domain controller, the server is referring to itself for Active Directory services.

You'll also notice that there is a check box to enable Exchange to Automatically Discover Servers. What this means is that Exchange will automatically discover the type of server selected in the Show list for the topology. When not selected,

Exchange will use the server you manually specify using the Add and Remove buttons.

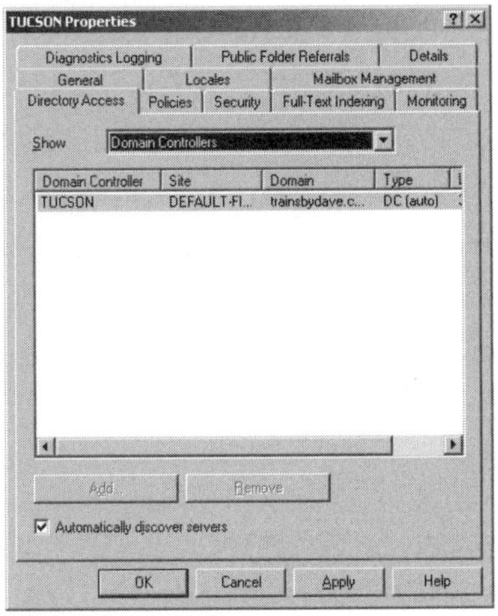

Figure 4-12. *Property sheet for the Tucson server.*

DSAccess

To reduce the number of calls to the Global Catalog server from your Exchange Server 2003, Exchange 2003 implements a directory access cache (DSAccess). This cache holds recent directory lookup information so that if the same information is requested within a specified period of time, the results can be returned to the client from the cache.

Increasing the cache size or the cache time will decrease the number of calls DSProxy and Outlook clients make to a Global Catalog server. You'll want to first measure the stress on the Global Catalog server and then, if necessary, modify the registry on the Exchange Server 2003.

The default parameters for cache size and cache time are a maximum of 4 MB of directory entries, which can be cached for up to 10 minutes. You can change these parameters in the registry of the Exchange Server 2003 as follows:

- To adjust the expiration time for cached entries, use the following registry entry:

  HKEY_LOCAL_MACHINE\System\CurrentControlSet\Services\MSExchangeDSAccess\Instance0
  Value Name: CacheTTL
  Value Type: Reg_WORD
  Value data: 0x*XXXX* (where *XXXX* = number of seconds desired)

- To adjust the size of the cache itself, use the following registry entry:

  HKEY_LOCAL_MACHINE\System\CurrentControlSet\Services
  \MSExchange
  DSAccess\Instance0
  Value name: MaxMemory
  Value Type: Reg_DWORD
  Value data: 0x*XXXX* (where *XXXX* = number of kilobytes desired)

- You can also specify the maximum number of entries in the cache, rather than its overall size, as follows:

  HKEY_LOCAL_MACHINE\System\CurrentControlSet\Services
  \MSExchangeDSAccess\Instance0
  Value name: Max Entries
  Value type: REG_DWORD
  Value data: 0x*XXXX* (where *XXXX* = number of entries)

Each cached entry requires about 3.6 KB of memory, and the overhead to run DSAccess is approximately 2.5 MB.

Configuration Partition and Directory Data

The two Active Directory services that an Exchange Server 2003 uses most often are the Global Catalog server for address book lookups and the configuration naming partition for routing information. It is possible that two different domain controllers will be referenced, depending on the type of request being made by the Exchange Server 2003.

When an Exchange Server 2003 boots up, it establishes a number of LDAP connections to domain controllers and Global Catalog servers. If it needs routing information to route a message, it can contact any domain controller to obtain this information, because each domain controller in the forest has a full copy of the configuration naming partition. If the Exchange Server 2003 needs to obtain the Global Address List, it will contact the closest Global Catalog server. Best practice is to place a Global Catalog server near the Exchange Server 2003 servers and make sure that they are in the same site and domain.

Manually Configuring Exchange Server 2003 for Global Catalog Lookups

You can hard-code which servers Exchange Server 2003 contacts to obtain data. This task involves merely specifying a preference for your Exchange Server 2003. Should the specified server be offline, Exchange fails over to standard DNS lookups.

To specify the domain controller to contact for configuration partition information, use the following registry key:

HKEY_LOCAL_MACHINE\System\CurrentControlSet\Services \MSExchangeDSAccess\Instance0
Value Name: ConfigDCHostName
Value type: REG_SZ
Value data: \\DirectoryServer.domain (for example, Tucson.hr.trains bydave.com)
Value name: ConfigDCPortNumber
Value type: REG_DWORD
Value data: 0x389 (the default LDAP port number is 389)

To specify the domain controller to contact for address book lookups, use this registry key:

HKEY_LOCAL_MACHINE\System\CurrentControlSet\Services \MSExchangeDSAccess\Profiles\Default
Value Name: UserGC1
Value type: REG_SZ
Value data: \\DirectoryServer.domain (for example, Tucson.hr.trainsby dave.com)
Value name: PortNumber
Value type: REG_DWORD
Value data: 0x3268 (the default port number for a GC server)
Value name: IsGC
Value type: REG_DWORD
Value data: 0x1 (always set to 1 if the server specified is a GC server)

Address Book Views

In Exchange 5.5, the view consistency checker (VCC) service runs in the background every 5 minutes, creating a new address book view (ABV) for each unique string of characters in the field that is being sorted. This method is not flexible for larger organizations and creates unwanted ABVs when words are misspelled or entered incorrectly.

Exchange Server 2003 eliminates ABVs and replaces them with address lists, which are created with build rules. These *build rules* use the LDAP search filter syntax defined in RFC 2254 and are extremely flexible. In fact, as Figure 4-13 shows, the Global Address List is built using a filter rule.

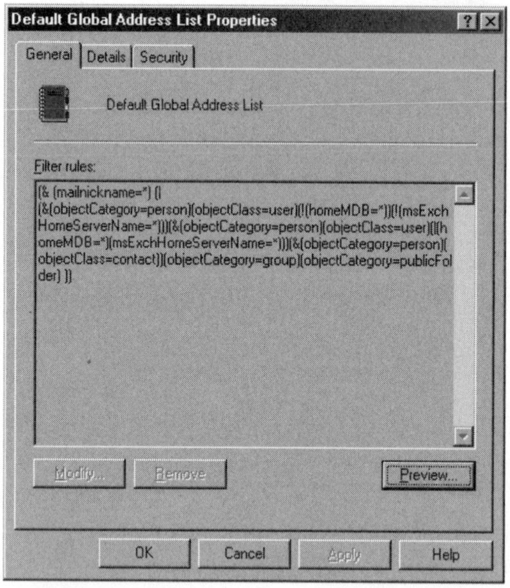

Figure 4-13. *Property sheet for the Global Address List, showing the filter rule.*

> **Tip** When you click the Preview button shown in Figure 4-13, you can test your build rule by having it used to search through the directory and find matching objects. If you get a list that isn't what you expected, you can modify your build rule. By testing your build rule here, you are not forced to close and open the address book properties multiple times to see the effects of a newly written rule.

Address lists are updated when the System Attendant service (Mad.exe) makes a call to Wldap32.dll. You can specify the frequency of this action on the property sheet in the Recipient Update service (Figure 4-14). To perform an update, the System Attendant service contacts a local domain controller, searches Active Directory for the objects and attributes specified in the build rule, and creates the new address list.

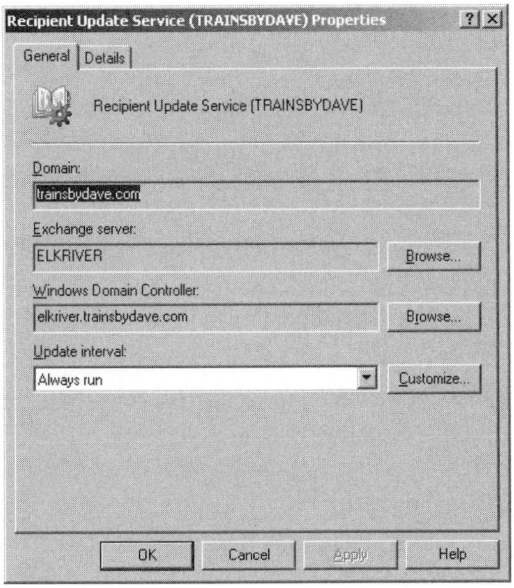

Figure 4-14. *Property sheet for the Recipient Update service.*

Several default address lists are configured in Exchange 2003. Table 4-3 lists the build rules for each of these default lists. Figure 4-15 shows where you can find the default lists in the Exchange System snap-in.

Table 4-3. Build rules for default address lists in Exchange 2003

<table>
<tr><th>Address List</th><th>Build Rule</th></tr>
<tr><td>Default Global Address List</td><td>(&(|mail=*)(proxyAddress=*)(textEncodedORAddress=*))(|(objectCategory=person)(objectCategory=group)(objectCategory=publicFolder)))</td></tr>
<tr><td>All users</td><td>(&(|mail=*)(proxyAddress=*)(textEncodedORAddress=*))(|(objectCategory=person)(objectClass=user))))</td></tr>
<tr><td>All groups</td><td>(&(|mail=*)(proxyAddress=*)(textEncodedORAddress=*))(|(objectCategory=group)))</td></tr>
<tr><td>All contacts</td><td>(&(|mail=*)(proxyAddress=*)(textEncodedORAddress=*))(|(objectCategory=person)(objectClass=contact))</td></tr>
<tr><td>Public folders</td><td>(&(|mail=*)(proxyAddress=*)(textEncodedORAddress=*))(|(objectCategory=publicFolder)))</td></tr>
<tr><td>All conference resources</td><td>M(msExchResourceGUID=*)</td></tr>
</table>

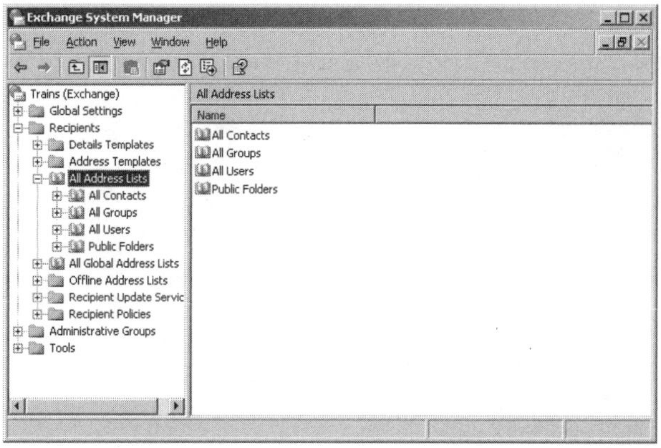

Figure 4-15. *Finding default address lists in the Exchange System snap-in.*

Integration with Internet Information Services 6.0

When Windows Server 2003 is installed, IIS is not installed by default. So before you can install Exchange 2003, you'll need to install IIS 6.0. The SMTP and other protocols that Exchange uses run inside the inetinfo.exe process and allow the abstraction of these protocols to dedicated servers, called front-end servers.

These protocols are basically transport stacks for the operating system, Windows Server 2003 no longer relies on RPCs. For instance, it is possible to have Active Directory information replicated over SMTP rather than RPCs.

> **Note** An RPC allows an application to execute code that resides on a remote machine. RPC-based applications use the network to transport the request. The client computer issues a call to "stub code" that takes the place of a local procedure. The stub code uses both communication and data conversion utilities to execute the request within the memory of the remote computer. Because RPC uses the network for its transport, TCP handshakes must be established for each new RPC between two machines, which results in high overhead on the network. RPC also requires permanent, high-bandwidth connectivity to ensure that the TCP connection can stay active. Compare this to SMTP, under which commands can be passed between servers in the form of messages. SMTP is thus more tolerant of lower-bandwidth environments and as a result is a better protocol over which to conduct server overhead functions, such as directory replication.

Given the ability to exploit Active Directory information via traditional Internet protocols, such as HTTP (and the improved version, WebDAV) and SMTP, as well as via Outlook Web Access (OWA), Web-based applications will become more popular, especially in environments where the work force is distributed but the information is centralized.

In addition, because IIS is now installed as part of the operating system and can run the transport protocols independently, the ability to host the protocols on different servers allows you to design an Exchange 2000 topology that will scale into the millions of users. Using a bank of front-end and back-end servers, Exchange 2000 can work with any size of installed base. For example, you can design your Exchange Server 2003 topology with a bank of front-end servers that allow non-MAPI clients, such as HTTP clients, to connect to virtual IP-addressable front-end servers while storing messages and collaboration data on separate back-end servers.

The protocols shipped with Exchange Server 2003, such as SMTP and NNTP, lead to services such as OWA, instant messaging, and data conferencing. These protocols and services are discussed in the sections that follow.

Simple Mail Transport Protocol

Exchange Server 2003 relies entirely on the Windows Server 2003 operating system to provide SMTP services. During the installation of Exchange Server 2003, the IIS SMTP protocol is extended to include additional command verbs that enable link state routing and other advanced features. In addition, an advanced queuing engine and an enhanced message categorization agent are installed. For more information on the SMTP protocol, see Chapter 20.

DNS Configuration

On the Internet (or on any TCP/IP network, for that matter), every device is represented by an IP address—using a four-part dotted-decimal notation, such as 192.168.0.1. A device with a TCP/IP address is called a *host* and is assigned a host name, which is a character-based name that is easier for humans to recognize and remember than its numeric IP address. The format of the host name is *hostname.domain.com*. When a host name identifies a resource on a TCP/IP network, computers must translate that host name into an IP address because computers communicate using only IP addresses. This translation is called *name resolution*.

There are two basic methods of resolving host names to IP addresses on a TCP/IP network. The first involves using a file called a Hosts file. The Hosts file is a single, flat file that simply lists hosts on a network and each host's IP address. To use the SMTP with a Hosts file, you must enter into that file the domain name and IP address of the hosts to which the IMS might need to transfer messages. As you might imagine, this process can be time-consuming.

The second method of resolving names is more efficient. It involves the Domain Name System (DNS), a hierarchical, distributed database of host names and IP addresses. In order to run Exchange Server 2003, you must have already installed Windows Server 2003 Active Directory and DNS services on your network. Although host files are still available in Windows Server 2003, given the dynamic nature of the new implementation of DNS, there are few times when you'll want to use them.

You are likely to want outside SMTP hosts to be able to transfer messages to your SMTP service. To enable this capability, you must create two records in the DNS database so that those outside hosts can resolve your server's IP address. The first record you must create is an address record, or A record for your Exchange Server 2003. This can be registered dynamically with DNS in Windows Server 2003. The second record is a mail exchanger record, or MX record, which is a standard DNS record type used to designate one or more hosts that process mail for an organization or site. This record must be entered manually in your DNS tables.

More Info This chapter provides a simple discussion of configuring TCP/IP and DNS, but these topics actually encompass a monstrous amount of material. If you need more information about using TCP/IP and DNS in the Windows Server 2003 environment, see *Microsoft Windows Server 2003 Administrator's Companion* by Charlie Russel, Sharon Crawford, and Jason Gerend (Microsoft Press).

Summary

This chapter described the ways in which Exchange Server 2003 is integrated with Windows Server 2003. It gave an overview of how Active Directory is structured and described how Exchange Server 2003 works with Active Directory. It also discussed the Internet information protocols installed with Windows Server 2003 as well as services available in Exchange Server 2003, such as Outlook Web Access, instant messaging, and data conferencing. In the next chapter, you'll learn how to assess your organization's needs as you begin the planning process for upgrading to Exchange Server 2003.

Part II
Planning

Chapter 5

Assessing Needs

Proper planning is valuable in any project, but in a Microsoft Exchange Server 2003 deployment, planning is especially critical. Many Exchange Server components are difficult or impossible to change after installation. Poor planning can cause problems that range from inadequate performance to outright failure of components.

We've broken our discussion of planning into two chapters. This chapter helps you gather the information you will need to plan your implementation of Exchange Server 2003. It looks at the business requirements of the enterprise, examines how to assess the needs of future Exchange users, and describes how to evaluate the resources of the current environment for the new messaging system. Chapter 6, "Planning for Development," discusses how to plan specific elements of your Exchange organization based on those assessments. Exchange Server is a complex program, but with suitable preparation, implementation of the new Exchange organization becomes a much easier task.

If you are reading this book from start to finish, you might want to skim these two planning chapters and then read the rest of the book. After you have a firm understanding of how the various components in an Exchange organization work, come back and read these two chapters more carefully. In the real world, planning should always come before implementation, but it helps to understand the implementation before working on your plan.

More Info This chapter and Chapter 6 provide an overview of planning an Exchange Server 2003 deployment that, coupled with the specific component knowledge you'll find throughout this book, should put you well on your way to designing an effective Exchange organization. If you are upgrading or migrating from a previous version of Exchange, you'll also be interested in Chapter 14, "Planning a Migration to Exchange Server 2003."

Defining User Needs

Your first step in designing any system should be to determine what that system needs to accomplish. In an Exchange system, this means asking yourself several questions:

- Will the system provide basic messaging services, that is, a way for users to send e-mail to one another?
- Will the system provide access to Internet resources? Can users send and receive Internet e-mail or participate in Internet newsgroups?
- Do you plan to offer public folders as a means of group discussion?
- Do you plan to offer wireless access or synchronization for your users?
- Are there any custom applications you want to use Exchange Server for? For instance, do you have a database of contact information that you want to make available as a public folder?

Your goals at this stage include gathering business requirements and understanding the corporate culture and technical environment—including the network topology and desktop systems—in which you will use Exchange Server 2003. When designing an Exchange organization, you must also find out what services and functionality your users require. After you've answered the questions presented in the following sections, you can effectively group users according to their needs. You can then use those groups to plan Exchange Server resources to accommodate user needs, as described in Chapter 6.

Messaging

Exchange Server 2003 is typically implemented as a messaging system. The odds are that your Exchange users will want to be able to send e-mail to one another. Ask the following questions to help describe the specific needs of your users:

- **To whom will most users be sending messages?** Messaging on most networks follows a fairly typical pattern. Users tend to send messages primarily to other users in their workgroup. Users also need to send messages to other workgroups or to outside recipients, such as people on the Internet. Developing a picture of these traffic patterns can help you plan user and server placement.
- **How much e-mail do users expect to generate and receive?** Some users rarely use e-mail; others send and receive dozens of messages per day. Knowing the average volume of messages for your users allows you to plan the capacity of your servers, the limits on your information stores, and the bandwidth requirements of your network.

- **Will users exchange scheduling and contact information?** Microsoft Outlook 2003 provides the ability to share scheduling and contact information dynamically between users. This generates extra messaging traffic and needs to be accounted for when designing your system.
- **What kind of messages and attachments will you allow users to send?** If your users will transfer large files to one another using e-mail, you must make allowances for this volume. Some organizations put limits on the amount of information that can be transmitted in a single message. Others put limits on the amount of space a single mailbox can consume. You can also apply different limits to different users. Executives, for example, might be given more flexibility than other employees.
- **Will user messages be stored primarily on an Exchange server or in local personal folders?** If server-based storage is to be the primary repository of user messages, how much space do you intend to allot for your mailbox stores? Your organization might have business policies that require e-mail to be stored for long periods of time. For example, some government units must store e-mail forever. Such information can help you plan hardware capacity for both servers and clients.
- **What kind of security will users need?** Do your users need to encrypt or digitally sign messages and attachments? If so, you will need to implement some sort of certificate server on your network, such as Microsoft Certificate Services. Exchange security is covered in Part VII, "Security."

Public Folders

Public folders are the foundation for collaboration within Exchange Server 2003. As you might recall, they enable public access to, and collaboration on, centralized messaging information. Public folders require considerable planning. In addition to planning storage capacity for the Exchange servers that will hold public folder replicas, you must plan public folder replication and user access to public folder servers. The following questions will assist you in assessing public folder usage in the new Exchange organization:

- **Which users will need access to which public folders?** Some workgroups will collaborate on certain documents and messages more than others. This information helps you decide where replicas of certain folders need to be placed and how often replication needs to occur.

- **Which users should be allowed to create public folders?** By default, top-level public folders in a public folder tree are created on the home server of the user who creates them. Subfolders are created on the same server as the top-level folder in which they are created. By restricting which users can create top-level folders, you can govern the placement of public folders on servers. Such restrictions also help you keep the structure of public folder trees manageable.
- **How much information do users expect to post within those public folders?** Both the type of information—documents, forms, executable files, or simple messages—and the size of a typical file help you determine the storage capacity required for public folder stores.
- **How long will the average message need to remain in a public folder?** This information helps you determine the storage space that your public folder stores will consume and the load that users will place on your servers when accessing the public folders.
- **How often will users access the public folders?** This information helps you further determine the load that your public folder servers will have to meet and to schedule public folder replication.
- **Will you use public folders to allow access to Internet newsgroups?** It's not uncommon to see thousands of messages come through an Internet newsgroup every day, and there are tens of thousands of groups available. You can create public folders that synchronize with Internet newsgroups, but you need to make sure your server can handle the message load.

Connections to Other Systems

Will any of your users need to access the Internet or a preexisting messaging system? Having this information can help you plan the placement of users and foreign messaging connectors. If one group of users tends to use a connector heavily, you might want to place those users on the server on which the connector is installed, to reduce the number of hops that messages have to take from your users to the foreign system. Any Exchange server can host a foreign messaging connector, and that messaging connector can be made available to all users in the organization. You might want to configure more than one connector to a foreign system to help balance the messaging load to that system.

You must decide between connector types when multiple connectors can support the same system. You will need to consider the types of foreign systems and the types of connectors they support, as well as the performance that those connectors will be expected to provide. For example, an X.400 Connector is highly reliable, but its reliability is due to a higher overhead that can affect performance. The X.400 Connector can also send and receive e-mail at scheduled times, thus reducing the impact e-mail has on other network applications.

Connectors also vary in the additional services they provide. A connector that enables the use of shared storage might be preferable to one that enables only e-mail between users. If you use a connector only to migrate from one version of Exchange Server to another, it will be a temporary addition to the Exchange organization. In such cases, choose the connector that makes the transition easiest for the users. In many cases, you can migrate the users transparently, with little interruption to their daily business, just by selecting the right connector. You'll learn more about connectors in Chapter 13, "Connecting Routing Groups," and Chapter 21, "Connecting to Other Messaging Systems with X.400."

Remote Access

Often, you will want to allow users to access private and public folders from a remote location. In planning an Exchange organization, you need to take the requirements of these remote users into account. This information can help you plan the placement of users, as well as plan a Routing and Remote Access Service (RRAS), virtual private network (VPN) access, or Internet-based access for your network. Various manufacturers offer solutions that can enable remote access to Exchange. This information is also valuable in security planning. Ask these questions to assess the remote access needs of the organization:

- Which users need to be able to access the Exchange organization remotely?
- Will users dial in to an RRAS server or access your network over the Internet? Dialing directly into an RRAS server usually provides better control and security. Accessing the network over the Internet is often much cheaper and more convenient, and new features such as RPC over HTTP do increase the level of security on Internet-based access.
- Where will you locate your RRAS server?
- On average, how many users will need simultaneous access to the network? This information helps you determine the number of RRAS servers you will need and the number of modems and phone lines.

Custom Applications

Do your users have special needs that can be met only by custom-tailored applications? If so, can the users themselves design these applications, or will you need to hire special personnel? The time to think about custom applications is during the planning stage. The use of custom applications could change many of the answers to the questions in this section.

Training and Support Services

Your users will likely need special training in using the new system. Don't make the mistake of assuming that e-mail is simple to use. Outlook 2003 and other messaging clients are sophisticated programs. Users might need to be taught how to use public folders or how to sign and encrypt messages. Do you plan to have users install the mail clients themselves? If so, they will need training, and you might need to set up a convenient way for them to do so.

Remember that users are often called upon to learn new things, including new versions of operating systems and software. Take the time to make sure that your users understand the system you are putting in place and know who their contact is for questions or problems. Public folders are a great place to store training materials so that they are available to all users. You could also use a public folder to list the contact information for support personnel. A public folder can use the same forms and views that are found in a user's mailbox folders. In this case, a public folder that stores contact information and uses the Exchange Contact form is ideal for a list of support personnel contacts.

Assessing Current Resources

Once you have determined the needs of your users, the next step in planning your organization is to assess your current resources. To make this assessment, you must put together three diagrams: one of your company's geographic profiles, another of your network topology, and a third of your Active Directory networking model.

Defining Your Geographic Profile

The easiest place to start your assessment is with a geographic profile of your company. Get out a pen and paper, and start drawing maps. If your network is global, start with all the countries in which your company has offices. Work your way down through states, cities, buildings, and even in-building locations.

Defining Your Software Environment

After you have a firm idea of how your company is laid out geographically, gather information on where users and resources are located within those geographical regions. This information helps you determine where the users are, where the computers are, whether the computers are ready for Exchange Server 2003 or your chosen messaging client, and how many licenses you are going to need. Consider the following along the way:

- Where are existing servers located?
- What are the servers' names and roles?
- What versions of which software are installed on the servers?
- How many workstations are in each location?
- What operating systems and software are used on those workstations?
- How many users are in each location?
- What are the users' needs?

Defining Your Network Topology

After you've created diagrams of your company's geographic profile, you need to diagram your company's network. Unlike the geographic profile, a network topology tells you exactly how your network is put together physically. When reviewing the geographic topology of the network, be sure to mark out the wide area network (WAN) links between the various locations and their bandwidths. This step helps you assess the network boundaries, the connectors required between locations, and the replication schedules. Figure 5-1 shows an example of a network diagram for a companywide WAN.

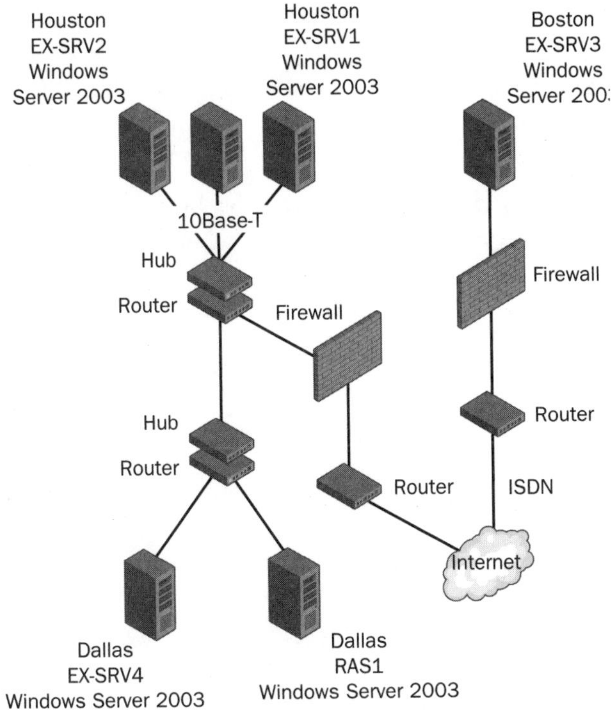

Figure 5-1. *Diagramming your network topology.*

Real World Systems Management Server

Ideally, you will already have a detailed inventory of your existing network assets. A comprehensive inventory includes a list of all the hardware and software on all of the computers on your network. The inventory should also take into account how your network is constructed and maybe even some of the network's use statistics.

If you don't already have a network inventory, you could go to all the computers on your network with a notebook in hand, but a better method is to use an automatic inventory system such as that built into Windows Server 2003 or, for larger networks, Microsoft Systems Management Server (SMS). You can use Windows and SMS to gather hardware and software information automatically from computers on your network. You can also use SMS to push installations of software (such as messaging clients) to workstations throughout the network from a central location, to control and support client software remotely, and even to keep track of licensing information on your network. SMS really is must-have software for any up-and-coming Exchange administrator.

Note, however, that SMS is not a simple install-and-run application. It is a comprehensive, enterprise-capable network management software package. SMS requires Microsoft SQL Server to provide the underlying database that captures and manages the network's data. To implement SMS and SQL Server, you should have defined and executed a project plan and systems design.

For more details on the systems management capabilities built into Windows Server 2003, see your product documentation. For more information on using Systems Management Server, check out the *Microsoft Systems Management Server 2003 Administrator's Companion* by Steven D. Kaczmarek (Microsoft Press).

A clear definition of your network's topology allows you to plan site boundaries, site connections, and server placement and to understand replication issues. Whether your network is a single local area network (LAN) within one office building or a WAN connecting thousands of users around the world, you should design the Exchange organization to optimize its messaging functions over the network topology.

Areas that can be optimized include the following:

- Routing group definition
- Server placement
- Message routing
- Public folder replication

The first step in defining a network topology is to determine the size of your network. The size of your network dictates how you will make many planning decisions. On a large WAN, for example, especially one that is geographically dispersed, you might want to consider setting up multiple routing groups. Using multiple routing groups means that you have to consider such things as messaging connectors, directory replication, and public folder replication among sites. If you are setting up a relatively small LAN, you might decide to configure only one routing group in your organization, which makes many of these decisions much easier.

In a small company, all your computers are likely to be connected on one high-speed LAN. In larger companies, networks usually consist of many small LANs connected in various ways to form larger, interconnected LANs or WANs. In your network topology diagram, you need to include all segments that make up your network. Figure 5-2 shows an example of a simple network diagram for a LAN.

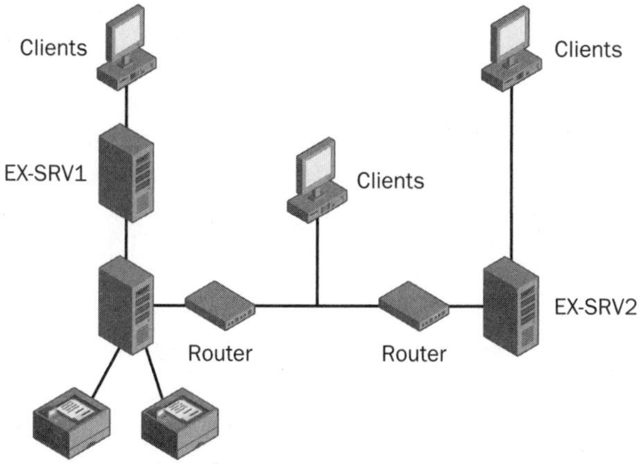

Figure 5-2. *Diagramming a LAN.*

For each segment, ask yourself the following questions:

- How big is the segment? How many computers are there? How large a geographic area does the segment cover?
- How is the segment wired? Does it use thin or thick Ethernet, shared or switched Ethernet, 10 Mbps or 100 Mbps, Fiber Distributed Data Interface (FDDI), token ring, or something else?
- What is the bandwidth of the segment? Determine the optimal bandwidth according to the type of network being used.
- How is the segment connected to other segments? Is the network segment connected to the rest of the network directly; is it connected through a router, switch, or bridge; or is it connected through a WAN link? Is the connection permanent or switched? What is the bandwidth of the connection?
- What protocols are used on the network?
- What are the traffic patterns on the network segment? At what times of day is network traffic within the segment heaviest? What application and operating system functions account for this traffic?
- What are the traffic patterns between this segment and other segments? At what times of day is network traffic heaviest between segments? What application and operating system functions account for this traffic?

Tip Although doing so can be somewhat tricky, you need to determine the available bandwidth of each segment of your network. The available bandwidth is the amount of bandwidth not consumed by average network activity. For example, if the throughput of a WAN link is 1.544 Mbps and the bandwidth consumed on that link can peak at 1.544 Mbps but averages around 512 Kbps (equivalent to 0.5 Mbps), the available bandwidth will be 1.544 Mbps through 0.5 Mbps, or 1.044 Mbps. You subtract the average value, not the peak value, because all network links experience peaks that don't represent the usual network bandwidth consumption.

Defining Your Active Directory Model

The final step in assessing your current resources is to document the Active Directory model in use on the network. Again, constructing a diagram is helpful. Whereas the topology diagram illustrates the physical layout of your network (cables, routers, and so on), the diagram of the networking model will illustrate the logical layout of your network. This logical layout includes how many domains your network has, how those domains are configured to interact, and the functions of those domains and the servers in them. Figure 5-3 shows a basic example of an Active Directory model.

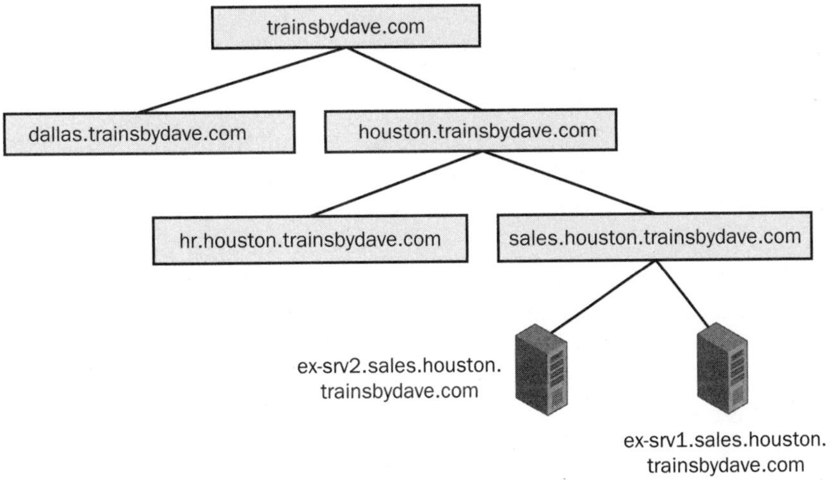

Figure 5-3. *Diagramming a networking model.*

Although Exchange Server routing and administrative groups differ from the sites and domains used in Active Directory, Exchange Server resources rely on domains and domain controllers to perform essential security operations. For example, to access an Exchange mailbox, a user must log in to a domain using a valid user account. Because Exchange Server services are Windows services, they too need to be authenticated by a domain controller before they can perform their functions. Each server in an Exchange organization is configured with a special user account called the Site Services account, which is used to validate Exchange services. For a detailed look at the integration of Exchange Server 2003 and Active Directory, see Chapter 4, "Understanding Windows Server 2003 Integration."

If your network contains only a single domain, the task of diagramming the networking model is easy. If your network consists of multiple domains, for each domain on your network, ask the following questions:

- What is the name of the domain?
- What is the function of the domain?
- Are any special trusts (i.e., cross-link trusts or one-way trusts) configured?
- How many user accounts are configured in this domain?

- What resources are configured in this domain?
- Who are the administrators of this domain?
- In what domain are the user accounts of the administrators configured?

Putting the Diagrams Together

After you've diagrammed your networking model, it's helpful to see how the networking model diagram, the geographic diagram, and the network topology diagram fit together. No real rule defines how Exchange routing or administrative groups should correspond to Active Directory domains. It is tempting, and sometimes appropriate, simply to create a routing and administrative group for each domain. However, this approach does not always work. A single domain might cover several geographic regions that a routing group might not be able to span, due to the topology of your network. You could end up with one group spanning several domains, or you cold end up with one domain spanning several groups. These decisions are more an art than science—an art that is the topic of the next chapter.

Defining Administrative Needs

Your last step in the assessment stage of the planning process is to determine how administration will be handled. In versions of Exchange Server prior to Exchange 2000 Server, Exchange administration was mostly separate from other forms of network management. With the introduction of Exchange 2000 Server came extensive integration with Active Directory and that continues in Exchange Server 2003; Windows and Exchange administrators must learn to get along.

In a small organization, one or two administrators will likely be able to handle administration for both Active Directory and the Exchange organization. Planning the administration of larger networks requires a bit more thought. Here are a few factors to consider:

- **User management** Since Exchange and Windows share Active Directory, it usually makes sense to let one person or group manage Active Directory users and their Exchange mailboxes (and usually other recipients, as well). Because the same interface is used to manage both, little extra training is required.

- **Routing** You will likely need one person or group to be responsible for managing routing in your organization. The administrative model in Exchange separates routing and administrative topologies. Servers can be grouped in administrative groups for permissions management and applying system policies, but they can belong to routing groups that span administrative groups for message routing. Responsibilities of this group include defining and maintaining routing and administrative groups, building and maintaining connectors between routing groups and to foreign systems, applying user and system policies, and managing permissions. You can think of this group as your core Exchange administrative unit.
- **Public folders** Designating a separate person or group to manage public folders and public folder replication is often useful. You might even want to designate a person to manage each distinct public folder tree. You can often leave basic administrative tasks on public folders up to expert users or to the people that manage the information stored in them.

Summary

Good planning can make or break your deployment of Exchange Server 2003. This chapter covered the first stage of planning an Exchange organization: assessing your current situation. It described how to assess the needs of your users and how to document your current resources by creating a geographic profile as well as profiles of the physical and logical layout of your current network. It also discussed considerations in planning how your Exchange system will be administered in an Active Directory environment. Now that you have collected the information you need, it's time to put that information to work. In Chapter 6, you will learn how to plan the actual Exchange organization.

Chapter 6
Planning for Development

In Chapter 5, "Assessing Needs," you learned how to assess the needs of your users and how to take stock of your current network situation. In this chapter, you'll learn how to put that information to use.

We divide the task of planning a Microsoft Exchange organization into three distinct subtasks: designing the overall Exchange organization, planning the location of Exchange routing groups, and placing individual Exchange servers in those groups to optimize the messaging system. This approach will provide you with a logical placement of resources developed with users' needs in mind.

Beginning at the organizational level, you'll establish organization-wide naming conventions, determine the number of routing groups you'll need and the boundaries of those groups, and plan how to link those groups. Next, at the routing group level, you'll plan the services that the group must provide. You'll also plan public folders and gateways. Finally, at the server level, you'll determine the functions each server will perform and plan the server hardware to accommodate those functions.

Planning the Organization

The best place to start planning an Exchange organization is at the top, that is, you determine how your system will look. Planning at this level primarily involves determining the number of routing groups and administrative groups that you need in the organization and deciding where the boundaries of those groups should be. You also need to plan any messaging links between those groups. Before you get started on these plans, however, you need to establish a convention for naming the various elements of the organization.

Establishing a Naming Convention

The requirement that names be unique is common to any system with a directory of users, resources, and servers. Because Exchange Server provides various migration tools, duplication can occur when different systems are migrated to an Exchange system. You should review the systems for possible duplication and take appropriate precautions—such as changing a name or deleting old accounts—before migrating multiple systems to Exchange Server.

Large Exchange systems can grow to include thousands of users worldwide and many routing groups and servers. Most names cannot be changed once an object has been created. Certain objects, such as user mailboxes, have different types of names as well. Before you install your first Exchange server, you need to establish a convention for naming the primary types of objects in your Exchange organization: the organization, groups, servers, and recipients.

Establishing a naming convention for distribution groups, as well as for users and contacts that appear in Active Directory, is a great help to Exchange users. Furthermore, distributing administration among multiple administrators in different regions can help to apply a naming standard to connectors and other Exchange objects.

> **Caution** Network and messaging systems should avoid using invalid characters in their names. Some systems do not understand invalid characters, and other systems misinterpret them as special codes (sometimes called escape sequences). This misinterpretation can cause these systems to try to interpret the remainder of a name as a command of some sort. The result, of course, is failure to communicate electronically and, perhaps, errors on the network or messaging systems. Although the list of invalid characters can vary, most systems consider some or all of the following, along with the space character (entered by pressing the spacebar on the keyboard), invalid characters:
>
> \ / [ ] : | < > + = ~ ! @ ; , " ( ) {}' # $ % ^ & * - _
>
> Avoid using invalid characters in any names, even if you find that Windows or Exchange Server will allow you to do so.

Organization Names

The organization is the largest element of an Exchange system, and its name should typically reflect the largest organizational element of your company. Usually, an organization is named after the enterprise itself, although it is possible to create multiple organizations in an enterprise and for the organizations to communicate with one another. Organization names can contain up to 64 characters, but to facilitate administration, limiting their length is good practice. Keep in mind that users of external messaging systems might need to enter the organization name manually, as part of the Exchange users' e-mail addresses.

Caution When you install the first production Exchange server, be sure that the organization name you specify is correct. If this means waiting for management's approval, so be it. Changing the organization name later is possible but requires a good bit of reconfiguration. Also, be aware that the Simple Mail Transport Protocol (SMTP) address space uses the organization and routing group names to construct e-mail addresses for the Internet. The SMTP address space can be changed, but doing so can be a hassle and a cause of confusion for other Exchange administrators later.

Routing Group Names

The convention for naming routing groups varies, depending on how the boundaries of the groups are established. In a typical Exchange system design, routing groups are named by geographic region or by department because routing group boundaries are determined based on wide area network (WAN) links and workgroup data flow. Like the organization name, routing group names can contain up to 64 characters, but keeping them as short as possible is best. Again, users of some external messaging systems might need to enter the name of the routing group as well as the organization name when sending e-mail to users of your Exchange system.

Server Names

The server name for an Exchange server is the same as the NetBIOS name of the Windows server on which Exchange Server 2003 is installed. Therefore, you should establish naming conventions for servers before installing Windows. You can determine the name of a Windows server on the Network Identification tab of the System utility in Control Panel. NetBIOS server names cannot be more than 15 characters long.

When installing an Exchange Server in an enterprise network, one recommendation for naming the server is to use its location or the type of function that the server will provide. You can end the name with one or two digits to allow multiple Windows servers in the same location providing the same network function. For example, an Exchange server in a company's London office could be named LON-EX01.

Recipient Names

Recipient names work a bit differently from the names of the other objects. Exchange Server allows several types of recipients, including users, contacts, groups, and public folders. (Public folders are discussed later in this chapter.) Each of the other types of recipients actually has four key names, which are shown on the General tab of the object's property sheet (Figure 6-1):

- **First Name** The full first name of the user.
- **Initials** The middle initial or initials of the user.
- **Last Name** The full last name of the user.
- **Display Name** A name that is automatically constructed from the user's first name, middle initial or initials, and last name. The display name appears in address books and in the Exchange System snap-in, so it is the primary way Exchange users search for other users. Display names can be up to 256 characters long.

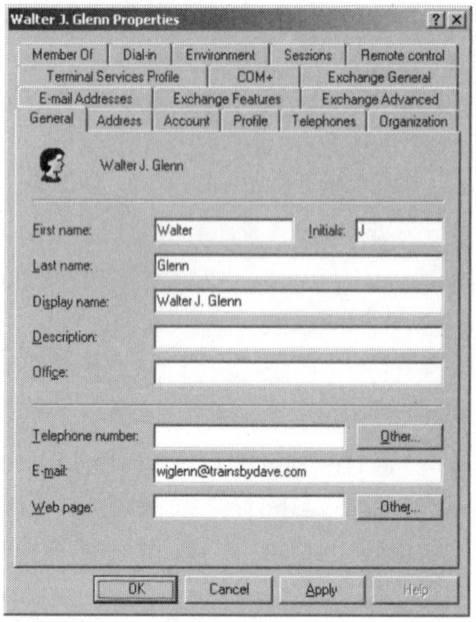

Figure 6-1. *Elements of a recipient's name.*

A naming convention should take into account the outside systems to which Exchange Server might be connecting. Many legacy messaging and scheduling systems restrict the length of recipient names within their address lists. Although Exchange Server allows longer mailbox names, the legacy system might truncate or reject them, resulting in duplicates or missing recipients. In addition, messages could show up in the wrong mailboxes or might not be transmitted at all. A common length restriction in legacy systems is eight characters. You can avoid many problems if you keep mailbox names to eight characters or fewer.

Real World Naming Conventions and Addressing

The names that you establish for objects in your Exchange organization determine the addresses that users of external messaging systems use to send messages to your recipients. Foreign systems do not always use the same addressing conventions as Exchange Server. Therefore, Exchange Server must have a way of determining where to send an inbound message from a foreign system. For each type of messaging system to which it is connected, Exchange Server maintains an address space consisting of information on how foreign addressing information should be used to deliver messages within the Exchange organization.

Suppose you set up Exchange Server so that your users can exchange e-mail with users on the Internet. In this situation, Exchange Server would support the SMTP address space by maintaining an SMTP address for each recipient object. A user on the Internet would then address messages to your users in the typical SMTP format—something like user@organization.com. (You will learn how this works in Chapter 13, "Connecting Routing Groups." For now, you need to understand that the way you name the objects in your organization has fairly far-reaching effects.)

Defining Routing Groups

In general, you want to keep the number of routing groups in your organization as low as possible. If you can get away with having just one routing group, you should do so. Many of the communications between servers in a group, such as message transfers, are configured and happen automatically, greatly reducing administration on your part. However, there are also many good reasons to use multiple routing groups. This section covers some of these considerations.

Geographic Considerations

If your company is spread over two or more geographic regions, you might want to implement a routing group for each region. The primary reason for doing so is to help manage network bandwidth consumption. A single routing group is easy to set up because much of the communication between the servers in a routing group occurs automatically. Unfortunately, this automatic communication consumes a considerable amount of bandwidth, which grows with the size of the routing group. If your network contains WAN links, which typically have a smaller amount of bandwidth available, it is best to divide the organization so that an Exchange routing group does not span a WAN link, because Exchange Server provides ways to limit and schedule the traffic between routing groups.

Network Considerations

Several physical factors determine the possible boundaries of a routing group. All Exchange servers within a routing group must be able to communicate with one another over a network that meets certain requirements:

- **Common Active Directory forest** All servers within a routing group must belong to the same Active Directory forest.
- **Persistent connectivity** Because of the constant and automatic communication between Exchange servers within a routing group, these servers must be able to communicate using SMTP over permanent connections—connections that are always on line and available. In addition, all servers within a routing group must be able to contact the routing group master at all times. If you have network segments that are connected by a switched virtual circuit (SVC) or a dial-up connection, you must implement separate routing groups for those segments.
- **Relatively high bandwidth** Servers in a routing group require enough bandwidth on the connections between them to support whatever traffic they generate. Microsoft recommends that the connection between servers support at least 128 Kbps. Keep in mind that if a network link is heavily used, 128 Kbps will not be sufficient for Exchange Server traffic. The network link should have a fair amount of bandwidth available for new traffic generated by Exchange Server, if an Exchange routing group will span that link.

Routing groups in Exchange Server—like sites in Exchange Server 5.5—are based on available bandwidth. However, Exchange Server uses SMTP, which is more tolerant of lower bandwidths and higher latency. This capability means that you can group servers into routing groups that you could not have grouped into sites in Exchange 5.5. You might want to divide Exchange servers into multiple routing groups for a number of reasons:

- The minimum requirements outlined previously are not met.
- The messaging path between servers must be altered from a single hop to multiple hops.
- The messages must be queued and sent according to a schedule.
- Bandwidth between servers is less than 16 Kbps, which means that the X.400 Connector is a better choice.
- You want to route client connections to specific public folder replicas since public folder connections are based on routing groups.

The most important factor to consider when planning your routing group boundaries is the stability of the network connection, not the overall bandwidth of the connection. If a connection is prone to failure or is often so saturated that the pragmatic effect is a loss of connectivity, you should place the servers that the connection serves in separate routing groups.

Be sure to have a Global Catalog server in each routing group and preferably in each Active Directory site. This arrangement decreases lookup traffic across your slower WAN links and makes the directory information for client lookups more available to your clients.

Planning Routing Group Connectors

After you've determined how many routing groups your organization will have and what the boundaries of those groups will be, you need to plan how those groups will be linked. Routing groups are linked by connectors that allow servers in the different groups to communicate. Exchange Server provides three connectors that you can use to link routing groups: the Routing Group Connector, the SMTP Connector, and the X.400 Connector. These connectors are covered in detail in Chapter 13. This section briefly describes the advantages and disadvantages of each connector.

Routing Group Connector

The Routing Group Connector (RGC) is used only to connect one routing group to another. The RGC is by far the easiest of the connectors to set up and, everything else being equal, is also the fastest. It has some of the strictest use requirements, however; it needs a stable, permanent connection that supplies relatively high bandwidth. SMTP is used as the native transport for the RGC.

The RGC works using bridgehead servers. A server in one routing group—a bridgehead server—is designated to send all messages to the other routing group. Other servers within the routing group send messages to the bridgehead server, which then sends the messages to a bridgehead server in the other routing group. That bridgehead server is then responsible for delivering the messages to the correct servers within the group. If you want, you can configure more than one bridgehead server in a routing group, for the purposes of fault tolerance and load balancing. Bridgehead servers let you control which servers transfer messages between routing groups.

SMTP Connector

The SMTP Connector can be used to connect two Exchange routing groups or to connect an Exchange organization to a foreign messaging system. It can also be used to connect two Exchange routing groups over the Internet. The SMTP Connector allows finer control over message transfer than the RGC, including the ability to authenticate remote domains before sending messages, to schedule specific transfer times, and to set multiple permission levels for different users on the connector.

X.400 Connector

The X.400 Connector can be used to connect two routing groups or to connect an Exchange organization to a foreign X.400 messaging system. In connecting two routing groups, the X.400 Connector is generally slower than an RGC because of additional communication overhead. Since the RGC allows scheduling and maximum message sizes, you most likely will not use an X.400 Connector to connect two Exchange routing groups.

Multiple Messaging Connectors

Generally speaking, it is simplest to configure only one connector between any two routing groups. You can, however, configure multiple connectors. Multiple connectors can be used to provide fault tolerance in case one connector fails or to balance the messaging load over different network connections. For example, you could create two X.400 Connectors between the same two sites using different pairs of messaging bridgehead servers. If one connector went down (most likely because one of the bridgehead servers in that pair failed), the other connector (and its designated bridgehead servers) would remain up.

A cost value is assigned to each connector you create on a routing group. Cost values range from 0 through 999. (There is no cost value assigned to the SMTP connector itself—only to the address spaces associated with the SMTP Connector.)

A messaging connector with a lower cost is always preferred over one with a higher cost. This approach allows you to designate primary and backup connectors between routing groups. When Exchange determines which connector it should use to send a message, it takes into account the cumulative cost of the entire messaging path. In Figure 6-2, for example, a message could move from group 1 to group 4 by being transmitted either through group 2 or through group 3. The path through group 2 has a cumulative cost of 4, whereas the path through group 3 has a cumulative cost of 2. Thus, Exchange Server will prefer the path through group 3 because it has the lowest cost.

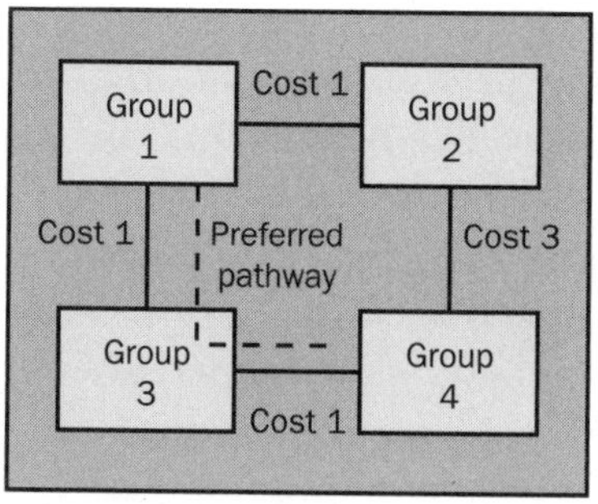

Figure 6-2. *Using costs to determine message routing.*

Use multiple connectors whenever the physical networking between routing groups is unreliable. For a small or medium-sized network with high-bandwidth links between routing groups, having a single connector between groups provides a consistent messaging pathway. This consistency is valuable in developing an accurate picture of network traffic and in troubleshooting message delivery problems. In medium to large networks that have inconsistent traffic patterns or restricted bandwidth availability as well as multiple, redundant links between groups, using multiple connectors between groups for backup or load balancing can enhance the messaging system's reliability.

Planning Routing Groups

After you've established the number of routing groups your organization will contain and determined how those groups will be linked, you're ready to design the groups themselves. Several elements go into a good routing group design. You need to establish a public folder strategy, and you also need to plan the services, such as foreign gateways, that your users will need. You will base many of these determinations on the assessment of user needs described in Chapter 5, "Assessing Needs."

Designing Your Routing Groups

A good portion of the work of designing an Exchange routing group involves planning the servers that will be members of that group. (Planning the Exchange servers themselves is the topic of a later section of this chapter.) The following guidelines can help you decide how to distribute the services among the servers in a routing group:

- If your goal is to isolate messaging traffic from other network traffic, put users and their home servers on the same network segment in a workgroup configuration. It is important to have high-bandwidth connections between mail clients and servers for the best performance.
- If your goal is to use a hierarchical physical network structure, in order to use its inherent security by grouping servers together, put servers on intermediate network segments that route traffic to the network backbone, and route traffic to the geographically located workgroup segments.
- Put the mailboxes for all users in a workgroup on the same server. Users tend to send the most e-mail to other users in their own workgroup. Keeping all of the mailboxes on the same server means lighter network traffic and lower consumption of server disk space.
- When possible, create duplicate services on multiple servers to provide fault tolerance. Always place Exchange servers on machines that have fault-tolerant hardware.

Planning Public Folders

Public folders in Exchange Server can be put to several uses, including as discussion forums, as public collections of documents, and even as the basis for custom applications. Exchange Server allows you to configure multiple public folder trees, each of which can contain any number of public folders. Folders created in the root level of a public folder tree are referred to as top-level folders. When a user creates a top-level folder, it is placed on that user's home server. When a user creates a lower-level folder, it is placed on the same server as the folder in which it is created. The contents of a public folder can be stored on a single server, or the contents can be replicated to other servers in the routing group and organization. (Chapter 10, "Using Public Folders," discusses the creation, storage, and replication of public folders in detail.) A few aspects of public folders are pertinent to routing group planning:

- Decide how many different public folder trees you want to maintain. For example, each department could manage its own tree, or you could have one companywide tree.
- Decide whether to distribute public folders on multiple servers throughout your routing group or to maintain them all on a single server.
- Decide whether to dedicate certain servers to public folders by having them contain only public folder stores or to have servers that contain both public folders in public folder stores and private folders such as mailboxes in mailbox stores.

- Determine which users will be using public folders for collaborative applications and whether those applications will require other services or special security.
- If users in remote routing groups need to access public folders in a local routing group, decide whether to replicate the contents to a server in the remote routing group to keep intergroup network traffic down.
- Consider which users should be allowed to create top-level folders in a public folder tree. Limiting the number of users who can create top-level folders allows you to control both the servers on which public folders are created and the basic organization of the public folder hierarchy.
- When naming public folders, you have a bit more license than with the names of other recipients. Public folder names can be up to 256 characters. However, when you name a folder, keep in mind that only a small portion of the name will actually display in your users' client software, and very long names could become a real hassle. Also, some users might occasionally need to type in the name of a public folder, and smaller names will be greatly appreciated.

Planning Gateways

Any server can be configured with a connector to a foreign system. All other servers in the organization will then be able to route messages over that gateway. When possible, you want to create a foreign messaging connector on the server that maintains the actual physical connection to the foreign system. Also, if one group of users makes primary use of a foreign connection, consider placing those users on the server on which the connector is installed.

Planning Servers

After you've planned the general structure of your organization and routing groups, you can plan your servers. The number of servers you need depends on the number of users in the routing group and the services that you plan to provide to those users. As you've learned throughout this chapter, you accomplish part of server planning while planning your organization and routing groups. After you have accomplished that, you should have a fairly good idea of the services that each routing group needs to offer and the number of servers that you need to have to offer those services.

Depending on your needs and resources, you are likely to have decided whether to concentrate your services on just a few powerful servers or instead to distribute the services among a larger number of less powerful servers. There really is no guideline for the number of servers that you need or the power of those servers. What is important is that you make a plan. After you make that plan, you can begin to estimate the hardware requirements for your servers.

When estimating the performance of an Exchange server, you need to consider four distinct categories of hardware: disk, processor, memory, and network. The sections that follow discuss each of these categories in turn.

Disk Considerations

Your server needs to have adequate disk space for Windows Server 2003, Exchange Server 2003, directory information, transaction logs, and information stores. The speed at which Exchange Server can access your disks is another important consideration.

SCSI drives are generally faster than IDE drives. Consider using a caching disk controller with a high-speed bus, such as PCI. Adding more drives and drive controllers allows Exchange Server to distribute the workload, reading and writing to multiple drives at the same time. Also consider placing your transaction logs on a separate physical disk so that the logs can be written sequentially, increasing performance.

Real World Calculating Disk Space

When you plan the amount of disk space your server will need, consider these factors:

- Windows Server 2003, Enterprise Edition (with Internet Information Services, Active Directory, and DNS), takes up about 1.5 GB, depending on the options you install.
- A standard installation of Exchange Server 2003 will take up an additional 180 MB.
- In addition to these figures, you need to factor in the number of user mailboxes and public folders on your server and the amount of space you plan to allow each type of store to consume.
- Transaction logs are relatively small (5 MB each), but you should use a separate drive for them.

Finally, you need to take into account any additional services you need to run on the server, including other major programs such as Microsoft SQL Server and Exchange extensions such as virus and filtering programs.

If you use multiple drives, you might also want to consider a hardware or software-based redundant array of independent disks (RAID), including disk striping with parity (RAID-5) or disk mirroring (RAID-1), to offer some level of fault tolerance. You can configure Windows software-based RAID in the Computer Management snap-in. Computer Management allows you to create a *volume set*, which is a group of hard disks that the Windows operating system treats like a single hard disk. Yet another option is to implement a form of hardware-based RAID, which can be costly but offers the best performance and fault tolerance available.

Although it might seem tempting to throw as much storage space at the Exchange server as you can, don't do it. Instead, think about the storage needs over time and the capability of the backup system. If the storage space might exceed the capacity of the backup system, you might need additional servers instead. Many gigabytes of data can accrue on an Exchange server over time. Eventually, the information stores can grow to be too large for the backup system. When defining the storage for a server, ensure that the backup system is adequate to fully back up the information stores, transaction logs, and operating system files. A large information store can take several tapes, and a very long time, to back up on a daily basis. A restore can take several hours. Multiple servers with smaller information stores provide an inherent tolerance to failure: the failure would affect fewer users for a shorter period of time because the restore process is shorter.

As the amount of data on an Exchange server grows, performance can diminish. Exchange Server manages a number of background tasks for the information stores. These tasks take longer to execute when there are more messages in the information store to manage; hence, performance degrades across the server as a whole. One way to keep the mailbox store from growing too large is to configure the server to limit the size of users' mailboxes. Another way is to configure multiple mailbox stores, which you learn how to do in Chapter 11, "Using Storage Groups."

Processor Considerations

Using multiple processors significantly increases a server's performance. Adding a second processor to a server, however, does not double its performance. The processors still share a motherboard, adapters, storage, and other components, and data can face a bottleneck in these components. However, Windows Server 2003 does support symmetric multiprocessing, and Exchange Server 2003 is a multithreaded application. Therefore, multiple pieces of the Exchange system can run simultaneously on different processors within the same system, significantly increasing response time.

Memory Considerations

Memory (RAM) is used to run active processes on a computer. When physical memory is not sufficient, the system supplements it by using a paging file on the computer's hard disk. Ideally, you should have enough physical memory on a server to avoid excessive use of the paging file. Right now, memory is the cheapest way to increase the performance of any computer. We recommend having at least 512 MB of RAM on any Exchange server as the bare minimum; use 1024 MB from the start if at all possible.

Network Considerations

The network interface cards on your servers should be fast enough to handle traffic coming from and going to clients and other servers. High-speed network adapters, such as those that use a PCI bus, are best. Fast servers can take advantage of multiple network interface cards, providing the ability to host connections to several other clients or servers at the same time. Furthermore, many server platforms allow you to merge network interface cards into a pool; then, should one of the cards in the pool fail, another card takes over. We recommend using high-speed PCI adapters that are capable of bus mastering whenever you can.

Ways to Add Fault Tolerance

Some standard precautions can be taken to ensure that Exchange servers stay on line, even when there are failures. An uninterruptible power supply (UPS) is a common way to ensure that the server does not go off line if the power in the building fails. A UPS can also prevent power surges from damaging the server components.

As we have already mentioned, a server can have multiple hard disks, multiple processors, and multiple network interface cards. These redundant components provide increased performance, load balancing, and failover options, depending on how they are configured. A server can also have dual power supplies, controller cards, and error-correcting RAM. Whenever a server has redundant internal components, it is better able to tolerate faults in those components. Server-class machines typically come with software that is able to monitor the servers' hardware components from a central management machine.

In addition to establishing redundancy for server components, you can establish redundancy for the server itself. Exchange servers can be configured to take advantage of a shared storage system using clustering. *Clustering* is a system in which multiple servers are configured in a cluster, so that if one server has a problem, the system fails over to the redundant server.

Summary

In this chapter, you learned how to use information about the needs of your users and the current assessment of your network to design an Exchange organization. The design of an organization happens at three distinct levels: the organizational level, the routing group level, and the server level.

Part II of this book, "Planning," has shown you how to collect and use information about your situation when planning your Exchange organization. Chapter 7, "Installing Exchange Server 2003," begins Part III, "Deployment," which looks at the deployment of Exchange Server 2003. In Chapter 7, you will learn how to install Exchange Server.

Part III

Deployment

Chapter 7

Installing Exchange Server 2003

So far, you've learned a bit about how Microsoft Exchange Server 2003 works and how to plan your Exchange organization. In this chapter, you'll actually get your hands dirty and install Exchange Server. You'll do this in four basic stages:

1. Make sure your server is prepared for the installation. The Exchange Deployment Tools will help you through this process.
2. Once preparation is finished, you'll run the Exchange Server 2003 Setup program from the Deployment Tools window, click a few buttons, and supply some information about your environment.
3. Verify that the new Exchange services are up and running.
4. Apply other software that might need to be integrated with Exchange Server, such as Exchange service packs, backup software, and virus-detection software.

Regardless of whether you're installing Exchange as the first server or as a subsequent server within the Exchange messaging system, you'll find that if you are prepared, Exchange Server 2003 is not difficult to install. If you are not prepared and choose the wrong options, however, you might end up having to reinstall the software or, worse, wreaking a bit of havoc on your existing system. For anyone involved in installing Exchange Server 2003, this is a critical chapter.

Preparing for the Installation

Although it's tempting (and easy enough) simply to insert the Exchange Server CD-ROM and go through the Setup routine, it's best to take care of a few chores first. You should verify that your server is correctly configured, gather some information, and set up special accounts. If you created a good deployment plan, you probably have all the information you need.

Real World **Taking Exchange Server 2003 for a Test Drive**

If you are considering upgrading your Exchange organization to Exchange Server 2003 from a previous version, we recommend trying the new version on a nonproduction server first to get a feel for its new features. You might also want to test-drive the software even if you are creating a new system rather than upgrading. Testing Exchange Server 2003 before deployment can help you plan the best ways to implement some of the features offered by the new version as those decisions come up during the "real" installation.

If you do decide to take Exchange Server 2003 for a test drive, we recommend setting up a test network that is physically separate from your actual network. If you do not have the resources for a separate network, you can test Exchange Server 2003 on a server on your existing network.

Gathering Information

The following is a checklist of critical questions you should ask yourself before starting an Exchange Server installation. The answers to some of them might seem a bit obvious, but taking the time to study them before you begin will prevent problems during or after installation:

- Does the computer on which you plan to install Exchange Server 2003 meet the hardware requirements? (See the next section, "Verifying Hardware Requirements.")
- Is the computer on which you plan to install Exchange Server 2003 running Windows Server 2003 or Windows 2000 Service Pack 3 or later?
- Does your server have access to a domain controller and Global Catalog server running Windows Server 2003 or Windows 2000 Service Pack 3 within the local Active Directory site?
- Do you have access to a user account with the appropriate administrative rights? You must be a local machine administrator on the server on which you will install Exchange Server 2003. You must be a member of the Domain Admins group if you need to run the domainprep tool as part of the installation. You must also be a member of both the Enterprise Admins and Schema Admins groups if you need to run the ForestPrep tool as part of the installation.
- Does your account have the right to modify the Windows 2000 Active Directory Schema? If not, you can have an administrator who does have rights modify the Schema before you begin installing Exchange Server 2003. (See the section "Installing Exchange Server 2003" later in this chapter.)

- Is Transmission Control Protocol/Internet Protocol (TCP/IP) correctly configured on your Windows server, and do you have access to DNS servers? (See the "TCP/IP" section later in this chapter.)
- What are the names of the organization and routing group you will create or join?
- If you are joining an existing routing group, what is its name?
- For what connectors will you need to install support during your Exchange Server setup?
- What is the disk configuration of the computer on which you are installing Exchange Server?
- Do you have the 25-digit key number from the back of the Exchange Server CD-ROM jewel case?
- Is Microsoft Internet Information Services (IIS) 5.0 or later running on the computer?

Tip The new Exchange Deployment Tools that run prior to Exchange setup provide a convenient checklist for making sure the preinstallation requirements are met. They also let you run many of the tools for setting up the environment before launching setup. You'll learn how to use them later in the chapter.

Verifying Hardware Requirements

Before installing Exchange Server 2003, you must make sure your machine meets the minimum hardware requirements. Table 7-1 details the Microsoft minimum and recommended configurations for a computer running Exchange Server 2003. Keep in mind that these requirements indicate the configurations on which Exchange Server will run, not those on which it will run *well*. Many Exchange servers require multiple processors and more memory to execute the desired services.

Table 7-1. Minimum and recommended hardware configurations

Hardware	Minimum	Recommended
Processor	133 MHz Pentium or compatible	733 MHz Pentium or compatible
Memory	256 MB	512 MB
Disk space	500 MB on the drive where you install Exchange 2003; 200 MB on the system drive	Space for e-mail and public folders; multiple physical disks configured as a stripe set or stripe set with parity
Drive	CD drive or network installation point	CD drive or network installation point
Display	VGA or higher	VGA or higher

Note To allow you to verify that your hardware and software are compatible with a given Microsoft product, Microsoft publishes hardware and software compatibility lists. Because these lists are published for various Microsoft operating systems and applications and are updated often, Microsoft publishes them online in searchable form at *http://www.microsoft.com/hcl/*.

Getting Service Packs

Microsoft provides its service packs online for free and on CD-ROM for a small charge. A *service pack* is an update to an operating system or application that encompasses the solutions for multiple problems. In contrast, hot fixes, or *patches*, are solutions to single, immediate problems with an operating system or application. A service pack will include all hot fixes up to the point that the service pack is released. Service packs and hot fixes assure you quick access to the latest improvements for your operating system or applications.

To get the latest service pack or set of hot fixes from Microsoft, downloading is the way to go. Be aware, however, that although hot fixes are usually small and quick to download, a service pack is typically many megabytes in size and can take a very long time to download, even with a fast Internet connection. Most—but not all—service packs include the contents of past service packs within them. Check to make sure that the service pack you are downloading does include past service packs if you do not already have them installed on your system. This information will be in the Readme file.

Once you have downloaded a service pack, it is important that you test it on another system before implementing it in your production environment. You should test it on the exact same type of hardware you have running in your environment.

Defining the Role of Your Server

Unfortunately, the Microsoft minimum configuration—a 133-MHz Pentium with 256 MB of RAM—is not sufficient for anything but a very small organization or test server, and even then, performance will depend on what you're doing with the server. For optimal performance, you should run Exchange Server 2003 on a computer that is not also functioning as an Active Directory domain controller for your network. All domain controllers experience some capacity loss because of the overhead required to manage security for the domain. The amount of this overhead is determined by the size and activity of the domain.

Although an Exchange server performs better if it is running on a machine that is dedicated to Exchange messaging, it is not uncommon in small networks to have one machine serve as both a domain controller and an Exchange server because it saves the expense of an extra machine. Saving on a machine, however, might result in meager performance for both Microsoft Windows Server and Exchange Server 2003.

If your computer needs to play the roles of both Exchange server and domain controller, you'll want more powerful hardware than that listed in Table 7-1. Also, running Exchange Server 2003 on the domain controller means that administrators of that machine must be administrators on all domain controllers.

The Exchange Server 2003 architecture was developed to participate in an Active Directory network. In fact, you can install Exchange Server 2003 only in an Active Directory domain; the Exchange server must also have access to a Global Catalog server. All domain controllers and Global Catalog servers that Exchange Server 2003 uses must be running Windows Server 2003 or Windows 2000 Service Pack 3.

You must also have Domain Name System (DNS) resolution running in your domain, as DNS is used as a service locator by Active Directory and Exchange Server 2003. For more on this subject, see Chapter 4, "Understanding Windows Server 2003 Integration." The network can have one or more Active Directory forests, each with multiple domain trees in it, and each domain tree can consist of one or more domains. Each Exchange server must be a member server or a domain controller. If it is a member server, the Exchange server must be able to access a domain controller in order to function.

Specifying the role of a server involves more than simply configuring it as a domain controller or as a member server. It also includes indicating the services that the server will provide to the network. One of these services is IIS. Hardware capacity is even more critical if your server is also running IIS or other network applications. IIS, which is required to install Exchange Server 2003, uses considerable memory and processing power; the exact requirements depend on its configuration. For example, if IIS is configured to provide File Transfer Protocol (FTP) service as well as the Simple Mail Transport Protocol (SMTP) and Network News Transfer Protocol (NNTP) services, it uses many more CPU cycles and much more hard disk space than if it did not provide those services. When determining your hardware requirements, you should list the services that the server will host and the hardware requirements of the various applications. Start with the application with the largest hardware requirements, and then increment the RAM, processor speed, and storage capacity for each additional service by about half of its own recommendation. You will then have a fair idea of your server's hardware needs. For more information on planning your server hardware, see Chapter 6, "Planning for Deployment."

Note When you install IIS on a Windows server (either during setup or afterward), make sure the NNTP and SMTP stacks are also installed. Neither is included in the default IIS installation, and both are necessary for installing the messaging components of Exchange Server 2003.

Optimizing Hardware Through Configuration

Increasing the speed of your processor and the amount of storage and memory on your computer are effective ways of making your Exchange server more powerful. You can also optimize your existing hardware to help boost the performance of an Exchange server if you configure the operating system in the following ways:

- If possible, use one physical disk and disk controller for your operating system and another for your pagefile. You can also increase the size of your pagefile to 50 MB or 100 MB beyond the size of your physical memory.
- After installing Exchange Server 2003, designate separate physical disks to house your information stores and transaction log files. This step allows your log files to be written more quickly to disk. The reason for this increase in speed is that logs are written to disk sequentially, while the Exchange database is written randomly. Having the logs and the database on the same physical disk affects hard disk performance because of the extra time required to continually reposition the head. Furthermore, keeping the logs on a separate disk can assist you if the database disk crashes because the logs are used to recover the database.
- You can also use a stripe set consisting of multiple physical disks to house the Exchange information stores and other main components, allowing the various components to be accessed most efficiently. Using a stripe set with parity has the additional advantage of providing fault tolerance. Because messaging data is considered critical to most businesses, you should avoid striping without parity because using it increases the chances of losing all data at once. Hardware RAID using striping with parity provides better performance than software RAID because the operating system does not have the burden of managing the disk activity.

Verifying System Requirements

In addition to making sure that your computer's hardware can handle Exchange Server 2003, you need to check certain other settings before proceeding with your setup.

Windows

Exchange Server 2003 can be installed only under Windows Server 2003 or Windows 2000 Service Pack 3. Make sure the NetBIOS name given to your Windows server is the name you want your Exchange server to have. It is simple enough to change the name of a member server before installing Exchange Server 2003, but it's more difficult to do so afterward. You can change the name beforehand by clicking the Change button on the Computer Name tab of the System Properties dialog box, which is accessed by clicking the System icon in Control Panel. This displays the Computer Name Changes dialog box, as shown in Figure 7-1. For more information on Exchange Server 2003's integration with Windows, see Chapter 4.

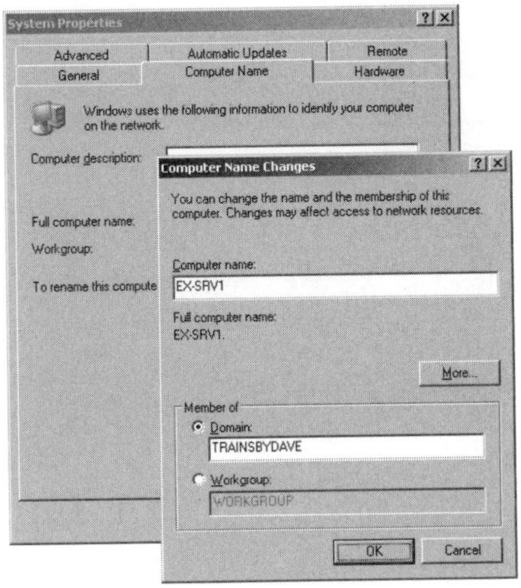

Figure 7-1. *Changing the name of your Windows server.*

Active Directory Domains

When you install the first Exchange server in an organization, you also create a new Exchange organization, routing group, and administrative group. If you are installing Exchange Server 2003 on a single-domain network or if your new Exchange routing group will not cross any domain boundaries, you should have no problems. However, if your new routing group will cross domain boundaries, you need to make sure appropriate security has been established before you start Setup.

TCP/IP

Exchange Server 2003 includes support for many Internet protocols, including SMTP, Network News Transfer Protocol (NNTP), and HTTP. All these protocols rely on the TCP/IP protocol suite to operate. In fact, SMTP is the default messaging transport mechanism in Exchange Server, meaning that TCP/IP must be properly configured on your Windows server before you install Exchange Server 2003. To configure TCP/IP on your Windows server, open the TCP/IP properties of the network connection you are using or use the Ipconfig utility, as shown in Figure 7-2. Note that each server's Ipconfig output reflects the actual IP configuration of that server—and varies widely from machine to machine.

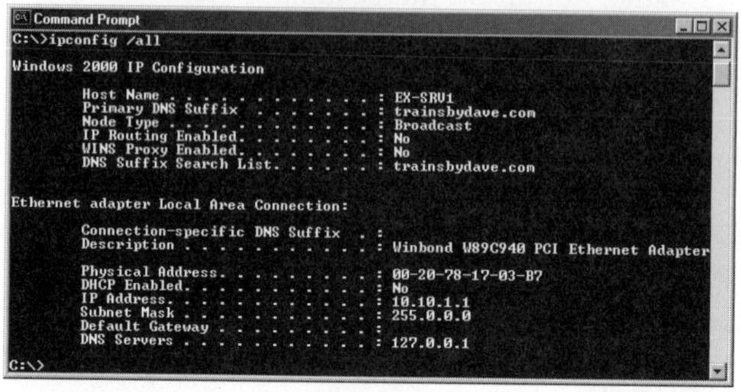
Command Prompt
C:\>ipconfig /all
Windows 2000 IP Configuration
Host Name . . . . : EX-SRV1
Primary DNS Suffix . . . . : trainsbydave.com
Node Type . . . . : Broadcast
IP Routing Enabled. . . . . : No
WINS Proxy Enabled. . . . . : No
DNS Suffix Search List. . . . . . : trainsbydave.com
Ethernet adapter Local Area Connection:
Connection-specific DNS Suffix . :
Description . . . . : Winbond W89C940 PCI Ethernet Adapter
Physical Address. . . . . : 00-20-78-17-03-B7
DHCP Enabled. . . . . : No
IP Address. . . . . : 10.10.1.1
Subnet Mask . . . . : 255.0.0.0
Default Gateway . . . . :
DNS Servers . . . . : 127.0.0.1
C:\>

Figure 7-2. *Using the Ipconfig /All command to verify TCP/IP configuration.*

> **More Info** For more information on configuring Windows networking, consult your Windows product documentation. You might also want to check out the *Microsoft Windows Server 2003 Administrator's Companion* by Charlie Russel, Sharon Crawford, and Jason Gerend (Microsoft Press).

Windows Clustering

Windows Server 2003 provides support for clustering technology, in which two Windows servers, called *nodes*, can be grouped to act as a single network unit. Clustering is designed to provide reliability through hardware redundancy. If one server in a cluster fails, another server in that cluster can take over, providing near-continuous access to network resources. To install Exchange Server 2003 in a clustered environment, you must ensure that a cluster has a single network name and IP address as well as a shared disk that is part of an external disk array. Whenever you add components to or remove components from the clustered Exchange server installation, you run the Setup program on the first node as usual. You must then run Setup again on the second node and choose the Upgrade Node option.

Creating the Exchange Administrator's Account

Exchange administration and Windows 2000 administration are handled separately. Just because an account has administrative privileges in Windows 2000 does not necessarily mean the account will have administrative privileges in

Exchange. When you install Exchange 2000 Server, one user account is given permission to administer Exchange: the account that you are logged on with when you start the installation. If you want to enable other Exchange administrators, you must do so manually, using the Exchange System snap-in.

For this reason, make sure that when you start Exchange Server Setup, you are logged on from the account you want to use for Exchange administration. This account can be the preconfigured Administrator account, your own account, or a special one you create just for the task. It should be a member of the following Active Directory security groups: Domain Admins, Enterprise Admins, and Schema Admins. Later, you can assign administrative privileges to other accounts or groups.

Alternately, you can have an enterprise administrator run the ForestPrep tool (discussed later in the chapter) and assign your account the Full Exchange Administrator permission. You will still need to have local administrative permissions on the server, as well.

Playing It Safe

It should go without saying, but we're going to say it anyway. Back up your system before you perform any action as major as installing Exchange Server 2003. You can use the Backup utility provided with Windows (which you can find in the Accessories folder). Just start the Automated System Recovery Wizard from the Welcome page of Backup to back up everything on the system and create a floppy disk you can use to start the restore process. You will need one formatted 1.44-MB floppy disk in addition to the media used in performing a backup. Should something go wrong during the installation, you'll be glad you took the extra time to perform a backup. Chapter 27, "Disaster Recovery of an Exchange 2000 Server," discusses the procedure for backing up an Exchange server by using Windows Backup. Although the procedure for backing up a Windows server is a bit different than the one described there, you can use that chapter as a tutorial for backing up your system prior to installing Exchange Server 2003 as well.

Installing Exchange Server 2003

Finally! After all the reading and planning, you actually get to run Exchange Server Setup. You can run Setup from either the Exchange Server 2003 CD-ROM or a shared network installation point. If you are using the CD-ROM, you have only to insert the disk and watch Setup start automatically. If you're installing over the network, you have to find and run the Setup program yourself. There could be multiple versions of the installation files for different encryption levels and for different languages. Be sure you find the right files for your situation. If you are performing a typical installation of Exchange Server 2003, you'll find the setup program in the root folder of the CD-ROM.

If you insert the Exchange Server 2003 CD-ROM and the Autorun feature is enabled on your system, a splash screen appears from which you can run the Exchange Deployment Tools and access other Exchange features, such as documentation and updated tools on the Web. If Autorun is disabled, you will need to run Setup.exe manually from the CD-ROM. In either case, the first thing you will see is the splash screen shown in Figure 7-3.

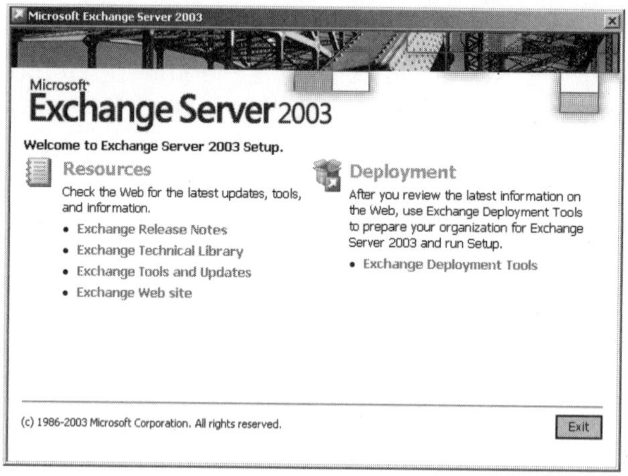

Figure 7-3. *The opening splash screen.*

Tip You should take advantage of the links to online resources provided on the splash screen. In particular, the Exchange Tools And Updates link gives you the opportunity to download updated management tools that are not available otherwise. There might even be an update available to the Exchange Deployment Tools.

Select the Exchange Deployment Tools option when you are ready to get started with your installation. The deployment tools are basically a set of reference documents that provide guided information for you to prepare your environment for Exchange installation, launch important tools like DomainPrep and ForestPrep, and then start the Exchange setup program.

Tip You don't have to use the Exchange Deployment Tools if you don't want to. Just browse to the setup\i386\ folder on the Exchange Server 2003 CD-ROM and run the setup.exe program. This method doesn't alleviate the responsibility of making sure your environment is properly prepared. It just means you can skip the guided deployment if you're already familiar with the process.

As you can see in Figure 7-4, you can use the deployment tools to perform four actions:

- Deploy the first Exchange server in an organization. That is the focus of this section.
- Deploy additional Exchange servers in an organization. We'll be covering that a bit later in the chapter, in the section "Installing in an Existing Organization."
- Perform post-installation steps. That topic is also covered later in the chapter.
- Install only the Exchange System Management Tools. This is the option to choose if, for the purposes of remote management, you want to install the management tools on a workstation or server other than the one on which Exchange is installed.

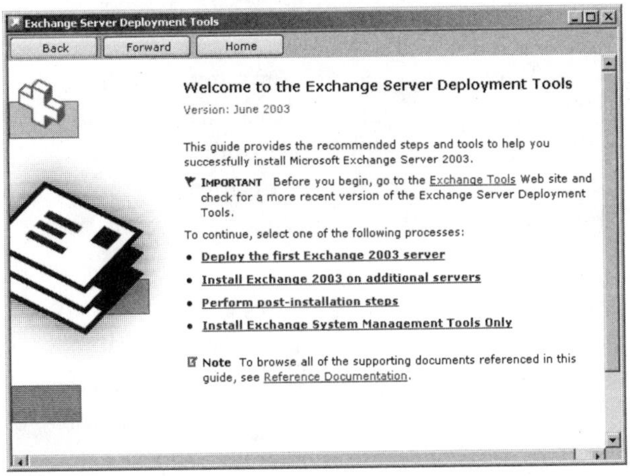

Figure 7-4. *Starting the Exchange Server Deployment Tools.*

Choose the Deploy The First Exchange 2003 Server option from the opening page and you are again presented with a list of choices. The first three options deal with Exchange 5.5 coexistence and upgrading Exchange servers; these options are covered in Part IV, "Upgrading and Migrating." The final option, New Exchange 2003 Installation, is what we're after here. Once you choose this option, you get to the real meat of the deployment tools. The resulting page presents a checklist of eight steps to complete to begin the installation of Exchange Server 2003. Check off each step as you go to make sure you are prepared for the installation. You can perform most of the steps without exiting the deployment tools. If you need to exit the deployment tools (such as to restart the server), any checks you have already filled in remain when you start the tools again. The eight steps include:

1. Verify that the server has Windows Server 2003 or Windows 2000 Service Pack 3 installed.
2. Verify that NNTP, SMTP, and WWW services are installed and running. If Windows Server 2003 is installed, also verify that ASP.NET is installed. None of these services is installed by default. Use the Add/Remove Programs Control Panel utility to install these services.
3. Install the Windows Support Tools from the Support folder on your Windows CD. These tools include the DCDiag and NetDIAG tools used in the next two steps.
4. Run the DCDiag (Domain Controller Diagnostics) tool to test network connectivity and DNS resolution for domain controllers. If you are running setup on a member server, add the option */s:*<domain controller> to specify a domain controller to test.
5. Run the NetDIAG (Network Diagnostics) tool to run a network diagnostics test on the server. This command runs a series of networking and DNS tests to ensure that the server is properly configured. The command is also run in the background during the installation of Exchange Server 2003, but a successful run now can save you the headache of a botched installation.
6. Run the ForestPrep tool to extend the Active Directory Schema with Exchange-specific classes and objects. You must be a member of the Enterprise Admins and the Schema Admins group to run this tool. The ForestPrep tool also creates a container for the Exchange organization. In the ForestPrep Wizard, you will select an account to be given the Exchange Full Administrator permission for the organization container. You must use an account with this permission to install Exchange Server 2003 or delegate permissions to install future Exchange servers. If you do not have the privileges needed to run ForestPrep, be sure to read the sidebar, "What If You're Not Allowed to Update the Schema?"
7. Run the DomainPrep tool once in each domain that will host an Exchange server. The DomainPrep tool performs a number of functions, the most important of which is creating the global security group Exchange Domain Servers and the domain local security group Exchange Enterprise Servers, which provide a context for providing permissions to Exchange servers. You must be a domain administrator to run DomainPrep.

8. Launch the Exchange Server 2003 setup program. This program is the focus of the next several sections.

> **Real World What If You're Not Allowed to Update the Schema?**
>
> In some large companies, or those with tight administrative policies, only a select few administrators might have permission to mess around with the Active Directory Schema. How, then, are you, a lowly Exchange administrator, to get your installation job done? Take heart—there is a way. You can run Exchange Setup from the command line, using a switch that causes Setup only to update the Active Directory Schema without actually installing any Exchange Server components. The command for doing this is Setup /forestprep. This means that you can hand the Exchange CD-ROM to an administrator who has permission to update the schema and let him or her update the schema for you. The administrator could also update the schema by using Exchange files on a shared network installation point. Once the schema has been updated, you can install Exchange Server 2003 yourself, provided the administrator gives your account the Full Exchange Administrator permission. There are two added bonuses to having someone else update the schema. The first is that you don't have to wait around for the update to finish. The second is that if something goes wrong, someone else gets the blame.

Once you have performed all the preinstallation tasks and launched the setup program, you'll see the welcome page of the Microsoft Exchange Installation Wizard. This page warns you to shut down any running applications before you continue. You've seen it before, but take the warning to heart. The most common reason that an Exchange Server installation fails at this point is that other MAPI-based applications are running in the background while Setup is running. These applications can include e-mail programs, Web browsers, and even components of Microsoft Office. Use the Processes tab of Task Manager to find and close any such applications. You also need to shut down all instances of System Monitor that are monitoring the server, whether they are running locally or on a remote machine. Finally, you need to make sure Event Viewer is not running on the server.

Choosing Components for Installation

After you've made sure no other programs are running, you will encounter one page of the wizard that asks you to read and accept the Microsoft End-User License Agreement and one page on which you enter the 25-digit key from the back of your Exchange CD jewel case. After you've completed these two steps and clicked Next, Setup searches for any components of Exchange Server that might already be installed on the computer. If Setup finds a previous installation of Exchange Server, you must choose whether you want to perform an upgrade. For more information about upgrading and coexisting with previous versions, see Part IV. If no previous installation is found, you are taken to the Component Selection page shown in Figure 7-5.

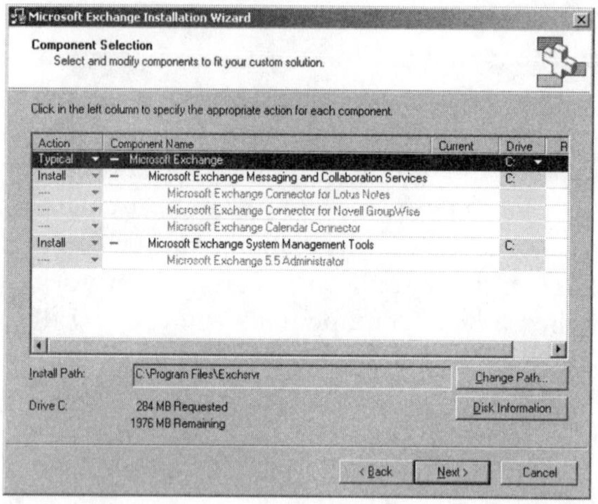

Figure 7-5. *Choosing components for an installation.*

Select one of three installation modes using the drop-down menu to the left of the Microsoft Exchange component. Typical mode (the default) installs all available components. Minimum mode installs the main Exchange component and messaging services but does not install System Manager. Custom mode lets you pick the components to install.

You can designate the drive on which you would like Exchange Server 2003 installed by selecting the Microsoft Exchange component and clicking the Drive drop-down menu to the right. You can also specify the installation path on that drive by clicking the Change Path button. All components you select to be installed are installed on the drive you choose; you cannot install individual components to different drives. Clicking the Disk Information button opens a dialog box that shows you all the drives on your system and the amount of space they have free.

If you are running Setup on a computer on which Exchange Server 2003 is already installed, you might see additional options as well, including Disaster Recovery, which attempts to reinstall the component, and Remove, which removes the component from an installation.

Note For a basic messaging system, it usually is best to install only Microsoft Exchange Messaging And Collaboration Services and Microsoft Exchange System Management Tools. However, you might want to go ahead and install the other available components if you think you might need them at some point. That way, you won't have to return to your CD-ROM to reinstall it.

Table 7-2 describes each of the components available on the Component Selection page. Once you have selected your components, click Next to go on to the next page of the Microsoft Exchange Installation Wizard.

Table 7-2. Components available in an Exchange Server 2003 installation

Component	Description
Microsoft Exchange	This is the primary node for the Exchange Server installation. To change the default drive on which other components will be installed, change the drive for this component.
Microsoft Exchange Messaging and Collaboration Services	Select Install on this node to install all the basic messaging components of Exchange, each of which is also described in this table. Once you select this component, all subcomponents are also selected. You must individually deselect any that you don't want installed.
Microsoft Exchange Connector for Lotus Notes	This item supports message and directory information transfer between Exchange Server 2003 and Lotus Notes.
Microsoft Exchange Connector for Novell GroupWise	This item supports message and directory information transfer between Exchange Server 2003 and Novell GroupWise.
Microsoft Exchange System Management Tools	This option installs the Exchange System snap-in. You must install this component to manage all Exchange components. You can also install it by itself to manage your Exchange organization remotely. For more information on using this utility, see Chapter 8, "Managing Exchange Server 2003."

Creating an Organization

In the next phase of installation, you create the organization you've been planning. First you must specify an installation type, as shown in Figure 7-6. You can choose either to create an Exchange organization or to join an existing Exchange 5.5 organization. If you will be joining an Exchange 5.5 organization, you will want to check out Part IV. If you want to create an Exchange organization, select the default option, Create A New Exchange Organization. After making your choice, click Next.

On the next page of the Installation Wizard, shown in Figure 7-7, you will name your organization. Do not take this task lightly. Although you can change an organization name later, it's better to get it right first. If you have not yet decided on the name, you haven't properly planned your organization. See Chapter 5, "Assessing Needs," and Chapter 6 for more information on planning and naming your organization. Click Next when you've entered the name.

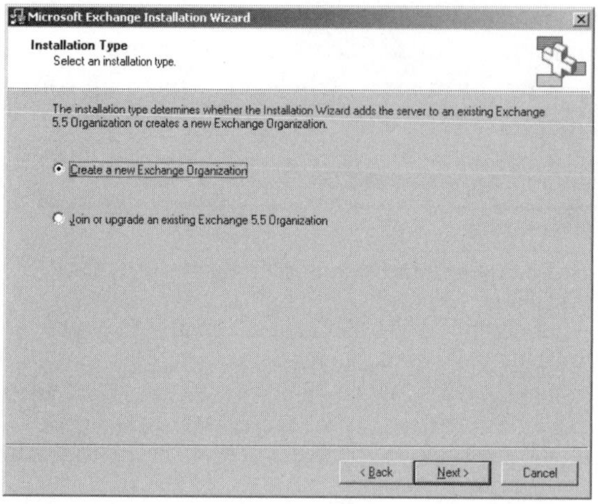

Figure 7-6. *Specifying an installation type.*

Note This section assumes that you're creating a new organization. If you're joining an existing Exchange organization, see the "Installing in an Existing Organization" section later in this chapter for a description of the slight differences between the two procedures.

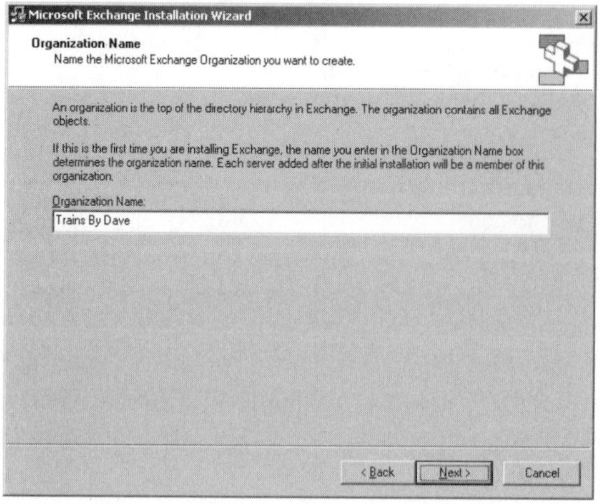

Figure 7-7. *Specifying a name for a new organization.*

Licensing

The next page of the Installation Wizard, shown in Figure 7-8, shows you the Per Seat licensing agreement. Exchange Server 2003 supports only Per Seat licensing, meaning that any client computer that connects to Exchange Server 2003 requires a Client Access License. For example, a computer that connects to Exchange Server 2003 using Microsoft Outlook 2003, one that connects using Outlook 2003 and Microsoft Internet Explorer, and one that connects using only Internet Explorer would each need one Client Access License. After you've agreed to the licensing agreement, click Next.

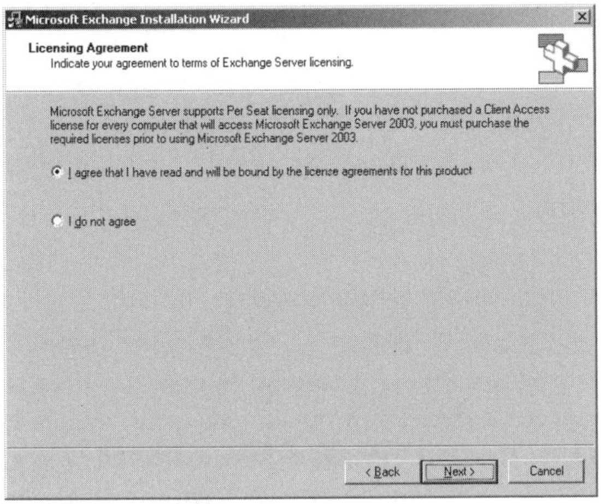

Figure 7-8. *The Per Seat licensing agreement.*

Confirming the Installation Choices

You're just about ready to start the actual installation. After you have designated a service account and clicked Next, you see an installation summary page that looks just like the Component Selection page (refer back to Figure 7-5), except that you cannot change anything. You can, however, back up through the pages in the wizard to change any information you want. When you're satisfied with the summary, click Next. Setup then begins copying files. Depending on the components you selected for installation, this can take several minutes.

During the process, Setup might notify you that it needs to extend the Active Directory Schema. This happens if you are installing Exchange Server 2003 and did not run the ForestPrep tool prior to installation. If you are logged on with a user account that has appropriate permissions to do this, go ahead and click OK. Don't be alarmed if it seems as though Setup is not getting anywhere. The schema updating process can take quite a bit of time (even hours), depending on your situation. (This might be a great chance to go get some lunch!) When Setup completes the task, the Installation Wizard will indicate that the installation was successful. Click Finish, and the new Exchange services will start.

Installing in an Existing Organization

Installing Exchange Server 2003 in an existing Exchange organization is nearly identical to installing it as the first server in an organization. You need to be aware of only a couple of small differences in the procedure. You start Setup the same way: from either the CD-ROM or a network installation point. The first difference you will notice is that you are not able to change the organization name. The name is displayed (refer back to Figure 7-7), but it is dimmed.

After you've chosen your administrative and routing groups, the rest of the process is no different from the one you used to install the first server in an organization. Make sure you select the Exchange service account used by other servers in the organization.

Real World Automating Exchange Server Setup 2003

If you plan to deploy a large number of Exchange servers in your enterprise or if you need to deploy servers remotely, you will be glad to know there is a way to automate the setup process. Setup places all the information that controls its file-copying process in a file named Setup.ini. The file is customized for a particular installation when you make choices in the various Installation Wizard pages described previously.

You can create your own Setup.ini files using tools and samples included in the Exchange Server 2003 Resource Kit. You can then create a batch script that runs the Setup program, using the information in your customized file. If you are deploying Exchange Server 2003 on existing Windows servers in your enterprise, you can also use Microsoft Systems Management Server or a similar application to further automate the process.

More Info To learn more about automating Exchange Server Setup, including all the parameters for customizing the Setup.ini files, consult the online product documentation.

Verifying Your Installation

You've installed Exchange Server, but don't pat yourself on the back just yet. You still need to perform some basic postinstallation tasks to make sure everything is running well. The first thing you should do is restart your server. After you've done so, check the Windows event log for any problems. Each Exchange component that makes up your new server runs as Windows services. You can verify that these services are running by using the Services tool, available from the Administrative Tools folder on the Start menu. Figure 7-9 shows the Services console window. You should see the following services listed:

- Microsoft Exchange Event
- Microsoft Exchange IMAP4
- Microsoft Exchange Information Store
- Microsoft Exchange Management
- Microsoft Exchange MTA Stacks
- Microsoft Exchange POP3
- Microsoft Exchange Routing Engine
- Microsoft Exchange Site Replication Service
- Microsoft Exchange System Attendant

Depending on the optional components you installed with Exchange Server 2003, you might also see several other Microsoft Exchange services running.

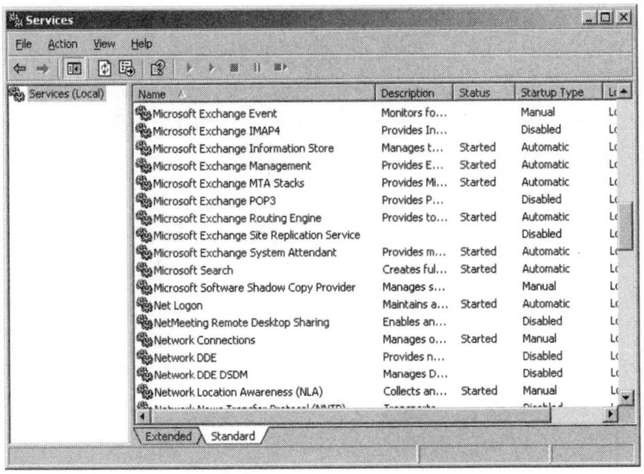

Figure 7-9. *The Services console window.*

Microsoft releases service packs for Exchange Server 2003, just as it does for Windows. To avoid possible problems later on, it is best to install the latest available Exchange Server 2003 service pack. See the "Getting Service Packs" section earlier in this chapter for more information. If you are concerned about the latest service pack introducing new problems (and they often do), consider testing the service pack on a nonproduction server first. After you've installed the service pack, you should restart the system again. When the server is back on line, check the Services console window again to ensure that the Exchange Server services are up and running. Your new Exchange server is ready to be configured. *Now* you can pat yourself on the back. And now that you've installed Exchange Server 2003, you're ready to apply the other software you need to integrate your Exchange environment, such as third-party backup software, virus-detection utilities, or content filtering applications.

> **Note** To verify that services are running on a remote Exchange Server, you can use the Connect To Another Computer feature of the Computer Management snap-in. You can also use server monitors to keep watch over services for you in the Exchange System snap-in. You'll learn how to set up these monitors in Chapter 26, "Monitoring Exchange Server 2003."

One of the first things you might be tempted to do after successfully installing Exchange Server 2003 is poke around the system to see what was put where. This is fine, of course, and it's a great way to learn more about how Exchange is laid out.

Summary

This chapter described how to install Exchange Server 2003. It discussed how to prepare your Windows server for the installation, including how to verify that the hardware on the server meets requirements for installing Exchange Server 2003 in the desired configuration. It then took you step by step through the installation process and described how to verify the installation once the setup routine is finished. Now that you have installed Exchange Server 2003, it is time to learn how to use it. Chapter 8 begins that process with a look at using the Microsoft Management Console and the Exchange System snap-in.

Chapter 8
Managing Exchange Server 2003

Now that you've installed Microsoft Exchange Server 2003, you're probably eager to start working with it. You'll want to begin creating users, groups, and other recipients, but first you need to know some basics of managing the Exchange system. For the most part, you will manage Exchange Server with tools called *snap-ins*, which work within Microsoft Management Console (MMC). The primary tool you will use is the Exchange System snap-in, which provides a graphical environment for configuring the various services and components of an Exchange organization. This chapter takes a look at the general workings of MMC and the Exchange System snap-in. Then, in the next chapter, you will learn how to use the Active Directory Users And Computers snap-in to set up and manage users, contacts, and groups.

Microsoft Management Console

Microsoft Management Console (MMC) provides a common environment for the management of various system and network resources. MMC is actually a framework that hosts modules called snap-ins, which provide the actual tools for managing a resource. For example, you will manage Exchange Server 2003 using the snap-in named Exchange System.

Note The start menu icon that loads the Exchange System snap-in is called *System Manager*, and you can do all your administration by selecting. This section, however, focuses on the Exchange System snap-in itself.

MMC itself does not provide any management functionality. Rather, the MMC environment provides for seamless integration between snap-ins. This allows administrators and other users to create custom management tools from snap-ins created by various vendors. Administrators can save the tools they have created for later use and share them with other administrators and users. This model gives administrators the ability to delegate administrative tasks by creating different tools of varying levels of complexity and giving them to the users who will perform the tasks. For example, you could create a custom console that allowed a user to add users, configure mailboxes, and create public folders only in an Exchange organization and nowhere else.

The MMC User Interface

When you first load MMC, you might notice that it looks a lot like Microsoft Windows Explorer. MMC uses a multiple-document interface, meaning that you can load and display multiple console windows in the MMC parent window simultaneously. Figure 8-1 shows the MMC parent window with the Exchange System snap-in loaded. The next few sections discuss the main parts of this window.

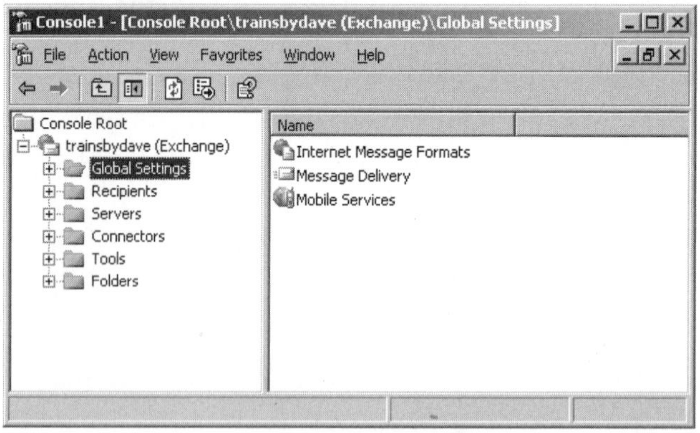

Figure 8-1. *MMC window with the Exchange System snap-in loaded.*

MMC Menu Bar

The main MMC menu bar always holds three menus: Console, Window, and Help. The Window and Help menus are pretty much what you would expect. The Window menu lets you manage console windows if you have more than one window open in MMC. The Help menu lets you access general MMC Help as well as Help for the snap-ins that are currently loaded. The Console menu is where most of the action is. From this menu, you can open and save consoles and even create new ones. You can also add snap-ins to and remove them from open consoles and set general MMC options. Options you can set include the following:

- **Console Title** Specifies the console name as it appears in the MMC title bar.
- **Console Mode** Author mode grants the user full access to all MMC functionality. User mode comes in three flavors: Full Access lets the user access all MMC commands but not add or remove snap-ins or

change console properties; Limited Access Multiple Window allows the user to access only the areas of the console tree that were visible when the console was saved and to open new windows; Limited Access Single Window works the same as Limited Access Multiple Window, except that users cannot open new windows.

Other options define whether users can access context menus on taskpads, save changes to the console, and customize views.

MMC Toolbar

The MMC toolbar is a standard Windows toolbar that provides access to commonly used MMC commands. By default, these commands include ones to open and save a console, create a new console, and open a new window.

Snap-in Action Bar

The snap-in action bar is actually a combination menu bar and toolbar; you can separate the two by dragging if you want. Although the actual menus (Action, View, and Favorites) remain the same no matter what console you have open, the commands on these menus can change a bit according to the open console.

The Action menu typically contains commands that apply to whatever container or object you have selected in your console. These commands duplicate the commands available on the shortcut menu that you see when you right-click an object. The Action menu lets you perform actions such as creating new views and objects in containers, opening an object's property sheet, and accessing tasks.

The View menu lets you control how information is displayed in the details pane of your console. You can, for example, change from icon to list view or customize the columns displayed.

The Favorites menu lets you add items to a list of favorites and organize that list into categories. The Favorites list can include shortcuts to tools, items in the console, or tasks.

The toolbar portion of the action bar provides quick access to some of the more commonly used actions associated with selected objects. Many icons on the toolbar change depending on the object selected in the scope pane or details pane of your console.

Scope Pane

The scope pane contains a hierarchy of containers referred to as a console tree. Some containers are displayed as unique icons that graphically represent the type of items they contain. Others are displayed as folders, simply indicating that they hold other objects. Click on the plus sign next to a container to expand it and display the objects inside. Click on the minus sign to collapse the container again.

Details Pane

The details pane changes to show the contents of the container selected in the scope pane. In other words, the details pane shows the results of the currently selected scope. The details pane can display information in a number of ways, referred to as *views*. You can access the standard views—large or small icon, list, and detail—through the View menu.

> **Note** The View menu also lets you customize the columns that are shown in the scope and details panes. In the details pane itself, you can rearrange columns and click a column heading to reorder rows alphabetically or chronologically.

In addition to the standard views, you can also create a taskpad view to show in the details pane. A taskpad view is a dynamic HTML (DHTML) page that presents shortcuts to commands available for a selected item in the scope pane. Each command is represented as a task that consists of an image, a label, a description, and a mechanism for instructing the snap-in to run that command. Users can run the commands by clicking a task.

You can use taskpad views to do the following:

- Include shortcuts to all the tasks a specific user might need to perform.
- Group tasks by function or user by creating multiple taskpad views in a console.
- Create simplified lists of tasks. For example, you can add tasks to a taskpad view and then hide the console tree.
- Simplify complex tasks. For example, if a user frequently performs a given task involving several snap-ins and other tools, you can organize, in a single location, shortcuts to those tasks that run the appropriate property sheets, command lines, dialog boxes, or scripts.

Snap-in Root Node

The snap-in root node is the uppermost node in the snap-in; it is usually named based on the product or task that it is associated with. MMC supports standalone and extension snap-ins. A standalone snap-in, such as Exchange System, provides management functionality without requiring support from another snap-in. Only one snap-in root node exists for each standalone snap-in. An extension snap-in requires a parent snap-in above it in the console tree. Extension snap-ins extend the functionality provided by other snap-ins.

Containers and Objects

Exchange Server 2003 is a great example of an object-based, hierarchical directory environment. All the little bits and pieces that make up Exchange are objects that interact with one another to some degree. The objects you see in the scope and details panes can be divided into two types:

- **Containers** Containers can contain both other containers and non-container objects. Container objects can also appear in the details pane. They are used to logically group all the objects that make up a management environment. An administrator uses the container objects to organize the tree and then to navigate through it.
- **Leaf objects** A leaf object is simply an object that cannot contain other objects. Some common leaf objects with which an administrator works daily include servers and connectors.

You manage all the objects in an MMC console through the use of property sheets. A *property sheet* is a dialog box you open by selecting an object and then choosing Properties from the Action menu. It consists of one or more tabs that contain controls for setting a group of related properties. Figure 8-2 shows the property sheet for a server object in the Exchange System snap-in.

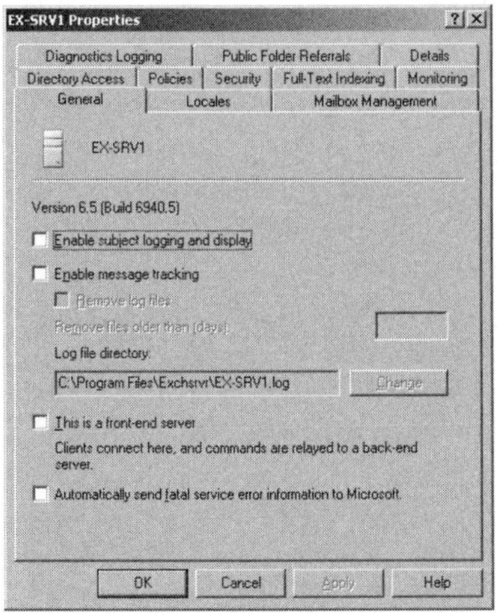

Figure 8-2. *Property sheet for a server object.*

How MMC Works

The MMC interface permits snap-ins to integrate within a common management console. This gives all snap-ins a similar look and feel, although they might perform their tasks in different ways. The console itself offers no management functions; it merely acts as a host to the snap-ins. Snap-ins always reside in a console; they do not run by themselves.

Snap-ins

Each MMC tool is built of a collection of instances of smaller tools called MMC snap-ins. A snap-in is the smallest unit of console extension and represents one unit of management behavior. The snap-in might call on other supporting controls and dynamic-link libraries (DLLs) to accomplish its task.

Snap-ins extend MMC by adding and enabling management behavior. They can provide this behavior in a number of ways. For example, a snap-in might add elements to the container tree, or it might extend a particular tool by adding shortcut menu items, toolbars, property sheet tabs, wizards, or Help to an existing snap-in. There are two basic types of snap-ins:

- **Standalone snap-ins** Provide management functionality even if they are alone in a console with no other supporting snap-ins. They do not rely on any other snap-ins being present. The Exchange System snap-in is an example of a standalone snap-in.
- **Extension snap-ins** Provide a variety of functionality, but only when used in conjunction with a parent snap-in. Some extend the console namespace, while others simply extend context menus or specific wizards.

Note Many snap-ins support both modes of operation, offering some standalone functionality and also extending the functionality of other snap-ins.

Packages

Snap-ins are usually shipped in groups called *packages*. For example, the Microsoft Windows operating system itself includes one or more packages of snap-ins. Additionally, other vendors might ship products composed entirely of packages of snap-ins. Grouping snap-ins into packages provides convenience for downloading and installation. It also permits several snap-ins to share core DLLs so that these DLLs do not have to be placed in every snap-in.

Custom Tools

MMC provides functionality for creating custom management tools. It allows administrators to create, save, and then delegate a customized console of multiple snap-ins tailored for specific tasks. Administrators can assemble these specific snap-ins into a tool (also called a *document*) that runs in one instance of MMC. For example, you can create a tool that manages many different aspects of the network—Active Directory, replication topology, file sharing, and so on. After assembling a tool, the administrator can save it in an .MSC file and then reload the file later to instantly re-create the tool. The .MSC file can also be e-mailed to another administrator, who can then load the file and use the tool.

Custom Consoles

One of the primary benefits of MMC is its support for customization of tools. You can build custom MMC consoles tailored for specific management tasks and then delegate those consoles to other administrators. These tools can focus on the particular management requirements of various administrator groups. For example, suppose that you have a group of administrators who need to be able to manage the connectors that let your Exchange organization communicate with a Lotus Notes organization. Suppose also that you do not want these administrators to have access to other management functionality in your Exchange organization. You could easily create a customized console that provided only the wanted capabilities. You could also extend any console already used by these administrators to include the additional management capabilities.

> **More Info** Obviously, there is a lot more to MMC than we can do justice to in a single chapter, especially when the chapter is really about using the Exchange System snap-in. For more information about MMC, start with the Help file available from any console window.

Using the Exchange System Snap-in

The Exchange System snap-in provides a graphical view of all the resources and components of an Exchange organization. No matter how many administrative and routing groups or servers you have set up, you can manage them all from a single Exchange System console window. Use this window, and the property sheets of all the objects in it, to navigate the Exchange organizational hierarchy and perform the various tasks associated with Exchange administration.

You will use both container and leaf objects to administer an Exchange organization. Most objects in the Exchange System console window—both container and leaf—have a property sheet that allows you to configure various parameters for that object and make it act in the way that will best serve the organization's needs. You can open an object's property sheet by selecting the object and choosing Properties from the Action menu. You can also right-click an object and choose Properties from its shortcut menu. You use property sheets to both configure and administer Exchange Server.

Real World Explore!

The sheer number of property sheets you will encounter when administering Exchange Server 2003 can seem daunting, but don't let them intimidate you. Take the time to play with the program. You probably won't be able to remember exactly where to go to accomplish every administrative task in Exchange Server, but it helps to think about what the task will involve. If you need to manage communication between two routing groups, find the Connectors container. If you need to manage communication between two servers, use the Servers container and check out the Message Transfer Agent (MTA). Each component handles a different aspect of the configuration, so multiple components might be involved with a single configuration or administrative task. As you use the program and get used to the Exchange environment, it will become easier to navigate the program and find exactly the object or objects you need to administer.

Learning the contents and layout of the various property sheets in the Exchange System snap-in is a key part of learning how Exchange Server works. Once you know how to organize tasks that match the way Exchange Server is structured, you will find that your administrative tasks flow more easily.

To administer an Exchange environment with the Exchange System snap-in, you must be logged on to Active Directory under a domain user account that has administrative privileges for Exchange Server. Until you specifically grant other user accounts privileges to administer Exchange Server, the only account with permission to do so is the account you were logged on with when you installed Exchange Server 2003.

Examining the Exchange Hierarchy

The top of the hierarchy in the scope pane of the Exchange System snap-in is the snap-in root node that represents the Exchange organization, as shown in Figure 8-3. In this example, the snap-in root node is named Trains By Dave (Exchange). All the Exchange containers are held within this node. There are six primary containers directly within the snap-in root node. The sections that follow describe each of these containers.

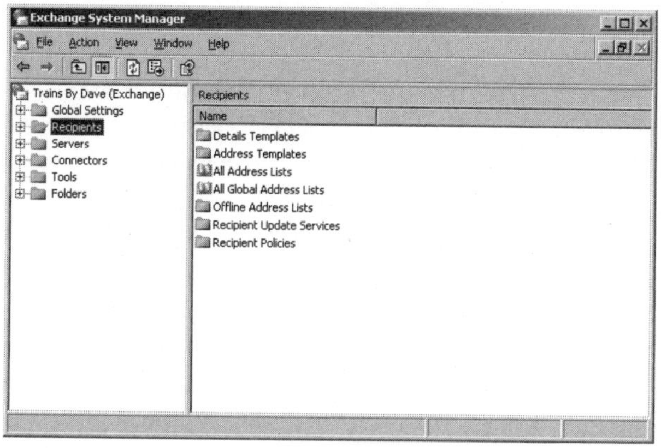

Figure 8-3. *The Exchange hierarchy.*

Note What you see in the main Exchange System scope pane depends on whether you have configured multiple administrative groups and whether you have configured the Exchange System snap-in to display administrative groups. If you have only one administrative group and have not changed the default settings, you will see the six containers discussed here. If you have multiple administrative groups and you have configured the Exchange System snap-in to display those groups, you will not see the Servers, Connectors, and Folders containers in the main display. Instead, you will see a container named Administrative Groups that in turn holds a container for each administrative group defined in your organization. Each of those administrative group containers will hold the five missing containers, because each of those items can be configured at the level of the administrative group. You will learn a lot more about working with administrative groups in Chapter 12, "Using Administrative and Routing Groups."

Global Settings Container

The Global Settings container holds objects governing settings that apply to your entire organization. Inside this container, you will find three objects. The first, Internet Message Formats, defines the formatting for SMTP messages sent over the Internet. Chapter 20, "Supporting Internet Protocols and SMTP," discusses the use of this object in detail.

The second object in the Global Settings container, Message Delivery, is used to configure message defaults for your organization. You can open the property sheet for this object by selecting the object and choosing Properties from the Action menu. The Defaults tab, shown in Figure 8-4, lets you set message limit defaults for your organization. You can set the maximum size, in kilobytes, for both incoming and outgoing messages, and you can set the maximum number of recipients that can exist on a server.

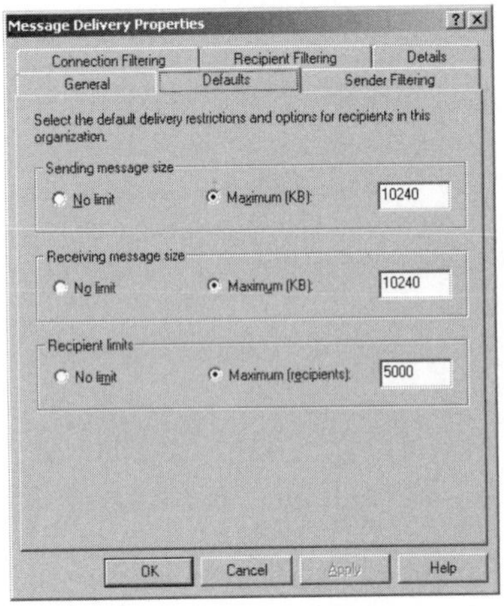

Figure 8-4. *Setting messaging defaults for your organization.*

The Filtering tabs let you create filters for handling messages from particular SMTP addresses, to particular recipients, or over particular connections. For each type of filter you create, you can specify whether messages should be deleted or dropped into custom folders. Filter provides a powerful method for blocking unwanted messages (spam) from reaching your recipients or to automatically group all suspect messages into a single location. You can learn more about this in Part VII, "Security."

The final object in the Global Settings container, Mobile Services, is used to configure wireless access and synchronization with the Exchange server. You'll learn more about this in Chapter 22, "Mobile Services in Exchange Server 2003."

Recipients Container

The Recipients container is used to manage server settings that apply to recipients in your organization. You can define recipient policies, manage address lists, and even modify address templates. All these actions are covered in Chapter 9, "Creating and Managing Recipients."

Servers Container

The configuration objects held within the Servers container will depend on how you have set up your organization. If your organization has only one administrative group, your Servers container holds one container for each of the servers in your organization. If your organization has more than one administrative group, you will find the containers for the individual servers inside those administrative group containers.

Regardless of how your organization is configured, the server containers are where you will perform a good bit of your Exchange administration. Within each server container, you will find configuration objects for managing the protocols, connectors, and storage groups configured on the server. The next several chapters of this book cover the various aspects of server management in detail and from a few different perspectives. In particular, you will learn to manage server components in Chapter 11, "Using Storage Groups," Chapter 12, and Chapter 13, "Connecting Routing Groups."

Connectors Container

The Connectors container holds configuration items for each of the connectors available within your organization. If you have only one administrative group, the Connectors container appears as a primary container under the organization. If you have multiple administrative groups, a Connectors container will appear for each group inside the group container.

The objects within the Connectors container represent both connectors between routing groups in your organization and connectors to foreign messaging systems. Chapter 13 covers connectors between routing groups, and Chapter 21, "Connecting to Other Messaging Systems with X.400," describes connectors to foreign messaging systems.

Tools Container

The Tools container holds objects that help you manage your Exchange organization. You'll find four containers within the Tools container. The Site Replication Services container lets you configure replication with existing Exchange 5.5 sites, using the Active Directory Connector. This topic is covered in Part IV, "Upgrading and Migrating."

The Message Tracking Center object is actually a shortcut for opening the Message Tracking Center, which lets you track specific messages in your organization. The Monitoring and Status container holds objects that let you monitor the status of servers and connections in your organization. Both of these objects are covered in Chapter 26, "Monitoring Exchange Server 2003."

The Mailbox Recovery Center allows you to simultaneously recover multiple disconnected mailboxes (for example, mailboxes no longer associated with a user). This feature is covered in Chapter 9.

Folders Container

The last container in the hierarchy is Folders. The Folders container holds the public folders hierarchy and the folders' properties, but not their contents. It also contains the system folders, a list of folders that Exchange users do not see. The system folders hold the Offline Address Book and other system configuration objects. If you have only one administrative group, the Folders container appears as a primary container under the organization. If you have multiple administrative groups, a Folders container will appear for each group inside the group container. You will learn more about configuring folders in Chapter 10, "Using Public Folders."

Customizing an Exchange System Console

The Exchange System snap-in is actually a saved console file that connects to a domain controller to get configuration information regarding your Exchange organization. In certain instances, however, you might want to direct the snap-ins to a particular domain or domain controller. For example, you might want to connect to a specific domain in an Active Directory forest or to different domain controllers in different forests to manage different companies or divisions. You might also want to create custom consoles for novice administrators or administrators to whom you want to give only limited access to Exchange resources. Fortunately, MMC makes all of this pretty easy.

To create a custom console or redirect an Exchange console to another domain controller, the first thing you need to do is to open MMC directly. The easiest way to do this is with the Run command on the Start menu. Enter *MMC* at the prompt. A blank MMC window opens, as shown in Figure 8-5. Next, choose Add/Remove Snap-In from the Console menu. This opens the dialog box shown in Figure 8-6. Here you can add any number of snap-ins to customize your console.

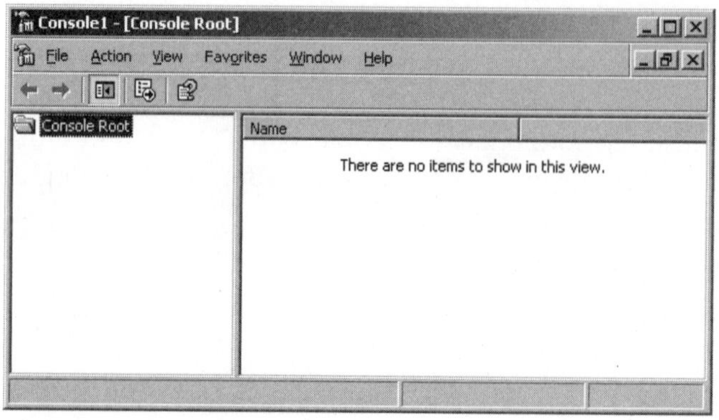

Figure 8-5. *Opening MMC directly.*

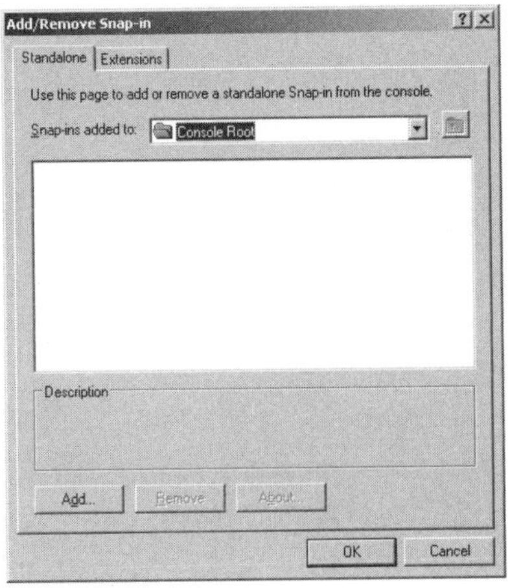

Figure 8-6. *Adding standalone snap-ins to a console.*

Real World Connection Requirements

The Exchange System snap-in interoperates with Exchange 2000 Server using local procedure calls (LPCs) or remote procedure calls (RPCs). A *procedure call* is an application programming interface (API) that connects to another program and runs using various data interface points. LPCs run on the same machine, so when you run the Exchange System snap-in on the Exchange server to which you are connected, you have invoked LPCs. RPCs run as a session-layer API between two different networked computers. RPCs are an open standard and can run over multiple protocols, such as NetBEUI, SPX, Banyan Vines, and TCP/IP. When you run the Exchange System snap-in on a computer that is different from the Exchange server to which you are connected, you have invoked RPCs. This means that to connect to a server, the Exchange System snap-in must be installed on the Exchange server itself or must be connected to an Exchange server via a network connection that supports RPCs.

Now let's look at creating a console that duplicates the functionality of the System Manager icon found on the Start menu, but allows you to redirect the connection to another domain controller. Click the Add button to open another dialog box that lists the standalone snap-ins available on your system. This dialog box is shown in Figure 8-7.

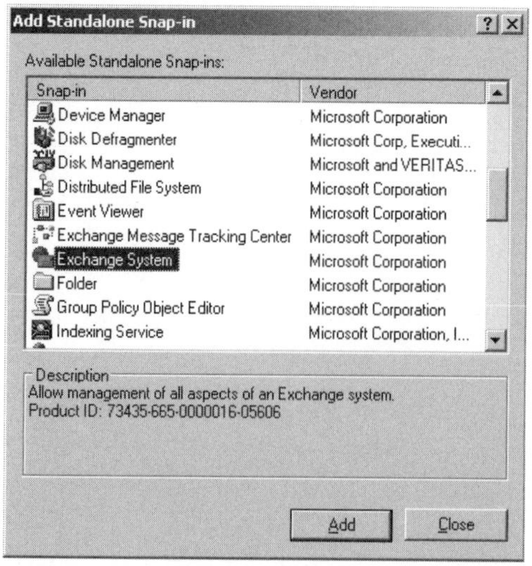

Figure 8-7. *Choosing from the available snap-ins.*

From the list of available snap-ins, choose Exchange System, and then click Add. The Change Domain Controller dialog box, shown in Figure 8-8, opens. In the list of domain controllers, choose the controller to which you want to direct the connection. You can also choose to direct the connection to any writable domain controller, in which case the connection will be made to the first domain controller to respond whenever you open the new console. When you are satisfied with your selection, click OK. Once you exit the remaining dialog boxes, you are taken back to the console window and can start using your new console. Remember to save it if it is a console you will want to use in the future.

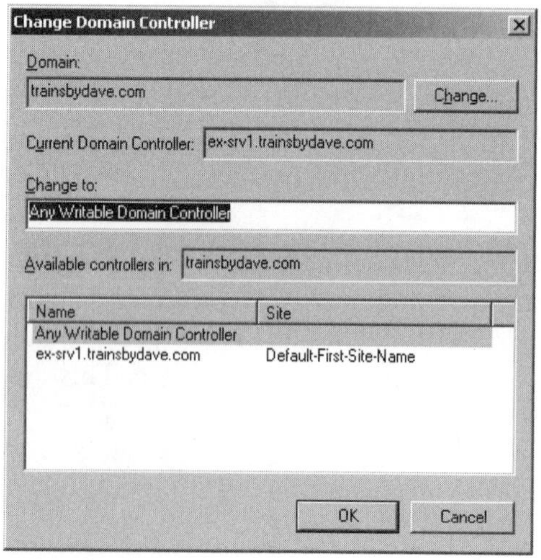

Figure 8-8. *Directing the connection to another domain controller.*

Instead of choosing the full Exchange System snap-in from the list in the Add Standalone Snap-In dialog box (refer back to Figure 8-7), you can choose one or more snap-ins that serve a more limited purpose:

- **Exchange Folders** Creates a console with only the tools for managing public folders. You can find more on this in Chapter 10.
- **Exchange Message Tracking Center** Creates a console displaying only the message tracking features. You'll learn more about using this tool in Chapter 23, "Security Policies and Exchange Server 2003."

Summary

This chapter provided a basic introduction to the tools used to administer an Exchange Server 2003 organization. The primary tool you will use to administer Microsoft Exchange Server 2003 is the Exchange System snap-in for the Microsoft Management Console, which provides a graphical environment for configuring the various services and components of an Exchange organization. Within this snap-in, you work primarily with the property sheets of objects. Chapter 9 begins a series of chapters that look at specific aspects of Exchange administration. In it, you will learn how to create and manage the basic Exchange recipients.

Chapter 9
Creating and Managing Recipients

Sending and receiving information is the foundation of messaging, groupware, and, of course, of Microsoft Exchange Server 2003. In this chapter, we start looking at the message transfer process within an Exchange system. Exchange Server 2003 is based on a multitude of messaging components, but with some analysis, it becomes apparent how these components interact to create an enterprise-wide messaging system.

Recipients are objects in the Active Directory directory service that reference resources that can receive messages through interaction with Exchange Server 2003. Such a resource might be a mailbox in the mailbox store in which one of your users gets e-mail, a public folder in which information is shared among many users, or even a newsgroup on the Internet.

No matter where a resource resides, however, a recipient object for that resource is always created within Active Directory on your network. One of your main tasks as an administrator is to create and maintain these recipient objects. Therefore, in addition to discussing mailboxes and message transfer, this chapter explains how to create and manage various types of messaging recipients. It also discusses tools that allow you to search for and organize recipients.

Understanding Recipient Types

Thinking of a recipient as a mailbox or simply as an object that can receive a message is tempting, and as you administer your organization, it might be convenient to take that view. But it is important to understand the ways in which the underlying architecture affects how you work with recipients in Exchange Server.

In Exchange Server, a recipient object does not receive messages. Instead, it is a reference to a resource that can receive messages. This is a subtle but important distinction. Recipient objects are contained in and maintained by Active Directory. The resources that those objects reference could be anywhere. One resource might be a mailbox for a user in your organization. A mailbox resource would be contained in the mailbox store of a particular Exchange server and maintained by its Information Store service. Another resource might be a user on the Internet. In this case, the recipient object would contain a reference to that resource, along with rules governing the transfer of messages. Five types of recipient objects are available in Exchange:

- **User** A user is any individual with logon privileges on the network. With regard to Exchange Server, each user in Active Directory can be mailbox-enabled, mail-enabled, or neither. As you'll recall from earlier chapters, a mailbox-enabled user has an associated mailbox on an Exchange server. Each user mailbox is a private storage area that allows an individual user to send, receive, and store messages. A mail-enabled user has an e-mail address and can receive, but not send, messages.
- **Contact** A contact is essentially a pointer to a mailbox in an external messaging system and is most likely used by a person outside the organization. This type of recipient points both to an address that will be used to deliver messages sent to that person and to the properties that govern how those messages are delivered. Contacts are most often used for connecting your organization to foreign messaging systems, such as Lotus Notes or the Internet. An administrator creates contacts so that frequently used e-mail addresses are available in the Global Address List as real names. This makes it easier to send e-mail because users do not need to guess cryptic e-mail addresses.
- **Group** A group is an object to which you can assign certain permissions and rights. Users who are placed in a group are automatically given the permissions and rights of the group. Exchange Server 2003 uses the concept of mail-enabled groups to form distribution lists. Messages sent to a group are redirected and sent to each member of that group. Groups can contain any combination of the other types of recipients, including other groups. These groups allow users to send messages to multiple recipients without having to address each recipient individually. A typical group is the one named Everyone. All Exchange recipients are made members of the Everyone group. When a public announcement is made, the sender of the announcement simply selects the Everyone group and is not forced to select every user's mailbox from the Global Address List.
- **Public folder** A public folder is a public storage area, typically open to all users in an organization. Users can post new messages or reply to existing messages in a public folder, creating an ongoing forum for discussion of topics. Public folders can also be used to store and provide access to just about any type of document. The concept of a public

folder as a recipient is sometimes difficult to grasp because the repository for information is shared. One way that a public folder is used as a recipient is when it is configured for a Network News Transfer Protocol (NNTP) news feed. Under this arrangement, the information from the newsgroup is sent to the public folder recipient and can then be viewed by Exchange users in the organization.

- ***InetOrgPerson*** The *InetOrgPerson* is a specialized user object that can be mail-enabled or mailbox-enabled. The object class is defined for use in LDAP and X.500 directories to hold information about people. In the Exchange and Active Directory world, however, the user object is typically associated with people. Support for the *InetOrgPerson* object has been added to Exchange Server 2003 mainly so that *InetOrgPerson* objects from other directory services can be easily migrated to an Exchange organization.

Although a public folder is a type of recipient, it performs many more functions than just transferring or receiving messages. For that reason, this chapter focuses on the other recipient types: users, contacts, and groups. Chapter 10, "Using Public Folders," is devoted to a full review of the features, functions, and administration requirements of public folders.

Users

As you are aware, Exchange Server 2003 is tightly integrated with Active Directory. In fact, the tool used to create user accounts, Active Directory Users and Computers, is also the tool used to create and manage mailboxes for your users. Exchange-related configuration details show up as extra tabs on the user's property sheet. This means that Exchange administrators and Active Directory administrators need to work together now more than ever. Although many administrators from the days of Exchange 5.5 hate the idea of giving up control of mailbox administration, doing so is usually the best course of action. Because all the user-related functions of mailboxes can now be managed from within Active Directory Users and Computers, letting one accounts administrator handle all user-related tasks from a single location makes sense. Users can have two possible e-mail configurations: the mailbox-enabled user and the mail-enabled user. Each of these configurations is detailed in the sections that follow.

Mailbox-Enabled Users

Mailboxes—the mainstay of any messaging system—are private, server-based storage areas in which user e-mail is kept. Every user in your organization must have access to a mailbox to send and receive messages because it is one of the primary methods of communication. In Exchange Server 2003, a user with a mailbox is referred to as a mailbox-enabled user. Mailbox-enabled users can send and receive messages as well as store messages on an Exchange server. One of your principal tasks as an administrator is to create and configure mailboxes for users.

Creating a New Mailbox-Enabled User

When Exchange Server 2003 is installed, several extensions for the Active Directory Users and Computers tool are installed as well. As a result, whenever you create a new user, you are automatically given the chance to create a mailbox for that user. To create a new user in Active Directory Users and Computers, make sure the Users container is selected, and then choose New User from the Action menu. This starts the New User Wizard, the first two screens of which are shown in Figure 9-1.

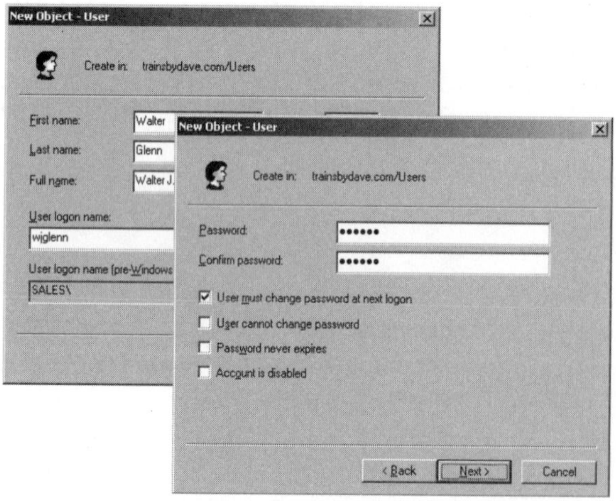

Figure 9-1. *Creating a new user account with Active Directory Users and Computers.*

If you have worked with Active Directory, you are probably familiar with the process of creating and naming a new user and giving that user a password. This is what you do in the first two screens of the wizard. However, Exchange adds a third screen for creating an Exchange mailbox, which appears after you enter the typical user information (Figure 9-2). Here you can choose whether to create a mailbox, and you can also enter an alias (an alternate means of addressing a user that is covered later in this section) and indicate the Exchange server and the storage group on that server where the new user's mailbox should be created. Once you are finished, click Next to display a summary screen for the new user. When you click Finish on this screen, the new user and mailbox are created.

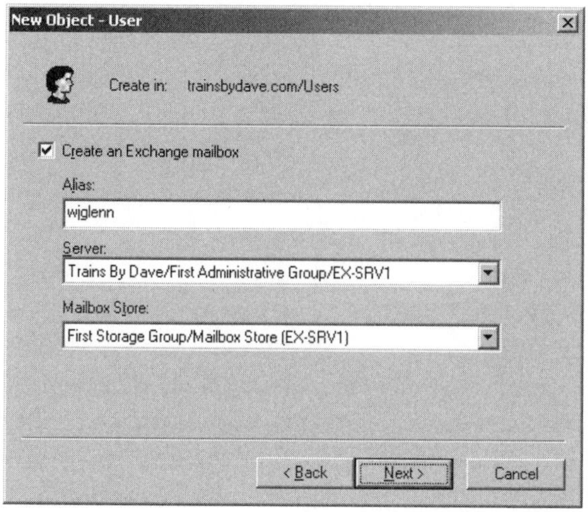

Figure 9-2. *Creating a mailbox for your new user.*

Creating a mailbox for an existing user is just as easy as creating one for a new user. Simply select any existing user in the Users folder in Active Directory Users and Computers, and choose Exchange Tasks from the Action menu. This command opens the Exchange Task Wizard, allowing you to add and configure the mailbox for the user.

Configuring Mailbox Properties

No matter which method you use to create mailboxes, you configure them in the same way—with the user object's property sheet. To do so, select any user object in Active Directory Users and Computers, and then choose Properties from the Action menu. The property sheet for a user has quite a few tabs. The next several sections cover the tabs that pertain to Exchange mailbox configuration.

> **Tip** Several tabs on the user object's property sheet hold advanced properties and are not displayed by default when you open a user's property sheet. To see these tabs, choose Advanced Features from the View menu of Active Directory Users and Computers before you open a property sheet.

General Tab

The General tab, shown in Figure 9-3, is where you configure basic user information. The first name, middle initial, and last name that you enter here are used to generate a display name, which is the name of the recipient as it appears in the Active Directory Users and Computers console. The rest of the information about this tab further identifies the recipient. All this information is available to users when they browse the Global Address List.

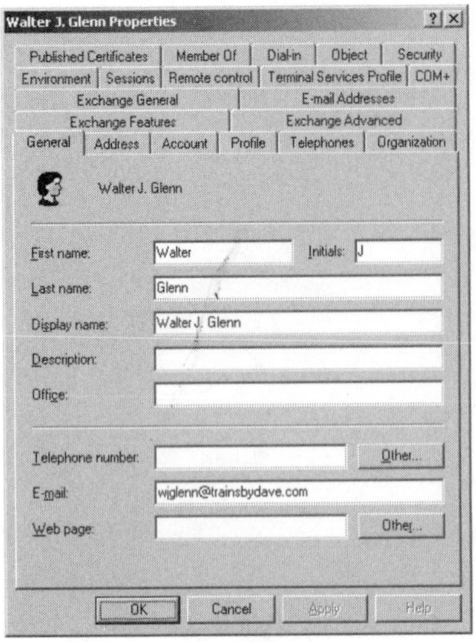

Figure 9-3. *Assigning user information on the General tab.*

Organization Tab

The Organization tab, shown in Figure 9-4, is used to configure additional information about the user's position in the company. You can use this tab to specify a user's manager and a list of people who report directly to the user. Click the Change button to display a list of recipients in the organization. All information configured on this tab is made available in the Global Address List.

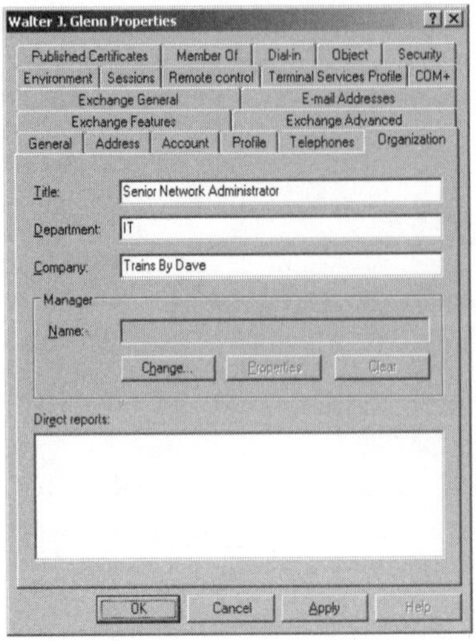

Figure 9-4. *Describing a user's position in the organization by using the Organization tab.*

Exchange General Tab

On the Exchange General tab, shown in Figure 9-5, you can configure general properties governing the Exchange mailbox associated with the user. The mailbox store that the user belongs to is displayed here but cannot be changed. The alias is an alternate means of addressing a user and is used by foreign messaging systems that cannot handle a full display name.

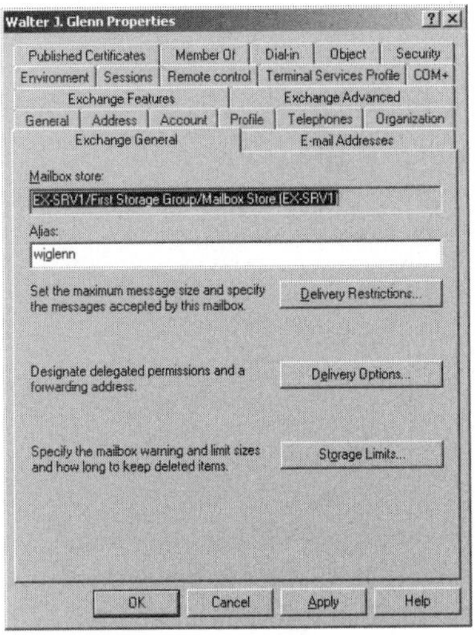

Figure 9-5. *Configuring general mailbox-related properties.*

You will also find three buttons on this tab that lead to more important settings. Click the Delivery Restrictions button to open the dialog box shown in Figure 9-6. You can set limits on the size of messages that can be transferred out of or into a particular mailbox. If an incoming or outgoing message exceeds its respective limit, it is not sent or received, and the sender of the message receives a nondelivery report. The Message Restrictions area allows you to restrict the messages coming into the selected mailbox. The default is to accept messages from everyone. You can specify that messages be accepted only from designated senders or that messages be accepted from everyone except a list of specific users. Choose the option you want, and click Add to select from recipients listed in Active Directory. You can also specify that messages be accepted only from authenticated users (that is, users with valid logon credentials for the network). This option works in conjunction with the other message restrictions you set.

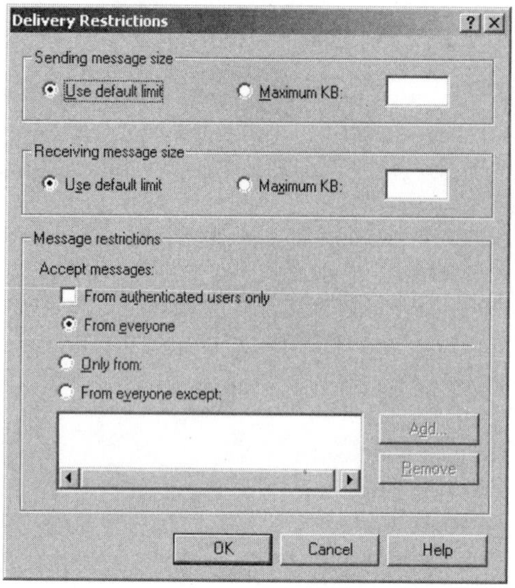

Figure 9-6. *Setting restrictions on a mailbox.*

Tip Setting general limits for an entire site or server at the same time is much more efficient than setting them for each individual user. Setting limits for a particular mailbox is one way of dealing with users who need to send large messages or who simply let messages accumulate.

Click the Delivery Options button on the Exchange General tab to open the dialog box shown in Figure 9-7. This dialog box allows you to give Exchange users other than the primary user *delegate access* to the mailbox. This type of delegate access is called Send On Behalf permission. By clicking the Add button, you can grant this permission to any recipient in Active Directory. Users included in this list can send messages that will appear as though they came from the selected mailbox. Any messages sent include the names of both the primary mailbox user and the user who actually sent the message. This permission might be used by an assistant who needs to send a message from a manager who is out of the office.

Note The Send On Behalf permission option can also be helpful in troubleshooting. If you assign this permission to yourself, as administrator, you can send test messages from any recipient in the organization. This practice can be a great way to test connections from remote servers. We recommend that you use test mailboxes created for this purpose and not actual user mailboxes. Many users would consider this type of extended access to their e-mail an intrusion.

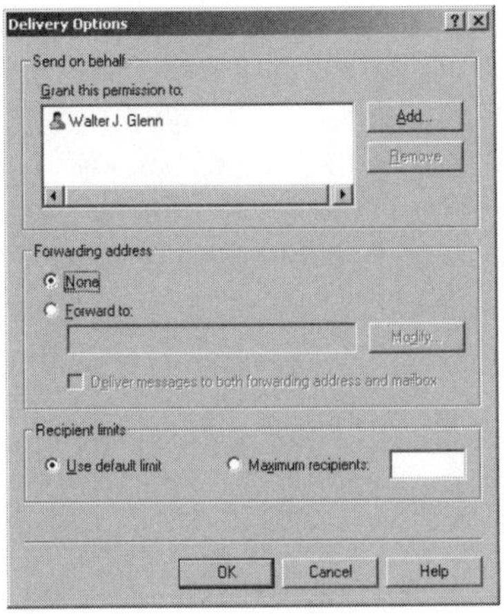

Figure 9-7. *Setting delivery options for a mailbox.*

You can also use the Delivery Options dialog box to assign a forwarding address for a mailbox. Any messages sent to the mailbox are routed to the mailbox of the designated alternate recipient. You can also specify that messages be sent both to the primary mailbox and to the alternate recipient. Exchange Server will deliver to each mailbox a separate reference to the message, so deleting the message from one mailbox does not cause it to be deleted from another. Finally, you can specify the maximum number of recipients to which a user can send a single message. By default, there is no limit.

Click the Storage Limits button on the Exchange General tab to open the dialog box shown in Figure 9-8. This dialog box lets you set parameters for storage limits and deleted item retention time. Often, users send and save huge attachments or are simply negligent about cleaning out their mailboxes. Either of these situations can cause a great deal of disk space to be consumed on your server. Fortunately, administrators can set any of three storage limits on a mailbox:

- **Issue Warning At (KB)** Specifies the mailbox size, in kilobytes, at which a warning is issued to the user to clean out the mailbox.
- **Prohibit Send At (KB)** Specifies the mailbox size, in kilobytes, at which the user is prohibited from sending any new e-mail. This prohibition ends as soon as the user clears enough space to fall back under the limit.
- **Prohibit Send And Receive At (KB)** Specifies the mailbox size, in kilobytes, at which the user is prohibited from sending, receiving, or even editing any e-mail. All the user can do is delete messages. This prohibition ends as soon as the user clears enough space to fall back under the limit. To do this, a user must delete items from his or her

mailbox and then empty the Deleted Items folder. When a user sends a message to a recipient who is prohibited from receiving any new messages, a nondelivery report is generated and returned to the sending user. Prohibiting the sending and receiving of e-mail is a pretty strong measure for an administrator to take. We recommend that you implement this solution only if you experience continued problems that you cannot otherwise resolve.

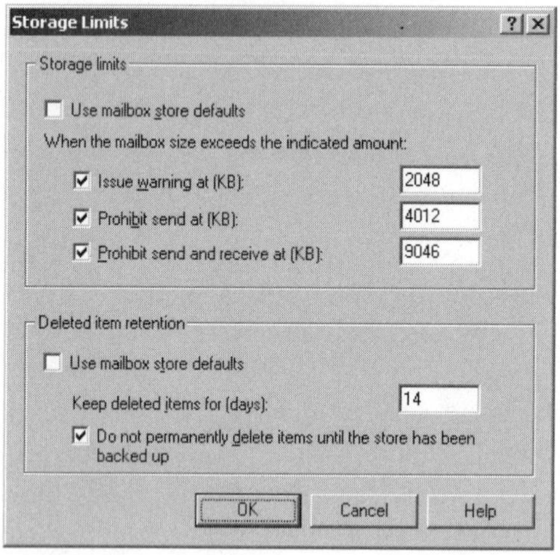

Figure 9-8. *Setting storage options for a mailbox.*

Exchange Server 2003 also includes a feature that gives users a certain amount of time to recover items that have been deleted from their Deleted Items folder. When a user deletes a message using a client application such as Microsoft Outlook, that message is placed in the user's Deleted Items folder. Only when the user deletes the item from the Deleted Items folder is it actually removed from the user's personal folders. However, the deleted item is still not actually deleted from the mailbox store. Instead, it is marked as hidden and is kept for a specified amount of time. During that period, the user can recover the item with the client application. Note that the ability to recover deleted items requires Outlook 97 or later.

The Deleted Item Retention area of the Storage Limits dialog box specifies the retention time for deleted items. You can either use the default value that is configured for the entire mailbox store or override it with a different value for the selected mailbox. If you choose to override the value, you can also specify that deleted messages not be permanently removed until the mailbox store has been backed up.

E-Mail Addresses Tab

The E-Mail Addresses tab, shown in Figure 9-9, lets you configure how the mailbox is addressed from different types of messaging systems. When you create a mailbox, two types of addresses are configured by default: SMTP and X.400. You can add, remove, or edit addresses as you please. A mailbox can have multiple addresses for a single type. For example, a mailbox for the Web site administrator Patricia Doyle might have two SMTP addresses: pdoyle@company.com and webmaster@company.com. E-mail addressed to these two addresses will be placed in the same mailbox. Although this tab provides a way to change addresses manually for each mailbox, a much easier way to change addresses for multiple mailboxes is with recipient policies, which are covered later in this chapter.

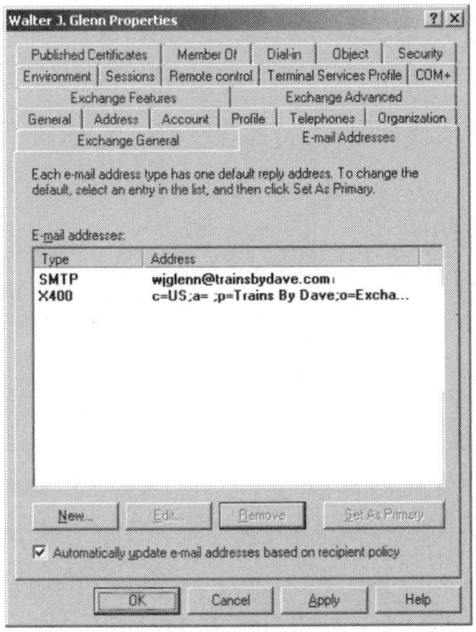

Figure 9-9. *Viewing e-mail addresses for a mailbox.*

Exchange Features Tab

The Exchange Features tab, shown in Figure 9-10, lets you enable and disable certain mobile services or particular protocols for an individual mailbox. For mobile services, you have only the option of enabling or disabling each service for the mailbox. For protocols, you can make these simple changes, as well as modify other parameters for that protocol. You will learn more about Internet protocols and how to configure them for sites, servers, and mailboxes in Chapter 20, "Supporting Internet Protocols and SMTP."

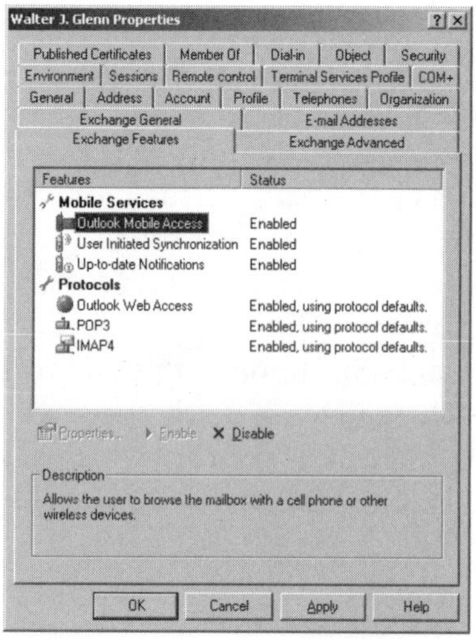

Figure 9-10. *Viewing Exchange features for a mailbox.*

Exchange Advanced Tab

The Exchange Advanced tab, shown in Figure 9-11, lets you configure a number of miscellaneous features that the Exchange designers decided were advanced.

The simple display name is an alternate name for the mailbox. It appears when the full display name cannot be shown for some reason. This situation often occurs when multiple language versions of the Exchange System snap-in are used on the same network.

By default, all recipients except public folders are visible to users via the Global Address List. You can select the Hide From Exchange Address Lists option to hide the mailbox from that list or from other lists created in the Exchange System snap-in. The mailbox will still be able to receive e-mail; it simply will not be included in address lists.

If you select the Downgrade High Priority Mail Bound For X.400 option, the current mailbox cannot send high-priority messages to X.400 systems. If the user sends a high-priority message, Exchange Server will downgrade it to normal priority.

In addition to these settings, you'll find three buttons on the Exchange Advanced tab that lead to separate dialog boxes with more configuration options. These buttons are covered in the sections that follow.

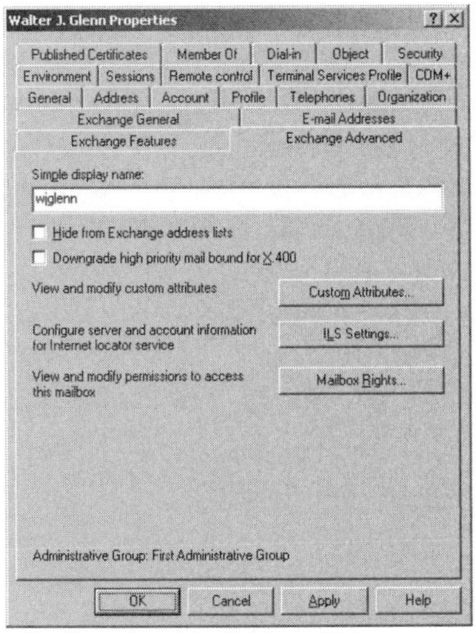

Figure 9-11. *Setting advanced Exchange mailbox features.*

Custom Attributes Button Clicking the Custom Attributes button displays the Exchange Custom Attributes dialog box, shown in Figure 9-12. This dialog box lets you enter information about a mailbox in 15 custom fields. These fields can be used for any information you need to include that isn't available on the other tabs. All these fields are available to users in the Global Address List. By default, these fields are labeled extensionAttribute1 through extensionAttribute15. Just select a field and click Edit to enter a new value. You can customize their names to suit your needs.

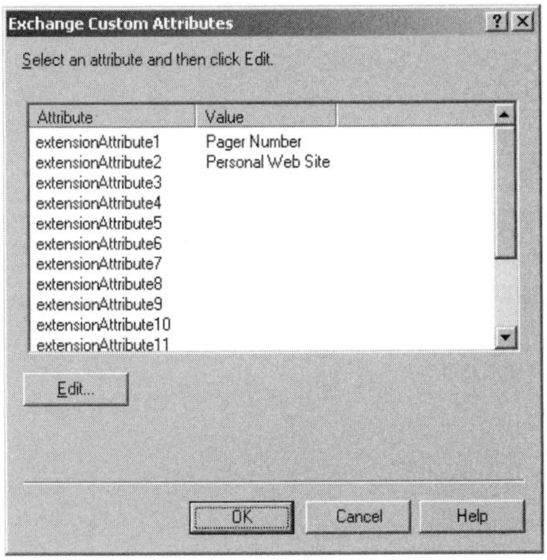

Figure 9-12. *Entering additional recipient information by using custom attribute fields.*

ILS Settings Button Click the ILS Settings button to display the ILS Settings dialog box. If you use Microsoft NetMeeting in your organization, this dialog box is for you. NetMeeting allows users to collaborate on documents by using audio, video, and a shared whiteboard. Use the ILS Settings dialog box to set up your Internet Locator Service (ILS) by configuring the ILS Server and Account fields. Once you've accomplished that, users can contact and set up meetings with the user of this mailbox.

Mailbox Rights Button The Permissions dialog box, shown in Figure 9-13, appears when you click the Mailbox Rights button. It lets you assign various access rights to a mailbox. By default, only the SELF group is given rights to the mailbox. You can add any user in Active Directory to this list by clicking the Add button.

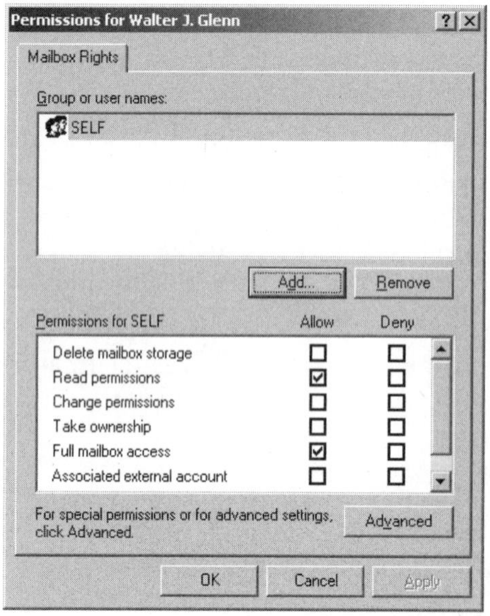

Figure 9-13. *Configuring rights on a mailbox.*

You modify the particular rights of any user in the list by selecting the user and selecting or clearing the Allow and Deny check boxes beside the individual mailbox rights. Here are the rights you can assign:

- **Delete Mailbox Storage** Allows a user to delete the actual mailbox from the information store. This right is given by default only to administrators.
- **Read Permissions** Lets the user read e-mail in the mailbox. You could use this right alone to allow a user to read another user's e-mail but not to send, change, or delete messages in the mailbox.

- **Change Permissions** Allows a user to delete or modify items in the primary user's mailbox.
- **Take Ownership** Allows a user to become the owner of a mailbox. By default, only administrators are given this permission.
- **Full Mailbox Access** Allows a user to access a mailbox and to read and delete messages. It also allows the user to send messages using the mailbox.
- **Associated eExternal Account** Provides a way to associate a Windows NT 4 user account with an Exchange 2003 mailbox.

Member Of Tab

The Member Of tab of a user's property sheet, shown in Figure 9-14, lists the groups to which the user currently belongs. You can add a group by clicking the Add button and then choosing from the available lists. Not only can you manage a group from a user's property sheet, but you can also manage a group from the group's property sheet. For more information, see the section titled "Groups" later in this chapter.

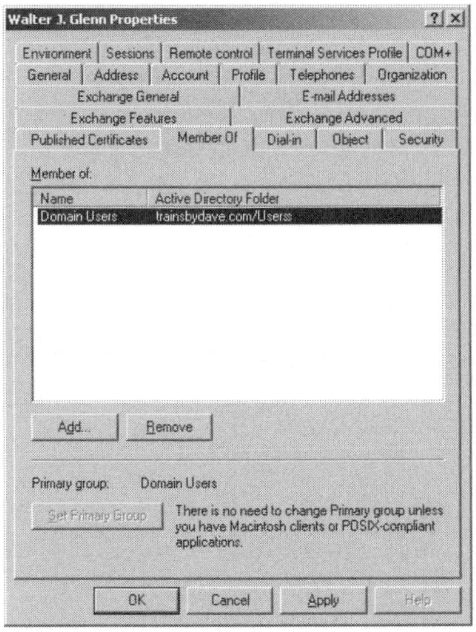

Figure 9-14. *Viewing the groups to which a mailbox belongs.*

Mail-Enabled Users

As you know, a mail-enabled user is simply a user that has an e-mail address but no mailbox on an Exchange server. This means that the user can receive e-mail through its custom address but cannot send e-mail using the Exchange system. You cannot enable e-mail for a user while creating the user. The only way to create a mail-enabled user is to first create a new user that is not mailbox-enabled, and then to enable e-mail for that user. To enable e-mail for an existing user, select that user in Active Directory Users and Computers, and choose Exchange Tasks from the Action menu. After going past the welcome page, select the Establish E-mail Address task and click Next. This opens the page shown in Figure 9-15. Simply enter an e-mail alias and click Modify to choose the type of e-mail address you want to enter for the user. You can create many popular types of addresses, such as SMTP, Microsoft Mail, and Lotus cc:Mail, or you can even create a custom address. Once you enable e-mail for a user, you can configure the e-mail settings just as you would for a mailbox-enabled user.

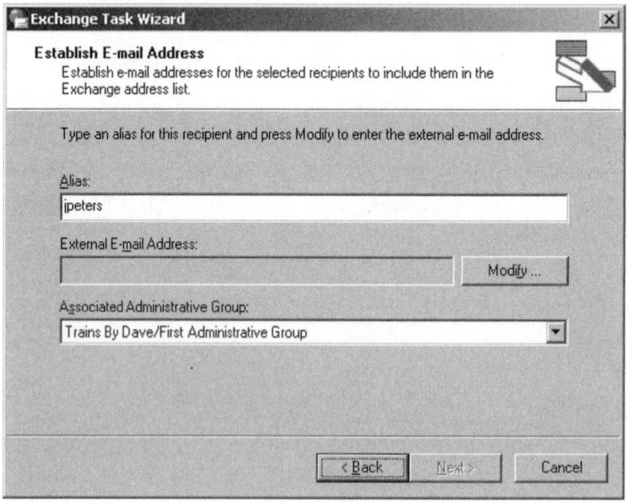

Figure 9-15. *Enabling e-mail for a user without giving the user a mailbox.*

Contacts

Contacts are objects that serve as pointers to resources outside an Exchange organization. You can think of a contact as an alias that contains an address for that outside resource and rules for handling the transmission of messages. Whenever a user sends a message to a contact, Exchange Server forwards the message to the appropriate foreign messaging system. Contacts have many of the same attributes as mailboxes and can be viewed in the Global Address List.

Creating a Contact

To create a new contact, choose New Contact from the Action menu of Active Directory Users and Computers. This command opens the New Object - Contact dialog box (Figure 9-16). Enter a full name and a display name, much as you would for a typical user.

When you click Next, the dialog box shown in Figure 9-17 opens. Enter a display name in the Alias field, click Modify, and select the type of foreign address you want to create. You can also select an administrative group that will hold the contact. If this seems like the same process you used to create a mail-enabled user previously, you are right. In fact, a contact is like a mail-enabled user that does not have the right to log on to the network. When you're finished, click Next to display a summary page. Click Finish on the summary page to create the new contact.

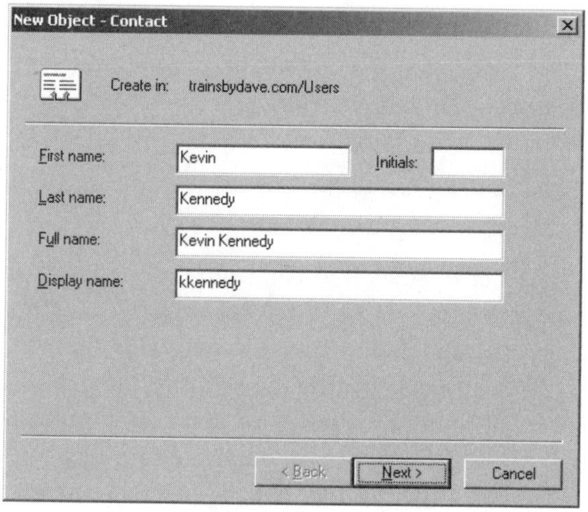

Figure 9-16. *Creating a new contact.*

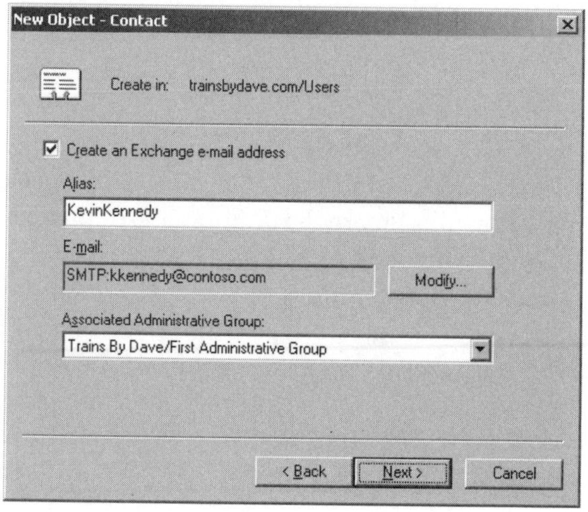

Figure 9-17. *Defining the contact's e-mail address.*

Configuring a Contact

Like all other objects in Active Directory, contacts are configured by means of a property sheet. Most of the tabs for contacts are identical to those for mailbox-enabled users, although contacts have noticeably fewer of them. You will, of course, encounter a number of differences:

- On the Exchange General tab of a contact's property sheet, you can change the alias and address. You can also set message restrictions. You cannot, however, set storage limits or delivery options, since contacts do not have storage on the Exchange server.
- On the Exchange Advanced tab, you cannot configure mailbox rights, since no mailbox is associated with the contact.
- There is no Exchange Features tab, meaning you cannot configure protocol settings or Mobile Access features for a contact.

Groups

In Active Directory, a *group* is a container of sorts that can hold users and other groups. You can assign permissions to a group that are inherited by all the objects that are members of that group. This makes the group a valuable security construct. Exchange Server 2003 also uses groups for another purpose. A group can be mail-enabled and then populated with other mail- or mailbox-enabled recipients to make a distribution list, a term you might be familiar with from earlier versions of Exchange Server. A group can contain users, contacts, public folders, and even other groups. When you send a message to a mail-enabled group, the message is sent to each member of the list individually. Groups are visible in the Global Address List.

Creating a Group

Creating a new mail-enabled group is easy. Choose New Group from the Action menu of Active Directory Users and Computers. This command opens the New Object - Group dialog box, shown in Figure 9-18. Enter a group name that describes the members the group will contain. You must also choose a group scope and a group type. The group scope defines the level at which the group will be available in Active Directory. The group type defines whether the group is for security or distribution purposes. A security group can be mail-enabled and used for distribution purposes, but a distribution group cannot be used for security purposes. When you're finished, click Next.

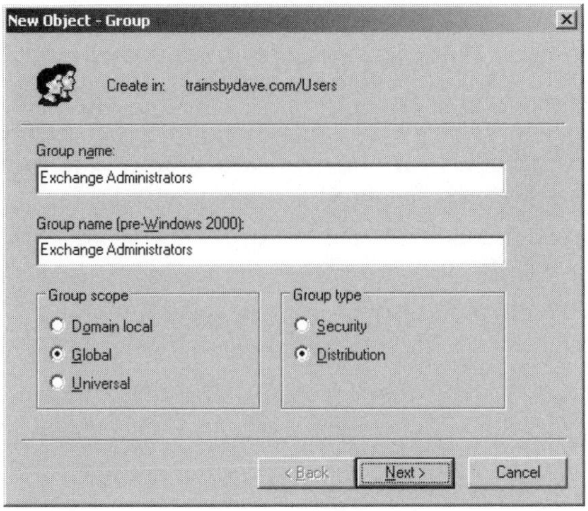

Figure 9-18. *Creating a distribution group.*

On the next page, you can specify whether an e-mail address should be created for the new group, and you can enter an alias name. If you are creating a group to be used as a distribution list, you must create an e-mail address. Once you click Finish in this screen, the new group is created and you are ready to add members. This process is described in the next section, along with other ways of configuring groups.

Configuring a Group

You configure a group in the same way that you configure other recipients—with a property sheet. Many of the tabs are identical to those of the same name for user objects; refer to the "Users" section earlier in this chapter for details on those tabs. Some of the tabs found on a user's property sheet simply don't exist for a group. This section covers the three Exchange-related tabs that do differ for a group.

Members Tab

The Members tab lists every member of the group. Click the Add button to access the Active Directory list, from which you can add new members to the group. You can click the Remove button to remove selected members. As mentioned earlier, groups can hold any other type of object, including users, contacts, public folders, and even other groups.

Managed By Tab

The Managed By tab, shown in Figure 9-19, lets you assign an owner to the group. The owner manages the group's membership. By default, the administrator who creates the group is the owner, but you can designate as owner any user, group, or contact in the Global Address List. If you give ownership to another user, that user can use Outlook to modify the group's membership and does not need access to Active Directory Users and Computers. You can relieve yourself of a great deal of work by specifying owners for the groups you create. As groups grow larger, they can consume a considerable amount of management time.

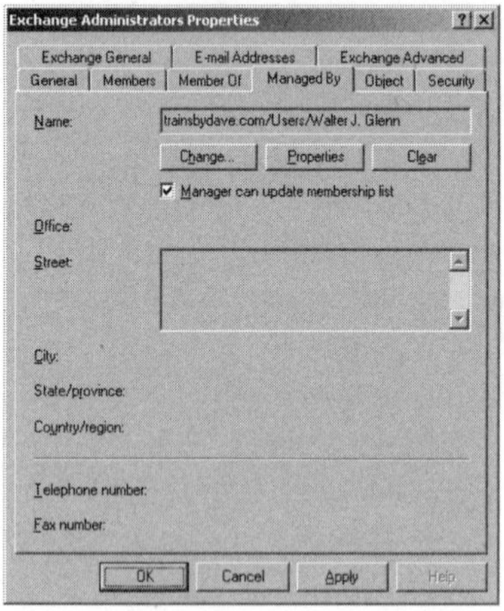

Figure 9-19. *Specifying a group owner.*

Exchange Advanced Tab

The Exchange Advanced tab, shown in Figure 9-20, holds several configuration options that might be familiar to you, such as Simple Display Name and the Custom Attributes button. You can also, however, configure several options that are specific to distribution lists:

- **Expansion Server** Whenever a message is sent to a group, the group must be expanded so that the message can be sent to each member of the group. The Message Transfer Agent (MTA) service of a single Exchange server performs this expansion. The default choice is Any Server In Site. This setting means that the home server of the user sending the message always expands the group. You can also designate a specific server to handle expanding the group, which is a good choice if you have a large group. In this case, expansion could consume a large amount of server resources, which can compromise performance for busy servers.

- **Hide Group From Exchange Address Lists** If you select this option, the group is not visible in the Global Address List.
- **Send Out-Of-Office Messages To Originator** If you select this option, users can configure Exchange clients to reply automatically to any messages received while they are away from their offices. When this option is selected, users who send messages to the group can receive these automatic messages. For particularly large groups, it's best not to allow out-of-office messages to be delivered because of the excess network traffic they generate.
- **Send Delivery Reports To Group Owner** If you select this option, the owner of the group is notified whenever an error occurs during the delivery of a message to the group or to one of its members. This option is not available when the group has not been assigned an owner.
- **Send Delivery Reports To Message Originator** If you select this option, any error notifications are sent to the user who sent a message to the group. If the Send Delivery Reports To Group Owner option is also selected, both the sender and the owner are notified.
- **Do Not Send Delivery Reports** If you select this option, no delivery reports are sent.

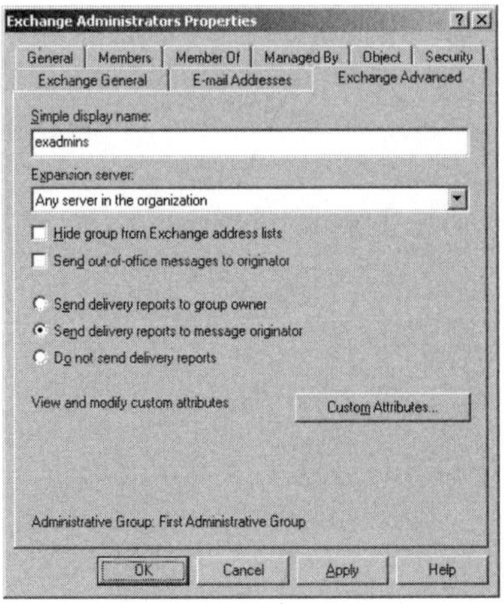

Figure 9-20. *Setting advanced properties for a group.*

Real World Using Message Restrictions on Groups

The Message Restrictions area on the Exchange General tab is often much more useful for groups than it is for individual users. In large organizations, groups can grow quite large, sometimes holding thousands of users. Because of the possibility of misuse, providing general access to groups this large is usually not a good idea. Imagine the increase in traffic if your users sent messages to thousands of users every time their kids had candy bars to sell or they found a good joke. Placing delivery restrictions on large groups allows you to limit access to the groups to a few select, responsible users.

Another potential risk is that someone from the Internet could e-mail everyone in your company, using a group's SMTP address. Imagine what your job would be like on the day that an anonymous person e-mailed malicious information to the entire company. Limiting access to the group will also help prevent this type of unwanted e-mail from occurring.

Creating Query-Based Distribution Groups

Exchange Server 2003 introduces a new type of object called a query-based distribution group—query-based because instead of making specific objects members of the group, the membership is dynamic and is based on general filters that you create. For example, you could create a query-based distribution group that included all mailbox-enabled Exchange users. No one has to manually update the membership of the group because whenever a message is sent to the list, the membership is generated on the fly.

Although query-based distribution groups are an exciting and useful addition to Exchange Server 2003, you do need to take a few limitations and costs into consideration:

- You can use query-based distribution groups only in a native-mode organization, meaning an organization in which no servers are running any version prior to Exchange 2000 Server. In addition, servers running Exchange 2000 Server should be updated to Exchange Service Pack 3 for the best reliability.
- The on-the-fly generation of members for a query-based distribution group generates additional overhead on the server that performs that generation—the expansion server. Expect the server to show increased CPU time and disk activity each time a message is sent to the group.
- The generation also causes increased network traffic and Active Directory utilization because the expansion server must send a query to

Active Directory to resolve the current membership each time a message is sent to the group.

Because of the additional overhead generated by query-based distribution groups, they are best used for making period announcements to important groups of users and are not intended as a replacement for standard distribution groups.

Creating a query-based distribution group is straightforward. In Active Directory Users and Computers, select the container in which you want to create the group and then choose New Query-Based Distribution Group from the Action menu. In the dialog box that opens, name the group, give it an alias, and click Next. On the next page, shown in Figure 9-21, you can choose from a number of predefined filters or create a customized filter. With a custom filter, you can specify a particular server or even a mailbox store for generating the membership. You can also build a custom list of fields from various objects used to generate the membership. For example, if your company uses the room number field when user objects are created, you could configure a query-based distribution group to send messages to everyone on the second floor.

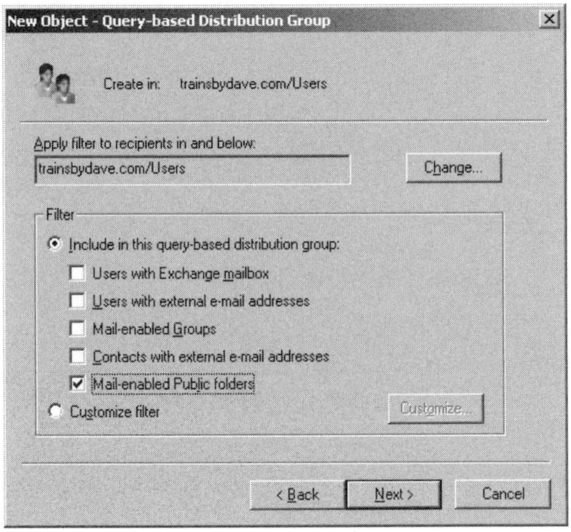

Figure 9-21. *Creating a query-based distribution group.*

Searching for Recipients

As your organization and the number of recipients in it grows, scrolling through lists of recipients to find the ones you need can become quite time-consuming. Fortunately, the Active Directory Users and Computers tool can help. This section describes how to use filtering and search tools to make finding a recipient easier.

Filtering Recipients

If you are looking for certain types of recipients, try filtering the recipient objects that are displayed in the Users folder. By default, all types of recipients are shown when you select the Users folder, including public folders. You can filter that view so that only selected types of recipients are shown. For example, you can choose to view only public folders or only contacts. Filtering your recipient view can be useful if you are looking for a specific recipient and the list based on recipient type is not very long, or if you need to select all recipients of a certain type.

To apply a filter, select the Users folder in Active Directory Users and Computers, and choose Filter Options from the View menu. You can also click the Filter Options button (the one that looks like a funnel) on the toolbar. The dialog box shown in Figure 9-22 opens. The default setting is to view recipients of all types. Select the Show Only The Following Types Of Objects option, and then select the types of recipients you want to view. When you click OK, the Users folder displays only those types of recipients.

The Filter Options dialog box also lets you specify how many recipients should be displayed per folder. Be careful with this one, however. If you set the number too low, many important items might not be shown. Also, keep in mind that the filter options you set apply to the entire Active Directory hierarchy, not just to the Users folder. This means that if you set the filter to show only users and groups, for example, no computers will show up in your Computers folder until you reset the filter.

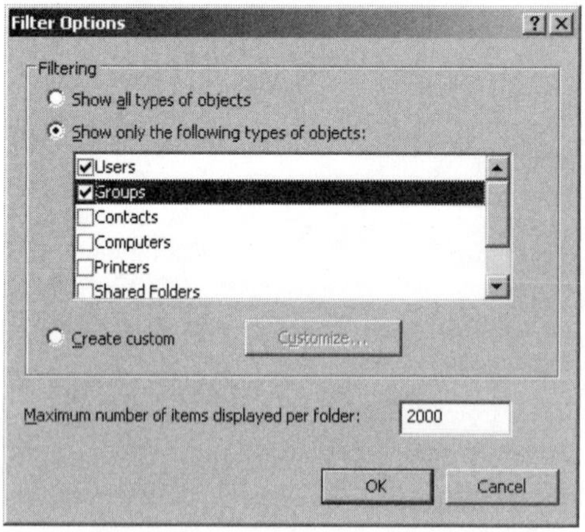

Figure 9-22. *Setting recipient filtering options.*

Another powerful service the Filter Options dialog box offers is the ability to configure custom filters. Select Create Custom and click the Customize button to open the dialog box shown in Figure 9-23. You can create a custom filter based on combinations of just about every field in all the tabs that you use to configure a recipient. Click the Field button to choose a field from the drop-down menu. Use the Condition drop-down menu to choose conditions, such as Begins With or Is (Exactly), and then enter the value under Value. Click Add to add your criterion to the list. You can enter multiple criteria for searching. Figure 9-23 shows a filter that will find all recipients whose city is Huntsville, whose department is Sales, and whose ILS settings are not present.

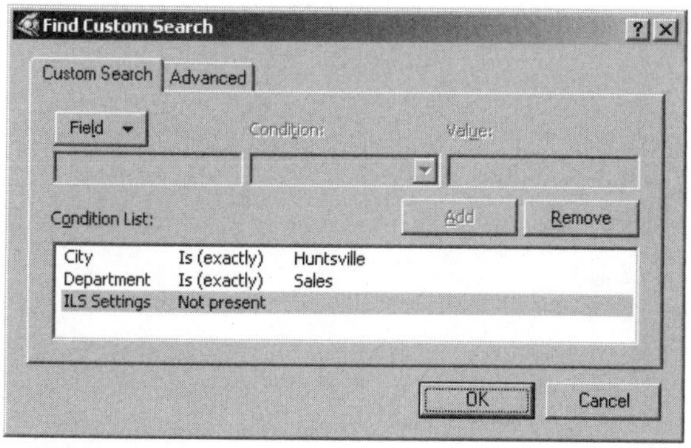

Figure 9-23. *Creating a custom filter.*

Finding Recipients

Active Directory Users and Computers also provides a recipient search tool that allows for some pretty sophisticated searching criteria. You open this tool by choosing Find from the Action menu. The Find Users, Contacts, And Groups dialog box appears (Figure 9-24).

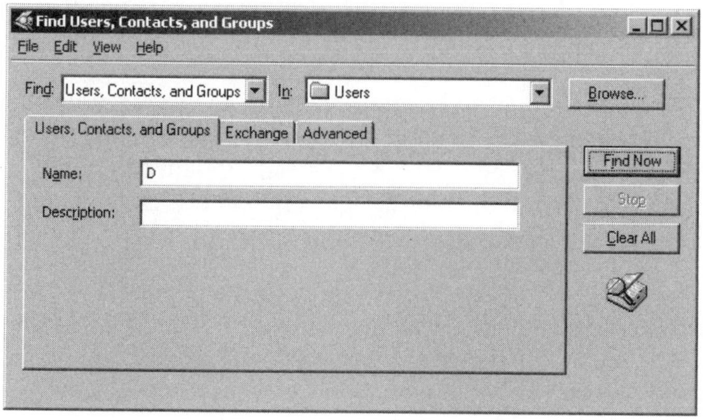

Figure 9-24. *Finding recipients in Active Directory Users and Computers.*

Use the Find field to specify what types of objects you want to find. The default is to find users, groups, and contacts. Use the In field to specify the folder in which you want to perform the search. The default is to search in the Users folder. Enter any part of a name or description and click Find Now to begin the search. The search shown in Figure 9-24 returns all users whose names begin with a "D." The dialog box expands to display the results (Figure 9-25). You can manipulate objects in the search results just as you would in the main Active Directory Users and Computers console by right-clicking them to access their shortcut menus.

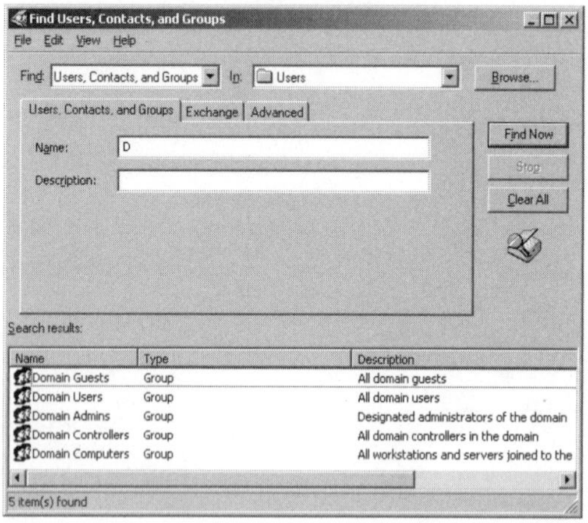

Figure 9-25. *Displaying the results of a search.*

You can also use a few advanced options to narrow down your search. The Exchange tab in the Find Users, Contacts, And Groups dialog box lets you specify that you want to view only Exchange recipients in your search results, and it even lets you set the specific types of recipients you want displayed. The Advanced tab provides custom filtering that works in same way as the custom filtering in the Filter Options dialog box, discussed in the previous section.

Tip The Find feature is one of the most useful tools in Active Directory Users and Computers. We find ourselves using it regularly to manage recipients. Using Find is much handier than using even the custom filtering choices, and it's certainly quicker than scrolling through long lists of recipients in the main Active Directory Users and Computers window.

Templates

A *template* is a recipient object that is used as a model for creating other recipient objects of that type. Every recipient type except public folders can serve as a template. To create a template, create a recipient object as you normally would. Enter any information that you want to use in the model. If, for example, you are creating a mailbox-enabled user template for new employees, you might enter all the organizational, phone, and address information for your company.

> **Note** When you create a recipient to use as a template, you will probably want to hide the recipient from the address book by using the Exchange Advanced tab on the template's property sheet. That way, users won't be able to view the template in the Global Address List. You will always be able to see it in Active Directory Users and Computers. You should also name your template in such a way that it is both easy to find and easy to distinguish from regular recipients. We like prefixing the name with "template" so that all templates are grouped together, or even with "ztemplate" so that they are shown at the end of the list.

To use a template to create an individual recipient, select the template in Active Directory Users and Computers and then choose Copy from the Action menu. The New Object Wizard opens, letting you create the new object. All the information that you entered as part of the template becomes part of the new object, and you can reconfigure the new object using its property sheet, as you would expect.

Recipient Policies

A *recipient policy* is a collection of configuration settings that can be applied across any number of recipients. Changing a policy enacts the change on every object to which the policy applies. Exchange Server 2003 offers two kinds of recipient policies:

- **E-Mail Address Policies** Use this type of policy to specify how e-mail addresses of various types should be formatted for the recipients linked to the policy.
- **Mailbox Management Policies** Use this type of policy to enforce restrictions on mailboxes, such as how long messages are retained or how large the mailbox can grow.

Exchange Server 2003 includes a single built-in recipient policy used to generate SMTP and X.400 e-mail addresses automatically for mail-enabled Exchange objects, such as users, groups, contacts, public folders, stores, and system attendants. You can create new policies at any time.

Recipient policies employ a "background apply" implementation to make configuration changes. You create a policy by defining the settings for that policy and associating that policy with one or more recipient objects in Active Directory. The policy is then applied at a later time, based on the schedule of the Address List service running under the System Attendant.

Creating a Recipient Policy

You create new recipient policies using the Exchange System snap-in. Open the Recipients folder, and then select the Recipient Policies folder inside it. Choose New Recipient Policy from the Action menu to create the new policy. This command opens a small dialog box that asks what property pages (tabs) you want to show on the property sheet for the new policy: E-Mail Addresses or Mailbox Manager Settings. You can use a policy to apply both types of settings, but it is our experience that policies are easier to manage when they are narrower in scope. Generally, you'll want to configure one policy to manage one setting or type of settings. For example, create one policy that formats e-mail addresses for a particular group. Create another policy that imposes mailbox restrictions on that group.

Once you decide on the type of policy to create, the property sheet for the new policy opens with the General tab showing (Figure 9-26).

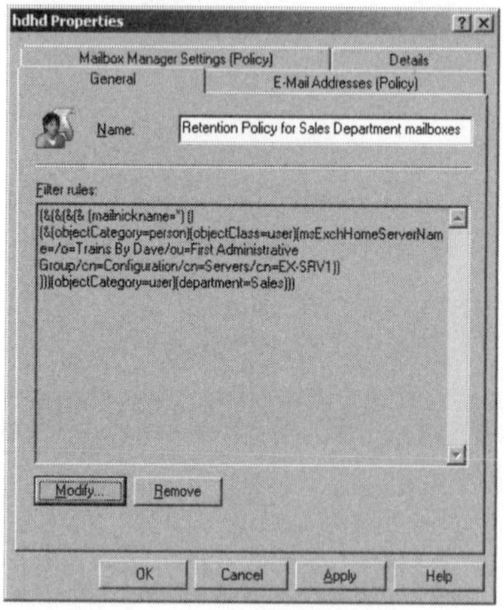

Figure 9-26. *Creating a new recipient policy.*

In the Name field, type a name for your recipient policy. Next, click the Modify button to open a Find dialog box similar to the Find Users, Contacts, And Groups dialog box. Select the types of recipients to which you want this new policy to apply on the General tab of this dialog box, and then, on the

Advanced tab, enter any custom filter settings you like, using field-level recipient attributes. Once you define your search criteria, click Finish to display the results in the Find window. Click OK when you finish defining your policy members. You then return to the General tab of the policy's property sheet, where you will see the filter rules you specified.

Use the options on the E-Mail Addresses (Policy) tab, shown in Figure 9-27, to configure rules for generating e-mail addresses for the members of the new recipient policy. The current rules are listed under Generation Rules. Make sure that the necessary addresses are selected for this set of recipients. Exchange Server uses the rules in this list to generate addresses automatically for any recipient to which this policy applies. You can create a new address generation rule by clicking the New button and choosing an address type, or you can modify an existing address generation rule by selecting the rule and clicking the Edit button. If you create a new address generation rule of the same e-mail type as an existing rule, you can make it the primary address for members of the policy.

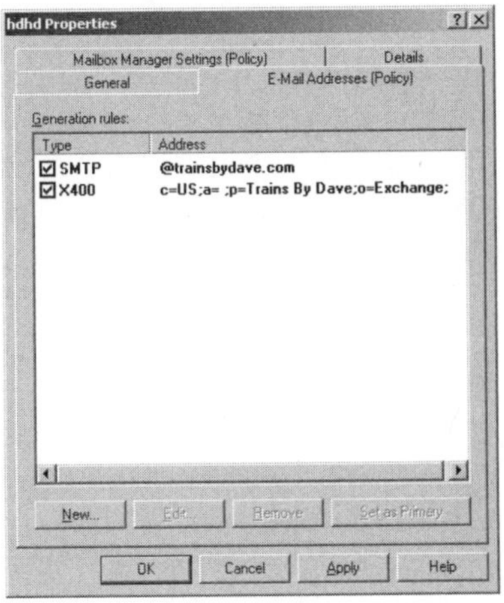

Figure 9-27. *Defining rules for generating e-mail addresses.*

Use the options on the Mailbox Manager Settings (Policy) tab, shown in Figure 9-28, to configure a retention limit and a size restriction for the various types of folders in a user's mailbox (Inbox, Sent Items, Tasks, and so on). The When Processing A Mailbox drop-down menu lets you choose what action should be taken when examining a mailbox affected by the policy. You can have Exchange generate a report, move items to the Deleted Items folder, move items to System Cleanup folders, or permanently delete items immediately. You can also create a message that is sent to users after their e-mail is processed (usually to let them know why their items might be missing). Finally, you can exclude specific message classes from deletion.

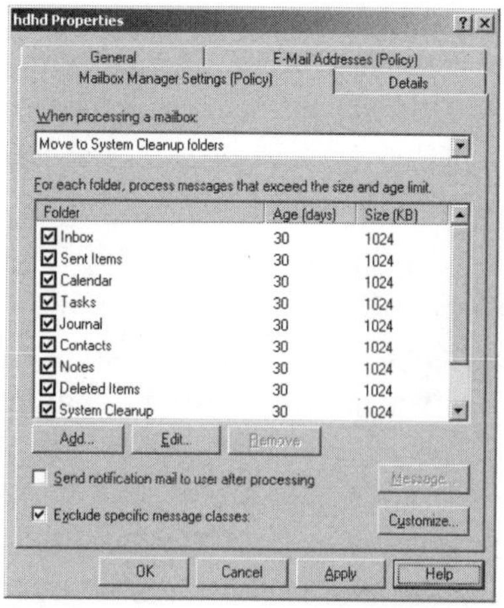

Figure 9-28. *Defining rules for generating e-mail addresses.*

Creating an Exception to a Policy

Once you have created a policy for a group of recipients, you can override the addressing settings for individual contacts. This is known as creating an *exception* to the policy. You do this using the Active Directory Users and Computers snap-in. Find the recipient or recipients for which you want to create an exception, and open their property sheets. Use the E-Mail Addresses tab to override e-mail address settings, and use the features on the Exchange General tab to override mailbox settings. This manual setting overrides any recipient policies in effect.

Address Lists

Address lists are a clever feature of Exchange Server 2003 that allow you to group recipients in the Global Address List according to attributes. Essentially, address lists allow you to add a hierarchical structure to the otherwise flat view provided by the Global Address List.

As you can see from the console shown in Figure 9-29, a number of address lists are preconfigured in the Exchange System snap-in. A separate list is configured for each type of recipient, including conferencing members, containing all the recipients of that type. There is also a Global Address List that displays all recipients in the organization. It is this list that client software typically uses to display an address book for the organization.

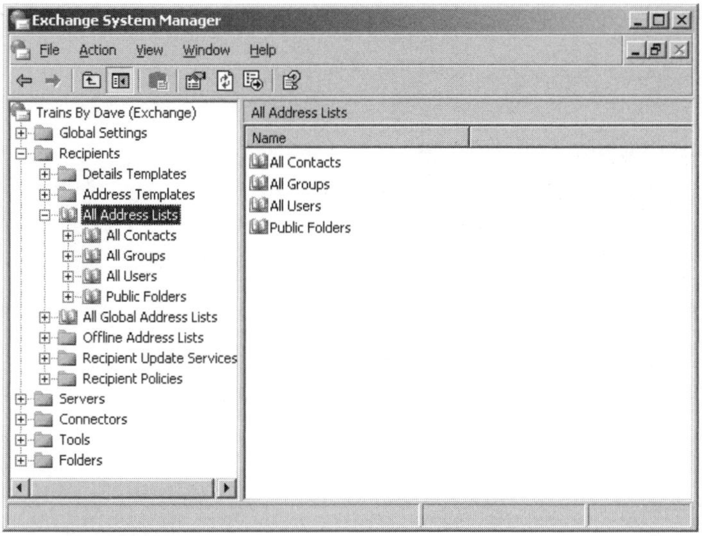

Figure 9-29. *Address lists that are preconfigured in the Exchange System snap-in.*

As you might have guessed, you can also create your own address lists that group recipients in any way you like, to make it easier for users to find the recipient they are looking for in your organization. You can create a new top-level address list right in the All Address Lists folder, or you can create an address list inside an existing address list.

Suppose you wanted to create a new regional address list structure that included only users with mailboxes and that grouped users first by state, then by city, and then by department. Your first step is to create a new top-level address list named Regional. To do this, you select the All Address Lists folder in the Exchange System snap-in and choose New Address List from the Action menu. This opens the dialog box shown in Figure 9-30.

In the Address List Name field, type *Regional*, and then click the Filter Rules button. This brings up the dialog box shown in Figure 9-31, which, if you've read the rest of this chapter, you should be getting comfortable with by now. On the General tab, select Users With Exchange Mailbox. When you are finished, click OK to return to the Create Exchange Address List dialog box. You have now created the folder that will hold the regional address lists you intend to create.

Next, you need to create a separate address list for each state. You do this by following the same procedure you used previously. Name each address list for the state, of course. When you get to the Find Exchange Recipients dialog box, in which you select user types, click the Advanced tab, shown in Figure 9-32. Here you can filter recipients based on field-level attributes. In the figure, we already selected the user attribute State, the condition Is (Exactly), and the value Alabama.

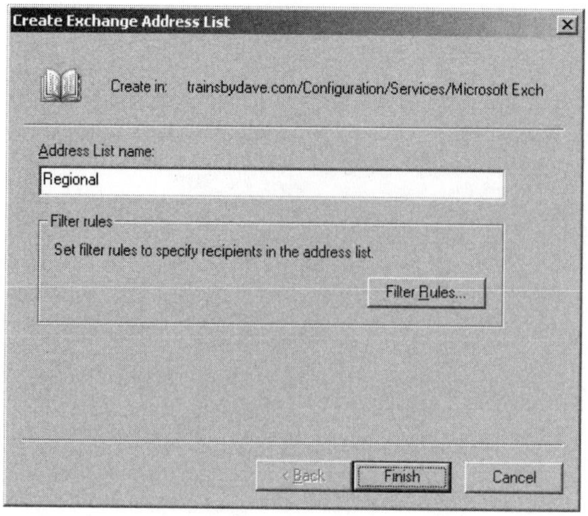

Figure 9-30. *Creating a new address list.*

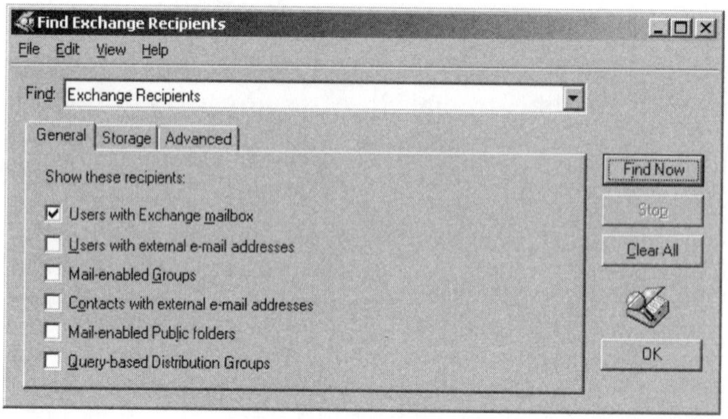

Figure 9-31. *Selecting the user types contained in an address list.*

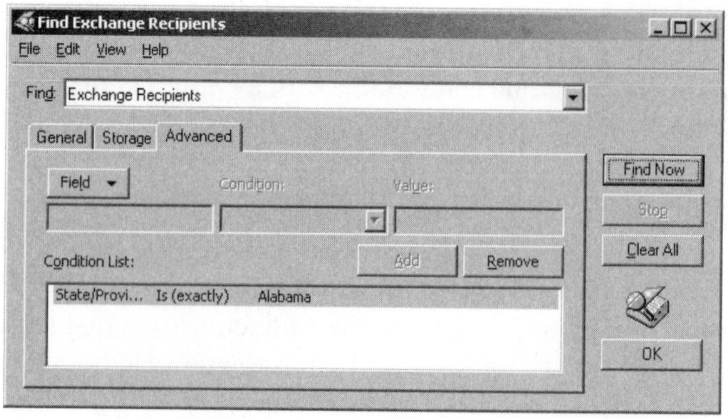

Figure 9-32. *Customizing a filter based on user attributes.*

Once you have configured the address lists for the states in your organization, you can create address lists for cities within those states, using the same procedure. Figure 9-33 shows an example of what the address list structure might look like when you're finished.

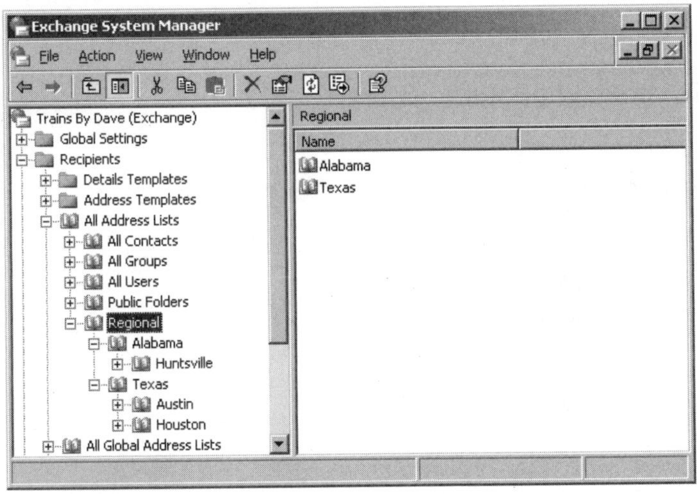

Figure 9-33. *Viewing your new address list structure.*

Address lists can be quite useful in large or complex organizations. Users can open these lists in client applications and find information about recipients quickly. Administrators can use the lists in the Exchange System snap-in to help organize recipients.

Summary

This chapter discussed how to create and work with recipients, the destination of all Exchange interactions. You learned about three of the five basic types of recipients in Exchange Server 2003—users, groups, and contacts—including how to create and configure each. You also learned how to search for recipients in various ways, create a template that can serve as a model for creating recipients, create policies that you apply to recipients, and create address lists that group recipients in different ways. Exchange clients use address lists to generate address books. The next chapter looks at the fourth type of recipient available in an Exchange organization: the public folder.

Chapter 10

Using Public Folders

Sharing information is a powerful means of facilitating workgroups and teams. When members of a team are located in geographically distant locations, the ability to share information is even more important. Microsoft Exchange Server 2003 offers that powerful groupware foundation through its implementation of public folders.

In Chapter 9, "Creating and Managing Recipients," you learned how to create and manage three of the four basic types of Exchange recipients: users, groups, and contacts. This chapter covers the fourth type of recipient: the public folder. To begin our look at the shared storage architecture of an Exchange Server system, this chapter explores how a user views shared storage and describes how to create, manage, replicate, store, and access public folders in an Exchange organization.

Understanding Public Folder Storage

Public folders are wonderful things, providing centralized storage of virtually any type of document or message and allowing controlled access by any user in the organization. Public folders provide the basis of workflow applications for Exchange Server 2003.

To perform the primary management of public folders, you will use the Exchange System snap-in. You can also use the Microsoft Outlook 2003 client to perform limited administrative duties. You can create and access public folders using either of these tools.

When you create a public folder, that folder is placed in the public folder store of a particular Exchange server. Any Exchange server that has a public folder store can host a public folder. A server might not have a public folder store if, for example, you have made it a mailbox server or dedicated it to some other specific task. A public folder is created in the public folder store of one server but can then be replicated to the public folder stores of multiple additional servers. In a typical organization, the public folders do not all exist on one server; rather, they are distributed across several servers.

An Exchange organization can host multiple *public folder trees*, with each tree consisting of a separate hierarchy of public folders. Within a public folder tree, the folders at the first level are referred to as top-level public folders. When a user creates a top-level public folder, it is placed in the public folder store on that user's home server. When a user creates a lower-level public folder, it is placed in the public folder store containing the parent folder in which the new folder is created. In addition, each public folder can be replicated to other servers in the organization. As you can see, this situation can get complicated. Public folders exist on different servers, and some public folders have instances on multiple servers.

Note In versions of Exchange Server prior to Exchange 2000 Server, an organization could have only one root-level public folder (and, therefore, one tree), named All Public Folders. In Exchange 2000 Server and Exchange Server 2003, you can create multiple root-level public folders, called public folder trees, that appear next to (or in place of) the All Public Folders tree. Each public folder tree uses a separate database on an Exchange server. Unfortunately, only the initial tree is visible from within MAPI clients such as Microsoft Outlook. Other trees can be viewed only from Microsoft Outlook Web Access (OWA), Microsoft Windows Explorer, or another application through the Installable File System (IFS). You will learn how to create new public folder trees later in this chapter.

To ensure that information about public folders is distributed throughout the Exchange system, Active Directory maintains a public folder hierarchy for each public folder tree. This is a single hierarchical structure that contains information about all public folders in that tree. The public folder hierarchies are automatically made available to every Exchange user in the organization.

A public folder is considered to have two parts. The first part is the public folder's place in the public folder hierarchy. The second part is the public folder content—the actual messages inside the public folder. The contents of a public folder exist on a single server, unless you specifically configure the content to be replicated to other servers.

Real World Dedicated Public Folder Servers

Some administrators prefer to use dedicated public folder servers. A *dedicated public folder server* is one from which the mailbox store has been removed. Dedicated public folder servers are useful in large organizations in which large amounts of public data and frequent access to that data consume a great deal of server resources. To use dedicated public folder servers in your organization, follow the steps outlined here. When you finish these steps, you're ready to create your public folders.

1. Decide which servers you want to have as your dedicated public folder servers.
2. Remove the mailbox store from the servers you've chosen to be dedicated public folder servers. To do so, find the Server container for the appropriate server in the Exchange System snap-in and delete the Mailbox Store configuration object for that server. Be careful when deleting the mailbox store from existing servers; any mailboxes in the store will also be deleted.
3. Delete the Public Folder Store object from all your organization's servers that will not host public folders. To do so, delete the Public Folder Store configuration object from the server's container. If the public folder store you want to remove already holds public folders, you must make sure that current replicas of those folders exist on other servers before deleting the object.

Using Public Folders in Microsoft Outlook 2003

Your users—and you—can use the Microsoft Outlook 2003 client both to create public folders and to manage certain public folder properties. This section covers both of these topics. You can also create and manage public folders using previous versions of the Outlook and Exchange clients. Although this section focuses on the use of Outlook 2003, most of the techniques described will work with these other clients as well.

Creating a Public Folder in Outlook

Creating a public folder using Microsoft Outlook is quite easy. Figure 10-1 shows the main Microsoft Outlook window with the folder list displayed and the Public Folders item expanded.

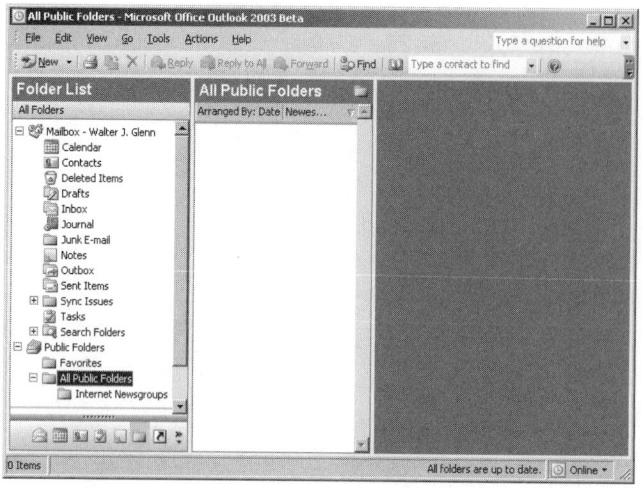

Figure 10-1. *The Outlook 2003 window, showing the public folder hierarchy.*

To create a public folder, ensure that the All Public Folders object (or the folder inside which you want to create the new folder) is selected and choose New Folder from the File menu. The Create New Folder dialog box opens (Figure 10-2). Enter the name of the public folder that you want to create, choose the type of items that folder should contain, select the folder in which it should be created, and click OK. You can set the types of messages that can be posted in a new folder, including calendar items, notes, tasks, contacts, and e-mail items. The default is the type of item that can be posted in the parent folder.

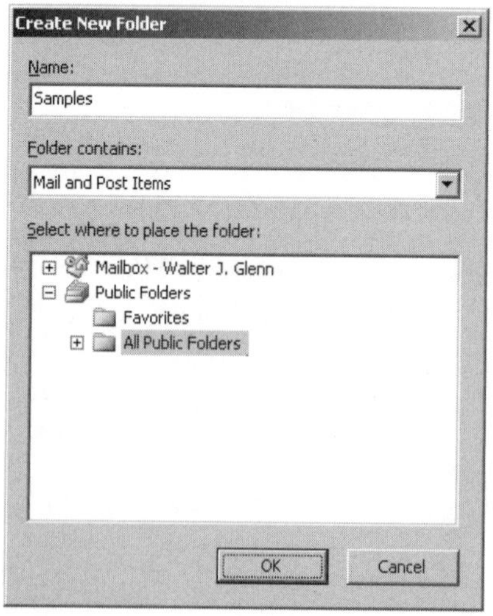

Figure 10-2. *Creating a public folder.*

Real World **Subscribing a Public Folder to a Mailing List**

A mailing list service is similar to a newsgroup but is run completely within e-mail. Each subscriber receives a copy of the other subscribers' comments in his or her own Inbox. A public folder has an e-mail address and can subscribe to a mailing list just like any other recipient, as long as your Exchange server has access to a list service server via Simple Mail Transport Protocol (SMTP). To create a public folder and have it subscribe to a mailing list, you need to have permission to add public folders. You also need to have Exchange administrative permissions.

First, create the public folder, following the procedure just described or using the one given in the "Creating a Public Folder in the Exchange System Snap-In" section later in this chapter. Next, use the Exchange System snap-in to assign yourself the Send As permission on the folder. Find the SMTP address of the folder (using the E-Mail Addresses tab on the folder's property sheet), and write it down. Then switch to the General tab and select the Show In Address Book option.

Go back to the Exchange client and create a "subscribe" message to the list service to which you want the public folder to subscribe. You will need to view the From field of the message box, so choose From Field from the View menu. In the From field, enter the SMTP e-mail address that you wrote down for the public folder. The list service might have specific instructions regarding what to place in the contents of the message. A typical message is Subscribe <folder>, where <folder> represents the name under which you want the public folder to subscribe. This name will appear in responses sent from the public folder to the mailing list. The list service should respond with a welcome message or a request for a confirmation message.

Now that the public folder is successfully subscribed to the list service, you can hide the public folder from the address book. It was shown only to ensure that the e-mail address would be resolved the first time that the list service responded.

Managing Public Folders in Outlook

After you create a public folder, you can configure it in several ways. The management of a public folder occurs in two places: the Outlook client and the Exchange System snap-in. Because users can create public folders, it is advantageous to allow them certain managerial responsibilities, which is why some management can occur in the client.

When a user creates a public folder, that user automatically becomes the folder's owner. The owner is responsible for the folder's basic design, which includes its access permissions, rules, and association of electronic forms. To perform this management, the user can simply open the property sheet for a particular public folder in Outlook.

General Tab

The General tab of a public folder's property sheet, shown in Figure 10-3, allows you to change the name of a public folder and enter an optional description of that folder. You can also choose the name of an electronic form that should be used to post new items to the folder. By default, the generic IPM.Post form is selected. Finally, you can specify that Exchange views of the folder be generated automatically. Exchange Client and Outlook process forms in different ways. This option provides compatibility in Exchange Client for folders created in Outlook.

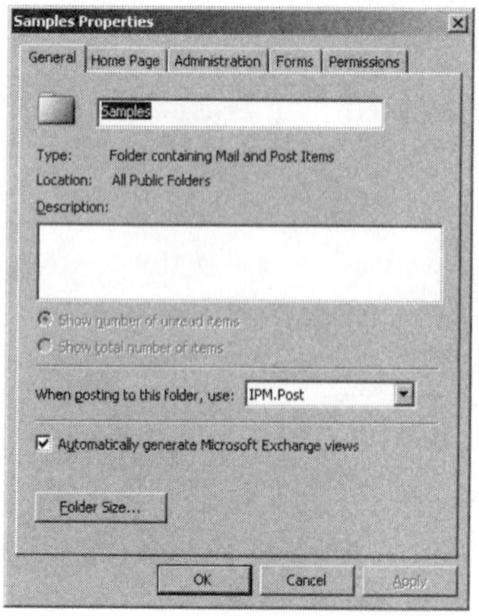

Figure 10-3. *The General tab of a public folder's property sheet in Outlook.*

Administration Tab

You use the Administration tab, shown in Figure 10-4, to set various options governing a public folder's use. The settings on this tab include the following:

- **Initial View On Folder** Specifies the initial Outlook view that is used whenever the public folder is opened. Available views include the default Normal threaded view as well as views grouped by discussion subject, topic, and poster.
- **Drag/Drop Posting Is A** Defines what happens when an item is dragged into a public folder. Options include Move/Copy and Forward.

- **Add Folder Address To** Adds the address of the folder as a contact to the Outlook Contacts folder.
- **This Folder Is Available To** Specifies whether the folder is accessible by anyone who has appropriate permissions or only by the folder owners.
- **Folder Assistant** Lets you create rules that apply to new items placed in the folder. Rules include such actions as automatically replying to or rejecting messages based on the posting user or subject.
- **Moderated Folder** Allows you to establish one or more moderators for the folder. A *moderated folder* is one in which a moderator must approve all newly posted items before they are made available to the public. Click this button to configure the folder's moderators. Keep in mind that users' posts to the folders will not appear immediately in a moderated folder. For this reason, you might want to configure an automatic reply to messages posted to moderated folders, letting users know that the moderator has received their message. You can do so by using the Reply To New Items With area and configuring either a standard or custom response.

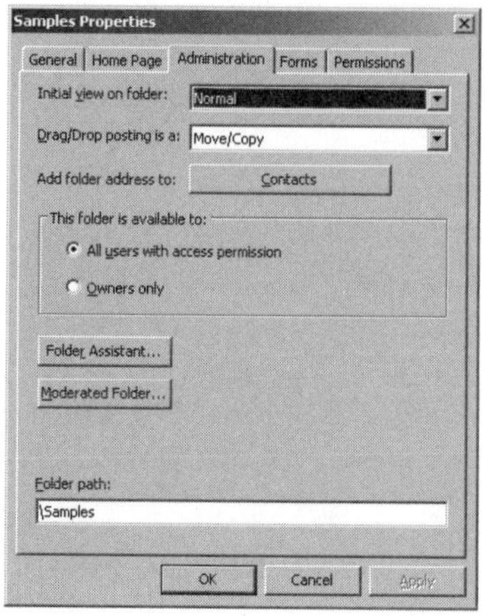

Figure 10-4. *The Administration tab of a public folder's property sheet in Outlook.*

Forms Tab

The Forms tab, shown in Figure 10-5, allows you to specify the forms that can be used in conjunction with the public folder. The forms specified on this tab appear as the choices in the drop-down list for the When Posting To This Folder option. Use this option on the General tab (refer back to Figure 10-3). You can also manage any associated form from this tab.

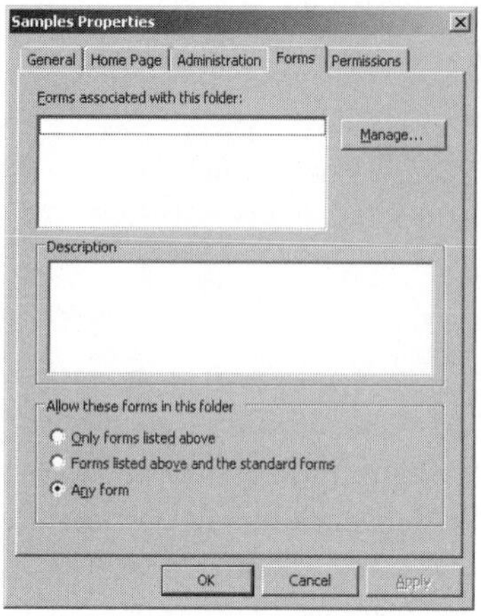

Figure 10-5. *The Forms tab of a public folder's property sheet in Outlook.*

More Info Some of this section's discussion of folder management in Outlook might seem cursory. This is because the subject of associating electronic forms with public folders is a bit outside the scope of this book. For excellent information about using Outlook and electronic forms, check out *Programming Microsoft Outlook and Microsoft Exchange 2003, Third Edition*, by Thomas Rizzo (Microsoft Press). This book provides information about using Outlook and Exchange Server to create custom collaborative environments. Although aimed at Exchange Server 2003 and Outlook 2003, many of the principles still apply. For specific coverage of Outlook 2002, check out the Second Edition of the book.

Permissions Tab

The Permissions tab, shown in Figure 10-6, allows you to assign permissions to users on the current public folder. Each user can be assigned one of several roles, and each role has a set of permissions associated with it. The available permissions are as follows:

- **Create Items** Allows the user to post items in the folder.
- **Read Items** Allows the user to open any item in the folder.
- **Create Subfolders** Allows the user to create subfolders within the folder.
- **Edit Items** Specifies which items in the folder the user can edit. The None option indicates that a user cannot edit items. The Own option

indicates that the user can edit only items that he or she created. The All option indicates that a user can edit any item in the folder.

- **Folder Owner** Grants the user all permissions in the folder, including the ability to assign permissions.
- **Folder Contact** Specifies that the user is to receive copies of any status messages regarding the folder, including non-delivery reports.
- **Folder Visible** Permits the user to see the folder in the public folder hierarchy.
- **Delete Items** Specifies which items in the folder the user can delete. The None option indicates that a user cannot delete items. The Own option indicates that the user can delete only items that he or she created. The All option indicates that a user can delete any item in the folder.

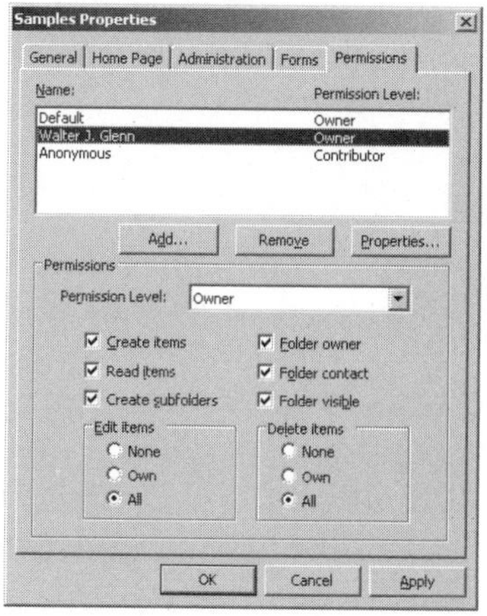

Figure 10-6. *The Permissions tab of a public folder's property sheet in Outlook.*

You can modify the permissions associated with any given role. Table 10-1 shows the available roles and the default permissions granted for each role.

Table 10-1. Default permissions for public folder roles

Role	Create	Read	Edit	Delete	Subfolders	Owner	Contact	Visible
Owner	Yes	Yes	All	All	Yes	Yes	Yes	Yes
Publishing editor	Yes	Yes	All	All	Yes	No	No	Yes
Editor	Yes	Yes	All	All	No	No	No	Yes
Publishing author	Yes	Yes	Own	Own	Yes	No	No	Yes

Table 10-1. Default permissions for public folder roles

Role	Create	Read	Edit	Delete	Subfolders	Owner	Contact	Visible
Author	Yes	Yes	Own	Own	No	No	No	Yes
Nonediting author	Yes	Yes	None	Own	No	No	No	Yes
Reviewer	No	Yes	None	None	No	No	No	Yes
Contributor	Yes	No	None	None	No	No	No	Yes
None	No	No	None	None	No	No	No	Yes

Using Public Folders in the Exchange System Snap-In

The previous section described how to configure public folders using the Outlook client. You can also create and configure public folders in the Exchange System snap-in. Certain tools for managing public folders are available only in this snap-in. In addition, only in Exchange System can you create and modify the top-level public folder hierarchies known as public folder trees.

Creating a Public Folder Tree

Creating a new public folder tree involves three steps. First, you must create a new top-level root folder that will house the new tree structure. Second, you must create a new public folder store on the server to hold the contents of that new tree structure. Finally, you must connect the new top-level folder to the new public folder store. The sections that follow describe these steps in detail.

Creating a New Top-Level Root Folder

The first step in creating a new public folder tree is to create a new top-level root folder. You should name this folder for the structure you wish to create. For example, if you are creating a tree for use only by executives, you might name the new top-level root folder Executives.

Each top-level root folder you create exists on the same level as the Public Folders tree and has its own database on each Exchange server that contains replicas of any of the folders in the tree's hierarchy. To create a new top-level root folder, first select the Folders container for the administrative group in which you want to create the folder, as shown in Figure 10-7. If you have only one administrative group, or if you have Exchange System set not to display administrative groups, the Folders container should appear directly under the root node.

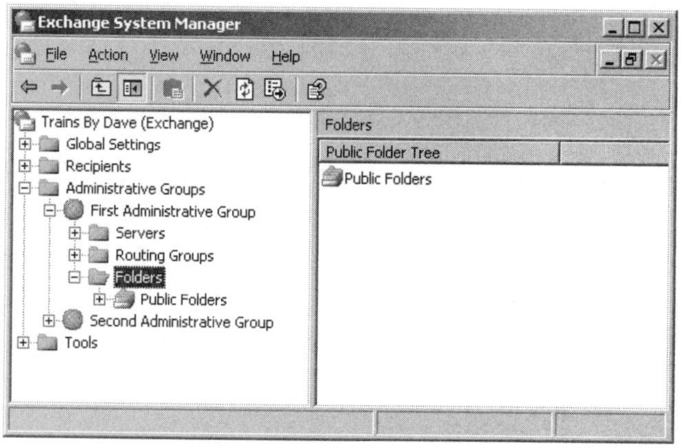

Figure 10-7. *Creating a new top-level root folder.*

Once you have selected the Folders container, choose New Public Folder Tree from the Action menu. This opens the property sheet for the new folder (Figure 10-8). Enter a name for the new tree in the Name field. After you are finished, click OK to close the property sheet and create the new public folder tree.

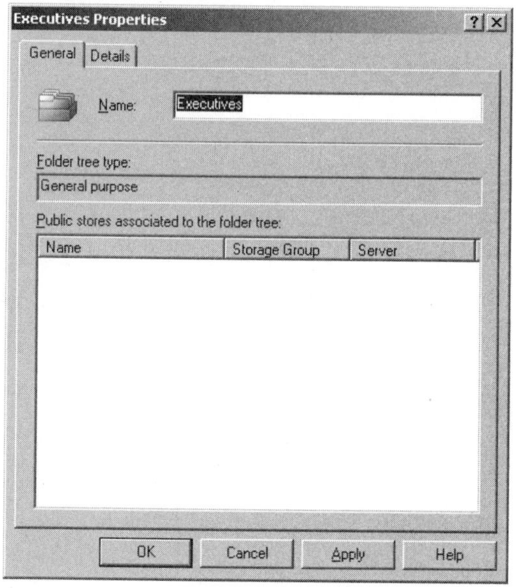

Figure 10-8. *Naming the new public folder tree.*

Creating a New Public Folder Store

Public folders reside in a public folder store. Each public folder tree uses its own database in the store. Once you've created the new top-level root folder for a tree, you must then create a new public folder store to hold that tree. In the Exchange System snap-in, locate the container for the storage group on the server on which you want to create the new tree, as shown in Figure 10-9. You will create the new public folder store in this storage group.

After you select the storage group, choose New Public Store from the Action menu. This opens the property sheet for the new store (Figure 10-10). Enter a name for the new store in the Name field. Click the Browse button to open a dialog box that lets you associate the new store with a public folder tree. Select the tree you created previously. Once you are finished, click OK to close the property sheet. Exchange System will prompt you to mount the new store once it has successfully been created. Click Yes to mount the new store.

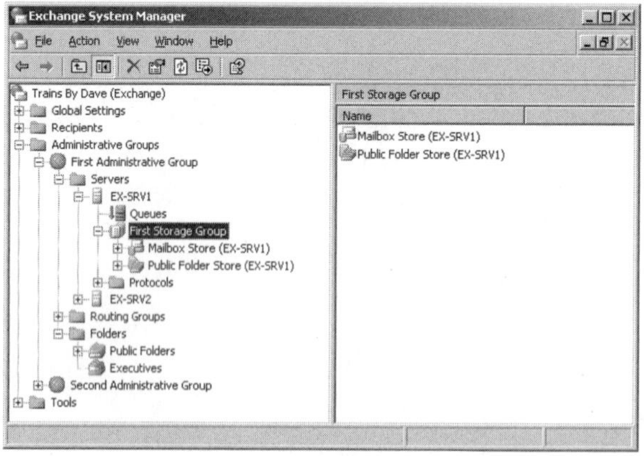

Figure 10-9. *Choosing the storage group for the new public folder store.*

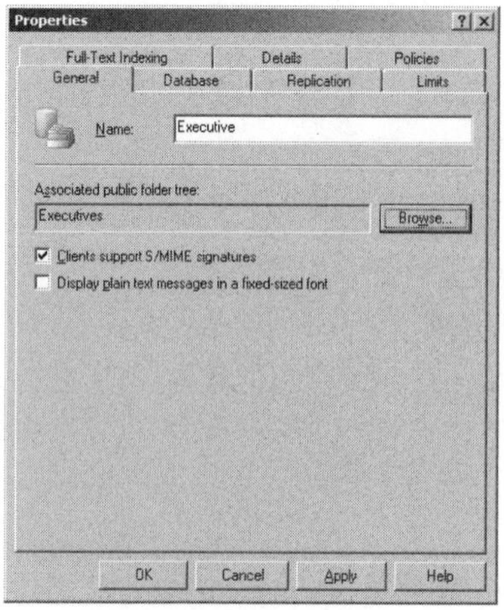

Figure 10-10. *Naming the new store and associating it with the public folder tree.*

Connecting to the Public Folder Store

The final step in creating the new public folder tree is to go back to the top-level root folder that you created earlier and associate it with the new public folder store. In the Exchange System snap-in, find and select the top-level root folder in the main Folders container. Then choose Connect To from the Action menu. This opens the dialog box shown in Figure 10-11, which displays the available public folder stores. You should see the one you just created. Select this store and click OK. The store is connected to the public folder tree and is listed on the Public Stores tab of the property sheet for the top-level root folder.

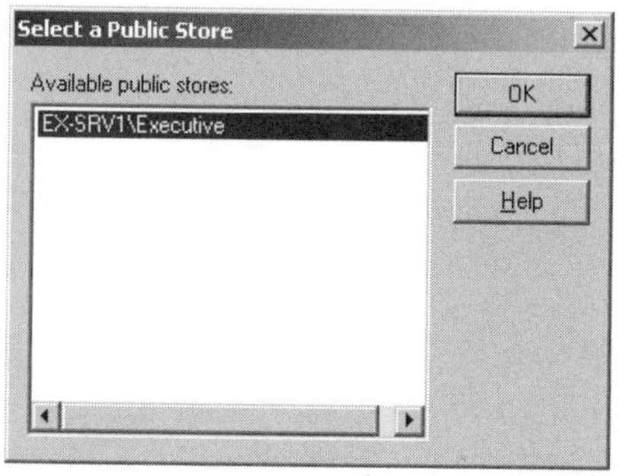

Figure 10-11. *Connecting the public folder tree to the public folder store.*

> **Tip** If you just created the new top-level root folder, you might find that the Connect To command is not available on the Action menu. If this happens, exit and restart the Exchange System snap-in to enable the Connect To command.

Once you have created and connected a new public folder tree, you might want to set permissions governing which users can make changes to the root level of that tree. To do so, just open the property sheet for the top-level folder and switch to the Security tab. By default, only the account used when creating the folder, the Domain Admins group, the Enterprise Admins group, and the Exchange Domain Servers group have permissions to modify the root folder. Click the Add button to specify permissions for additional users.

Creating a Public Folder in the Exchange System Snap-In

The first step in creating a new public folder is deciding where to create it. In the Exchange System snap-in, select the public folder tree in which you want to create a new folder. If you want to make a new top-level folder in that tree, create the folder right in the top-level root folder. Otherwise, select the folder in the tree in which you want to create a new subfolder, as shown in Figure 10-12.

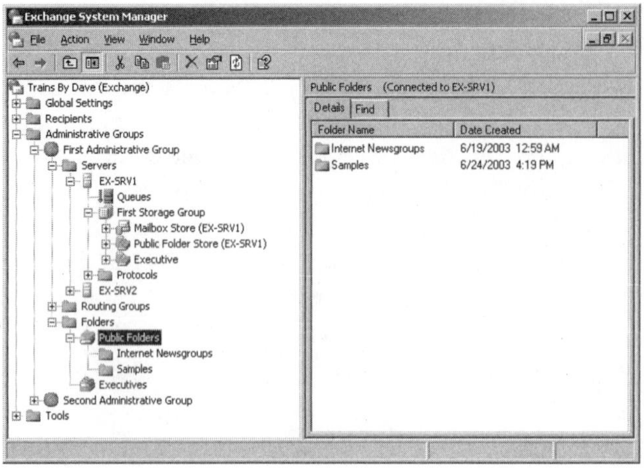

Figure 10-12. *Selecting a location for the new public folder.*

When you have selected the parent folder, choose New Public Folder from the Action menu. This command opens the property sheet for the new public folder (Figure 10-13). All you really have to do to create a new public folder is enter a name in the Name field and click OK. The Exchange System snap-in creates the new folder, and users with the appropriate permissions should find it immediately accessible. If you like, you can also enter a description for the new folder.

At the bottom of the General tab for a public folder, you'll also find an option named Maintain Per-User Read And Unread Information For This Folder. If you select this option, the folder itself will keep track of messages (and mark as read) each individual user of the folder has read. Since most clients (including Outlook) keep track of this information themselves, it is usually not necessary to enable this option.

Once you have created a new public folder, you still need to mail-enable the folder and configure the public folder's e-mail-related settings for your organization. To mail-enable a folder, select the folder in Exchange System and choose All Tasks Mail Enable from the Action menu. The command should take effect immediately, although you will get no feedback from Exchange System after executing it. Once you have mail-enabled a folder, that folder's property sheet will include several extra mail-related tabs, including Exchange General, E-Mail Addresses, and Exchange Advanced. These tabs work like the equivalent tabs for other recipients and allow you to perform such functions as setting delivery options and restrictions, changing the display name and alias, and setting custom attributes. Because Chapter 9 covers the use of these tabs with other types of recipients, we won't describe them here.

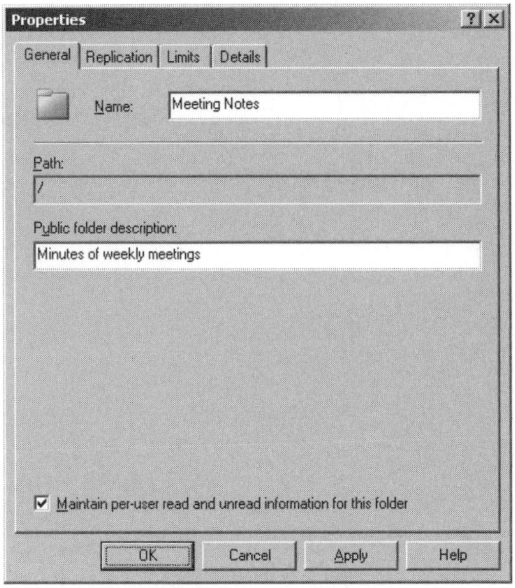

Figure 10-13. *Naming a new public folder.*

You should, however, be aware of an important setting that is added to the General tab of a folder's property sheet when you mail-enable that folder. This setting governs whether you want the name for the folder that is visible in address books to be the same as the public folder name or a different name that you specify.

Managing Public Folders in the Exchange System Snap-In

You manage public folders at two levels within Exchange System. At the level of the public folder store, you specify general parameters for how that public folder store should handle public folders. At the level of the public folder itself, you specify properties that govern that folder and often override settings made at the store level.

Managing Public Folders at the Public Folder Store Level

The properties of public folders that you manage at the public folder store level govern the default behavior of all of the public folders in the public folder store. You access these properties using the property sheet of the Public Folder Store object, found in the container for the storage group in which the public folder store is configured. Most of the tabs on this property sheet govern public folder replication, which is discussed in detail later in this chapter. The tab that we are concerned with here is named Limits and is shown in Figure 10-14.

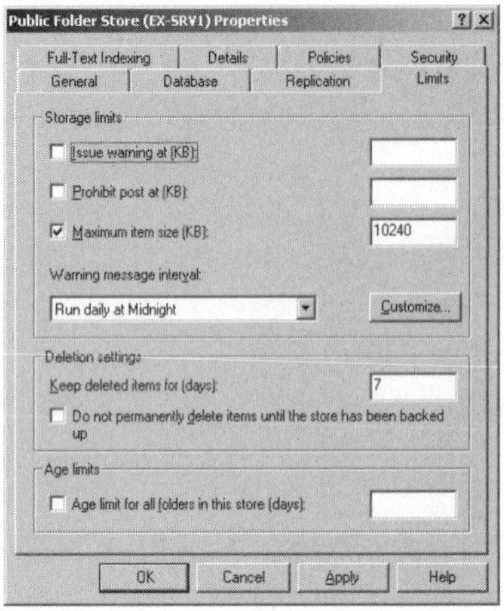

Figure 10-14. *Configuring limits for a public folder store.*

You can use the Limits tab to set default storage limits for all public folders in the public folder store. This storage limit indicates how large (in kilobytes) a public folder can become before certain actions are taken, including issuing a warning to the folder's contacts and prohibiting the posting of new messages. You can also limit the maximum size of messages (with attachments) that users can post. You can override any of these storage limits at the folder level for individual folders, as you'll see a bit later in this chapter.

Exchange Server 2003 also supports a great feature called deleted-item recovery. When a user deletes a message from a folder, that message is marked as hidden and is actually retained for a certain number of days on the server before being permanently deleted. Within that period, known as the *deleted-item retention time*, the user can recover the item. To do so, however, the user must be using Outlook 97 or later (which includes Outlook 97, 2000, 2002, and 2003). To enable this feature for the public folder store, simply set the number of days that you want to keep deleted items on the server. The default setting is *0*. In addition, you can specify that items not be permanently removed from the public folder store until at least one backup has occurred.

The final limit that you can set on the Limits tab is the default number of days for which items are kept in the public folders in the public folder store. The default is no age limit at all.

Note Although age limits make sense for folders that have time-sensitive data, such as an internal classified ads folder or a newsfeed from the Internet, they should be used with caution because most Exchange users expect to retrieve their data indefinitely. Note that public folder age limits work in combination with deleted-item retention time. Suppose that you set a 20-day age limit on your public folders and a 10-day deleted-item retention period. Then suppose that a user deletes an item on day 19—one day before it would automatically expire. The deleted-item retention period, which applies only to user-deleted messages, starts at this point. If the item is recovered within the deleted-item retention period, the age limit for the newly recovered item is reset to add 20 more days.

Managing Public Folders at the Folder Level

You can also manage public folders in Exchange System on a folder-by-folder basis, using the folder's property sheet. Some of the tabs on a folder's property sheet deal only with public folder replication, which is covered later in this chapter. The General tab, which you saw previously in the discussion of creating a public folder, lets you change the description of the folder and the option for maintaining per-user read and unread information. As with the public folder store's property sheet, we are interested primarily in the Limits tab (Figure 10-15) at this point. As you can see, the information on this tab is identical to the Limits tab of the Public Information Store. Any setting you make at the public folder level overrides the setting made at the public folder store level.

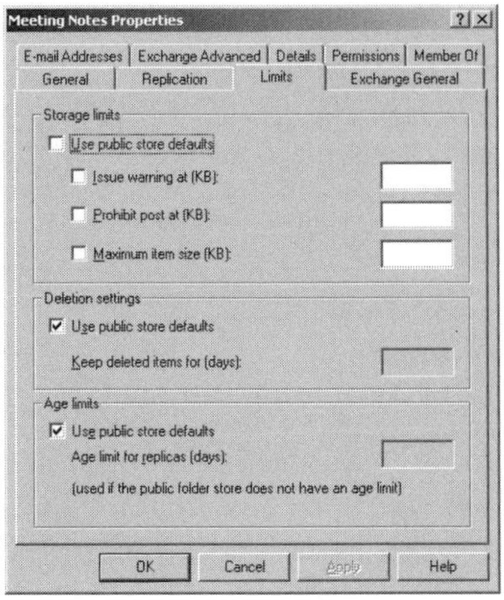

Figure 10-15. *Configuring limits for a single public folder.*

Note Exchange System provides a way to propagate the configuration settings for a parent folder to all of its subfolders. Select the parent folder in Exchange System and choose the All Tasks Propagate Settings command from the Action menu. A dialog box appears that lets you choose the settings that you want to propagate to all subfolders. Once you've propagated the settings to the subfolders, you can change the settings for any particular child folder.

Replicating a Public Folder

The contents of public folders are not replicated to other public folder stores in your organization automatically. If you want replication to occur, you must set it up manually, on a per-folder basis. You can configure each public folder individually to have replicas on multiple public folder stores. When you set up replication for a parent folder, its child folders are also replicated by default, although you can change this for individual child folders.

Public folder replication follows the multimaster replication model, in which every replica of a public folder is considered a master copy. In fact, there is no easy way to distinguish a replica from the original after replication occurs.

Creating a Replica

After you've decided which folders you want to replicate, you manually create and configure the replicas. The method for doing this involves pushing replicas from one public folder store to other public folder stores, using the property sheet of the public folder that you want to replicate. To set up replication for a public folder, open its property sheet in Exchange System and then switch to the Replication tab (Figure 10-16).

This tab lists any public stores that already contain a replica of the public folder. Click the Add button to open a dialog box that lists the available public stores in your organization that do not have replicas of the folder. Select the store to which you want to replicate the folder and click OK. The public store is added to the list of stores that contain replicas.

Below the list of public folder stores, you'll find a drop-down menu named Public Folder Replication Interval. Use this menu to schedule the replication of the public folder to the other public folder stores. You have several options here:

- **Never Run** Essentially turns off replication of the public folder, which is handy if you want to stop the replication temporarily to do something like troubleshoot a bad connector.

- **Always Run** Essentially keeps replication going all the time. Because this option would cause excessive traffic, it is generally a poor choice. However, it can be useful when you first configure a new replica and you want it to be created as soon as possible. In this situation, turning on the Always Run option ensures that the content will be replicated quickly. Be sure to set the schedule to something more reasonable afterward, however.
- **Run Every 1, 2, or 4 Hours** Causes replication to occur at the defined interval.
- **Use Custom Schedule** Allows you to define a custom schedule for replication. Click the Customize button to bring up a dialog box with a calendar of hours you can use to set up the replication schedule.
- **Use Public Store Schedule** Causes the folder to replicate according to the default replication schedule set for the public folder store to which the public folder belongs. This option is the default.

Other options on the Replication tab let you see the last replication message Exchange Server generated regarding the current public folder (the Details button) and set the priority that replication messages concerning this folder should have in your Exchange system.

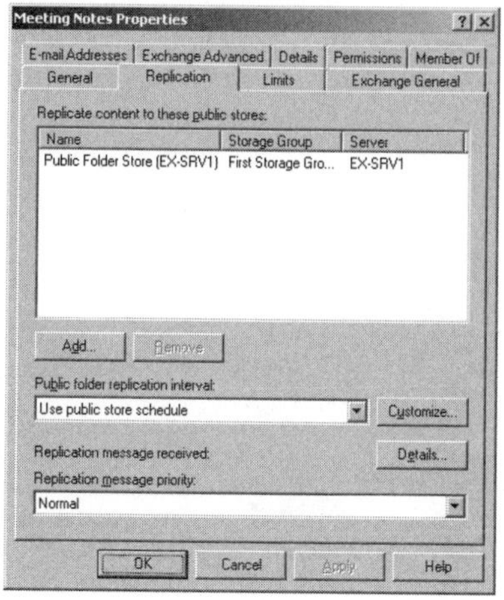

Figure 10-16. *Configuring replication for an individual public folder.*

You can quickly check the replication status of any folder by selecting it in the System Manager snap-in and viewing the Replication tab in the right-hand pane. You'll find the name of the servers the information was replicated to along with the replication status and last received time. You can also use the Status tab to check the current status of the public store. This information includes statistics on each public information store configured in the administrative group, including the size of the folder, the number of items it contains, when it was last accessed, and when the last replication information was received.

Configuring Replication at the Public Folder Store

Once you have created replicas of a public folder and configured how replication should behave at the folder level, you can also configure how replication should behave at the public folder store level. To do this, open the property sheet for the Public Folder Store object and switch to the Replication tab (Figure 10-17).

You can take two actions on this tab. The first is to configure a default interval for replication that applies to all of the folders in that store. You do this with a drop-down menu like the one used to configure a schedule for an individual folder, as described in the previous section. The value you specify here will apply to all the folders in the store, unless you specify something other than the Use Public Store Schedule setting on an individual folder's property sheet. In other words, if you set a schedule for an individual folder, that schedule overrides the setting on this tab.

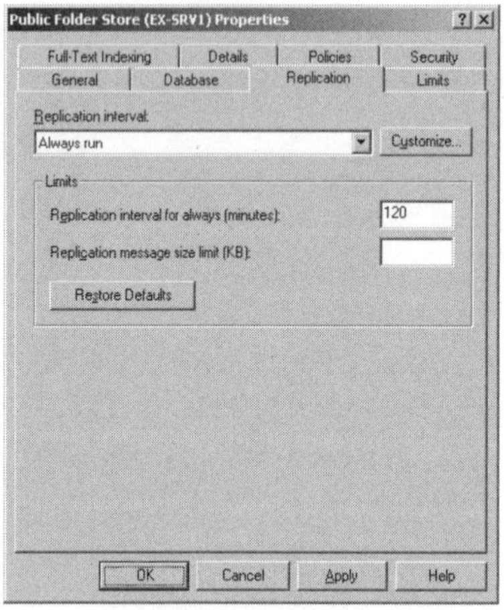

Figure 10-17. *Configuring replication for an entire public folder store.*

The second action you can take on the Replication tab of a public folder store's property sheet is to define limits for replication. By default, no limits are defined. If bandwidth between servers is a consideration, you can specify the maximum time, in minutes, that replication is allowed to go on when it occurs. You can also define the maximum size, in kilobytes, of a single replication message.

Note When folders are replicated, conflicts are possible if users work with different replicas. Exchange has a way to handle replica conflicts intelligently and automatically. The Exchange server allocates revision numbers to all messages posted in a public folder. Using the assigned revision number, the server identifies conflicts as they occur. A conflict might occur when two revisions of the same message are sent from two separate servers to a single server during replication. The server places the conflicting revisions in the replica so that you can resolve the conflict yourself by integrating the revisions or, better yet, by having the authors of the messages work it out themselves. The server then replicates these revisions throughout the organization.

Public Folder Referrals

Users don't really care which replica of a public folder they connect to. However, we administrators do care for a variety of reasons. When a client requests a public folder, the request is processed in a certain order:

1. The client checks the default public store configured for its Mailbox store to which it belongs.
2. If no replica of the folder is found in the client's default public folder, the client next checks any Exchange server to which it has an existing connection.
3. The client then checks every other server that is in the same routing group as the client's home public folder server.
4. The client then checks servers in other routing groups, starting with the lowest cost connections.

As administrator, you can use two strategies to modify the way in which public folder referrals are handled. First, you can configure connectors between routing groups to refuse public folder referrals. The following connectors have the ability to refuse public folder referrals: Routing Group, SMTP, X.400, and X.25. Connectors are discussed in further detail in Chapter 13, "Connecting Routing Groups."

The second strategy you have for modifying referrals is to customize the list of servers that any particular server can refer a client to. Just open the Property sheet for the server in the Exchange System snap-in, switch to the Public Folder Referrals tab, and configure a custom list of servers.

Synchronizing Public Folder Replicas

Public folder replication follows the multimaster replication model, in which every replica of a public folder is considered a master copy. When you decide which folders you want to replicate, you manually create and configure those replicas. Any change made to a public folder is automatically replicated to other copies of that folder by the Exchange Public Folder Replication Agent (PFRA) service. These copies are based on settings you configure. Replication is an e-mail-based process that uses SMTP as its transport mechanism.

The PFRA uses three primary constructs to keep track of replication throughout an organization and to determine whether a public folder is synchronized. These constructs include the following:

- **Change Number** The change number is made up of a globally unique identifier for the Information Store and a change counter that is specific to the server on which a public folder resides. When a user modifies (or creates) a message in a public folder, the PFRA for that Information Store assigns a new change number to the message.
- **Time Stamp** The PFRA stamps messages with the time and date as soon as they arrive in a public folder and applies a new time stamp whenever a message is modified.
- **Predecessor Change List** This is a list of all of the Information Stores that have made changes to a message and the most recent change number assigned by each Information Store on the list.

Together, these constructs are referred to as *message state information* and play a role in message creation, deletion, and modification.

Message Creation

When a new message is created in a folder, the Information Store receiving the message assigns a change number to the message and deposits it in the folder. The message is replicated to other replicas of the folder during the normal replication schedule.

Message Deletion

When a message is deleted from a folder, the Information Store running the replica in which the message is deleted sends a replication message to all other Information Stores that host a replica of the folder. When each Information Store receives the replication message, it removes the deleted message from its own replica.

Message Expiration

When a message expires (reaches the configured age limit for messages in the folder), the Information Store deletes the message from the folder but does not send a replication message to other Information Stores. Each Information Store removes expired messages from its own folders based on settings made for that particular store and for the folder. Thus, it is possible for different stores to expire a message at different times.

Message Modification

When a change is made to a message in one replica of a public folder, the PFRA for that Information Store updates the message state information for that message and sends a replication message to other Information Stores on which replicas of the folder exist. This replication message contains the modified message and all its attachments.

When another Information Store receives such a replication message, the modified message inside is used to replace the original message in that store if the message state information determines that the message is indeed newer than the original.

Even though the PFRA sends out replication messages, there is no mechanism in place for ensuring that replication messages reach their destination. The logic behind this is that generating an extra confirmation message for each replication message would unnecessarily double the amount of traffic involved in replication. Thus, it is possible for a message in different replicas of a public folder to become out of sync. A process known as backfill is used to remedy this situation. During regular maintenance, status messages are sent between servers, and change numbers for messages on different replicas are compared. If a server is found to be out of sync, it then generates a *backfill* request for any changes that have not yet been received.

Summary

Public folders provide centralized storage of virtually any type of document or message and allow controlled access by any user in the organization. As such, they provide the basis of workflow applications for Exchange Server 2003. In this chapter, you learned what you need to know to set up a good public folder system in your Exchange organization, including how to create public folders, how to manage them with the Outlook client as well as with the Exchange System snap-in, and how to create multiple public folder trees in your Exchange organization. You also learned how to set up replication so that your public folders can be copied to public folder stores on other servers. Now it's time to turn to another aspect of the Exchange storage architecture. In Chapter 11, "Using Storage Groups," you will learn how to configure and manage Exchange Server 2003 storage groups.

Chapter 11

Using Storage Groups

In the previous two chapters, you learned how to create and manage the various types of recipients in Microsoft Exchange Server 2003. In this chapter, we turn our attention to storage groups. We'll look at the issues involved in planning multiple databases and discuss when you should and should not use circular logging, how to create a storage group, how to create and delete a store, and how to mount and dismount a store.

Review of Exchange 2003 Storage Architecture

Chapter 2, "Exchange Server Storage Architecture," described the storage architecture of Exchange Server 2003. This section will refresh your memory by summarizing the main points of that architecture. Refer to Chapter 2 if you need more details.

A storage group in an Exchange system consists of a set of up to five databases for the Enterprise Edition, and two for the Standard Edition. All the databases in a storage group use the same transaction log files. Each database in Exchange Server 2003 comprises two files: the rich text file (the .EDB file); and the native content file, or streaming file (the .STM file). Both of these files are managed as one unit by the Information Store service. The native content file can hold any type of content in its original form. Information is read into and out of the native content file by the Exchange Installable File System (ExIFS), a kernel mode component that provides very fast streaming.

Benefits of Using Storage Groups

These days, it is not uncommon to find Exchange 5.5 databases that are well over 20 GB in size. The time necessary to back up these databases can exceed several hours. The problem with this is not the time it takes to back up the database, but the time it takes to *restore* such a large database. During the restoration, of course, your users' productivity goes down the drain. In Exchange database planning, the old cliché is a good one: *Always plan for failure so that you can succeed*. You'll find that prudent use of storage groups will help you succeed during disaster recovery.

In implementing storage groups and allowing multiple databases per Exchange server, Microsoft has made some tremendous changes to the Extensible Storage Engine (ESE) database architecture since Exchange Server 5.5. These changes significantly enhance recoverability and maximize productivity when an Exchange database becomes corrupted. In addition, storage groups offer several key benefits, which are listed here and discussed in the sections that follow:

- Each server can host more users than before.
- Each database can be backed up and restored individually.
- Each server can host multiple businesses.
- A separate store can be used for special mailboxes.
- Circular logging can apply to individual storage groups.

Increased User Support

Probably the largest benefit of storage groups is that they allow you to spread users across databases and storage groups on the same Exchange Server 2003. This provides three advantages:

- You can support more users on a single server than was possible in Exchange 5.5.
- You'll have less downtime when a database becomes corrupted.
- You can host more users on an Exchange server because you can keep your databases to a manageable size.

As mentioned earlier, within a storage group, you can have up to five databases. Each server can house up to four storage groups. Thus, each server can have a maximum of 20 databases.

However, when you run the Information Store Integrity Checker (Isinteg.exe) on a database, you must dismount that database. In addition, Isinteg.exe needs a second database for temporary use. Therefore, if you have five databases operating in a given storage group, you will have to dismount a second database so that Isinteg.exe can run properly. If you limit the number of operating databases to four in a single storage group, you will always have room to run Isinteg.exe without having to dismount a second store.

Having your users spread out across multiple databases means that only a subset of your users is affected if one of your databases goes off line for some reason.

The other users can continue to work because their databases are up and running. A database that is offline is considered to be *dismounted*. Its icon appears with a red down arrow in the Exchange System snap-in, as shown in Figure 11-1.

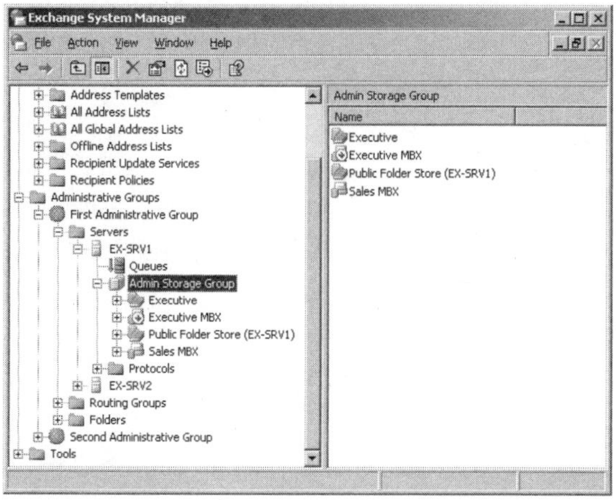

Figure 11-1. *Online databases and an offline database (Executive MBX) in a storage group.*

Individual Backup and Restore

Because each individual database can be mounted or dismounted, you can back up and restore databases individually while other databases in the same storage group are mounted and running. Consider a scenario in which you have created four mailbox stores in the same storage group, one for each of four departments. If one of those stores becomes corrupted, the other three can remain mounted while you restore the fourth store from backup and then mount it again. You are not required to dismount all the stores in a storage group in order to restore one of them. And if one store becomes corrupted and cannot be mounted, it does not stop other stores in the same storage group from being mounted and available to users.

Note In addition to the five databases allowed in each storage group, a special sixth storage group named the recovery storage group is also allowed. The recovery storage group is intended as a temporary group that you can bring online for use in performing recovery operations. For example, you could bring the recovery storage group online, restore mailboxes to it, and allow users to access it while you resolve any problems with the original storage group. You could then merge the mailboxes of the storage recovery group back into the original storage group. The use of the recovery storage group is detailed in Chapter 27, "Disaster Recovery of an Exchange Server 2003 Database."

Hosting of Multiple Businesses

If you manage e-mail for multiple businesses, you can host them on a single server. You can create an individual store for each business or even devote a storage group to a business, if needed. In either case, Exchange Server 2003 keeps the information for each business completely separate in its respective store, unlike Exchange Server 5.5.

Separate, distinct stores allow you to set up different administrative schedules for the businesses. For instance, some administrators might want to have full backups performed every day, while others might need only weekly full backups. Some might want to have each department hosted in a separate store, while others might be happy to house all their users in the same store. This flexibility makes it easier to meet your customer's needs.

Support for Special Mailboxes

Although it is not widely recommended, you can take a special mailbox or set of mailboxes and create them in their own store. One instance when this might be useful would be for a journalizing recipient who receives copies of all appropriate e-mails in your organization to ensure they comply with local laws or industry-specific regulations. Another instance might be for a project team who is working with highly sensitive and mission-critical company information. Their work might warrant the use of a separate store or public folder tree.

Circular Logging for a Single Storage Group

You might need to control the transaction logs for some storage groups because of limited disk space. It could be the case, for example, that information held in one native content file is expendable while information held in a different native content file is not. Because you are limited to recovery at the last full backup when using circular logging, you could place your expendable information (such as a history of companywide memos) in one public folder in one storage group for which you permit circular logging, and you could place your users' e-mails in a different storage group that has circular logging turned off. That way, you'd be able to focus your disaster recovery efforts on the most important information. For a description of how circular logging works, refer to Chapter 2.

Planning Storage Groups

In most new implementations, whether they are migrations or clean installations, planning is the part that gets the least attention and yet deserves the most. We can't emphasize enough that poor planning leads to poor implementation and increased administration over the long term. If you were to record the types of support activities you perform each day for a month and then review them, you might find that 50 percent or more of them could have been avoided with better planning and implementation. I know you're thinking that you don't have the time to do good planning. But if you don't, you'll end up using the time you saved dealing with the unforeseen troubles caused by your migration to Exchange Server 2003.

Real World Network Administration at Its Best

We know of one Exchange administrator who faithfully accomplishes the following activities on a regular basis. He developed this list by taking a thorough look at his daily activities and proactively planning ways to avoid common "fires." Needless to say, his Exchange network runs smoothly and he feels ready for any disaster that might occur. To some of you, these tasks might seem like overkill. But we would encourage you to withhold your judgment as you examine these steps. We think this is nothing less than outstanding administration.

On a daily basis, he checks his logs—all of them. He checks the application, security, system, directory, and other logs. If he sees any warnings or cautions, he checks them out and resolves them that day, if possible. He also checks his backup software logs each day to make sure the backups worked. He performs an incremental backup every day except Friday. In addition, he uses a monitor or critical services on his Exchange servers and sends bounce messages every hour to his company's regular vendors and customers. In all, eight Internet SMTP servers are sent bounce messages. If the link goes down, he often knows about it before anyone else and can troubleshoot it and (sometimes) fix it before his users even know something is wrong. (To learn more about Link Monitor and Server Monitor, see Chapter 27.)

On a weekly basis, he performs a full backup of all of his servers and makes sure on Monday that they were successful. If not, he starts another full backup on Monday as he is leaving work. He also checks his antivirus software for updates and uses their network software to update his servers and his users' workstations.

Every month, he runs a series of System Monitor charts, logs the activities, and then prints a report for each server, placing it into an ever-expanding notebook. These charts measure the health of his servers and run for three days at 10-minute intervals. With them, he is able to predict how the addition of a service or a new group of users will affect each of his servers. And when he requests new hardware, he has the numbers and the credibility to back up his request.

In addition, each month he performs a trial restore for each tape backup device that he uses. Since he performs backups on three different servers, he does three trial restores. Here is how he does it. He takes 15 percent of the information that is currently being backed up and copies it to another location on the same server. Often, he'll create a temporary folder named Test. Then he backs up this temporary folder, noting the size and number of files. After the backup and verify operation is complete, he deletes the Test folder and then restores it from the tape backup. When the restore is complete, he compares the size and number of files in the restored folder to those in the original Test folder. If they match, he knows his tape backup system is working. If they don't match, he has some troubleshooting to do.

Once a month, he also restores his Exchange databases to an offline server that is configured in roughly the same way as his production server. He then makes sure that those databases work on the offline server. This exercise has given him the confidence to know that he can do a solid restore quickly and efficiently, and the knowledge that his backup system really is working. The time to learn how to restore your Exchange databases is not when the storm is raging and you're on the phone with Microsoft technical support. It's better to learn when everything is calm and you can make mistakes with an offline server.

Also, every four to six weeks, he offers user training, usually on topics that have dominated his support calls. This type of "customer service" approach has led to a steady decline in help desk calls because he has developed smarter users who can perform some very basic troubleshooting themselves, such as making sure that everything is plugged in or that the printer is on line.

On a quarterly basis, he drains his uninterruptible power supply (UPS) batteries and makes sure that his UPS software cleanly shuts down his servers. It's better to find out that your UPS software isn't working during a test than during a power outage. A good way to corrupt your Exchange database is to experience an unexpected power outage and have your UPS cut power to your Exchange server instead of shutting it down cleanly.

Moreover, on a quarterly basis, he checks for firmware updates and revisions for all of his servers. If there is a new update, he installs it. For his users, he'll check for updates or service packs for the various applications that his firm uses. If new updates or service packs have been released, he tests them with a few trusted users and, barring anything negative, pushes the updates out to the rest of his network. Finally, he checks the cooling fans on all his servers quarterly to make sure they aren't getting weak.

Because of his good planning, he has the trust of his superiors. He has taken the time to tell them what he is doing and why. Consequently, he has been able, over time, to implement many standards that have contributed to a smoothly running network. Being proactive in his planning has helped him achieve a situation in which he spends a good portion of his time being proactive about the upcoming changes his network will experience instead of just putting out fires.

Planning for Disk Space

Let's take a look at some planning issues. We'll trust you to not skim this section. Since this chapter focuses on storage groups, we'll confine our discussion to planning for disk space, multiple databases, and multiple storage groups. (For a broader look at how to plan for Exchange Server 2003, refer to Chapter 5, "Assessing Needs," and Chapter 6, "Planning for Development.") When planning disk space capacities for your Exchange 2003 server, you need to consider several key factors:

- The number of users to be housed on a given Exchange server
- The types of users to be housed on a given Exchange server
- The average size of an e-mail and an attachment, and the number of attachments that your users will need to send and receive
- The number and size of public folders

The next two sections describe how to calculate the disk space needs of your Exchange server.

Calculating Disk Space for E-Mails and Attachments

Messaging activity by your users is going to be difficult to forecast. Some users send and receive only a few e-mails each day. Others are at the opposite end of the spectrum, sending and receiving lots of e-mails each day, some with large attachments. Obviously, given the same hardware specifications, you can house more light users in a single mailbox store than you can heavy users. Although it might seem trivial to do so, it's best to develop some type of classification system for your environment and then run the numbers to determine how many users you want per store, per storage group, and finally, per server. If you can get a semi-accurate picture of your current messaging usage, you'll be better able to predict hardware and storage group needs.

A good way to do this is to pick a random sample of your users—at least 15 percent—and then conduct an audit of their current e-mail usage. Be sure they are saving copies of their sent e-mails in the Sent Items folder so that you can get an idea as to how many e-mails they are sending each day and the size of their e-mails. You can also see how many e-mails had attachments and, by opening the e-mails, you can see the sizes of the attachments. Security concerns might keep you from getting the information you need from some users, and in those cases you can give them a short survey to fill out.

Once you've collected your data, you need to analyze it. This part simply involves running some numbers. Consider this example: Assume that you conducted your analysis on 45 users (out of 300 users) over a 60-day period, and you find that the average number of e-mails per day for each user is 14, with 2 attachments. Let's further assume that the average size of each e-mail is 1 KB and the average size of each attachment is 200 KB. The numbers would look like this:

- 14 e-mails × 1 KB = 14 KB per day in e-mail.
- 2 attachments × 200 KB = 400 KB per day in attachments.
- Total average disk space usage: 828 KB per day (414 KB for the store, 414 KB for the transaction logs).
- 828 KB × 300 users = 248,400 KB, or 248.4 MB, of disk space per day for all 300 users. Over a two-month (60-day) period, there will be 44 working days, so 10,929 MB, or 10.9 GB, of disk space will be needed.

This final figure of 10.9 GB is somewhat misleading because the transaction logs will not be retained forever and some of the e-mails will be deleted. Eventually, the ESE will delete the old logs, freeing up disk space to be used again by the transaction logs. Therefore, let's assume that the ESE keeps only a week's worth of logs, or 5 × 414 KB = 2070 KB. Thus, after two months of activity, you will need only 5,466,870 KB, or 5.4 GB (44 days × 414 KB average usage × 300 users, plus 2070 KB for the logs) of disk space to run Exchange 2000 Server.

We're not finished yet. All we have established is the amount of disk space needed to record e-mails and attachments. We still need to look at public folders and backup throughput.

Calculating Disk Space for Public Folders

To illustrate how to determine the space needed for the public folders, let's assume that each user posts an average of three documents per day to your public folders, each with an average size of 6 KB. (Although this document size might seem large, refer to Chapter 2's discussion of storage architecture. You will see storage of multiple types of documents in Exchange happening more and more.) We would calculate the public folder disk space like this: 3 posts × 300 users × 6 KB × 2 (because each post is recorded once in the store and once in the transaction log). This scenario comes out to 10,800 KB (10.8 MB) per day of disk space for your users to post to their public folders. Over 44 days, you will need 237,600 KB (237.6 MB) plus 27,000 KB for the transaction logs (3 posts × 300 users × 6 KB average size × 5 days), giving you a grand total over a two-month period of 264,600 KB (264.6 MB) of disk space needed for your public folders. Thus, you would need 5.46 GB for e-mails and 264.6 MB for public folders, or approximately 5.7 GB of total disk space for a two-month period. We're still not finished, however. We now need to see how to use these numbers in planning for our storage groups.

Planning for Multiple Storage Groups

Once you've gotten a handle on your disk space needs, you need to consider how many storage groups you need. One factor you need to think about is the varying priorities of the work your users do. Let's assume that 20 of your 300 users perform work that is absolutely mission-critical. Perhaps they are sales staff who take orders over the phone or who process customer orders that are placed in a public folder that is exposed on your Web site. Let's assume that if these users are down for even 15 minutes, your company loses in excess of $50,000. In this type of situation, you should consider splitting these users into two groups and hosting each group in its own mailbox and public folder store. Hosting them in their own storage group, however, is not necessary.

The reasoning behind this recommendation is that if the other databases become corrupted, these users could continue to operate without disruption because you can dismount and restore one or any combination of stores while another store runs in the same storage group. And if one group's database needs to be restored, it would be a fast restore because it would be much smaller than the companywide database in which the other 280 users are hosted. In addition, since these users are spread over two databases, the other half of the group can continue to work and remain productive. Hence, plan your storage groups with disaster recovery in mind more than disk space usage considerations.

Planning for Backup Throughput

Another consideration when planning your storage groups is the type of throughput you need when you do a restore. Let's assume that you have purchased a tape drive with a maximum throughput of 10 GB per hour, or 166.6 MB per minute. At that rate, restoring the databases from tape backup would take about 35 minutes, if all the users were housed in the same database. When you factor in the time needed to diagnose the problem, find the tapes, and do the backup, you can reasonably assume that your users would be without e-mail and public folders for one to two hours, depending on the nature of the problem and how fast you can get to a point at which a restore operation can be performed.

In some companies, being down for one or two hours is no big deal. In others, it could spell disaster. Therefore, you'll need to determine how long your users can be without Exchange services while you are performing a restore. Discussions with your manager can help you formulate the amount of downtime that is acceptable in the event of a disaster.

Suppose that as a result of these discussions, you determine that no one is to be without Exchange services for more than 30 minutes. To plan how to stay within this maximum downtime, you would take the restore time you calculated in the previous section and divide it by the maximum downtime allowed by management policy. This calculation will determine the number of stores you'll need to create on your Exchange server. To determine the minimum number of storage groups you will need, divide the number of stores by 5 (the number of stores per storage group).

In our example, we know that it will take 35 minutes to restore data for 300 users. However, this number reflects keeping data for only two months. Most companies keep data much longer than this. So, if in our running example, we set our data retention policy to a more realistic period of one year, we'll need to multiply our previous numbers by 6 to gain an accurate restore picture for one year's worth of data. Thus, restoring databases holding a year's worth of information would take 210 minutes, or 3.5 hours. Now, how would you handle this? Well, you'll want to be able to restore the databases within 15 minutes to give yourself plenty of time to meet your company's 30-minute downtime policy. Therefore, you would need to create a minimum of 14 separate mailbox stores and 14 separate public folder stores (210/15). This assumes, of course, that the databases will be relatively the same size. If some databases turn out to be much larger than the restore time goal, it would be wise to create additional stores or move some users' mailboxes to create store sizes that will meet your goals.

In this scenario, you would need at least five storage groups to accommodate 28 stores. Since we have a maximum of four storage groups per server, you'll need two Exchange servers to accommodate these databases. It would be best to load balance the databases as much as possible between the two servers. Also, since the system uses one set of transaction logs per storage group, increasing the number of storage groups would prevent the buildup of a large number of transaction logs per storage group, although it would cause an overall increase in the number of transaction logs for the entire system.

Creating Storage Groups

Creating a storage group is quick and painless. Remember that you cannot create more than four storage groups on any given Exchange 2003 server. Attempts to do so will result in an error message.

To create a storage group, open the Exchange System snap-in and navigate to your server object. Right-click the server object, point to New, and choose Storage Group from the submenu (Figure 11-2). The property sheet for the new storage group appears (Figure 11-3). As you type in the name of the storage group, you'll notice that it is entered in all three fields simultaneously. This step ensures that there aren't any mistakes in the transaction log location or the system path location.

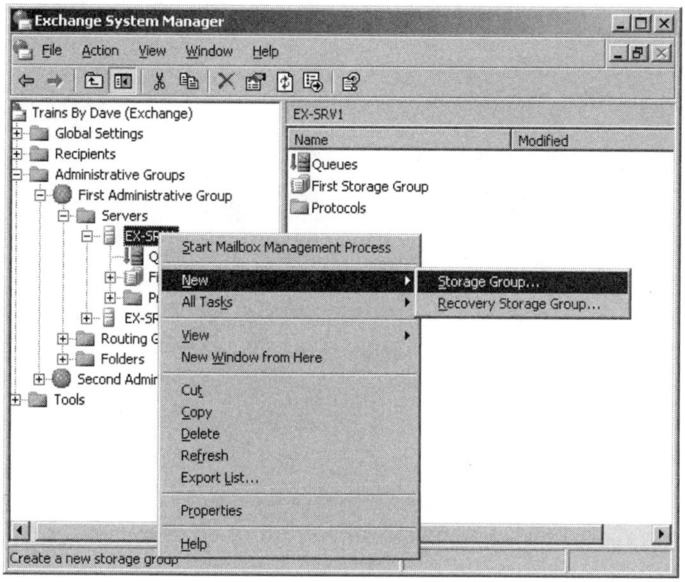

Figure 11-2. *Creating a storage group.*

The property sheet also allows you to select the Zero Out Deleted Database Pages and Enable Circular Logging options. The Zero Out Deleted Database Pages option tells the storage group to write zeros to deleted pages within all of the stores inside the storage group during an online backup. Select this option if you want to be sure that deleted data cannot be recovered. This will add overhead to your backup process and slow down your backup routine, but it will increase the security of your deleted data. The Log File Prefix field can be used to specify a prefix to be placed at the beginning of each log file. This feature allows you to store all your log files in the same location and still identify which logs go with which storage groups.

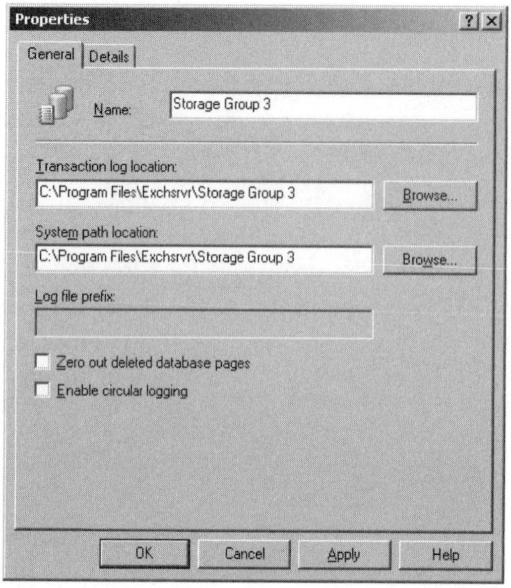

Figure 11-3. *Property sheet for a new storage group.*

The Enable Circular Logging option enables circular logging for the storage group. Consider enabling this feature only for those storage groups that do not hold mission-critical data. Circular logging does reduce the number of transaction logs created by the ESE's Store process, but it eliminates the ability to recover your databases up to the point of a disaster. With circular logging enabled, you can recover only to the last full backup. Consider carefully the full implications of losing the most recent data in your Exchange databases before selecting this option.

The Details tab of the storage group's property sheet allows you to enter notes about the storage group, such as who created it and what its purpose is.

Creating Stores

You can create two kinds of stores in a storage group, a *mailbox* store for messages and a *public folder* store for public folder use. Each store will have its own .EDB and .STM files. You can't create a store until you have created a storage group. When you first install Exchange Server 2003, it creates a storage group named First Storage Group (which you can rename by right-clicking it and choosing Rename) as well as a mailbox store and a public folder store inside that storage group.

Creating a Mailbox Store

To create a new mailbox store, right-click the storage group in which you would like to create the store, point to New, and then choose Mailbox Store. Figure 11-4 shows the property sheet that appears. On the General tab, enter the name of the mailbox store, and then click the Browse button next to the Default Public Store field to see a list of public folder stores with which you can associate the mailbox store (Figure 11-5). Choose a public folder store from the list, and click OK.

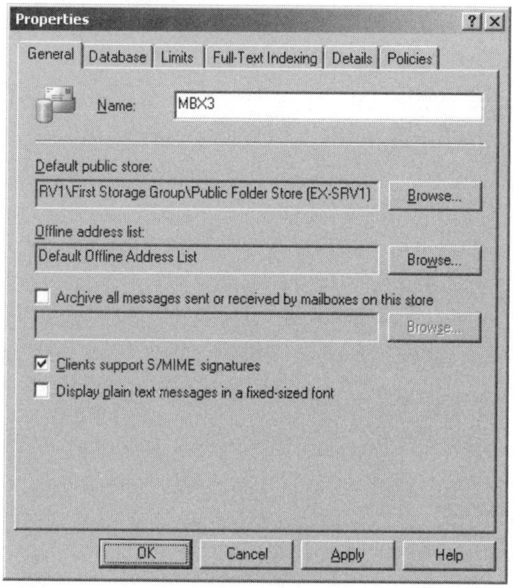

Figure 11-4. *General tab of the property sheet for a new mailbox store.*

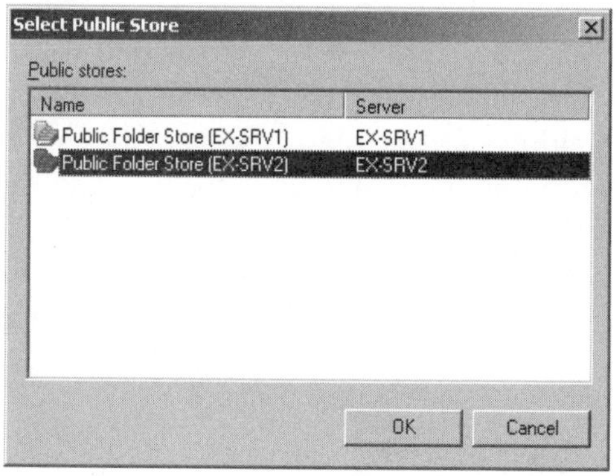

Figure 11-5. *Selecting a default public folder store for the new mailbox store.*

Note Selecting a public folder store to associate with the new mailbox is required because each Exchange user must have a default public folder store for public folder access. Selecting a public folder store here does not limit the user's ability to access other public folder stores or public folder trees. Instead, it provides an entry point into the whole public folder area.

After selecting a public folder store to associate with your mailbox store, click Browse next to the Default Offline Address List field to choose a default offline address list for users homed in this store (Figure 11-6). Users will still be able to download other offline address lists; this option simply specifies the default.

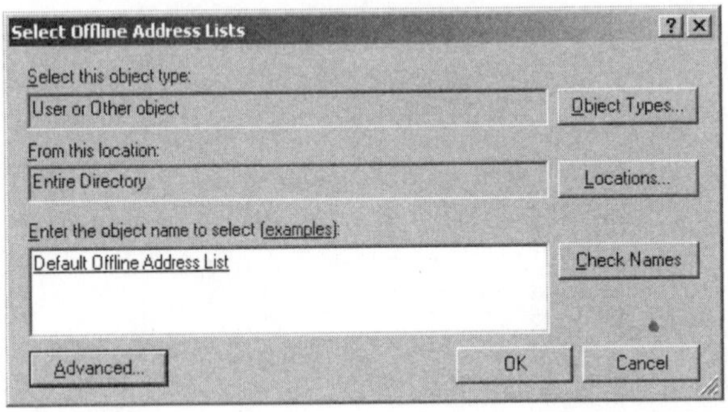

Figure 11-6. *Selecting a default offline address list for the new mailbox store.*

If you want the mailbox store to support Secure/Multipurpose Internet Mail Extensions (S/MIME), select the Clients Support S/MIME Signatures check box. (See Part IV, "Upgrading and Migrating," to learn more about S/MIME and when you would want to use it.) And if you want all incoming messages converted to 10-point Courier, select the Display Plain Text Messages In A Fixed-Sized Font option.

On the Database tab of the property sheet (Figure 11-7), you can specify where you want the two files that make up this store to be physically located. Even though you can navigate to a remote share point on another server, Exchange Server 2003 will not allow you to map either of your files to a network share. However, you can create a volume mount point and specify it as the location for either of your files. This can be helpful if you know that a particular database will house large files or many files, since you can create a special partition for them. You can also specify the time at which you want the store maintenance utilities to run for this particular store.

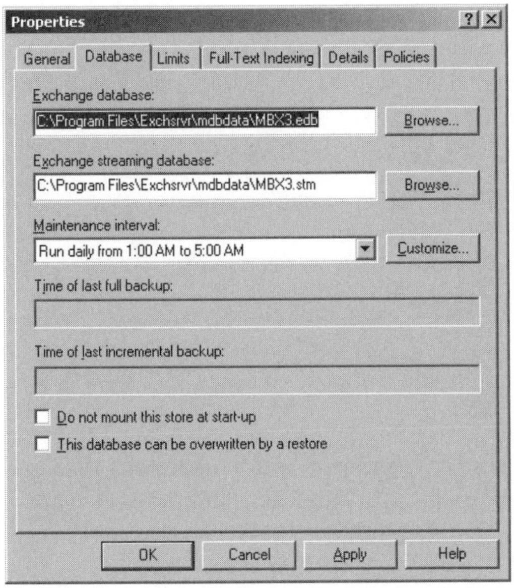

Figure 11-7. *Database tab of the property sheet for a new mailbox store.*

The Do Not Mount This Store At Start-Up check box allows you to specify that the store not be mounted at startup. This is useful if you need to perform administrative functions on the store, such as moving mailboxes from another store or creating policies before mounting the store. The default is to have the store mounted when Exchange services start. Finally, you can select the This Database Can Be Overwritten By A Restore check box. This option relates to the database's globally unique identifier (GUID).

Each database has a GUID. This GUID is stored in the ESE database in one of the general purpose tables. (For more information about ESE, consult Chapter 2.) The database GUID, along with its physical path on the hard disk drive, is also stored in Active Directory. When the Store.exe process starts, one of its tasks is to attempt to mount the database. Before mounting the database, however, the Store.exe process compares the database GUID it finds in the database to the database GUID for that database in Active Directory. The directory paths are also compared.

If everything matches, the database is mounted. If there is a mismatch in any of the information, the Store.exe process refuses to start up the database. This failure can occur if the database files are moved from a different server or directory to their present location. The reason the Store.exe process requires the GUID to match is to prevent a database from being accidentally moved to a different location and having it start up under a different storage group with different transaction logs.

If the This Database Can Be Overwritten By A Restore option is selected, the Store.exe process assumes you really want to move the database to this present location. So at startup, the Store.exe process will "fix" the database by changing the GUID in the database to the GUID that is in Active Directory; then at the next mounting, the GUIDs will match and the database will mount. Finally, the option is cleared as part of this process.

> **Note** If no database is found in the path when the Store.exe process is trying to mount the database, the process will prompt you with an option to create a new database. The This Database Can Be Overwritten By A Restore option is really only invoked when the Store.exe process finds a database in the path it is instructed to look in and finds what it believes is the *wrong* database because the GUID is different.

The This Database Can Be Overwritten By A Restore option functions similarly during a restore. During the *AddDatabase()* call, Windows Backup passes in the GUID, database name, and storage group name to the Store.exe process. If these match, the Store.exe process passes back the locations where the files should be restored. If the GUID doesn't match, the Store.exe process looks at this check box, and if selected, it passes the database back to the backup process where the database files should be written.

> **Note** By moving databases around and selecting the This Database Can Be Overwritten By A Restore check box, you can create multiple, different databases with the same GUID on your Exchange Server. If you try to mount both databases, only one will mount because of the conflicting GUIDs. Under no circumstances does Microsoft recommend keeping two databases with the same GUID or "swapping" databases for any reason. Unexpected and undesirable results can occur.

The Limits tab (Figure 11-8) allows you to set deleted-item retention times and storage warning limits for the mailbox store. You can also set these options globally by creating a mailbox store policy under the Policies container. Values set via a policy cannot be overridden at the server level.

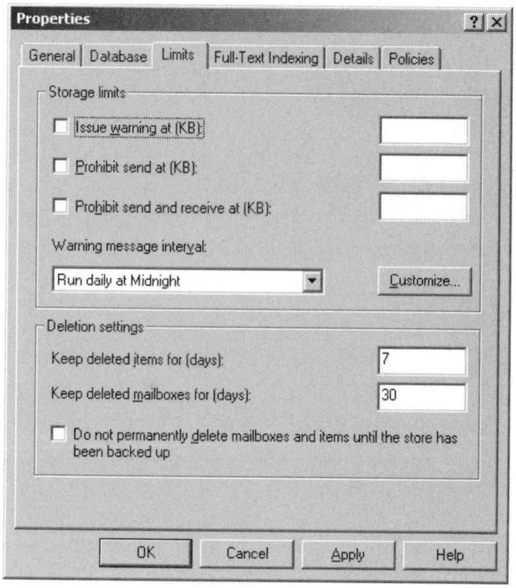

Figure 11-8. *Limits tab of the property sheet for a new mailbox store.*

Features on the Full-Text Indexing tab are unavailable during the creation of your mailbox store. However, after the store has been created, you can enable full-text indexing by right-clicking the store in the Exchange System snap-in, pointing to All Tasks, and choosing Create Full Text Index. Once this index is created, additional objects appear under the Full-Text Indexing container (Figure 11-9) and the features on the Full-Text Indexing tab will be available for configuration. For more information about the architecture of full-text indexing, see Chapter 2. To learn more about how to work with full-text indexing, see "Creating a Full-Text Index" later in this chapter.

On the Details tab of the mailbox store's property sheet, you can enter administrative notes about the mailbox store, such as who created it and its purpose. The Security tab, which will show up only on the property sheet of a successfully created mailbox store, lists the permissions for the users and groups that have access to the mailbox store. It's best to leave these at their default values unless you have specific reasons for altering them. Finally, the Policies tab lists any group policies that apply to this database. You cannot configure the group policy from this location, however.

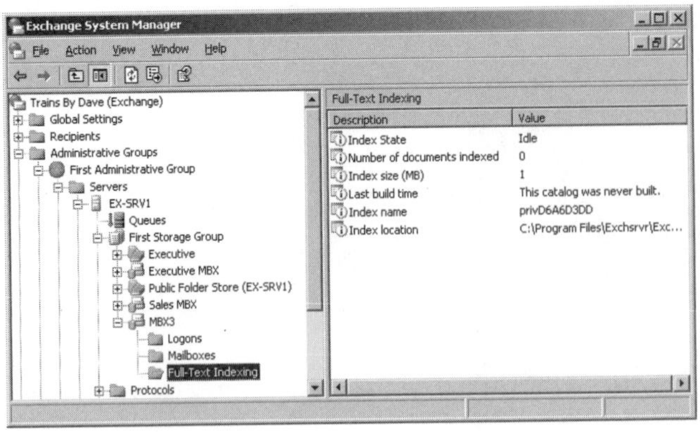

Figure 11-9. *Objects in the Full-Text Indexing container for Mailbox Store.*

Note You can create new public folder stores in a storage group. This process is covered in Chapter 10, "Using Public Folders."

Moving Transaction Log Files and Database Files

In Exchange Server 5.5, Microsoft provided the Microsoft Exchange Optimizer, a graphical wizard that enabled the movement of databases from one location to another. In Exchange Server 2003, moving log and database files is a manual process that requires careful attention on your part as you move your files. Because all of the stores reference the same set of transaction logs, you can't move a single store in a storage group to another location without moving all the other stores along with it. However, you can move individual files within a database to a separate location, which we will discuss in just a moment.

When you attempt to move either the transaction log file location for a storage group or the stores within a storage group, you'll see a message that warns you that your current backups will be useless after the move. The reason moving a database invalidates current backups is that the transaction logs that have been backed up have the database path hard-coded in their headers. If you move a database, the headers in the backed-up copies of the transaction logs will still point to the old location for the database. Thus, a recovery process won't work because it won't be able to find the database that the transaction logs were supporting. (See Chapter 2 for more information about this topic.)

Since Microsoft recommends that your transaction log and stores be held on different spindles, you can relocate your transaction log files, your store databases, or both by using the General tab of the property sheet for the storage group in question (refer to Figure 11-3). Select the new location where you want the files or databases to reside, and the following happens:

1. All the stores are dismounted.
2. The selected files or databases are moved.
3. The stores are remounted.

As we mentioned previously, you can select a store's database files to reside in two different places. To relocate a store's database files, use the Database tab on the store's property sheet (refer to Figure 11-7). First dismount the store, and then enter the new directory location for the database files. You are not required to place them both in the same location. And, as we mentioned earlier, you can host databases on a volume mount point. Once you've chosen the new directory location and selected OK, the databases will be moved and Active Directory will be updated. This action also updates the headers in the transaction files automatically. The store should mount as it normally would.

Deleting Stores or Storage Groups

Before you can delete a store or storage group, you must first remove its contents. Therefore, you'll need to delete your mailbox and public folder stores before deleting a storage group.

Deleting a Mailbox Store

Before you delete a mailbox store, you should first back up all its data to ensure that you can later restore any important information that was inadvertently deleted. After finishing your backup, make sure that you have moved to another store any mailboxes you need to keep. If you're going to delete only one store, you can move its mailboxes to another store in the same storage group. Of course, if you're planning to delete the entire storage group, plan to move the mailboxes to a store in a different storage group. You can delete the mailbox store by right-clicking it in the Exchange System snap-in and choosing Delete.

If any messages in the SMTP queue are awaiting outbound delivery, you will receive an error message informing you of this circumstance. If you choose to delete anyway, you will be given the option of selecting a new store to be used as the inbound queue for the SMTP messages.

Deleting a Public Folder Store

Deleting a public folder store is a bit more complicated than deleting a mailbox store. First, the store you are deleting must not be the last or only store that contains the public folder tree. If it is, you will not be able to delete the public folder store. Second, this store must not be the default public folder store for any mailbox stores or users. To determine whether this is the case, you'll need to look at the property sheet of each mailbox store to see if any of them are using the store you want to delete as their default public folder store. If any are, you'll want to reconfigure the mailbox store to use a different default public folder store. Third, if the public folder store to be deleted maintains the only replica of one or more folders, you will receive a warning that all data will be lost if you do not first replicate the data to another store.

Deleting a Storage Group

When there are no longer any stores associated with the storage group, you can delete it by right-clicking the group in the Exchange System snap-in and choosing Delete.

Creating a Full-Text Index

The information store creates and manages indexes for common key fields for faster lookups and searches. When you enable full-text indexing, the index is built before the client search, thus permitting faster searches. Full-text indexing makes it easy for Outlook users to search for documents, including text attachments, in the information store. Each information store can be indexed individually for flexibility. For a discussion about how indexing works, refer to Chapter 2.

To enable indexing, right-click the store you want to index, point to All Tasks, and choose Create Full-Text Index. Even though your selection is Create Full-Text Index, all you are doing at this point is enabling the indexing feature for this store. You'll be prompted for a location in which to create the catalog. Once you have specified the location, click OK and the indexing objects are created. You will see these new objects inside the Full-Text Indexing object (refer to Figure 11-9).

Initially, the Index State object will indicate that no full-text index was ever created for this store. In addition, the Last Build Time object will indicate that the catalog was never built. Thus, even though the indexing objects have been created, you still don't have a full-text index.

To create a full-text index, right-click the store object, point to All Tasks, and then choose either Start Full Population or Start Incremental Population. Start Full Population indexes all existing data, and Start Incremental Population indexes only information that is new or modified since the last full population. Depending on the amount of information in your store, this process could take from several minutes to several hours.

Once the index is populated, you will see that the value for the Number Of Documents Indexed rises, as does the value for the Index Size (MB). You will also be able to discern when the last build time was for this store and the current location of your index databases.

Summary

This chapter has given you the information you need to administer storage groups in your Exchange organization. You should now understand the storage group architecture and be able to create and manage storage groups and stores. You should also know how to enable indexing and create a full-text index for a store. In the next chapter, you will learn how to implement and administer routing groups.

Chapter 12
Using Administrative and Routing Groups

In versions of Microsoft Exchange Server prior to Exchange 2000 Server, both the routing boundaries and the administrative boundaries were defined by the concept of a site. In Exchange Server 2003, these two functions are broken out into administrative groups and routing groups. Administrative groups are purely logical and are used to group individual administrative roles together to fit a company's organizational criteria. A *routing group* is a collection of Exchange servers that enjoy permanent, high-bandwidth connectivity. Routing groups are most often based on the physical topology of your network. In this chapter, you will learn how to define and manage administrative groups and routing groups in Exchange Server 2003.

Administrative Group Concepts

Administrative groups are used to define the administrative topology for large companies with many locations, departments, divisions, Exchange servers, and Exchange administrators. They are logical in nature, which means that you can define a group based on geography, department, division, or function. For instance, if your company has 14 offices in 14 countries, you will likely have one or more Exchange servers in each location, with an Exchange administrator in each location as well. It might be best, in this scenario, to create an administrative group for each of your 14 locations so that the local Exchange administrator can manage the local Exchange servers. Another possible arrangement would be for one group to manage all the routing group functions, another to manage all the public folder functions, and still another to manage all the system policy functions. With administrative groups, members of the larger Exchange administration team can specialize in one area of administration, even if your Exchange organization is worldwide.

An administrative group makes it easier to assign administrative permissions. After you set the permissions for the administrative group object, any objects that are created or moved into the object will inherit its permissions. Hence, it is easiest to set permissions for an administrative group first and then to create objects inside the group and have them inherit the group's permissions. As always, it's best to set permissions at the highest object level and then have those permissions flow down the object hierarchy. Objects that you can create in an administrative group include the following:

- Servers
- Routing groups
- Public folder trees
- System policies

Choosing an Administrative Model

Essentially, you can use one of three administrative models to organize your administrative groups: centralized, decentralized, and mixed. For the purposes of our discussion, we'll create a fictitious company called Trains By Dave. Trains By Dave has seven offices in three regions, as shown in Figure 12-1.

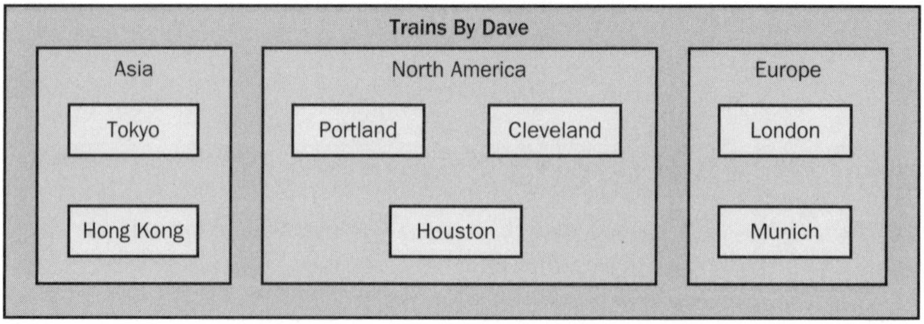

Figure 12-1. *Trains By Dave.*

Centralized Administrative Model

In the centralized administrative model, one group maintains complete control over all the Exchange servers. You might have only one group or a few tightly controlled groups for administrative purposes. Your routing group topology does not need to be the same as the administrative topology, which means that you can have multiple routing groups that reflect your physical topology while maintaining centralized administrative control in one administrative group. Figure 12-2 illustrates how this would work for Trains By Dave.

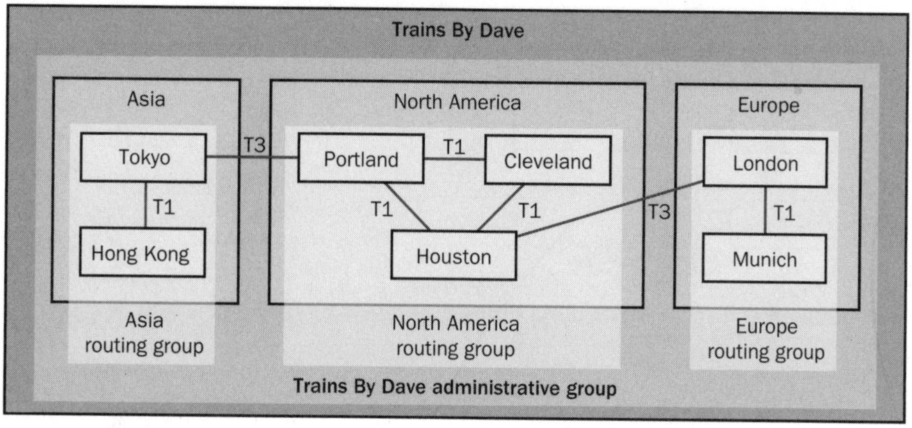

Figure 12-2. *Centralized administrative model.*

> **Note** The fact that a high-speed connection exists between each of these geographical locations has no impact on the administrative model. All the servers could be in the same administrative group, even if there was only an 8-Kbps connection between each location.

Decentralized Administrative Model

In the decentralized administrative model, each location has its own team of Exchange administrators and allows them administrative control over any objects placed inside their administrative group. These groups are often based on geographical locations or on the departmental needs of the company. Each of these groups can contain policies, servers, public folder trees, and other objects specific to the group. Figure 12-3 illustrates how this would work for Trains By Dave. We would set up an administrative group for each of the three continents and have a group of Exchange administrators, each of whom manages the Exchange servers in his or her own geographical area.

If you are migrating from Exchange Server 5.5 and you had multiple sites in your Exchange 5.5 organization, you will be forced into using a decentralized model of administration during the migration. Each Exchange 5.5 site will be created as a separate administrative group in Exchange Server 2003.

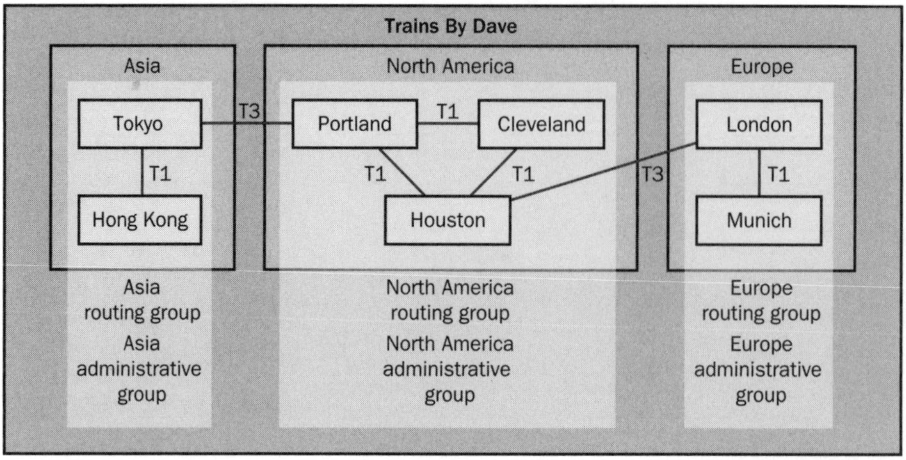

Figure 12-3. *Decentralized administrative model.*

If you would like to centralize administration for both your Exchange 2003 servers and your Exchange 5.5 servers, you'll need to set permissions on the administrative groups that limit administration of that group to those whom you specify. This action won't really incorporate the Exchange 5.5 servers into one administrative group, but it will limit administration to one group of administrators. The only way to really achieve the centralized model described previously is to migrate all your Exchange 5.5 servers to Exchange Server 2003.

Note *Native mode* means that no more legacy Exchange servers are running on your network (that is, all servers run Exchange 2000 Server or Exchange Server 2003). Native mode for Exchange Server 2003 is separate and distinct from native mode for Microsoft Windows 2000 or the higher functional levels of Windows Server 2003. For more information about native mode—what it is and how it works in Exchange Server 2003—see Chapter 16, "Coexisting with Previous Versions of Exchange."

Mixed Administrative Model

The mixed administrative model is best for restricting certain administrative functions to certain people while not creating specializations for every administrative function. In this model, you create administrative groups by function rather than by geographical location or departmental boundaries. For instance, you might create an administrative group whose only child object is policies. In this scenario, you can restrict to a handful of people the ability to create new policies or alter existing policies for your Exchange organization. However, all other administrative functions could remain under the default First Administrative Group and not be placed in their own administrative group.

You can also use this model to combine specialized administrative functions and geographical considerations into one administrative model. For instance, you might create an administrative group to manage the routing groups, a second group to manage policies, a third group for the Atlantic division, a fourth group for the European group, and a fifth group to manage all the public folder trees. Figure 12-4 illustrates what this would look like for Trains By Dave, retaining a decentralized model for day-to-day administration but centralizing the public folder trees into one administrative group and the policies into another administrative group.

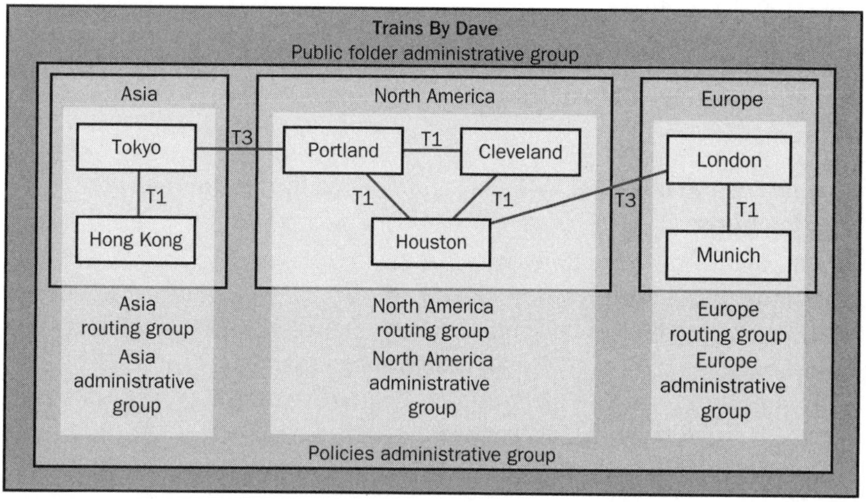

Figure 12-4. *Mixed administrative model.*

Administrative Groups and Permissions

Exchange Server 2003 permissions are based on the Active Directory permissions model. This means that you can assign permissions to a user or group by object, child object, or object class.

When you create an object in Active Directory, that object inherits its parent's permissions by default. Inheritance allows permissions to flow down the object hierarchy so that you don't have to assign permissions to child objects manually. In addition, when you need to change permissions for an entire range of objects, all you need to do is change the permissions for the parent object to make the child objects inherit those permissions automatically.

The permissions model in Exchange Server 2003 gives administrators a large amount of control over how permissions flow to containers and objects. This control is accomplished through customized inheritance, which allows you to specify that only certain objects can inherit permissions. You can specify inheritance for the following:

- This object only
- Inherit only
- This object and subcontainers
- This object and children objects
- Subcontainers only
- Children objects only
- This object, subcontainers, and children objects
- Subcontainers and children objects

Real World Be Aware of How Permissions Flow in the Configuration Naming Partition

By default, members of the Enterprise Admins group have full control over your administrative groups. Members of the Domain Admins group also have significant permissions on these objects. Figure 12-5 shows an Active Directory Services Interface (ADSI) Edit console window that illustrates how these permissions are ultimately inherited from the configuration context. (ADSI Edit is an MMC snap-in.)

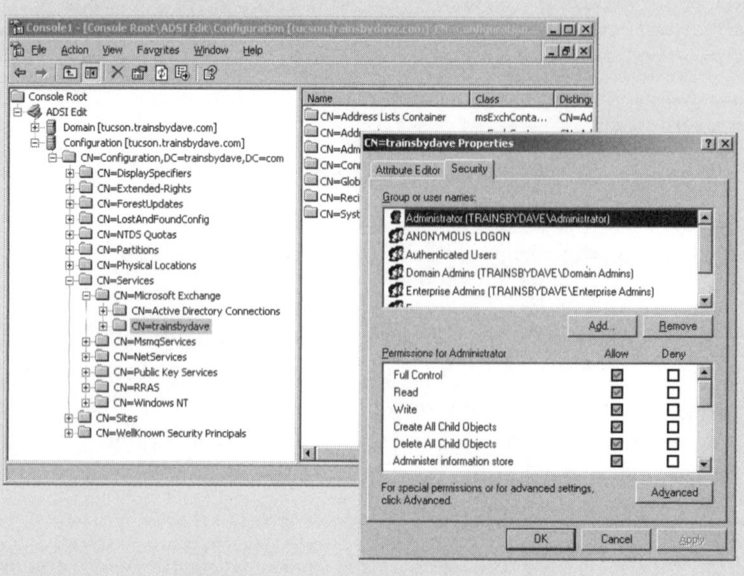

Figure 12-5. *ADSI Edit console, showing permissions inheritance for administrative groups.*

Because Exchange Server 2003 holds much of its information in the configuration partition of Active Directory, your Exchange organization is created in this partition. To Active Directory, the organization object is just another object to which default permissions flow.

If your climate is such that there is a sharp division between the activities of the Exchange administrators and the domain administrators, you'll need to create an Exchange Admins group and give this group full control over all aspects of your Exchange organization, and limit the depth and scope of permissions for the Domain Admins group. You will have to do this manually for the organization object itself. In addition, you'll need to block inheritance of permissions from the Active Directory configuration partition and reassign permissions at the organization level for all of your Exchange Server objects.

More Info For additional information about how to block permissions inheritance, refer to *Microsoft Windows Server 2003 Security Administrator's Companion*, by Roberta Bragg (Microsoft Press).

Creating an Administrative Group

Because Exchange Server 2003 is installed in many small and medium-sized companies, the Administrative and Routing Group interface is disabled by default. To see these groups, navigate to the General tab of the organization's property sheet, as shown in Figure 12-6, and then, in the Administrative Views section, select the Display Routing Groups and Display Administrative Groups options, as desired.

Note Although Figure 12-6 shows the interface in native mode, you can also select these configurations in mixed mode. You do not need to be in native mode to see the routing and administrative groups.

Note that if your Exchange 2003 server is installed in an existing Exchange 5.5 site, the Administrative and Routing Group interface is enabled by default. Each Exchange 5.5 site appears as a separate administrative group in the Exchange System snap-in. For more information about how Exchange 2003 and Exchange 5.5 servers can coexist, refer to Chapter 16.

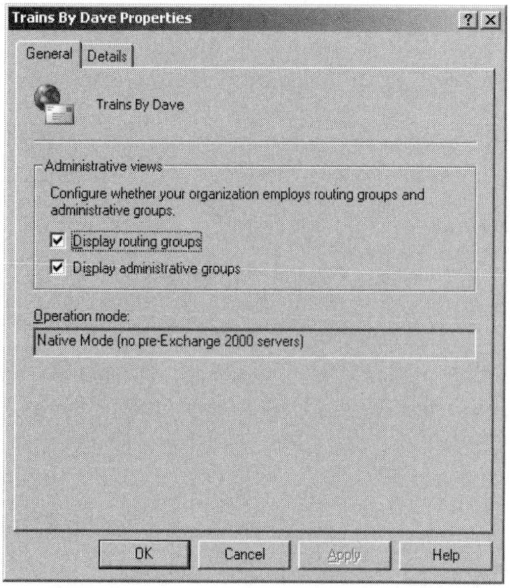

Figure 12-6. *Enabling the Administrative and Routing Group interface.*

Once you enable the display of administrative and routing groups, you can begin to set up your administrative groups. To do so, open the Exchange System snap-in, right-click the Administrative Groups container, point to New, and choose Administrative Group. Figure 12-7 shows the property sheet you will be working with. Simply enter your administrative group name and make any notes you desire on the Details tab, and you're finished. You've created an administrative group.

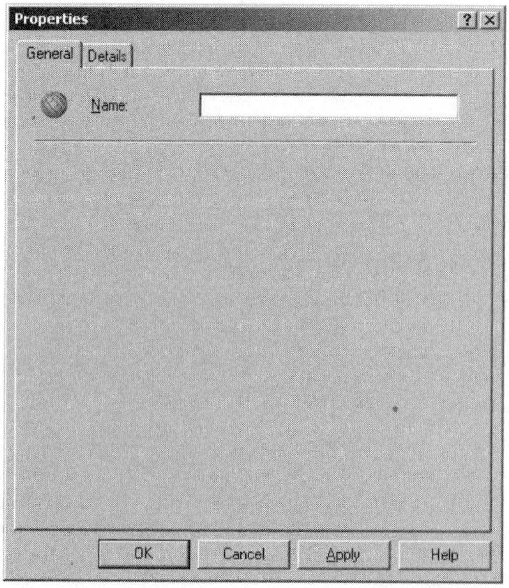

Figure 12-7. *Property sheet for a new administrative group.*

Once you create an administrative group, you can turn your attention to creating child objects for the group. By default, no objects are created in the group. When you right-click the group, the shortcut menu allows you to create three new types of containers:

- Routing Groups container
- System Policy container
- Public Folders container

Creating a New Container

To create a new container that this administrative group will administer, choose the type of container you want to create from the shortcut menu (Figure 12-8). Once you make your selection, the container is created for you inside the administrative group. No wizard appears to create any of these containers. You'll also find that there are no properties to set because this is just a container. You can think of the container as a box that will hold other boxes—nothing more, nothing less. Once created, the actual properties will be set on the routing groups themselves.

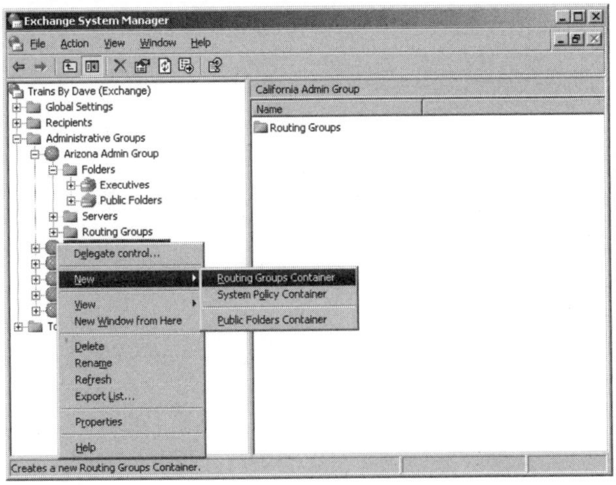

Figure 12-8. *Shortcut menu for a new administrative group, showing the types of containers you can create.*

Note Although Figure 12-8 shows three choices, sometimes you will see only two. The option to create a Public Folders container will not appear if the administrative group is new and no other containers have yet been created inside it. Once you create a new container such as a new Routing Groups container, when you attempt to create a second container, you'll see the option to add a Public Folders container. The option to create a Public Folders container will also not appear if you have already created a container of this type, since each administrative group needs only one Public Folders container.

Server Objects and Administrative Groups

In Exchange Server 2003, servers are always installed by default into the First Administrative group under the Server container. (The First Administrative group is given this name by default; you can change the name to fit your overall naming convention for administrative groups by simply right-clicking it.) You'll notice that we don't have the option to create a Server container under a new administrative group and then move servers from the First Administrative group into the new administrative group. This is by design.

When a new administrative group is created, a Server container for the group is automatically created but not displayed in the Exchange System snap-in. This can be seen in our example with the Hawaii Admin group. In Figure 12-9, if we look at this administrative group in the Active Directory Sites and Services snap-in (running Show Services Node), you can see that both a server container and an advanced security container have been created in the Hawaii Admin group, even though these don't appear in the Exchange System snap-in. However, once a server is installed into the administrative group, the server object will appear in the Exchange System snap-in. Therefore, you must create your administrative groups before installing your Exchange 2003 servers if you plan to have those servers spread across multiple administrative groups.

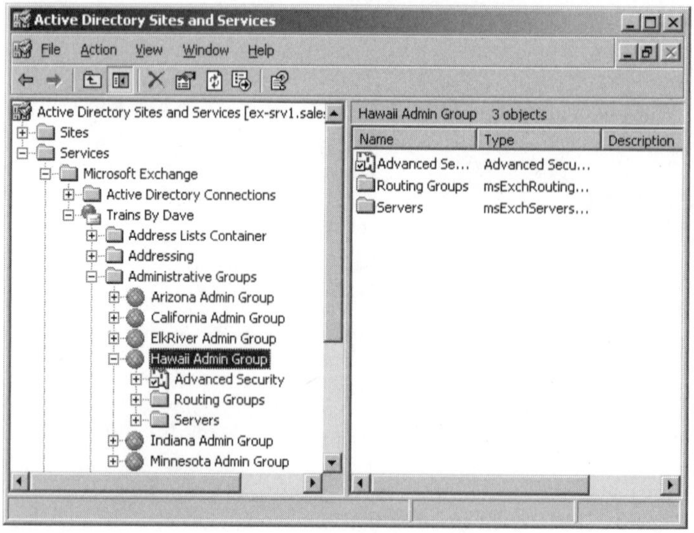

Figure 12-9. *Server object under the Hawaii Admin group in Active Directory Sites and Services.*

Exchange 2003 Policies

Policies in Exchange Server 2003 are designed to increase administrative flexibility while reducing administrative effort. A *policy* is a set of configuration parameters that applies to one or more Exchange objects in the same class. For example, you can create a policy that affects certain settings on some or all of your Exchange servers. If you want to change these settings, all you need to do is modify the policy, and the modification will be applied to the appropriate server's organization.

There are two types of policies: recipient policies and system policies. *Recipient policies* apply to mail-enabled objects and specify how to generate e-mail addresses. Recipient policies are covered in Chapter 9, "Creating and Managing Recipients." *System policies* apply to a server, a mailbox store, or a public folder store. These policies appear in the Policies container under the administrative group responsible for administering the policy (Figure 12-10).

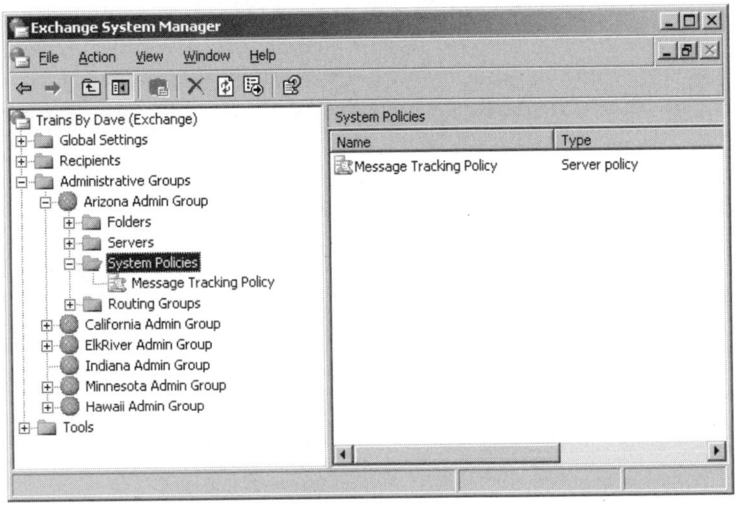

Figure 12-10. *System policy object.*

Note No default container is created for system policies when Exchange Server 2003 is installed. You must create one before you can start building system policies. Right-click the administrative group in which you want to create the policy folder, point to New, and select System Policy Container.

Creating a System Policy

Generally speaking, creating a system policy involves navigating to the appropriate System Policies container, right-clicking the container, and then selecting the kind of policy you want to create: a server policy, a mailbox store policy, or a public store policy.

When working with system policies, be sure to create the policy object in the administrative group that will be responsible for administering the policy. Failure to do so could lead to the wrong people having administrative control over your critical policies. Let's take a look at how to create each of the three types of system policies, starting with server policies.

Creating a Server Policy

A server policy enforces message tracking and log file maintenance settings. It is not used to enforce security or other settings on the servers in the administrative group. To create a server policy, right-click the System Policies container, point to New, and then choose Server Policy. You will see the New Policy dialog box (Figure 12-11), where you specify the tabs that will appear in the policy's property sheet. With a server policy, you'll have only one choice: the General tab. Select the check box for this tab, and then click OK. You'll see the configuration box where the policy will be created.

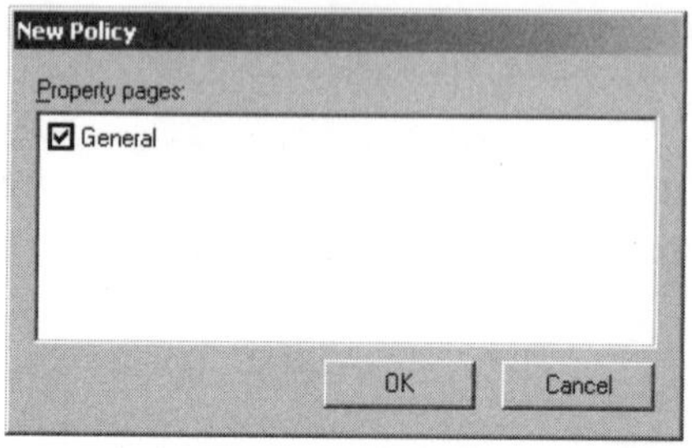

Figure 12-11. *New Policy dialog box.*

Next, you need to enter the name of your policy on the General tab of the policy's property sheet. As Figure 12-12 shows, there are actually two General tabs. The first is for naming the policy. Choose a name that describes the task the policy is intended to accomplish, such as Message Tracking Policy or Enable Subject Logging Policy. Good naming at this stage will save you time in the long run because you won't need to look at the policy's properties to determine what the policy does.

The General (Policy) tab (Figure 12-13) is the actual policy that is applied to the Exchange servers in your organization. It is named General (Policy) because you are potentially configuring the General tabs of the property sheets of all of your servers. (We discuss how to apply this policy to servers throughout your organization later in this chapter.) If you compare this tab to the General tab in a server's property sheet, you will find that they are identical, except for the identifying information at the top of the tab.

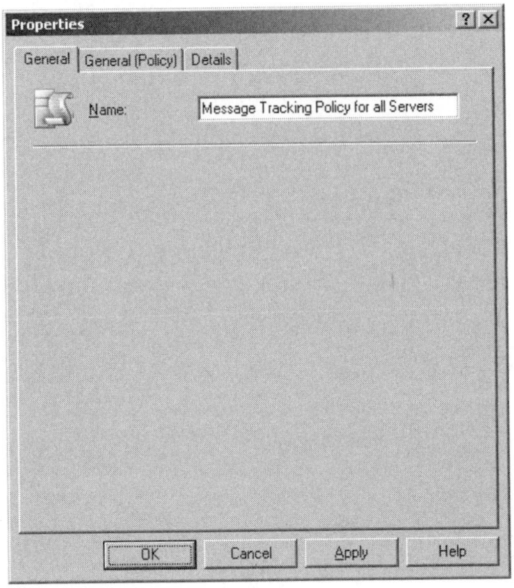

Figure 12-12. *Naming a policy on the General tab.*

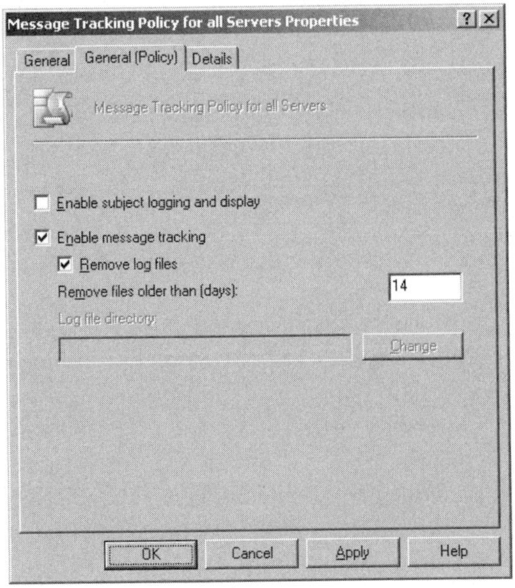

Figure 12-13. *General (Policy) tab.*

On the General (Policy) tab, you can enable subject logging and display for all Exchange servers attached to the policy. This setting works in tandem with the Enable Message Tracking option. Together, these two settings ensure that messages passed in your organization can be tracked. Enabling these two options is useful for troubleshooting if some users are not receiving messages from other users. You can track the message through your organization to determine where it is getting stuck to pinpoint where your transport problems exist. For more information about message tracking and subject logging, refer to Chapter 26, "Monitoring Exchange Server 2003."

Once a policy is in force, it cannot be overridden at the local server level. The message tracking policy we've been using as an example was set on the EX-SRV1 server in the Arizona administrative group. Figure 12-14 illustrates that the message tracking options are dimmed in the property sheet for the EX-SRV1 server because these values have been set by a policy.

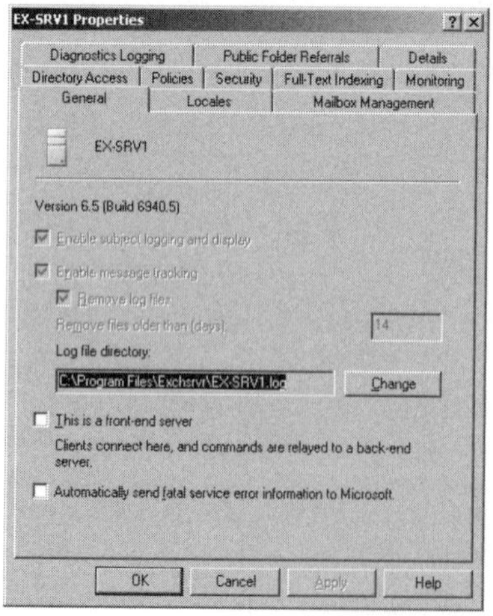

Figure 12-14. *Property sheet for the EX-SRV1 server, showing dimmed message tracking options.*

At this point, you might be wondering how we applied the policy to our servers. Here are the steps you need to take to apply a policy after you create it. Simply right-click the new policy, and then choose Add Server. A dialog box opens that lets you choose any combination of servers in your Exchange organization. After you select the servers, click OK, and the policy is attached to those servers. To verify this, select the policy object you just created in the Exchange System snap-in. The servers you added should appear in the details pane (Figure 12-15). You can also check out all the policies that are currently applied to a server using the Policies tab on the server's property sheet.

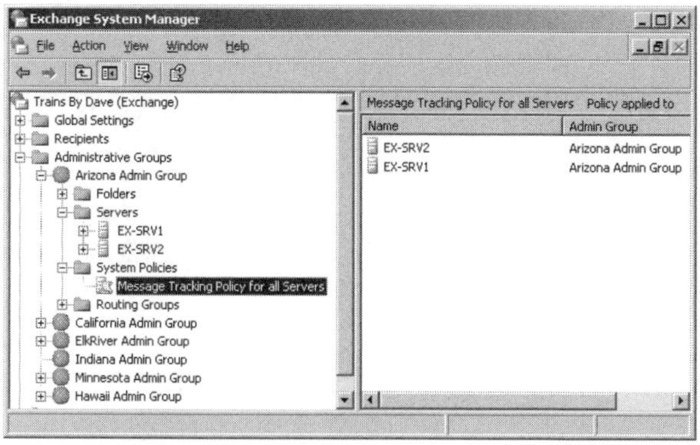

Figure 12-15. *Servers to which the selected policy applies.*

To remove a server from a policy, navigate to the server policy object in the Exchange System snap-in. Highlight the server you want to remove in the details pane. Right-click the server and choose Remove From Policy.

If you make changes to an existing policy after you save your changes, you will be presented with a message box asking whether you want to apply the changes in the policy to all the objects immediately. You can select either Yes or No. Selecting Yes will force the policy to be applied immediately to the target objects. Selecting No will cause the policy changes to be applied at normal replication intervals.

Creating a Public Store Policy

Public store policies encompass a number of configuration options, including maintenance schedules, limits, and full-text indexing. They are applied on a per-store basis across public folder tree boundaries.

The procedure for creating a public store policy is similar to the one for creating a server policy, described in the previous section. However, you have the option of specifying five tabs on the property sheet for a public folder store policy:

- **General (Policy)** You can enable support for Secure/Multipurpose Internet Mail Extensions (S/MIME) and specify that text should be converted to a fixed-sized font (10-point Courier).
- **Database (Policy)** You can specify when you would like daily maintenance to run on your public folders.
- **Replication (Policy)** You can specify how often you would like replication of public folders to occur as well as the replication size limit and the number of minutes that equates to the Always interval.

- **Full-Text Indexing (Policy)** You can specify the update interval and the rebuild interval for your public folders.
- **Limits (Policy)** You can specify storage limits, deletion settings, and age limits for all items in all folders in the public folder store (Figure 12-16).

You can learn more about the details of public store settings in Chapter 10, "Using Public Folders."

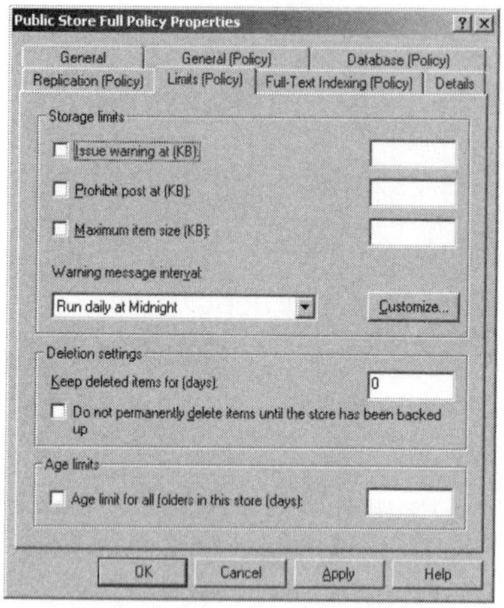

Figure 12-16. *The Limits (Policy) tab of the property sheet for a public folder store policy.*

To apply the policy to your public folders, you'll need to associate the policy with the folders just as you did for the server policy in the previous section. By default, no policy is actually applied to its intended recipient; you must associate it with the object by choosing Add Public Store from the policy's shortcut menu.

Unlike server policies, which have only one tab on their property sheets, a public store policy can have up to seven tabs. This doesn't mean that you have to use all the tabs in a given policy. If you would like to add tabs to or delete tabs from an existing public store policy, all you need to do is right-click the policy and choose Change Property Pages. Then choose the tabs you want to add or delete, and configure them as needed.

Creating a Mailbox Store Policy

A mailbox store policy allows you to configure a number of settings for mailboxes, including the default public folder store, the maintenance schedule, a message journaling recipient that will receive copies of all e-mails that flow through the organization, and full-text indexing. When creating a mailbox store policy, you can choose to include the General, Database, Limits, and Full-Text Indexing tabs in the policy's property sheet.

> **Note** Message journaling is a concept that was introduced with Exchange 5.5, Service Pack 1. Essentially, it sends copies of most e-mails to a common recipient for use later in either legal or governmental proceedings. This feature is most often enabled when a company is forced to retain all its e-mails to meet government regulations or for legal purposes.

On the General (Policy) tab, you can specify a default public folder store for the mailbox stores that will be associated with this policy. This ability is very handy when you need to create a large number of mailbox stores and want to associate most or all of them with a particular public folder store. The General (Policy) tab also allows you to specify the default offline address list that your selected mailbox stores will use. You can choose to archive messages on this store. In addition, you can enable client support of S/MIME signatures and a fixed-sized font for all incoming messages.

The only item you can set on the Database (Policy) tab is the time at which daily maintenance will run. If you are creating a public folder store policy as well, consider staggering their maintenance times to allow for better system performance during the online maintenance routine. In your planning, be sure to consider other routines that run during off-hours too, including backup programs, online defragmentation of the database, and replication.

> **Note** The major tasks that the store runs for online maintenance include making sure that the correct free/busy and offline address book folders exist for an administrative group and, if they don't exist, creating them; purging database indexes that were previously created but haven't been used recently; deleting items over the time limit that have exceeded the deleted items retention time (called a hard delete); expiring items in public folders over their age limit; purging deleted mailboxes from the store that are over their retention limit; and detecting mailboxes that are no longer connected to a user object as well as detecting mailboxes that have been reconnected to a user.

On the Limits (Policy) tab (Figure 12-17), you can specify storage limits and deletion settings. Based on mailbox size, you can also choose when you would like the System Attendant service to notify users that they have exceeded their limits. Using the Customize button to create a customized schedule allows you to set more than one time during a 24-hour period when users exceeding their limits will be notified by system e-mail that they need to take action to reduce the size of their mailboxes.

When you apply a mailbox store policy, you do so on a store-by-store basis, not on a per-storage-group or per-server basis. Also, the mailbox store does not need to be mounted for you to be able to associate it with the policy. You can learn more about the details of mailbox store settings in Chapter 11, "Using Storage Groups."

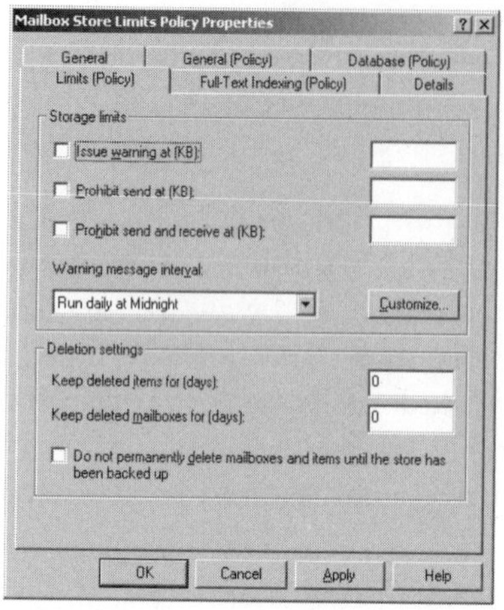

Figure 12-17. *The Limits (Policy) tab of the property sheet for a mailbox store policy.*

Managing Policy Conflicts

Two different policies can conflict when applied to the same object. When this occurs, the typical behavior is for the newer policy to override the older policy. However, at times the newer policy will not be able to override the older policy and you will receive a message indicating that the object has been placed under the control of a conflicting policy. You will then be asked whether you want to remove the object from the control of the conflicting policies. Choosing Yes will apply the new policy, and choosing No will keep the old policy.

Creating and Managing Routing Groups

As you've seen, an administrative group is a collection of objects that are grouped together to allow you to assign administrative tasks to groups of administrators conveniently. By contrast, a routing group is a collection of servers that enjoy permanent, high-bandwidth connectivity. The links between routing groups are assumed to be either slow or unreliable. *Connectors* are used to connect routing groups over these slow wide area network (WAN) links. Thus, while administrative groups are logical in nature, routing groups are determined by the physical topology of your network.

Routing groups allow you to specify the routes that messages will take to get from the sender to the recipient within your organization. By implementing costs on the connectors, you can channel the physical path you want messaging to take in your organization. For more information about the architecture of routing groups, refer to Chapter 3, "Understanding Exchange Server Routing Architecture."

Creating a Routing Group

You will need to create routing groups if you have two or more servers that are connected over a slow or unreliable WAN link. You can create routing groups in either mixed mode or native mode. Although routing groups do not need to be mapped to administrative group boundaries in native mode, they cannot span administrative groups in mixed mode. This limitation is imposed by the way in which Exchange 5.5 interoperates with Exchange Server 2003. As long as Exchange Server 2003 is in mixed mode, it retains its ability to interoperate with Exchange 5.5. And since you cannot move servers between sites in Exchange 5.5, you cannot move them between routing groups or administrative groups in Exchange Server 2003 in mixed mode.

You'll create your routing groups inside the Routing Groups container. If your situation warrants it, you can create new Routing Groups containers in other administrative groups. You can create only one Routing Groups container per administrative group, but you can create multiple routing groups in each Routing Groups container.

To create a routing group, simply right-click the Routing Groups container, point to New, and then select Routing Group. Enter the name of the new routing group on the General tab, and click OK.

Your new routing group will consist of two child objects, Connectors and Members (Figure 12-18). The Connectors container is where you will create your Routing Group Connectors (for details, see Chapter 13, "Connecting Routing Groups"), and the Members container is where you will place the server objects that are members of the routing group.

If you need to connect to a foreign e-mail system, you can do so by installing either an X.400 Connector or an SMTP Connector, most likely the former. (See Chapter 21, "Connecting to Other Messaging Systems with X.400," for information about how to connect to a foreign system.) These connectors can also be used to connect routing groups within your organization, but it is best to use the Routing Group Connector for this purpose. The Routing Group Connector can be used only inside your organization to connect your routing groups. It cannot be used to connect to a foreign e-mail system.

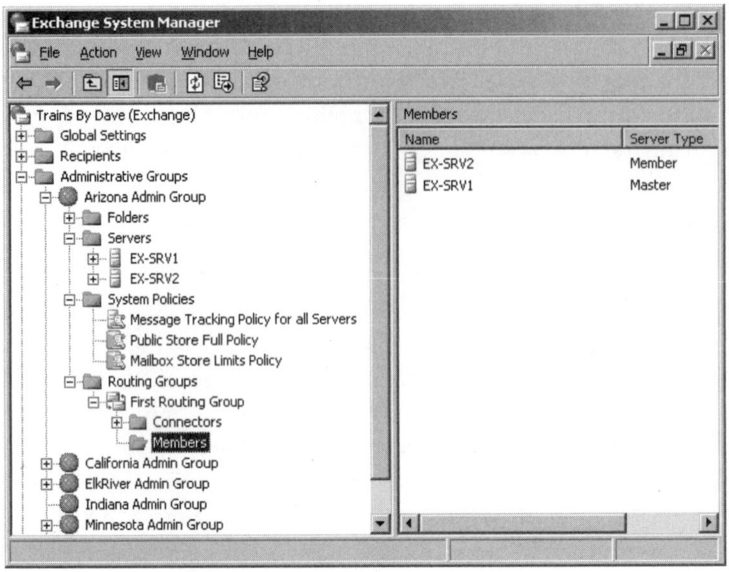

Figure 12-18. *Objects in a new routing group.*

Managing a Routing Group

Two of the primary tasks in managing a routing group are to create new routing groups and to add one or more servers to a routing group. When you add a server to a routing group, you are, in effect, telling Exchange Server 2003 that the server being added has high-speed, permanent connectivity to the other servers in the group. Although no minimum bandwidth floor is hard-coded into the Exchange operating system, the suggested absolute minimum is a 64-Kbps connection that is available at all times.

Note Be sure to test your WAN links before implementing Exchange Server 2003. A leased line of 64 Kbps might offer more permanent bandwidth than a T1 that is often saturated with non-Exchange traffic. A prudent approach is to account for all other traffic on your WAN links and then use the amount of bandwidth left over to determine whether you have permanent, high-bandwidth connectivity.

To add a server to a routing group, navigate to and select the Members container for the routing group to which the server currently belongs (by default, the First Routing Group). Drag the server into the Members container of the destination routing group.

Note When you remove a server from a routing group, you are actually removing the SMTP virtual server or the X.400 service through which that server communicates and having the service re-created in the new routing group.

By default, all the servers created in your organization belong to the first routing group, which is the default routing group that is created when Exchange Server 2003 is initially installed. However, you might well need additional routing groups based on your physical topology.

To rename a routing group object, simply right-click the routing group, choose Rename, and enter the new name. To delete a routing group, you must first move all the servers that are members of the doomed routing group to other routing groups. You cannot delete a routing group that has server objects residing in the Members container. After you move all the servers, right-click the routing group and choose Delete. Click Yes to confirm the routing group deletion.

Summary

In this chapter, you have seen how to create and manage both administrative and routing groups. When it comes to routing groups, the containers themselves are not that difficult to manage. However, creating and managing the connectors between routing groups is not always easy and often presents additional challenges to the administrator. In the next chapter, we'll turn our attention to the challenges of routing group connectors.

Chapter 13

Connecting Routing Groups

Chapter 3, "Understanding Exchange Server Routing Architecture," discussed the message-routing architecture of a Microsoft Exchange Server 2003 organization. That chapter also discussed routing groups and how you can use them to group together servers that enjoy permanent, high-speed connectivity. Further, it described the link state algorithm, which is a link propagation protocol that replaces and improves upon the Gateway Address Routing Table (GWART) of Exchange Server 5.5. In Chapter 12, "Using Administrative and Routing Groups," you learned how to create and manage administrative groups and routing groups. What you need to know now to make it all work is how to create and manage the individual connectors that link routing groups together, and how to use the automatically generated link state information that pertains to those links. That is the focus of this chapter.

You can really use only three connectors to connect your routing groups:

- **Routing Group Connector (RGC)** The Routing Group Connector (RGC) is the main connector used to connect routing groups and is the simplest to configure. It uses SMTP as its default transport mechanism, but it might also use a remote procedure call (RPC) if required.
- **SMTP Connector** The SMTP connector takes a bit more work to set up than the RGC and sports some different features. It is mainly used to connect routing groups where you want to force SMTP to be used for the transport mechanism. The SMTP connector can also be used to connect an Exchange organization to a foreign messaging system (like the Internet) using SMTP.
- **X.400 Connector** The X.400 Connector can be used to connect routing groups and to connect to a foreign system. When used for connecting routing groups, its primary advantage is that it can be used over extremely low bandwidth and in fairly unreliable connections. The X.400 Connector is discussed in Chapter 21, "Connecting to Other Messaging Systems with X.400."

Routing Group Connector

In most environments, the Routing Group Connector is the best choice for connecting routing groups because it is fast, reliable, and easy to set up. The RGC uses the Simple Mail Transport Protocol (SMTP), which means that it can be used even when bandwidth is slow or unreliable.

The Routing Group Connector is a unidirectional connection from one server in one routing group to another server in a different routing group. Therefore, if bidirectional communication is necessary (it usually is), you'll need to create two connectors to form the logical, bidirectional link between the two routing groups.

Fortunately, System Manager offers to automatically configure the other end of a link for you when you create the first connector. If you take advantage of this, the connector that Exchange creates in the remote routing group inherits the settings you choose for the local connector, with two major exceptions.

The first exception is evident on the General tab of the Routing Group Connector property sheet (Figure 13-1). If the remote routing group has more than one server, Exchange Server selects the These Servers Can Send Mail Over This Connector option and then selects each SMTP virtual server for this configuration. If any of the virtual servers created on the target servers are incompatible with message transfer over this connector, you'll need to either manually remove those servers from this list or manually configure the other connector.

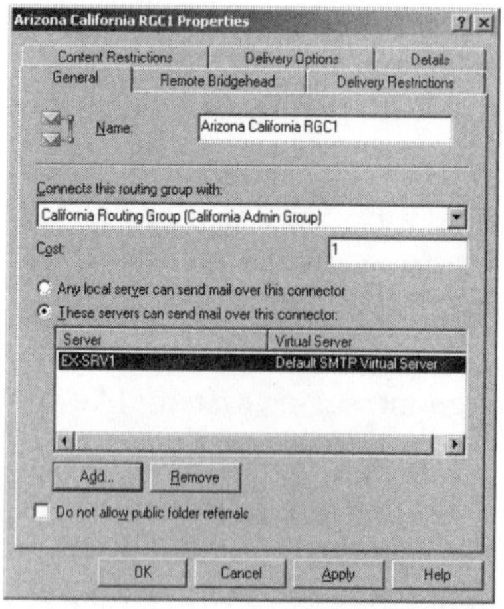

Figure 13-1. *Specifying servers that can send e-mail over this connector.*

The second exception to inherited settings is evident on the Remote Bridgehead tab (Figure 13-2). Exchange Server lists all the SMTP virtual servers as target servers. Again, if you have an SMTP virtual server that should not be a target server, you'll need to either remove the server from the list or configure the connector manually.

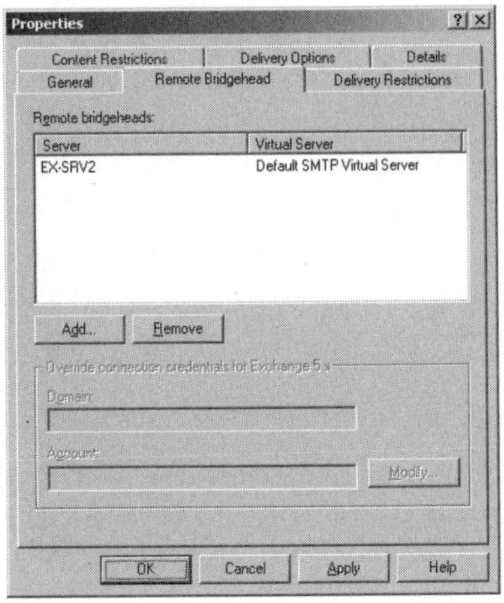

Figure 13-2. *Specifying target servers for this connector.*

Note If your Exchange organization includes Exchange 5.x servers and those servers reside in a separate Microsoft Windows NT 4 domain, you can have a Routing Group Connector connect as an account in the NT 4 domain. Remember that a Routing Group Connector looks like a site connector in the Exchange 5.x organization and that it functions in the same way.

The Routing Group Connector uses a bridgehead server that acts as the gateway through which messages flow into and out of the routing group. The RGC offers a level of fault-tolerance by allowing multiple source and destination bridgehead servers. Bridgehead servers can be used in one of three ways:

- No bridgehead server is designated and all servers in the routing group function as bridgehead servers for message transmission.
- One bridgehead server is designated and all e-mail destined for other routing groups flows through that one server. This gives the administrator great control over messaging configuration.
- Multiple bridgehead servers are used and all e-mail flows over one of these designated servers. This configuration offers the advantages of load balancing and fault-tolerance. If one bridgehead server is unavailable for message transport, another will be available.

Note Microsoft recommends having at least 64 Kbps of available bandwidth for a connection handled by a Routing Group Connector. Also, no encryption is currently available between the bridgehead servers.

Real World Resolving Target Server IP Addresses for Bridgehead Servers

When a bridgehead server (BHS) that hosts a Routing Group Connector receives a message destined for a server in the other routing group, the BHS takes several steps to resolve the IP address of the target BHS. The BHS contacts DNS and attempts to resolve the IP address of the host (A) record of the target machine. If multiple records exist, DNS considers the preference values when deciding which BHS to resolve to. When using Windows DNS, all Windows-based servers automatically register A records in DNS. If no A record exists, the BHS attempts to resolve the IP address using the NetBIOS name resolution process.

More Info To learn more about the DNS and Windows Server 2003, refer to *Microsoft Windows Server 2003 Administrator's Companion* by Charlie Russel, Sharon Crawford, and Jason Gerend (Microsoft Press) and *Active Directory for Microsoft Windows Server 2003 Technical Reference* (Microsoft Press).

Creating a Routing Group Connector

To create a new Routing Group Connector, right-click the Connectors container located under the routing group container in the Exchange System snap-in, point to New, and then select Routing Group Connector. On the General tab, enter the name of the connector and then select the routing group to which you would like this connector to connect (Figure 13-3).

You can also select either the Any Local Server Can Send Mail Over This Connector or the These Servers Can Send Mail Over This Connector option. The first option is the default and allows any server in the routing group to use the connector for sending messages destined for a server in the other routing group. The second option is a way to reserve the connector for certain virtual servers in the routing group. When you select this option, you'll be able to specify the virtual servers in the routing group that can use this connector.

Tip Be sure to select a virtual server that will send e-mail to the destination routing group. For example, assume that you have a group of external users who send their messages into the organization using Transport Layer Security (TLS) and that you've set up an SMTP virtual server to accept e-mail on a second IP address over port 25. This SMTP virtual server requires a certificate for authentication. Let's now assume that there are no such configurations for the local users on your LAN. If you were to choose this virtual server as the only server to send e-mail over the Routing Group Connector you are creating, messages sent by the local users would be rejected because the message would be routed back to the second IP address of the server, and the SMTP server would be looking for TLS security and certificates. In this scenario, you want to be sure you *don't* select this virtual server for your Routing Group Connector.

At the bottom of the General tab is a Do Not Allow Public Folder Referrals option. Selecting this option means that if a client cannot access or find a public folder replica in the local routing group, the client will not be referred servers in other routing groups over this Routing Group Connector.

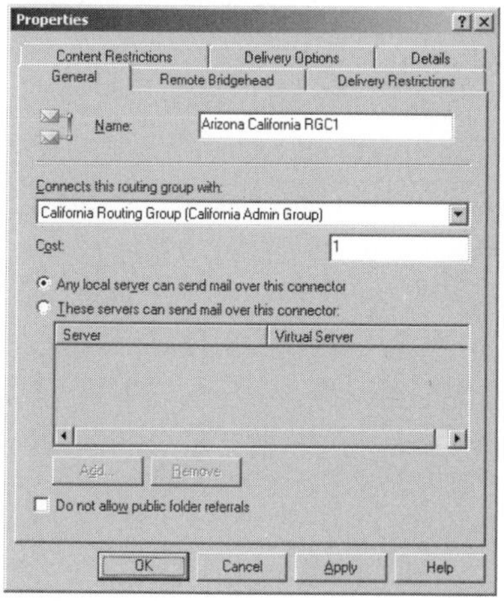

Figure 13-3. *General tab of the Routing Group Connector's property sheet.*

Remote Bridgehead Tab

On the Remote Bridgehead tab (refer to Figure 13-2), you can specify one or more servers in the remote routing group to serve as target bridgehead servers. The connector will attempt to establish a connection with each target server before sending messages. The servers are contacted in order, starting with the server at the top of the list. Also, if the destination server has more than one SMTP virtual server configured, you'll need to select the one that will allow messages to be sent across the connector you are setting up.

Delivery Restrictions Tab

On the Delivery Restrictions tab (Figure 13-4), you can indicate who can use this connector, either by specifying that all messages are to be rejected except for those from a select list of users or by specifying that all messages are to be accepted except those from a select list of users. You'll find that you cannot enter groups here. Instead, you can enter only mail-enabled users and contacts.

Tip To select more than one user from Active Directory, highlight the first user in the Select Recipient list and then use the down or up arrow on your keyboard to select a contiguous list of users. To select a discontiguous list of users, hold down the Ctrl key and then use your mouse to highlight all the users you want to add to this list.

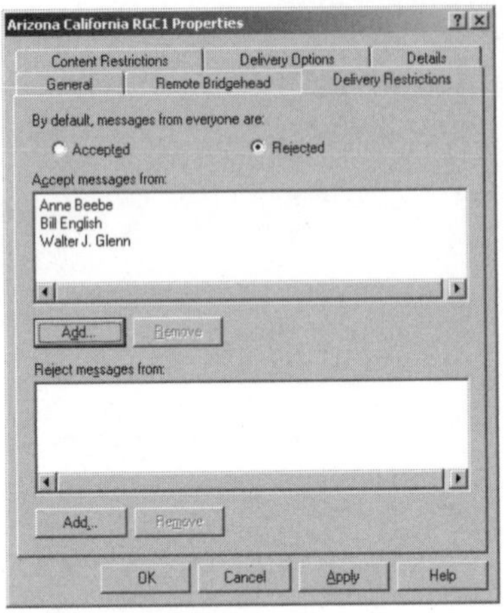

Figure 13-4. *Delivery Restrictions tab of the Routing Group Connector's property sheet.*

Real World Giving Priority to Messages from Certain Users

When used in conjunction with the cost assigned to the connector, the Delivery Restrictions tab can be configured to give a higher priority to messages sent via the Routing Group Connector from a certain group of users than it would to messages sent from other users. For instance, suppose that your sales staff and pre-sales support staff are located in two different cities that also represent two different routing groups. Let's further assume that most of your orders come in over the telephone and that when members of your sales staff have a technical question about a product, they need to send that question via e-mail to the pre-sales support staff. In this scenario, you might want to set up two Routing Group Connectors. The first would be a connector with a cost of 100 that would accept messages from any user and forward them on as appropriate but would reject messages from members of the sales staff. The second connector would have a cost of 1, and it would reject all users except for the members of the sales staff, who would be listed on the Delivery Restrictions tab. This arrangement would cause the sales staff's messages to be sent to the other routing group faster than messages from other users.

Delivery Options Tab

The Delivery Options tab, shown in Figure 13-5, allows you to specify when messages can flow through the connector. This ability is especially helpful when you're using the connector over a slow or unreliable WAN link, or over a link for which you are charged different rates at different times of the day. By selecting the Use Different Delivery Times For Oversize Messages check box, you can hold larger messages until the times you set, presumably when the connector is experiencing little traffic.

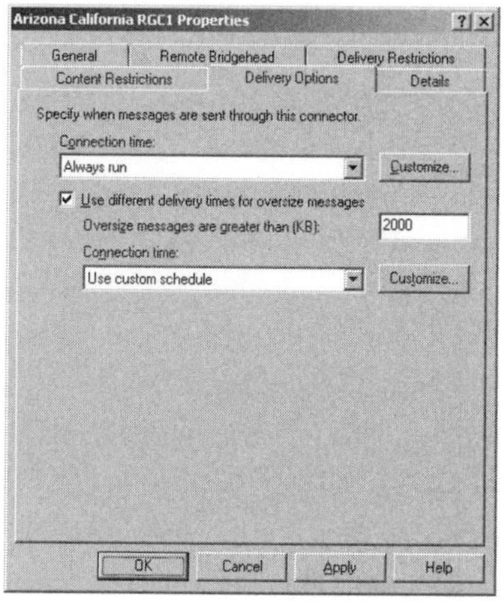

Figure 13-5. *Delivery Options tab for the Routing Group Connector's property sheet.*

Content Restrictions Tab

On the Content Restrictions tab, shown in Figure 13-6, you can set the priorities, types, and sizes of messages that can pass over this Routing Group Connector. The Allowed Priorities section lets you select which priority messages are allowed over the connection. This is a great way to establish connectors dedicated, for example, to passing high priority messages. In the Allowed Types section, selecting the System Messages option allows the transmission of all non-user-generated messages, including directory replication, public folder replication, network monitoring, and delivery and nondelivery report (NDR) messages. In the Allowed Sizes area, you can restrict messages to those smaller than a specified size.

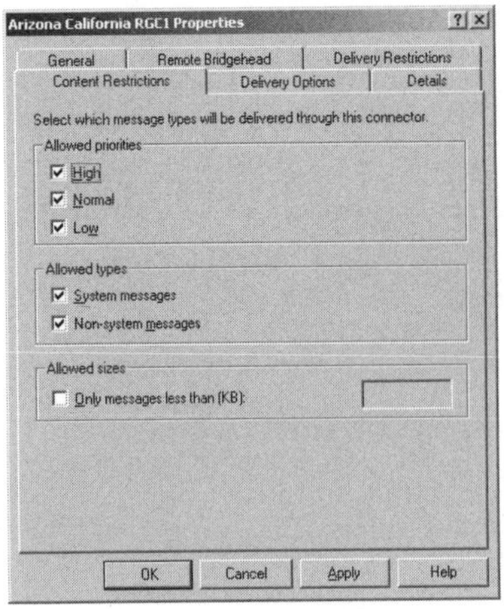

Figure 13-6. *Content Restrictions tab for the Routing Group Connector's property sheet.*

Real World **Comparing the Routing Group Connector with the Exchange 5.5 Site Connector**

The Routing Group Connector uses SMTP as its transport protocol, giving it a higher tolerance than the Site Connector in Exchange Server 5.x for lower-bandwidth and higher-latency environments. The Site Connector uses TCP to initiate and maintain a connection to the target bridgehead server and then uses remote procedure calls to invoke the connector's functions. RPCs incur much overhead and require higher bandwidth and greater permanency to maintain their bindings. In contrast, although the Routing Group Connector passes SMTP commands through a TCP session, the commands don't make RPC calls to the target server. Instead, SMTP sends a series of discreet commands that can tolerate lower bandwidth and less permanency than RPCs. For a more complete discussion of SMTP, please see Chapter 20, "Supporting Internet Protocols and SMTP."

When you upgrade an Exchange 5.5 bridgehead server that is configured with a Site Connector, you'll find that the connector is upgraded to a Routing Group Connector that communicates over RPC to Exchange 5.x servers, yet it uses SMTP to communicate with other Exchange 2003 servers.

The Routing Group Connector contains two features not available in the Site Connector in Exchange Server 5.5. First, you can create a schedule to define when messages pass over the connector. Second, you can schedule messages based on size (for instance, any message over 2 MB) so that you can send them when bandwidth usage is lower.

SMTP Connector

Although the RGC uses SMTP as its native transport mechanism, Exchange Server 2003 also provides an SMTP connector that can be used to link routing groups. You might want to use an SMTP connector instead of an RGC for three reasons:

- The SMTP connector is more configurable than the RGC and offers a greater ability to fine-tune the connection. The SMTP connector also offers the ability to issue authentication before sending e-mail, use TLS encryption, and remove e-mail from queues on remote servers.
- The SMTP connector always has to use SMTP. When you are connecting an Exchange 2003 server with an Exchange 5.5 server, the Routing Group Connector uses remote procedure calls to communicate because it has no way of knowing whether the Exchange 5.5 Server is configured to use SMTP, which was provided through the Internet Mail Service in previous versions of Exchange. There is no way to force the RGC to use SMTP, so an SMTP connector can be used instead.
- The SMTP connector is also capable of connecting independent Exchange forests within an organization so that messages can be transferred.

Even though the SMTP connector can be useful for linking routing groups in certain circumstances, its primary use in Exchange Server 2003 is for external communication—linking either to the Internet or to a non-Exchange environment. Like the Routing Group Connector, it is a unidirectional connector, so you must configure a connector at each end of the link.

When connected to the Internet, the SMTP connector uses a smart host (another SMTP server to which messages are sent for routing) or MX records in DNS for next-hop routing. When configured internally between two routing groups, the connector relays link state information between routing groups but still depends on the MX records in DNS for next-hop information.

Arguably the biggest difference between the SMTP connector and the Routing Group Connector is that the SMTP connector can use encryption and authentication. If encryption is necessary for some of your messages, you'll need to use the SMTP connector. Another feature of the SMTP connector is its ability to authenticate in a remote domain before sending a message to it. Like the Routing Group Connector, the SMTP connector lets you schedule messages to be sent at a time when bandwidth usage is low.

The SMTP connector allows you to create scopes that permit only certain servers in your Exchange organization to use the connector. Instead of limiting the replication of this connector to the servers inside the scope, you can now choose to allow either all servers in the organization to use this connector or only the servers in the local routing group (Figure 13-7).

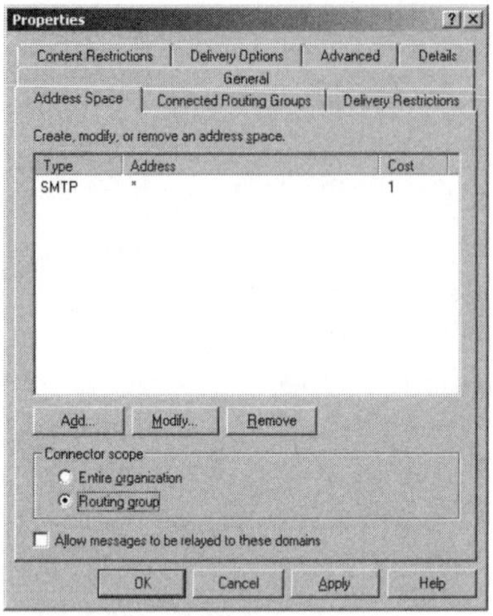

Figure 13-7. *Configuring the scope of the SMTP connector.*

Finally, you'll want to use the SMTP connector if your bandwidth is less than 64 Kbps or higher than 16 Kbps. If your sole reason for choosing the SMTP connector is that you want to use SMTP between your routing groups, choose the Routing Group Connector instead. The Routing Group Connector uses SMTP as its transport protocol.

Creating an SMTP Connector

You create an SMTP connector in the same manner as you create a Routing Group Connector: right-click the routing group, point to New, and choose SMTP connector. Once you've done so, you're presented with the connector's property sheet with the General tab displayed (Figure 13-8), in which you will name the connector and make some choices regarding DNS. The Use DNS To Route To Each Address Space On This Connector option causes the connector itself to work with DNS to make direct connections to the destination SMTP server, based on the MX records and preference values. If you would rather forward e-mail upstream because multiple direct connections either take too long or are too costly, select the Forward All Mail Through This Connector To The Following Smart Host option. You can enter either the fully qualified domain name (FQDN) of the smart host or its IP address here. If you choose to enter the IP address, you must place it inside brackets—for example, [192.168.2.200].

Also, the value you specify here will override the value in the Smart Host setting in the Advanced Delivery dialog box, which you display by clicking Advanced on the Delivery tab of the SMTP virtual server's property sheet.

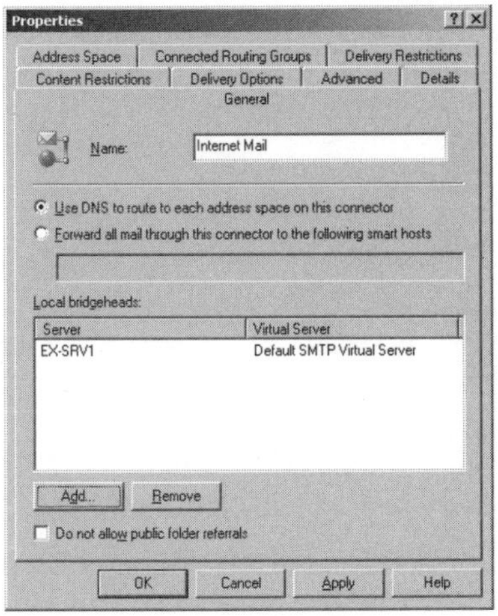

Figure 13-8. *General tab of the SMTP connector's property sheet.*

Delivery Options Tab

The Delivery Options tab of the SMTP connector's property sheet has one feature that the property sheet for the Routing Group Connector (refer to Figure 13-5) doesn't have: Queue Mail For Remote Triggered Delivery. This feature allows clients to connect periodically to your Exchange server and download messages. To make this process secure, your clients must connect using an account in your domain. When you click the Add button to specify the accounts that are authorized to use TURN/ATRN, you'll find that only local domain accounts are available. This restriction occurs because it is your Exchange server that is holding e-mail for others to retrieve, and hence they need to be authenticated in your domain. Therefore, you need to specify which Active Directory accounts can download e-mail. The client must issue a TURN command to trigger the download from Exchange Server 2003.

Advanced Tab

Figure 13-9 shows the Advanced tab of the SMTP connector's property sheet, which has a number of important configuration options that you'll need to consider as you set up the connector. First, you can set the SMTP connector to send HELO instead of EHLO. Traditionally, when an SMTP client connects to an SMTP server, the first command that is sent is the HELO command. This command starts the session and identifies the sender of the coming message. By default, Exchange Server 2003 sends the EHLO command, which is a start command that also indicates that the Exchange server is able to use the Extended SMTP (ESMTP) commands. Not all SMTP servers are capable of communicating using these extended commands. If you need to connect to an SMTP server that doesn't understand ESMTP commands, select this check box to have Exchange Server send the HELO start command instead. To see a list of SMTP commands, refer to Chapter 20.

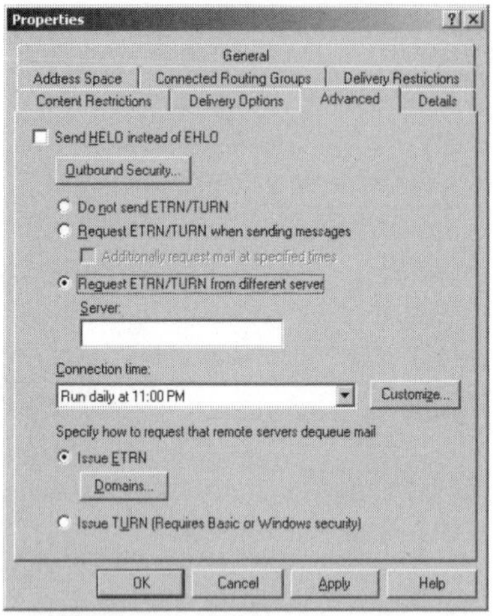

Figure 13-9. *Advanced tab of the SMTP connector's property sheet.*

Also on the Advanced tab, you can click the Outbound Security button to provide authentication credentials to the remote domain. The Do Not Send ETRN/TURN option prevents this connector from requesting a dequeuing off a remote server. This option is selected by default. When selected, it permits this connector to be used only for basic sending and receiving of messages via SMTP; no remote dequeuing requests can be made. You'll want to leave this option selected most of the time.

If you want to send a dequeuing message along with other messages that are being sent to an SMTP server, select the Request ETRN/TURN When Sending Messages option. If you choose this option, you can also request dequeuing at certain times by selecting the Additionally Request Mail At Specified Times check box and then choosing the dequeuing time under Connection Time. You would use these settings, for example, when your Exchange server connects to another Exchange server via a dial-up connection. Once connected, your Exchange server would send any e-mail destined for the receiving server. Within the same session, a request would be sent to the other Exchange server to dequeue any messages that are destined for mailboxes located within your Exchange environment.

To request dequeuing from a server other than the one to whom the message was sent, select the Request ETRN/TURN From Different Server option and then enter the server's name. Select this option when you have one server that will handle your outbound messages and another server that holds your inbound messages for your organization.

If you would like to request that dequeuing occur at certain times, select the Connection Time drop-down list and choose one of the default options, or click the Customize button and set the schedule that is needed. You might use this setting if your Exchange server did not have a permanent connection to the Internet and you wanted to retrieve your e-mail from your ISP periodically, using a dial-up connection.

Finally, under Specify How To Request That Remote Servers Dequeue Mail, select either the Issue ETRN option or the Issue TURN option. To use ETRN, you must have a static IP address, whereas with TURN, you do not need a static IP address. In addition, ETRN requires that the domain to be dequeued be specified, so if you click on the Domains button, you can add the local domain name that you want dequeued.

Address Space Tab

When you connect to a foreign system, you must specify an address space that the connector will use. An *address space* is a set of address information associated with a connector or gateway that specifies the domains to which this connector will send messages. Typically, an address space is a subset of a complete address; usually, it is just the domain name.

You specify the address space on the Address Space tab of the connector's property sheet (Figure 13-10). If this SMTP connector will be used for your organization's Internet e-mail, you can choose "*" as the address space, which means that any string of characters will be valid, and messages can be routed to any domain over this connector.

You can specify address spaces for SMTP, X.400, Lotus cc:Mail, Microsoft Mail, Lotus Notes, and Novell GroupWise types of addresses. If the address space that you need to use is not one of these types, select Other and enter the address space.

You can prevent messaging relay by not selecting the Allow Messages To Be Relayed To These Domains check box. This will ensure that unsolicited e-mails cannot be routed through your SMTP server back out to the Internet. However, if this SMTP connector is being used as a relay point between two foreign SMTP systems, select this check box and add to the address space area the destination name of the domain to which messages should be relayed.

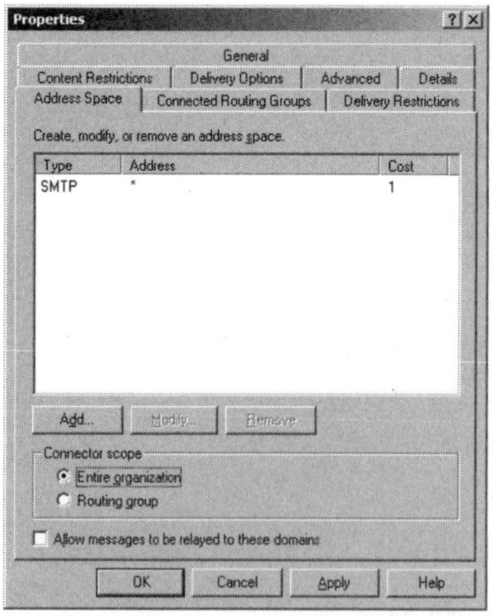

Figure 13-10. *Address Space tab of the SMTP connector's property sheet.*

Finally, if you want to limit the use of this SMTP connector to those servers that are members of the same routing group, select the Routing Group option in the Connector Scope area. The default is to allow all servers in the organization to use this connector. Since servers that are not in the same routing group are assumed to exist across either a slow connection or a nondedicated connection, it is a good idea to enable this setting to keep servers in remote routing groups from routing messages to the Internet or a foreign e-mail system over this connector.

Real World **Setting Up the SMTP Server as a Relay Server**

Let's assume that your organization is known by two different names in the marketplace: trainsbydave.com and contoso.com. Let's further assume that you want all messages to enter the organization through the SMTP connector on a server that is a member of the trainsbydave.com domain. Here are the steps you would take to make sure that all messages for both domain names are routed correctly:

1. Enter an A record in DNS for this server's host name and IP address.
2. Enter two MX records in DNS, one for each domain, both pointing to this server's IP address.
3. Create the SMTP connector for the trainsbydave.com domain.
4. Add contoso.com as a valid address space.
5. Select the Allow Messages To Be Relayed To These Domains check box.

(continued)

6. Create an MX record and an A record in your internal DNS tables to point to the internal SMTP server that is serving the contoso.com domain.

Now messages addressed to either contoso.com or trainsbydave.com will be routed to the same server, and those messages addressed to sugarmaple.com will be relayed to the contoso.com Exchange server.

Connected Routing Groups Tab

If you do not configure an address space on the Address Space tab, you must use the Connected Routing Groups tab to indicate which routing groups are connected to the local routing group. The purpose here is to inform the connector of which routing groups are adjacent to it to enable internal routing of messages. The routing groups are recorded by administrative group membership, so your choice will always involve selecting the administrative group as well. If your organization is small, with one routing group and one administrative group, enter an address space on the Address Space tab and leave this tab blank.

Link State Administration

This section takes a look at how to manage the link state information for your Exchange system. (Refer to Chapter 3 for a discussion of how the link state protocol works.) Administration of link state information takes place inside the Queues container for a server and is mainly a function of queue management. We will be most concerned with the SMTP protocol (Figure 13-11), since it is used by both the Routing Group Connector and the SMTP connector.

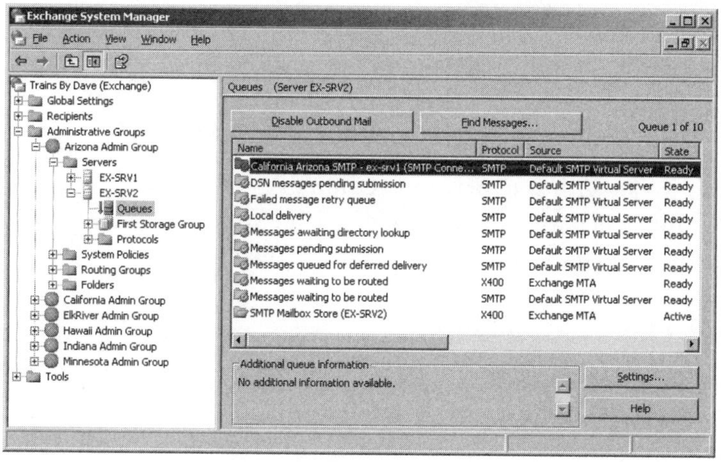

Figure 13-11. *Queues in Exchange System.*

Before launching into our discussion, let's look at the topology for a network that we will use as an example. Figure 13-12 shows that our fictitious company, hr.trainsbydave.com, has offices in four cities: Folsom, Tucson, Minneapolis, and Indianapolis. It also shows the user located in each city that we will use to illustrate messaging and connectivity. We are assuming that each connector's cost is equal to 1. Furthermore, the Routing Group Connectors are named by state, such as California Arizona RGC for the link between Folsom, California, and Tucson, Arizona. And finally, the servers are named after their location, so we have four servers: Tucson, Folsom, Minneapolis, and Indianapolis.

It is important to note that each server's display of the overall routing topology will be different because not all routes or connectors are displayed in Exchange System for any given server. Take a moment to familiarize yourself with this topology before reading on.

When ssmith sends a message to benglish, it must pass through the Folsom server. The message does not pass through Minneapolis because it does not represent the lowest-cost route. By default, routing will occur over the route with the lowest cost, which in this case is Indianapolis to Folsom to Tucson, for a total cost of 2.

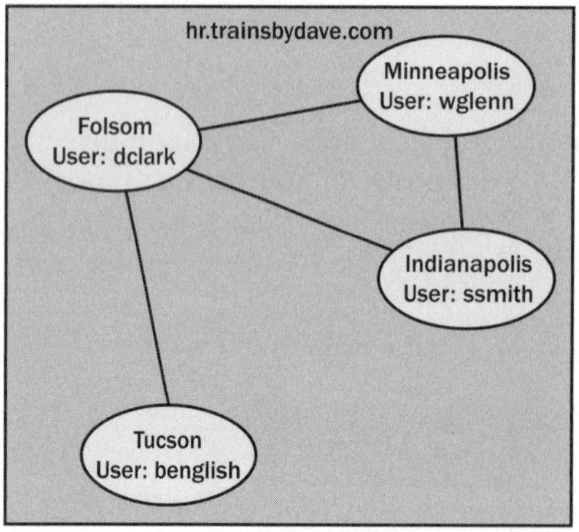

Figure 13-12. *Routing topology for hr.trainsbydave.com.*

Now that you are familiar with our fictitious company, let's look at how the link state protocol works when a link goes down. We'll cover four different scenarios and illustrate how the link state protocol is administered.

Scenario 1: First Link Is Unavailable

Normally, a message sent from benglish to ssmith would have to travel over two separate links (Indianapolis/Folsom and Folsom/Tucson) and through three different servers (Tucson, Folsom, and Indianapolis). However, let's assume that the Folsom server has gone offline for some reason and that benglish sends a message to ssmith. As Figure 13-13 shows, messages are initially placed in the outbound queue for the RGC.

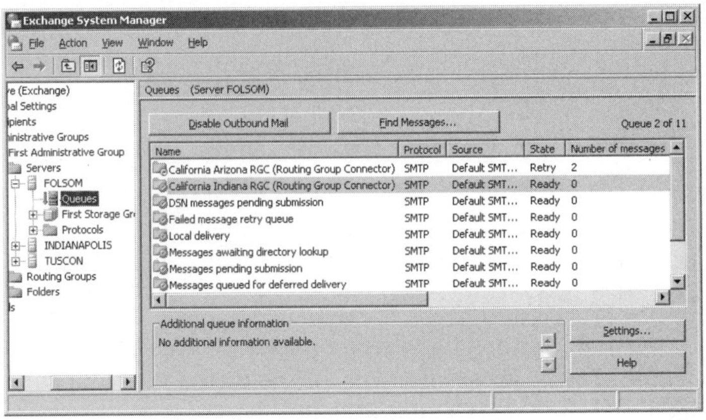

Figure 13-13. *Messages held in the outbound queue of the California Arizona RGC.*

Managing Messages in Outbound Queues

Microsoft has given us a handy way of knowing that something is wrong with the queue—icons. As you can see in Figure 13-13, the icon in the results pane (the right pane) for the California Arizona routing group queue has changed to show that it is in the retry state (a small blue arrow on the icon).

You can manage queues and the messages inside in several ways. First, you can freeze a queue by right-clicking it and choosing Freeze. If you do so, messages in the queue remain there even if the link starts working again. Freezing a queue can be a good way of making sure that message delivery is not attempted while you troubleshoot a problem. If you double-click a queue to find the actual messages inside, you'll find that you can also freeze individual messages. Freezing a message is handy if you know that a particular message in the queue is either quite large or very unimportant and you want to hold it back until the rest of the messages have been sent. You can unfreeze a queue or an individual message by right-clicking the object and choosing Unfreeze. When you unfreeze a queue or message, message delivery resumes immediately.

You can also delete any individual message in an outbound queue by right-clicking it and choosing Delete (or just by clicking it and pressing the Delete key). When doing so, you can specify whether or not to send a nondelivery report to the originator.

Resuming Normal Operation

Just because the messages have been sent doesn't mean that the link state information is back to normal. Once a server is up and running, the messages might transfer, yet the connector icon will still show the link as being in a retry state. This is nothing to be alarmed about. Wait a few minutes and check the queue again; you'll usually find that the icon shows the queue in a normal state.

Scenario 2: Destination Link Is Unavailable

We've seen what happens to a message when the first hop becomes unavailable. Now let's take a look at what happens to a message when the final hop becomes unavailable. In this scenario, benglish sends another message to ssmith, but this time the Indianapolis server is unavailable.

When benglish sends the message, it is routed from Tucson to Folsom, where it waits until the Indianapolis server comes back up or the message's expiration time is reached, in which case the user is sent an NDR.

Scenario 3: Alternate, Higher-Cost Route Is Available

One feature of the link state protocol is its ability to detect when part of the overall route is down and reroute a message over a higher-cost link. Recall from Chapter 3, though, that improvements to the link state protocol in Exchange Server 2003 mean that links are not marked as unavailable if they are the only link between two locations or if the link state is oscillating.

For this scenario, let's increase the connector cost between Folsom and Indianapolis to 100. Figure 13-14 shows the new topology. Now suppose that benglish in Tucson sends a message to ssmith in Indianapolis.

Given the connector costs, normal routing for this message would flow through Minneapolis. Let's say, however, that the link between the Minneapolis and Folsom routing groups is down. This will force messages to be routed over the higher-cost link between Indianapolis and Folsom.

Note If you are ever in doubt as to which path a message has taken, track the message. For more information about how to do so, consult Chapter 26, "Monitoring Exchange Server 2003."

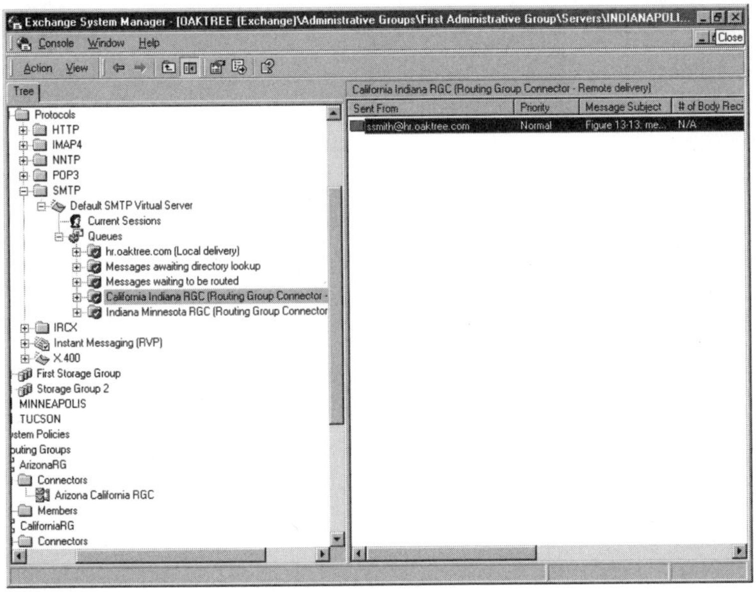

Figure 13-14. *New topology for hr.trainsbydave.com.*

Scenario 4: Message Has Multiple Destinations

If a message is sent to both internal and external recipients, a temporary queue is set up for each external domain name as well as each internal Exchange Server 2003 that hosts a recipient of the message. For instance, suppose that we've sent a message to a group of fictitious domain names. When the message is sent, the advanced queuing engine creates the necessary queues. The link state protocol does not concern itself with these outbound SMTP queues to external domains. Its only concern is keeping link state information current for the internal servers.

Summary

In this chapter, you learned how to administer and manage the Routing Group Connector and the SMTP connector. In addition, you saw how link state information enables message routing for different situations. For instance, you saw that the link state protocol is smart enough to know when a link is down and hold messages until it comes up again.

The link state protocol is one of the most powerful features of Exchange Server 2003. Another feature of Exchange Server 2003 is its ability to coexist with Exchange 5.x servers. If your organization is running Windows NT 4 and Exchange 5.5, the issues of upgrading and coexisting with Windows Server 2003 and Exchange Server 2003 during a migration will be important to you. These issues are the subject of Part IV, "Upgrading and Migrating."

Part IV
Upgrading and Migrating

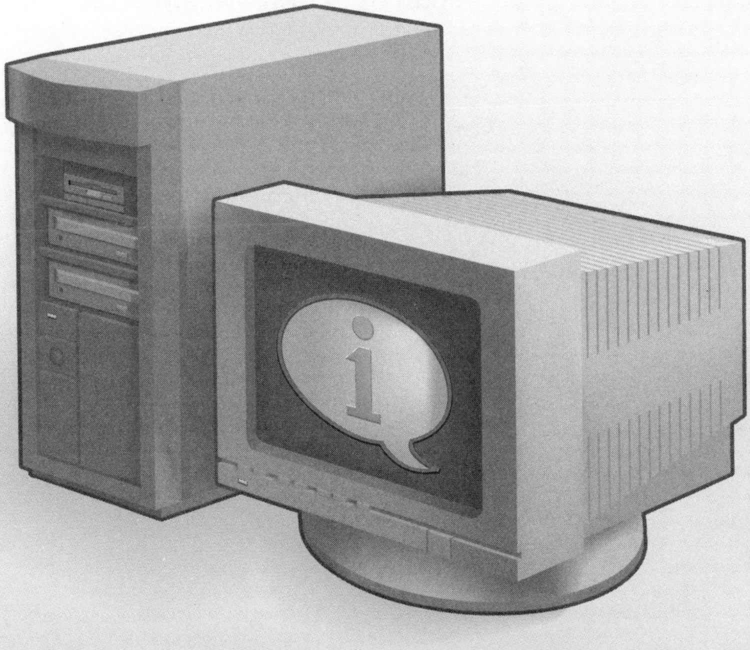

Chapter 14

Planning a Migration to Exchange Server 2003

At the time of this writing, a very large install base of Microsoft Exchange 5.5 Server still exists, and many users will want to migrate to Microsoft Windows Server 2003 and Microsoft Exchange Server 2003. Some will be running Exchange 5.5 on Windows 2000 Server; others will be running Microsoft Windows NT as their base operating system.

Whatever your present environment is, you'll need to do some planning before migrating to Exchange Server 2003. This chapter is written at a very high level and only just touches the surface of our topic, so we'll focus here on the decisions you must make and the strategies you must lay out before you start your migration. You probably feel about this chapter like you do about other planning chapters, and you'll have a strong urge to skim it and think that you're ready to perform your migration. But we want to emphasize that *failure to plan well for your migration will lead to problems and mistakes in the real migration.*

Differentiating Between Migration and Upgrade

Out of the chute, let's differentiate between a migration and an upgrade. A *migration* is the process of moving your existing information from one server or organization to another—in our case, to the Exchange 2003 platform. An *upgrade* is the process of converting the current software on your Exchange server to a new platform, such as Exchange Server 2003, while using the same hardware. This is sometimes referred to as an in-place upgrade. Whether you migrate or upgrade, you'll be changing platforms, but the hallmark is the introduction of new hardware, and in most cases, a new forest and Active Directory too. (Chapter 15, "Migrating to Exchange Server 2003," provides more details about upgrading.)

The cost of upgrading is less expensive than the cost of migrating. Often in a migration, administrators choose to restructure their user accounts, mailboxes, and other Exchange information, although in smaller environments, there might be no reason to do this. An upgrade is less complex and provides the fastest and easiest path to Exchange Server 2003.

A migration is usually more expensive but also offers more alternatives and benefits, such as restructuring the forest and providing a new administrative structure for your Exchange organization. Depending on how the information is migrated, you might need to touch each desktop to reconfigure the Microsoft Outlook profiles—not fun! But the consolidation, new design benefits, and new administrative flexibilities that a restructuring operation offers are often compelling reasons for organizations to opt to endure the pain of a migration instead of the (relatively) painless in-place upgrade.

Planning the Migration Strategy

A well-planned migration must take into account all aspects of Exchange Server, such as the following:

- Mailboxes
- Distribution lists
- Public folders
- Messages
- Attachments
- Calendars
- E-mail addresses

In addition, a well-planned migration strategy takes into consideration the business and technical reasons for the migration as well as emphasizing communication about the migration process. You can't focus only on the technical aspects of the migration; you also need to inform key stakeholders. Those with a business interest in the migration should have input into the plan's goals and outline the business reasons that underlie the migration. Key players on the business side of the migration project might include the following individuals:

- Human resources
- Customer management
- Sales

- Marketing
- Administration
- Manufacturing
- Executives

Common business goals for a migration can include better internal routing of e-mail; a development environment that leverages Active Directory; compatibility with mission-critical, industry-specific software; or simply ensuring that your company stays current with its technology. Less tangible goals, such as increasing user productivity or increasing e-mail efficiency, come into play as well.

Technical goals should be listed in concert with the business goals for the project. Common technical goals include the following:

- More secure e-mail platform
- Better or more flexible management of the Exchange system
- Higher availability of Exchange services
- Better scalability as the organization grows
- Integration with other applications that the organization is using now or in the future

It is imperative that the key stakeholders understand what you hope to accomplish through the migration. A cost is associated with migrating to any new system, and establishing clear, measurable goals is a good way to ensure that the cost is justified. The reason for this is simple: the more objective and measurable the goals for the project, the more easily you can define the project's success.

Taking a Current Snapshot

One important task you must accomplish when writing the migration plan is taking an inventory of your current network. You need to know how your various locations are connected, how each location is wired, and how the underlying Windows Server 2003 infrastructure is laid out. Here are a few of the more important aspects of your system that you must describe:

- Current network performance and types of connectivity.
- Current Windows Server 2003 domain and global catalog topology. If you're running Microsoft Windows NT 4, detail the proposed Windows Server 2003 topology.

- Network-layer diagram that shows the subnets, hosts per subnet, and other IP addressing information.
- DNS-oriented diagram that outlines name resolution on your network and on the Internet.

Plan to expand these diagrams with information about the migration so that you are not caught off-guard by an unforeseen situation.

Choosing Network Migration Tools

Microsoft has provided a number of important tools for your migration. In this chapter and the next, we'll discuss how to use them when migrating from Exchange 5.5 Server to Exchange Server 2003. Three tools in particular have the potential to help you with your migration process: Move Server Wizard, Exmerge, and Exchange Migration Wizard. Another more comprehensive tool, called the Active Directory Migration Tool, can help you with planning your migration to Active Directory.

As part of your migration strategy, you'll need to decide whether you're going to migrate all the information at the same time or in stages. If you decide to migrate in stages, you'll need to ensure that messages flow between your systems, Global Address Lists are updated appropriately, and public folder access is not diminished.

Move Server Wizard

Move Server Wizard enables you to collapse your Exchange 5.5 organization into fewer source sites—that is, move smaller sites of servers into larger ones—so that the migration is more easily accomplished.

We should mention from the outset that this tool can be complex to use, and you might need to do substantial groundwork on your Exchange 5.5 server before you can use the tool. In many scenarios, Move Server Wizard won't meet your needs.

Here are the key features of this tool:

- **Uses same hardware** All operations are performed on the same server. Mailboxes are not moved to a new server.
- **Moves directory information** Directory information associated with a mailbox is moved to a new site.
- **Moves distribution lists and contacts** Distribution lists (DLs) and contacts are moved to the target site.

- **Cleans up the source site** Objects that have been moved to the new site are deleted in the source site automatically.
- **Preserves addressing information** The Reply-To addressing information in the properties of the moved objects are preserved.

As with nearly all tools, Move Server Wizard has some drawbacks. The first is that your Outlook profiles will need to be reset after the server moves—there is no getting around this. Second, public folders are not preserved. Hence, you'll need to re-home your public folders before you use Move Server Wizard so that you don't have any orphaned folders in the source site. And finally, access control security settings are not preserved, so you'll need to reconfigure them before using the Move Server Wizard.

Two more issues might indicate that this tool is not the best choice in your situation. First, once you start your migration to Exchange 2003, you cannot use Move Server Wizard and there is no rollback that will allow you to use it. Second, using this tool requires a fair amount of planning and effort, and you might find that using it costs you more time and effort than using other tools, approaches, and migration paths to achieve your ultimate goal. Specifically, you must verify the following list of issues before you use the tool:

- Public folders (including system folders) are re-homed on another server in the same site.
- No users default to this server for public folder access.
- News feeds are re-homed.
- INS (Internet News Service) is removed completely.
- KMS (Key Management Server) isn't installed.
- IMS (Internet Mail Service) isn't installed.
- Event service isn't installed.
- No connectors are installed.
- Server is not the routing calculation server for the site.
- There is no target server on a connector.
- There is no messaging BHS (Bridgehead Server).
- There is no Directory Replication BHS (DRBHS).
- You must be running Exchange 5.5 SP2 or later.
- There is no cluster server.
- Server monitors can't shut down the moved server or any server in the original or destination site.

- Directory replication is complete.
- Full online backup is complete.

Exmerge

Exmerge (Exchange Server Mailbox Merge) is a very flexible tool that helps you perform bulk export and import actions on mailboxes, and during a migration scenario, you would use it to move a large number of mailboxes between servers in different organizations without moving the servers as well. Essentially, this tool exports an individual mailbox to a .pst (Personal Store) file for importing into an Exchange 2003 mailbox. (We know of more than a few environments that also use this tool for disaster recovery of individual mailboxes.) Exmerge can work in the Exchange 5.5, Exchange 2000, or Exchange 2003 environments.

One of the tool's drawbacks is its inability to move directory information when the mailbox is moved. Also, a mailbox must exist on the target system into which the .pst file can be imported, and Exmerge does not preserve reply-to capabilities. In addition, the Outlook profile will need to be reconfigured at the client after the mailbox information is moved to the new mailbox. (We illustrate how to use this tool in Chapter 15.)

Exchange Migration Wizard

Exchange Migration Wizard is another tool for moving mailboxes between servers and organizations. This tool uses a single-step process to export mailboxes from an Exchange 5.5 Server and import them into an Exchange Server 2003 and can be also be used to migrate system information to and from the Exchange 5.5 server to the Exchange 2003 server. Exchange Migration Wizard will preserve mailbox directory information during the migration and populate Active Directory with new information as needed. Reply-to abilities are maintained along with the X.500 Distinguished Name (DN) of the mailbox.

Like all tools, Exchange Migration Wizard has some drawbacks. First, it does not clean up accounts in the Exchange 5.5 directory after the migration. You will need to do this manually. Second, it will not move distribution lists, and you will need to reconfigure each client's Outlook profile after the move is completed.

Active Directory Migration Tool

Active Directory Migration Tool is a handy, comprehensive tool that, when used properly, ensures you have a clean, error-free migration to Active Directory. (We highlight this tool in Chapter 15.)

Active Directory Migration Tool is a Microsoft Management Console (MMC) snap-in that provides wizards to automate migration tasks such as moving users, groups, and computers between or within forests. This tool can also migrate trusts and perform security translations.

Using ADMT, you can migrate user and machine accounts from Windows NT to Active Directory and upload Exchange 5.5 directory information to Active Directory to supplement account attributes. This tool offers a trial mode, which logs all activity that takes place but does not actually perform the task at hand. This allows you to test your migration plan and see the results without actually performing the migration.

Creating the Migration Team

In very small organizations, migration is a solo activity. But in medium and larger organizations, a team approach to the migration is essential to success. If your employer believes that you can conduct an Exchange migration all by yourself or if you believe this, expectations need to be adjusted. Table 14-1 describes the individuals who should be involved in the migration and their corresponding duties.

Table 14-1. Migration team responsibilities

Job Title	Migration Duties
System architect	Coordinates the design, testing, and implementation of Exchange at each site.
Hardware installation and support personnel	Upgrades server and client computers.
Windows NT Server and Exchange Server administrator	Keeps the servers running and backed up. Performs the migration tasks of moving information to the Exchange 2003 platform.
Desktop support staff	Solves client problems, such as creating new Outlook profiles.
Help desk support staff	Trains the support staff on new features of Outlook and Exchange and offers the first line telephone support.
User trainer	Performs training of end users.
Testing and implementation specialist	Tests the migration plan, and documents problems and methods.
Coexistence specialist	Understands the existing system and how it interacts with Exchange Server 2003.

As you can see from Table 14-1, your migration team must handle many functions. The team needs to communicate well and work together to get the migration done on schedule and according to plan. Again, planning is the key.

Deciding When to Move Users

You can either move your users all at once, a process called *single-phase migration*, or move them in groups, a process called *multi-phase migration*. Single-phase migration can be good for your organization if you're not moving data from your existing system, you have the capability to move everyone at the same time, and you have all the hardware you need to run your Exchange 2003 systems. In larger environments, single-phase migration is the better choice merely because of the resource constraints when moving large numbers of mailboxes, distribution lists, and other Exchange information in a single effort.

The multi-phase migration is better when your organization cannot upgrade all departments at the same time, you need to free up hardware for redeployment during the latter stages of the migration, or your organization can't migrate everyone within an acceptable downtime period. A multi-phase migration will necessitate coexistence. (We discuss coexistence issues from an architectural perspective in Chapter 16, "Coexisting with Previous Versions of Exchange.") Coexistence is the term used to describe a scenario in which two different platforms (in this case, Exchange 5.5 and Exchange 2003) need to exist side by side and interoperate seamlessly.

Maintaining Connections During Coexistence

You must consider a plethora of issues when living in a dual-platform environment. We'll discuss them now.

Connectors Between Platforms

To connect dissimilar platforms, you need some type of connection between the platforms during the migration period. If you're moving from Exchange 5.5 to Exchange Server 2003, you can use the Active Directory Connector (ADC). If you're coming from another system, you can use an SMTP Connector or an X.400 Connector. The essential point to understand here is that Exchange 2003 will work with most connectors, and you should plan the way that messages will be transferred internally between groups during the migration period.

Maintaining External Addresses

If your users receive e-mail from other systems in your organization or from outside your organization, your users' external e-mail addresses should be preserved. With good planning, you can attach these addresses to the migrated mailboxes, which we'll discuss in Chapter 15. If you elect to not do this, your users will need to inform others of their e-mail addresses.

Naming Conventions

You'll need to take a look at naming conventions. Both your current conventions and the ones you'd like to use in Exchange 2003 should be discussed and formalized before starting the migration.

Directory Names The directory name is also known as the common name. This *common name* is used by Active Directory to create the unique full directory name of a mailbox. It is visible only in the Exchange System Manager (ESM). The default directory name is the same as the alias name but without spaces. Directory names cannot be changed after they are created, so be sure you like your convention before creating the mailbox.

Display Names The display name appears in the address book and can be changed at any time. Migrated messages use the display names of the senders and recipients. If you change the display names during the migration, replies to migrated e-mail can fail if an association between the old and new display names cannot be established.

By default, the first and last names are used to create the X.400 e-mail addresses. The alias is used to create the SMTP address. The alias is visible to the public and can contain spaces, unlike the directory name. Be sure that your naming convention states whether the nickname should be used for the first name or the display name. You'll also need to consider how to handle duplicate names and hyphenated names.

Managing Migrated Messages

After a mailbox is migrated, the old mailbox can contain messages that were sent during the mailbox migration. In Exchange 5.5, you can configure the old mailbox to forward e-mail to the new mailbox. However, if you are running a system that doesn't support e-mail forwarding or if you haven't configured the Exchange 5.5 mailbox to forward e-mail, your users will need to connect to the old mailbox to retrieve any messages that still appear there. You can ask your users to perform this task before their Outlook profiles are reconfigured to point to the new mailbox.

You must consider a few issues so that users can avoid problems when replying to migrated messages. First, if only one display name matches the display name in the message, Exchange can resolve the address and forward the message without a problem. However, if more than one display name matches the display name in the message, the user is presented with a dialog box requesting her to select one name from a list of display names. This can be confusing for users when the display name in Exchange 5.5 matches the display name in Exchange

2003 and mailboxes exist in both platforms for the same user. You can easily see how such a scenario can cause trouble for you.

Second, if no display name in the address book matches the display name in the message, the user must find the new address in the address list. If you are changing your naming conventions in Exchange 2003, you must educate your users about how to find other members of the organization by their new display names in the address book. This education will be key to your successful migration.

For a user to be able to reply to a migrated message, the display name must appear in the address list either as a custom recipient or as a mailbox, but not as both.

Migrating Distribution Lists

During a multi-phase migration, in which addresses are constantly changing, migrating distribution lists can be a hassle. You can ensure correct routing to the members of a distribution list by planning to use one of the approaches in the following list. Each approach has benefits and limitations, and none is free of error, so you'll need to test the approach you want to use before starting your migration.

- Migrate the distribution lists before migrating any mailboxes.
- Set up a forward scheme for each distribution list to a distribution group in Windows Server 2003.
- Maintain two lists on both systems. You must do this manually, and it is probably the least desirable option.
- Disable your distribution lists in Exchange 5.5 and create new distribution groups in Exchange 2003 after the migration is complete.

Creating a Deployment Plan

After considering all the various issues involved in your migration and forming the migration team, you are ready to write the plan. A rough plan formulated in your head is not enough. Your plan must be detailed on paper, and all team members should review it for holes and problems before you move forward.

A test environment that can simulate your current platform and determine the viability of your plan is essential. Such an environment gives you two important advantages. First, you see whether your plan will work. Second, you have a chance to practice your skills at migrating the information. You'll become familiar with the screens, choices, and options. Learning about the migration from a semi-real-world scenario will help eliminate surprises.

Most smaller and medium-sized organizations don't have the funds or space to create a simulated environment. But those organizations that do have space and can afford a testing lab will be miles ahead in resolving problems and can even prevent problems from occurring during the real migration.

As part of this migration process, you should create a contingency plan that gives you options in case of failure, disaster, or unexpected results. A contingency plan should include the following:

- Outline of anticipated problems and methods to solve them
- Rollback plans at each stage of the migration process
- Clear definition of the point at which a rollback is no longer desirable or is impossible
- Method and order for migrating DRBHS, BHS, and public folders
- Method of decommissioning old servers
- When to and who will move the Exchange Server 2003 into Native Mode

Sample Migration Plan Outline

In this section, we provide part of a sample outline for your migration plan. Migration plans will vary greatly across regions, countries, and organizations, so use this outline as a starting point for developing your own.

I. Migration plan name

II. Migration project name

III. Scope of migration plan

IV. Reasons for migrating to Exchange Server 2003

  A. Business reasons

    1. Cost projections
    2. Expected ROI
    3. Productivity issues
    4. Other reasons

  B. Technical reasons

    1. Increased security
    2. More administrative flexibility
    3. Other reasons

- C. Benefits of migrating to Exchange Server 2003
- D. Definition of success
  1. Objective/measurable goals
  2. Definition of when each goal is attained

V. The Migration Team

- A. Members' contact information
- B. Team roles and responsibilities
- C. Communication between members
- D. Communication between members and stakeholders

VI. Current network snapshot

- A. Physical layer diagram and discussion
  1. Areas to improve before migration
- B. Network layer diagram and discussion
  1. Areas to improve before migration
- C. Name resolution
- D. DHCP
- E. Windows Server 2003 topology
  1. Domain controller placement
  2. Global catalog placement
  3. Windows Server 2003 site topology
- F. Security structure
  1. Firewall topology
  2. IDS and security applications
  3. Proposed location for front-end servers
- G. Hardware discussions
  1. Current hardware
  2. Proposed hardware with cost projections
  3. Resource recovery for decommissioned servers

H. Homegrown applications for Exchange
    1. Description of how these applications will change with Exchange 2003
    2. Method for regression and quality testing

VII. The Proposed Network Topology after the Migration
    A. Active Directory design
    B. Exchange administrative design
    C. User mailbox and database design
    D. Public folder design
    E. DNS, DHCP, domain controller, and global catalog design
    F. Remote Access and Outlook Web Access design
    G. Security design incorporating Exchange 2003 features

VIII. The migration plan
    A. Active Directory design and preparation
    B. Moving users to Active Directory
    C. Moving directory information to Active Directory
    D. Moving mailboxes to Active Directory
    E. Moving distribution lists to Active Directory
    F. Moving public folders to Active Directory
    G. Upgrading the clients to Outlook 2003
    H. Decommissioning old Exchange servers
    I. Moving to native mode

IX. Assessment and evaluation

Summary

In this chapter, we briefly discussed how to plan for a migration to Exchange Server 2003. Planning is essential to the success of your migration; however, it isn't enough. In the next chapter, we demonstrate how to move from a Windows NT 4.0/Exchange 5.5 environment to a Windows Server 2003/Exchange Server 2003 environment and illustrate some of the tools we've discussed in this chapter.

Chapter 15

Migrating to Exchange Server 2003

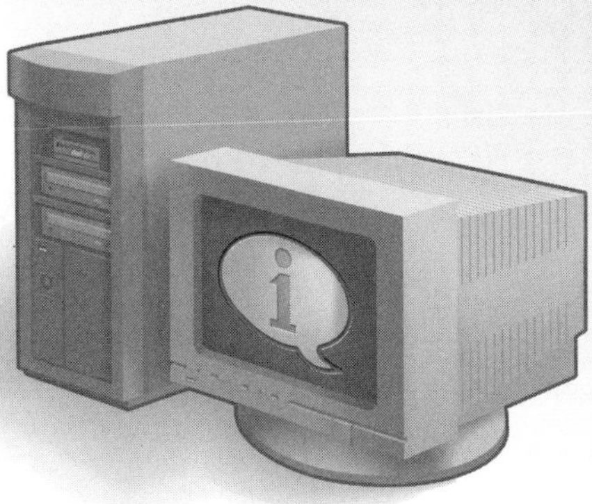

In this chapter, we guide you through a migration from Microsoft Exchange 5.5 to Microsoft Exchange Server 2003. We illustrate how to move users and discuss migrating public folders to Exchange 2003. At the end of this chapter, we examine rollback scenarios and outline the decisions you'll confront along the way. When appropriate, we provide our thoughts on the pros and cons of each decision.

A thorough book on migration would be at least as long as this entire book, so we discuss the more common tools and hope that doing so provides a sufficient roadmap for your migration journey from Exchange 5.5 to Exchange Server 2003.

The Example Scenario

We describe the migration process in the context of a particular scenario, so you need to know some preliminary details. We start with a Microsoft Windows NT 4, Service Pack 6A environment. Here is the other relevant data:

- The Windows NT domain name is Trains. The Exchange 5.5 organization is named Trains.
- The PDC is named PDC1 and is running Exchange 5.5, Service Pack 4 in the Corp Site.
- A Windows NT Member Server in the Trains domain is named MNExch01. This server is running Exchange 5.5, Service Pack 4 in the Minnesota Site.
- A second Windows NT Member Server in the Trains domain is named CAExch01 in the California site. It is also running Exchange 5.5, Service Pack 4.

- A Microsoft Windows Server 2003 Active Directory forest is running and is named Trainsbydave. The Domain Name System (DNS) name is trainsbydave.com. The domain controller is named ElkRiver.
- A member server in the trainsbydave domain is named Indianapolis. It will host the Exchange Server 2003 when it is time to install Exchange 2003.

The migration process can be broken down into a few major objectives. Here is what you will accomplish in this chapter, in order:

1. Move all the mailboxes on the three Trains Exchange 5.5 servers to a single Exchange Server 2003 in the trainsbydave.com forest.
2. Move all the user accounts from Windows NT 4 to Active Directory directory service. Move all the user accounts from the Exchange 5.5 directory to Active Directory. Do both in such a way as to not create duplicate accounts.
3. Join the Exchange Server 2003 to the Exchange 5.5 organization.
4. Consolidate Exchange administration and information onto a single server.

Notice that in our scenario, the Windows Server 2003 forest already exists. This is the preferred approach to upgrading from Windows NT to Windows Server 2003—upgrading the user accounts to Windows Server 2003 before upgrading the Exchange platform is cleaner and easier. You could do the reverse, but remember that to upgrade to Exchange 2003, you *must* have a Windows Server 2003 forest, even if you must create one just for Exchange 2003. If you must create a Windows Server 2003 forest, it makes sense to first migrate the user accounts from Windows NT to Active Directory. In most scenarios, this approach will make the most sense.

> **Note** If you are running earlier versions of software such as Novell GroupWise or IBM Lotus Notes, you should consider starting fresh with Exchange 2003 and making the previous e-mail system available for a period of time after Exchange 2003 is up and running.

Understanding the Big Picture

You need to understand the big picture before you can grasp each part of the migration process. The overarching goal of your migration is to merge two different user account databases into a single database (Figure 15-1). This is important to understand because you will use different tools to migrate different databases to Active Directory. Also, understanding where information resides in Active

Directory is essential to performing a migration. Fundamentally, you must understand where you're coming from as well as where you're going. Figure 15-2 illustrates where the Exchange information resides in Active Directory.

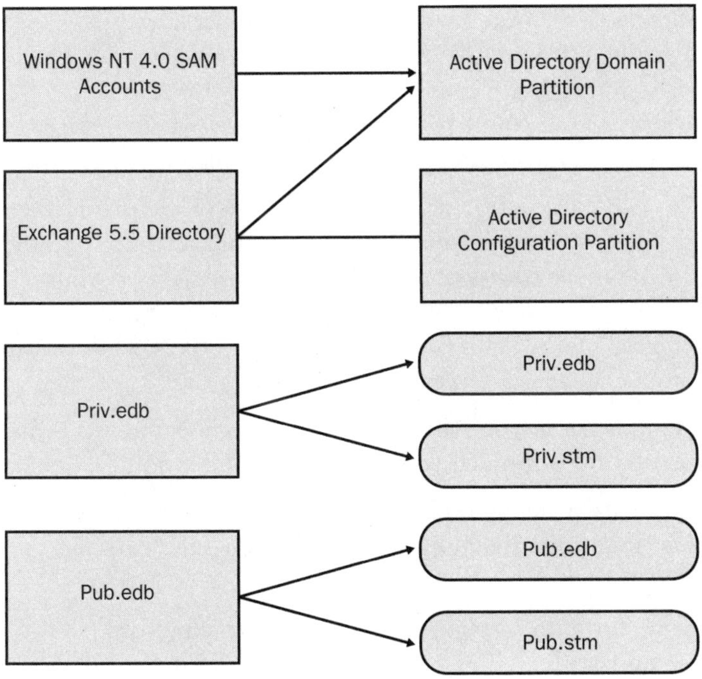

Figure 15-1. *Database migrations.*

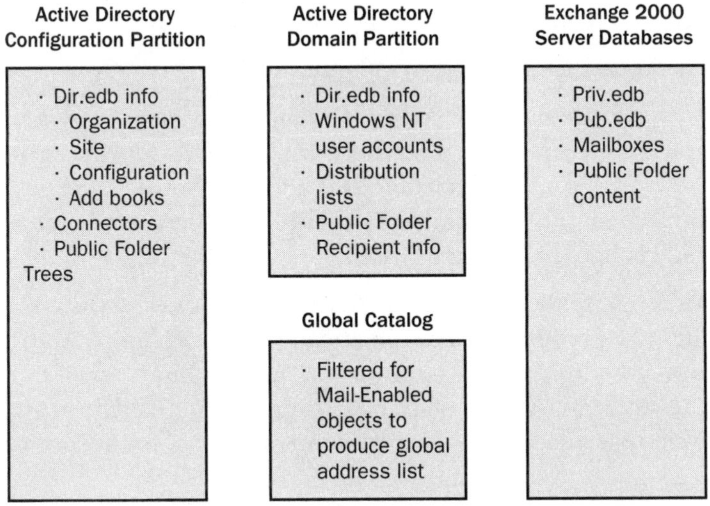

Figure 15-2. *Where Exchange information resides in Active Directory.*

To avoid creating duplicate accounts, you migrate your Windows NT 4 user accounts before you migrate your Exchange user accounts by using the Active Directory Connector (ADC). In Windows NT 4, even though the mailbox is tied to a primary account (or could be tied to a primary account) in the Windows NT account database, a separate user account also exists in the Exchange 5.5 directory for that mailbox. If you migrate the user accounts to Active Directory via the ADC before migrating the user accounts from the Windows NT accounts database, a new user account is created in Active Directory for that Exchange 5.5 account. The default setting is to create a disabled user account.

Even though the ADC can create user accounts in Active Directory for the Exchange 5.5 accounts, you will need to migrate the domain accounts from the Windows NT account database to preserve the Security Identifiers (SIDs) of each user account in Windows NT (which means preserving access to resources). Such resources include the Exchange 5.5 mailboxes while those mailboxes reside on an Exchange 5.5 server.

In this first stage of the migration, you will need to make some initial decisions that will have an impact on the approach you take to your migration:

- Whether you will create a new Exchange organization in the Active Directory forest or join your Exchange 2003 servers to the existing Exchange 5.5 organization
- Whether you will perform an in-place upgrade of your Windows NT primary domain controller (PDC) or move your Windows NT accounts to Active Directory
- Whether you will need to allow access to resources in the Windows NT domains after the accounts have been moved to Active Directory
- Whether you will expire the old Windows NT accounts

If you choose to join your Exchange 2003 servers to your Exchange 5.5 organization, you'll be able to move your mailboxes between the servers as the main method of migrating the mailboxes to Exchange 2003. If you choose to create a new organization, you'll need to use the utilities provided by Microsoft to move the mailboxes to the Exchange 2003 organization.

Likewise, if you choose to upgrade the PDC as your first Windows Server 2003 domain controller, the user accounts will automatically be upgraded to Active Directory and there will be no need to migrate the user accounts to Active Directory. However, if you want a clean start with your new Active Directory, you must use the utilities provided by Microsoft to migrate the accounts out of the Security Account Manager (SAM) database into Active Directory.

If you are running a single Exchange server hosted on a single domain controller, the easiest migration approach is to perform an in-place upgrade. In this scenario, you upgrade the PDC and then upgrade Exchange 5.5, all on the same box. The common problem with this scenario is hardware—most of the hardware that was purchased to run Windows NT and Exchange 5.5 will not be adequate to run Windows Server 2003 and Exchange 2003. Therefore, even in a single-server environment, the chances are good that you'll need to perform some type of migration to a new Active Directory and that an in-place upgrade will not be feasible.

> **Note** You could take a new server, make it a backup domain controller (BDC), promote it to a PDC, install Exchange 5.5 on it, move the mailboxes and other information, and then perform an in-place upgrade. But this process really just re-invents the wheel: your actions are very similar to installing Windows Server 2003 and then doing a migration. Our advice is to perform a migration rather than an in-place upgrade unless you're in the unusual position of having hardware that will accommodate future in-place upgrades.

The advantage of installing Exchange 2003 on an Exchange 5.5 site is that the mailboxes, public folders, connectors, and system folders can all be moved to the Exchange 2003 server without using any migration tools provided by Microsoft. In many scenarios, this will be the best way to perform the migration.

In our running example, we redesign our Exchange system, starting with migrating the user accounts from the Windows NT SAM to the Active Directory. Our redesign focuses on going from three Exchange servers in three sites to one Exchange server in the forest. However, we install our Exchange Server 2003 into the Exchange 5.5 organization.

The first step in our migration scenario is to create a Windows Server 2003 forest, which we have already done (but did not illustrate here). Then we migrate the Windows NT accounts to Active Directory. If you do this correctly, you won't encounter any duplicate accounts in Active Directory.

Migrating Windows NT Accounts to Active Directory

In this section, we migrate Windows NT accounts to Active Directory. The first tool we use is the Active Directory Migration Tool (ADMT), which migrates accounts from the Windows NT SAM to the Windows Server 2003 forest. Install the ADMT tool on the Windows Server 2003, and then run the tool on the server. ADMT installs its snap-in under the Administration Tools for the server.

To run the ADMT tool, open the snap-in and then right-click the Active Directory Migration Tool folder. Figure 15-3 shows the default options. We'll discuss the User Account Migration Wizard option in detail.

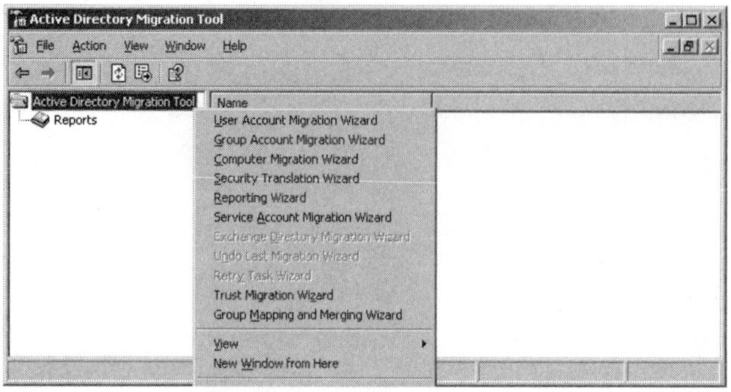

Figure 15-3. *Default set of wizard choices in ADMT.*

When you run the wizard, the first page asks whether you want to do the migration or just perform a test. Select the test option (Figure 15-4) and then click Next. You want to perform a test first to ensure that enough trial migrations are run to eliminate any problems before performing the actual migration.

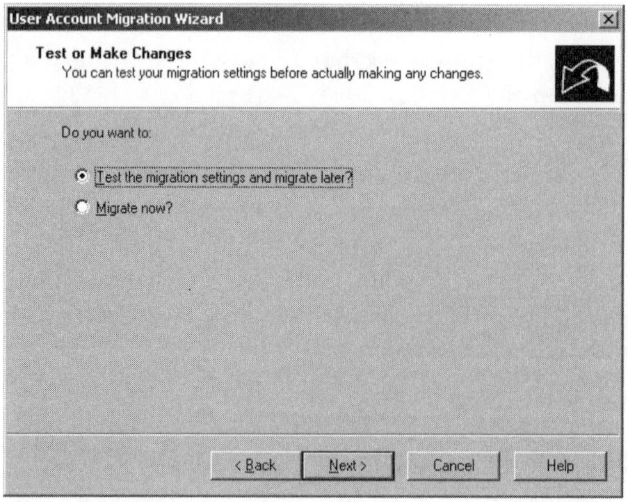

Figure 15-4. *Selecting the test option in the User Migration Account Wizard.*

The Domain Selection page (Figure 15-5) appears next. This is where you select the source and target domains to perform the migration. This is also where this tool starts to shine. Until now, we've done very little (if any) prepping of either domain for the migration. A helpful aspect of this tool is that it will not run until both domains are adequately prepped and ready for a migration and, if necessary, the tool itself will perform the necessary configuration changes to prep each domain. When we click Next on the Domain Selection page, ADMT performs an internal audit of both domains and informs us that our Windows Server 2003 target domain (Trainsbydave) is not in native mode. Before you can migrate user accounts from Windows NT to Active Directory, your Active Directory domain will need to be in native mode.

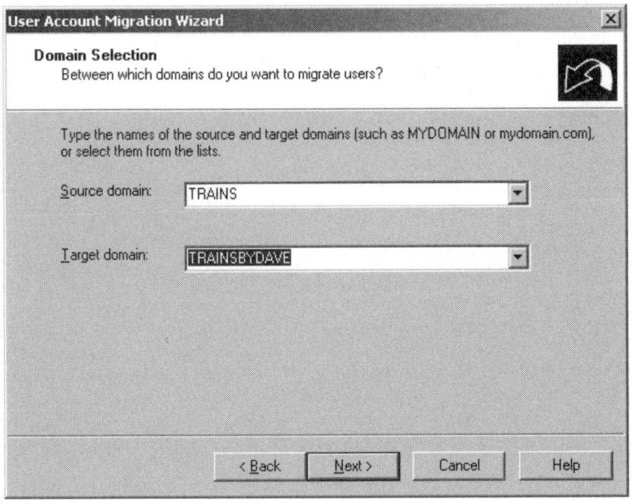

Figure 15-5. *Domain Selection page in the User Account Migration Wizard.*

After you switch your Windows Server 2003 domain into native mode, you encounter the User Selection page. On the User Selection page, click the Add button to bring up the Select Users dialog box (Figure 15-6). In the Select Users dialog box, you can select the object type, source location, and names to migrate.

To display the source domain names, you can either enter them manually or click the Advanced button and the Find Now button (Figure 15-7), and then select the names for inclusion in the test migration.

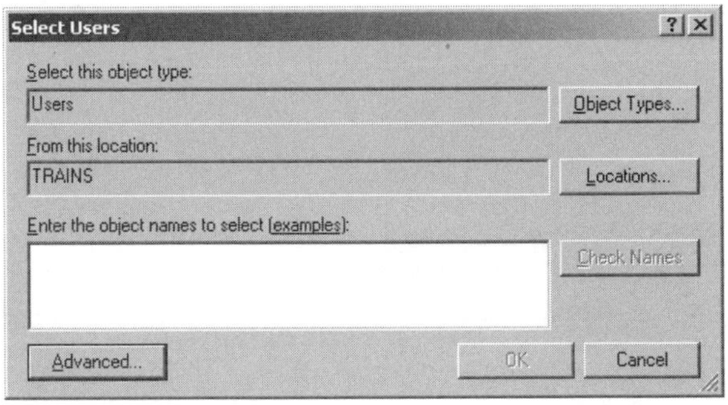

Figure 15-6. *Entering source domain names manually on the User Selection page.*

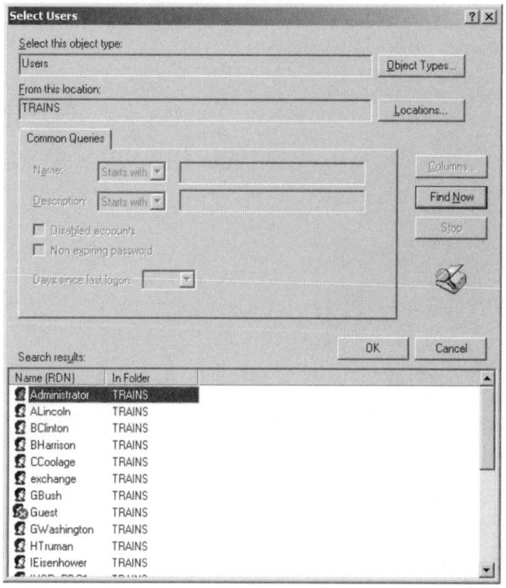

Figure 15-7. *Using the Find Now button to gather the user accounts from the Trains domain.*

After you select the accounts, they appear in the User Selection page. Click Next to move to the Organizational Unit Selection page (Figure 15-8). Browse to select the target organizational unit (OU) named Employees, and then click Next.

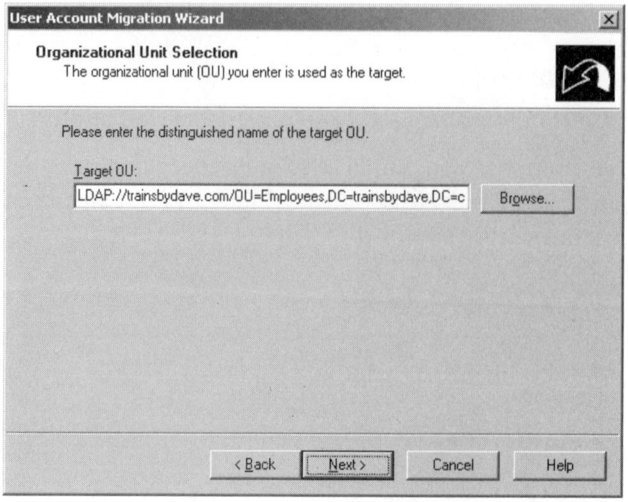

Figure 15-8. *Selecting the target organizational unit.*

The next page is the Password Options page (Figure 15-9). This is where ADMT really shines. Notice in Figure 15-9 that you can select to have new passwords assigned to the migrated accounts, or you can migrate the account passwords, which eases your work because you don't have to communicate new passwords to each of your users. For account passwords to migrate, you will need to do the following:

- Change the Default Domain Controllers Policy to enable the Let Everyone permission to apply to anonymous users.
- Add the Everyone security group to the built-in group Pre-Windows 2000 Compatibility Access security group.
- Verify that the passwords of the source domain user accounts match the password policy of the target domain.
- Save the password file encryption key in the directory in which ADMT is installed using this syntax: *admt key* sourcedomainname driveletter-andpath *[*password*]*. The password file that is created is randomly named with a .PES extension.
- In the source domain, run the pwdmig.exe tool, which is found on the Windows Server 2003 server CD in the \i386\admt directory. After installing this tool on your Windows NT PDC, reboot the server. You need the .PES file that you created earlier to get through this Password Migration Wizard.
- On the export server in the source domain, change the parameter of the HKLM/System/CurrentControlSet/Control/Lsa key from *0* to *1* for the AllowPasswordExport (REG_DWORD) value.

After completing each of the preceding steps, choose to migrate all the passwords. Then click Next.

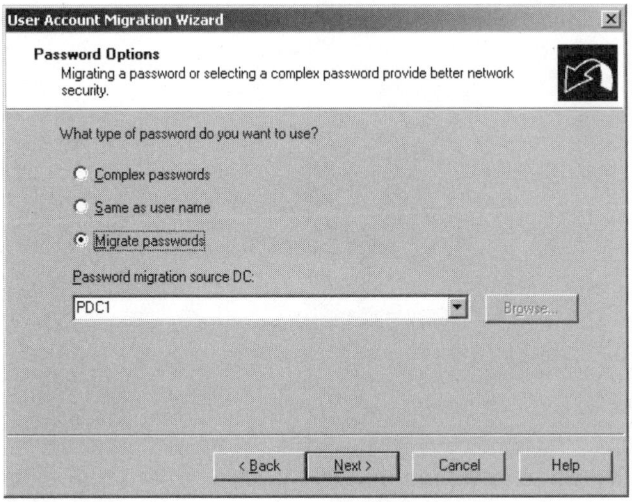

Figure 15-9. *Options for migrating passwords.*

The Account Transition Options page (Figure 15-10) appears next. On this page, you can configure the target account state (as enabled or disabled, or make it the same as the source account), configure the disabling values on the source account, and/or migrate the source account SIDs.

When the SIDs are migrated, they do not become the primary SIDs on the new account in Active Directory. Instead, a new SID is created when the new account is created, and the Windows NT SID is added to the SID *History* attribute of the account. This SID is still used to help build the user's access token, but it is not the primary SID on the new user account.

Migrating the SIDs is important for a couple of reasons. First, if your users will be authenticating in the next Windows Server 2003 domain but need access to resources in your Windows NT domain, migrating the SIDs enables them to access resources in the Windows NT domain, without additional configuration or administrative effort on your part, while being authenticated in your Windows Server 2003 domain. Second, if the users will be authenticating in the Windows Server 2003 domain and still use their Exchange 5.5 mailbox for a period of time, migrating the SIDs will make this configuration seamless and transparent to them. We advise migrating the SIDs of each account unless you have a specific reason not to.

In our example, choose to enable the target accounts so that your users start authenticating in the target domain right away. Also choose to expire the Windows NT accounts after 60 days so that your users can use their old accounts if necessary during the transition period. Also migrate the SIDs.

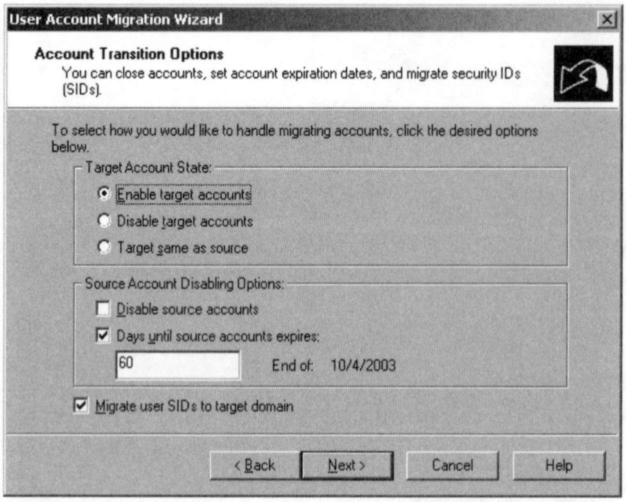

Figure 15-10. *Configuring account information.*

When you click Next in the Account Transition Options page, ADMT initiates a further audit of both the target and source domains. Because we have done very little prepping of either domain, ADMT notifies you of the following and offers to make these configuration changes for you:

- Auditing in the source and target domains must be enabled to migrate the SIDs.
- A local security group called *domainname$$$* must exist in the source domain to migrate the SIDs. ADMT will create this group.
- Addition of the TcpipClientSupport registry key in the source domain. Again, SIDs will not be migrated without this registry key.

After you allow these configuration changes to be implemented by ADMT, the wizard will want to reboot the PDC. Be sure you reboot.

The next page is the User Account page (Figure 15-11). This page needs to be populated with a user account that has administrative rights on the source domain. Enter the appropriate information and click Next. ADMT will validate this account, so if you entered incorrect information, you'll be prompted to re-enter the data.

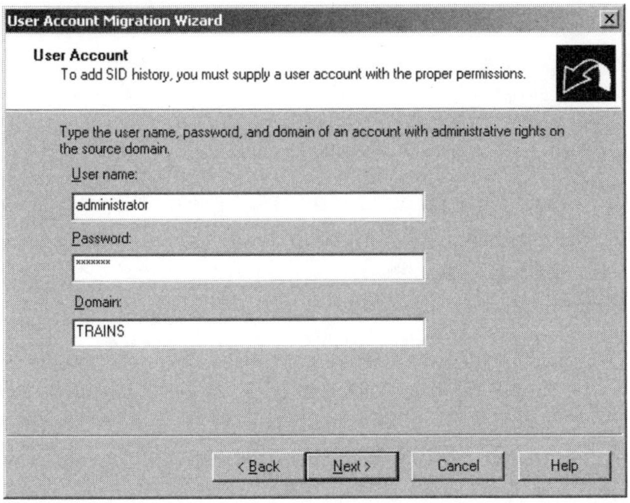

Figure 15-11. *Entering a user account with proper administrative permissions.*

The next page is the User Options page (Figure 15-12). This is where you can configure roaming profiles, update user rights, migrate user groups as well as the user accounts that the accounts are members of, and rename migrated accounts with a prefix or suffix. You have several options, some of which are obvious choices in certain scenarios.

For example, if most of your users use roaming profiles, select the check box to translate those roaming profiles into a Windows Server 2003 platform version. The Fix Users' Group Memberships option adds migrated user accounts to a target domain group if those users were members of that group when their accounts were in the source domain. A way to ensure that users don't lose their group memberships is to select the Migrate Associated User Groups option, which migrates the groups that migrated user accounts belong to. This option should be used to maintain the group membership information in the target domain.

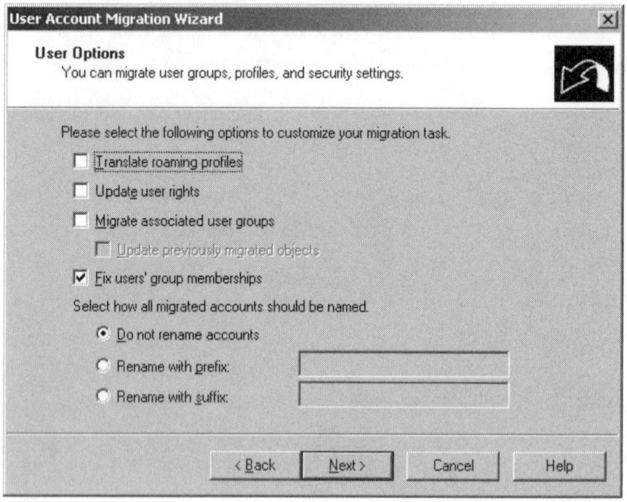

Figure 15-12. *Migrating user groups, profiles, and security settings.*

When you click Next in the User Options page, you'll be presented with the Naming Conflicts page, shown in Figure 15-13. You have three choices: ignore conflicting accounts, replace conflicting accounts, or append a prefix or suffix to conflicting accounts. What you are really doing is telling ADMT how to handle a migrated account if that account already exists in Active Directory.

You might wonder why an account would be pre-existing. If, for example, we used the Active Directory Connector before running ADMT, the ADC would have created disabled user accounts in Active Directory. When ADMT was run to migrate the same account, we would have a duplicate or conflicting account already existing in Active Directory.

If you want to know which accounts are in conflict, rename your accounts with a prefix of "aaa" so that they are listed first in the preview pane of Active Directory Users and Computers (ADUC). In our example, let's rename conflicting accounts by adding the "aaa" prefix to them even though we don't expect any conflicting accounts.

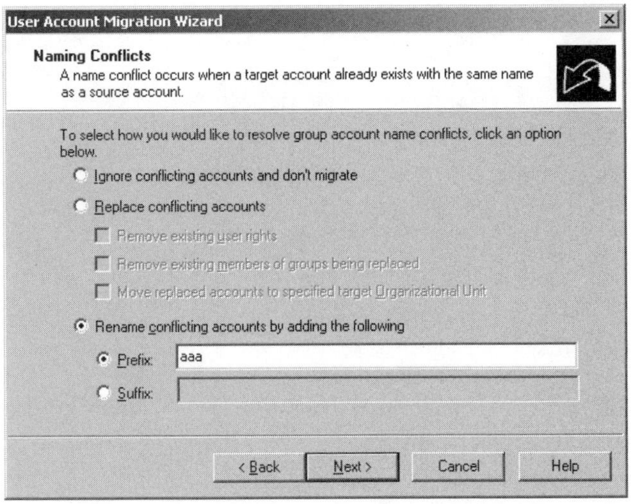

Figure 15-13. *Choosing how to handle conflicting accounts.*

Click Next to display the Finish page. Click the Finish button to begin the migration. During the migration, a status box appears (Figure 15-14) that identifies the number of users, groups, and computers that were migrated. When the migration is over, the Status line displays Completed. Now you're ready to move on to the next phase of the migration.

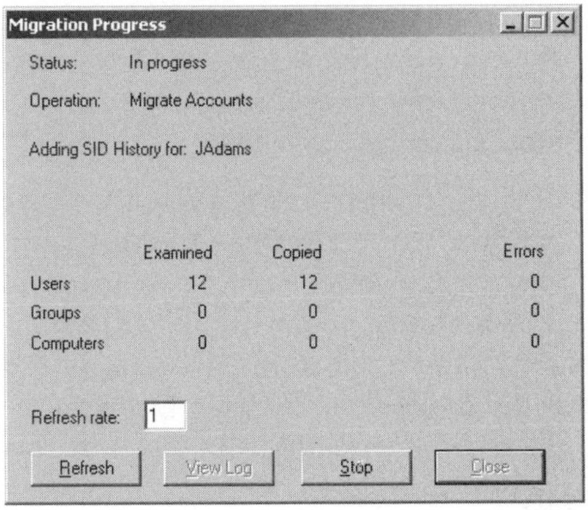

Figure 15-14. *Reviewing the status of the migration.*

Because we experienced no errors in our test migration, let's migrate the user accounts to Active Directory. You can see in Figure 15-15 that these accounts now exist in Active Directory in the Employees OU. (To learn how to manage duplicate accounts, see the "Managing Duplicate Accounts" section later in this chapter.)

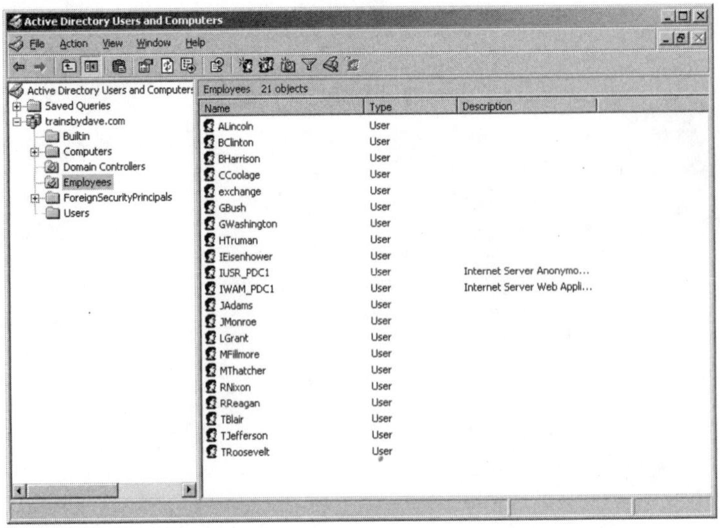

Figure 15-15. *Migrating accounts in the Employee organizational unit.*

Migrating Exchange Account Information

So far in this migration, we've moved the user accounts (commonly referred to as *cloning*) from the Windows NT account database to Active Directory. If we were to open the properties of a migrated account at this point, we would not see any Exchange-related attributes on the account. To populate the Exchange-related attributes on the Active Directory account, we need to use the ADC to move Exchange 5.5 account directory information to Active Directory.

If this process is a bit confusing, think of it this way: our goal is to have a user account in Active Directory that has both regular Active Directory and Exchange account information. We also want to use the same accounts we're using in Windows NT and Exchange 5.5. What we are doing is taking the Windows NT account information from the Windows NT account database and then supplementing that account with the Exchange 5.5 account directory information. We use ADMT to move the base account information to Active Directory, and we use the ADC to move the Exchange 5.5 account directory information to form a complete user account in Active Directory.

Before we can use the ADC to move account information, we need to run forestprep and domainprep to prepare the Windows Server 2003 Active Directory to accept Exchange-related information from the Exchange 5.5 directory. All we are doing at this point is moving account information. We have not yet touched the users' mailboxes, public folders, or any other connectors.

After you run both forestprep and domainprep, you must install the ADC on the Windows Server 2003 domain controller so that you can upload the Exchange 5.5 directory information. You will find the ADC installation program on the Exchange Server 2003 CD ROM in the ADC folder.

When you run setup, you are presented first with a Welcome screen and then the licensing agreement, with which you'll need to agree. The third screen (Figure 15-16) will ask you whether you want to install the connector service component and/or the ADC management components. The first selection installs the ADC service, and the second selection installs the console.

Caution It is important to note that the ADC is a service that runs on the Windows Server 2003 domain controller, not on the Exchange 5.5 or Exchange 2003 server. This service is administered from Windows Server 2003 via a snap-in in the Microsoft Management Console (MMC).

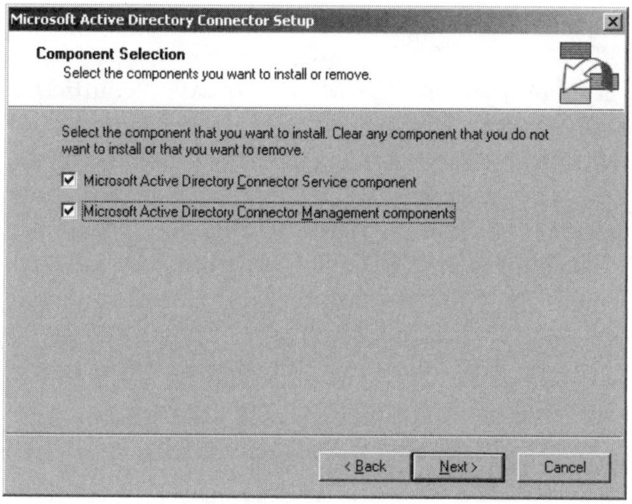

Figure 15-16. *Selecting the components you want to install.*

The next screen asks where you want to install the ADC files, the default location being c:\program files\msadc. You can select the default or enter your own path. We've chosen to use the default path.

The Service Account screen appears next. Here you enter the service account information to configure the security context in which the service will run. Be sure to select an account that has write privileges to Active Directory. After you click Next on the Service Account screen, the installation of the ADC service and snap-in begins. When the installation is finished, you are presented with a Finish screen. Click the Finish button to finish the ADC installation.

More Info For information about how to configure and manage the ADC service, refer to Chapter 16, "Coexisting with Previous Versions of Exchange."

After the ADC service is installed, you can create a Connection Agreement (CA) to your Exchange 5.5 server. In our scenario, we create a Connection Agreement to PDC1 and move over only the user accounts in the Corp site's recipient container. Once this is accomplished, the properties of your accounts in Active Directory have Exchange attributes added to them.

Before we continue with our migration scenario, you must understand what happens when you move accounts out of the Exchange 5.5 directory first and then out of the Windows NT accounts database: you produce duplicate accounts. Let's discuss duplicate accounts in more detail.

Managing Duplicate Accounts

Duplicate accounts are synonymous with what Microsoft calls "conflicting accounts." Essentially, these accounts are created when the Windows NT accounts are moved to Active Directory after the Exchange 5.5 directory information has been uploaded to Active Directory. By default, when an Exchange 5.5 directory account is uploaded without a corresponding user account in Active Directory, a disabled account is automatically created in Active Directory. This is illustrated in Figure 15-17, in which we used the ADC to upload account information from the Corp site's recipient container before moving the corresponding Windows NT accounts to Active Directory. As you can see, each account is disabled.

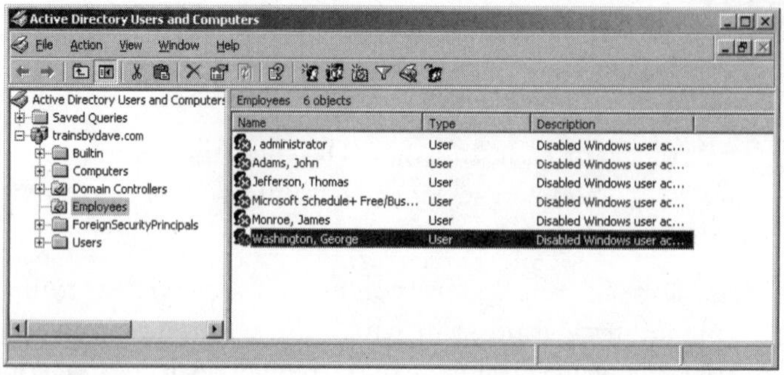

Figure 15-17. *Disabled accounts in the Employees OU.*

If you migrate the Windows NT accounts as illustrated earlier, you find that conflicting accounts do exist in the directory. Some accounts are listed twice—for example, James Monroe and jmonroe, which are therefore conflicting accounts. As is often the case, the naming conventions in a Windows NT accounts database are different from those in an Exchange 5.5 directory, hence, not all conflicting accounts will appear with the prefix or suffix that is specified for conflicting accounts in the User Account Migration Wizard.

To merge conflicting accounts, run the Active Directory Account Clean-up Wizard, or ADCLEAN. You can find this wizard in the \setup\i386\exchange\bin directory. Run it directly from the Exchange Server 2003 CD. Following the Welcome page is the Identify Merging Accounts page (Figure 15-18), which allows you to pinpoint where you want ADCLEAN to search for conflicting accounts. You can even specify whether you want to search only those accounts with Exchange mailboxes. Because we have yet to migrate any mailbox information, clear the Search Based On Exchange Mailboxes Only check box and accept the default to Search The Entire Directory.

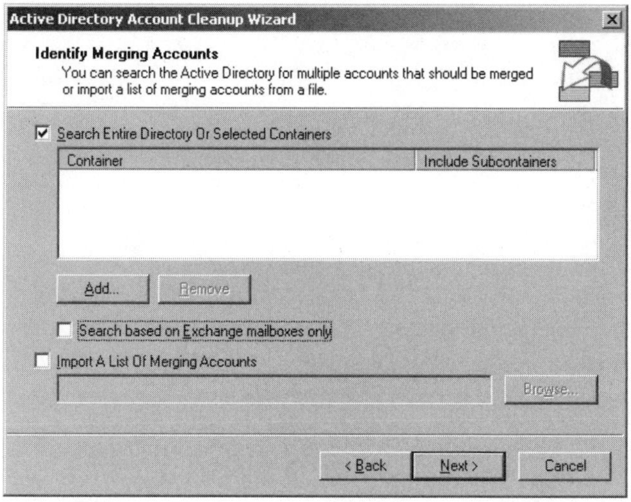

Figure 15-18. *Searching for conflicting accounts to merge.*

When you click Next, you are presented with a list of conflicting accounts. Notice in Figure 15-19 that our search has yielded four conflicting accounts, and that each has a different display name. To examine information for a particular account, such as the display name or logon ID, highlight the desired account and click the Account Information button (Figure 15-20).

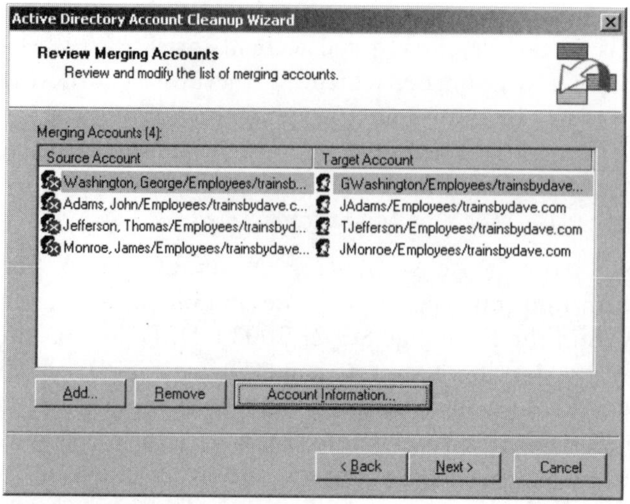

Figure 15-19. *Conflicting accounts in ADCLEAN.*

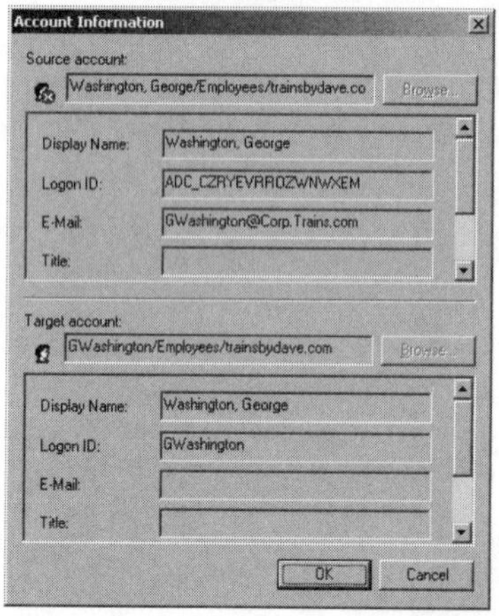

Figure 15-20. *Informational box providing details about a particular account.*

If you want to export the list of accounts to be merged to a spreadsheet for further analysis and modification, click Next. If you do not want to export the list, select the Begin The Merge Process Now check box (Figure 15-21) and then click Next to begin the merge process. A pop-up box will appear reminding you that merged accounts cannot be unmerged. Just click Yes and continue with the merge. After the merge is completed, the Account Merge Results box appears explaining how many accounts were found and how many were merged successfully (Figure 15-22).

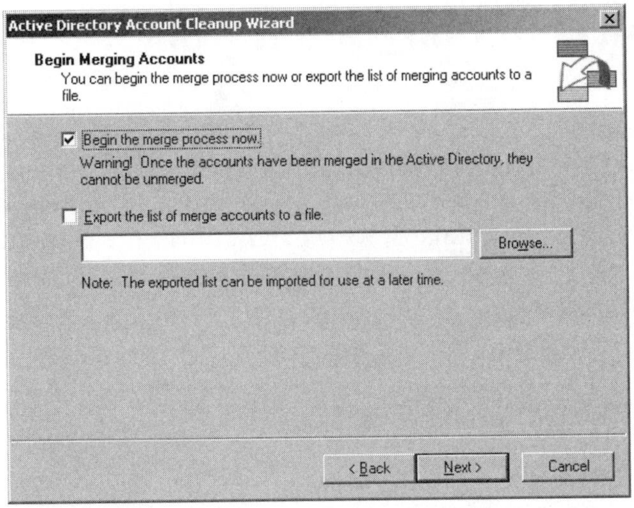

Figure 15-21. *Beginning the merge process.*

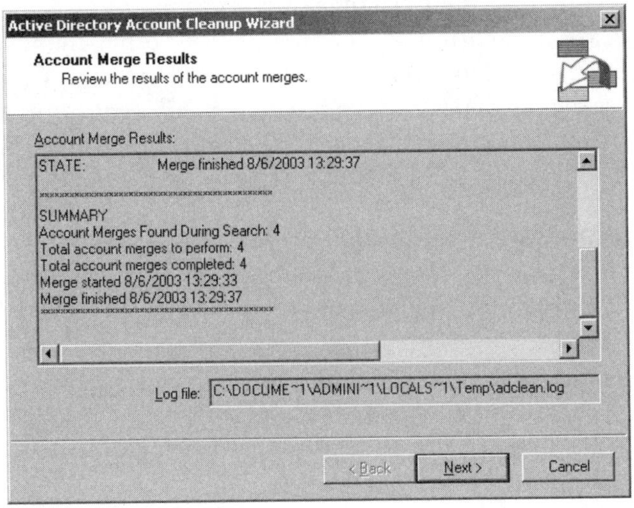

Figure 15-22. *Informational box indicating that the four accounts were merged successfully.*

Now no accounts should have conflicts. If conflicts remain, you should know why and have some idea about how to further troubleshoot those accounts. If you can't get an account to merge, try deleting it in Active Directory and running your migrations on it again. When you do, check the UAMW and ADCLEAN log files to learn about why an account isn't merging or migrating successfully.

Finishing the Account Migration from Exchange 5.5

At this point in our migration, you've performed only Exchange 5.5 directory uploads from the Corp site's recipient container. Our Active Directory accounts still do not have any Exchange information. Now you must create Connection Agreements with the other two Exchange 5.5 sites and upload the account information for the recipients in those sites. That will complete the account migration portion of the overall migration to Exchange Server 2003.

Installing Exchange 2003 into the Exchange 5.5 Site

We now have to install an Exchange Server 2003 in our Windows Server 2003 forest, so we'll need to run forestprep and domainprep. If you used the ADSIEdit tool, you'd find at this juncture that the Exchange organization object is not yet defined in the configuration partition of Active Directory other than to have a globally unique identifier (GUID), as Figure 15-23 illustrates. After installing the first Exchange Server 2003 into the Exchange 5.5 organization, this organization object is renamed to the Exchange 5.5 organization name—in our scenario, Trains.

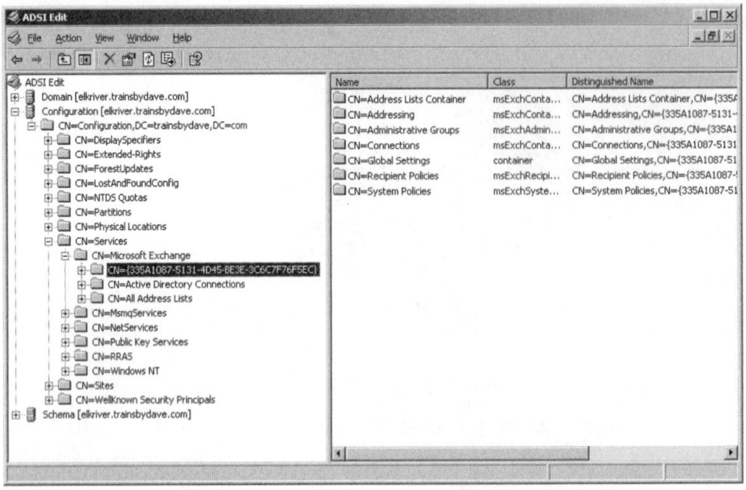

Figure 15-23. *Exchange organization object, defined so far in Active Directory with only a GUID.*

Let's start the Exchange Server 2003 installation in the Windows Server 2003 forest. Because we have the ADC installed, this installation will vary from a new installation of Exchange 2003 in that after the Component Selection page, you are presented with an Installation Type page in which you can choose to join an existing Exchange 5.5 organization or create a new organization. The choice you make here will have an impact on the rest of your migration. There is no rollback option, and you cannot change your mind later, so be sure you know exactly what you want to do.

If you choose to create a new organization, you are forced to use another utility to migrate the mailboxes. If you install Exchange Server 2003 into an Exchange 5.5 site, you can use the Move Mailbox tool and re-home your public folders to migrate information to Exchange 2003, as shown in Figure 15-24. Using Move Mailbox avoids a lot of headaches and saves you time, and it is our preferred approach.

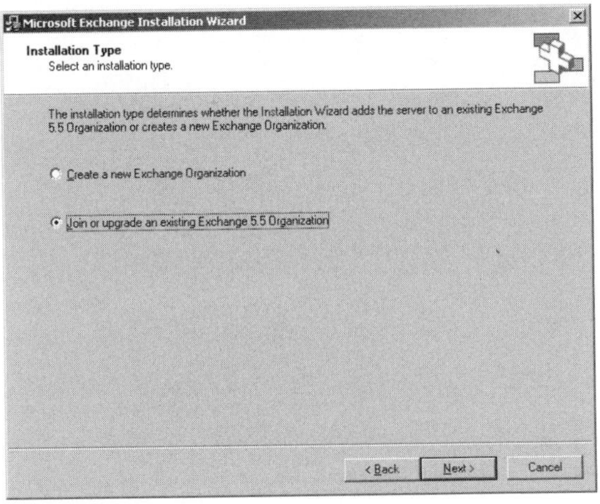

Figure 15-24. *Choosing to install Exchange Server 2003 into an Exchange 5.5 organization.*

In the next page, you are asked to enter the name of an Exchange 5.5 server so that you can join the Exchange 5.5 site. We'll enter the PDC1 server name to install our Exchange Server 2003 into the Corp 5.5 site. Click Next.

Remember that to install the Exchange Server 2003 into any Exchange 5.5 site, the account under which you are installing Exchange 2003 must have administrator permissions on the site and configuration objects in the target Exchange 5.5 site; thus, a trust relationship must be established between your forest and the host Windows NT domain for the Exchange 5.5 site. You also will want to add the Active Directory Domain Admins security group to the local Administrators group on the Windows NT server. Finally, to finish the Exchange 2003 installation, you'll need the Exchange 5.5 service account password. You can run through the rest of the Exchange 2003 installation without explanation since each page is self-explanatory.

> **Tip** Before finishing the Exchange 2003 installation, if you want to, you can install the Exchange 5.5 Administrator tool on your Exchange Server 2003 so that you can manage both environments from the same location. To do this, select a Custom installation in the Components Selection page, and then select to install the Exchange 5.5 Administrator tool.

After Exchange 2003 is finished installing, you will notice two things immediately. First, in the Exchange System Manager (ESM), the First Administrative Group is named after the site into which you installed Exchange Server 2003, which, in this case, is Corp. Second, the Exchange 5.5 Server appears as a transparent object. The transparency is a visual reminder that the server is running Exchange 5.5, not Exchange 2003 (Figure 15-25).

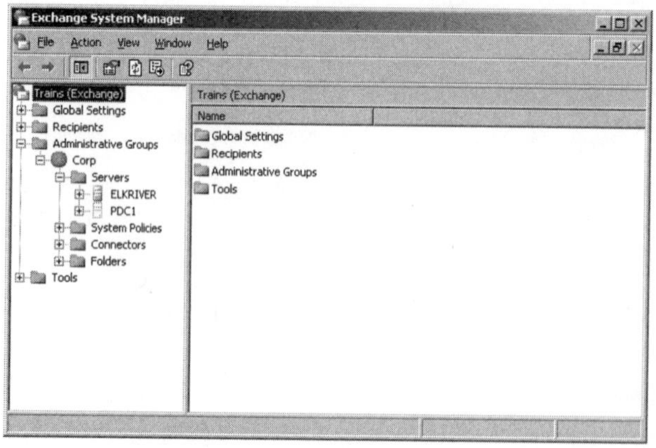

Figure 15-25. *ESM for Exchange 2003.*

Also notice in ADSI Edit that the organization object has been renamed to the same name as the Exchange 5.5 organization, in this case, Trains (Figure 15-26).

> **Planning** If you want a different organization name, you must rename the Exchange 5.5 organization *before* you install the first Exchange 2003 server into the organization. You can do this using the Raw Properties option of the Exchange 5.5 Administrator. To run the Administrator in this mode, navigate to the \exchsrvr\bin directory from a command prompt, and type *admin /r*. From there, you should be able to open the properties of the organization object and change the display name of the organization. Exchange 2003 picks up this display name and uses it for the organization name in Active Directory.

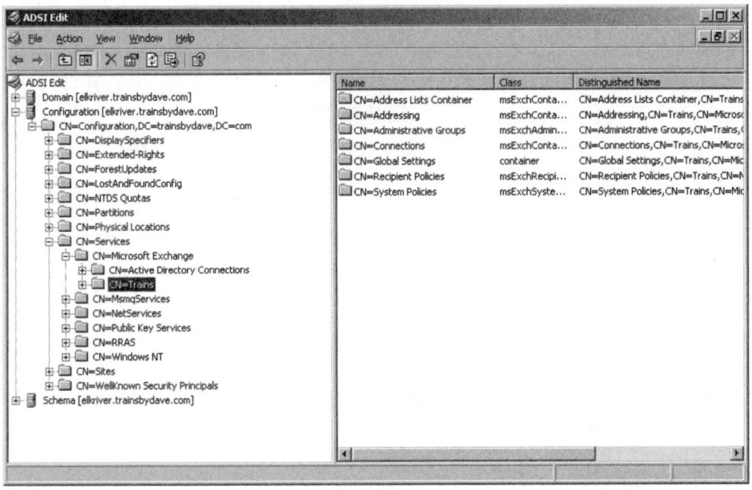

Figure 15-26. *The organization object renamed to the same name as the Exchange 5.5 organization—in this case, Trains.*

In the Exchange 5.5 Administrator, the Exchange Server 2003 appears in the Corp site as another server. Also, when the Exchange Server 2003 is highlighted, in the right pane appears (with other objects) the Site Replication Service (SRS). (We discuss the SRS in Chapter 16, but briefly, the SRS acts like the directory service on an Exchange 5.5 server but replicates site and configuration information back to the Active Directory configuration partition.) Because of the SRS's involvement in the ESM, other sites in the Exchange 5.5 organization appear as Administrative Groups (Figure 15-27), and the objects appear as transparent to indicate they are Exchange 5.5 objects.

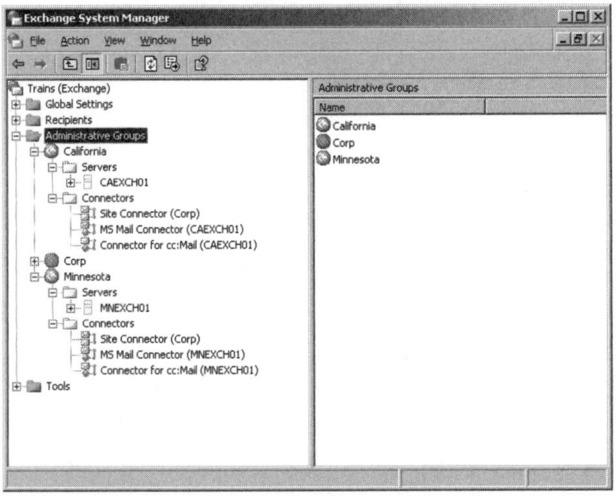

Figure 15-27. *ESM illustration of other Exchange 5.5 sites appearing as transparent objects.*

Your next step in the migration is to use the Move Mailbox feature in ADUC to transfer the mailboxes from the Exchange 5.5 server in the Corp site to the ElkRiver Exchange 2003 server. In the Exchange Tasks Wizard shown in Figure 15-28, the Exchange 5.5 servers (PDC1, MNEXCH01, and CAEXCH01) are listed with the Exchange Server 2003 (ElkRiver). This gives you the ability to use the same interface to move mailboxes between Exchange 2003 and Exchange 5.5 servers—very nice!

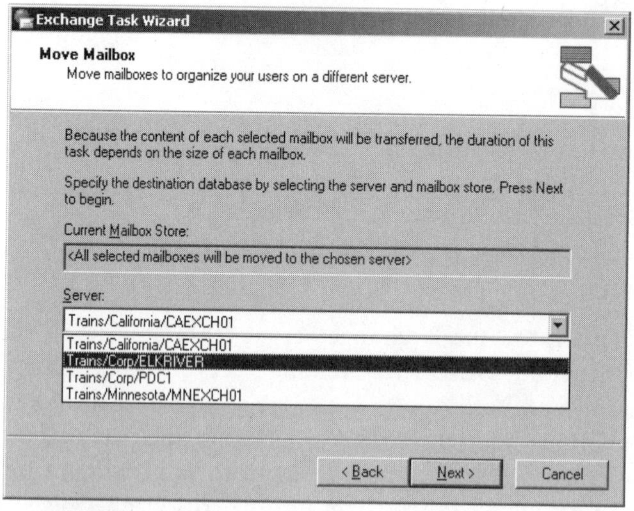

Figure 15-28. *Move Mailbox page in the Exchange Task Wizard in ADUC.*

Tip Depending on the number and size of mailboxes to be moved, the actual move can take minutes or hours. Since the user cannot access his mailbox while it is being used, best practice here is to perform this activity during off-business hours.

Using Exmerge

So far, you have moved the mailboxes from the Corp site to the Exchange Server 2003 and migrated all the user accounts. Now you must contend with the mailboxes that exist in the other two Exchange 5.5 sites. Our plan is to consolidate mailboxes from three sites into one Exchange server, but it is impossible to install two more Exchange 2003 servers into those sites and then use Move Mailbox to move those mailboxes to Exchange 2003 since our design calls for only one Exchange Server 2003.

This is when Exmerge (Microsoft Exchange Mailbox Merge Wizard) comes in handy. It is a sophisticated tool that offers multiple applications and configuration choices, but in our migration scenario, we will use it to export the contents of a mailbox in Exchange 5.5 to a .PST file. The contents can then be imported into a new mailbox for that user in Exchange 2003. Note that we'll need to do this for each site in a separate administrative action.

Note When migrating mailbox content between organizations or from an Exchange 5.5 site to an Exchange Server 2003 site that has no 2003 server installed in that site, Exmerge is really your only choice.

For Exmerge to run properly, the following must be handled:

- The account under which this tool is run must have invasive permissions on the source mailboxes.
- The target mailboxes must be previously created in Exchange 2003 and initialized. This means that creating the mailbox is not enough. You must also do one of two things: send e-mail to that mailbox to initialize it, and/or have the user connect to the mailbox using her Microsoft Outlook client.
- The account under which this tool is run must have Send As and Receive As permissions on the Exchange 2003 mailbox store. These permissions are denied by default, so you'll need to block permissions inheritance at the store level, copy the permissions so that the store retains its permissions, then change the default to allow this account these permissions. You'll also need to do this for any group of which the account is a member that has also been denied these permissions. For example, if you run this tool as the Administrator, you'll need to allow these permissions for the Administrator account and also for the Domain Admins and Enterprise Admins security groups.
- Do not run the ADC to upload Exchange 5.5 directory information for any of the accounts for which you will run Exmerge. In our scenario, when ADC was run, the Exchange 5.5 directory information pointed the Active Directory account back to the Exchange 5.5 server for mailbox information. Hence, we were unable to create a new mailbox in the 2003 databases because the account was already configured with a mailbox in the Exchange 5.5 databases. In this scenario, even though the mailbox can be exported to a .PST file, there is no method of importation. The only workaround is to not upload the Exchange 5.5 directory information and, after creating a new mailbox for that Active Directory account in the Exchange 2003 databases, use Exmerge to migrate the mailbox data.

Tip Common error messages are well documented in both TechNet (*http://www.microsoft.com/technet/*) and the document that accompanies Exmerge. Be sure to use these tools to help you troubleshoot your use of Exmerge.

Also note that in our scenario, we did not use the ADC to upload Exchange 5.5 directory information about those accounts outside the Corp site. Instead, we created mailboxes for them in our Exchange 2003 databases and then initialized each mailbox by sending an e-mail to it. We'll illustrate using Exmerge with three accounts instead of the 15 or more accounts that we have been using in our example.

To run Exmerge, start the program and move past the Welcome page. On the next page, choose to perform the extraction and importation in one step. Note that we are also selecting to delete the .PST file after it has been imported (Figure 15-29).

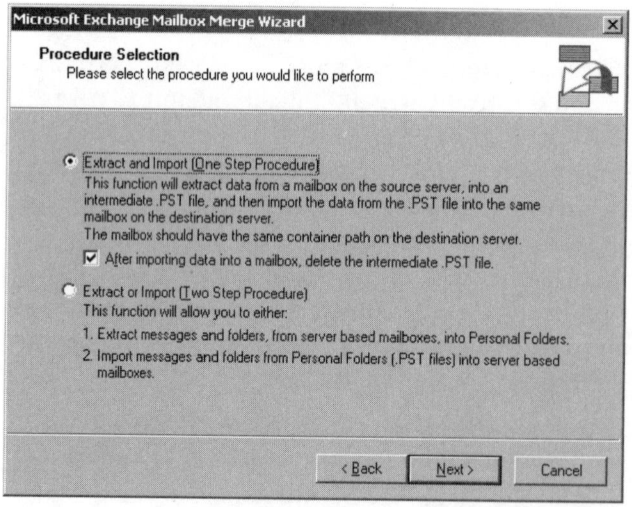

Figure 15-29. *The Procedure Selection page in the Exmerge Wizard.*

The next two pages you encounter ask for the source and target server information. After these pages are populated, we confirm the options we want by clicking the Options button:

- Select User Messages and Folders on the Data tab.
- Select Merge Data Into The Target Store on the Import Procedure tab.

- Leave the default on the Folders tab (no folders are ignored).
- Accept the default of All Dates on the Dates tab.
- Leave all input boxes empty on the Message Details tab.

After entering the server information, click Next to display the Mailbox Selection page (Figure 15-30). If your permissions are configured correctly on the source server, a list of mailboxes is shown. Highlight the mailboxes you want to migrate. In our example, we selected three mailboxes to migrate. Click Next.

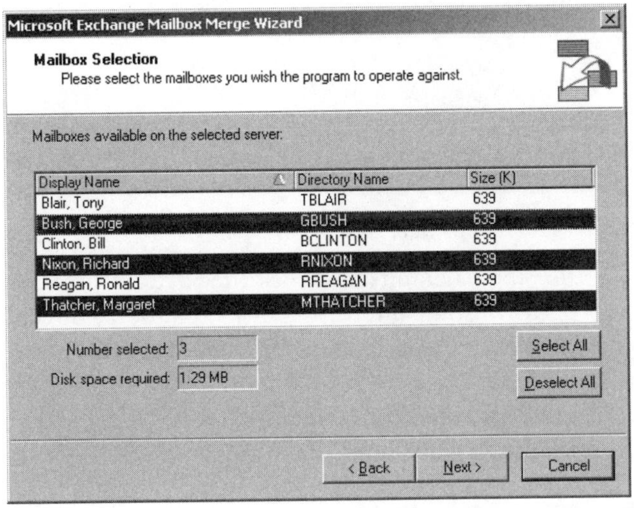

Figure 15-30. *Selecting the mailboxes to be merged using the Exmerge Wizard.*

The next page prompts you for the locale you want to use. Accept the default and move on to the Target Directory page, which asks you to enter the location where the .PST files are to be written. We created a unique path to ensure that the .PST files can be easily found. To do this, click the Change Folder button and select a folder. In our example (Figure 15-31), we selected the folder named pstfiles. Note that we selected a partition that could easily hold the amount of information we are migrating.

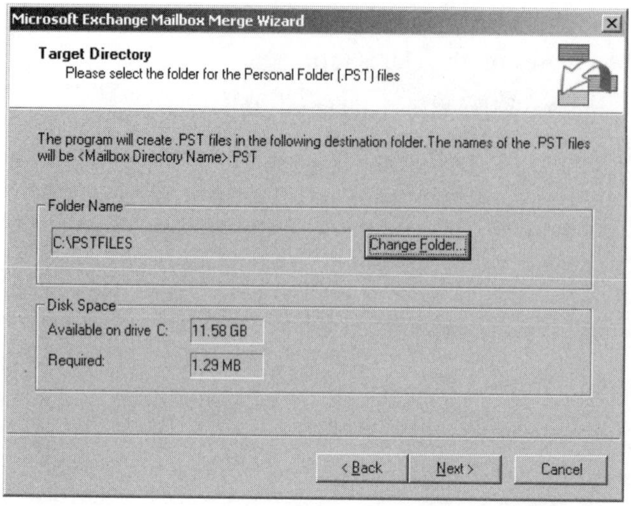

Figure 15-31. *Selecting the folder where .PST files will be written.*

On the next page, accept the File Name defaults and click the Save Settings button. (From this page, you can perform some interesting tasks that don't directly relate to our migration scenario. You can read more about what the page has to offer in the Exmerge documentation.) Click Next to start the migration of the user's mailbox data to the .PST file and then to the mailbox in Exchange 2003. A status box (Figure 15-32) provides details about the migration.

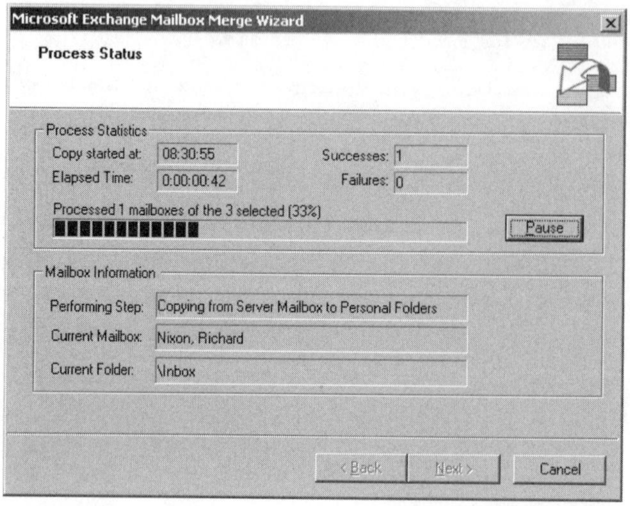

Figure 15-32. *Migration status box in the Exmerge Wizard.*

Finally, you can verify that the data has been transferred by looking at the user's mailbox information in the ESM and seeing that mailboxes both exist and have items inside them (Figure 15-33).

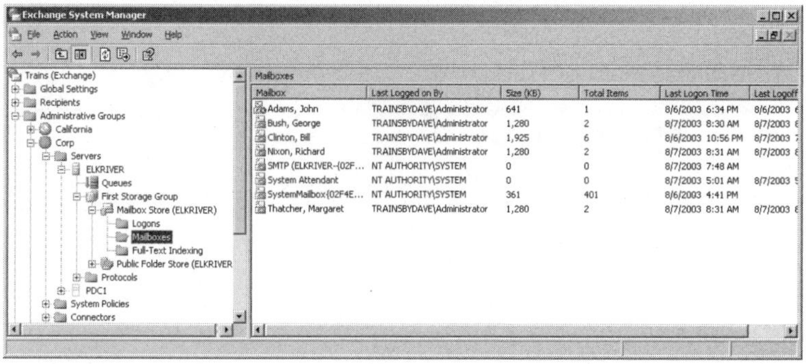

Figure 15-33. *Mailbox item information in the ESM.*

You might have a few problems the first time you use Exmerge, but eventually you'll find this tool easy to use and very reliable. Using this tool will require some extra administrative effort on your part if you are migrating hundreds or thousands of mailboxes, but the effort will pay off when the contents are migrated to the new mailboxes and your users find their mailbox information to be in order.

Migrating Public Folders

In our scenario, the best way to migrate public folder information is to perform two basic steps:

1. Replicate and re-home all the public folders in the Exchange 5.5 system to the Corp site.
2. Replicate and re-home all the public folders in the Corp site to the ElkRiver Exchange 2003 server.

Installing an Exchange 2003 server into the Exchange 5.5 organization allows you to use replication to move public folder information to the new Exchange platform rather than use the Public Folder Connector Agreement in the ADC. Replication is the preferred method of migrating public folder information to the Exchange 2003 system.

Don't forget to replicate all public folders with content, the Schedule+ Free Busy folders, the Offline Address Book folder, and the Organizational forms folder. Pay attention to all your system public folders. For example, if you don't replicate the Schedule+ Free Busy folder, calendar information will be lost.

Re-homing public folders in Exchange 2003 is not difficult. Just replicate the folders to Exchange 2003 and then remove the Exchange 5.5 server from the replication tab. Because public folders in Exchange 2003 have no "home," all that is needed is a single read/write replication of the folder in the Exchange 2003 environment.

Finishing the Migration

To finish the migration, you have to complete a few final tasks:

1. Upgrade your connectors.
2. Upgrade the Internet Mail Connector.
3. Upgrade foreign connectors, if necessary.
4. Replace the Gateway Address Routing Table (GWART) with the Link State Table (LST).

Connector Upgrades

If you are in a multi-site, multi-routing group environment and need to upgrade your connectors, you must upgrade them to be Routing Group Connectors (RGCs). This process will work fine because Exchange 2003 servers use RPCs to talk to a Site Connector and SMTP to talk to a Routing Group Connector.

If you are upgrading an X.400 Connector, you'll be happy to learn that the X.400 Connector is preserved, but TP4 information isn't preserved because TP4 is not supported in Windows Server 2003.

Internet Mail Connector Upgrade

If you are upgrading an Internet Mail Connector (IMC), you need to know that the IMC is upgraded to an SMTP Connector. The configuration information is preserved in the connector. However, the SMTP Connector isn't necessary for normal SMTP traffic: the SMTP Virtual Server (VS) can handle this function quite well.

If you need to remove the IMC from your mixed environment or reroute your Exchange 2003 server incoming e-mail at the firewall, perform the following steps. First, swap Exchange 2003 server IP addresses with IP addresses of the Exchange 5.5 IMC server. Then run Ipconfig /flushdns and Ipconfig /registerdns at the command prompt to re-register Exchange 2003 with DNS. Restart the Net Logon service on Exchange 2003 and update your MX records to reflect any changes. Once you accomplish this, remove the IMC on the Exchange 5.5

server. After the IMC is removed, recalculate the Gateway Address Routing Table (GWART) in Exchange 5.5.

Upgrading Foreign Connectors

Foreign connectors such as MSMail, IBM Lotus cc:Mail, and Lotus Notes are preserved along with their configuration information. Any other connectors, such as TP4, RAS, SNADS, OfficeVision, and connectors developed using the Exchange 2000 Server Resource Kit, are not preserved or supported in Exchange 2003. If you need them after the upgrade, leave Exchange 2003 in mixed mode and keep an Exchange 5.5 server on hand to run them. You'll need to preserve an Exchange 5.5 server until the connectors are no longer needed.

GWART and LST

Regarding keeping track of link state information, the LST is smarter, faster, and better at it than the GWART and thus replaces the GWART. The ADC and the SRS replicate Exchange 5.5 routing information to the LST, but the state information on Exchange 5.5 connectors won't be available in the LST. In addition, the GWART isn't sophisticated enough to include state information from the LST.

Decommissioning and Removing the Last Exchange 5.5 Server and Site

After all the information has been migrated to Exchange 2003, you need to decommission the Exchange 5.5 servers before switching to native mode in Exchange Server 2003. Do not skip this part of the process, or the configuration information in Exchange 2003 will always refer to Exchange 5.5 servers that no longer exist.

To remove the last Exchange 5.5 server in a site and to remove the last Exchange 5.5 site in the organization, stop the Exchange 5.5 Exchange services and disable the System Attendant on each Exchange 5.5 server. Then, from the Exchange 2003 server, use the Exchange 5.5 Admin Program to connect to the Exchange Server 2003 server. (This might seem a bit counterintuitive.)

Delete the Exchange 5.5 server from the site and then force replication on the Connection Agreement for that site. Wait for the Exchange 5.5 server to disappear. After you have done this for all the Exchange 5.5 Servers, use the ESM to delete the SRS. Then delete the recipient and public folder Connection

Agreements in the ADC snap-in. After doing this, remove the ADC in Add/Remove Programs.

Points to Remember

Here are some points to note:

- You can't use the ESM to remove Exchange 5.5 servers from an Admin Group; you must use the Exchange 5.5 Admin program.
- You must log on with an account that has Full Exchange Administrator permissions in Exchange 2003 and Service Account Admin permissions on the Exchange 5.5 site. You might want to create a special account for this purpose.
- You can't delete an Exchange 5.5 server that you're connected to using the Admin program.

After all the Exchange 5.5 Servers are removed, you can switch to native mode in Exchange Server 2003. Until then, you must remain in mixed mode to safely remove all the Exchange 5.5 servers.

Considering a Rollback

If you need to roll back changes, you can do so to some degree but it will require a great deal of effort. If you are performing an in-place upgrade, you must restore the server from tape backup. Be sure to replace all files. This is the only way to roll back an in-place upgrade.

To roll back partially upgraded organizations, you'll need to do the following:

- Move all mailboxes back to the 5.5 servers.
- Remove entries on the Address Space tab in all connectors for all Exchange 2003 servers.
- Rebuild the GWART.
- Re-home public folders on Exchange 5.5 servers.

The point of no return on a rollback for partially upgraded organizations is not clearly defined, but it is something that you need to consider. The farther into the migration process you go, the more difficult rolling back to Exchange 5.5 will be. And there will be a point at which it will be easier to fix the current problems in Exchange 2003 than to roll back to Exchange 5.5.

Recommendations

Here are a few recommendations:

- Perform the migration in a lab environment and take note of how you would roll back at each point along the way.
- When you join an Exchange 2003 server with the Exchange 5.5 organization, you've really reached a watershed that is difficult to roll back because the configuration of both Exchange platforms has been replicated to the Exchange 5.5 directory and Active Directory. It is difficult, but not impossible, to cleanly remove all this replicated information.
- It is very easy to delete and re-migrate user accounts using ADMT and the ADC. If you don't like the results of your account migration with ADMT, just delete them in Active Directory and start over.
- After accounts, mailboxes, and public folder information has been successfully migrated to Exchange 2003, rollback will be very time-consuming and probably not worth the effort.
- In your plan, note the point at which you will no longer consider a rollback to Exchange 5.5 to be feasible and then work out contingency plans to fix unforeseen problems after that point.

Summary

In this chapter, you learned how to perform a migration from Exchange 5.5 to Exchange Server 2003. We described the ADC, the ADMT, and Exmerge, and provided recommendations for decisions that will affect your migration. In the next chapter, we'll discuss Exchange Server 2003 and Exchange 5.5 coexistence issues.

Chapter 16

Coexisting with Previous Versions of Exchange

Many of you who pick up this book are facing coexistence—that is, interoperability—with previous versions of Microsoft Exchange. You might be migrating from Microsoft Exchange Server 5.5 to Microsoft Exchange Server 2003, or upgrading from Exchange Server 2003. In either case, the upgrades or migrations will at some point take place over a period of time, and you will need to contend with coexistence issues.

To make the migration go more smoothly and enable a seamless coexistence with Exchange Server 5.x, Microsoft has created a couple of services—enhanced connectors that make it possible for two different versions of Exchange to exist together in the same environment. Knowing how to use these two tools will go a long way toward making the migration straightforward and relatively painless for both you and your users.

In this chapter, the word "coexistence" describes a configuration in which different versions of Exchange Server are installed in the same Exchange organization at the same time. This type of configuration is known as a *mixed-mode* configuration. Running Exchange Server 2003 in mixed mode means that Exchange Server 2003 can interoperate with previous versions of Exchange Server and accommodate the differences between the various versions.

When running in mixed mode, rules that apply to earlier versions of Exchange Server also apply to Exchange Server 2003. Moreover, after you install Exchange Server 2003, you can install earlier versions of Exchange into the organization and experience interoperability between the platforms.

If you move Exchange 2003 to *native mode*, you're removing interoperability between previous versions of Exchange and Exchange 2003 in your organization. Because this is a one-time, no-going-back decision, before you switch to native mode, you must be certain that you'll never again need to interoperate with an earlier version of Exchange.

Real World Mixed Mode vs. Native Mode

Although running Exchange Server 2003 in mixed mode allows you to interoperate with Exchange 5.5 systems, running Exchange 2003 in native mode means that you've closed the door on interoperability with previous versions of Exchange. Here are some guidelines to determine whether you are ready to switch to native mode:

- You no longer have Exchange 5.5 servers in your organization.
- You have no plans to add Exchange 5.5 servers to your organization in the future—for example, as a result of a merger or the acquisition of a company with Exchange 5.5 servers.
- Your organization will never require interoperability between your Exchange 2003 servers and previous versions of Exchange Server. (Connectors can provide connectivity between your servers; however, administration of servers is limited to Exchange 2003 servers.)
- Your organization does not use any connectors or gateway applications that run only on Exchange Server 5.5.

To switch to native mode in the Exchange System snap-in, navigate to the organization that you want to switch to native mode, right-click the organization's name, and select Properties. On the General tab of the organization property sheet, change the operation mode to Native Mode.

It is important to remember that once you have switched to native mode, your Exchange 2003 organization is no longer interoperable with Exchange 5.5 systems and the change cannot be reversed.

If you are currently running Exchange 5.5, during the Exchange Server 2003 setup, you are given the option of either joining the existing site or creating a new organization. Because you can have only one Exchange 2003 organization per Active Directory forest, you'll need to decide whether you should install your first Exchange 2003 server into your Exchange 5.x site. If you do, the existing Exchange 5.x organization name will be replicated to Active Directory as the Exchange 2003 organization name. If you choose not to install Exchange Server 2003 into your Exchange 5.x organization, you'll need to choose a unique organization name, and you'll be forced to use a connector to transfer messages between the two organizations. In this case, you will have two separate Exchange organizations, and they will connect to each other as foreign e-mail systems.

In a mixed-mode organization, the Exchange System snap-in shows all Exchange servers installed in the organization, but non–Exchange 2003 servers appear as transparent objects. For example, in Figure 16-1, the PDC1 server is an Exchange 5.5 server.

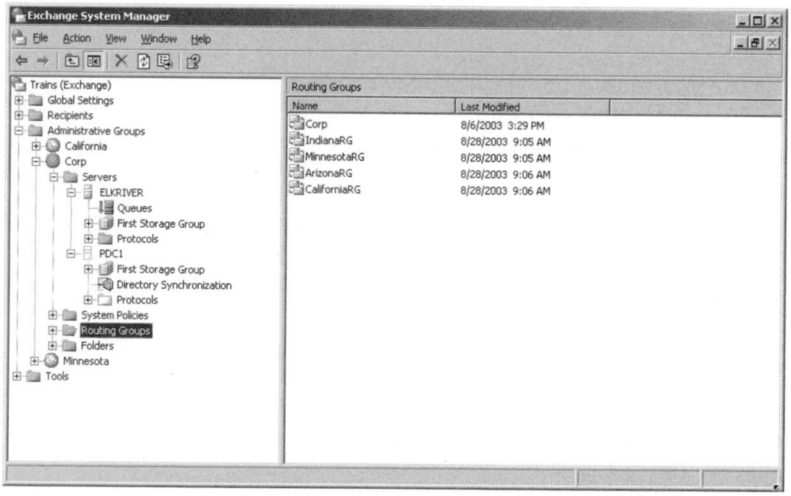

Figure 16-1. *An Exchange 5.5 server (PDC1) in the Exchange System snap-in.*

When the first Exchange 2003 server is installed into an existing Exchange 4.x or 5.x organization, two additional services are installed automatically: Site Replication Service (SRS) and the Active Directory Connector (ADC) service. These two components work together to provide replication between the Exchange 4.x and 5.x servers and Exchange Server 2003. *Intrasite replication* occurs using remote procedure calls (RPCs), and *intersite replication* is handled via directory services (mail-based) transfer. A connection agreement is automatically established in the ADC service between Active Directory and the SRS database to allow directory replication to occur. (Connection agreements are discussed later in this chapter, in the section "Active Directory Connector.") The other Exchange 4.x and 5.x servers will see the Exchange 2003 server as just another 5.x server.

Coexisting with the Exchange 5.x Directory

As we discussed in Chapter 4, "Understanding Windows Server 2003 Integration," Active Directory has three naming partitions: configuration, schema, and domain. In this section, we will primarily be concerned with the configuration and domain naming partitions of Active Directory and how SRS and the ADC service allow the Exchange 5.x directory and the configuration and domain partitions of Active Directory to coexist. (The authors recognize that Exchange 4.x is built on directory services as well. However, for the sake of this discussion, we will use the phrase "Exchange 5.x" to refer to all previous Exchange systems, including both the 4.x and 5.x platforms.) Let's spend some time looking at each of these services.

Site Replication Service

Site Replication Service is responsible for replicating Exchange 5.x site and configuration information to the configuration naming partition of Active Directory when an Exchange 2003 server belongs to an existing Exchange 5.5 site. This allows the Exchange 2003 server to be represented in the Exchange site server list so that earlier versions of Exchange Server can send messages to and receive messages from the Exchange 2003 server.

SRS consists of a service that is activated and a database that is initialized when the first Exchange 2003 server is introduced into a legacy Exchange site. Activation can also occur when an Exchange 5.5 directory replication bridgehead server is upgraded to Exchange Server 2003. If you install additional Exchange 2003 servers into the Exchange 5.5 organization, these servers will include SRS, but SRS will be disabled. The components of SRS are as follows:

- Site Replication Service application (Srsmain.exe)
- Site Consistency Checker (runs as part of Srs.exe)
- SRS database (Srs.edb) and transaction logs (ESE98 format)

Even though SRS is similar to the Exchange 5.5 directory service, its Name Service Provider Interface (NSPI) is disabled to prevent Microsoft Outlook clients from connecting to and using the Exchange 2003 directory for name resolution. If the NSPI were activated, Outlook clients could attempt name resolution in the wrong directory, leading to name resolution errors.

SRS must also run LDAP in order to communicate with Active Directory. Because the Microsoft Windows Server 2003 operating system also uses LDAP and locks the well-known port 389 for its own use, SRS defaults to using port 379 for its LDAP communications. No special configuration is needed for SRS to communicate with Active Directory using LDAP.

Unlike the ADC service, which we will discuss in a moment, SRS automatically installs its own connection agreement (Config CA). The agreement is between

SRS and Active Directory rather than between Active Directory and the Exchange 5.5 directory. Config CA is the pathway through which SRS on the Exchange 2003 server passes configuration-naming data to Active Directory. This is a read-only agreement, and it can be seen in the Active Directory Connector Management snap-in, shown in Figure 16-2. (Read-only and other types of agreements are discussed more fully later in this chapter in the section "Active Directory Connector.")

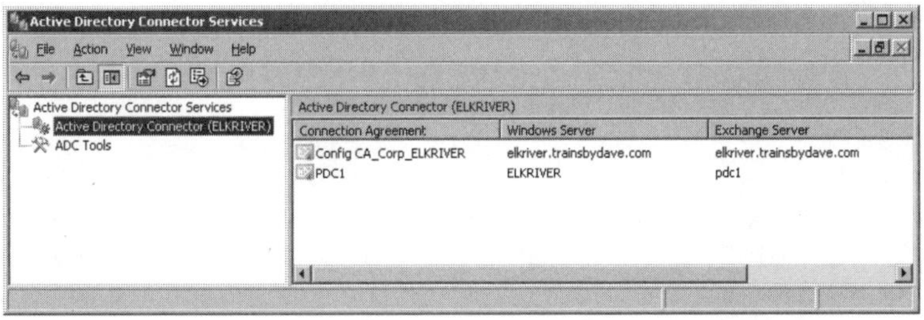

Figure 16-2. *Read-only connection agreement in the Active Directory Connector Management snap-in.*

To communicate with Exchange 5.x servers, SRS uses RPCs. Thus, to the Exchange 5.x servers, Exchange Server 2003, via SRS, looks like another Exchange 5.x server. If an Exchange 5.x bridgehead server is upgraded to Exchange Server 2003, SRS will notice this and communicate with that bridgehead server using SMTP.

Since SRS is a read-only service, meaning that it can't be configured, there isn't a great deal to manage. However, a couple of points are worth noting. First, this is a two-way connection agreement that cannot be modified. Second, recall that the agreement is between Active Directory and SRS. This can look confusing when you first encounter the interface because the agreement reports the Exchange server and the Windows Server 2003 server as the same server. You'll be creating a connection "between" the same server because the server hosting the Exchange 2003 server that is installed into your Exchange 5.5 site is also a domain controller in the Windows Server 2003 Active Directory. This is most clearly seen on the Connections tab of the property sheet for the connection agreement, as illustrated in Figure 16-3.

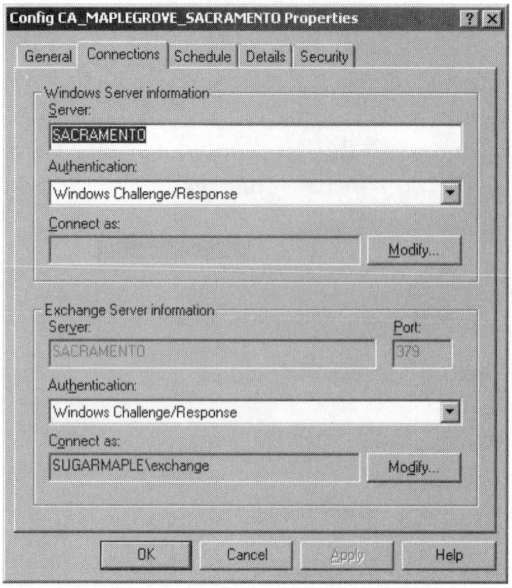

Figure 16-3. *Connection agreement "between" the same server.*

Site Consistency Checker

The Site Consistency Checker (SCC) is an updated version of the Knowledge Consistency Checker from Exchange Server 5.5 and runs inside SRS. It ensures that knowledge consistency is maintained for sites and administrative groups when interoperating between Exchange Server 5.5 and Exchange Server 2003. In addition, in a large organization with many Exchange 5.5 sites, a triangulation of replication links, which would create duplicate replication paths, could be created as sites are migrated from Exchange Server 5.5 to Exchange Server 2003. The SCC ensures that as new replication links are created, triangulation is avoided in the link topology.

SRS Database

SRS uses the Extensible Storage Engine (ESE) database technology. You'll find that it installs the same set of databases and transaction logs as a storage group. By default, these files are stored in the Exchsrv\srsdata folder. Unlike the stores in a storage group, the SRS database cannot be mounted or dismounted, but you can start and stop SRS in the Services utility.

Active Directory Connector

The Active Directory Connector is a service that runs on your Windows Server 2003 domain controller and allows you to synchronize your Exchange Server 5.5 and Windows Server 2003 directories. Unlike SRS, which replicates information between an Exchange 5.x organization and the configuration naming partition in Active Directory, the ADC service replicates information between the Exchange 5.x directory and the domain partition in Active Directory.

The ADC service comes in two versions: one ships with Windows Server 2003, and the other ships with Exchange Server 2003. The Windows Server 2003 version of the ADC service allows directory information in your Exchange Server 5.5 organization to be replicated to the Windows Server 2003 Active Directory. The Exchange 2003 version of the ADC service lets you synchronize Exchange Server 5.5 directory information with Windows Server 2003. It also works with SRS. If you've installed the Active Directory Connector in Windows Server 2003, Exchange Server automatically updates it to the Exchange 2003 version when you install Exchange Server 2003.

After you've synchronized the directories, as described in the sections that follow, Windows Server 2003 Active Directory generates the Global Address List of mail-enabled users for those users who connect to the Exchange 2003 server. Users connecting to the Exchange Server 5.5 directory will continue to access the Global Address List from the Exchange Directory Store.

Planning Connection Agreements in Active Directory Connector Service

You configure synchronization between your two directories by defining connection agreements that the ADC service manages. A *connection agreement* is just that—an agreement that you manually instantiate to define how directory information is synchronized between the two directories. You will define at least one primary connection agreement and one or more nonprimary connection agreements. The agreements must contain server names, objects to synchronize, target containers, and a synchronization schedule.

Connection agreements are either one-way or two-way. As the name implies, a *one-way connection agreement* allows directory information to flow in only one direction—from the directory you specify to the directory to which the connection agreement connects. For example, if a connection agreement is configured as one-way from directory D1 to directory D2, any changes made to objects in the D1 directory will be replicated to the D2 directory. However, changes made to objects in the D2 directory will not be replicated to the D1 directory. A *two-way connection agreement* allows replication to flow in both directions. Hence, changes made to objects in either directory are replicated.

When setting up your connection agreements, strive to match one or more containers in one directory with one or more containers in the other directory. Your environment, future plans, and network administrative model will all affect your choice. For instance, you can synchronize the default Recipients container in your Exchange 5.5 site with one Active Directory container—perhaps the Users organizational unit (OU). In this scenario, any subcontainers in the Recipients container will be created automatically under the Users OU, as shown in Figure 16-4.

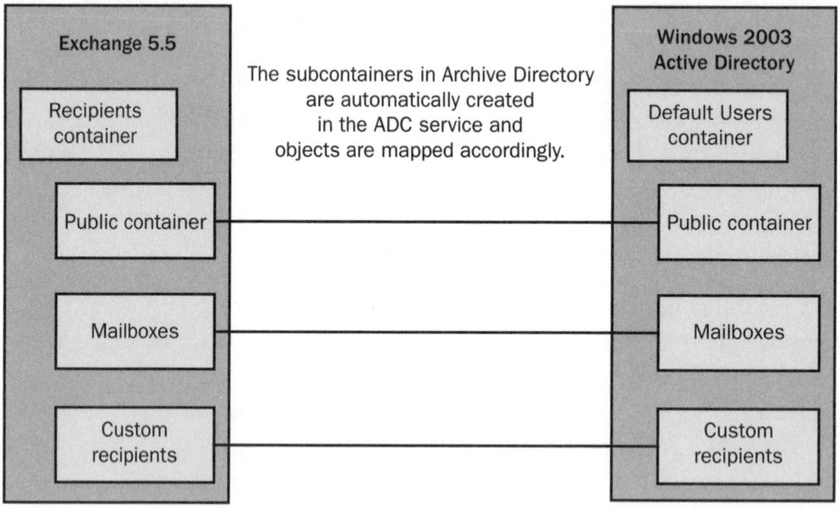

Figure 16-4. *Container synchronization.*

You can also synchronize from one Exchange container to multiple Active Directory containers by choosing to replicate one object class to one Active Directory OU and another object class to another Active Directory OU. For instance, if all your Exchange 5.5 recipients were created in the default Recipients container, you could choose to replicate your user objects to a Users OU in Active Directory and your custom recipients to a Contacts OU, as shown in Figure 16-5.

By the same token, you can synchronize multiple Exchange containers with multiple Active Directory containers or synchronize multiple Active Directory containers with multiple Exchange containers. Moreover, you can configure each connection agreement to synchronize single or multiple object types. This service gives you the opportunity to rearrange your object hierarchy in Active Directory.

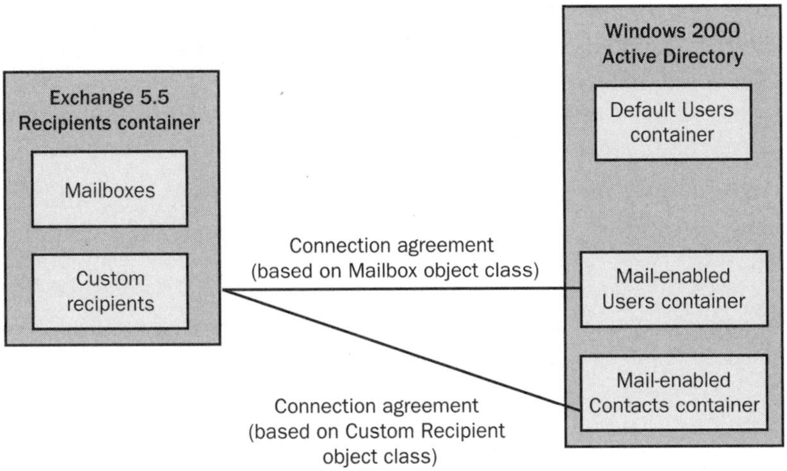

Figure 16-5. *Object class synchronization.*

Installing the ADC Service

You install the ADC service from the ADC folder on the Exchange 2003 companion CD-ROM. During the installation, the installation wizard prompts you to choose the Microsoft Active Directory Connector Service Component, the Microsoft Active Directory Connector Management Components, or both (Figure 16-6). Selecting Microsoft Active Directory Connector Service Component installs the ADC service (Adc.exe). Selecting Microsoft Active Directory Connector Management Components installs the Active Directory Connector Management snap-in into a separate Microsoft Management Console (MMC).

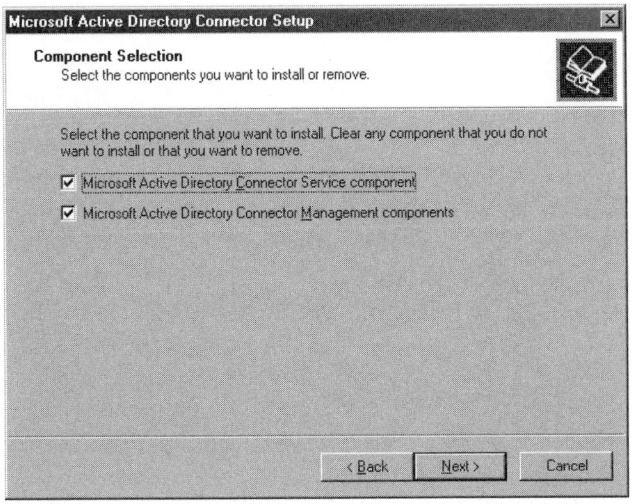

Figure 16-6. *ADC service installation choices.*

The user account that you log on with to install the ADC service must have the ability to modify the schema; otherwise, you'll receive an error message. However, if Exchange Server 2003 is already installed somewhere in your Windows Server 2003 forest, schema modifications are not necessary when installing the ADC service, since the schema has already been extended.

Next, the installation wizard asks for a location for the installation files and for the administrator name and password in the Windows Server 2003 domain. The final installation screen asks you to finish the installation.

> **Tip** After you've migrated all of your directory information to Windows Server 2003 and fully implemented Exchange Server 2003, you'll no longer need the Active Directory Connector service because you'll no longer have any Exchange 5.5 servers. If you choose to uninstall the ADC service, you must first delete all the connection agreements you defined on the local server. Best practice would be to do this after you have switched your Exchange 2003 organization to native mode.

Configuring the Active Directory Connector Service

Once you've installed the ADC service, you'll need to create the primary connection agreement. To do so, launch the ADC service snap-in by choosing Active Directory Connector from the Microsoft Exchange menu. Right-click the server name, point to New, and choose either Recipient Connection Agreement or Public Folder Connection Agreement. For our discussion in this chapter, we'll use Recipient Connection Agreement. You'll need to give your connection agreement a name that describes the function it will serve. Figure 16-7 illustrates how to name a two-way agreement.

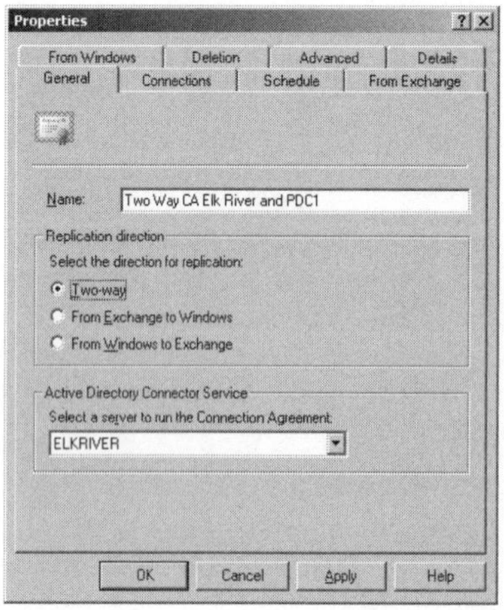

Figure 16-7. *Naming a two-way connection agreement.*

Connections Tab On the Connections tab shown in Figure 16-8, we've configured the Connect As values for each server because these two servers are in different domains and we are writing from each directory to each directory. If you have different domains, which will usually be the case when migrating from Exchange Server 5.x to Exchange 2003, you will need to enter Connect As values for each directory to which you would like to write information that is generated in the other directory.

You can also specify the port number that will be used by Exchange Server 5.5. You'll need to change this port number if your Exchange 5.5 server is running on a Windows Server 2003 domain controller. When Windows Server 2003 boots up, the Active Directory LDAP services start before any Exchange services, and the LDAP service locks port 389 (the default LDAP port) for its own use. If you leave the port number at 389 for the ADC service to use in this scenario, the ADC will fail to bind to the Exchange directory because of a port number conflict. Most administrators choose port 390 in this situation.

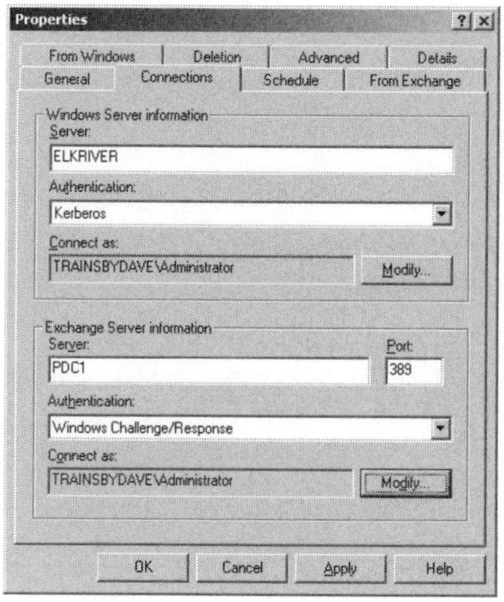

Figure 16-8. *Connections tab of the ADC service property sheet.*

Tip If you're running Exchange Server 5.5 on a Microsoft Windows NT 4 server, be sure to specify the domain name in front of the Windows NT 4 user name that you use to log on to the domain (for example, *domain name\username*). If you don't specify the domain name, you'll receive an 8026 error message in the Event Viewer application log informing you that the bind was unsuccessful.

Schedule Tab You configure the replication interval for the connection agreement on the Schedule tab (Figure 16-9). Setting the replication interval to Always will cause the connection agreement to replicate every 15 minutes. You can force the entire directory to replicate the next time the software runs the agreement, whether it runs on a predetermined schedule or not, by selecting the Replicate The Entire Directory The Next Time The Agreement Is Run check box. Selecting this option sets the *msExchServerXHighestUSN* attribute to 0 and the *msExchDoFullReplication* attribute to True for the connection agreement.

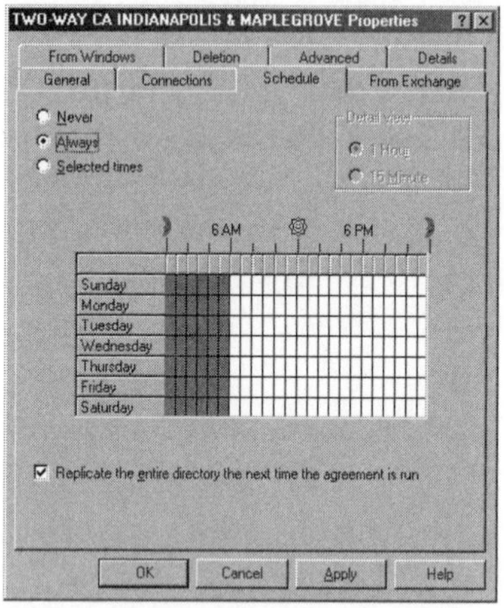

Figure 16-9. *Schedule tab of the ADC service property sheet.*

From Exchange and From Windows Tabs The From Exchange tab (Figure 16-10) and the From Windows tab (Figure 16-11) let you set which containers and objects in your Exchange 5.5 site will replicate to Windows Server 2003 Active Directory and vice versa.

By default, each Exchange site has one Recipients container. If you've created multiple subcontainers under the Recipients container, you have several options for replicating your objects to Windows Server 2003. If you want to retain the same container structure in Active Directory, create one connection agreement and choose the Exchange site as the source container. Active Directory will automatically create the same container structure in its directory and populate it accordingly. If you want to consolidate several Exchange containers into one container in Active Directory, create one connection agreement and individually choose each of the containers as the source, pointing them to the same container in Active Directory.

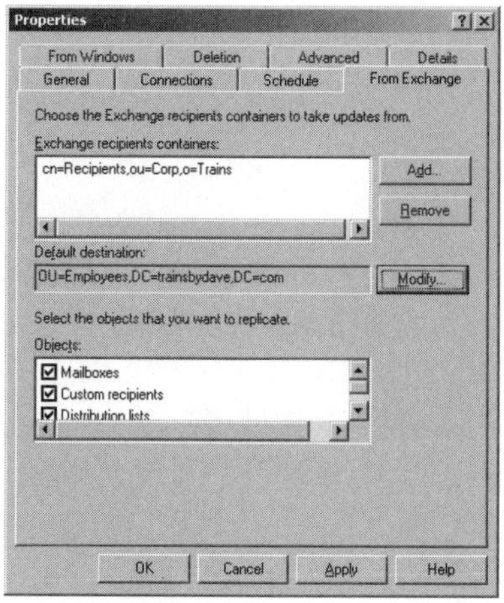

Figure 16-10. *From Exchange tab of the ADC service property sheet.*

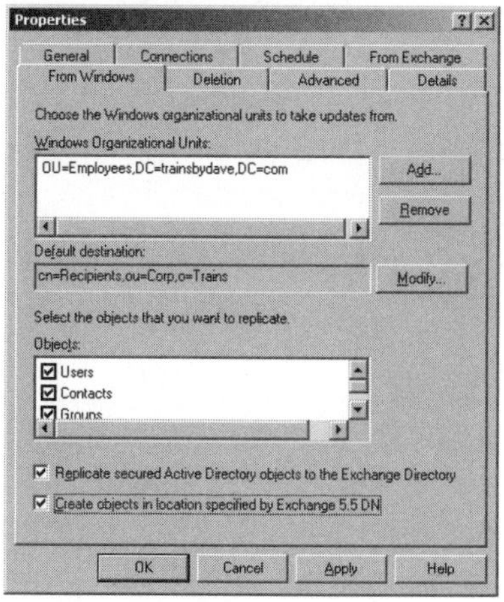

Figure 16-11. *From Windows tab of the ADC service property sheet.*

If you want to have complete control over each container (for example, if you want to have the mailbox container replicate every 30 minutes but have the custom recipient container replicate every 12 hours), create a separate connection agreement for each container, specifying your source and target containers.

If you want to change your recipient structure entirely in Active Directory from what it was in Exchange 5.x, you have two options:

- You can choose one connection agreement, replicate your Exchange containers to one Active Directory container, and then manually move the objects within the Windows Server 2003 containers after they exist in the Active Directory.
- You can create multiple connection agreements and have each connection agreement process one Recipients container (or object type) and point it to a specific OU in Active Directory. Generally speaking, unless you have a specific reason to choose the previous option, it's best to use this technique, since it is both easier and limits the possibility of human error when moving objects from one container to another.

On the From Windows tab, you can select the Replicate Secured Active Directory Objects To The Exchange Directory check box. Normally, any object with any Deny access control entry (ACE) set would not be replicated to your Exchange 5.5 directory. Selecting this check box disables the filtering of objects based on the specified Deny ACE so that those objects are replicated from Windows to your Exchange 5.5 directory. Deny ACEs can be set on the Security tab of the object in question.

Deletion Tab The Deletion tab (Figure 16-12) lets you specify how you want the target directory to manage deleted objects in the source directory. You can either have the deleted object replicated to the target directory or have it cataloged in the appropriate import file format. If you choose to delete the objects, the target directory's tombstone setting will determine when the object will be deleted. If you choose to catalog the deletion list, you'll need to manually perform a directory import and choose to have all the objects being imported deleted during the import process.

> **Note** *Tombstoning* affixes a future date and time to an object after deletion so that all copies of the object in the directory will be deleted at the same time. This practice prevents replication services from backfilling a deleted object into the directory and presenting it as though it had never been deleted.

Remember that Windows Server 2003 strips an object of its permissions after you delete it. If you think you might want to use a deleted object again, keep it in the deletion list and then import it again when you need the object.

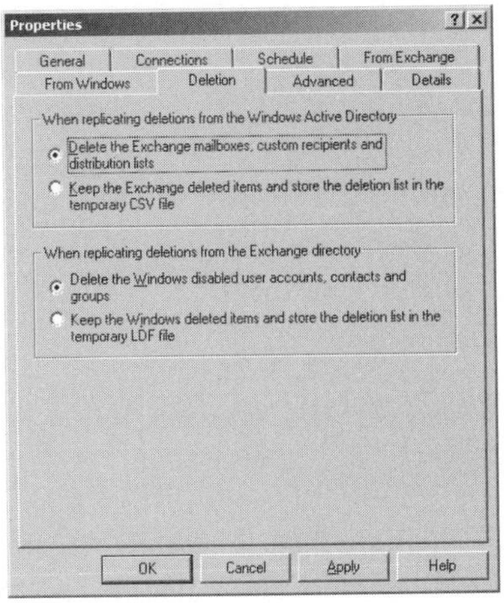

Figure 16-12. *Deletion tab of the ADC service property sheet.*

Advanced Tab On the Advanced tab (Figure 16-13), you need to configure several important values. First, in the Paged Results area, you can change the number of entries per LDAP page. Increase this value if your Exchange 5.5 server is running on a Windows Server 2003 domain controller. You want to do this because both Active Directory and the ADC service will be using LDAP to send and receive queries. Paging improves performance by grouping together objects to be replicated before each replication request. Larger page sizes (containing more objects per page) require fewer LDAP requests to complete replication of all objects, but they also require more memory to operate. Setting the page size to 0 results in no replication; do this only if you want to disable the connection agreement.

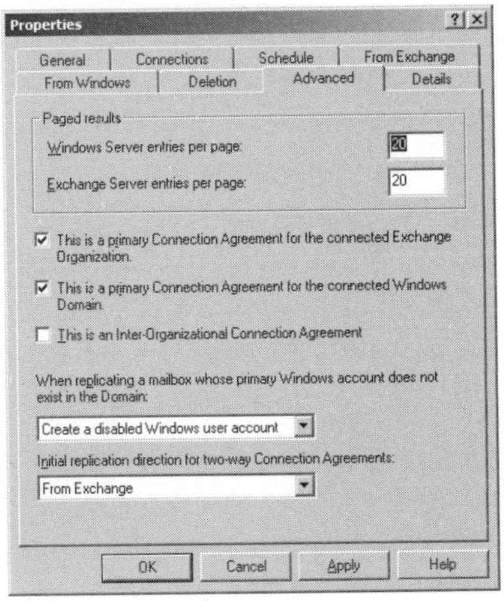

Figure 16-13. *Advanced tab of the ADC service property sheet.*

Be sure to give careful attention to the check boxes for configuring primary agreements. The This Is A Primary Connection Agreement For The Connected Exchange Organization option is the default. A *primary connection agreement* will attempt to create new objects in the target directory when synchronizing objects from one directory to another. Furthermore, if a mailbox in Exchange Server 5.5 has no primary user account, and no corresponding Windows Server 2003 user account exists in Active Directory, a primary connection agreement will create a new user account as part of the replication of the mailbox.

A *nonprimary connection agreement* doesn't create new objects in the Exchange Server 5.5 directory and instead replicates only attributes between the Exchange Server 5.5 mailbox and its corresponding Windows Server 2003 user object. Furthermore, if the connection agreement is nonprimary, the ADC service establishes replication only if you've designated a primary user account on the mailbox's General tab. If no primary user account is designated for the Exchange 5.5 mailbox and no corresponding Windows Server 2003 user object exists, a nonprimary connection agreement won't attempt to create the user object in Active Directory.

Having multiple two-way, primary connection agreements to multiple Exchange Server 5.5 sites from one Active Directory container means that each new object you create in the Active Directory container will replicate to each Exchange Server 5.5 site directory. This scenario will create multiple instances of the same object in your Exchange Server 5.5 organization. The Exchange 5.5 Directory Service will then replicate these objects throughout the organization. If you need to synchronize multiple Exchange sites with one container in Active Directory, configure your connection agreements as one-way from Exchange, with only one two-way connection agreement. This configuration will allow newly created objects in Active Directory to be replicated to your Exchange 5.5 directory without incurring multiple instances of that object.

If you want to create multiple connection agreements from the Active Directory to the Exchange Server 5.5 directory, it's best to set only one connection agreement as primary and the rest as nonprimary. Do this by clearing the This Is A Primary Connection Agreement For The Connected Windows Domain check box on all but one of your connection agreements. The overall effect will be that an object created in Active Directory will be created only once in the Exchange 5.5 directory. You'll need to consider which Exchange 5.5 sites should receive the newly created Active Directory objects.

The most complicated scenario is one in which you need to have certain objects that are created in Active Directory replicated to certain Exchange 5.5 sites and other objects created in Active Directory replicated to other Exchange 5.5 sites. If this is your situation, consider creating separate primary connection agreements from different Active Directory containers to each Exchange 5.5 site. Although doing so will increase the complexity of your ADC service administration, it will allow you to specify which Active Directory objects are replicated to which Exchange 5.5 site.

Associated with the This Is A Primary Connection Agreement For The Connected Windows Domain check box is the setting This Is The Primary Connection Agreement For The Connected Exchange Organization check box, used for replicating a mailbox object that has no corresponding primary user account in Active Directory. This check box controls whether an object is created in the Windows Server 2003 domain if no user account match exists between the two directories. The When Replicating A Mailbox Whose Primary Windows Account Does Not Exist In The Domain drop-down list becomes unavailable if you clear the check box. Use this setting if you need to migrate several mailboxes and you're sure that some of the mailboxes don't have user accounts in Active Directory.

The This Is An Inter-Organizational Connection Agreement check box should be selected if the connection agreement is being made between two Exchange organizations, which would be the case when uploading directory information from an Exchange 5.x organization to a Windows Server 2003 Active Directory whose schema has already been extended with an Exchange 2003 directory. It is also selected when you are replicating your 5.x information to an Active Directory that has *no* Exchange 2003 organization defined, and thus whose schema has not been extended to include Exchange 2003 objects.

You would not want to select this option if you have installed an Exchange 2003 server into an existing Exchange 5.5 organization. In this case, the Exchange 2003 organization and the Exchange 5.5 organization are the same.

When replication is scheduled to occur within a two-way connection agreement, you can choose the direction in which replication will occur first in the Initial Replication Direction For Two-Way Connection Agreements check box.

Summary of ADC Options

Because this can be a bit confusing, we thought we'd make a quick reference list available to you as you think through your CA options:

- If you're coming from a single Exchange 5.5 site, create one connection agreement to retain the same container structure in Active Directory.
- To consolidate multiple Exchange Server 5.5 containers into one container in Active Directory, create one connection agreement and choose each of the Exchange containers individually as a source.
- To have complete control over the synchronization of each Exchange 5.5 container as it replicates to Windows Server 2003 Active Directory, create a connection agreement for each source container.
- To substantially change your container model, either configure one connection agreement, move all your source objects into one Windows Server 2003 container, and then manually move the objects within the Active Directory; or set up multiple connection agreements that specify each source and destination container.

Setting the Default Policy for the ADC Service

By right-clicking the Active Directory Connector Management snap-in in the MMC, you can configure which attributes of each object you want to replicate to the other directory. As was mentioned previously, a nonprimary connection agreement replicates only the attributes of an object to the other directory. This property sheet lets you choose the attributes you want to replicate.

Working with Sites, Administrative Groups, and Routing Groups

For Exchange 2003 and Exchange 5.x organizations to coexist, you will need to leave Exchange Server 2003 in mixed mode. Remember that there is no direct relationship between mixed mode and native mode in Windows Server 2003 and mixed mode and native mode in Exchange Server 2003. In other words, you can have all your servers running Windows Server 2003 in native mode but still have Exchange Server 2003 running in mixed mode to permit interoperability with one or more Exchange 5.x servers.

Mixed mode offers compatibility with previous versions of Exchange Server, but it also has its limitations. Be aware of these, which include the following:

- Exchange 5.x sites appear as administrative groups in the Exchange System snap-in.
- You cannot move mailboxes easily between administrative groups.
- You cannot move servers between administrative groups.
- Members of a routing group must come from the same administrative group.
- Exchange 2003 Administrative Groups will appear as sites in the Exchange 5.5 Administrator.
- The Exchange 5.5 Administrator will not recognize routing groups in Exchange Server 2003.

In other words, when running in mixed mode, Exchange 2003 administration is similar to Exchange 5.x administration, with the site boundaries defining your routing and administrative boundaries.

The last bullet point in the preceding list is particularly important. In mixed mode, each routing group must be created in the administrative group in which the servers exist. This is because Exchange 5.x sites have a one-to-one relationship with administrative groups. Although you can place your Exchange 2003 servers into routing groups that exist in different administrative groups, you cannot assign a server to a routing group that is held under a different administrative group than the administrative group of which the server is a member. For example, if Server1 was created in the Minneapolis administrative group, it cannot be a member of the Arizona routing group unless the Arizona routing group is created inside the Minneapolis administrative group. (See Chapter 12, "Using Administrative and Routing Groups," and Chapter 13, "Connecting Routing Groups," for a discussion about how to implement administrative and routing groups.)

Real World Increasing Administrative Flexibility

One way to increase your administrative flexibility in mixed mode is to subdivide an Exchange 5.x site. Assume that sufficient bandwidth exists between three locations, each hosting three Exchange servers, to place all the servers in the same Exchange 5.5 site. Let's further assume that of these nine servers, five are running Exchange Server 2003 and four are running Exchange Server 5.5.

(continued)

When a user on an Exchange 5.5 server sends a message to a user on an Exchange 2003 server, the Exchange 5.5 Message Transfer Agent (MTA) routes the message directly to the Exchange 2003 server. From an Exchange 5.5 server's perspective, the routing process works the same as it always has. Now suppose that a user on an Exchange 2003 server sends a message to a user on an Exchange 5.5 server. Because Exchange Server 2003 can operate under different rules, you can subdivide the administrative group into several routing groups and force the message from the Exchange 2003 user to travel along a certain path before it gets to the Exchange 5.5 server. This works because the ADC service and SRS do not replicate routing groups and intra-administrative group connectors to the Exchange 5.5 environment.

After switching your organization into native mode, your servers and routing groups will no longer be tied to the administrative group. Thereafter, you'll have full flexibility in routing messages in your environment and in the kind of administrative model you implement.

Handling Other Coexistence Issues

Let's take a brief look at some other issues surrounding coexistence between Exchange Server 5.5 and Exchange Server 2003.

Proxy Address

After a server joins an existing Exchange site, the proxy address settings for addresses such as SMTP, X.400, cc:Mail, and Microsoft Mail are copied to a recipient policy for users in that administrative group. This ensures that the same proxy addresses are generated for all users in the administrative group. This policy cannot be removed, and it will be the highest-priority policy in the system, meaning that any other recipient policies that conflict with it will not be enforced.

Foreign E-Mail Connection

Because SRS replicates site and configuration information between the Exchange 5.x and Exchange 2003 systems, it is possible for users in one system to use a connector in the other system to send messages. For instance, Exchange Server 2003does not ship with a connector for Professional Office System (PROFS). If you need connectivity between Exchange Server 2003 and a PROFS system, you'll have to retain an Exchange 5.x server and use its connector to send and receive messages with your Exchange 2003 organization. Exchange 5.x will act as the transport backbone in this situation.

Messages

Messaging works between Exchange Server 5.x and Exchange Server 2003 because Exchange Server 2003 retains an instance of the MTA in its default installation. Exchange Server 2003 does have its own version of the MTA, with the main difference being that the Exchange 2003 MTA uses LDAP to perform directory lookups, rather than the Directory API (DAPI) used by the Exchange 5.5 MTA.

If two or more Exchange 2003 servers are installed into the same site, they will detect each other automatically and use SMTP as their message transport. This allows them to take advantage of such features as the advanced queuing engine, routing, and link state algorithms. In addition, remember that SMTP is asynchronous and can operate at very low bandwidth.

> **Tip** If two or more Exchange 5.x sites exist with low bandwidth between them, you can use the SMTP routing in Exchange Server 2003 to your advantage. First, install an Exchange 2003 server into each site, and then increase the connector cost on the current Exchange 5.x site connectors. Subdivide your Exchange 5.x site, and place each Exchange 2003 server in its own routing group. Then create a Routing Group Connector between the two routing groups. This path will now be available to the Exchange 5.5 servers, and these servers will use this new, low-cost path to route messages from one to the other.

The advantage of this technique is that it allows you to use the link state information and the asynchronous nature of SMTP to route messages between your Exchange 5.5 servers. Since SMTP is more tolerant of low bandwidth and high latency, you might find this to be a good method to reduce the number of non-delivery reports (NDRs) to your users and ensure a better transfer success rate over slow or unreliable connections.

User Data

When working in a mixed-mode environment, you need to consider a few issues related to private and public user data. One deployment issue is that of delegate access to another's private mailbox. In a mixed mode environment, delegate access can be established in Exchange Server 5.5 only when users are in the same private information store on a single server or when the delegate's mailbox and the origination mailbox are on different servers. The Emsmdb32 DLL will not allow delegate access between users' mailboxes if they reside in different mailbox stores on the same physical server.

You can replicate individual public folders between Exchange 5.5 and Exchange 2003, and clients can access either replica because there is very little difference between public folders in the two systems. In addition, the public folder hierarchy is replicated between all versions of Exchange Server.

Recall that Exchange 2003 supports multiple public folder trees, whereas Exchange 5.5 has one monolithic tree. The default public folder tree in Exchange 2003, Public Folders, can be seen by MAPI clients such as Microsoft Outlook. Other public folder trees cannot be seen by these clients.

The data content of a public folder can also be replicated between public folders, but note that permissions set in Exchange Server 2003 are not represented in Exchange 5.5. If you need to house secure information in your public folder trees in Exchange 2003, migrate the users who will need access to that information to Exchange 2003 as well, and then set up an independent tree and secure it accordingly.

Summary

In this chapter, you learned about some coexistence issues between Exchange 5.5 and Exchange 2003. We discussed the SRS, the SCC, and the SRS databases. We also discussed the ADC service and planning issues surrounding the ADC, and illustrated how to install the ADC service. Finally, we outlined other coexistence issues, such as handling proxy addresses and foreign e-mail connections, and managing user data. This chapter also caps a three-chapter overview of migrations and updates. In the next chapter, we'll turn our attention to the clients for Exchange Server 2003.

Part V
Clients

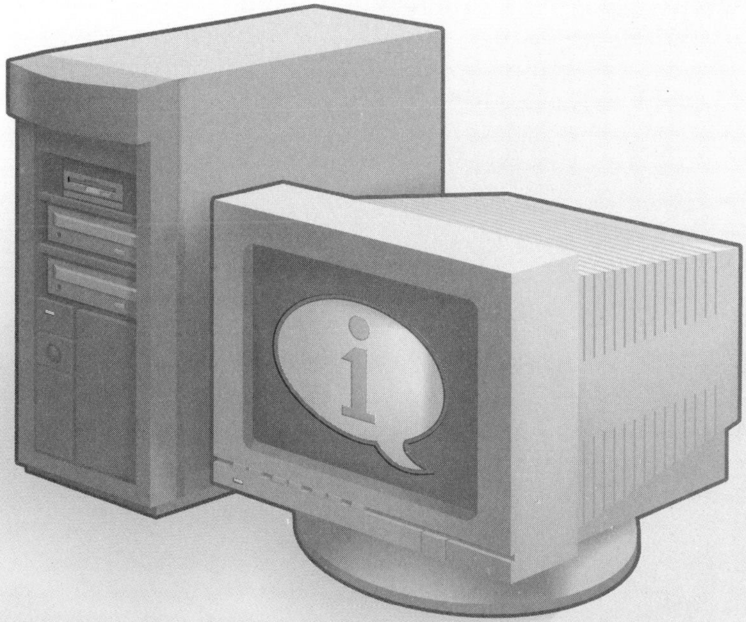

Chapter 17

Overview of Exchange Clients

Up to this point, we have focused primarily on the server aspect of the Exchange environment, because this book is primarily about administering Microsoft Exchange Server 2003. However, a server does not operate in a void; clients must connect to it to complete the picture.

This is the first of four chapters that examine the deployment of clients in an Exchange organization. This chapter introduces you to the main types of clients that you might find in your Exchange environment:

- Microsoft Outlook
- Microsoft Outlook Express
- Microsoft Outlook Web Access
- Exchange Client
- Microsoft Schedule+
- Standard Internet e-mail clients
- UNIX clients
- Macintosh clients

Each of these can be used as a client in an Exchange organization. Because the focus of this book is Exchange Server 2003, and because each of these clients has a wide range of functionality and features, we do not describe each client in depth. Instead, this chapter simply introduces the major types of Exchange client software. Chapter 18, "Deploying Outlook 2003," covers the deployment of the standard desktop client, Outlook 2003, in more detail. Chapter 19, "Supporting Outlook Web Access," focuses on Outlook Web Access; and Chapter 20, "Supporting Internet Protocols and SMTP," looks at using other types of Internet Protocols to access Exchange Server 2003.

Microsoft Outlook

Microsoft Outlook 2003 is the latest version of Microsoft's premier messaging client. Originally introduced with Exchange Server 5, Outlook combines the functionality of Exchange Client and Schedule+ (both of which are described later in this chapter) to deliver a complete messaging, scheduling, and contact management solution. As you learned in Chapter 10, "Using Public Folders," Outlook clients can also work with public folders to share information.

In addition to providing all the functionality that formerly required both Schedule+ and Exchange Client, Outlook supports add-ins. *Add-ins* are program modules that, as their name implies, can be seamlessly added to the Outlook environment to extend the functionality of the product. The Schedule+ add-in, for example, provides compatibility between Schedule+ and the Outlook Calendar. The ability to use add-ins makes Outlook a strategic product for Microsoft because third-party developers can use Outlook as an application development platform. One example of a third-party add-in is a product named Pretty Good Privacy (PGP), which allows a user to send encrypted and signed messages using the PGP protocol. PGP is used mainly for Internet e-mail.

Outlook 2003 is a component of Microsoft Office 2003 and will become widely used as organizations upgrade to this newest version of the popular office suite. It is included in all Microsoft Office 2003 editions: Microsoft Office Small Business Edition 2003, Microsoft Office Standard Edition 2003, Microsoft Office Professional Edition 2003, and Microsoft Office Student and Teacher Edition 2003. Outlook 2003 is also shipped with Exchange Server 2003. As shown in Figure 17-1, Outlook 2003 looks much like previous versions of Outlook. However, it includes several new features, including the ability to do the following:

- Block junk e-mail and unwanted attachments
- Use a new Cached Exchange Mode so that users can read messages even when disconnected from the Exchange Server
- Adapt its display preferences depending on network connection quality
- Access shared team calendars and view them side by side
- Accept ink markup when running on Tablet PCs

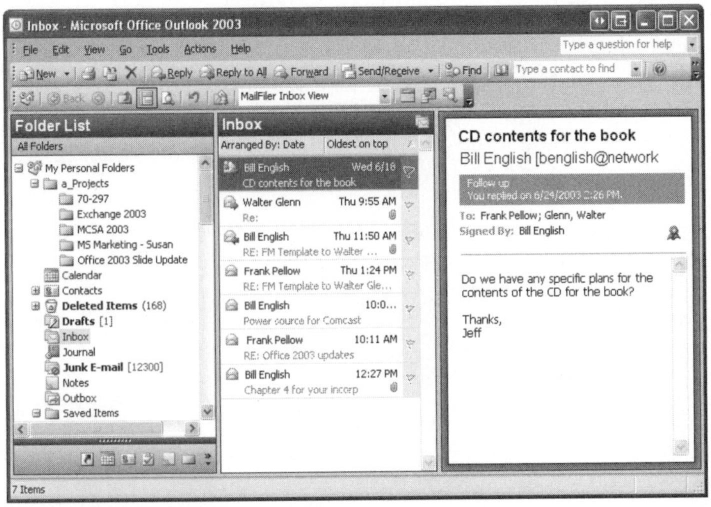

Figure 17-1. *The basic Outlook 2003 client.*

Although this book focuses on using Outlook 2003 with Exchange Server 2003, let's look at all the features that Outlook provides on its own:

- **Messaging** E-mail has become a way of life. Outlook provides a single, universal Inbox for all the user's messaging needs. Users can send and receive messages using a variety of servers. The servers supported are Exchange Server; Microsoft Mail; Internet-based HTTP, SMTP, POP3, and IMAP4; and a variety of third-party messaging servers. Messages can be created in three formats: plain text, rich text, and HTML.
- **Scheduling** Life today is so fast-paced that most people use some kind of calendar/planner. Outlook's Calendar feature allows you to manage appointments and recurring events for yourself or another user on an Exchange server. You can even schedule users across the Internet through the use of iCalendar group scheduling.
- **Contact management** Too many people keep track of their contact information for friends, relatives, and co-workers in a paper-based phone book that has scratched-out entries and entries with arrows pointing to other entries with more updated information. In essence, it is an inefficient and messy method. You can keep track of clients, staff, or any other category of people and their contact information within Outlook. This information can include phone numbers, addresses, birthdays, anniversaries, and anything else you might need to make note of for a contact.

- **Journaling** There's an old business quip that is often used to settle business disputes: The person with the most documentation wins. Having a record of every type of contact with a co-worker, a client, or anyone else could come in handy later on. Outlook's Journal Feature can keep track of every phone call, fax, and e-mail sent and associate it with a specific contact.
- **Notes** We have all been in situations in which we've had to jot down an address or phone number but had no paper and pen handy. The Notes feature of Outlook gives you the electronic equivalent of sticky notes. Use Notes to record information you need to keep that doesn't exactly belong in a contact, a calendar, or an e-mail item.
- **Tasks** Did you forget to call someone back? What about that report you promised your boss—it was due today! Outlook's Tasks feature gives you the ability to create tasks, assign them to yourself or others, and establish due dates. You'll never miss that important deadline again.

More Info For more details on installing, using, and supporting Outlook 2003, see *Microsoft Outlook 2003 Inside Out* by Jim Boyce (Microsoft Press).

Outlook Today

By default, a page named Outlook Today appears first when you start Outlook 2003, as shown in Figure 17-2. Outlook Today presents a sort of snapshot view of Outlook, including your new messages, active tasks, and some calendar information. You can customize Outlook Today to show the information you want.

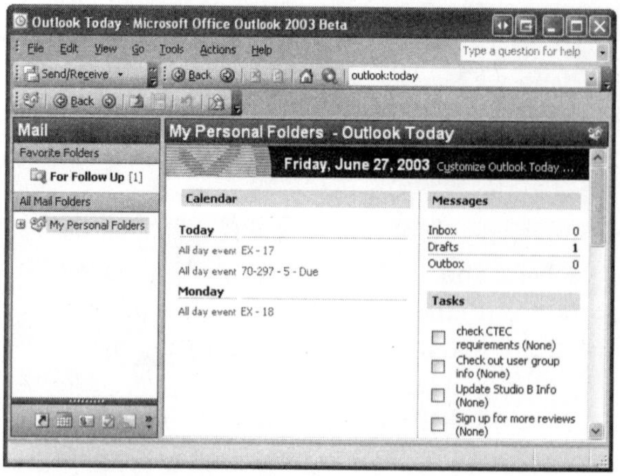

Figure 17-2. *Using Outlook Today.*

Microsoft Outlook Express

Outlook Express, shown in Figure 17-3, is a subset of the standard Outlook product. It ships and installs with Microsoft Internet Explorer and is the default e-mail reader for all versions of Microsoft Windows without Outlook or other e-mail client installed. It allows users to retrieve and send e-mail messages, participate in Internet newsgroups, and access directory information over standard Internet-based protocols. Outlook Express cannot take advantage of most of the collaboration features that Exchange Server 2003 provides, such as native access to public folders and calendaring. Let's look at its three main capabilities—messaging, news reading, and directory service lookup—and see how they differ from their counterparts in Outlook.

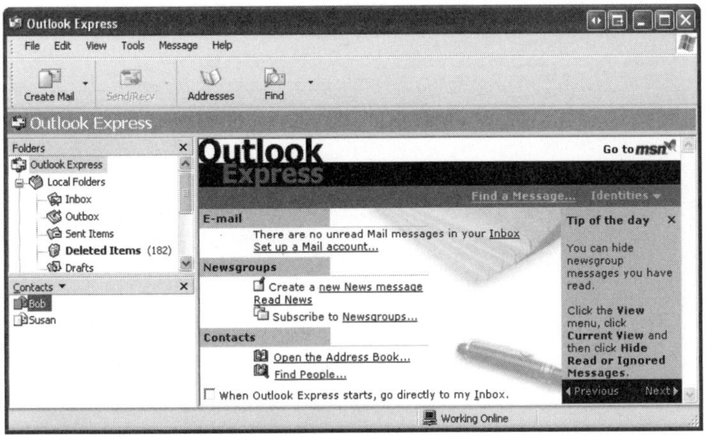

Figure 17-3. *Outlook Express.*

Messaging

E-mail support within Outlook Express is similar to that of the Internet Mail Only option in Outlook: only messaging over the HTTP, POP3, IMAP4, and SMTP protocols is supported. When Outlook Express interacts with Exchange Server 2003 for retrieving messages, it does so over either the POP3 or IMAP4 protocol. This means that although Outlook Express can use Exchange Server 2003 as its messaging server, Outlook Express is not a native Exchange 2003 client. In addition, using Outlook Express to access an Exchange 2003 mailbox does not provide the groupware messaging present in Outlook, such as native access to public folders and Outlook forms.

Outlook Express provides support for multiple e-mail accounts, letting users retrieve messages from multiple servers and view them all in a single Inbox. It also allows multiple users to have their own individual identities for messages, contacts, and tasks. Some basic rules functionality (Figure 17-4) is available through the Create Rule From Message command on the Messages menu. Outlook Express can impose some client-side rules for handling incoming e-mail, but you cannot use it to create server-side rules, as you can with the Rules Wizard in the full Outlook 2003 product.

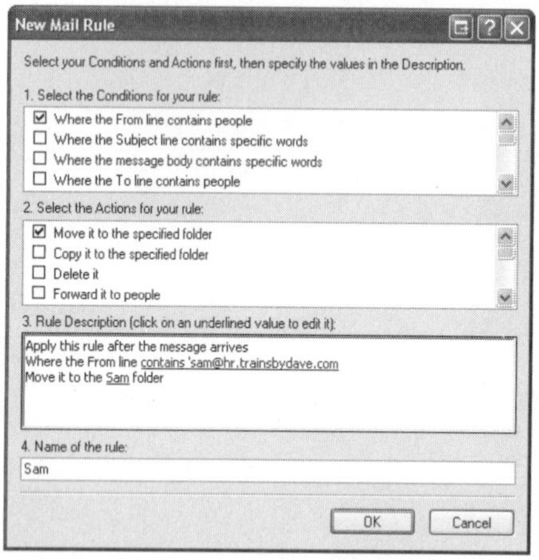

Figure 17-4. *Creating a rule in Outlook Express 6.*

News Reading

Outlook Express can act as a news reader for Internet newsgroups via any NNTP-compliant news server, such as Exchange Server 2003. It can access Exchange 2003 public folders as newsgroups over NNTP. However, when using Outlook Express to access Exchange 2003 public folders, you need to consider the client application that created the entry in the public folder. If the entry was created by an NNTP-compliant news reader such as Outlook Express, all contents of the entry are available to Outlook Express. If, however, the entry was created by a native Exchange client such as Outlook 2003, access to that entry with Outlook Express (and with any other NNTP-compliant news reader) is really effective only with public folders containing standard post items (using the IM.Post form). When Outlook Express accesses a public folder as a newsgroup containing any other Exchange message type (contact item, calendar item, journal item, or task item), it shows only the name of the entry and the information found in the notes portion at the bottom of all Outlook message types.

Performing Directory Service Lookups

Many companies on the Internet provide information about various Internet users. For instance, if you wanted to find out the e-mail address of John Smith, you could query various directory service providers to see whether they had any record of his e-mail address or other information about him. Outlook Express makes the directory service queries via Lightweight Directory Access Protocol (LDAP).

Outlook Express does not access LDAP-based information by querying an Exchange 2003 server specifically. Because Exchange Server 2003 relies heavily on Active Directory, to seek information about a user, an LDAP query would be directed to Active Directory via LDAP over TCP port 389. The client could be configured to present any LDAP queries to an Exchange 2003 server or to any domain controller in Active Directory. For more information about LDAP, POP3, IMAP 4, and NNTP, see Chapter 20.

Outlook Web Access

Outlook Web Access (OWA) is a way of accessing e-mail and scheduling information from an Exchange server, just as you would from Outlook, through a standard Web browser such as Microsoft Internet Explorer or Netscape Navigator. OWA is present in two versions:

- Rich Experience Outlook Web Access, which takes advantage of features in Internet Explorer 5 (or later) to provide features such as secure messaging, rules, spell-checking, and reminders
- Basic Outlook Web Access, which can be used with any Web browser but does not support all the features of the Rich Experience Outlook Web Access

OWA is really just a way to access e-mail over port 80 from a browser (or whatever port your browser and network are set to use). OWA support is configured when you install Exchange Server 2003. Thereafter, a user can use his browser to access many of the functions ordinarily available through Outlook. Users have access to basic e-mail, calendar and group scheduling, basic public folders, and collaborative applications. OWA is more powerful than it ever has been and could certainly be used as a primary Exchange client by someone who didn't need access to advanced features. However, some features are not available when using either the Rich Experience or the Basic version of OWA, including the following:

- Personal address books (because they are stored on your workstation)
- Searching for messages

- WordMail and Microsoft Office integration
- Viewing free/busy details of others
- Outlook forms
- Synchronizing local offline folders with server folders
- Access to your .PST file

The universality of the browser client makes OWA an attractive choice in environments with diverse clients (such as Windows, Macintosh, and UNIX) and that require a shared messaging client. OWA is extremely beneficial for users, such as information systems staff, who move around to different workstations frequently during the day. They can simply check their e-mail using OWA instead of creating an e-mail profile on each workstation. You'll learn more about supporting and using OWA in Chapter 19.

Exchange Client

Exchange Client was the default client for Exchange Server from the first release of the Exchange product until Exchange Server 5.5 was released. It is available in 32-bit Windows, 16-bit Windows, MS-DOS, and Macintosh versions. Exchange Client delivers many of the functions that are inherent in the Exchange system, such as messaging and the ability to access public folders. It does not have scheduling capabilities built into it, so it depends on Schedule+ (covered in the following section) to provide this capability.

The versions of Exchange Client for Macintosh and for 16-bit Windows are not comparable, feature for feature, to the 32-bit Windows version of Exchange Client. However, both the Macintosh and 16-bit Windows versions do include e-mail, personal calendaring, tasks lists, and group scheduling. If you have been using Exchange Server in your environment for a while, you might have Exchange Client on some, most, or all of your client machines. Exchange Server 2003 fully supports Exchange Client, but the client will not be enhanced in subsequent releases of Exchange Server, and it does not allow access to some of Exchange Server 2003's more advanced features.

Schedule+

Schedule+ was the default program used for scheduling and contact management for Exchange Server until Exchange Server 5.5, when it was replaced by the group collaboration capabilities of Outlook. Both Schedule+ 1 and Schedule+ 7 are available in 32-bit Windows, 16-bit Windows, and Macintosh versions. Users moving to Outlook from Schedule+ can import their existing calendar data so that nothing is lost in the transition.

Schedule+ clients can still be used with Exchange Server 2003, but Schedule+ will not be enhanced in subsequent releases of Exchange Server. You can use Schedule+ in an Exchange environment that also includes Outlook users. The two client applications can access the same calendaring information, but Outlook provides some additional functionality, such as the following:

- Journal feature
- Notes feature
- Integrated contacts
- Additional views
- Advanced custom view capabilities
- Task delegation
- Advanced printing options
- Public folder with calendars

Standard Internet E-Mail Clients

One of the goals of Exchange Server 2003 is to continue to comply with the standards being used by the Internet community. Because Exchange Server 2003 is compliant with several popular Internet protocols, it can be used as the messaging server for third-party e-mail clients, provided that the clients are also compliant with those protocols.

If you are running third-party Internet e-mail client software as either a POP3 client or an IMAP 4 client, you can use Exchange Server 2003 as your messaging server. Although Outlook Express is a Microsoft product, it is a good example of the type of software we're talking about here. Outlook Express really has nothing specifically to do with Exchange Server; you could use it to get your e-mail from your local ISP and to read newsgroup messages from a UNIX-based news server somewhere on the Internet. In the case of Outlook Express, Exchange Server might never even enter the picture.

Non-Windows Platforms

In our discussions of clients using Exchange Server 2003, we usually assume that they're running on a Windows operating system. How do non-Windows operating systems connect with Exchange Server? Let's look at two other popular operating systems: UNIX and Macintosh.

UNIX Clients

No Outlook client exists for the UNIX operating system, so UNIX users have one of two choices for connecting to Exchange Server 2003:

- **Internet e-mail client** A UNIX-based, third-party Internet e-mail client can be used to access messages from Exchange Server 2003 over either the POP3 or IMAP4 protocols.
- **Outlook Web Access** Because the basic version of OWA runs in a standard browser, UNIX users can access their e-mail using their own Web browser.

Macintosh Clients

Macintosh clients have three choices for accessing Exchange Server 2003:

- **Outlook 2001 for Mac** Microsoft's Outlook client for Macintosh provides functionality similar to that of its 32-bit Windows counterpart. There are also plans to provide Exchange Server support for the e-mail client that is part of Microsoft Office for Macintosh—Entourage.
- **Internet e-mail client** Like UNIX users, Macintosh users can access Exchange Server 2003 with their own POP3 or IMAP4 e-mail clients.
- **Outlook Web Access** OWA is also accessible from a Macintosh-based Web browser.

As you can see, the client choices for the UNIX and Macintosh operating systems are extensive, mainly due to Exchange's support for industry-standard protocols. Exchange Server 2003 gives the user a variety of ways to access messages, regardless of the operating system.

Choosing a Client for Exchange Server

Philosophically, choosing a client for Exchange Server is easy. Outlook 2003 is the most current version of the Outlook client, it provides the greatest amount of functionality, and it is designated by Microsoft as the official client for Exchange Server 2003. Outlook 2003 is bundled with Microsoft Office 2003 and with Exchange Server 2003. Although Exchange Client and Schedule+ are supported by Exchange Server 2003, they are no longer being enhanced with new features and cannot access all the services that Exchange Server 2003 provides. Standard Internet e-mail clients also miss a great deal of the functionality that Exchange offers, but they are fast enough to be used efficiently over the Internet.

As they say, however, your mileage may vary. You might have a large installed base of Exchange Client users, and upgrading them can be a significant administrative task. Some or all of the people in your organization might already have an e-mail program that they like and, rather than going through the pain of change, they might choose to forgo the advanced features available with Outlook. Any of these factors might contribute to a decision to support non-Outlook clients as part of your Exchange environment or to use Outlook Web Access.

You might also have such a widespread mix of client platforms that you need to use the most generic client possible: the Outlook Web Access client. Or you might need to use OWA to service the messaging needs of some of your users and use the complete Outlook product for other users. Client machines can also use standard Internet POP3 and OWA clients to access your Exchange Inbox over the Internet.

The bottom line is that Outlook 2003 allows you to take advantage of all that Exchange Server 2003 has to offer, but other preexisting clients, although potentially missing some newer features, are supported and work with Exchange Server 2003 as well.

Summary

Exchange Server 2003 supports a wide variety of clients, including Outlook, Outlook Express, Outlook Web Access, Exchange Client, Schedule+, and standard Internet e-mail clients. Outlook 2003 is the current standard client for Exchange Server 2003 because it provides the most functionality and is the clear upgrade path for forthcoming Exchange clients.

Outlook Express is a capable client for Exchange Server 2003 as long as the server supports the POP3 or IMAP4 protocol. Outlook Web Access is a good client to use when your organization supports non-Windows-based clients such as UNIX and Macintosh, or when your users need to access the server over the Internet. The new version of Outlook Web Access makes great strides in becoming more useable. Exchange Client and Schedule+ are still functional alternatives in the Exchange environment, although upgrading to Outlook gives you more functionality. The next chapter takes a more in-depth look at deploying and using Outlook 2003.

Chapter 18

Deploying Outlook 2003

Microsoft Outlook 2003 is the latest version of Outlook. Because it is a component of Microsoft Office 2003, Outlook 2003 will become widely used as organizations upgrade to this newest version of the popular Office suite. It is included in all Office 2003 editions and is also shipped with Microsoft Exchange Server 2003. This chapter looks at some of the issues an administrator faces when deploying Outlook 2003, including installation, using Outlook 2003 offline, and enabling multiple users.

Installing Outlook 2003

Installing client software is among the more repetitive tasks you face as an administrator. However, it's one that you've got to perform because a client/server system such as Exchange Server 2003 will not work unless both sides of the equation are in place.

Because this book focuses on Exchange Server, we will not provide detailed instructions for installing Outlook 2003. We'll simply give an overview of the installation methods available, explaining some of the options you or your users have when performing a standard Outlook installation on an individual machine. We'll then introduce the Office Custom Installation Wizard, which allows you to create customized installations for your users.

More Info This chapter provides an overview of the concerns regarding Outlook 2003 from an administrator's view, but Outlook is a pretty complex program. If you want to learn more about using Outlook 2003, read *Microsoft Outlook 2003 Inside Out* by Jim Boyce (Microsoft Press, 2003). To learn more about Office 2003 deployment, check out the *Microsoft Office 2003 Resource Kit* (Microsoft Press, 2003).

Standard Outlook Installation

Like most Microsoft programs, Outlook 2003 installs with a setup wizard regardless of whether you are installing Outlook as part of Office 2003 or as a standalone installation. You can customize just about every aspect of an installation, including adding and removing components during or after an installation. Figure 18-1 shows the component selection process for Outlook 2003 during a custom installation of Office 2003. (The list of Outlook components is the same when installing only Outlook.) For each component of Outlook 2003, you can elect to perform one of the following actions:

- Install the component to run from the local hard disk. If disk space is abundant, many administrators choose to install every available component to run in this way.
- Install all subcomponents of the component to run from the local hard disk. This essentially chooses the previous option for an entire group of components.
- Set the component to install the first time the user attempts to use it. If a user never uses a certain component of Outlook, the component is never installed and doesn't waste space. On the other hand, constantly used components are installed locally. This option also saves time during the initial install.
- Make the component unavailable. This simply means that the user will have to run the installer again to install the component. You can also use this option to prevent the user from installing certain components, as long as you don't make the installation files available.

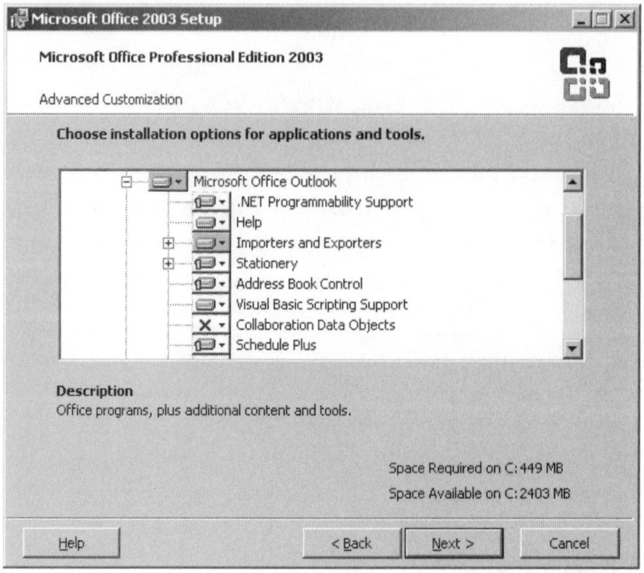

Figure 18-1. *Specifying which Outlook 2003 components to install.*

After you've selected the components to install, Windows Installer takes care of the rest of the installation with little or no intervention on your part.

The first time a user runs Outlook 2003 following a standard installation, Outlook starts up and prompts the user to configure the user's e-mail account. In an Exchange organization, this configuration involves providing the name of the Exchange server and the user name.

Customizing Outlook Installation

As an administrator, you can customize the setup of Outlook 2003 in three ways. You can run the setup program with command-line switches, use a setup information file to answer various setup questions and then specify the setup information file using command-line switches, and customize an installation of Outlook with the Office Custom Installation Wizard. The following sections briefly discuss these options.

Using Command-Line Switches

You can customize the setup of Outlook somewhat by using various switches. Most of the switches involve the use of a Microsoft Installer (.MSI) package file. Table 18-1 lists the available command-line switches.

More Info For more information about using switches to modify your Outlook installations, see the setup.htm file on the Outlook 2003 or Office 2003 installation CD-ROM.

Table 18-1. Command-line switches for installing Outlook 2003

Switch	Use
/a <msifile>	Creates an administrative install point using the .MSI file for client installations.
/f [options] <msifile>	Repairs the Outlook installation using various repair modes.
/i <msifile>	Specifies the name of the .MSI file to be used during installation. This switch cannot be used with the */a* switch.
/j [options] <msifile>	Creates an icon that can be used later to install a feature not configured during setup.
/l [options] <logfile>	Specifies the log file used during installation and also switches to be passed to the Windows Installer.
/noreboot	Specifies that the computer not reboot or display a dialog box asking the user to reboot when the installation is finished.
/x <msifile>	Uninstalls Outlook.
/q [options]	Specifies the amount of information to be presented on screen during the installation.
/wait	Indicates that the installer should wait for the installation to complete before exiting.
/settings	Specifies the path and settings file to be used for the automated installation.

Using a Setup Information File

If a file named Setup.ini exists in the same directory as Setup.exe, or if the */settings <inifile>* switch specifies an .INI file with a different name, that file will be used to modify the default behavior of the setup. Because this file can specify all the parameters you would normally provide at the command line, it is useful for a number of reasons:

- You can avoid typographical errors at the command line.
- You are not subject to limitations on the length of the command.
- You can enforce specific settings, even with an interactive installation.

The file is merely a text document and can be opened with Microsoft Notepad or any other text editor. Like other .INI files, each line represents one aspect of the installation. To include a comment, type a semicolon at the beginning of each comment line.

Using the Office Custom Installation Wizard

The Office Custom Installation Wizard, shown in Figure 18-2, works with Windows Installer to let you tweak almost every detail of the installation process. Using the Custom Installation Wizard, you can perform the following actions:

- Define the path where Outlook 2003 is installed on client computers.
- Set the installation options (Run From Hard Disk, Install On First Use, Don't Install) for individual components of Outlook 2003.
- Define a list of network servers for Windows Installer to use when the primary installation server is unavailable.
- Specify other products to install or other programs to run on the user's computer when the Outlook installation is done.
- Hide selected options from users during setup.
- Add custom files and Windows registry settings to the installation.
- Customize desktop shortcuts for Outlook 2003.
- Set user default options.
- Use Office profile settings created with the Profile Wizard for Office 2003 to preset user options.

To accomplish all this, the Windows Installer uses two types of files: an installer package (an .MSI file) and an installer transform file (an .MST file). The installer package contains a database that describes the configuration information. The installer transform file contains modifications that are to be made as Windows Installer installs Outlook. The package file never changes; it is essentially a database that helps Windows Installer relate various features to actual installation files. The transform file is what the Office Custom Installation Wizard helps you create. It allows you to create unique setup scenarios that use the same installation files. In other words, you could create different installation routines for different departments but use only one network installation point.

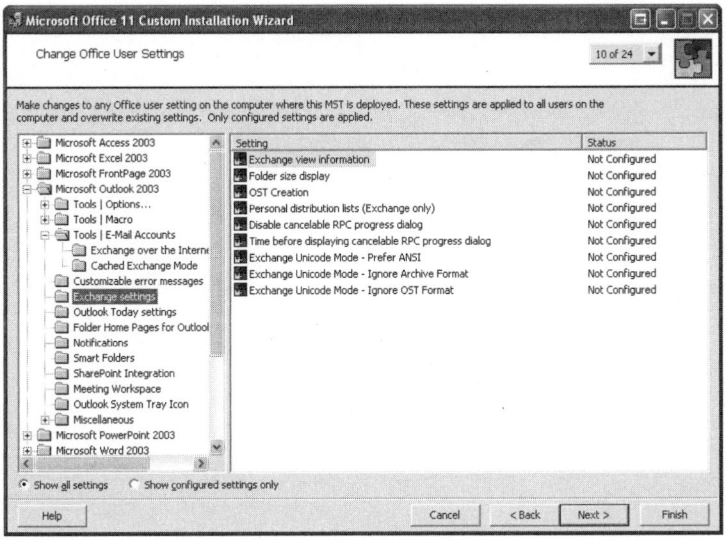

Figure 18-2. *Customizing an Outlook installation with the Office Custom Installation Wizard.*

More Info The Office Custom Installation Wizard is included on the CD-ROM that accompanies the *Microsoft Office 2000 Resource Kit* (Microsoft Press). It is also available online at *http://www.microsoft.com/office/ork/xp/default.htm*. The resource kit provides detailed information about using the wizard.

Systems Management Server

Systems Management Server (SMS) is a Microsoft application specifically designed to help administrators address the needs of larger user communities. The *Microsoft Office 2003 Resource Kit* (Microsoft Press), which is available in both book form and online, contains instructions for creating installation packages and configuration files that can be used by SMS. The resource kit also contains a sample package definition file (PDF) that can be used with SMS to distribute the customized version of the executable client setup file to the users on your network. The PDF is a text file (with an .SMS extension) that includes the setup parameters necessary to install Outlook 2003 using SMS. The sample PDF is as follows:

```
[PDF]
Version=2.0

[Package Definition]
Publisher=Microsoft
Name=Office 2003 Applications
Version=11.0
Language=English
Programs=Typical, Manual, Custom, Uninstall
MIFName=off11

[Typical]
Name=Typical (quiet)
CommandLine=setup.exe /qb- /m off11
AdminRightsRequired=True
UserInputRequired=False
DriveLetterConnection=False
CanRunWhen=AnyUserStatus
RemoveProgram=False
SupportedClients=Win NT (I386)
Win NT (I386) MinVersion1=5.00.0000.0
Win NT (I386) MaxVersion1=9.99.9999.9999

[Manual]
Name=Manual
CommandLine=setup.exe /m off11
UserInputRequired=True
AdminRightsRequired=True
DriveLetterConnection=False
RemoveProgram=False
SupportedClients=Win NT (I386)
Win NT (I386) MinVersion1=5.00.0000.0
Win NT (I386) MaxVersion1=9.99.9999.9999

[Custom]
Name=Custom (quiet)
CommandLine=setup.exe /qb- TRANSFORMS="New Custom Setup File.MST" /m off11
AdminRightsRequired=True
UserInputRequired=False
DriveLetterConnection=False
CanRunWhen=AnyUserStatus
RemoveProgram=False
SupportedClients=Win NT (I386)
Win NT (I386) MinVersion1=5.00.0000.0
Win NT (I386) MaxVersion1=9.99.9999.9999

[Uninstall]
Name=Uninstall
CommandLine=setup.exe /qb- REBOOT=ReallySuppress /m off11 /x
AdminRightsRequired=False
UserInputRequired=False
DriveLetterConnection=False
CanRunWhen=AnyUserStatus
SupportedClients=Win NT (I386)
Win NT (I386) MinVersion1=5.00.0000.0
Win NT (I386) MaxVersion1=9.99.9999.9999
```

You must accomplish two steps before distributing Outlook 2003 to your client systems. First, you must create a package. The package consists of the PDF just discussed and a package source folder containing all the files necessary for the installation. After you've created the package, the second step is to create an advertisement to distribute the package. An advertisement consists of the package as well as a list of all client systems on which you want the package installed (called a *collection*). SMS provides flexibility and granularity so that you can install the package only where you want it. For example, you might decide to install the package only on client systems that meet minimum memory and hard disk parameters and ignore all other systems. The job can also be set to run only after a certain time period and, if not voluntarily accepted by the user within that time frame, the job can be configured to become a mandatory installation that the user cannot stop or defer to a later time period.

Supporting Outlook 2003

Many features of Outlook 2003 are especially relevant in a book about Exchange Server 2003 because they involve interaction between the Outlook 2003 client and Exchange Server. These features include the ability to work while disconnected from the Exchange server and to let more than one user work with a specific computer.

Using Cached Exchange Mode

Exchange Server and Outlook form the two ends of a powerful communications system. Most of the time, people communicate while the programs are in direct contact with each other so that the give and take of the process can proceed freely.

However, recall from Chapter 1, "Introducing Exchange Server 2003," that communication with messaging systems such as Exchange Server is *asynchronous*, which means that one party can send a message without the other party's being available to receive the message. Even though messages and replies might fly through your Exchange Server environment as rapidly as a conversation transpires on the telephone, the recipient is not required to be available when a message is sent, and the sender does not have to be online when the message is received.

This simple fact means that you can also use the Outlook 2003 client without being connected to the Exchange server. You can read messages in the local folders or create messages that are stored in your Outbox and sent when you reconnect to Exchange Server. This powerful feature makes users more productive in many situations that are typically thought of as downtime. (For example, you've probably seen people sitting on planes answering their e-mail.)

You can work offline with Outlook 2003 without modifying the software in any way. In fact, if you start Outlook 2003 when you are disconnected from the network, the environment looks almost the same as it does when you are connected to an Exchange server. The folder list displays all the folders for your mailbox, and you can create messages as though you were connected. Of course, the Outlook 2003 client must previously have been connected to the Exchange Server at some point.

All this is accomplished through a feature called *Cached Exchange Mode*, which, when enabled, stores a copy of your Exchange mailbox on the local computer. This copy is stored in a file called an offline storage (OST) file. When a client computer is offline (either deliberately or due to a network error), Outlook 2003 automatically switches over to a disconnected mode, during which it periodically attempts to restore the connection. While the connection is unavailable, all the data inside the OST file is available to the user.

By default, however, public folders are not displayed in the folder list when you are working offline. The main reason for this is that public folders tend to be both numerous and large. Synchronizing public folders by default would cause a lot of undue network traffic. As such, you have to manually select public folders to be synchronized by first placing them in your Public Folder Favorites folder and then setting up Outlook to download Public Folder Favorites. You'll see how to configure all this in the upcoming sections.

Configuring Cached Exchange Mode

Cached Exchange Mode is enabled by default when you install Outlook 2003 and set up an Exchange mailbox, and little configuration is necessary. However, you can change the connection setting used in this mode and also disable Cached Exchange Mode.

Changing Cached Exchange Mode Connection Settings To change the connection settings used by Outlook 2003 for Cached Exchange Mode, use the commands on the Cached Exchange Mode submenu on Outlook's File menu. The following connection settings are available:

- **Download headers and then full items** This setting causes Outlook to download all the headers of messages first, and then download the complete items. The result is that the user sees the full list of messages more quickly in the Outlook client.
- **Download full items** This setting causes Outlook to download the header, body, and attachments of all messages at once. The presentation of messages is a bit slower when using this setting, because each message is displayed in the client only when the previous message is finished downloading.

- **Download headers** This setting causes Outlook to download only the headers of new messages. The body of the message and any attachments are downloaded only when you open the item.
- **On slow connections download only headers** This setting differs in that you can select it in addition to one of the three previous settings. Outlook 2003 has the ability to detect a slow network connection state. When the setting is enabled, Outlook switches to downloading only headers when it detects a slow link—no matter which of the previous three settings is selected.

Disabling Cached Exchange Mode Whenever you enable your Outlook 2003 client for offline use, you automatically enable the standard folders in your mailbox for offline use. The only way to disable offline use of your mailbox folders is to disable Cached Exchange Mode for your Outlook client. You can disable offline use by choosing the E-Mail Accounts option from the Tools menu in Outlook 2003. Select the View or Change Existing E-mail Accounts option, click Next, select the Exchange account, and click Change. On the window that opens, click the More Settings button, switch to the Advanced tab, and disable the Use Cached Exchange Mode option.

Note Outlook 2003 and Exchange Server 2003 support the use of offline folders without using Cached Exchange Mode. Just disable the Cached Exchange Mode option and make sure an offline folder file is configured. The only reason you might want offline folder access is to limit the synchronization of particular Exchange folders—something most users won't need to deal with. You can learn more about this in *Microsoft Outlook 2003 Inside Out* by Jim Boyce (Microsoft Press).

After you disable Cached Exchange Mode, you will no longer be able to use Outlook 2003 with the contents of any of your Exchange-based folders if you are not connected to an Exchange server. If you open Outlook with offline access disabled when you are not connected to an Exchange server, you receive a message that Outlook could not open your default e-mail folders, and Outlook opens with your default file system instead.

Note Disabling offline access after you've created an offline folder does not delete the offline folder. It is not deleted until you explicitly delete it.

Synchronizing a Mailbox

Synchronizing a mailbox is a simple process from the user's perspective, but the system must perform several complex tasks to accomplish it. When you start Outlook 2003, the system determines whether the client computer is connected to an Exchange server. You can create messages, delete messages, and perform other standard functions while offline. The next time you start Outlook and connect to an Exchange server, Outlook and Exchange Server automatically synchronize the contents of your offline folder. When Exchange Server synchronizes the contents of a folder on an Outlook 2003 client machine with the contents of the matching folder on the Exchange server, the system makes a copy of any messages that exist in only one location and places them in the other location. Exchange also synchronizes messages that have been deleted in one location but not in the other location.

The standard, default folders in your Outlook mailbox (Inbox, Outbox, Deleted Items, Calendar, Sent Items, Contacts, Tasks, Drafts, Journal, and Notes) are synchronized automatically, as long as you set up a location in which to store their contents.

Real World When Synchronization Doesn't Work

Even though you've configured everything correctly on your Outlook 2003 client, at times your folders might not synchronize automatically when you reconnect. If Outlook determines that you have a slow connection, it automatically stops synchronization from occurring. You can still synchronize either all folders or a specific folder by using any of the synchronize commands on the Tools menu.

Other errors might also prevent synchronization. A synchronization log file is always placed in the Deleted Items folder of the offline folder. Check this log for error codes that can help you solve synchronization problems.

Synchronizing Public Folders

As we mentioned earlier in this chapter, the standard mailbox folders are automatically enabled for offline access. You can verify this capability by displaying the property sheet for one of the folders in the mailbox, such as your Inbox. One of the tabs in the property sheet is labeled Synchronization. (This tab is discussed in the section titled "Shaping Synchronization.") However, if you display the property sheet for a public folder, you do not see the Synchronization tab, because public folders, by default, are not enabled for offline access. Public folders typically contain large amounts of information that would clog your client machine. In addition, the contents of public folders are often subject to change, making synchronization difficult. (See the Real World sidebar "Public Folder Synchronization Conflicts" later in this chapter.)

You can, however, easily enable a public folder for offline access. Simply move the public folder to the Favorites list in the Public Folders container of the folder list. You can make this change by dragging the folder into the Favorites folder or by pointing to Folder on the File menu and choosing Add To Public Folder Favorites. When you drag a public folder to the Favorites folder, the folder has the same name as the original public folder.

When you designate a public folder as a Favorite, you do not move it from its established place in the public folder hierarchy; you simply add the folder to your list of Favorites. When a public folder is in the Favorites list, the property sheet for the folder contains a Synchronization tab. You can remove a folder from the Favorites list by selecting and then deleting it.

Real World Public Folder Synchronization Conflicts

Conflicts can arise when more than one person is using and modifying the items in a public folder offline. If you change an item in a public folder while you are offline, when you synchronize that folder, Exchange Server checks the timestamp for the existing version of the item. If the timestamp for the existing version is later than the original timestamp for the item you changed, someone changed the contents of the folder item since you last downloaded it. If this type of conflict occurs, you receive a message that includes copies of all conflicting versions of the item. It is up to you to resolve the conflict, either by combining all versions of an item into a single version and then clicking Keep This Item or by clicking Keep All to keep all versions of the message.

This procedure is more complicated than it sounds. A user might find it difficult to decide whether to keep an existing item or overwrite it, and the wrong decision could have negative results. For this reason, you should place controls on who is allowed to download and modify public folders by using the standard Exchange security system.

Shaping Synchronization

After you enable offline access for your Outlook client, you can shape the way that each folder synchronizes with Exchange. If a folder is enabled for offline use, the property sheet for the folder contains a Synchronization tab, as shown in Figure 18-3.

Click the Filter button to display a dialog box that allows you to define filtering conditions (Figure 18-4). This dialog box has several tabs that allow you to define a complex condition. After you set up a filter, Outlook uses the conditions described in the filter to control which messages are synchronized between the Outlook client and the corresponding folders in Exchange Server. Keep in mind that these limits are imposed on all future synchronization attempts but have no effect on any messages that currently reside in the offline message store.

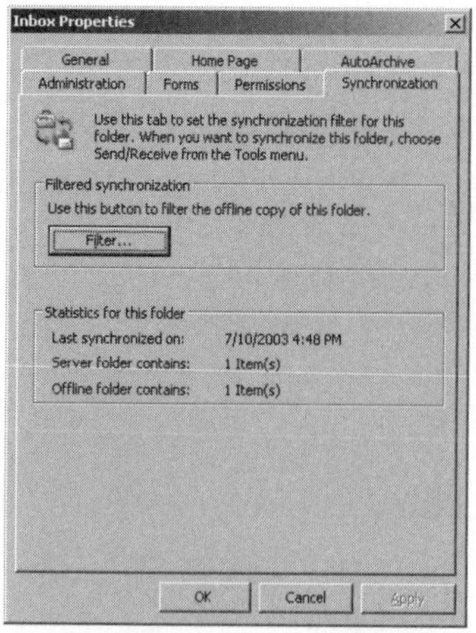

Figure 18-3. *Synchronization tab of a folder's property sheet.*

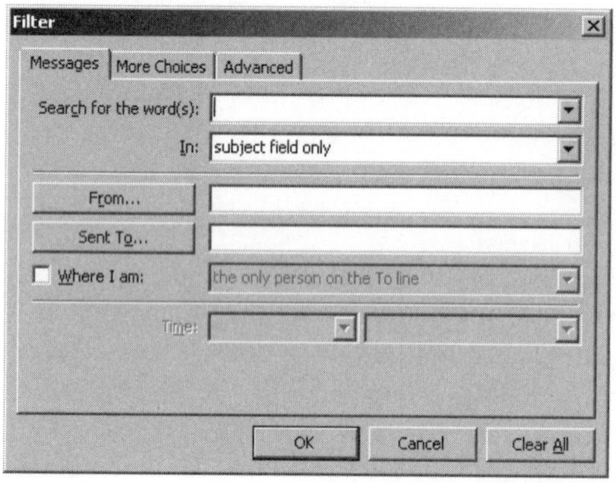

Figure 18-4. *Filtering messages to be synchronized.*

Filtering is an enormously useful tool for getting all the benefits of offline access without incurring the excessive overhead caused by synchronizing less important messages. You could create a filter that disables synchronization for any messages that have large file attachments, for example, or you could synchronize only messages from your boss. Be careful to remember when you have synchronization filters on. In an offline folder, there is no indication that the messages presented in the folder are not the complete set of messages stored in the matching Exchange folder.

Deciding Whether to Copy or Synchronize Public Folders

Synchronization is no more than a sophisticated way to copy messages automatically between folders on the Exchange server and the offline folder on an Outlook 2003 client. For your Inbox, Outbox, and other mailbox folders, synchronization works well. But should you use the process for public folders?

Public folders can serve a wide variety of purposes. A public folder can be a simple repository of static information, such as a library, or it can be a dynamically changing discussion group. You can copy the contents of a public folder to your mailbox simply by dragging the folder into the Mailbox container in your Outlook folder list. When should you copy and when should you synchronize the contents of a public folder?

The longer you have the contents of a public folder away from the Exchange server, the more likely it is that you will have a conflict when you reconnect—that is, you might make changes to your offline copy while others are changing the version on the Exchange server. Although public folders do have a way to detect conflicts, as we described earlier, you must resolve those conflicts manually, which can be time-consuming.

When deciding whether to copy or synchronize a public folder, you should carefully analyze how the folder is intended to be used offline. If its contents are meant only to be read, you probably will find that a simple copy operation works well. If you will be making changes in the contents of the folder, you should seriously consider preventing later conflicts by applying filters to the synchronization process so that you modify only the messages that are unlikely to be modified by other users.

Enabling Multiple Users in Outlook 2003

The capabilities of Outlook 2003 and the capabilities of Exchange 2003 work in conjunction with each other. Outlook is a client, and Exchange is a server. When an Outlook client is connected to an Exchange server, the client is representing a single user. In some situations, however, the same Outlook client can be used to support multiple users at different times. This section explores the scenarios in which this situation can occur.

Understanding Outlook Profiles, Exchange Mailboxes, and User Accounts

Before you learn how to implement multiple users with Outlook, you need to understand the differences between an Outlook profile and an Exchange mailbox as well as how both of these entities interact with user accounts.

A *profile* is a client-side configuration. An Outlook profile is a set of information services configured for a particular user or purpose. The Exchange Server information service in a profile includes a reference to an associated Exchange server and mailbox. When a user starts Outlook, he or she uses the information in an Outlook profile to establish a connection with a particular Exchange server.

Normally, each client machine has a single default Outlook 2003 profile. When a user starts Outlook on that machine, the default profile is used to determine which Exchange mailbox will be used on the server side of the environment. If a user is starting Outlook for the first time or is using a machine that does not have a profile, he or she is prompted to create a profile before fully logging on to the associated Exchange server. To see the profile that your Outlook client is currently using, choose E-Mail Accounts from the Tools menu of Outlook 2003, and then select View or Change Existing E-mail Accounts. You will see the dialog box shown in Figure 18-5.

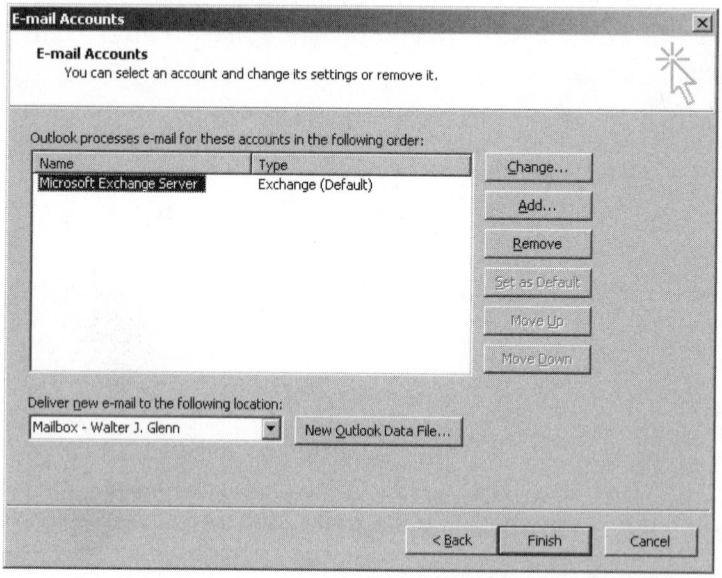

Figure 18-5. *Viewing the current profile from Outlook 2003.*

Creating Multiple Profiles with Outlook 2003

Sometimes a single profile on an Outlook client is not enough. You might want to use more than one Outlook profile for any of several reasons. Perhaps you are using Outlook on a machine that you share with other users. Having separate profiles allows each profile to reflect the various mailboxes and configuration information for a given user. You might also be using a machine under different circumstances (such as in the office and on the road), making it desirable to be able to select a profile based on your current situation.

When you first log on to Outlook 2003, you are prompted to create a profile, which is used as the default profile. To create an additional profile, open the Windows Control Panel and double-click the Mail icon; then choose Show Profiles. Clicking this button displays a list of the profiles on the machine, as shown in Figure 18-6.

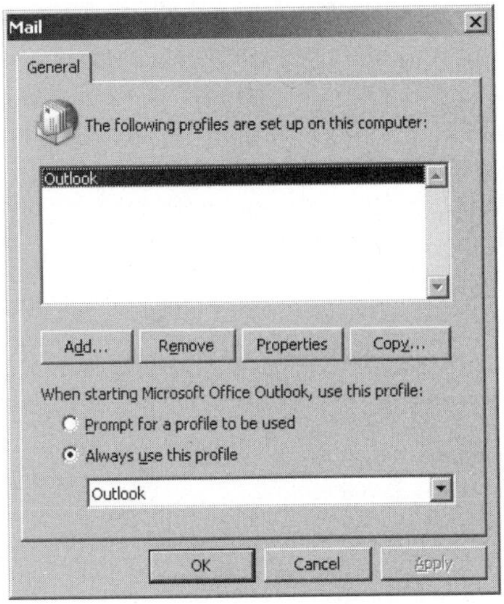

Figure 18-6. *A list of e-mail profiles.*

To add a new profile, simply click the Add button, which starts the New Profile Wizard. This wizard prompts you for the values needed for a profile, including the name of the target Exchange server and the mailbox that the profile will use on that server. The Inbox Setup Wizard also asks whether you will be using this machine while traveling, and if so, the wizard sets up an offline folder. You can also delete or modify existing profiles in this dialog box.

At the bottom of the Mail dialog box, you can specify a user profile to be used as the default profile for this client machine. Outlook uses this default profile to connect to an Exchange server unless you specify otherwise. The use of a default profile can be somewhat cumbersome, however, because it requires you to display the Outlook property sheet when you want to use a different profile. Alternately, you can have Outlook prompt you for a profile every time you start Outlook. If you select this option, a dialog box appears every time you start Outlook, allowing you to select the profile to use.

Providing Access to Different Exchange Mailboxes

The Outlook profile described in the preceding section includes client-side configuration information. But remember that Outlook is the client portion of a client/server system. You still need the appropriate user privileges to access the server side of the equation in Exchange Server.

Exchange security is based on the Windows Server 2003 security model. Each Exchange object has an access control list (ACL) consisting of a discretionary access control list (DACL) and a system access control list (SACL). These lists are used in conjunction with the user's access token to either grant or deny access. For instance, before an Outlook client can access an Exchange server, the user must log on to a network and receive a ticket from the domain controller. This ticket is used to gain entrance to the Exchange server. Figure 18-7 illustrates this process.

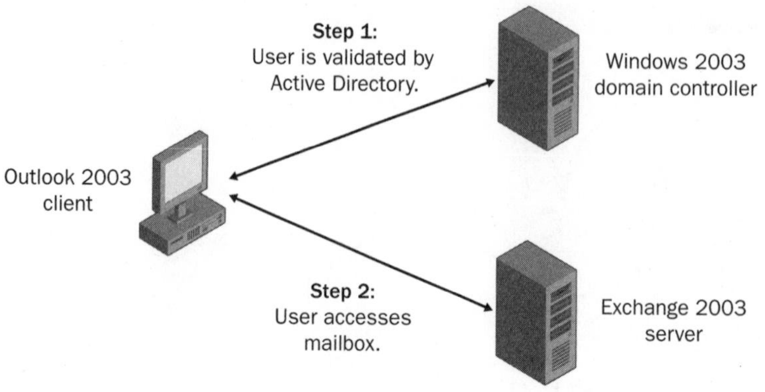

Figure 18-7. *Using the Outlook client to connect to an Exchange 2003 server.*

If you specify a different user name with each profile, you can use multiple Outlook profiles to access different Exchange mailboxes. In some situations, however, you might want to allow an individual to access different Exchange mailboxes while using the same user name. For example, you might want a receptionist to be able to open the mailbox of another receptionist who has called in sick for the day.

A mailbox in Exchange is really just a storage place in an Exchange server's private store provided for a mailbox-enabled user. When you create a mailbox, you can give other users permission to access it. You can grant this permission from the Active Directory Users and Computers snap-in by opening the property sheet for the user and then displaying the Exchange Advanced tab. On this tab, click the Mailbox Rights button to open the Permissions dialog box shown in Figure 18-8. When you click the Add button, you see a list of users and groups. You can select one or more of these entities and then click OK to grant them access to the mailbox. You can also delete accounts from the list, but you can never delete the primary account for the mailbox.

> **Tip** If you do not see the Exchange Advanced tab, you need to enable the Advanced view in Microsoft Management Console by choosing the Advanced command from the View menu.

You can also allow other users to see any folder in your mailbox by granting them permission through the standard property sheet for a folder in Outlook. If users have permission for a specific folder or their user accounts have been granted permissions on the mailbox, they can open the folder by choosing Other User's Folders from the Open submenu of the main File menu. They can also add the mailbox to their profile by using the option on the Advanced tab of the Microsoft Exchange Server property sheet. They simply click the Add button in the top portion of the Advanced tab and select the mailbox they want to add.

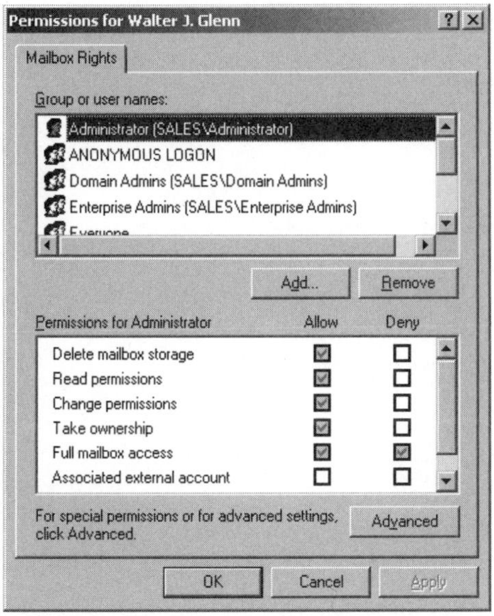

Figure 18-8. *Granting permissions to other users.*

Using Outlook to Delegate Mailbox Access

The previous section described how the administrator controls access to another user's mailbox using Active Directory Users and Computers. Using Outlook, users can grant privileges to other users without contacting the administrator. They can grant these privileges by right-clicking the folder (such as Calendar), choosing Properties, and then adding the appropriate user on the Permissions tab, as shown in Figure 18-9. These permissions are similar in nature to ACLs, except that they are Exchange-specific and can be assigned only to certain mail-enabled Active Directory objects. There is no one-to-one correlation between the permissions you see here and the Windows permissions.

In addition, a user can use the Delegates tab of the Options dialog box (available from the Tools menu) to delegate access to the folders in his or her mailbox. The user can also assign different levels of permissions for each folder. The person being granted delegate access will receive e-mail indicating that permissions have been granted and detailing what level those permissions are.

Once the privileges have been assigned to another user, that user can access the folders by pointing to Open on the File menu and choosing Other User's

Folder In Microsoft Outlook. This option is commonly used by administrative assistants checking their bosses' schedules or in situations in which a mailbox represents a conference room, a TV, a company car, or any other resource that can be checked out. In these cases, the Calendar is used to track resource use. By providing a few users with the ability to modify the resource's Calendar—and the rest of the company the ability to review the calendar—you can maintain a centralized location for companywide resource tracking.

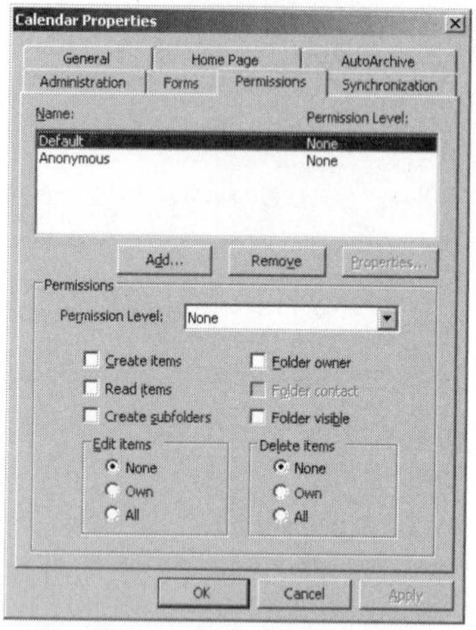

Figure 18-9. *Granting access using Outlook.*

Setting Up Roving Users

A *roving user* is a user who does not have a fixed physical location and might consequently log on to many different machines. (In Windows parlance, these users have *roaming profiles*. Exchange Server calls them *roving profiles*.) To accommodate such a user, you could set up a user profile on each of the machines he or she might use, but this solution might be impractical. Another way to address this situation is by creating a roving user profile.

The configuration information for a roving user is stored on a shared disk on a network server, allowing this information to be accessed from any machine that can connect to the network. When you set up a roving user profile on a machine running Windows Server 2003, client machines that log on to the network with that profile look on the shared disk for configuration information. The common access to the storage of a roving profile eliminates the need to have this profile stored on many machines. When you enable roving users in Windows, that's all you have to do. Outlook 2003 automatically supports roving Exchange users. For more information about setting up a shared user profile on Windows Server 2003 and various clients, refer to the documentation for those products.

You can also accommodate roving users through Microsoft Outlook Web Access and the Web Store. These features are discussed in Chapter 19, "Supporting Outlook Web Access."

HTTP Access from Outlook

When used with the Microsoft Windows Server 2003 RPC Proxy Service and Exchange 2003, Outlook 2003 clients can connect to an Exchange server using HTTP or HTTPS instead of a direct RPC. This reduces the need for virtual private networks (VPNs) or dial-up remote access to the network, and thus reduces cost for remote Outlook access in the process. Using HTTP Access also provides for increased security by ensuring that remote Outlook users don't need access to the entire network. This unifies the connection methods also found in Microsoft Office Outlook Web Access and Outlook Mobile Access.

To connect to an Exchange 2003 server, the following requirements must be met:

- The client must be running Microsoft Windows XP with Service Pack 1 and the Q331320 hotfix (or later) and Outlook 2003.
- The user must have a mailbox on a server running Microsoft Exchange Server 2003 and Microsoft Windows Server 2003.
- The Microsoft Windows Server 2003 RPC Proxy Service must be enabled and configured.

To set up an Outlook client to connect to an Exchange server over HTTP, you'll need the URL for the server running the RPC Proxy service.

> **More Info** For more information on configuring Outlook 2003 to connect to an Exchange server using RPC over HTTP, check out the *Microsoft Office 2003 Resource Kit* (Microsoft Press, 2003) or find the information on the Web at *http://www.microsoft.com/office/ork/2003/three/ch8/outc07.htm*.

Summary

Outlook 2003 is the preferred client for Exchange Server 2003. This chapter covered how to deploy Outlook 2003 in your organization, describing the various installation options, how to support offline use of Outlook 2003, and how to set up profiles and provide access to other users' mailboxes. Outlook is a full-featured client that can be used in conjunction with Exchange Server, even when the client machine is not directly connected to an Exchange Server. A single Outlook client can support many users, and a single user can roam to different machines and use Outlook on each of those machines to check his or her e-mail.

The next chapter looks at how to access e-mail, public folders, and calendars over the Web using Outlook Web Access.

Chapter 19

Supporting Outlook Web Access

This chapter focuses on Microsoft Outlook Web Access (OWA). Because the need for remote access to e-mail has greatly increased, use of OWA will also only increase as time goes by. Understanding the advantages and limitations of OWA will benefit your planning, implementation, and troubleshooting efforts. In the following sections, we'll examine the new OWA features in Microsoft Exchange Server 2003, how to manage OWA, and how to deploy this technology. There is much here to discuss, so let's get started.

Features of OWA

OWA provides an environment for users to access both public folder store data and mailbox store data using a browser. With OWA, clients based on UNIX, Macintosh, and Microsoft Windows can view and work with any public folder, mailbox, Global Address List (GAL), and calendar. (For UNIX users, OWA is the primary Outlook solution for e-mail, calendar, and collaboration functionality.)

Among the many navigation, view, and workflow improvements that have an impact on performance and functionality of OWA in Exchange Server 2003 are the following:

- Two different versions of OWA
- New customized logon page
- Cookie-based validation in which the OWA cookie is invalid after the user logs out or becomes inactive for a configured period of time
- Starting with Microsoft Internet Explorer (IE) 6 with Service Pack 1, the credentials cache is cleared after logout
- Better user interface
- User-configured window size that persists during an OWA session
- Preview pane can be to the right of messages and attachments that are open directly in the pane

- Spelling checker is provided for e-mail messages
- Server-based e-mail handling rules that are created and managed by the user

In spite of all these new features, OWA does retain some limitations. Therefore, before you deploy OWA, you must consider what will not be accommodated:

- **Offline use** A user must connect to an Exchange server to view information.
- **No access to offline folders** There is no synchronization of local offline folders with server folders.

Logon/Logoff Improvements

You can enable a new logon page for OWA that will store the user's user name and password in a cookie instead of in the browser. When the user leaves his OWA session or after a configured period of inactivity, the cookie is cleared. In either scenario, a user must re-authenticate to use OWA again. Note that the sessions do not timeout during the creation of a message.

This logon improvement is not enabled by default. To enable the logon page, open the properties of the HTTP Virtual Server and select the Enable Forms Based Authentication For Outlook Web Access check box (Figure 19-1). Note that before you can use this feature, you must have Secure Sockets Layer (SSL) configured in Microsoft Internet Information Services (IIS).

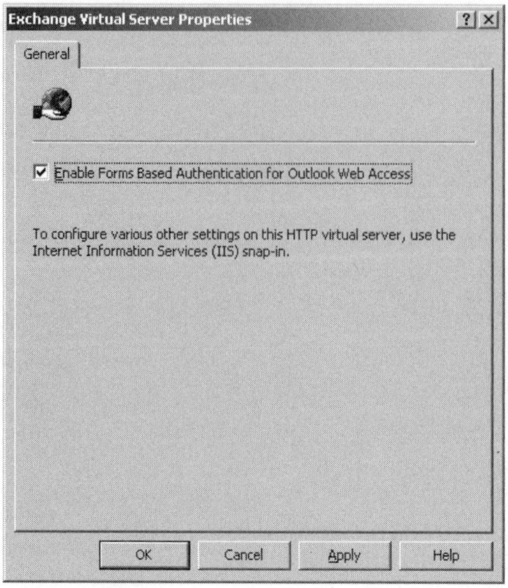

Figure 19-1. *Enabling logon authentication.*

To configure SSL, you must either install Certificate Services on your Windows Server 2003 and generate a certificate for the OWA Web site, or purchase an SSL certificate from a third-party source. After you install the SSL certificate and require SSL on your Web site that is hosting OWA, you will be presented with the new logon screen shown in Figure 19-2.

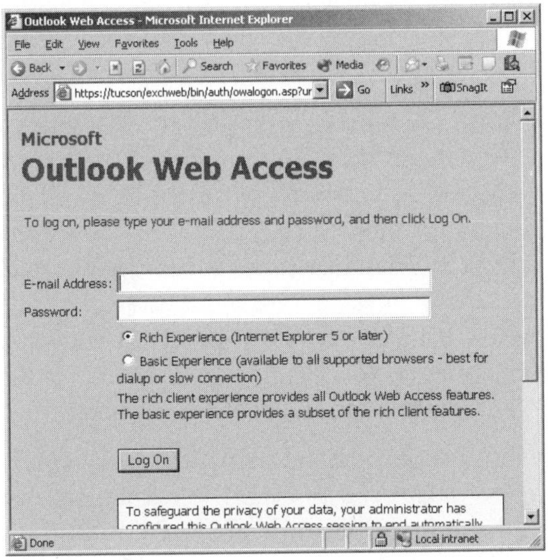

Figure 19-2. *Exchange 2003 OWA logon screen.*

The new logon improvement has three other features. First, users cannot accidentally enable the Remember My Password check box. Also, when the user logs off, the user has no way to access her inbox unless she re-authenticates. Finally, the OWA toolbars and graphics are downloaded in a hidden frame during the logon process to give a peppier logon experience to the user.

Notice that during the logon process, the user can choose from two interface experiences: Rich and Basic. The Rich experience includes all OWA features. The Basic experience does not and is meant for users who are connecting over a slow wide area network (WAN) link and need only the essentials of OWA. For users with faster connection speeds, the Rich experience is preferred.

As an administrator, you can configure the registry of the OWA for timeout settings. Think also in terms of a public computer and a trusted computer. A *public computer* is one that is available to the general public, for instance, a kiosk in a public area that supplies OWA. If the Public setting is selected, the timeout will be set to 15 minutes. This timeout setting can be overridden by a server-side registry setting:

```
Location: HKEY_LOCAL_MACHINE\System\CurrentControlSet\Services\MSExchangeWEB\OWA
Parameter: PublicClientTimeout
Type: REG_DWORD
Value: <number of minutes>
```

This registry key assumes a 15-minute timeout setting. The minimum value is *1*, and the maximum value is *43200* (30 days).

The *trusted computer* setting is meant for those computers that sit on your internal network. The default value for this setting is assumed to be *1440* minutes, or 24 hours. If you want to change this setting, use the same registry key you would for the Public computer but use the parameter *TrustedClientTimeout*. The minimum and maximum values for *PublicClientTimeout* and *TrustedClientTimeout* are the same.

You need to know about some issues with the timeout setting. First, the cookie-based timeout setting is not absolute—it triggers between the value of the setting and 1.5×<*setting*>. In other words, if you set the timeout value as 10 minutes, the timeout actually triggers between 10 and 15 minutes (10 × 1.5 = 15). Since the default setting for the trusted computer is 1440 minutes, the actual timeout will trigger somewhere between 1440 and 2160 minutes, or 24–36 hours. Such a wide window for a timeout trigger might not be compatible with your security policies. Unfortunately, the formula is not configurable, so you might be forced to lower the default value on trusted computers if your information security policies dictate this.

The second issue you need to be aware of is that the *TrustedClientTimeout* setting cannot be lower than the *PublicClientTimeout* setting. Even when you set the trusted value lower than the public value, Exchange 2003 will automatically adjust the trusted value to be equal to the public setting. This automatic configuration change will kick in regardless of which value you incorrectly set. So whether you set the trusted value too low or the public value too high, you'll end up with the trusted value being automatically set to be equal to the public value.

Another security feature implemented in Exchange 2003 OWA is that by default, the user cannot change his password. If you upgrade from Microsoft Exchange 2000 to Exchange 2003, the Exchange 2000 setting that allows users to change passwords will be retained. You can set this parameter in the Exchange server's registry:

```
Key:  HKEY_LOCAL_MACHINE\System\CurrentControlSet\Services\MSExchangeWEB\OWA
Parameter:  DisablePassword
Type: REG_DWORD
Value:  0x0000001= users cannot change passwords, 0x00000000=users can change
    passwords
```

Securing Outlook Web Access Client Traffic

To secure the transmission of messages between Exchange 2003 OWA and a client, you must decide how to authenticate the client and whether you want client traffic encrypted or signed.

You can authenticate your client in one of three ways: Anonymous, Basic, and Integrated Windows. The *Anonymous* setting is the least secure authentication scheme, providing limited access for specific public folders and directory information. Anonymous authentication is supported by all clients and is the preferred method of allowing general public access to specific public folders.

Basic authentication uses clear text to authenticate the client with a domain controller. Basic authentication requires the user to enter the user name, the domain name, and the password. Because the user name and password are sent in clear text between the server and the client, using SSL to encrypt the user name and password is recommended to ensure safer transmissions.

Integrated Windows Authentication (IWA) is meant for clients running Internet Explorer 5 or later. IWA uses Kerberos to perform authentication and offers the highest level of security. In IWA, the user's password is not sent on the line in clear text. Instead it is encrypted so that even when the password's packets are sniffed, the attacker cannot read the password. We'll discuss how to implement these concepts later in this chapter in the section titled "Deploying OWA."

Managing OWA

You can manage OWA in several ways. If you need to manage OWA for individual users, use Active Directory Users and Computers. Use the Exchange Features tab (Figure 19-3) to enable or disable user access to the user's mailbox via OWA.

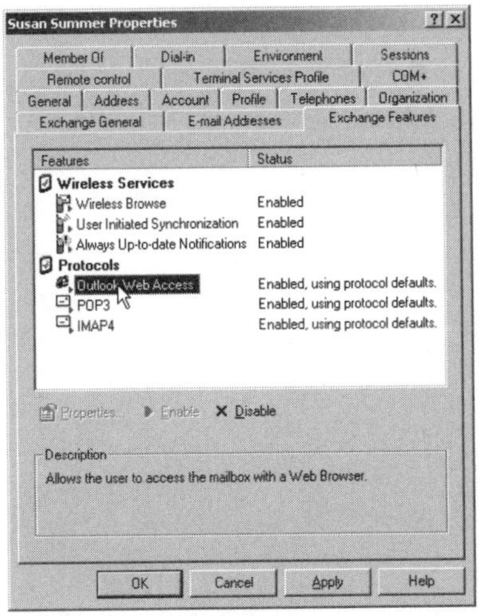

Figure 19-3. *Enabling OWA in a user's account properties.*

To manage the OWA server, you use two administrative tools: the Exchange System Manager (ESM) and the Internet Services Manager (ISM).

Exchange System Manager

With the Exchange System Manager snap-in, you can create new virtual servers or virtual directories that will appear in the Internet Services Manager snap-in. Each virtual server requires its own unique IP address and port number combination. You will create more than one virtual server when you have users with different authentication needs in OWA—for example, when only certain users need to read their e-mail using SSL; or when you host e-mail for more than one domain name and you want to ensure that each domain name has its own OWA configurations.

You create more than one virtual server using the HTTP virtual server in the Exchange System Manager. The virtual server itself has only one property to configure, indicating that this object is not the primary one in which we configure OWA settings—particularly security settings. You can find the HTTP virtual server in the Protocols folder in the ESM (Figure 19-4).

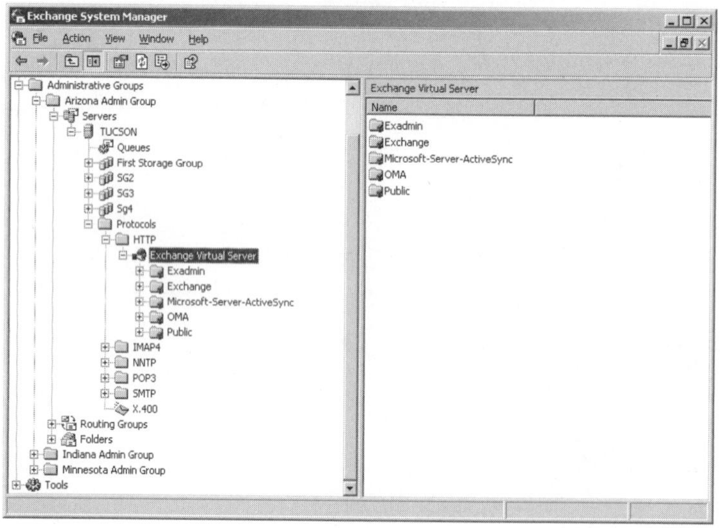

Figure 19-4. *The HTTP virtual server in the Exchange System Manager snap-in.*

Internet Information Services

You administer many parts of OWA through the Internet Information Services snap-in. After you open the Internet Information Services snap-in and expand your server to see its subordinate objects, you see several virtual roots that Exchange creates when it is installed:

- **Exchange** (*http://server/exchange*) This root points to the Exchange mailboxes.
- **Public** (*http://server/public*) This root points to the public folders.

- **Exadmin** (*http://server/exadmin*) This root is for Web-based Exchange administration.
- **OMA (Outlook Mobile Access)** This root works with mobile clients to enable them to access their mailboxes and public folders.
- **Exchange Active Sync** This root is used to synchronize information with mobile clients and their devices.

These virtual roots point to the databases via the ExIFS (Exchange Installable File System). In Exchange 2000 Server, the Exchange databases were exposed as another virtual file system to operating system. Hence, the operating system can read and write files to the Exchange databases similarly to the way it does to a FAT (File Allocation Table), FAT32, or NTFS file system. Because Microsoft is moving to hosting files in a SQL database rather than in the Web Storage System, they decided to leave the ExIFS mounted in Exchange 2003 but not expose it as the (default) M:\ drive, as they did in Exchange 2000. All this means is that the virtual roots in Exchange 2003 are still pointing to the Exchange databases, but the databases are not exposed in the interface as another file system.

Each of these virtual roots can be individually managed in IIS. You can set security, content expiration, and other settings for each part of Exchange using the Internet Information Services snap-in. When you manage these virtual roots in IIS, you are managing the HTTP virtual server in Exchange.

Deploying OWA

We will cover two basic deployment scenarios: the single-server scenario, and the front-end/back-end scenario.

Single-Server Scenario

In the single-server scenario, there is only one Exchange server. Users connect directly to IIS on the single Exchange server and access their mailboxes on the Exchange server. For many smaller environments, this will be the topology used. This is also the most simple and straightforward approach to implementing OWA.

Front-End/Back-End Scenario

In the front-end/back-end scenario, at least one front-end (FE) server hosts the Exchange protocols in a bank of IIS servers. In the back-end (BE), at least one Exchange database server is running. The FE servers proxy client calls to the BE servers to give them access to their mailboxes or public folders.

The protocols that can be offered using this scenario include POP3 (Post Office Protocol version 3), IMAP4 (Internet Messaging Application Protocol version 4),

NNTP (Network News Transfer Protocol), and HTTP (Hyper Text Transfer Protocol). For a detailed discussion of these protocols, refer to Chapter 20, "Supporting Internet Protocols and SMTP."

Both the enterprise and standard versions of Exchange 2003 support this front-end/back-end scenario. Front-end servers will not host a mailbox or a public folder store. Front-end servers forward client requests to back-end servers that are also running Exchange 2003. A back-end server maintains at least one mailbox or public folder store. Note that you can use an Exchange 2003 FE to proxy to an Exchange 2000 BE server, but the functionality will be limited to the Exchange 2000 feature set. If you want the full set of features that ships with Exchange 2003, you need to use Exchange 2003 at both ends.

The back-end/front-end configuration gives you several advantages:

- **Single namespace** Because you can use protocols such as Network Load Balancing (NLB), no matter how many IIS servers you place in the cluster, the clients will have only a single name and IP address to remember when they want to connect to their mailboxes over HTTP.
- **Offload processing** If you choose to implement SSL or some other type of encryption, the front-end servers will handle all the encryption and decryption processing, thus offloading this work from the BE database servers.
- **Better security** You can select where you want your FE servers to reside—inside a firewall, outside a firewall, or perhaps in a perimeter network. FE servers can be configured to authenticate users before proxying their requests to BE servers.
- **Scalability** Because you can add new servers to the FE load-balancing cluster, each added server represents additional capacity to manage new and existing client requests. And because clients do not need to know which BE server hosts their mailboxes, you can move a client's mailbox to a new server, and that move will be transparent to the client. This architecture is very scalable and can accommodate millions of users.

NLB is a server that ships with Windows 2003 that dynamically distributes client calls for services between multiple FE servers. Notice that we are talking about the client request level, not the client session level. Sessions aren't load-balanced; all the individual client calls are. This load balancing is achieved through the virtualization of the Media Access Control (MAC) and IP addresses on each Network Interface Card (NIC) on each server in the cluster. Hence, as each call comes into the servers, that call has the same host name, IP address, and MAC card combination as the other calls, making it much easier to load-balance the traffic load, not just session load, between servers.

More Info To learn more about network load balancing, refer to the *Network Load Balancing Technical Overview* white paper, which can be found in TechNet or the MSDN Library.

You can always use a third-party hardware solution for load balancing, or you can implement the Domain Name System (DNS) round-robin scheme.

Microsoft has some other guidelines for implementing the FE/BE architecture. First, place at least two servers in the NLB cluster for each protocol you want to offer using this architecture. Each FE server will determine where the user's mailbox resides by using the user's directory information from Windows 2003 server.

Second, if you need broad availability for your Exchange databases, implement a clustering solution for these databases. Doing so will ensure you achieve as much up-time as possible.

Finally, do not allow direct access to the BE servers. It will defeat your purpose in creating FE servers in the first place, and it will place unnecessary load on those BE servers.

Configuring an OWA FE Server

The default configuration for Exchange 2003 is that no additional configurations are required on an FE server other than selecting the Front End server check box. This box is available in the server's properties. Once selected, the Exchange server is ready to run as an FE server.

If you host multiple domain names or multiple public folder trees, create additional virtual servers or directories. To create a new virtual server, open the ESM and navigate to the HTTP protocol folder. Then right-click the folder, point to New, and select HTTP Virtual Server. You need to name the server, so enter a unique IP address and port number combination (Figure 19-5), and set your access and authentication values on the Access tab. After you finish, the new virtual server will be created and you can start the server.

Note The virtual server in Exchange and the Web site in IIS will need to be started separately. Note that if you select the same IP address as the default virtual server and select a different port number, you'll need to manually configure the port number on the new Web site in IIS in order to get both the Web site and the virtual server to start. Also, an FE server cannot be the Recipient Update Server for any domain controllers in your organization.

When you create a new virtual server, that server is associated with the default domain name for your Exchange organization, so you'll need to associate the new virtual server with a specific SMTP domain name. You can do this in the virtual server's properties in the ESM, as shown in Figure 19-5. Click the Modify button and select the domain name for this virtual server to manage. If you don't change the association, users will be unable to log on to the front-end server unless they also have e-mail addresses from the default domain. If the domain name that you need to assign to the virtual server does not appear in the list, add it in as an additional SMTP domain for your Exchange organization in the Recipient Policies.

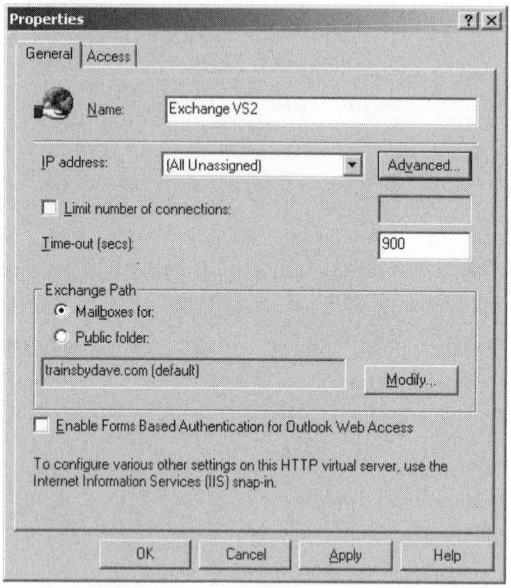

Figure 19-5. *Adding a new HTTP Virtual Server.*

To host multiple domain names using virtual directories instead of new virtual servers, add a virtual directory under the default Exchange HTTP virtual server by right-clicking the Exchange Virtual Server, pointing to New, and selecting Virtual Directory. You can select the domain name you'd like the virtual directory to service by clicking the Modify button (Figure 19-6). Once selected, this virtual directory can service client requests for e-mail or public folder access.

You would want to use virtual directories over virtual servers when you need to either browse or synchronize e-mail with OMA clients. When you want to access e-mail over Port 80 using the same IP address for each domain name, virtual directories are your answer. Let's look at how this works using an example. Your default domain name is trainsbydave.com and you want to host e-mail for Networknowledge. By using virtual directories, the URL for Networknowledge would be *www.trainsbydave.com/Networknowledge*.

If you have additional IP addresses available, using a virtual server for each additional hosted domain might make more sense, because each virtual server would be assigned a unique IP address and the URL would be domain-specific: *www.networknowledge.com/exchange* or *www.trainsbydave.com/exchange*. Remembering one domain name in the URL might be easier for your users than remembering two different domain names.

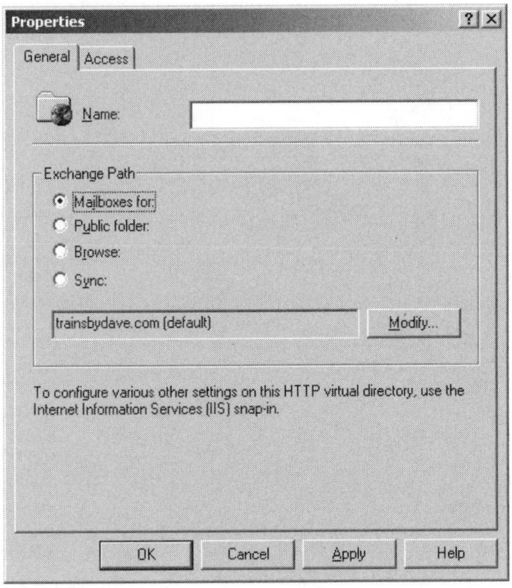

Figure 19-6. *Configuring a virtual directory and assigning it to a domain name for an HTTP Virtual Server.*

Unlike with the virtual server, you have two additional selections: Browse and Sync. The Sync selection dims the Modify button and inserts the Outlook Mobile Access selection to allow synchronization of your OMA clients. This virtual directory inherits the parent virtual server's SMTP domain assignment. Hence, if you need to synchronize e-mail with OMA clients for five different domain names, you'll need to have five different HTTP virtual servers set up, each assigned to a different SMTP domain name.

Note When you configure additional virtual servers or directories on the FE servers, you need to do the same on the BE servers so that the FE/BE topology works properly. This is because the address through which the client browser accesses the FE server is forwarded by the FE server to the BE server, so the BE server must be aware of every name a client might use to read the FE server. Note that when your BE servers are clustered, you must use the cluster group name.

Firewalls and FE Servers

Consider your firewall topology when you plan the placement of your FE servers. You have only three placement choices: place the FE server inside your firewall, place the FE server outside your firewall, or place the FE server between two firewalls. Each configuration has pros and cons. Let's discuss each one individually.

Placing an FE Server Inside a Single Firewall

When you place an FE server inside your firewall, you have a single firewall separating your FE server and the network from the Internet. The positive aspect of this topology is the cost savings as well as the offering of some security to your FE server and network. You need to open the client access ports to the FE server, such as port 110 for POP3, 143 for IMAP4, 119 for NNTP, and 80 for HTTP.

The downside to this topology is that once the firewall has been compromised or traversed, your entire network is exposed. This isn't just an issue with the FE server—it is an issue of having only one firewall. Many smaller organizations will choose a single firewall because of the financial savings. However, if at all possible, implement two firewalls and a perimeter network.

Place the FE Server Outside Your Firewall

Placing your FE server outside of a single firewall is probably the least desirable configuration because your FE server is entirely exposed, and the number of ports you must open on your firewall to allow the FE server to talk with the BE server makes the firewall look like Swiss cheese.

To have a firewall between your FE and BE server, you need to open the following ports:

- 389 and 3268 for Lightweight Directory Access Protocol (LDAP) lookups to a domain controller and global catalog server
- 80 for regular HTTP traffic
- 53 for DNS traffic
- 135 and 1024+ for remote procedure call (RPC) traffic
- 445 for Netlogon traffic
- 88 for Kerberos traffic

Some of these port openings can be mitigated by using Hosts file entries on each FE server. In addition, you can configure the FE server to use specific domain controllers and global catalog servers by modifying the entries on the Directory Access tab in the server's properties. This will enable you to close the RPC ports. On this tab, be sure you deselect the Automatically Discover Servers check box (Figure 19-7) to disable the option.

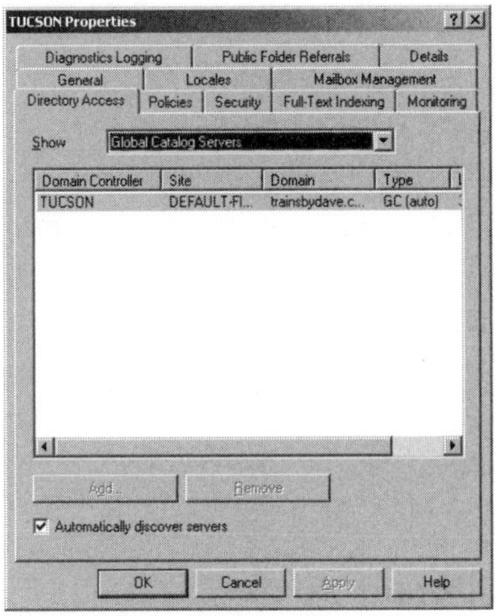

Figure 19-7. *The Directory Access tab in the server's properties.*

Placing the FE Server Between Two Firewalls

Placing the FE server between two firewalls is the preferred method of implementing the FE/BE topology. The FE server is protected by the Internet firewall, and only the client access ports are open on the Internet firewall. The required ports of 135, 1024+, 445, and the ports we just discussed will need to be opened on the intranet firewall between your FE and BE servers, or else the Hosts file and the Directory Access modifications will need to be made, but this is certainly better than opening these ports on your external firewall.

If you place an FE server in a perimeter network to service HTTP requests, then on the Internet firewall, open only port 80. On the firewall between your FE and BE servers, open the ports discussed in the previous section or make the Hosts file and DSAccess modifications as described.

You'll also want to configure two other registry keys. The first is the DisableNetlogonCheck registry key. DSAccess connects to Active Directory to check available disk space, time synchronization, and replication participation using NetLogon over RPC. If you chose to not allow RPC traffic over your firewall, you should stop this NetLogon check. Here is the DisableNetlogonCheck registry key information:

```
Key:  HKEY_LOCAL_MACHINE\System\CurrentControlSet\Services\MSExchangeDSAccess
Value Name:  DisableNetlogonCheck
Data Type:  REG_DWORD
Value Data: 1
```

On the FE servers, you should also create a registry key to prevent DSAccess from pinging domain controllers, and you do this by editing the LdapKeepAliveSecs key. Create this registry key as follows:

```
Key location:  HKEY_LOCAL_MACHINE\System\CurrentControlSet\Services\
    MSExchangeDSAccess
Value Name:  LdapKeepAliveSecs
Data Type: REG_DWORD
Value Data: 0
```

Although you can't use SSL (443) between the FE and BE servers, you can implement Internet Protocol Security (IPSec) at the network layer. IPSec can be configured to either require the security or simply to ask for the security.

More Info For step-by-step instructions about how to create IPSec filters between your FE and BE servers, refer to Chapter 4 of *Securing Exchange Communications in the Security Operations Guide for Exchange 2000*. This guide can be found in TechNet (*www.microsoft.com/technet*).

OWA User Features

In this section, we'll cover the OWA user interface and discuss some of the features that are unique to Exchange 2003 Server.

When the user opens OWA, the default interface is very similar to Outlook 2003 (Figure 19-8), in which the panes have a vertical format. The user desiring a more traditional view of Outlook can change this default presentation by clicking the Show/Hide Preview Pane button.

Through the OWA interface, users can also set configuration options for the following:

- Out of Office Assistant
- Messaging
- Spelling
- Secure messaging
- Privacy and junk e-mail prevention
- Date and time formats
- Calendar
- Reminders

- Contacts
- Changing the password (if enabled on the server)
- Recovering deleted items

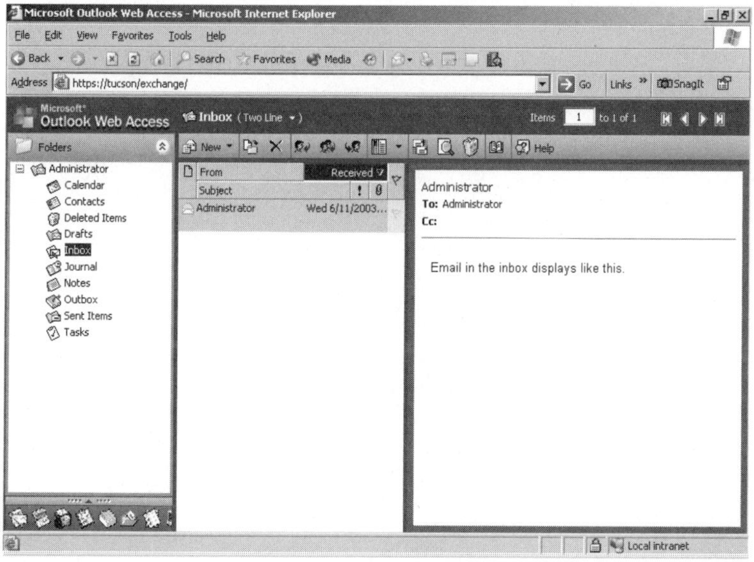

Figure 19-8. *The default OWA interface focused on the user's inbox.*

The options presented in the OWA interface are not as robust as those in the Outlook client. Many options will be missing, but some of the more important ones will be available to your OWA users through the browser interface. There is also a limited rules wizard that will enable OWA users to manage messages based on a predefined set of criteria.

OWA Segmentation

OWA *segmentation* provides the ability to selectively enable or disable OWA features in the user's browser interface. For example, you can enable or disable calendaring, contacts, and public folders. Segmentation can occur on either a per-user or a per-server basis. User settings override server settings when a conflict arises.

Segmentation is useful when you want to limit client functionality due to training constraints or other organization-specific policies; charge a premium for certain functionalities; or lessen the performance impact of certain features on the server, the network, or a slow WAN connection from the client. To enable segmentation on the server, modify the registry as follows:

```
Key:  HKEY_LOCAL_MACHINE\System\CurrentControlSet\Services\MSExchangeWEB\OWA
Data Type:  REG_DWORD
Value Name:  DefaultMailboxFolderSet
Value:  Varies
```

We say the registry key value "varies" because the value you enter depends on the features you want to display in the OWA interface. For each feature you want to include, you must sum the values and enter the total into the registry. The values are presented in a table that we've taken directly from the Exchange 2000 help file (Figure 19-9).

Feature	Value (Decimal)									
	512	256	128	64	32	16	8	4	2	1
Messaging	0	0	0	0	0	0	0	0	0	1
Calendar	0	0	0	0	0	0	0	0	1	1
Contacts	0	0	0	0	0	0	0	1	0	1
Tasks	0	0	0	0	0	0	1	0	0	1
Journal	0	0	0	0	0	1	0	0	0	1
Sticky Notes	0	0	0	0	1	0	0	0	0	1
Public Folders	0	0	0	1	0	0	0	0	0	1
Reminders	0	0	1	0	0	0	0	0	1	1
New Mail	0	1	0	0	0	0	0	0	0	1
IE5 Rich UI	1	0	0	0	0	0	0	0	0	1
All	1	1	1	1	1	1	1	1	1	1

Figure 19-9. *Server-Side OWA segmentation values matrix from the Exchange 2000 help file.*

Let's look at an example and refer to Figure 19-9. Suppose you want to enable only the user's inbox, new mail, and calendaring functions. You would add the decimal value for each function as follows:

1 (inbox) + 256 (new mail) + 2 (calendaring) = 259

The decimal summation is 259. In the registry entry (Figure 19-10), you select Decimal and then enter **259**. After you click OK, the decimal is automatically converted to hex and is displayed, as illustrated in Figure 19-11.

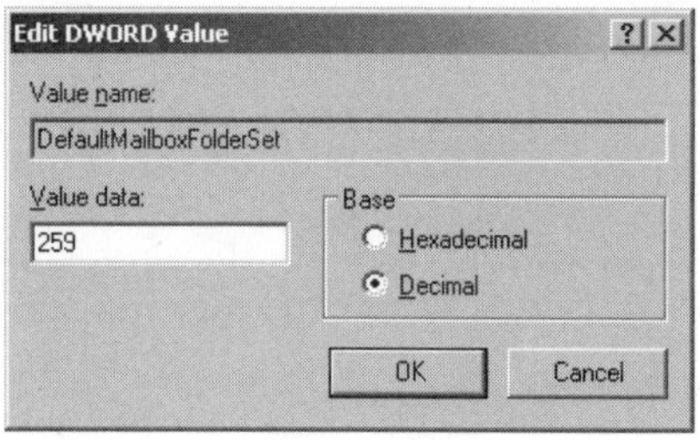

Figure 19-10. *Entering a decimal value for the DefaultMailboxFolderSet registry key.*

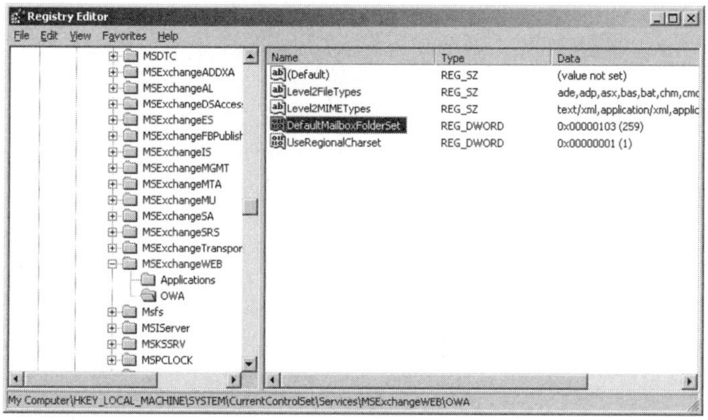

Figure 19-11. *Observing the value of 259 for the DefaultMailboxFolderSet registry key in the Registry Editor.*

You can see the effect of entering the decimal summation in Figure 19-12, in which the user's default folder set for OWA is now vastly different because only the Inbox, Calendar, and Options folders are available—Tasks, Journal, Notes, and other folders do not appear. In this illustration, the Folders folder merely points back to the available folders in this view, and the Options section cannot be turned off. However, the Options menus are limited too. For example, in this illustration, since we didn't select to display Contacts, the Contacts Options in the Options menu is not displayed.

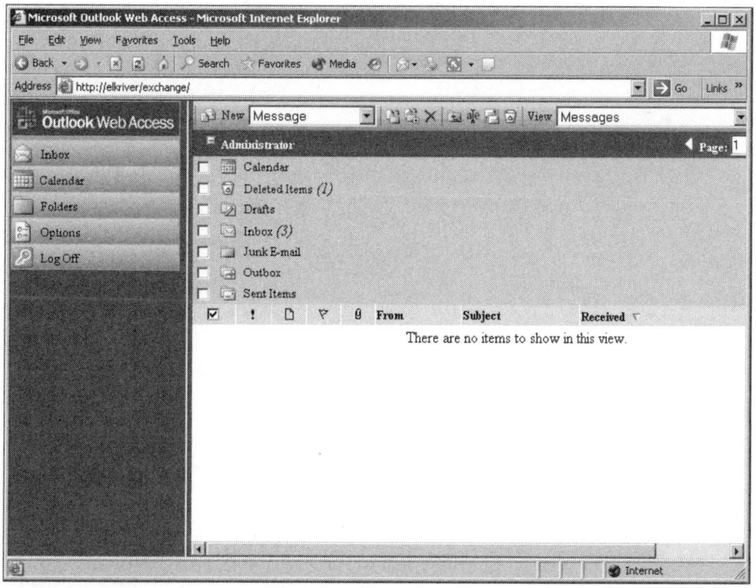

Figure 19-12. *The OWA interface with the limited* DefaultMailboxFolderSet *value applied.*

If you need to enable these interface limitations on a per-user basis, add the Active Directory attribute *msExchMailboxFolderSet*. You must extend the schema to add this attribute by importing the owa-schema.ldf file. This file can be found in the Exchange 2000 Service Pack 2 or Service Pack 3 file set and is in the Support\Owaschema folder. Included with this file is the Owa-Schema.vbs script which, when run, will take care of extending the schema for you.

Once you have extended the schema, you can modify *msExchMailboxFolderSet* on the user account in Active Directory by using the ADSI Edit tool. You use the values in Figure 19-13 to establish the folder set you want displayed for a particular user in OWA. You find the user's account in the domain partition (Figure 19-14). Simply open the account properties, double-click the *msExchMailboxFolderSet* attribute, and enter the value in the dialog box provided.

Feature	Value (Decimal)									
	512	256	128	64	32	16	8	4	2	1
Messaging	0	0	0	0	0	0	0	0	0	1
Calendar	0	0	0	0	0	0	0	0	1	1
Contacts	0	0	0	0	0	0	0	1	0	1
Tasks	0	0	0	0	0	0	1	0	0	1
Journal	0	0	0	0	0	1	0	0	0	1
Sticky Notes	0	0	0	0	1	0	0	0	0	1
Public Folders	0	0	0	1	0	0	0	0	0	1
Reminders	0	0	1	0	0	0	0	0	1	1
New Mail	0	1	0	0	0	0	0	0	0	1
IE5 Rich UI	1	0	0	0	0	0	0	0	0	1
All	1	1	1	1	1	1	1	1	1	1

Figure 19-13. *Per-client OWA segmentation values matrix from the Exchange 2000 help file.*

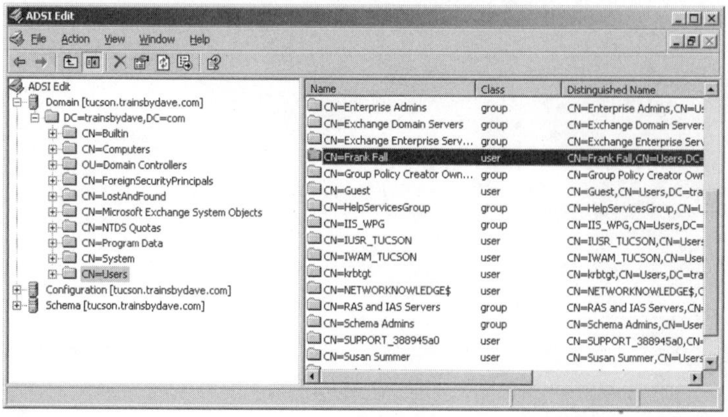

Figure 19-14. *A user account highlighted in ADSI Edit inside the domain partition.*

Summary

In this chapter, you learned about the features of OWA, how to implement OWA, and how to secure client transactions. You also learned how to limit the OWA interface both at the server and user account levels. In the next chapter, we'll look at the various Exchange protocols, such as POP3, IMAP4, and SMTP. We'll also discuss the SMTP Virtual Server and how to configure it.

Chapter 20

Supporting Internet Protocols and SMTP

This chapter covers the Simple Mail Transfer Protocol (SMTP), Post Office Protocol version 3 (POP3), Internet Message Access Protocol version 4 (IMAP4), and Microsoft Outlook Web Access (OWA). At first glance, these might seem the sort of dry topics that only a true geek would appreciate. In reality, however, a good understanding of the basic Internet protocols will greatly assist your efforts in troubleshooting and understanding the Microsoft Exchange Server 2003 architecture.

SMTP is the native transport protocol for Microsoft Exchange Server 2003 and is used by the Routing Group Connector, by the SMTP Connector, and for general communications between Exchange 2003 servers. The other protocols—POP3, IMAP4, and OWA—are considered different ways to access the Store process. Understanding the advantages and limitations of each protocol will benefit your planning, implementation, and troubleshooting efforts.

Simple Mail Transfer Protocol

Because it is impossible to provide an in-depth analysis of SMTP in this book, this section concentrates on the parts of SMTP that are most relevant to administering and troubleshooting Exchange Server 2003.

Simple Mail Transfer Protocol (SMTP) has its roots in the File Transfer Protocol (FTP). Before SMTP was originally defined in RFC 561, it was customary to copy messages to their destinations as simple files, using FTP. The problem with this technique was that it was sometimes difficult to discern who had sent the file and to whom the file was being sent, due to the lack of identifying information. What was needed was the ability to pass information between two hosts while identifying who the sender and recipient were.

In 1973, the beginnings of such a message structure were defined, containing some header fields and the body of the text. Further refinements came in RFCs 680, 724, and 733 before the current standard in RFC 822 was issued. Now each header line consists of a field name terminated by a colon and followed by a field body. For a message to be valid, the creation time, source, and destination fields must be filled in. Other optional fields, such as received, subject, reply-to, and return-path, can be filled in as well. As the message passes from one Message Transfer Agent (MTA) to the next, these required fields are enumerated and then added to the message header, allowing the recipient to see how the message was transferred through the mail system.

> **More Info** For more information about the standards for transferring messages, refer to *"F.400/X.400 Standard: Data Networks and Open System Communication Message Handling Systems,"* from the International Telecommunication Union at *http://www.itu.org*.

The SMTP design is based on a communication model that follows these basic steps:

1. The user makes an e-mail request to a sender-SMTP.
2. The sender-SMTP establishes a two-way transmission channel to a receiver-SMTP.
3. The sender-SMTP generates SMTP commands and sends them to the receiver-SMTP.
4. The receiver-SMTP sends response commands to the sender-SMTP.

For example, if User1 wants to send e-mail to User2 over SMTP, the sequence of events would be as follows (assuming that both users are running the SMTP service on their computers):

1. User1 contacts User2 and establishes a two-way transmission channel over TCP port 25, using the HELO command.
2. User1 sends a MAIL command indicating the sender of the e-mail. This is how we know who sent the e-mail.
3. User2 sends an OK reply.
4. User1 sends a RCPT command identifying the recipient of the e-mail. This is how we know who the recipient of the e-mail is.
5. User2 sends an OK reply.
6. User1 sends the e-mail.
7. User2 sends an OK reply.
8. User1 sends the QUIT command.
9. User2 sends an OK reply and then terminates the connection.

The commands from the sender and receiver are always sent one at a time, and one reply is sent for each command. SMTP does not support multiple commands sent as a batch to another SMTP host. Table 20-1 lists the more common SMTP commands and their purpose.

Table 20-1. Summary of SMTP commands

Command	Description
HELO	Identifies the sender-SMTP to the receiver-SMTP based on host names.
MAIL	Initiates e-mail transfer with indication of originator (reverse path argument). If routed through a relay agent, the first host in the list is the most recent relay agent. Non-delivery reports generated by the receiver-SMTP are sent back using this command.
RCPT	Identifies one of the recipients (forward path argument). Multiple recipients are specified by multiple use of this command. The forward path can optionally include a list of relay hosts, but it must include the final destination mailbox.
DATA	Indicates that message data is ready to be sent in 128-ASCII-character codes.
RSET	Resets e-mail transfer. Received e-mail data is discarded.
VRFY	Asks the receiver-SMTP to verify that the e-mail address identifies a user.
EXPN	Asks the receiver-SMTP to confirm the identity of a mailing list and return the membership of that list.
HELP	Requests help on a command.
NOOP	Requests the receiver-SMTP to send an OK.
TURN	Reverses roles of sender and receiver.
QUIT	Requests termination of connection. The receiver-SMTP must send an OK and then close the transmission channel.

7-Bit ASCII Character Set

SMTP commands are sent in the American Standard Code for Information Interchange (ASCII) 7-bit character set. This fact is important because the TCP architecture assumes an 8-bits-per-byte transmission channel.

E-mail started in the United States and at first was used to send text only. Because the entire English alphabet and standard English punctuation marks can fit into the 128 (2^7) possible combinations of 7 bits, the 8th bit was used as a parity bit, giving some extra redundancy in error checking.

The first 128 characters in the ASCII character set define the 26 letters of the English alphabet in both lowercase and uppercase and the more common punctuation marks that might be used in everyday messaging. Messages that use only these characters are said to be 7-bit ASCII.

Extended ASCII Character Set

Because there are many more than 128 characters in the international alphabets, the extended ASCII character set defines 256 characters, accommodating most European alphabets. Defining this many characters means using the 8th bit for character generation instead of for parity. The problem with doing so is that SMTP doesn't permit the use of the 8th bit. Thus, even if you could find an SMTP MTA that would pass all 8 bits, the 8th one would be lost because the protocol itself works only with 7 bits. The solution to this problem has been to fit 8 bits into 7 bits at the sending end and then extract them at the receiving end. Since bits don't compress very well, we add some extra bytes so that the bit combination is cleanly divisible by 7.

We accomplish this task by taking 7 bytes, each with its underlying 8 bits, lining them up sequentially at the bit level, repackaging the bits so that 7 bits equals 1 byte, and then sending the bytes across the line. For instance, if you have 7 bytes, each with 8 bits, you could line up the bits and create 8 bytes of 7 bits each. At the receiving end, the bits are repackaged into 7 bytes of 8 bits each.

Uuencode is a UNIX-based utility that repackages a file with 8-bit data into another file with 7-bit data so that it can be ported across SMTP. The recipient invokes uudecode to convert the data back to an 8-bit standard.

MIME Format

In today's world, we aren't just sending text back and forth—we are sending files from a wide variety of PC applications and languages. This level of complexity is where Multipurpose Internet Mail Extension (MIME) comes in. MIME provides a way to send more than just text across the Internet. It is a standard that allows multiple files of various content types to be encapsulated into one message. RFCs 2045 through 2049 currently define MIME and are considered to be a single standard.

MIME works by concatenating all the attachments, placing separators between them. Each body part specifies a content type that indicates the kind of file it represents, and it also indicates how the file is encoded for transfer through the e-mail system.

Each content type consists of both a top-level media type and a corresponding subtype. It is possible to define additional types other than those specified in the RFCs to accommodate proprietary formats. Table 20-2 lists the more common top-level types and their corresponding subtypes. Each of the five discrete types corresponds to a single file. The composite types can encapsulate discrete or other composite contents.

Exchange Server 5.5 is based on the X.400 protocol, which is considered to be a closed backbone message transfer system. By *closed* we mean that in an X.400 backbone, you need to explicitly define all peer MTAs on the network or over the Internet. SMTP, on the other hand, is considered to be an *open* message transfer system because any computer running SMTP will generally accept connections from any other computer running SMTP, and these peer connections do not need to be specified in advance. Because the default transport protocol for Exchange Server 2003 is SMTP, Exchange Server 2003 has greater interoperability with foreign e-mail systems than Exchange Server 5.5.

Table 20-2. Top-level media types

Media Type	Subtypes
Discrete	
Text	Plain, rich text, enriched
Image	Jpeg, gif
Audio	Basic
Video	Mpeg
Application	Octet-stream, Postscript
Composite	
Multipart Message	Mixed
	RFC 822

Each SMTP server routes messages to the next SMTP server based on the e-mail exchanger (MX) records it finds in the DNS. SMTP transfers messages over a TCP port 25 connection. If you're coming from a Microsoft Exchange 5.5 Server environment, you might be surprised to learn that the MTA is not involved in SMTP message transfers. In Exchange 2003 (and Exchange 2000), the MTA does not play a prominent role when it comes to message transfers. The MTA still exists for connections to other MTA-based systems, such as Exchange 5.5 or Lotus cc:Mail, and it is still used for e-mail that travels over an X.400 Connector, but the core protocol for moving messages around your Exchange 2003 environment is SMTP, not the MTA.

SMTP Service Extensions

In November 1995, RFC 1869 was published, containing several extensions to the SMTP command structure. These extensions, which are registered with the Internet Assigned Number Authority (IANA), allow the receiver-SMTP to inform the sender-SMTP of the service extensions it supports. The purpose of this revision in the SMTP standard was to make SMTP adaptable in the coming years. When SMTP is extended, it is referred to as ESMTP.

When working with extensions, the sender-SMTP sends an EHLO command in place of the HELO command. The receiver-SMTP can respond by indicating which extensions it supports. If it does not support any extensions, it sends an error response.

Exchange Server 2003 takes advantage of these extensions by using the ETRN command, which is the extended version of the TURN command. This command asks the computers not only to reverse roles but also to verify the remote host name so that hosts other than the one for which the messages are intended cannot retrieve the messages. Because of the host name verification, which includes the domain name, ETRN is used to trigger e-mail delivery for a specific domain rather than for a specific host.

Exchange Server 2003 and the SMTP Service

SMTP is really the heart of Exchange 2003 transport services. The SMTP service installed by Exchange 2003 supports many of the ESMTP commands. Although there is only one SMTP service, you can configure multiple virtual SMTP servers on each Exchange 2003 server. Each virtual server can be started, stopped, or paused independently of other virtual servers. However, stopping or pausing the SMTP service itself will affect all the virtual servers. (See the next section, "SMTP Virtual Servers," for more information.)

When the SMTP service is running, new connections can be accepted from users. When it is stopped, all users' connections are severed. When the SMTP service is paused, each virtual server continues to service currently connected users but will not accept new users.

Installing Exchange Server 2003 extends the base SMTP service to add functionality, including the following:

- Commands to support link state information (X-LINK2STATE)
- The advanced queuing engine
- The enhanced message categorization agent
- The Installable File System (IFS) store driver

Note Even though the IFS is installed and running in Exchange Server 2003, the databases are not exposed via the M: drive by default as they were in Exchange 2000 Server. So, the IFS is loaded and running whether or not you see the M: drive in Exchange 2003.

Figure 20-1 shows a sample log file for the SMTP service as it records the sending of a message from the local server to a remote server. Some of the commands, such as X-LINK2STATE and XEXCH50, are unique to Exchange Server 2003 and are considered ESMTP commands. You can see how the log file allows you to use the SMTP commands to troubleshoot SMTP services.

More Info The log file is discussed further in the "Configuring and Administering a Virtual Server" section, later in this chapter.

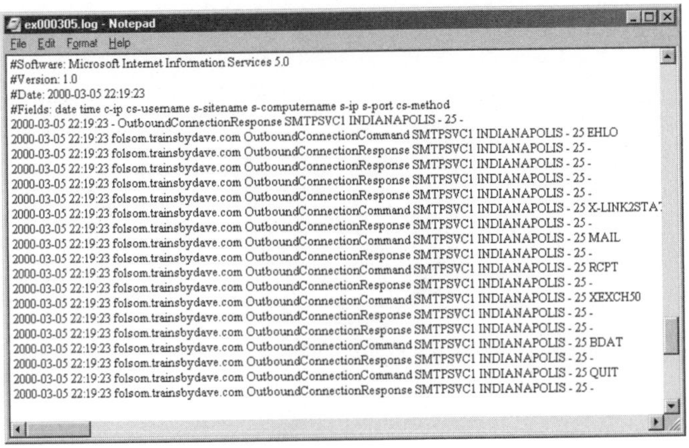
ex000305.log - Notepad

File Edit Format Help

```
#Software: Microsoft Internet Information Services 5.0
#Version: 1.0
#Date: 2000-03-05 22:19:23
#Fields: date time c-ip cs-username s-sitename s-computername s-ip s-port cs-method
2000-03-05 22:19:23 - OutboundConnectionResponse SMTPSVC1 INDIANAPOLIS - 25 -
2000-03-05 22:19:23 folsom.trainsbydave.com OutboundConnectionCommand SMTPSVC1 INDIANAPOLIS - 25 EHLO
2000-03-05 22:19:23 folsom.trainsbydave.com OutboundConnectionResponse SMTPSVC1 INDIANAPOLIS - 25 -
2000-03-05 22:19:23 folsom.trainsbydave.com OutboundConnectionResponse SMTPSVC1 INDIANAPOLIS - 25 -
2000-03-05 22:19:23 folsom.trainsbydave.com OutboundConnectionResponse SMTPSVC1 INDIANAPOLIS - 25 -
2000-03-05 22:19:23 folsom.trainsbydave.com OutboundConnectionResponse SMTPSVC1 INDIANAPOLIS - 25 -
2000-03-05 22:19:23 folsom.trainsbydave.com OutboundConnectionCommand SMTPSVC1 INDIANAPOLIS - 25 X-LINK2STA
2000-03-05 22:19:23 folsom.trainsbydave.com OutboundConnectionResponse SMTPSVC1 INDIANAPOLIS - 25 -
2000-03-05 22:19:23 folsom.trainsbydave.com OutboundConnectionCommand SMTPSVC1 INDIANAPOLIS - 25 MAIL
2000-03-05 22:19:23 folsom.trainsbydave.com OutboundConnectionResponse SMTPSVC1 INDIANAPOLIS - 25 -
2000-03-05 22:19:23 folsom.trainsbydave.com OutboundConnectionCommand SMTPSVC1 INDIANAPOLIS - 25 RCPT
2000-03-05 22:19:23 folsom.trainsbydave.com OutboundConnectionResponse SMTPSVC1 INDIANAPOLIS - 25 -
2000-03-05 22:19:23 folsom.trainsbydave.com OutboundConnectionCommand SMTPSVC1 INDIANAPOLIS - 25 XEXCH50
2000-03-05 22:19:23 folsom.trainsbydave.com OutboundConnectionResponse SMTPSVC1 INDIANAPOLIS - 25 -
2000-03-05 22:19:23 folsom.trainsbydave.com OutboundConnectionResponse SMTPSVC1 INDIANAPOLIS - 25 -
2000-03-05 22:19:23 folsom.trainsbydave.com OutboundConnectionCommand SMTPSVC1 INDIANAPOLIS - 25 BDAT
2000-03-05 22:19:23 folsom.trainsbydave.com OutboundConnectionResponse SMTPSVC1 INDIANAPOLIS - 25 -
2000-03-05 22:19:23 folsom.trainsbydave.com OutboundConnectionCommand SMTPSVC1 INDIANAPOLIS - 25 QUIT
2000-03-05 22:19:23 folsom.trainsbydave.com OutboundConnectionResponse SMTPSVC1 INDIANAPOLIS - 25 -
```

Figure 20-1. *Sample log file.*

SMTP Virtual Servers

As we mentioned earlier, in Exchange Server 2003, you can create multiple SMTP virtual servers on the same physical server to provide separate configurations for different messaging services. In most cases, additional virtual servers are not needed. However, if you are hosting multiple domains or want to have more than one default domain name, you can create multiple virtual servers to meet your needs. From the user's perspective, each virtual server appears as a separate SMTP server.

Another reason to create multiple virtual servers is to satisfy different authentication requirements for different groups of users. You can create as many virtual servers as you need to handle the different configurations. Every virtual server on any one physical server must belong to the same routing group. Multiple virtual servers won't increase your throughput, but they are very handy if you need to configure different options for different sets of users.

Each virtual server has its own distinct configuration, including IP address, port number, and authentication settings. By default, each Exchange 2003 server has at least one virtual server that listens on port 25 on all IP addresses. This can be changed, of course, but the default SMTP Virtual Server (VS) is coded to do this out of the box.

There are two ways to create a new SMTP VS. The first approach involves launching the Exchange System snap-in. Then, under the server object, navigate to and expand the Protocols container. Right-click the SMTP container, point to New, and then choose New SMTP Virtual Server. The New SMTP Virtual Server Wizard starts (Figure 20-2) and asks you to enter the name of the virtual server. Choose a descriptive name because this is the name the object will have within Exchange System.

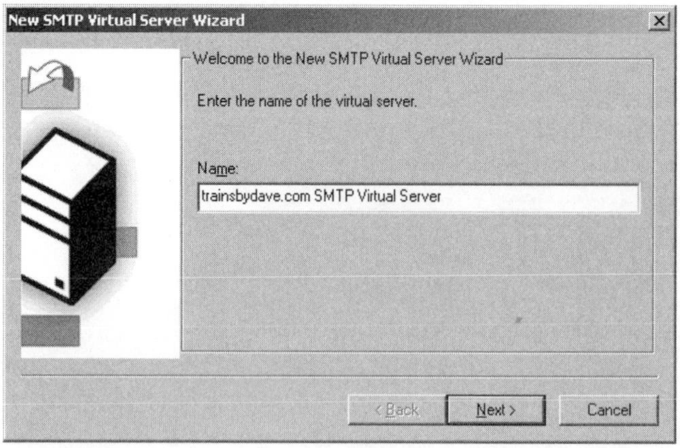

Figure 20-2. *First page of the New SMTP Virtual Server Wizard, in which you name the virtual server.*

The next page of the wizard asks you to select an IP address for this new virtual server (Figure 20-3). Be sure to select an address that is different from the IP address of the default SMTP server. Each virtual server requires a unique IP/port number combination. Once you've made your selection, click Finish to create the new virtual server.

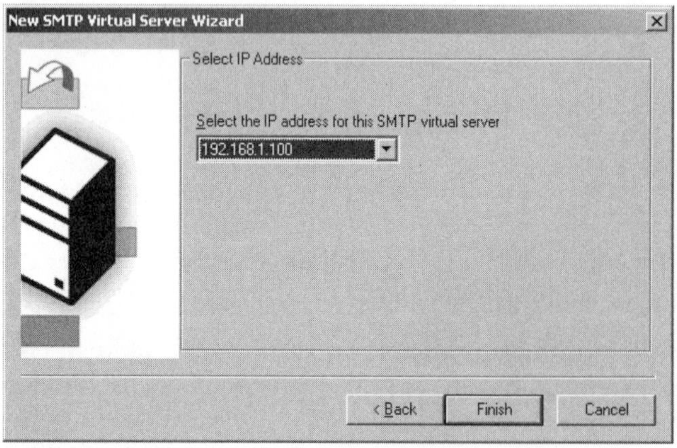

Figure 20-3. *Selecting an IP address for the new virtual sever.*

> **Tip** The IP address you specify will need to have been bound to the server before you attempt to create the virtual server. Also, be sure to add an address (A) record and an MX record in DNS for this virtual server.

The second way to create a new virtual server is through the new Internet Mail Wizard (IMW). You run the IMW by right-clicking the Organization object and then following the screen prompts. If you're coming from an Exchange 5.5

environment, you'll find this wizard to be similar in concept to the Internet Mail Connector Wizard. The IMW is intended for those who are less familiar with the SMTP server in Exchange 2003 and who either don't have the time or are uninterested in learning how to configure the SMTP VS manually for inbound and outbound Internet e-mail.

In those environments with a dedicated Exchange or messaging staff, this wizard will be of little value because the staff will possess the skills to create and manage the SMTP virtual servers without additional help. If you work in an environment in which individuals have minimal Exchange skills and you want to ensure e-mail delivery for both inbound and outbound e-mail, the wizard will help you get e-mail moving.

Be aware of the following considerations when using the IMW:

- It is intended primarily for small and medium companies with less complex environments.
- It will create an SMTP Connector.
- If you have any connectors or additional SMTP virtual servers, the wizard will not run.
- You cannot use this tool to configure an Exchange 5.5 or earlier server.

To run the Internet Mail Connector Wizard, right-click the Organization object, and select Internet Mail Wizard. The second screen after the Welcome screen lists the following prerequisites for configuring the default virtual server:

- You have a registered domain name on the Internet.
- You have an Internet-assigned IP address.
- You configured DNS with an MX record that points to your Internet IP address.

If you have already implemented the prerequisites, getting e-mail in and out of your organization using the default SMTP VS will be straightforward. By default, the SMTP VS is set up to transfer messages in and out of your organization.

After you ensure the prerequisites are configured correctly, you select the server on the Server Selection page (Figure 20-4) and click Next.

The next page in the Internet Mail Wizard runs a check on that server (Figure 20-5) for compliance with requirements. For example, the server cannot be a member of a load-balancing cluster, and the server cannot act as a router between two networks.

On the Internet E-Mail Functions page, you can select whether you want the VS to receive and/or send Internet e-mail. Make your selections, and then click Next.

Note that the default SMTP VS is set up to both send and receive e-mail, but the IMW lets you set the default SMTP VS to only send or only receive e-mail. For example, if your users download their e-mail from a POP3 server, you can set up the SMTP VS to only send e-mail, not receive it. Only sending mail is becoming a rare scenario, but it prompted the creation of the IMW for the novice or busy Exchange administrator.

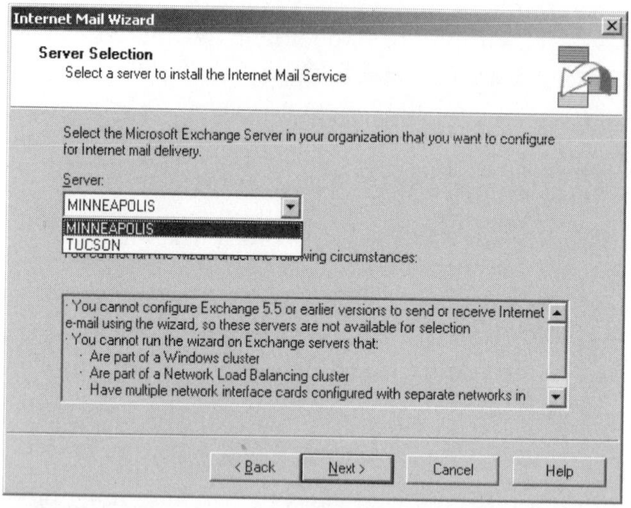

Figure 20-4. *The Server Selection page.*

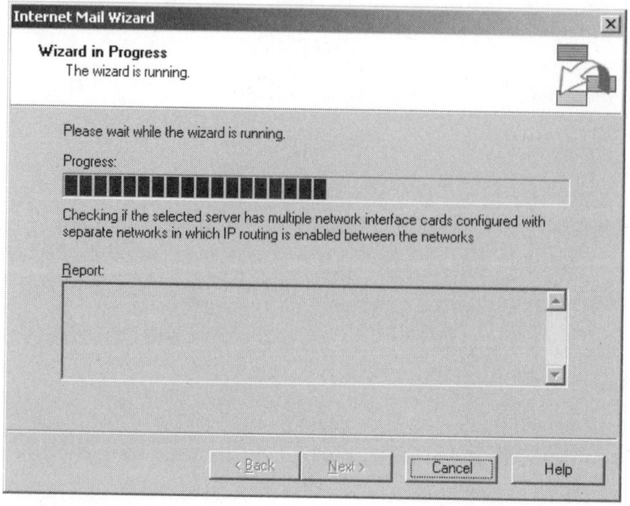

Figure 20-5. *Wizard In Progress page that runs the compliance checks.*

When you have an Exchange server that is dual-homed with one card assigned an Internet IP address and the other assigned a private IP address, the Configure Your

Server page will appear next in the IMW (Figure 20-6). If you select Yes at this juncture, a second SMTP VS is created for Internet Mail using the Internet-assigned IP address. The default SMTP VS is assigned to listen for SMTP traffic on the private IP address. In our example, we'll select Yes so that you can see the effect.

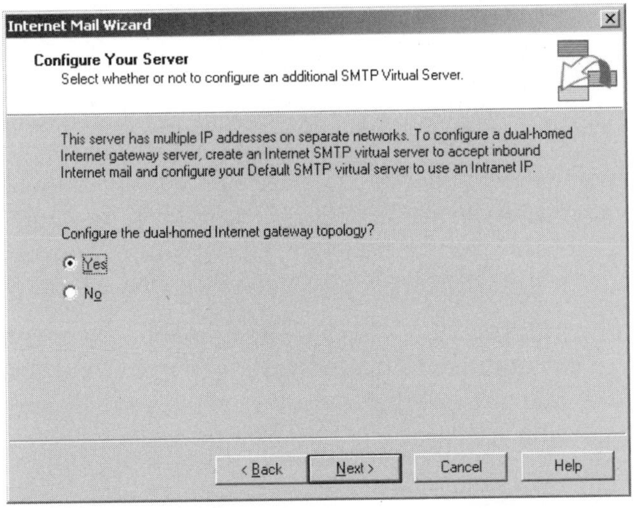

Figure 20-6. *The Configure Your Server page.*

The next page (Figure 20-7) is the Create Two SMTP Virtual Servers page. You need to assign an IP address to each VS. The internal VS will receive the private IP address and the other VS will be assigned the Internet IP address. We'll discuss the effect of doing this in just a moment.

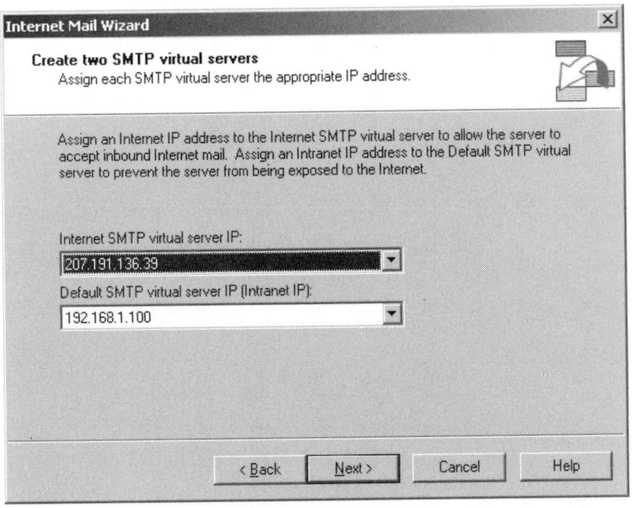

Figure 20-7. *The Create Two SMTP Virtual Servers page.*

More Info Some IP address ranges have been set aside by the Internet authorities for use *only* on an intranet that is protected or disconnected from the Internet. Hence, these ranges of IP addresses are described as *private*. One such range is 192.168.0.0 with a subnet mask of 255.255.0.0. To better understand the terms "private" IP address and "Internet" IP address, read the *Microsoft Windows Server 2003 TCP/IP Protocols and Services Technical Reference* (Microsoft Press).

After you decide to create an additional VS, you must indicate the domains on which these virtual servers will be transferring e-mail on the SMTP Domains for Inbound Email screen. Enter the domain names using the Add button and then click Next. The default domain name for the Exchange server will appear automatically. To receive e-mail for more than one domain, enter the configuration value on this screen.

The next screen is the Outbound Bridgehead Server (BHS) screen. Here you select which server will act as the outbound BHS for the SMTP Connector that is created by the IMW. The default SMTP VS of the server you are configuring will appear here. Accept the default selection, and then click Next.

The Outbound Mail Configuration page (Figure 20-8) appears next. This page allows you to select two different settings for outbound e-mail:

- Resolve outbound e-mail destination domain names using DNS.
- Forward all outbound e-mail to a smart host and let that smart host resolve and send your e-mail to the destination SMTP servers.

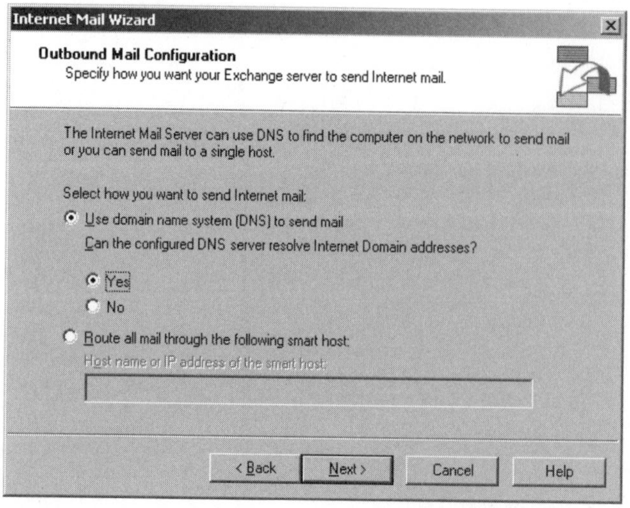

Figure 20-8. *The Outbound Mail Configuration.*

If you make the first selection but then select the associated No option, the next screen will ask you to give the wizard a DNS server to reference that can resolve the destination domain names to their IP addresses. If the DNS server that the Exchange server you're configuring can resolve the destination DNS domain names for outbound e-mail, select the Yes option.

The next page in the wizard is the Outbound SMTP Domain Restrictions page, which allows you to configure restrictions for particular destination domains that this SMTP VS will be allowed to transfer e-mail to. The default is to deliver e-mail to all domains as addressed by your users, which is, by far, the most common choice.

The final page is a Configuration Summary page. Here you can review your choices. It is important to note that no configuration changes have occurred during the course of running this wizard—your changes are not written to the Exchange server until you click Next. After you click Next, the configurations are written and the needed virtual servers are created. Finally, you are presented with the Completing The Internet Mail Wizard page, so click Finish to close the wizard.

In our example, we used the wizard to work with a dual-homed Exchange server that had one Internet and one private IP address. What changes were written to Exchange? First, each VS is now assigned to a single IP address, and the default VS is no longer configured to use All Assigned IP addresses. Second, an SMTP Connector was created that uses the internal VS as its BHS. Because the server we used was dual-homed, we were given the option of creating a VS for each unique IP address and port number combination that was available. In this instance, we were allowed to create a VS for the Internet IP address and one for the external IP address, even though both used port 25. Without dual network cards, we would not have been able to create the second VS using the IMW.

Configuring and Administering a Virtual Server

Once you've created the virtual server, you can configure its property sheet by right-clicking the virtual server and choosing Properties. On the General tab (Figure 20-9), you can enable logging on this virtual server so that you can track user connections. Four formats are available for log files:

- **W3C extended log file format** The default log file format for IIS and SMTP. Information is written to an ASCII text file. Unlike other formats, you can choose what is written into the log and can limit the size of the log file itself. There are usually multiple entries for a single transmission.
- **Microsoft IIS log file format** Information is written to a comma-delimited ASCII text file. Once the data is written it cannot be changed,

and the log format is not customizable. There are usually multiple records for a single transmission.

- **NCSA common log file format** Information is written to an ASCII text file in the National Center for Computing Applications (NCSA) format. Once the data is written, it cannot be changed, and the log format is not customizable. There are usually multiple records for a single transmission.
- **ODBC logging** Information is written to an open database connectivity (ODBC)-compliant database.

On the General tab, you can also limit the number of users who connect to this virtual server by selecting the Limit Number Of Connections To check box and then entering the desired limit. You can also limit idle connections to a certain number of minutes to conserve system resources.

Finally, the General tab (Figure 20-9) allows you to change the IP address to which the virtual server is bound without creating a new virtual server. If you need to change the port number, click the Advanced button, and then make your changes in the Advanced dialog box (Figure 20-10). You can also assign multiple combinations of IP address and port number to the same virtual server, which gives you maximum administrative flexibility. Selecting All Unassigned allows the virtual server to respond to any requests that are not handled by other services.

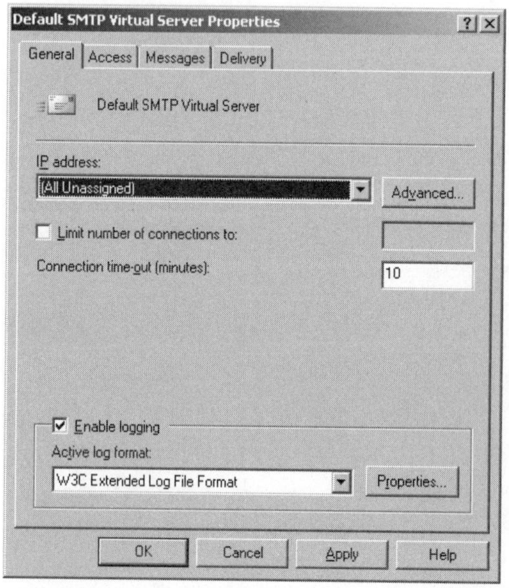

Figure 20-9. *General tab of the property sheet for a virtual server.*

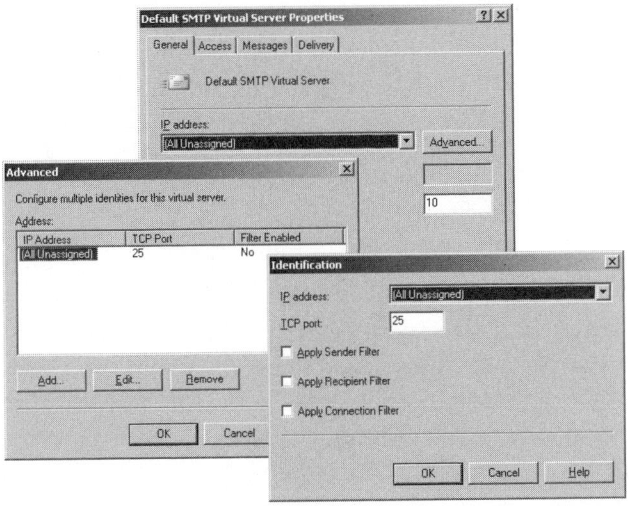

Figure 20-10. *Changing the port number of a virtual server.*

Enabling message filtering The Filter Enabled column in the Advanced dialog box indicates whether message filtering is enabled. You can enable filtering by selecting the Apply Filter options in the Identification dialog box (Figure 20-10), which you display by clicking either Add or Edit in the Advanced dialog box. When message filtering is enabled on an SMTP virtual server, the server will not accept e-mail from any domain on the message filtering list. Message filtering is defined globally but is enabled for individual IP addresses. Before you can enable message filtering, you must first create a message filter list (Figure 20-11). You can choose to filter from the senders list, the recipients list, or a connections list.

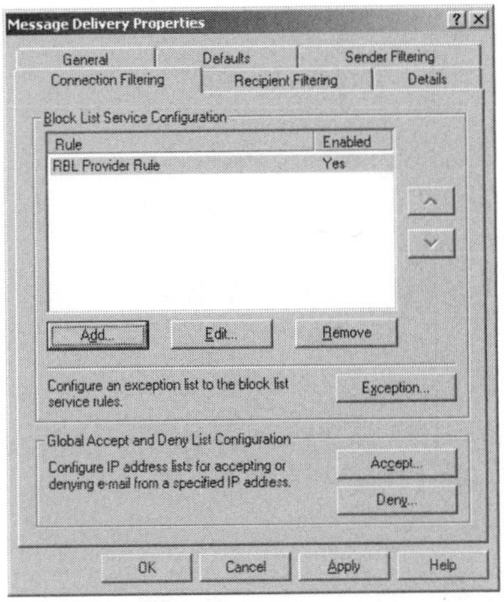

Figure 20-11. *Connection Filtering tab in properties of the Global Settings/Message Delivery object.*

To create a message filter list, open the Exchange System snap-in, and select the Global Settings container. Right-click Message Delivery, and choose Properties. You'll see three filtering tabs: Recipient, Sender, and Connection. Select the filtering types you want to configure, and then select the tab to enter your rules.

Connection Filtering

Exchange 2003 supports connection filtering based on Real-Time Black Lists (RBLs). This feature uses externally-based services to identify three categories of offenders based on their IP addresses: unsolicited e-mail, dial-up user account lists, and servers that open for relay. Exchange allows you to check incoming e-mail, resolve the originating domain name to an IP address, and then check that IP address and/or domain name to an RBL. If a match is found, the SMTP server issues a "550 5.*x*.*x*" error in response to the RCPT TO: command.

Connection filters are implemented using rules. These rules include the ability to do the following:

- Set the rule display name
- Enter the DNS suffix of the RBL provider
- Return a custom error message instead of the default 550 error message
- Customize the return status code from the RBL provider
- Disable the rule without deleting it
- Enter exceptions to all rules using global settings
- Configure exceptions to all rules using a separate exceptions list

You configure your connection filtering rules on the Connection Filtering tab in the properties of the Global Settings/Message Delivery object (Figure 20-11).

To create a connection filter, click the Add button to invoke the Connection Filtering Rule dialog box (Figure 20-12) on the Connection Filter tab. Type a display name for the filter, and then type the DNS suffix of the RBL provider. Enter a custom error message for the sender or select the Return Status Code by clicking on the Return Status Code button.

When an e-mail sender is found to be in one of the offending categories defined by Black List (or in a subcategory to which you have subscribed), a default error message is returned to the sender. You can customize the error message as follows:

- %0 = connecting IP address

- %1 = Rule Name
- %2 = the RBL Provider

For example, suppose you wanted your error message to read as follows:

You have sent an e-mail message to <my_company>. Your IP address <IP Address> was blocked by <RBL Provider> and is considered unsolicited e-mail.

You would enter the following in the Custom Error Message To Return field (Figure 20-12):

You have sent an e-mail message to <My_Company>. Your IP address %0 was blocked by %2 and is considered unsolicited e-mail.

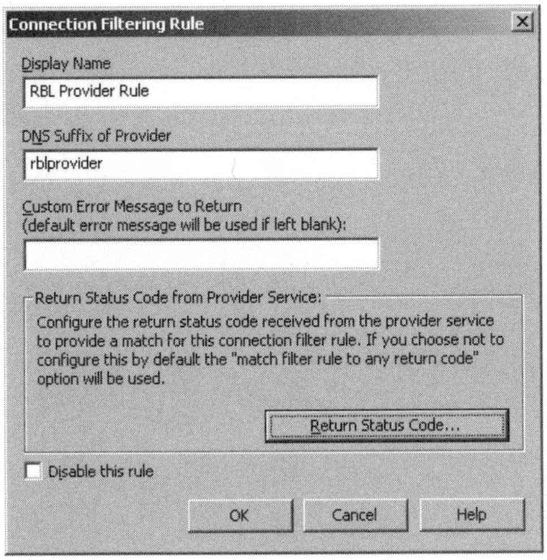

Figure 20-12. *Connection Filtering Rule dialog box.*

Return Status Codes (RTC) work with the 127.*x*.*x*.*x* IP address range to give your e-mail server a status report on the e-mail that is received. When your e-mail server receives an e-mail, Exchange contacts the RBL provider. The RBL provider uses the sender's information in the headers of the e-mail to check for an A (Address) record in DNS for the originating e-mail server. A reverse lookup is initiated and, if the IP address is found on the provider's list, the RBL provider returns a 127.0.0.*x* status code that indicates the e-mail is coming from an offending IP address. The code also indicates the type of offense. For instance, if the IP address returned is 127.0.0.3, and your RBL provider has indicated that a "3" in the last octet, the e-mail is coming from a known source of unsolicited e-mail. When that status code is returned, Exchange filters the e-mail.

The RBL provider might return a bitmask, which is a return message that can serve more than one purpose. For instance, IP addresses might be a member of more than one list. If "3" means unsolicited e-mail and "4" means a known relay server, a return status code of "7" would indicate that the IP address is a member of both lists. However, you can enter a bitmask for the return status codes, as Figure 20-13 suggests. If you enter 0.0.0.4, and your RBL has indicated that "4" is for known relay servers, this rule filters only for IP addresses that are known SMTP relay servers. Furthermore, if your RBL provider has indicated that a "3" is the return status code for known sources of unsolicited e-mail, a bitmask of 0.0.0.4 will *not* filter unsolicited e-mail. Bitmasks are used to filter for a specific type of IP address. You do have the option to create multiple rules, each with an individual bitmask that filters for a specific type of IP address. Note that a bitmask checks only against a single value. If you set a bitmask value that is returned when an IP address appears on two lists, the mask will match only IP addresses that satisfy both settings. For example, if you set a bitmask of 0.0.0.7, the IP address will be filtered only when the IP address appears on the 0.0.0.3 and 0.0.0.4 lists.

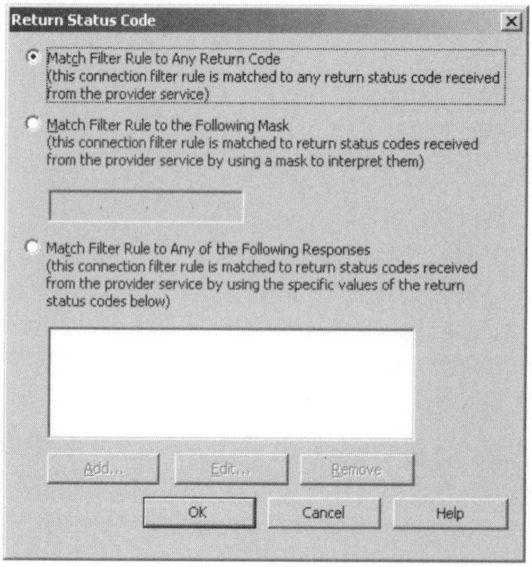

Figure 20-13. *Return Status Code dialog box.*

You have three choices when deciding what type of return status code you want. We've already discussed one option: Match Filter Rule To The Following Mask. Another option is Match Filter To Any Return Code. This selection is the most broad; any return status code will invoke this filter rule. Your last option is Match Filter Rule To Any Of The Following Reponses, which allows you to enter custom bitmasks supplied by your RBL provider.

Your RBL provider will give you all the codes you need for work with their system so that Exchange can filter for the IP addresses you specify by entering multiple rules in this area.

In the Connection Filtering Rule dialog box, you can also specify exceptions to the connection filtering rules, which means that you can force the acceptance of e-mail from blacklisted sources or reject e-mail from sources who are not blacklisted. You might use the exceptions feature when you want to allow delivery of messages to specific recipients, such as the postmaster, or from a specific server, regardless of the RSC from your provider.

After you create your filter rules, you must apply them to a specific SMTP VS. You accomplish this in the properties of the SMTP VS. On the General tab, click the Advanced button to display the Advanced dialog box, and then click the Edit button to display the Identification dialog box (Figure 20-14). Here you select the type of filtering for this particular VS. You can select from any of the three types of filtering that are available in Exchange Server 2003.

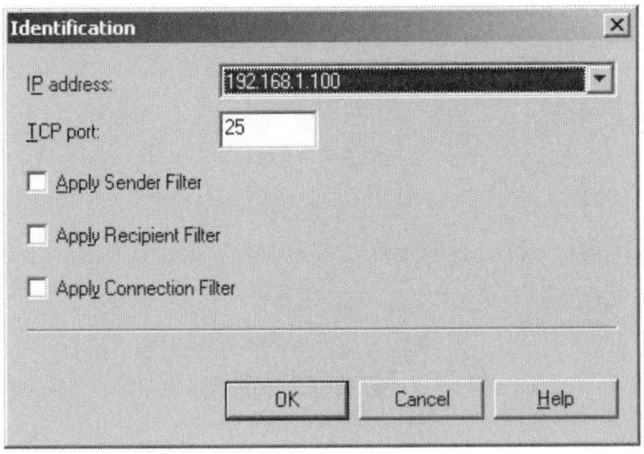

Figure 20-14. *Selecting the type of filtering for a particular VS.*

Recipient Filtering

Recipient filtering allows you to block an e-mail message based on its destination. You can block based on invalid recipients in your organization or develop a recipient filter list for outbound e-mail. (Note that recipient filtering only applies to anonymous connections. Authenticated users and Exchange servers bypass recipient filtering.)

You can block inbound e-mail based on invalid Active Directory user lookups, meaning that the target user doesn't exist in your organization. But you can also block inbound e-mail based on who has permissions to send e-mail to that user.

To enter a recipient for the recipient filtering list, click the Add button on the Recipient Filter tab in the properties of the Message Delivery global object (Figure 20-15). To filter all messages for a particular domain, enter ***@*<domain_name>*.com** or just **@*<domain_name>*.com**. Otherwise, enter the specific e-mail address that should be included in this filter list.

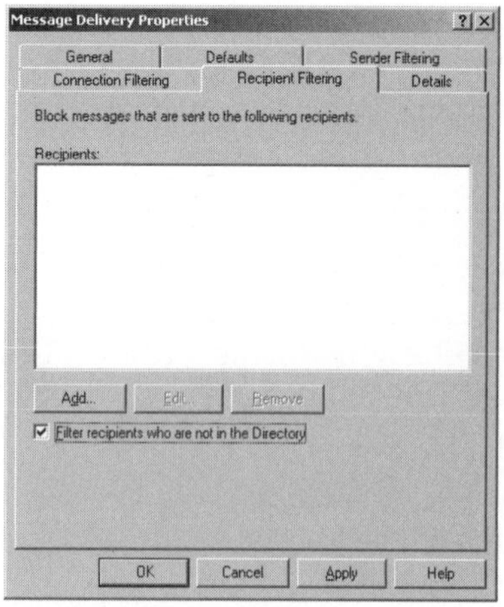

Figure 20-15. *Entering a recipient for the recipient filtering list.*

To filter outbound recipients, select the Filter Recipients Who Are Not In The Directory check box. Doing so filters e-mail addresses that are not in your Active Directory. You must consider two issues when choosing this option. First, Exchange will perform filtering only on domain names for which it is authoritative. You'll need to set this in the Recipient Policies global object. Second, enabling this feature causes Exchange to return different status codes for valid and invalid recipients. E-mail abusers can use such codes to discover valid e-mail addresses in your organization.

After you create the recipient filter, be sure to apply it to the SMTP VS. Otherwise, it won't do you much good!

Sender Filtering

Sender filtering filters messages based on the sender of the message. On the Sender Filtering tab (Figure 20-16), enter the e-mail addresses you want to filter, or configure individual options. Note that you can block based on entire domain names as well by entering the individual domain name as follows: *@<*domain_name*.com>.

If you choose the Archive Filtered Messages option, each message is archived. Be certain you want to select this option because the archive can fill up rather quickly. And since clearing messages from the archive is not a routine matter, you'll need to schedule the manual removal of them from the archive on a regular basis.

You can also filter messages that have a black FROM field. Some automated junk e-mail scripts and sources of unsolicited e-mail do not populate this field. This action is not turned on by default but in most cases should be.

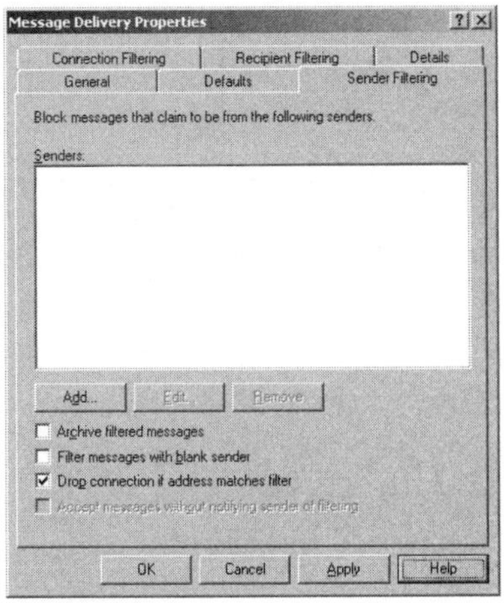

Figure 20-16. *Filtering messages based on the sender of the message.*

The Drop Connection If Address Matches Filter options is selected by default. This option forces Exchange to immediately drop the TCP connection when a sender's address matches an address on the filter.

Finally, the Accept Messages Without Notifying Sender Of Filtering option (dimmed in Figure 20-16) ensures that the originators of messages being filtered are *not* notified with an NDR (non-delivery Report) that their messages were not delivered. If you have a large amount of spam e-mail, selecting this option can improve server performance.

Note Any changes you make to a virtual server won't take effect for a few minutes because the metabase update service needs time to replicate the changes to the IIS metabase. This update service replicates changes made in Active Directory to the IIS metabase, allowing you to make changes to a virtual server without a permanent connection to each system involved in the update.

Configuring access properties On the Access tab (Figure 20-17) of the virtual server's property sheet, you'll find a number of important configuration options. Clicking the Authentication button displays a dialog box that allows you to choose Basic authentication, anonymous access, Integrated Windows Authentication (IWA), or a combination of these options. You can also specify here that Transport Layer Security (TLS) encryption be enforced based on the domain name that you enter.

Note Integrated Windows Authentication requires a valid Windows Server 2003 user name and password. It authenticates users by relaying their information directly to the domain controller. Once users are authenticated, they access objects in their security context. IWA was called Windows NT Challenge/Response in IIS 4.

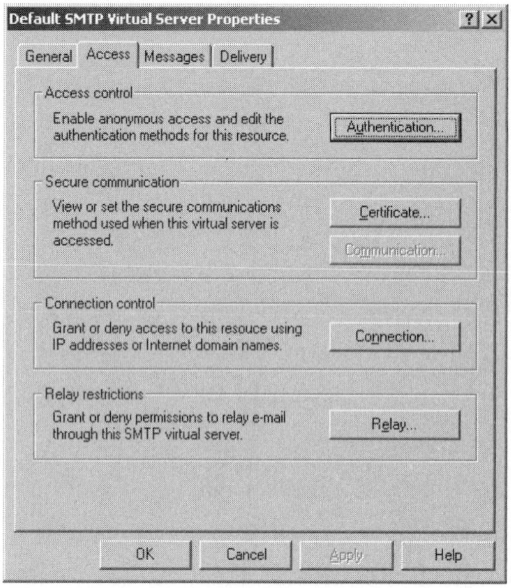

Figure 20-17. *Access tab of a virtual server's property sheet.*

The Secure Communication area of the Access tab has two buttons: Certificate and Communication. If a certificate is not yet installed on this server, you can create a default one, using a wizard that you start by clicking the Certificate button. Once a valid certificate is installed, you can require that communication take place over a secure channel. You do so by clicking the Communication button. In the Security dialog box (Figure 20-18), you can require both secure channel communication and 128-bit encryption. If external users who need high security are sending e-mails to this virtual server, consider using both encryption and certificates.

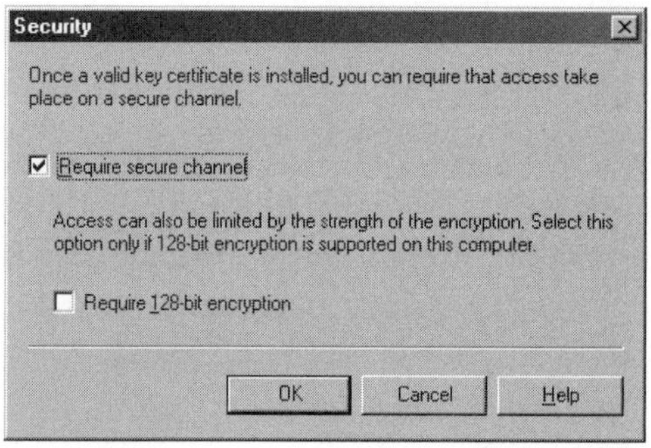

Figure 20-18. *Configuring security requirements.*

By clicking the Connection button in the Connection Control area of the Access tab (Figure 20-17), you can specify the domain name or IP address of computers to be given access to or excluded from the virtual server (Figure 20-19).

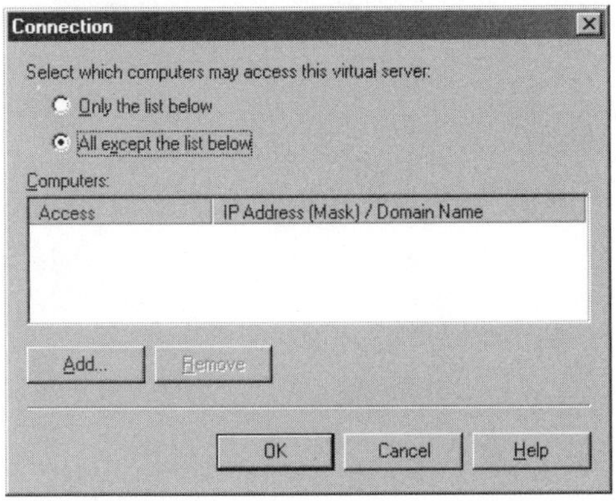

Figure 20-19. *Connection dialog box.*

Finally, clicking the Relay button in the Relay Restrictions area of the Access tab allows you to indicate which SMTP servers can relay messages through this virtual server (Figure 20-20). You can specify the servers by domain name or IP address. You can also establish an exception to these restrictions by selecting the Allow All Computers Which Successfully Authenticate To Relay, Regardless Of The List Above check box. This option could be used to allow vendors outside your company (each with their own SMTP domain name) to use your Exchange server as their messaging relay to the Internet once they authenticate to prove they have permission to do so.

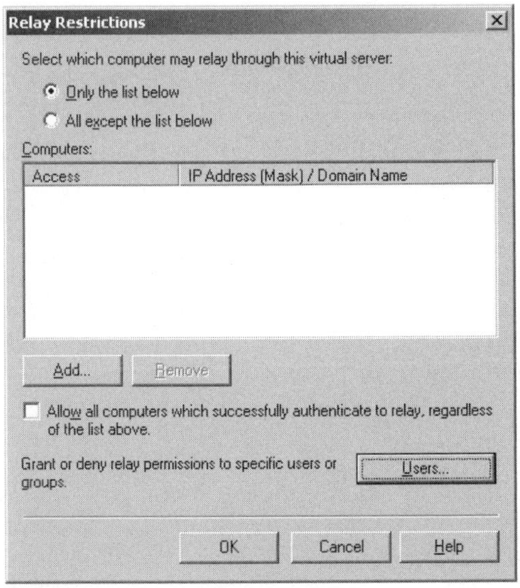

Figure 20-20. *Relay Restrictions dialog box.*

You can also allow a select group of users to relay e-mail to the Internet by configuring the Grant Or Deny Relay Permissions To Specific Users Or Groups. To do this, first clear the Allow All Computers Which Successfully Authenticate To Relay check box, click the Users button, and then enter your configuration values. Note that the default is to allow users to submit e-mail. But you can enter another Active Directory group and give those users the Relay permission (Figure 20-21).

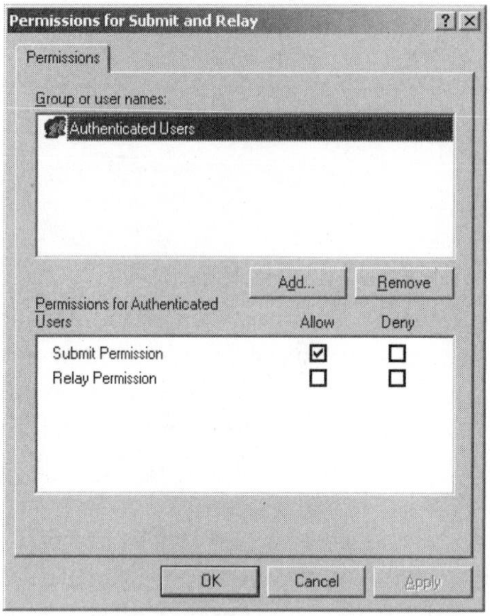

Figure 20-21. *Permissions For Submit And Relay dialog box.*

You can restrict relay abilities based on a single IP address, a range of IP addresses, or a domain name (Figure 20-22). You must choose one method per entry in the restrictions list, so if you want to restrict message relay based on both IP address and domain name, you'll need to make two entries.

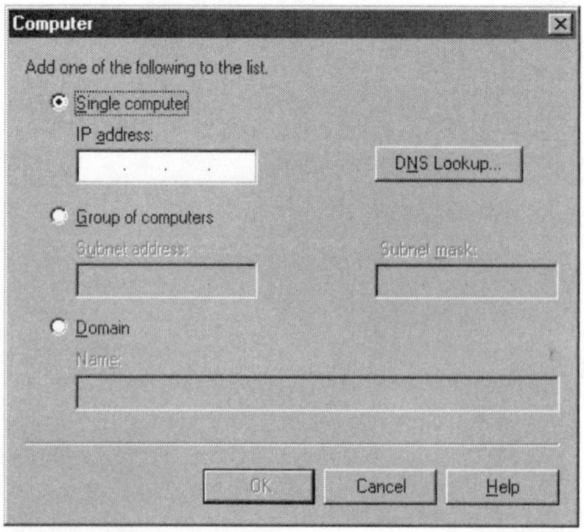

Figure 20-22. *Adding a computer to the relay restrictions list.*

Configuring messaging limits and badmail behavior The Messages tab of the property sheet (Figure 20-23) for a virtual server holds configuration choices governing message size limits and badmail behavior. *Badmail* is defined as e-mail that cannot be delivered or returned. The default directory for badmail is \Exchsrvr*mailroot\vsi* #\badmail (where *vsi* # is the specific virtual server; for instance, *vsi 1* is the default SMTP virtual server). You can change the location of the badmail directory and the queue directory by clicking on the Browse button and then selecting a different location. Usually, when a message is undeliverable, the sender receives a non-delivery report (NDR). You can also designate that a copy of all NDRs be sent to the e-mail address of your choice.

Caution Do not select the M: drive for your badmail directory. Doing so will cause conflicts with Exchange administration and transport services and will cause messages to stop flowing.

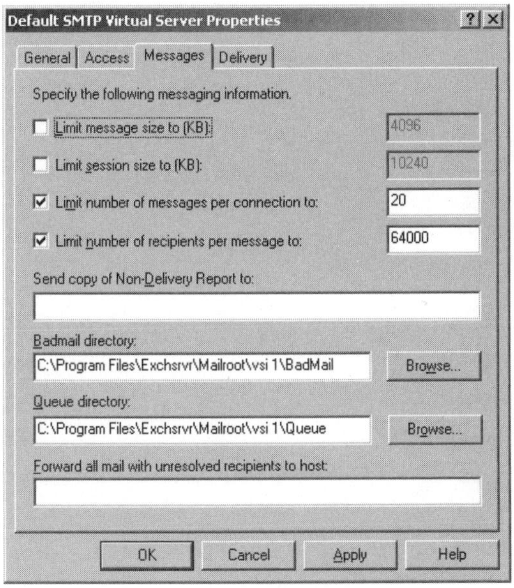

Figure 20-23. *Messages tab of a virtual server's property sheet.*

If you have another e-mail server in your organization, such as a UNIX-based server, that handles the same domain as your SMTP virtual server, enter the host name for that server in the Forward All Mail With Unresolved Recipients To Host text box. When your Exchange server receives e-mail for a user that it can't resolve, it will forward the e-mail to this host. For example, if the SMTP virtual server and a UNIX e-mail server both serve the trainsbydave.com domain, Exchange Server might receive e-mail intended for UNIX users. When Exchange Server can't find these users, it will know to forward these messages to the designated host in the other system.

Configuring delivery information The Delivery tab of the virtual server's property sheet lets you configure outbound e-mail retry and expiration values as well as outbound connection values and security information. If this virtual server will be connecting to another virtual server, be sure to make the outbound security settings match the inbound security settings on the other virtual server.

The Advanced Delivery dialog box (Figure 20-24), displayed by clicking Advanced on the Delivery tab, has several interesting options. The Masquerade Domain option allows you to indicate a different domain name to be placed in both the Mail From and From fields of all outgoing messages. The Mail From field is found within the SMTP message header and denotes the domain the message came from, whereas the From field is found in the body of the message and denotes who the message is from. When a message's Mail From field is modified, the modification remains through delivery.

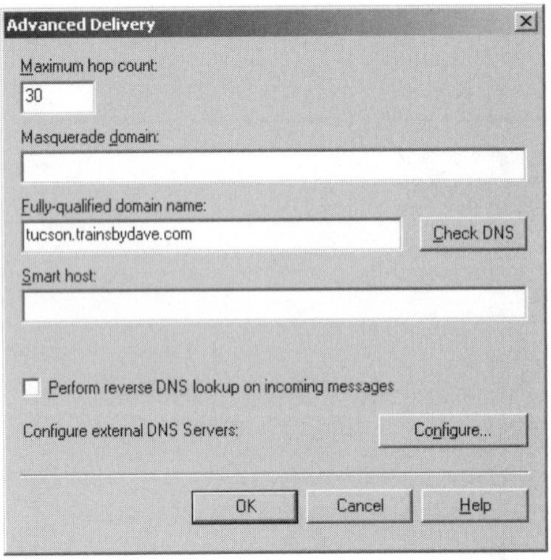

Figure 20-24. *Advanced Delivery dialog box.*

For instance, if your server is hosting the sales.hr.trainsbydave.com domain inside of the trainsbydave.com domain, the default entry in the Mail From field would be sales.hr.trainsbydave.com. If you would like to change this to trainsbydave.com, enter that information in the Masquerade Domain field. All outgoing messages will then appear to come from the trainsbydave.com domain, and any NDRs will be sent back to the trainsbydave.com domain.

In contrast, the From field, which the Masquerade Domain field also modifies to denote (in our example) the alternate domain of trainsbydave.com, applies only to the first hop. This means that if the message has to pass through a number of messaging systems to reach its destination, it will revert to its original domain name after the first hop. The Maximum Hop Count option, which sets the maximum number of Received header lines that an SMTP server will accept on incoming messages before returning an NDR to the message originator, is configured here too.

Selecting the Perform Reverse DNS Lookup On Incoming Messages option causes Exchange 2003 Server to attempt to verify that the client's IP address matches the domain name submitted by the client in the HELO/EHLO command. If the reverse DNS lookup is successful, the Received header is not changed. If it is unsuccessful, the Received header indicates "unverified" after the IP address. If reverse DNS lookups are affecting performance, consider clearing this check box. This feature is disabled by default.

Troubleshooting SMTP

There are several ways to troubleshoot problems with SMTP. First, make sure that the virtual server settings are correct. For instance, be sure that the IP address and port number assignments do not conflict with those of other virtual servers. Second, enable logging on the SMTP server, and then read the log files to see whether an error code or error reply has been recorded. This information can help you pinpoint the cause of your problem. Finally, use Telnet to connect to the SMTP server, and then send the SMTP commands to the server to see its response. This is the most granular and effective way to troubleshoot an SMTP server. For example, if you want to test an Exchange server to ensure that it is not open for relay, follow these steps:

1. Use the command prompt to open a Telnet session by entering the following command: *open <server_name> 25* (Figure 20-25). You will receive information from the SMTP server indicating the server name, the e-mail service it is running, and the version along with the date and time the message was generated (Figure 20-26).

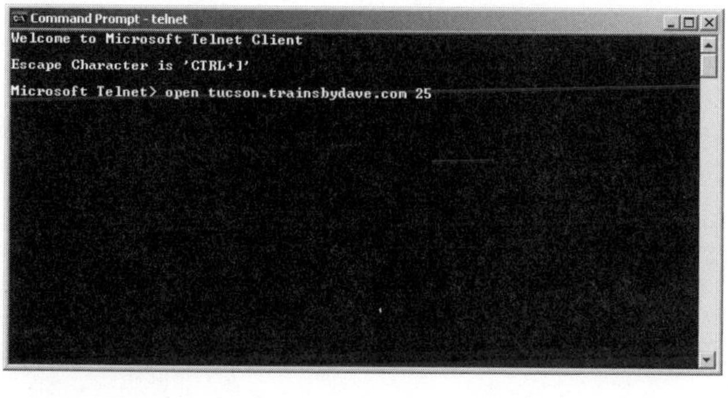

Figure 20-25. *Telnet command to open a Telnet session to SMTP server Tucson.trainsbydave.com over port 25.*

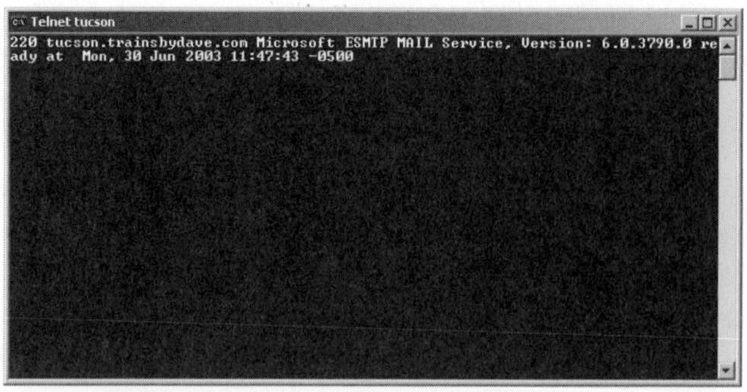
Telnet tucson
220 tucson.trainsbydave.com Microsoft ESMTP MAIL Service, Version: 6.0.3790.0 re
ady at Mon, 30 Jun 2003 11:47:43 -0500

Figure 20-26. *Response from the Tucson server allowing the Telnet connection.*

2. Enter the EHLO command. You'll receive the list of commands supported by the server.
3. Enter the following command: **mail from: <president@whitehouse.gov>**
4. Enter this command: **rcpt to: <*your_e-mail_address*>**

   If your Exchange server is not open for relaying, you'll receive a 550 5.7.1 error message: "Unable to relay for <*your_e-mail_address*>" (Figure 20-27).

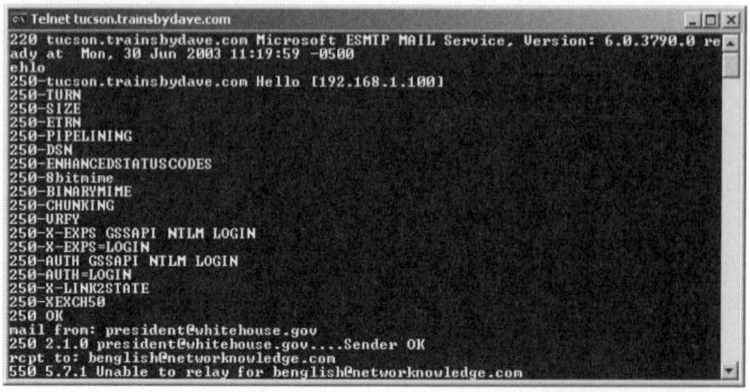
Telnet tucson.trainsbydave.com
220 tucson.trainsbydave.com Microsoft ESMTP MAIL Service, Version: 6.0.3790.0 re
ady at Mon, 30 Jun 2003 11:19:59 -0500
ehlo
250-tucson.trainsbydave.com Hello [192.168.1.100]
250-TURN
250-SIZE
250-ETRN
250-PIPELINING
250-DSN
250-ENHANCEDSTATUSCODES
250-8bitmime
250-BINARYMIME
250-CHUNKING
250-VRFY
250-X-EXPS GSSAPI NTLM LOGIN
250-X-EXPS=LOGIN
250-AUTH GSSAPI NTLM LOGIN
250-AUTH=LOGIN
250-X-LINK2STATE
250-XEXCH50
250 OK
mail from: president@whitehouse.gov
250 2.1.0 president@whitehouse.gov....Sender OK
rcpt to: benglish@networknowledge.com
550 5.7.1 Unable to relay for benglish@networknowledge.com

Figure 20-27. *Telnet session using commands to test for abilities to relay through the Tucson server.*

You can open a Telnet session to any Exchange server and then use the SMTP commands and the Extended SMTP commands to test the SMTP service on that server. Getting a good handle on how to use these commands will help you troubleshoot the SMTP service when you suspect messages are not being transferred correctly.

Post Office Protocol 3

POP3 was developed in response to SMTP and is designed for workstations that don't have the resources to maintain both SMTP services and a message transfer system. In addition, continuous connectivity to the network for each workstation, which is necessary for an SMTP host to operate correctly, is impractical in many instances.

POP3 permits a workstation to dynamically access a server that is holding e-mail for it. It does not allow extensive manipulation of e-mail on the server. Instead, it is used to download e-mail from the server. Once the e-mail has been downloaded, the server deletes its copy of the messages unless you have set your POP3 client to keep a copy of the message on the server. POP3 is a very small, fast, lean protocol that is really for e-mail retrieval only. To send e-mail, a POP3 client uses a normal SMTP connection to the destination e-mail server or a local SMTP relay server.

POP3 has both a client side and a server side. The server starts the POP3 service by listening on TCP port 110. When a POP3 client wants to use this service, it establishes a TCP connection with the server and then receives a greeting from the server. The client and server then exchange commands and responses until the connection is either closed or aborted. Like SMTP commands, POP3 commands are not case sensitive and can contain one or more arguments. A POP3 session between the server and the client will progress through several stages:

1. Once the TCP connection has been opened and the POP3 server has sent a greeting, the session enters the Authorization state. In this state, the client must identify itself to the POP3 server.
2. Once the client has successfully been authenticated, the session enters the Transaction state. During this phase, the server gathers the client's e-mail and, in response to requests from the client, sends e-mail to the client. The client's mailbox is locked to prevent messages from being modified or removed until the session enters the Update state. A series of commands and responses usually passes between the client and server during this phase.
3. When the client issues a QUIT command, the session enters the Update state. In this state, the POP3 server releases any resources it is holding on behalf of the client and sends a good-bye message. Messages are then deleted from the server, and the TCP session is terminated.

Table 20-3 summarizes the POP3 commands.

Table 20-3. Summary of POP3 commands

Command	Description
USER	Supplies user name for mailbox
PASS	Supplies password for mailbox
STAT	Requests the number of messages and total size of message
LIST	Lists the index and size of all messages
RETR	Retrieves the specified messages
DELE	Deletes the specified message
NOOP	No action required
RSET	Rolls back message deletion
QUIT	Updates (commit) message deletion and terminates connection

Administering POP3 in Exchange Server 2003 simply involves choosing the number of users that can connect to each POP3 virtual server, indicating whether POP3 is assigned to a specific IP address or to All Unassigned, and setting message encoding instructions for the virtual server. All these settings in the POP3 virtual server work the same as in other protocols and are described throughout this chapter.

Internet Messaging Access Protocol 4

In POP3, once a message has been downloaded from the server, it is, by default, deleted from the server. This deletion is a real disadvantage for users who move from workstation to workstation because e-mail they have already downloaded remains on the workstation to which they downloaded it. IMAP4 was developed to allow users to leave their e-mail on the server and to allow remote access to messages. Thus, IMAP4 extends the functionality of POP3 to allow both offline and online storage of messages.

In addition, IMAP4 allows user-initiated storage of messages and nonmail messages, permits users to manage their own configurations, and allows the sharing of mailboxes. This protocol allows a client to manipulate e-mail messages on a server as though it were a local mailbox, unlike POP3, which can do little more than copy a message from a POP3 server to a local mailbox.

When a client connects to an IMAP4 server, it does so over TCP port 143. The IMAP4 server is always in one of four states. For each state, the client can issue a limited number of commands to the server. Some commands transition the server into the next state. It is a protocol error for the client to issue a command that is not appropriate to the present state of the server. Figure 20-28 shows the IMAP4 states for an IMAP4 server as they are described in RFC 2060. Table 20-4 lists the more common IMAP4 commands.

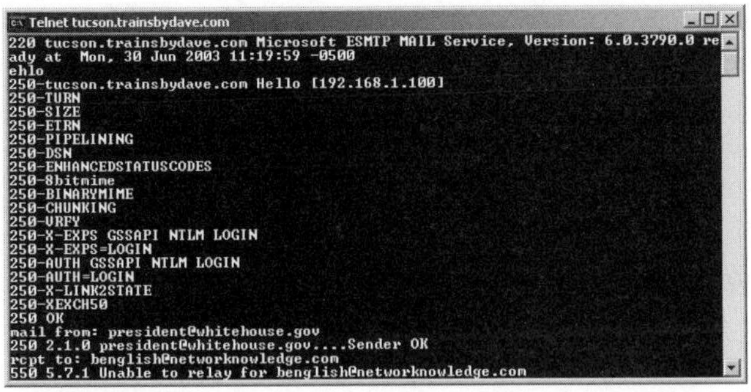
Telnet tucson.trainsbydave.com
220 tucson.trainsbydave.com Microsoft ESMTP MAIL Service, Version: 6.0.3790.0 re
ady at Mon, 30 Jun 2003 11:19:59 -0500
ehlo
250-tucson.trainsbydave.com Hello [192.168.1.100]
250-TURN
250-SIZE
250-ETRN
250-PIPELINING
250-DSN
250-ENHANCEDSTATUSCODES
250-8bitmime
250-BINARYMIME
250-CHUNKING
250-VRFY
250-X-EXPS GSSAPI NTLM LOGIN
250-X-EXPS=LOGIN
250-AUTH GSSAPI NTLM LOGIN
250-AUTH=LOGIN
250-X-LINK2STATE
250-XEXCH50
250 OK
mail from: president@whitehouse.gov
250 2.1.0 president@whitehouse.gov....Sender OK
rcpt to: benglish@networknowledge.com
550 5.7.1 Unable to relay for benglish@networknowledge.com

Figure 20-28. *IMAP4 states as described in RFC 2060.*

Table 20-4. IMAP4 commands

Command	Description
CAPABILITY	Requests a listing of the functionality of the server
AUTHENTICATE	Indicates an authentication mechanism
LOGIN	Identifies a client with user name and password
SELECT	Selects the mailbox to use
EXAMINE	Selects a mailbox in read-only mode
CREATE	Creates a mailbox
DELETE	Deletes a mailbox
RENAME	Renames a mailbox
SUBSCRIBE	Adds a mailbox to the server's set of active mailboxes
UNSUBSCRIBE	Removes a mailbox from the server's set of active mailboxes
LIST	Lists a set or subset of mailboxes
LSUB	Lists subscribed mailboxes
STATUS	Requests the status of a mailbox
APPEND	Adds a message to a mailbox
CLOSE	Effects pending deletions and closes a mailbox
EXPUNGE	Effects pending deletions
SEARCH	Searches a mailbox for messages satisfying a given criterion
FETCH	Fetches specified body parts for a given message
STORE	Changes the data of specified messages in a mailbox
COPY	Copies a message to another mailbox
NOOP	No action required
LOGOUT	Closes the connection

Administering IMAP4

IMAP4 is, for the most part, self-administering. You might want to consider a couple of items, however. Figure 20-29 shows the General tab of the property sheet for the IMAP4 default virtual server. Because IMAP4 has the ability to request public folders, Microsoft's implementation of this protocol lets you choose whether to show public folders to the client. In addition, you can enable fast message retrieval here, which will cause Exchange Server to approximate the message sizes, rather than calculate their exact size. This estimation is done only when the clients do not need to know the exact message sizes for retrieval.

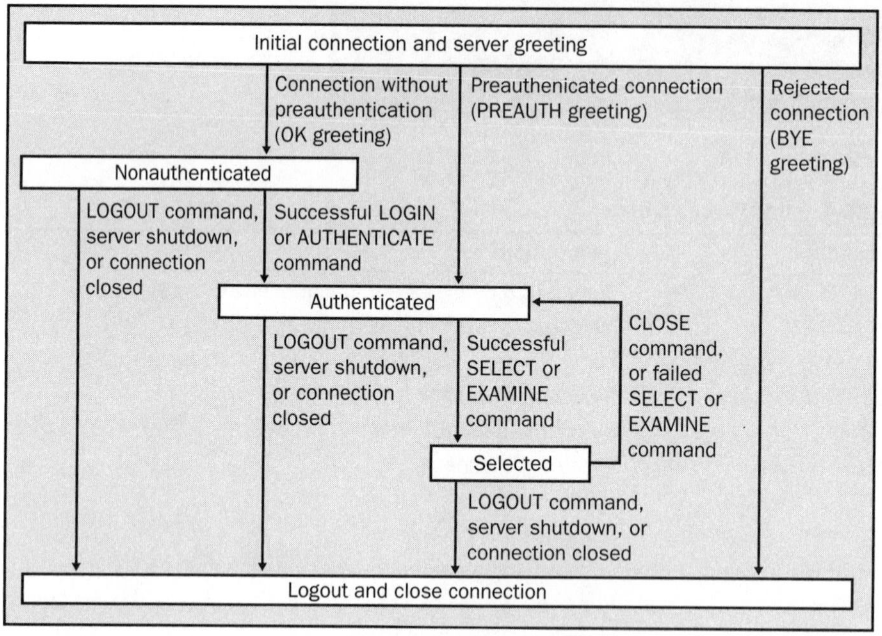

Figure 20-29. *IMAP4 default virtual server properties.*

Network News Transfer Protocol

Because Network News Transfer Protocol (NNTP) is growing in popularity, it would be wise for us to take a brief look at the architecture of this protocol. We'll then discuss the more pragmatic aspects of administering NNTP on your network.

NNTP Architecture

NNTP specifies a way to distribute, query, retrieve, and post news articles on the Internet. A client wanting to retrieve a subset of articles from the database is called a *subscriber*. NNTP allows a subscriber to request a subset of articles rather than requiring the retrieval of all articles from the database. Before NNTP was developed, two methods of distributing news items were popular: Internet mailing lists and the Usenet news system.

An Internet mailing list, commonly known as a *list server*, distributes news by the use of distribution e-mail lists. A subscriber sends a message to the distribution list, and the message is e-mailed to all members of the list. But sending a separate copy of an e-mail to each subscriber can consume a large amount of disk space, bandwidth, and CPU resources. In addition, full distribution of the message can take from several minutes to several hours, depending on the size of the list and the physical resources available to propagate it. Maintaining the subscriber list also involves significant administrative effort, unless a third-party program is used to automate this function.

Storing and retrieving messages from a central location instead of sending an e-mail to each subscriber can significantly reduce the use of these resources. The Usenet news system provides this alternative. In addition, Usenet allows a subscriber to select only those messages he or she wants to read and also provides indexing, cross-referencing, and message expiration.

NNTP is modeled on the Usenet news specifications in RFC 850, but it is designed to make fewer demands on the structure, content, and storage of the news articles. It runs as a background service on one host and can accept connections from other hosts on the LAN or over the Internet.

When a subscriber connects to an NNTP server, the subscriber issues the NEWSGROUPS command to determine whether any new newsgroups have been created on the server. If so, the server notifies the subscriber and gives the subscriber the opportunity to subscribe to the new newsgroups. After this, the subscriber is connected to the desired newsgroup and can use the NEWNEWS command to ask the server whether any new articles have been posted since the subscriber's last connection. The subscriber receives a list of new articles from the server and can request transmission of some or all of those articles. Finally, the subscriber can either reply to a news article or post a new article to the server by using the POST command.

NNTP uses TCP for its connections and SMTP-like commands and responses. The default TCP port for NNTP is 119. An NNTP command consists of a command word followed in some cases by a parameter. Commands are not case sensitive. Each line can contain only one command and cannot exceed 512 characters, including spaces, punctuation, and the trailing CR–LF (carriage return/line feed) command. Commands cannot be continued on the next line.

Responses from the server can take the form of a text response or a status response. Text responses are displayed in the subscriber's client program, whereas status responses are interpreted by the client program before any display occurs.

Each status response line begins with a three-digit numeric code. The first digit of the response indicates the success, failure, or progress of the previous command. Table 20-5 lists the meaning of different values for the first digit. The second digit in the code indicates the function response category. These categories are listed in Table 20-6. The third digit indicates the specific response.

Table 20-5. Meaning of first digit of status response code

First Digit	Meaning
1*xx*	Informative message
2*xx*	Command OK
3*xx*	Command OK so far; send the rest of it
4*xx*	Command was correct but couldn't be performed for some reason
5*xx*	Command not implemented or incorrect or a serious program error occurred

Table 20-6. Meaning of second digit of status response code

Second Digit	Meaning
*x*0*x*	Connection, setup, and miscellaneous messages
*x*1*x*	Newsgroup selection
*x*2*x*	Article selection
*x*3*x*	Distribution functions
*x*4*x*	Posting
*x*8*x*	Nonstandard (private implementation) extensions
*x*9*x*	Debugging output

In general, the 2*xx* codes are sent upon initial connection to the NNTP server, depending on the posting permissions. Code 400 is sent when the NNTP server discontinues service, and the 5*xx* codes indicate that the command could not be performed for some unusual reason. Table 20-7 lists some common codes you might encounter when troubleshooting NNTP connections.

Table 20-7. Common NNTP status response codes

Code	Meaning
100	Help text
190–199	Debug output
200	Server ready; posting allowed
201	Server ready; no posting allowed
400	Service discontinued
500	Command not recognized
501	Command syntax error
502	Access restriction or permission denied
503	Program fault; command not performed

NNTP Commands

It isn't possible here to go into detail about each NNTP command. However, several of the commands that you will see in both the event log and the output log file are worth describing in case you ever need to troubleshoot an NNTP connection. Figure 20-30 illustrates some of these commands.

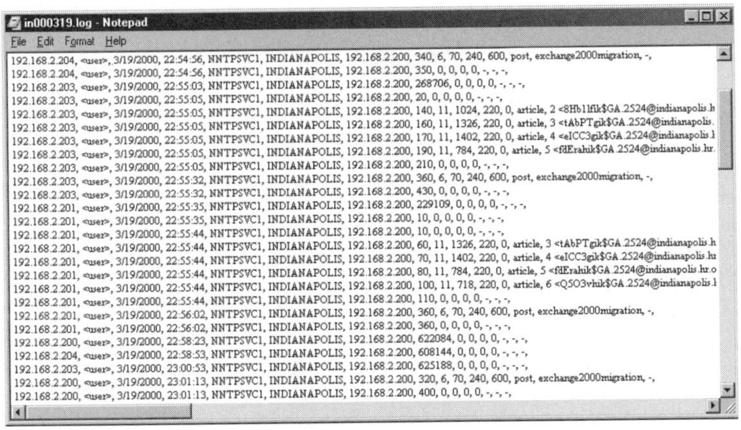

Figure 20-30. *Log file for NNTP service.*

The ARTICLE, BODY, HEAD, and STAT commands refer to the retrieval and transmission of a news article. The HEAD and BODY commands are identical to the ARTICLE command, except that they return either the header lines (HEAD) or the body text (BODY) of the article. No text is returned with the STAT command. Instead, this command returns the message ID to the subscriber.

The ARTICLE command has two forms: one that is followed by the message ID of the article to display and one that is followed by either a parameter or no parameter. In the first form, the ARTICLE command displays the header, a blank line, and then the body text of the specified article. The subscriber obtains the message ID from a list that is provided in response to the NEWNEWS command.

The second form of the command, ARTICLE *<message-id>*, displays the header, a blank line, and then the body text of the message. The subscriber chooses the message number from the range of articles provided when the newsgroup was selected. If the number is omitted, the current article is assumed. Some of the error responses that might occur with this command include the following:

- "420 no current article has been selected"
- "423 no such article number in this group"
- "430 no such article found"

The GROUP command must be followed by the name of a newsgroup. Newsgroup names are not case sensitive. If the group requested no longer exists, the subscriber receives the error message "411 no such news group." If the requested group does exist, the subscriber receives the article numbers of the first and last articles in the group, along with an estimate of the number of articles in the group. This number is not guaranteed to be accurate.

The LIST command returns a list of valid newsgroups and associated information. Each newsgroup is sent as a line of text that looks like this:

<group> <last> <first> <p>

where

- *<group>* is the name of the newsgroup.
- *<last>* is the number of the last known article currently in that newsgroup.
- *<first>* is the number of the first article currently in the newsgroup.
- *<p>* is either "y" or "n," where "y" indicates that posting is allowed and "n" indicates that posting is not allowed.

It might be possible to receive a "y" in the *<p>* portion of the response and still not be able to post to that newsgroup because the newsgroup is moderated, is restricted, or has gone offline for some reason.

The NEWSGROUPS command is followed by the date, the time, and then an optional *<distributions>* parameter. It lists newsgroups that have been created since the date and time specified. The date is specified as six digits in the *yymmdd* format. For the year, the closest century is assumed as the first two digits. Hence, 86 would mean 1986, and 30 would mean 2030. The time parameter is sent as six digits in *hhmmss* format, with the hours calculated on a 24-hour time clock. The time zone is assumed to be the server's time zone unless the token GMT appears, in which case both the date and the time are evaluated at the 0 meridian.

The optional *<distributions>* parameter is a list of distribution groups. For instance, the distribution portion of net.trainsbydave is "net." This parameter causes the distribution portion of the article to be examined for a match with the distribution groups listed. Only those that match the specified groups will be listed.

Administering NNTP

NNTP in Exchange Server 2003 is used to create asynchronous group discussions. You can configure it to communicate with external NNTP servers to make popular Usenet groups available internally to your users. NNTP in IIS replaces the Internet News Service in Exchange Server 5.5. Installing Exchange Server 2003 enhances NNTP in Windows Server 2003, giving NNTP the ability to communicate with other news servers through newsfeeds.

You can create multiple NNTP servers within your organization in a master-subordinate layout. This enables clients to connect to a collection of servers and still maintain accurate views of newsgroup content. Creating a collection of servers provides scalability for a large user base, such as an ISP, and fault tolerance if a subordinate server should go offline.

Even though the master server controls the article numbers and maintains synchronization with the subordinate servers, clients always connect to the subordinate news server. DNS configuration automatically distributes the client load equally across subordinate servers. Since each subordinate server provides a newsfeed to the master server, a newly posted article will first be sent to the master server and will not appear on the subordinate server until the master server sends the article to all subordinate servers.

Real World Setting Up a Master-Subordinate Newsfeed

To set up a master-subordinate newsfeed, perform the following steps:

1. Create the newsgroup on the master server.
2. Create the newsgroups on the subordinate servers.
3. Create a newsfeed from the master server to each subordinate server.
4. Create a newsfeed from each subordinate server to the master server.

Configuring an NNTP Virtual Server

To configure the NNTP virtual server in the Exchange System snap-in, navigate to your server object, expand the Protocols container and then the NNTP container, and right-click the default virtual server. Figure 20-31 shows the General tab of the NNTP virtual server's property sheet.

By default, an NNTP server communicates over TCP port 119 or via Secure Sockets Layer (SSL) using TCP port 563. When multiple virtual NNTP servers are present, each must be assigned a unique IP address and/or TCP/SSL port combination.

The default number of connections to an NNTP server from other NNTP hosts is 5000. Adjust this number based on your server's resources and the number of concurrent NNTP connections you expect. The Path Header text box enables you to specify the name of the server to append to the NNTP path header. The default is the fully qualified domain name (FQDN) of the computer. A client can examine the path header to see the route a message has traveled from a source client through various news servers to the destination news server.

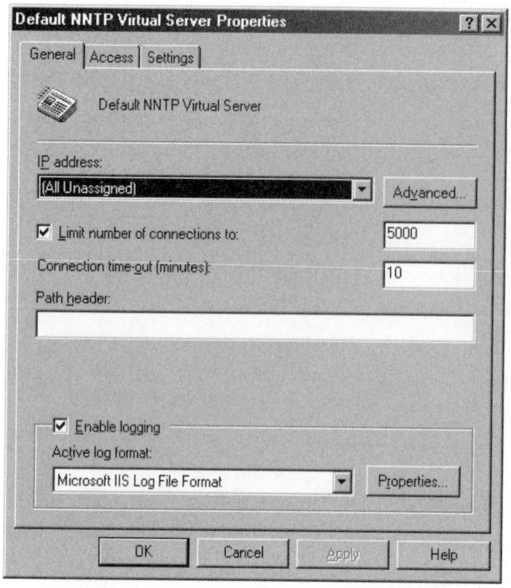

Figure 20-31. *General tab of an NNTP virtual server's property sheet.*

The Settings tab allows you to set limits on articles that are posted and to enable control messages and moderated newsgroups (Figure 20-32). This tab also allows you to prevent other servers from pulling articles from this server. The default is to allow them to do so.

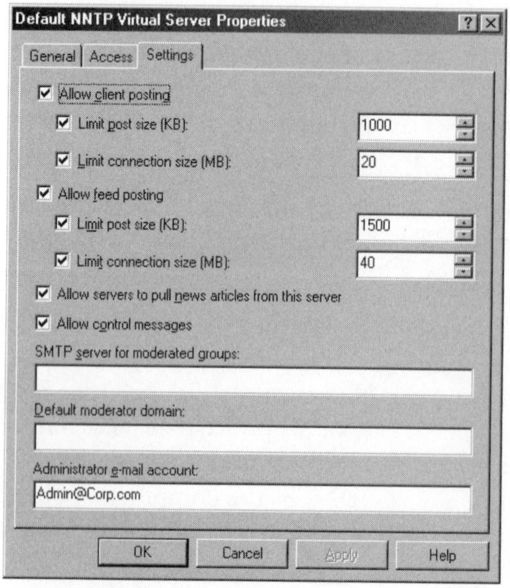

Figure 20-32. *Settings tab of an NNTP virtual server's property sheet.*

NNTP hosts use *control messages* to communicate with one another, to create and remove newsgroups, and to cancel messages that have already been posted. For example, if you create a new newsgroup, the host providing the newsfeed sends a control message to hosts receiving the newsfeed, indicating that a new newsgroup has been created. NNTP then uses this information to determine whether a new newsgroup should be added under the newsgroup object.

The Administrator E-Mail Account text box on the Settings tab lets you specify an e-mail address that will receive NDRs when messages are not successfully delivered to the newsgroup moderator. To enable the sending of NDRs, create a new DWORD value named *MailFromHeader* with a value of *1* in the registry key HKEY_LOCAL_MACHINE\SYSTEM\CurrentControlSet\Services\NntpSvc \Parameters\.

NNTP Server Objects

Listed underneath the NNTP virtual server in the Exchange System scope pane are five objects, as shown in Figure 20-33. Let's take a brief look at each one.

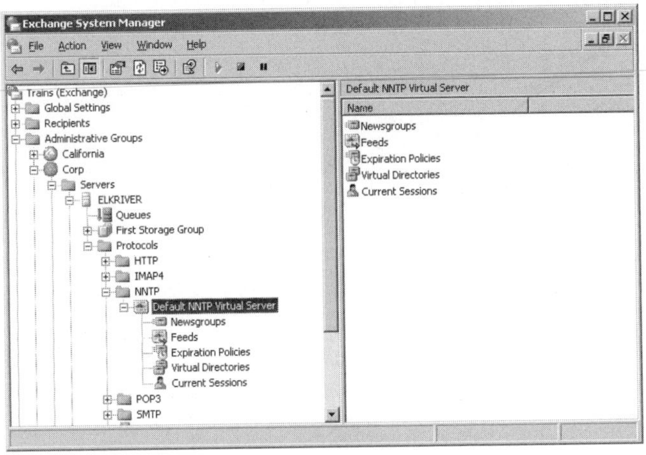

Figure 20-33. *NNTP server objects.*

The Newsgroups object lists the newsgroups that are currently configured on this server, plus the three control newsgroups.

The Feeds object lists inbound and outbound feeds. You set up each feed with a wizard that asks, in part, which role you want the feed to play: Peer, Master, or Slave. By default, each feed uses the asterisk (*) as a wildcard to denote that all newsgroups on the remote server will be involved with the feed. You can enter individual newsgroups manually if you're interested only in a subset of the newsgroups on the remote server.

By right-clicking the Expiration Policies object, pointing to New, and then choosing Expiration Policy, you can run through a simple wizard to specify how long newsgroup messages should be retained. The time interval is set in hours and can be a maximum of 9999 hours, or just under 14 months.

The Virtual Directories object allows you to set up a virtual root and then map that root to a file system, a remote share, or an Exchange public folder database (Figure 20-34). Start the wizard by right-clicking the Virtual Directories container, pointing to New, and then choosing Virtual Directory. This wizard allows you to select a different server to which this virtual root will write. Using this option, you can have the root written to the file system of a remote server.

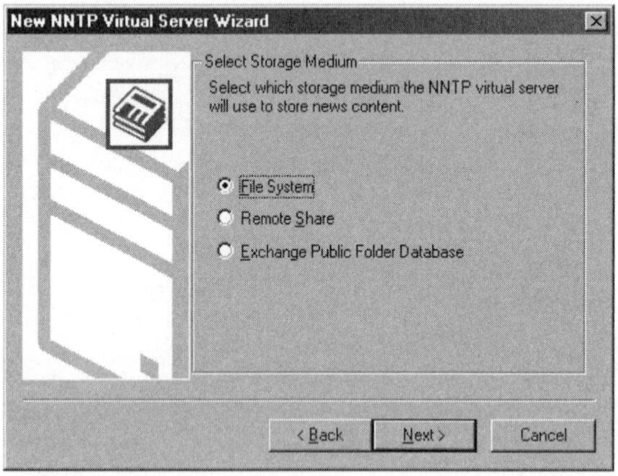

Figure 20-34. *Mapping a virtual root to a file system.*

Finally, you can monitor users' current sessions with the Current Sessions object. Simply highlight the Current Sessions object to see all users who are engaged in a current session with this NNTP virtual server listed in the details pane. From here, you can forcibly disconnect individual users by right-clicking the user and choosing Terminate. You can forcibly disconnect all users at once by right-clicking any user in the list and choosing Terminate All.

Lightweight Directory Access Protocol

Lightweight Directory Access Protocol (LDAP), although not unique to Exchange Server 2003, is still a foundational protocol without which it could not operate. LDAP has its roots in the X.500 Directory services and was first defined in RFC 1487. By now LDAP has been through three revisions, and the current standard is defined in RFC 2251.

The X.500 Directory Access Protocol (DAP) originally required an OSI stack. The current version of LDAP runs over TCP/IP and is thus more adaptable in today's market. In addition, an LDAP server can query a non-LDAP server. Earlier versions of LDAP provided for a client to send queries to a front-end processor at the server that converted the LDAP query to a DAP query and presented that to the server. Version 3 no longer requires this conversion. Moreover, earlier versions of LDAP specified the object classes and attributes as part of the protocol, making the directory static and nonextensible. With LDAP version 3, clients can query a server to discover the object classes and attributes, and the protocol no longer defines what you have come to know as the schema.

LDAP version 3 also allows for X.509 certificates as well as Connectionless LDAP (CLDAP), which is well suited for applications that need to make simple queries and get fast responses. CLDAP uses user datagram protocol (UDP) as the transport protocol at the transport layer.

In LDAP version 3, the client transmits a request to the server describing the query to be performed on the directory. The server performs the query and returns the results to the client. There is no requirement in the RFC for synchronous behavior by either the server or the client, which means that multiple requests and responses can be passed between the client and server in any order, provided that the client eventually receives a response for every request.

An LDAP client assumes that there are one or more servers that jointly provide access to a Directory Information Tree (DIT). The tree is composed of entries with names, each of which must have one or more attribute values that form its Relative Distinguished Name (RDN), which must be unique among all its siblings. The concatenation of the object hierarchy names above the RDN form the entry's Distinguished Name (DN), which is, by default, unique in the tree. An example of a DN is: *CN=Bill English,DC=HR,DC=Trainsbydave,DC=com.*

Each attribute is actually a set of attributes, each of which is a defined type that has one or more associated values. The attribute type is identified by a short, descriptive name and an Object Identifier (OID). The attribute type governs whether there can be more than one value entered in a given attribute field, what rules the syntax must conform to, and other functions. The schema is a collection of attribute type definitions, object class definitions, and other information.

An LDAP server must provide information about itself and other LDAP servers hosting the same directory. This information is represented as a group of attributes located in the root DSA-Specific Entry (DSE), which is named with the zero-length LDAP DN. You can retrieve these attributes by performing a base object search of the root with the filter "objectClass=*". The root DSE *must not* be included if the query performed is focused on a subtree as its starting point.

All message exchanges are encapsulated in a common envelope, the *LDAPMessage*. The only common fields in the envelope are the message ID and the controls. The following list offers the commands for LDAP version 3 that are sent inside the LDAPMessage:

- BindRequest
- BindResponse
- UnbindRequest
- SearchRequest
- SearchResultEntry
- SearchResultDone
- SearchResultReference
- ModifyRequest
- ModifyResponse
- AddRequest
- AddResponse
- DelRequest
- DelResponse
- ModifyDNRequest
- ModifyDNResponse
- CompareRequest
- CompareResponse
- AbandonRequest
- ExtendedRequest
- ExtendedResponse

If the LDAP search is operating over a connection-oriented transport such as TCP, the server returns a sequence of responses in separate LDAP messages containing zero or more SearchResultEntry responses, one for each entry found during the search. The client knows that the server has returned all the results when the server sends the SearchResultDone message. Each entry in a SearchResultEntry contains all the attributes specified in the field of the search request. Return of any attribute is subject to access control and other administrative policies.

Summary

In this chapter, you learned some of the basics of SMTP, IMAP4, POP3, and NNTP. You learned how to read the more common commands of these protocols and how to log the interaction between the server and client for troubleshooting purposes. You also learned how to filter messages to reduce SPAM in your environment. In the next chapter, you'll learn the basics of connecting Exchange Server 2003 to other messaging systems using the X.400 Connector.

Part VI
Functionality

Chapter 21

Connecting to Other Messaging Systems with X.400

Microsoft Exchange Server 2003 can connect to a multitude of modern and legacy messaging systems. Until this point, we have focused primarily on working within the Microsoft Exchange Server 2003 environment. You have set up your Exchange system and learned how to deploy and administer all of its components—from routing groups to clients to clustered servers. Exchange Server 2003 is not the only messaging system out there, however. Many types of messaging systems are available today, and you might have to connect your Exchange system to one or more of them. You might, for example, be upgrading from a legacy system or need to establish communications with another company. Even though Exchange Server 2003 provides connectors for connecting to proprietary systems like Lotus Notes and Novel GroupWise, you can also use a standard X.400 Connector to connect to systems that support X.400. This chapter covers the basics of connecting Exchange Server 2003 to other messaging systems, referred to as *foreign systems*, using the X.400 Connector.

> **Note** Exchange Server 2003 no longer supports the Connector for Microsoft Mail, which was included with previous versions. The Exchange System Manager included with Exchange Server 2003 does support the management of Connectors for Microsoft Mail that are installed on servers in your organization running Exchange 2000 Server. However, you cannot configure the connector on a server running Exchange Server 2003.

Overview of X.400

X.400 is a messaging standard that is used by many messaging systems. An enterprise that implements X.400-compliant e-mail systems can support a heterogeneous messaging environment. X.400 uses a strict addressing method that reflects a hierarchical environment. An X.400 address reflects the recipient's position in a messaging hierarchy. For example, the X.400 address for Denise Smith at the Phoenix location of a company named Contoso might be "c=US;a=;p=Contoso;o=Phoenix;s=Smith;g=Denise." Each of these parameters represents a particular X.400 value or hierarchical placement: "c=" stands for the country; "a=" represents the Administrative Management Domain; "p=" represents the Private Management Domain and is equivalent to the Exchange organization; "o=" stands for the X.400 organization, the equivalent of an Exchange administrative group; "s=" stands for the surname, or last name; and "g=" stands for the given name, or first name.

You can use the X.400 Connector to connect Exchange Server 2003 to any foreign messaging system that supports the X.400 standard.

More Info To find out more about the X.400 standard, look at Request for Comments 1330 (RFC 1330). You can find this online at several Web sites, including *http://www.cis.ohio-state.edu/hypertext/information/rfc.html*.

Real World **Using Other Foreign Gateways**

Many messaging systems use gateways to connect to dissimilar messaging systems. Exchange Server 2003 supports many gateways in the form of connectors. The X.400 Connector, the Lotus Notes Connector, and the Novell GroupWise Connector are examples of gateways that are built into Exchange Server 2003. Other vendors provide a variety of gateways for connecting Exchange Server 2003 to external, proprietary electronic mail, fax, voice mail, and other types of systems.

Many connectors are available for Exchange Server, either included with the Exchange Server software from Microsoft or offered separately by other vendors. It is not possible to discuss here every connector that can be used to connect Exchange Server 2003 to foreign systems. For that reason, we're limiting our discussion to the X.400 Connector because of its wide acceptance as a messaging standard. If you need to know the specifics of connecting Exchange Server 2003 to a particular messaging system, consult the Exchange Server 2003 product documentation.

Creating an MTA Service Transport Stack

Creating an X.400 Connector to link Exchange Server 2003 to a foreign X.400 system is not too difficult. The one thing you must remember is that each end of an X.400 Connector must be configured separately. This chapter assumes that the administrator of the foreign system will configure the connector in the foreign system appropriately.

To configure the X.400 Connector in Exchange Server 2003, you must first create a Message Transfer Agent (MTA) service transport stack. This transport stack is configured for a particular Exchange server and is basically a set of information about the software and hardware that make up the underlying network. The transport stack allows for a layer of abstraction between the X.400 Connector and the network itself.

> **Note** Transport stacks exist at the server level, and each is associated with a particular Exchange server. In contrast, the connector or connectors that use the transport stack exist at the routing group level. What this means to you is that you can configure multiple MTA transport stacks and X.400 Connectors within a routing group, giving you the ability to balance the load placed on servers by messaging connectors.

There are two different types of MTA transport stacks, each defined by the type of network hardware or software you have configured:

- **TP0/X.25** Uses an Eicon port adapter to provide both dial-up and direct communication in compliance with the Open Systems Interconnection (OSI) X.25 recommendation.
- **TCP/IP** Defines specifications for running OSI software, such as X.400 messaging systems, over a TCP/IP-based network. Exchange Server 2003 uses Windows 2003 TCP/IP services.

Because TCP/IP is easily the most commonly installed type of MTA transport stack, we will use it as an example here. However, the configuration process is nearly identical for the X.25 MTA transport stack.

You create an MTA transport stack with the Exchange System snap-in. First navigate to the X.400 object in the Protocols container of the server on which you want to install the stack, as shown in Figure 21-1. Right-click the Microsoft MTA object, point to New on the shortcut menu, and choose TCP/IP X.400 Service Transport Stack. This opens the property sheet for the new MTA transport stack. You will use this property sheet to configure the stack. You're already familiar with the Details tab, which lets you enter an administrative note regarding the object. The other two tabs are discussed in the sections that follow.

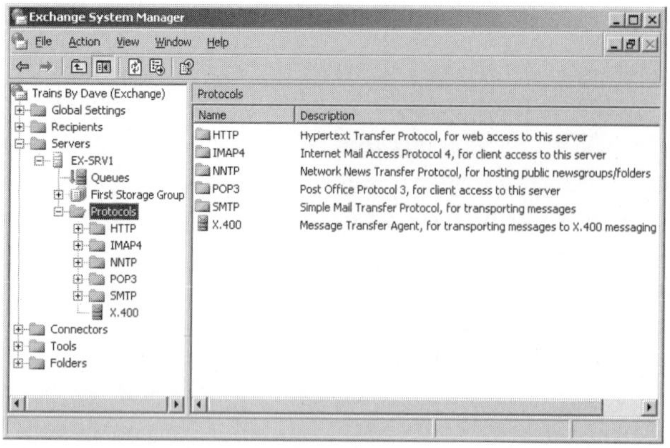

Figure 21-1. *Creating a new MTA transport stack.*

General Tab

Use the General tab, shown in Figure 21-2, to change the display name for the MTA transport stack and to configure OSI addressing information. Unless you plan to allow other applications besides Exchange Server 2003 to use the MTA transport stack, you do not need to worry about the OSI addressing values.

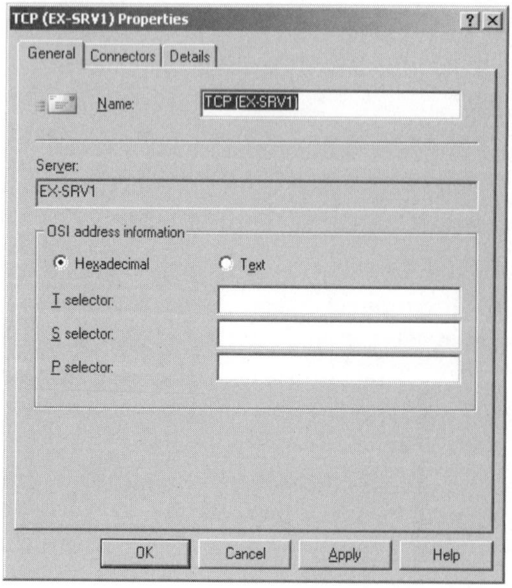

Figure 21-2. *Configuring general properties for an MTA transport stack.*

Connectors Tab

The Connectors tab, shown in Figure 21-3, lists all the messaging connectors in the routing group that are configured to use the current MTA transport stack. When you first create a stack, this list is blank. As you create new connectors that use the MTA transport stack, these connectors are added to the list. After you've created the MTA transport stack, you can find its configuration object in the Microsoft MTA container of the server on which the transport stack was created.

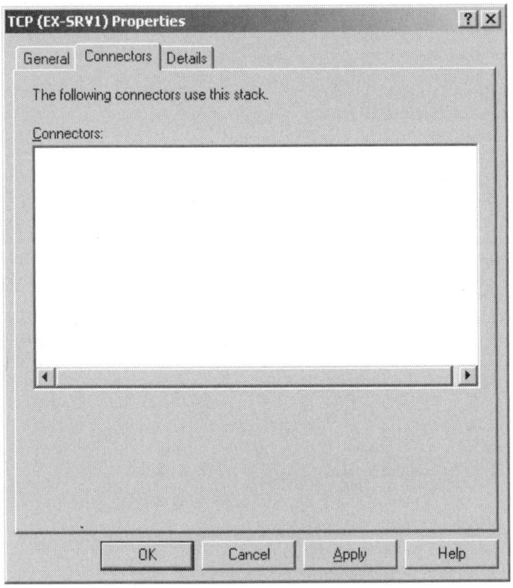

Figure 21-3. *Viewing the connectors that use an MTA transport stack.*

Creating an X.400 Connector

After you've created an MTA transport stack, you must create the X.400 Connector itself. To do so, in the Exchange System snap-in, navigate to the Connectors container of the routing group in which you want to create the connector, as shown in Figure 21-4. Choose New TCP X.400 Connector from the Action menu. This opens the property sheet for the new X.400 Connector. The next several sections discuss the tabs on this property sheet.

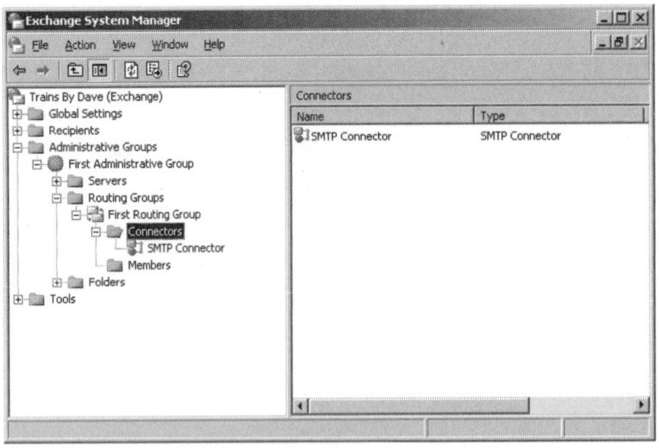

Figure 21-4. *Finding the Connectors container.*

General Tab

The General tab, shown in Figure 21-5, defines basic naming and connection information for the connector. You can configure the following settings on this property sheet:

- **Name** Gives the name of the connector as it will appear in the Exchange System snap-in. Notice that there is no default value here, as there is for the display names of most other configuration objects. We suggest using a name that includes the type of connector (X.400) and the routing groups, servers, or locations you are connecting. An example might be to type *X.400 Rgroup1 -> Atlanta X.400*.
- **Remote X.400 Name** Indicates the name of the remote server to which the local connector will connect. Click the Modify button to change the remote X.400 name and password. The password can be specified to prevent unauthorized connectors from opening an association to it. If a remote connector has been assigned such a password, you must enter it in this field.
- **X.400 Transport Stack** Indicates the connector transport stack that the X.400 Connector is currently configured to use. You can change the stack used at any time.
- **Message Text Word-Wrap** Contains options that enable or disable word wrap on outgoing messages. Some messaging systems do not allow messages to use word wrap, in which words automatically wrap to the next line rather than trailing off the right edge of a message window when windows are resized. Select Never to disable word wrap on all outgoing messages. This is the default. Select At Column and enter

a number to have Exchange Server automatically insert a carriage return at the specified column on all outgoing messages.

- **Remote Clients Support MAPI** When selected, indicates that the remote messaging system and clients support Messaging Application Programming Interface (MAPI). Exchange Server will transmit rich text and MAPI characteristics along with messages.
- **Do Not Allow Public Folder Referrals** When selected, prevents users of the remote system from accessing public folders configured in the local routing group.

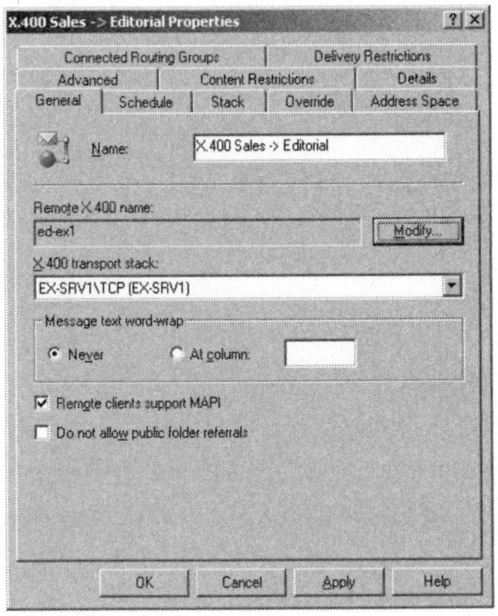

Figure 21-5. *Configuring general connection properties for a new X.400 Connector.*

Schedule Tab

The Schedule tab on X.400 Connector's property sheet, shown in Figure 21-6, lets you restrict the times at which the X.400 Connector can be used. By default, the X.400 Connector can be used at any time (Always); for the most part, you will want to leave this value alone. There might be times, however, when you want to limit connectivity, such as on a very busy network or when you need to bring a network down for maintenance.

You can set an X.400 Connector schedule to one of four values:

- **Never** Disables the connector altogether. This setting is useful for bringing the connector down while performing maintenance.
- **Always** Allows connections to be made to and from the server at any time.

- **Selected Times** Allows you to define specific times at which the X.400 Connector is available. This setting can be useful on a busy network. If immediate messaging is not a concern, you can schedule messages to be sent only at specific periods during the day, when network traffic is otherwise low.
- **Remote Initiated** Allows remote servers to connect to the current server, but does not allow the local server to initiate a connection. This setting can be useful if sending outgoing messages immediately is not a big concern but receiving incoming messages is.

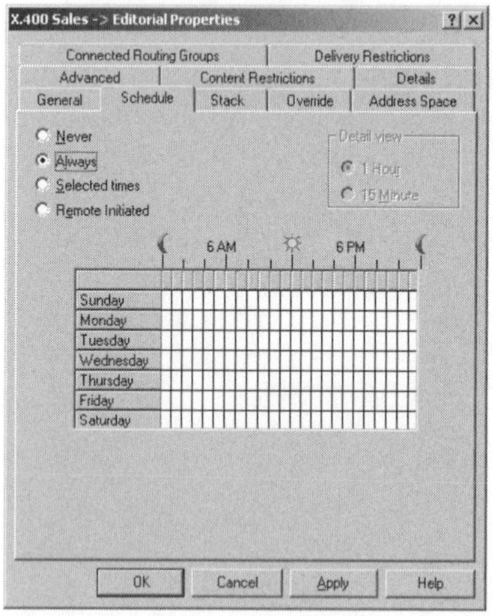

Figure 21-6. *Scheduling the availability of an X.400 Connector.*

Stack Tab

Use the Stack tab, shown in Figure 21-7, to specify transport address information about the foreign X.400 system. After you've specified the host name or IP address of the foreign system, you can provide outgoing OSI addressing information, if necessary, for the foreign system to which you are connecting.

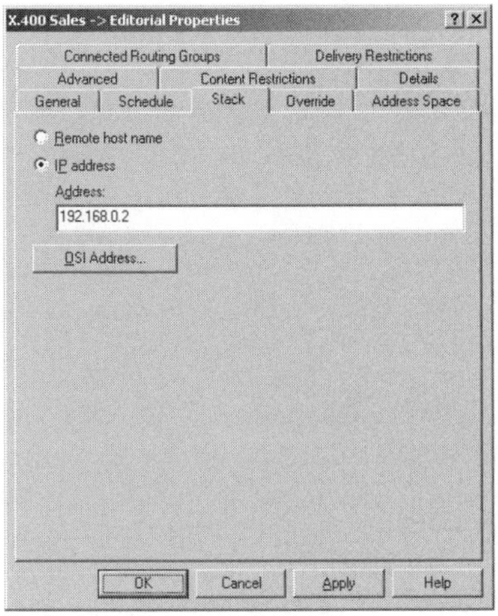

Figure 21-7. *Configuring transport address information for the foreign X.400 system.*

Override Tab

The Override tab, shown in Figure 21-8, lets you configure certain settings that override the local MTA settings when messages are sent over the X.400 Connector. For the most part, you can leave these advanced settings alone, particularly if you are using the X.400 Connector to connect to another Exchange routing group. If you are connecting to a foreign X.400 system, that system's administrator will be able to tell you whether you need to adjust any of these settings.

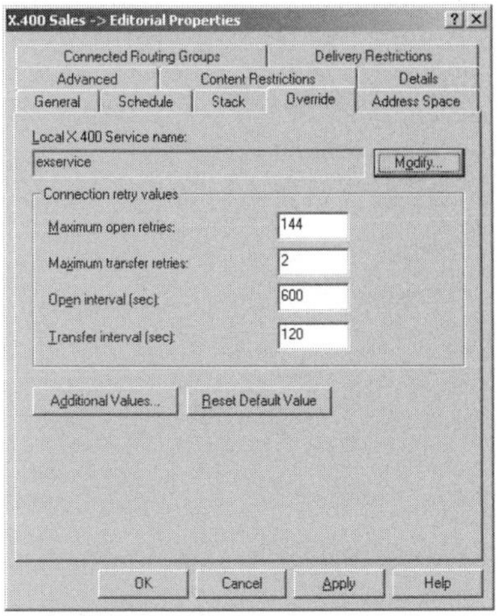

Figure 21-8. *Overriding values for local MTA information.*

You can also override the name and password of your local MTA on this tab. These options are used mainly when the name and password of the local MTA are too long or when they use characters or spaces that MTAs on foreign systems cannot accept. The overriding values are used only for the X.400 connection.

Address Space Tab

Foreign systems typically do not use the same addressing scheme as Exchange Server 2003. For this reason, the Exchange MTA relies on address spaces to choose foreign gateways over which messages should be sent. An *address space* is the part of an address that designates the system that should receive the message. For example, a typical Internet address takes the form *user@company.com*. Everything after the @ sign is the address space. The format of the address space is enough to tell the MTA that the message should be sent via SMTP.

The Address Space tab, shown in Figure 21-9, allows you to configure an address space for the foreign X.400 system to which you are building a connection. The Exchange MTA compares the destination address of outgoing messages with this address space to determine whether the outgoing messages should be sent over the X.400 Connector.

To add an address space, click Add. The Add Address Space dialog box opens (Figure 21-10). This dialog box allows you to specify the type of address space you want to add. Because you are connecting to a foreign X.400 system, you will want to configure an X.400 address space. Click OK.

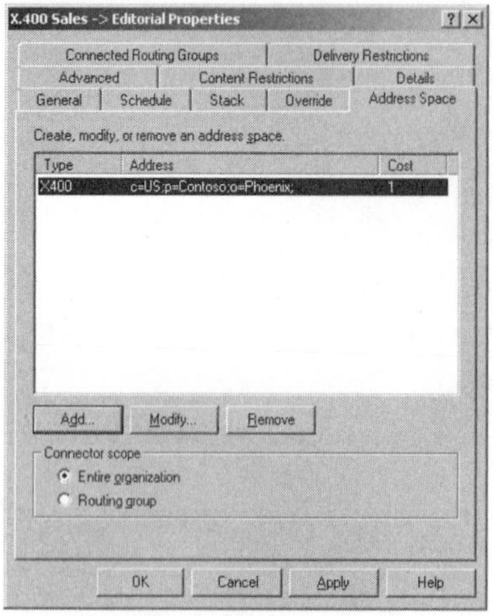

Figure 21-9. *Configuring an address space for the X.400 Connector.*

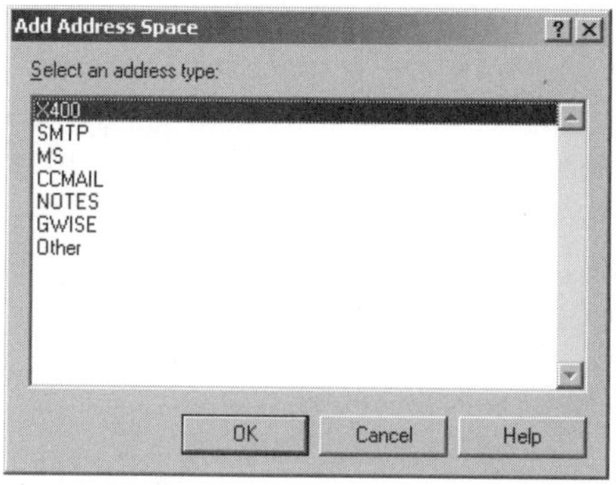

Figure 21-10. *Choosing the type of address space.*

The X.400 Address Space Properties screen appears, as shown in Figure 21-11. The administrator of the foreign system should be able to provide the addressing information that you need to configure here. X.400 addresses are case-sensitive and need to be typed exactly as provided.

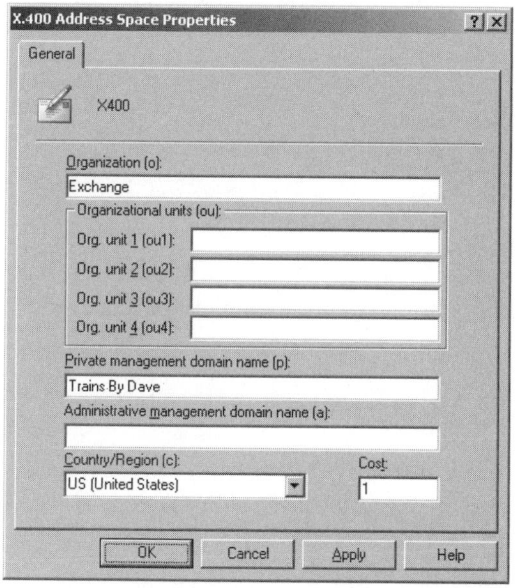

Figure 21-11. *Configuring the new X.400 address space information.*

Connected Routing Groups Tab

The Connected Routing Groups tab of the X.400 Connector's property sheet, shown in Figure 21-12, is used only when you are using an X.400 Connector to connect an Exchange 2003 routing group with an Exchange 5.5 site. (Remember, the Exchange 2003 Routing Group is the equivalent of an Exchange 5.5

site.) Although messaging between the groups can work if you leave the Connected Routing Group tab blank and configure an address space for the remote server, Exchange Server will not know that it is communicating with an Exchange 5.5 site. As a result, the two environments will not allow each other access to their public folders. Click New to display a dialog box in which you can enter the name of the Exchange 5.5 site to which you are connecting. When you add a routing group, an address space for that group is generated.

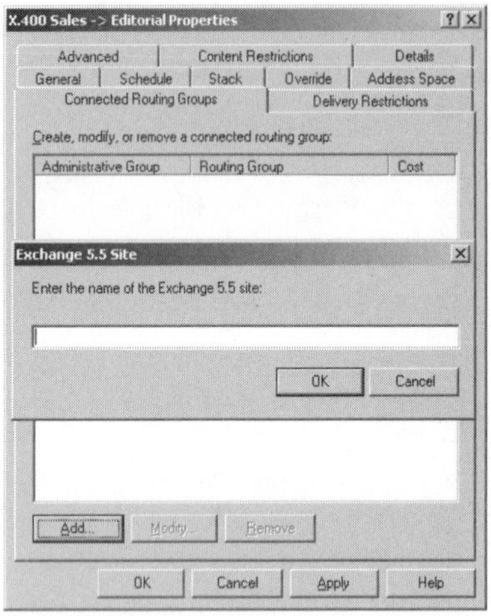

Figure 21-12. *Letting Exchange Server know that you are connecting to an Exchange 5.5 site.*

Exchange MTA compares the destination address of outgoing messages with this address space to determine whether the outgoing messages should be sent over the X.400 Connector.

Delivery Restrictions Tab

The Delivery Restrictions tab, shown in Figure 21-13, gives you control over which users can and cannot send messages over the X.400 Connector. You can control this in one of two ways:

- You can choose to prohibit all users from transferring messages over the X.400 Connector except for those whom you specifically allow. This option is represented on the top part of the tab. By default, all users are allowed to use the connector. To allow only certain users, click the Add button and select the users from the address book.
- You can choose to permit all users to transfer messages over the X.400 Connector except for those whom you specifically disallow. This option is represented on the bottom part of the tab. By default, no

users are disallowed. To disallow certain users, click the Add button and select the users from the address book.

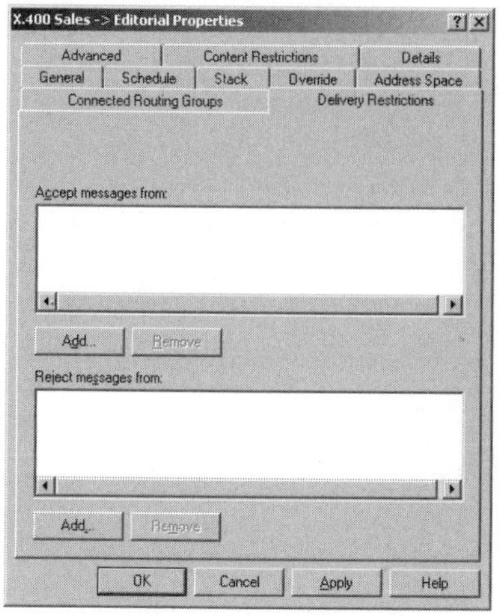

Figure 21-13. *Restricting the use of an X.400 Connector.*

Advanced Tab

The Advanced tab, shown in Figure 21-14, is used to specify options for MTA conformance, links, and message attributes. The settings depend primarily on the specifications of the foreign system to which you are connecting. The following options are available:

- **Allow BP-15 (In Addition To BP-14)** The Body Part 15 (BP-15) standard is part of the 1988 X.400 recommendation and supports several advanced messaging features, such as the encoding of binary attachments. The Body Part 14 (BP-14) standard is part of the older 1984 X.400 recommendation, which supports fewer features. If you do not select the Allow BP-15 option, only the BP-14 standard will be used.
- **Allow Exchange Contents** Exchange Server supports the use of Extended MAPI–compliant clients, which in turn support such features as rich text format. Make sure that any foreign X.400 system to which you are connecting supports such features before you allow them to be transferred.
- **Two-Way Alternate** The two-way alternate specification is an X.400 standard in which two connected X.400 systems take turns transmitting and receiving information. If the foreign system to which you are connecting supports this option, enabling it can greatly improve transmission speed.

- **X.400 Bodypart For Message Text** This option specifies how message text should be formatted. Unless you are communicating with foreign systems that use foreign-language applications, leave this value at its default setting, International Alphabet 5 (IA5).
- **X.400 Conformance** X.400 standards are published periodically as recommendations. Exchange Server 2003 supports the two primary recommendations: those issued in 1984 and those issued in 1988. Updates have been made to the standard since 1988, but they don't really form a new recommendation. The 1988 recommendation has two versions: normal mode and X.410 mode. The default setting is 1988 normal mode, and you can expect it to work with most foreign X.400 systems.
- **Global Domain Identifier** The global domain identifier (GDI) is a section of the X.400 address space of the target system. It is used to prevent message loops that can occur with outgoing messages. The administrator of the foreign X.400 system will let you know whether you need to modify these values.

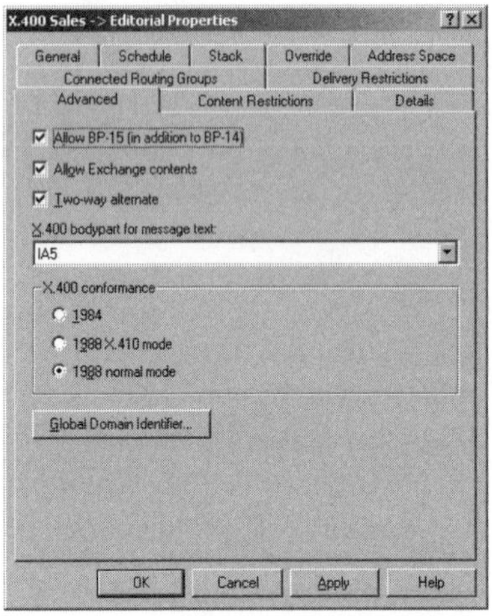

Figure 21-14. *Configuring advanced X.400 properties.*

Content Restrictions Tab

The Content Restrictions tab, shown in Figure 21-15, is used to restrict certain types of messages. The following options are available:

- **Allowed Priorities** Messages sent across this connector can be restricted by message size.

- **Allowed Types** You can choose whether this connector supports system messages (like public folder replication messages) or nonsystem messages (like standard interpersonal messages).
- **Allowed Sizes** Messages sent across this connector can be restricted by message size.

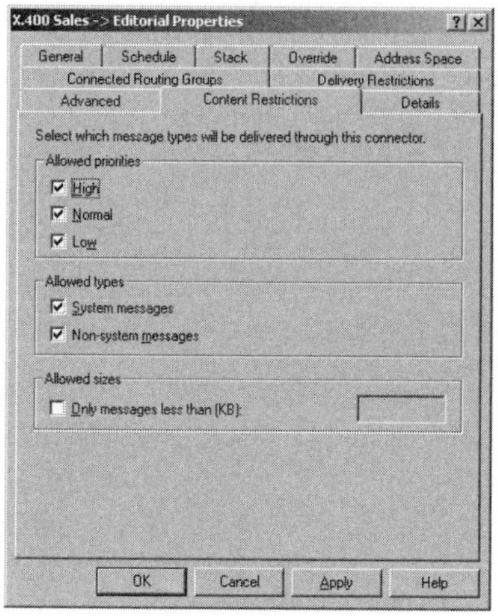

Figure 21-15. *Content Restrictions tab.*

Summary

In this chapter, you learned how to configure Exchange Server 2003 to transfer messages and synchronize directory information with foreign messaging systems that use X.400. In particular, you learned how to set up an X.400 Connector to transfer messages with any X.400-compliant messaging system. The next chapter discusses mobile services in Exchange Server 2003.

Chapter 22

Mobile Services in Exchange Server 2003

Modern workers are more on the go than ever, and timely access to the constantly increasing amount of information about corporate networks has never been more important. The mobile services built into Microsoft Exchange Server 2003 provide access to most Exchange services by mobile devices, such as Pocket PCs and SmartPhones.

Exchange Server 2003 provides mobile services through two mechanisms:

- **Exchange ActiveSync** Exchange ActiveSync allows users of Microsoft Windows–powered mobile devices (such as the Pocket PC, Pocket PC Phone Edition, or SmartPhone) to synchronize data with an Exchange server. Users access the information using powerful client software such as Microsoft Pocket Outlook, which provides a rich user experience and duplicates much of the functionality of Microsoft Outlook 2003 or Microsoft Outlook Web Access.
- **Outlook Mobile Access** Outlook Mobile Access (OMA) provides access to the Exchange environment through the use of Web browsers and mobile microbrowsers (such as Microsoft Pocket Internet Explorer) using HTML, Extensible HTML (XHTML), and compressed HTML (CHTML). OMA provides access to a wider class of clients (basically any that can use a browser) than using Exchange ActiveSync with Pocket Outlook does, but OMA does not provide as sophisticated an experience.

The mobile services now provided in Exchange Server 2003 were previously supplied by a product named Microsoft Mobile Information Server (MIS). Wrapping many of the mobile services from MIS with Exchange Server 2003 into a single product provides a logical consolidation of services for client access to corporate information. This consolidation allows you to have a single planning and deployment phase as you implement your messaging environment, rather than forcing you to first install Exchange Server 2003 and then install and configure a separate product like MIS.

This consolidation also offers another large advantage. Simply put, the use of Exchange along with MIS (and often third-party products as well) really didn't work that well, at least not without a lot of hair pulling. The design goal behind including mobile services in Exchange Server 2003 was to make mobile clients able to connect to Exchange directly following installation with little configuration necessary—and to a large degree, this goal is realized.

Note In a mixed Exchange environment, you must use Exchange Server 2003 for both the front-end and the back-end servers to gain access to mailboxes by using Outlook Mobile Access and Exchange ActiveSync. For mailboxes that are stored on a server that is running Exchange 5.5 and Exchange 2000, deploy Microsoft Mobile Information Server.

Exchange ActiveSync

Microsoft ActiveSync is a program shipped with mobile devices such as Pocket PC 2002 (which includes the standard Pocket PC, Pocket PC Phone Edition, and SmartPhones) and Microsoft Windows Mobile 2003 (the newest version of the Pocket PC line). One version of ActiveSync runs on the mobile device and another version runs on the user's desktop. The user can create a partnership between the mobile device and a desktop computer using a serial cable, USB cable, infrared, or other wireless connection. Once this partnership is created, ActiveSync synchronizes data between the computer and the mobile device.

Exchange ActiveSync is a service running on an Exchange server that allows the client-based ActiveSync program to synchronize between the mobile device and a user's Exchange Server folders. Users can connect to Exchange ActiveSync using any type of connection that provides access to the local network. The mobile device can be connected to a desktop computer, connected to the local network through a wireless access point, or connected via a mobile carrier.

Unlike previous versions of Exchange ActiveSync (which required that users have Outlook running on the desktop and use Outlook to synchronize and connect to the Exchange Server), Exchange ActiveSync in Exchange Server 2003 lets users synchronize directly to Exchange. It can still be integrated with the desktop version of ActiveSync, so any settings that a user has created from the desktop translate over to the device and can be altered there. However, the use of the desktop version of ActiveSync is not mandatory.

Setting Up Exchange Server 2003 for Exchange ActiveSync

Configuring Exchange ActiveSync on the Exchange server side really couldn't be simpler. To start with, the service is enabled automatically during the installation of Exchange Server 2003, so mobile device users can configure their devices and start accessing Exchange information right away. (This is covered in the following section, "Setting Up a Mobile Device for Exchange ActiveSync.")

To manage mobile services for the Exchange organization, expand the Global Settings container in System Manager, right-click the Mobile Services container, and choose Properties. This opens the Mobile Services property sheet shown in Figure 22-1.

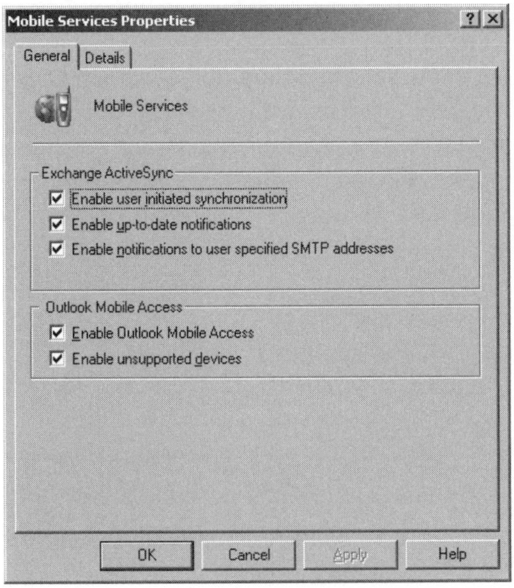

Figure 22-1. *Configuring mobile services for an Exchange organization.*

The Mobile Services property sheet holds three options relating to Exchange ActiveSync:

- **Enable User Initiated Synchronization** This option lets users start the synchronization process from their mobile devices. Disable this option to disable Exchange ActiveSync for all users.
- **Enable Up-To-Date Notifications** Mobile devices that use Windows Mobile 2003 or later are able to receive special notifications from Exchange indicating that new information is available on the Exchange server and initiating synchronization automatically. Use this option to enable these notifications. Note that this option is not available unless the Enable User Initiated Synchronization option is also enabled.

- **Enable Notifications To User Specified SMTP Addresses** This option lets users configure their own SMTP carrier for notifications instead of using the carrier configured at the Exchange server. With this feature enabled, when a new message arrives in a user's mailbox, up-to-date notifications allow a synchronization to occur on a user's device. Enable this feature when you have users who are using mobile devices to synchronize, and you do not want to specify the carrier. This option is also not available unless the Enable User Initiated Synchronization *and* Enable Up-To-Date Notifications options are also enabled.

You can also configure mobile services on a per-user basis. Assuming that Exchange ActiveSync is enabled globally (i.e., that the Enable User Initiated Synchronization option is enabled in System Manager), you can configure the first two options discussed on the previous list (enabling synchronization and enabling notifications) using the Exchange Features tab on a user's account property sheet in Active Directory Users and Computers, as shown in Figure 22-2. You can use this feature to disable mobile service options for individual users when those options are enabled at the global level. However, you cannot use this feature to enable options for individual users when the options are disabled at the global level.

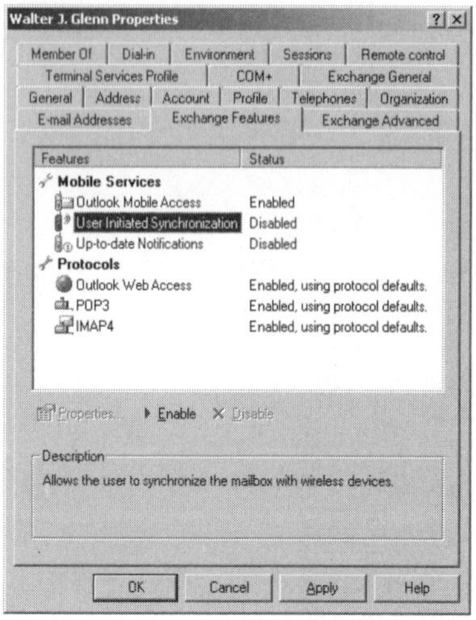

Figure 22-2. *Configuring mobile services for an individual user.*

Setting Up a Mobile Device for Exchange ActiveSync

Setting up a mobile device that uses Microsoft ActiveSync to access Exchange ActiveSync is also a straightforward process. First, you'll need to configure the device to access the network. Devices can connect in any of the following ways:

- Wirelessly through an access point on the network, using a networking protocol like 802.11
- Wirelessly through a mobile carrier that can connect to the network
- Using a docking cradle and a PC that is connected to the network as a gateway through which to connect

Once the device is configured so that it can access the network (and that is usually the trickiest part), you'll need to configure Microsoft ActiveSync on the device to connect to Exchange. To do this, use the following steps:

Note The procedures and figures in this section are based on the standard Pocket PC 2002 and might differ just a bit from those you'll see on other Windows-powered mobile devices. However, the configuration and use will be similar across all these devices.

1. On the mobile device, tap Start, and then tap ActiveSync. This opens the ActiveSync window shown in Figure 22-3.

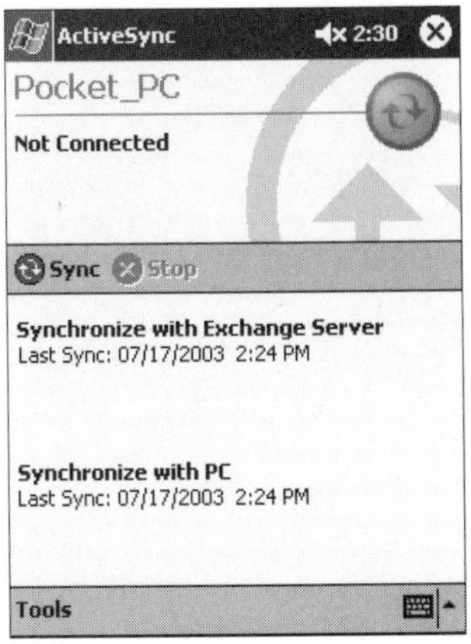

Figure 22-3. *ActiveSync for Pocket PC 2002.*

2. Tap the Tools menu, and then tap Options to open the ActiveSync options window.

3. Switch to the Server tab, shown in Figure 22-4.

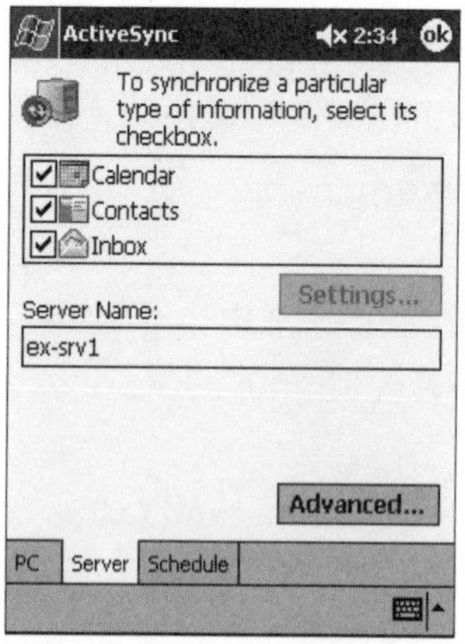

Figure 22-4. *Configuring an Exchange server in ActiveSync.*

4. In the Server Name field, enter the name of the Exchange server to which you want to connect.
5. Tap the Advanced button to open the Advanced Connection Options window, shown in Figure 22-5.

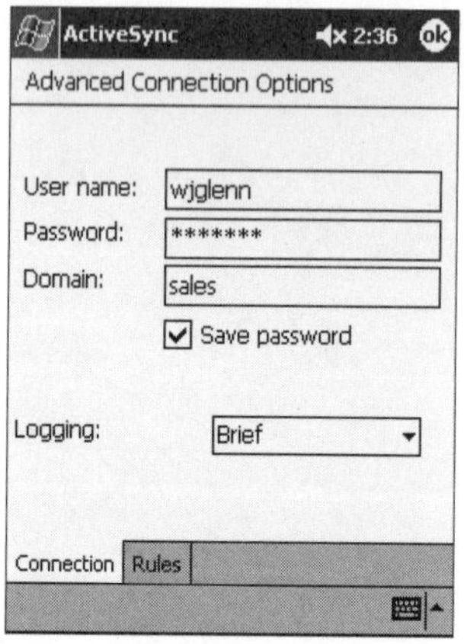

Figure 22-5. *Configuring advanced connection options in ActiveSync.*

6. Enter your user name, password, and domain name.
7. Switch to the Rules tab and specify how ActiveSync should handle conflicts (when the same item appears on both the mobile device and the Exchange server). You can have ActiveSync either replace the item on the device or replace the item on the server.
8. Click OK, and then click OK again to return to the ActiveSync main window.

After you are connected and have synchronized information with the Exchange server, you can access that information within applications on the mobile device. Pocket Outlook, for example, synchronizes your Inbox by default and any additional subfolders that you specify. The Calendar application synchronizes with scheduling information from Exchange, Contacts with your contact information, and so on. Figure 22-6 shows views of these programs in Pocket PC 2002.

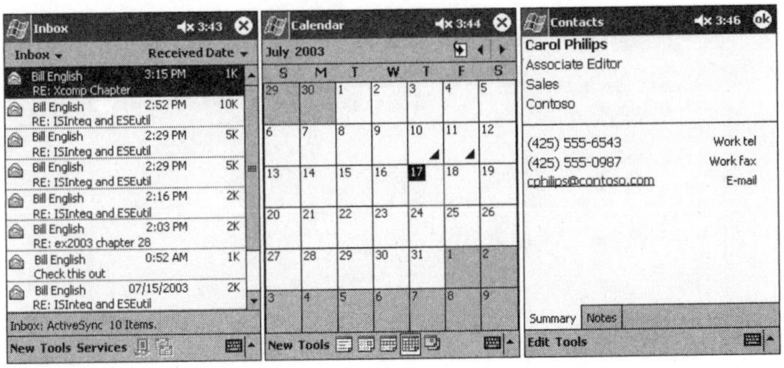

Figure 22-6. *Using pocket applications on a Pocket PC.*

More Info You can learn more about using Microsoft ActiveSync 3.7, Exchange ActiveSync, and Pocket PC at the Windows Mobile page at *http://www.microsoft.com/windowsmobile/default.mspx.*

Outlook Mobile Access

Outlook Mobile Access (OMA) provides a way to access Exchange using a browser or mobile microbrowser that uses HTML, Extensible HTML, Wireless Application Protocol 2.*x*, and compressed HTML, which is used in Japan. Outlook Mobile Access provides rudimentary, text-based access to Inbox, Calendar, Contacts, and Tasks. OMA also provides a search support for Inbox folders and the Global Address List.

Outlook Mobile Access is intended to provide the lowest common denominator mobile access to Exchange information. Non-Microsoft devices that don't have ActiveSync built in and that don't use Outlook can still access Exchange Server 2003 directly from the device using a compliant browser.

Tip OMA uses a virtual directory to provide user access that works the same way as the Outlook Web Access (OWA) virtual directory. In fact, you should follow the same configuration guidelines for setting up OMA on a server as when setting up OWA on a server. Check out Chapter 19, "Supporting Outlook Web Access," for more information about OWA.

OMA differs from Outlook Web Access in that OWA is customized for a full-sized monitor, decent bandwidth, and a keyboard. OMA is customized for small-screen, low-bandwidth environments. OMA uses a text-only interface, so you don't have to worry about downloading large images, as shown in Figure 22-7.

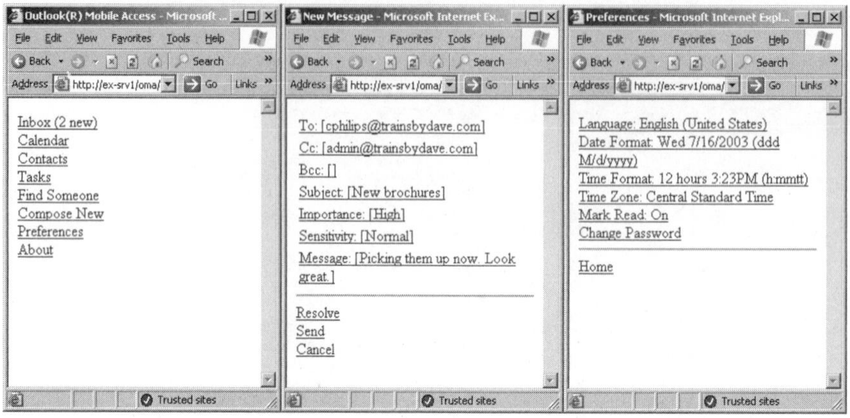

Figure 22-7. *Home page, message interface, and configuration page of OMA.*

As you can see, OMA provides a familiar interface for working with Exchange information, including Inbox, Calendar, Contacts, Tasks, and other features you'd expect. OMA also provides complete access to the Exchange folder system, not just the main folders. You can read, reply to, and forward messages, as well as mark them read and unread. Most of the basic functions for working with other items are also present, meaning you will not have to provide a lot of extra training to users—once they are connected, they will be in a familiar environment.

Configuring Outlook Mobile Access in Exchange Server 2003

Outlook Mobile Access is installed automatically during the installation of Exchange Server 2003, but it is disabled. You can enable OMA using the same Mobile Services property sheet you use to configure Exchange ActiveSync, as shown in Figure 22-8. In System Manager, expand the Global Settings container, right-click the Mobile Services container, and choose Properties. Select the Enable Outlook Mobile Access option to turn the service on. Once the service is turned on, users can connect to OMA using the address *http://servername/oma*.

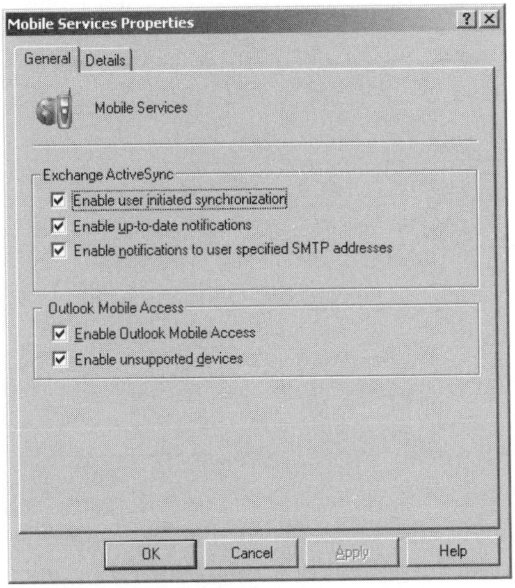

Figure 22-8. *Enabling OMA in System Manager.*

Enabling Unsupported Devices in OMA

The other OMA option available on the Mobile Services property sheet (Figure 22-8) is to enable unsupported devices. The mobile devices that are supported by OMA are determined by the Device Update package that is installed on the Exchange Server 2003 computer. An initial Device Update package is installed on the server during the installation of Exchange Server 2003. Devices supported by the package available at the initial release of Exchange Server 2003 are listed in Table 22-1.

Table 22-1. Mobile devices supported by OMA in initial Exchange Server 2003 release

Device	Rendering Language
Casio Cassiopeia E-2000	HTML
Compaq i-PAQ 3630	HTML
Microsoft Pocket PC Phone Edition	HTML
Microsoft SmartPhone	HTML
NEC N503is	cHTML
Panasonic P503is	cHTML
Panasonic P504i	cHTML

Table 22-1. Mobile devices supported by OMA in initial Exchange Server 2003 release

Device	Rendering Language
Fujitsu F504i	cHTML
Mitsubishi D503iS	cHTML
Sony SO503iS	cHTML
Mitsubishi D503iS	cHTML
NEC N504i	cHTML
Sony EricssonT68i	xHTML
Sanyo A3011SA	xHTML-mp (WAP2.0)
Toshiba C5001T	xHTML-mp (WAP2.0)
Sharp J-SH51 MML	MML (HTML)
Toshiba J-T51	MML (HTML)

Supported devices are really just those that have been tested by Microsoft and approved for use. However, just because a device is not on the supported devices list does not mean it won't work. Though we don't recommend supporting devices that are not on the list as a general policy, you might find through your own testing that some devices in use in your company work just fine. Select the Enable Unsupported Devices option on the Mobile Services property sheet to configure Exchange to accept connections from devices that are not in the Device Update package currently in use on your server.

Note An updated Device Update package will be available for download from Microsoft approximately every six months. The updated Device Update package adds support for additional mobile devices for use with Outlook Mobile Access in Exchange Server 2003. To obtain the latest Device Update package for Exchange Server 2003, visit the following Microsoft Web site: *http://www.microsoft.com/exchange*.

Summary

This chapter looked at the two mobile services available in Exchange Server 2003: Exchange ActiveSync and Outlook Mobile Access. Exchange ActiveSync provides users with Windows-powered mobile devices a way to synchronize directly with Exchange servers. Outlook Mobile Access provides simple, text-based browser access to Exchange services.

In the next part of this book, you will begin your look at security in Exchange Server 2003. Chapter 23, "Security Policies and Exchange Server 2003," focuses on planning security policies.

Part VII
Security

Chapter 23

Security Policies and Exchange Server 2003

You might be wondering why a chapter on security policies is in a technical book. The reason is simple: you can't effectively implement security for your Microsoft Exchange 2003 server until you implement security policies that instruct your organization about how to manage information held on that server. By defining what you are trying to secure and why, you can write information security policies that will form the foundation for the security technology you purchase and the electronic policies (e-policies) you create and implement. Figure 23-1 illustrates how information security policies lead to electronic policies. Figure 23-2 shows an example of how this would work.

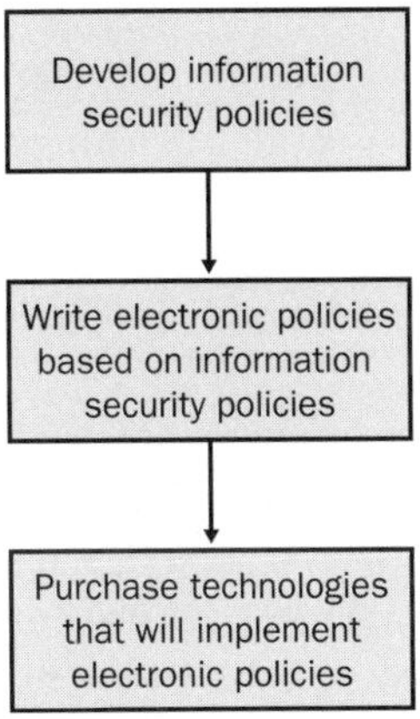

Figure 23-1. *How information security policies ultimately translate into electronic policies.*

> **More Info** If you want an outstanding book on writing information security policies, please reference *Information Security Policies Made Easy*, by Charles Cresson Wood (PentaSafe).

In most environments, the implementation of a security technology is the result of conversations between the IT department and other interested parties. What is often lacking in the initial planning stages is an explicit rationale for the security technology in the form of a written policy. Writing down your policy objectives and strategies will go a long way toward garnering support for your information security plan. In this chapter, we help you accomplish this by outlining the issues you need to consider when creating your information security policies and explaining why these issues are important.

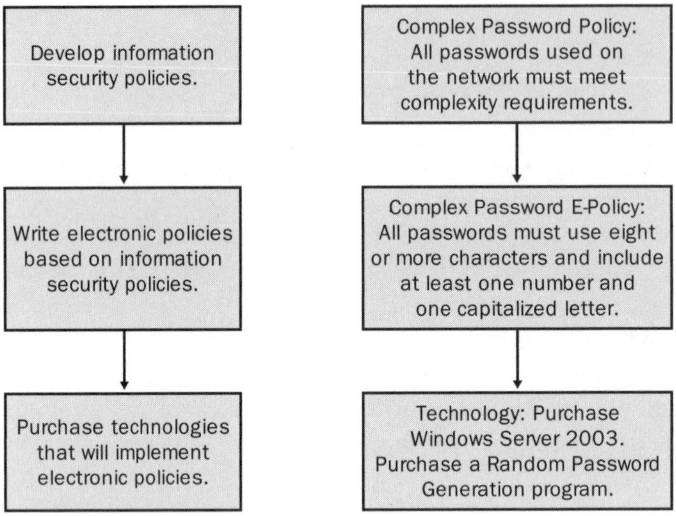

Figure 23-2. *Password policy example.*

Why Are Information Security Policies Important?

Your greatest weakness is not your security technology—it is the people you work with every day. Each member of your organization is a hacker's potential access point to sensitive information in your company. And, conversely, each member of your organization could potentially become an internal hacker. Information security policies define acceptable and unacceptable behavior for handling information and thus help ensure that information is not accidentally leaked, compromised, or destroyed.

You might find our assertion to be a bit paranoid, because you likely know and trust many people in your organization. However, abuse of company resources does occur, even in smaller firms. For example, one individual we know is a consultant for a small company with roughly 35 employees. One employee was discovered to be running his own online used car sales company from his workstation as well as his own Web site, using the firm's e-mail address for his own purposes. Security policies can curtail this type of activity. By the way, this firm implemented a new security policy stating that use of the company's computers for personal or side businesses was strictly prohibited. This action stopped one other employee from engaging in an online trading business over the lunch hour.

The process of outlining security policies forces management to define how much risk they are willing to accept relative to their most critical information assets. Specifically, it answers these questions:

- What is the most critical information?
- Where does this critical information reside?
- Who will be able to access this information?
- What are the costs to the organization if the information is compromised or destroyed?
- What measures will the company take to ensure the information's privacy and integrity?

Explicit information security policies assure the purchase and implementation of the proper security technologies. Failure to establish an adequate organizational infrastructure for information security can lead to costly mistakes—in terms of money, time, and unexpected vulnerability. Your organization must document the following thoroughly: who assumes responsibility for certain actions, policies, standards, operational procedures, enforcement mechanisms, risk analysis, the security incident response team, the information security budget, and the planning team.

One other very important reason to implement information security policies is the growing body of case law that essentially says management and sometimes technical staff can be held liable for inadequately addressing information security matters. The basis of such liability can be negligence, breach of fiduciary duty, failing to use the same security measures found in other organizations in the same industry, failing to exercise due care, or failure to act after a real notice has occurred. Be sure to speak with your legal counsel about the level of exposure you currently have regarding the security in your organization.

Information Security Policies and Electronic Policies

In the previous section, we suggested that more than one document was necessary to implement security in your organization. One of those documents will be an e-policy document. *E-policies* translate information security policies into specific, measurable objectives for your IT staff. Table 23-1 provides some examples.

Table 23-1. E-Policy examples

Information Security Policy	Electronic Policy
Administrative and Service Account passwords must never be in a readable form outside the servers or a physically secure environment.	Administrative and Service Account passwords can never be written down unless such documentation is secured in the IT vault. Passwords can be read and communicated only to members of the Administration team.
Unless specifically authorized, users cannot acquire, possess, or use hardware or software tools that could be used to compromise information systems security.	Only members of the administrative team are authorized to acquire, possess, and use hardware or software tools that can be used to compromise information systems security. These tools will not be used without the approval of the Director of Technology, and the approval must be in writing. The tools will be used only for specific, time-limited functions and then their use must be stopped.
Users will not use company computers for personal use.	IT personnel are authorized to uninstall non-supported programs or programs installed for personal use. IT personnel are authorized to delete any data files, without warning to the owner of those files, that are clearly created and used for non-company activities.

After the information security policies are written, you must write the e-policies. Only then will you be ready to implement security technologies, which we will discuss in the Chapter 24, "Exchange Server Security," and Chapter 25, "Securing Exchange Server 2003 Messages."

Information Security Policies for Exchange Server 2003

The next few sections outline policies that relate to messaging and that should be a part of your overall information security policies. We've listed several examples to help illustrate our points.

Password Policies

Because users will need to authenticate to an Exchange 2003 server, and because they will need to be authenticated in the Microsoft Windows Server 2003 Active Directory environment, you will need password policies. Such policies could include the following topics:

- Minimum password length
- Password complexity
- Re-use of old passwords prohibited
- User-selected passwords prohibited

- Storage of passwords
- Anonymous user IDs prohibited (consider Microsoft Outlook Web Access)
- Displaying and printing of passwords
- Periodic password changes
- Transmission of passwords to remote users
- Limits on consecutive attempts to log on using a bad password
- Help desk password resets
- Encryption of passwords
- Use of passwords in scripts, code, and other electronic forms
- Use of duress passwords
- Disclosing passwords to consultants and contractors
- Password sharing prohibitions
- Forced change of all passwords after system compromise

This list isn't comprehensive—some topics might or might not be in your password information security policies—but it should get you started. Here are two examples of the way these topics can be expanded into information security policies:

- **Password sharing prohibited** Users are prohibited from sharing their passwords in any form with other users in this company or anyone outside this company. If a member of the IT department needs to log on under your user account, that member must obtain a password re-set on your user account before logging on.
- **Use of duress password** The information about Server X is highly sensitive and, if leaked to non-authorized personnel, would irrevocably and significantly damage the purpose and work of our organization. Therefore, only the Director of Technology is allowed to log on to this server and perform administrative functions. Should the Director of Technology be logging on to the server under a situation of duress, the Director must enter the duress password. This password must execute code that will immediately destroy all data on the server.

The second example is a bit extreme and would be implemented only in environments requiring extremely high security. However, the policy illustrates what must occur in a given scenario. An electronic policy would stipulate how the information was to be deleted. The information security policy dictates only that the information must be deleted.

Logon Policies

Because each user will need to authenticate to Active Directory before using any of the Exchange 2003 services, you will need to focus on your logon policies as part of the Exchange 2003 information security policy development. Here are some ideas for what your policies can cover:

- Requirement of a user ID and password to access services on your network
- Use of separate user IDs for internal and external logons
- No sharing of user IDs and passwords
- A security notice in the system logon banner indicating who is authorized to log on to your network
- The displaying of the last user name that was used to log on
- Limitation on the daily number of logons to prevent unauthorized use of the system
- Restriction against multiple logon sessions at multiple nodes
- Restriction against automatic logon processes
- Automatic logoff process
- Requirement to log off when you have left your desk (as opposed to locking the workstation)

Here is an example of an information security policy for the network logon banner in the preceding list:

- This system is for the exclusive use of authorized personnel only. If you are not an authorized user, you are instructed to not attempt to log on and to leave this terminal. All activities on this terminal will be monitored and recorded by system personnel. Improper use of this system is strictly prohibited and could result in termination of employment. Criminal activity will also be prosecuted to the fullest extent of the law.

Many locations don't employ such a banner, but it can be invaluable in court when an unauthorized user logs on to your system and commits criminal activity.

Acceptable Use Policies

Some acceptable use policies directly affect the use of Exchange services. In this section, we list the policies that you should consider implementing, with your Exchange 2003 server in mind:

- Prohibition of storage of personal e-mail on company servers
- Use of e-mail system for business purposes only

- Incidental use of company e-mail system for personal use
- Prohibition of using e-mail system for non-approved activities
- Permissible uses of company e-mail system
- Non-employee use of company e-mail system
- Termination of employee and mailbox retention
- Voluntary leaving of employee and mailbox retention
- Access to e-mail via Outlook Web Access
- Use of company e-mail address in e-mail lists
- Transference of e-mail to portable devices
- Requirement of digital signatures for sensitive e-mails
- Requirement of encryption of e-mails for sensitive data
- Requirement of SSL for browser-based access to e-mail

As you can see, you have much to consider when writing security policies for e-mail. You won't end up including every item in this list in your security policies, but you should consider and discuss each one. There might also be other policy items not included here that would be suitable for your environment.

As security becomes more and more important in our business transactions, you might need to clarify when e-mails should be encrypted and signed. Saying that all e-mails should encrypted and signed is the easy answer but might not be warranted. In many scenarios, specifying that only some types of content should be encrypted and/or signed when sent is more appropriate treatment. You might even need to specify a policy regarding which third-party Certificate Authorities (CA) can be trusted.

Computer Viruses, Trojans, and Worms

Because most computer viruses, Trojans, and worms (which we'll refer to generically as *viruses* in our discussion) are spread though the use of e-mail, you must write information security policies about the viruses. Simply installing antivirus software is often not enough protection. Users should be told how to treat suspicious e-mails, what and what not to do when they suspect they have been infected, and how to avoid committing actions that would introduce viruses on your network. Here is a list of items to consider when writing security policies about viruses and e-mail:

- Users must not attempt to clean viruses on their own
- Duty to report suspicious e-mail
- Antivirus software must be installed and working on all network nodes

- Prohibition against downloading software from third-party sources
- Prohibition against using unapproved antivirus software
- All outbound e-mail and attachments must be virus-free
- Virus checking at firewalls, servers, workstations, and other network devices
- Use of multiple antivirus software packages from different vendors
- Virus checking of all software downloaded from third-party sources
- Updating of virus definitions on firewalls, servers, desktops, laptops, and other network devices
- Prohibition against use of personal floppy disks without virus checking
- Antivirus software must be current
- Prohibition against scanning of Exchange databases and transaction logs with virus-checking software
- Content must be decrypted before checking for viruses
- Backup or imaging of servers before cleaning for viruses
- All user involvement with computer viruses prohibited

Caution Do not scan Exchange databases and transaction logs by antivirus software. Scanning the Exchange databases and/or transaction logs with the file-based antivirus scanning utilities *will, at some point, corrupt your databases or transaction logs*. Never directly scan the Exchange databases or transaction logs with antivirus scanning software. Some of the patterns of 1s and 0s will look like a virus signature and, if the software attempts to clean the file, the file will become corrupted.

Caution Use antivirus software written specifically for Exchange server to avoid database and transaction log corruption. Use this software to scan the databases and use the normal file-based scanning software to scan everything on your Exchange server except the databases (*.stm and *.edb) and their supporting transaction logs (E*******.log).

Schema Extensions by Exchange Server 2003

Because the installation of Exchange Server 2003 extends the schema in your organization, you should include a few security policies about this extension. Consider the following requirements:

- The schema extension by Exchange Server 2003 should be tested in a laboratory environment first.

- All "home-grown" applications must be tested for quality assurance and compatibility with the schema extensions introduced by Exchange Server 2003.
- Installing Exchange 2003 in your production environment before all quality assurance and compatibility tests have been successfully passed is strictly prohibited.

Since Exchange is also a development environment, here are some issues that should be discussed regarding ongoing development on your Exchange Server 2003:

- Separation between testing and production environments
- Development Staff has administrative access to testing environment but not to production environment
- No testing by developers in production environment
- Use of images or backups of production servers on test servers
- Formal change control procedure required for all production servers
- Production system changes must be consistent with security policies and architecture
- Requirement to document all changes to production system
- Requirement to test all production system changes for security vulnerabilities in test environment first
- Movement of software from test environment to production environment

Third-party applications will be installed on your Exchange 2003 server, so consider the following issues when writing your information security policies:

- Test third-party applications for Exchange Server 2003 in the test environment first.
- Assess third-party applications for security vulnerabilities.
- Installing third-party applications if known security vulnerabilities cannot be fixed is prohibited.
- Running non-essential services on servers and workstations is prohibited.
- Conduct periodic operating system and application audit on all servers.
- Implement security patches and fixes promptly.
- Test all security patches and fixes in test environment before installing in production environment.
- Run the same service pack levels and same security fixes on all Exchange servers.

- Management approval is required for installation of service packs and security fixes on all Exchange servers after the software has been successfully tested in the test environment.
- Set the timing of changes to production systems that cause a re-boot of production servers.
- Back up or image Exchange production servers before installing new software.
- Third-party software vendors must supply a written integrity statement.

As you can see, overall change and control procedures are important. Also, most of these policy items assume the company has invested in a development environment in which new software can be tested. Creating a list of standards against which new software can be measured is difficult, but you can use the following standards as a starting point for developing your own quality and compatibility measurements:

- Ability to send and receive e-mail
- Ability to send and receive signed e-mail
- Ability to send and receive encrypted e-mail
- Ability to send and receive signed and encrypted e-mail
- Ability to access public folder
- Ability to post to a public folder
- Ability to run custom applications presented via a public folder
- Ability to perform all mailbox functions, such as calendaring, tasks, and journals
- Ability to enforce inbox rules
- Ability to use Out Of Office Assistant
- Ability to recover a mailbox

Test the more common functions and check the newsgroups (*news.microsoft.com*) for any complaints or bugs that were found in the new software. If the new software is from a third-party source, find out from its company whether there are any known issues with this software and Exchange Server 2003.

Data Security

Because Exchange will host critical and sensitive information, consider the following for Exchange Server 2003:

- Statement that information is an important company asset

- Legal ownership of e-mail and messages
- Requirement of disclaimer notices on all e-mail
- Prohibition of downloaded company e-mail to personal home computers
- Use of company information for non-business uses
- Using e-mail to transfer company information to third-parties
- Right of company to examine e-mail content at any time
- Right of company to monitor use of e-mail
- All e-mail activity monitored and reported to management
- Prohibition of disclosure of confidential information via e-mail
- Prohibition of responding to e-mail receipts
- Acceptable use of e-mail receipts
- Prohibition of stationary in e-mails
- Use of signatures in e-mail
- Confidentiality e-mail agreements required for all employees
- New confidentiality e-mail agreement required for change in employment status
- Prohibition against giving non-employees e-mail accounts on production system
- Data classification scheme
- Acceptable retention of hardcopy e-mails
- Removal of sensitive information from the company's network via e-mail
- Permission required to take secret information off company's premises
- Scrubbing Exchange databases after backup that hold secret information
- Shredders required to dispose of hardcopies of e-mail
- Dissemination of confidential or secret information prohibited via distribution lists or e-mail server lists

Data security encompasses many issues. Let's discuss a few of them. First, if you can define a data classification scheme such as public, private, confidential, or secret, you can tie the encryption and signing of e-mail to certain levels of content. For example, you could require that all e-mail containing confidential information be signed, and all e-mail containing secret information be both signed and encrypted. Spelling this requirement out in a set of policies will help your users know when to use these advanced methods of sending and receiving messages and protect your company.

Second, check with your legal counsel regarding ownership and monitoring of e-mail. A user can assert a right of privacy for their company-given e-mail account unless the company clearly informs the user that e-mail hosted on a company server is company property.

Finally, if your users send out confidential or sensitive content in their e-mails, it may be a good idea to add a disclaimer to all outgoing e-mails to protect the user and the company in the event the e-mail is accidentally sent to the wrong recipient. Check with your legal counsel.

Legal Exposure to Unwanted E-Mail Content

This section focuses on adult or offensive content that is received by employees in your company. A set of information security policies should be developed with these security issues in mind:

- No company endorsement of unwanted, received e-mail content
- Requirement to make reasonable efforts to block all offensive e-mail
- Requirement of user to notify management of received offensive e-mail
- Prohibition of sending or forwarding offensive content, such as jokes, in e-mail
- Right of company to remove offensive material and e-mail without warning
- Disclaimer of responsibility or liability for message contents
- Requirement of disclaimer that personal statements do not necessarily reflect the company's views, positions, and opinions
- Prohibition of using e-mail to engage in sexual, ethnic, or racial harassment
- Prohibition of using outbound e-mail to engage in sexual, ethnic, or racial harassment

Every element of this list should be included in your security policies, because, for example, adult spam likely violates your sexual harassment policies, and jokes innocently passed between co-workers might leave your company exposed to unnecessary sexual harassment liability.

Backing Up and Archiving Exchange Databases

Surprisingly, some organizations do not guard their backup tapes and media very well. Most organizations view the backup of databases as a routine software procedure. However, more thought needs to be given to the backing up and storage of Exchange databases. Here are some elements to consider when writing security policies in this area:

- Acceptable archival storage media

- Regular testing of archival storage media
- Backup media stored in separate fire zones from Exchange servers
- Backup media rooms must be fire-proofed
- Backup media rooms must be physically secure
- Offsite storage of backup media required
- Specification of backup process and frequency
- Users notified that Exchange data is routinely backed up
- Requirement to encrypt backup media
- Two copies of backup media required for confidential or secret information
- Two copies of backup media stored offsite for confidential or secret information
- Monthly trial backup and restore required to test backup processes and media
- Quarterly audit of backup processes required
- Minimum information retention period for mailboxes
- Minimum backup media retention period
- Regular purging of old e-mails or outdated information for all user's mailboxes
- Requirement to retain a copy of all e-mail

You can move a user's mailbox between databases, so you can place those users who send and receive the most sensitive e-mails in a single database and then require multiple backups of that database along with message journaling, increasing the chance that information can be recovered in the event of a disaster.

In certain industries, laws and rules might stipulate that you implement a certain backup and retention policy. Some of this work might have been done for you already in industry standards. Be sure to pay attention to those standards.

E-Mail Integrity

In this section, we outline some issues that you should consider regarding e-mail integrity:

- E-mail address changes confirmed via previous address
- E-mail originator must be clearly identified
- E-mail system must reject all e-mail that does not have a verifiable originator

- Employees must make truthful statements in their messages
- Prohibition against misrepresentation of identity in e-mail system
- Employee contact information must be consistently represented
- Right to free speech does not apply to company's e-mail system
- Contracts cannot be signed using digital signatures
- Only designated employees can form contracts via e-mail and digital signatures
- Prohibition of use of encryption technologies that cannot be decrypted by system personnel
- No trusting of non-approved certificate authorities
- Maximum life for all encryption keys
- Process for generating encryption keys
- Requirement of minimum key length
- Protection of private keys

We understand there is positive case law regarding contracts that can be formed and signed using a digital signature. However, you need to check with your legal counsel on whether you want to allow this to occur.

Also, check with your legal counsel regarding whether a person's First Amendment rights can be curbed by the company. This free speech issue could potentially be controversial, so clarify it and be proactive.

Finally, because we are encrypting more and more, specifying which CAs can be trusted is important. Also, specify which encryption methods are acceptable in your organization and prohibit the encryption of data that can't be decrypted by your company.

Miscellaneous Elements to Consider

The information security issues listed in the preceding lists aren't comprehensive, so we've provided one last list of items that didn't quite fit in our categories. Although we're calling the items in the following list miscellaneous, these items are critical for you to consider when writing information security policies for your organization:

- Prohibiting the use of e-mail addresses other than official company addresses for company use
- Forwarding company e-mail to non-company addresses prohibited
- No use of the e-mail system as an electronic database

- Periodic destruction of archived e-mail databases employed without warning
- Owner authorization required to read e-mail messages of other workers
- Prohibiting the altering of e-mail message headers
- Prohibiting the sending of unsolicited bulk e-mail
- User must stop sending e-mail messages after request to stop has been received
- Authorization to send e-mail to distribution lists required
- Prohibition against opening attachments unless they are expected
- Use of e-mail system requires attendance at authorized training sessions

Some of you are going to love the element in this list about not using the e-mail system as an electronic database. We have heard more than a few Exchange administrators complain about users filing and saving every e-mail forever. Perhaps this element alone will pique your interest in writing these information security policies!

Several of these elements ensure users don't use your company system for spam. If your marketing department or sales department sends out bulk e-mail, you'll want to word the policy such that authorization is required and that all bulk e-mail is not inherently prohibited.

Forwarding company e-mail to personal e-mail accounts is often prohibited. This policy will ensure that those who work with sensitive information cannot send that information to their own e-mail account and then sell the information to your company's competitors. Auditing the mailboxes of these users will ensure that they follow the policy. A written policy, in and of itself, can't keep someone from doing anything prohibited, but it can give you cover to monitor user activities and expose the user if a policy is being violated.

Summary

In this chapter, we outlined some security policy elements that related to e-mail and Exchange that should be included in your overall security policy manual. The creation of such policies forms the foundation for creating electronic policies that, in turn, inform our security technology decisions and purchases. In reality, a great security implementation starts with information security policies that are comprehensive in nature and that specify acceptable and unacceptable behavior in a number of areas, including messaging.

In Chapter 24 and Chapter 25, we outline how to implement specific security technologies, including firewall planning, certificates, encryption of e-mail, and using digital signatures.

Chapter 24

Exchange Server Security

In July of 2000, *Information Week* stated that "The bill to 50,000 US firms this year for viruses and computer hacking will amount to $266 billion, or 2.5 percent of USA's GDP." These numbers are only going up. Security has become so central to the administrator's role that we've decided to devote a large portion of this book to discussing it.

In this chapter, we offer ideas about how to add complexity and create hindrances to those who wish to attack your network over port 25. Unfortunately, when attempting to secure your system, you must accept the 80 percent rule: you can make your data only about 80 percent secure. If someone really wants to get at your server, given enough time and effort, he or she will succeed. However, if you have good strategies in place and sophisticated tools to assist you, you can anticipate and thwart most attacks.

The Scope of Security

We've all heard the old phrase "a chain is only as strong as its weakest link." You can easily apply that thinking to security: "a network is only as secure as its least secured link." You should always consider e-mail to be one of those "weakest links" on your network because it is an obvious entry point. Attackers use e-mail to wreak havoc because it's easy: no matter how well you secure your network, chances are good that you have port 25 open on your firewall and that a Simple Mail Transport Protocol (SMTP) server is ready to work with e-mail when it comes in.

When you begin thinking about security strategies, you should always answer the following question: "What am I securing Exchange Server 2003 against?" The answers to this question are varied and can be grouped into six categories:

- Social security
- Physical security
- Administrative security

- SMTP security
- Platform security
- IIS security

We discussed the first category, social security, in depth in Chapter 23, "Security Policies and Exchange Server 2003." In this chapter, we'll touch on the other five security categories.

Motivations of an Attacker

Although a lot of literature has been written about the technical aspects of securing a network, not much is available about who your enemies are and what motivates them to attack you. Before you can determine how to protect your organization, you must learn to think like a hacker, figure out where you're vulnerable, and then develop a game plan to reduce your exposure. If you can understand who would want to do you harm and what they would gain from such harm, you can better protect your company and your information. You must make the following assumptions:

- You do have enemies.
- You are on their target list.
- You will be attacked some day.
- You cannot afford to be complacent.

One of the most difficult realities for an organization to accept is the presence of enemies who might attempt to harm them by using technology. *Every organization has enemies*. This is not an overstatement. It does not matter how noble or sincere your efforts and goals are: somebody in the world doesn't like what you are doing and could decide to cause you harm by compromising your network.

The motivations of hackers can be varied and complex. Hackers are often motivated, in part, by their invisibleness. On the Internet, a hacker can "peek" into a company's private world—its network—and learn a lot while remaining anonymous.

Some individuals are just curious to see what they can learn about your company or individuals within your company. These hackers often don't have any malicious intent and are unaware that their actions violate security policy or criminal codes.

Others hackers are simply trying to help. You've probably been in this category once or twice yourself. In your zeal to be helpful, you bypass security policies to fix problems or accomplish emergency assignments. You might even believe that your efforts are more efficient than following established guidelines and policies. Nevertheless, the bypassing of known security policies is one element of hacking a network.

Some individuals act with malicious intent, engaging in acts of sabotage, espionage, or other criminal activities. They can become moles, stealing information to sell to competitors or foreign groups. Some simply enjoy destroying the work of others as well as their own work. Others act out of revenge for a real or perceived wrong committed against them, or believe they are acting in line with a strongly held belief system. Still others are more methodical and hardened and turn hacking into a career: they might even take employment just to do your company harm.

Although their motivations for invading the privacy of your company are varied, most hackers share certain personality traits. According to the *Diagnostic and Statistical Manual of Mental Disorders IV*, published by the American Psychiatric Association, the motivations just described are often triggered by traits that psychologists say are part of the Anti-Social personality. The essential feature of this personality is a pervasive pattern of disregard for, and violation of, the rights and sensibilities of others. These people are characterized by the following traits:

- Failure to conform to lawful behavior by repeatedly performing acts that are grounds for arrest
- Deceitfulness, evidenced in acts such as repeated lying, use of aliases, or conning others for personal gain
- Impulsivity
- Irritability and (in some cases) physical aggressiveness
- Consistent irresponsibility
- Lack of remorse, as indicated by being indifferent to or rationalizing the hurt and damage they have caused others

In addition, most hackers feel a sense of entitlement, and think they should be treated differently because they perceive themselves as being special or above the rules. They are typically bright and curious, and enjoy a challenge.

Individuals exhibiting these traits might be working in your organization. Such people can be, at times, nice, enjoyable, funny, witty, and pleasant, so don't classify people based on one or two incidents.

Real World Think Globally When Diagnosing a Security Problem

Recently, a US firm with national visibility in its industry was attacked by a group based outside of the US. The attacking group used its Exchange Server to send out spam messages (in its own language) to addresses all over the world. At first, this problem looked like a virus, but then the company realized the attackers had planted a program on the Exchange server that was launching the outgoing e-mails.

By the time the US firm had figured out the problem, outbound SMTP queues had nearly 100,000 messages sitting in them, ready to be sent.

How Hackers Work

Hackers start by learning that an e-mail server exists, which generic scanning tools can tell them. Coupled with the public information of your Domain Name System (DNS) records, hackers can quickly know a lot about your network.

Finding company information is easy for anyone. You can do it. Simply open a command prompt and type **nslookup**. Set the type of the record you're looking for to a mail exchanger (MX) record by typing **set type=mx**. Enter a domain name. In our example, we'll type in **Microsoft.com**. Figure 24-1 gives us the results.

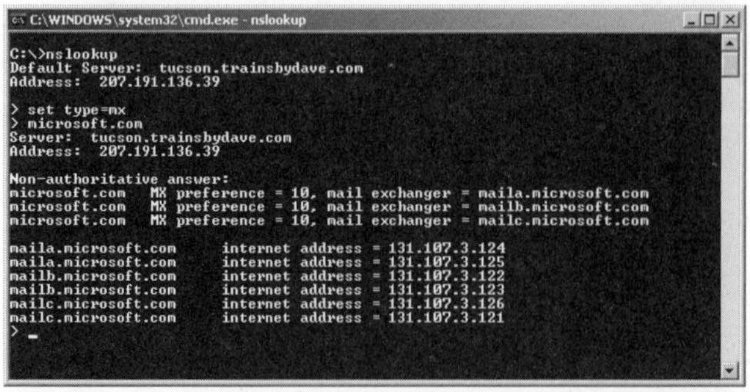

C:\WINDOWS\system32\cmd.exe - nslookup
C:\>nslookup
Default Server: tucson.trainsbydave.com
Address: 207.191.136.39
> set type=mx
> microsoft.com
Server: tucson.trainsbydave.com
Address: 207.191.136.39
Non-authoritative answer:
microsoft.com MX preference = 10, mail exchanger = maila.microsoft.com
microsoft.com MX preference = 10, mail exchanger = mailb.microsoft.com
microsoft.com MX preference = 10, mail exchanger = mailc.microsoft.com
maila.microsoft.com internet address = 131.107.3.124
maila.microsoft.com internet address = 131.107.3.125
mailb.microsoft.com internet address = 131.107.3.122
mailb.microsoft.com internet address = 131.107.3.123
mailc.microsoft.com internet address = 131.107.3.126
mailc.microsoft.com internet address = 131.107.3.121
>

Figure 24-1. *Using the NSLookup tool to find the public MX records for Microsoft.com.*

Next, the hacker determines the platform of your SMTP server in one of two ways. In the first approach, the hacker can use Telnet to open a session to your server over port 25 and then read the banner, which by default includes the version of the Exchange server you're running (Figure 24-2). Notice that the software version is displayed in the banner. The main version number, 6.0, means Exchange Server 2003. An Exchange 2000 Server registers with a main version number of 5.0. A SendMail server has its name and the version of SendMail software used by the company displayed in the header as well as the operating system (OS).

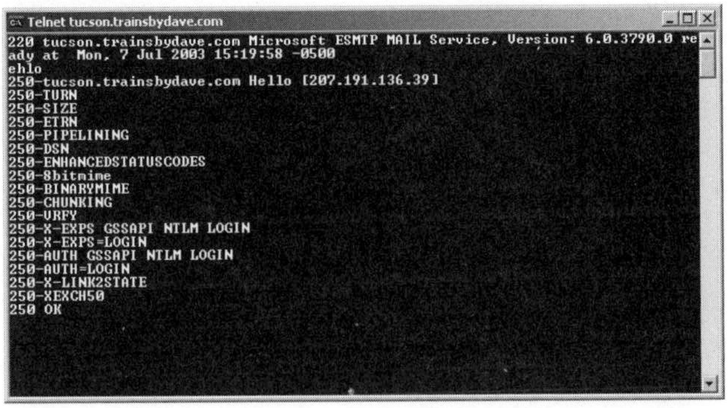
Telnet tucson.trainsbydave.com
220 tucson.trainsbydave.com Microsoft ESMTP MAIL Service, Version: 6.0.3790.0 re
ady at Mon, 7 Jul 2003 15:19:58 -0500
ehlo
250-tucson.trainsbydave.com Hello [207.191.136.39]
250-TURN
250-SIZE
250-ETRN
250-PIPELINING
250-DSN
250-ENHANCEDSTATUSCODES
250-8bitmime
250-BINARYMIME
250-CHUNKING
250-VRFY
250-X-EXPS GSSAPI NTLM LOGIN
250-X-EXPS=LOGIN
250-AUTH GSSAPI NTLM LOGIN
250-AUTH=LOGIN
250-X-LINK2STATE
250-XEXCH50
250 OK

Figure 24-2. *Opening a Telnet session to the Tucson server running Exchange Server 2003.*

The second way to determine your e-mail server platform is to send a bogus e-mail to your server. This is accomplished by sending a message to an unlikely e-mail address such as lskdfjsliej34@trainsbydave.com. The non-delivery report (NDR) returned will have the e-mail server information in its header. The following sample is a message header that we've sent to our own Exchange server at Networknowledge.com. Notice that the platform and version of the Exchange server is embedded in the message header (look for the XmimeOLE line):

```
Received: by snoopy.networknowledge.com
id <01C344CB.DE8D6CE0@snoopy.networknowledge.com>; Mon,7Jul 2003 16:08:09 -0500
X-DSNContext: 335a7efd - 4457 - 00000001 - 80040546
content-class: urn:content-classes:dsn
Subject: Undeliverable: test
MIME-Version: 1.0
Content-Type: multipart/report;
   report-type=delivery-status;
   boundary="----_=_NextPart_001_01C344CB.DE8D6CE0"
Date: Mon, 7 Jul 2003 16:08:09 -0500
Message-ID: <byVPMZ7VY0000000a@snoopy.networknowledge.com>
X-MS-Has-Attach: yes
X-MimeOLE: Produced By Microsoft Exchange V6.0.6249.0
X-MS-TNEF-Correlator:
Thread-Topic: test
Thread-Index: AcNEy94N8s377i5iQE+RNH2oOBoKPgAAACD7
From: "System Administrator" <postmaster@networknowledge.com>
To: "Aenglish" <Administrator@networknowledge.com>

This is a multi-part message in MIME format.
```

Now that the hacker knows which e-mail server software you're running, he or she checks known databases to find vulnerabilities to exploit. The known vulnerabilities for Exchange Server 2003 are listed in Microsoft's Security Bulletins and can be found at *www.microsoft.com/security*. Some of the vulnerabilities will involve Microsoft Internet Information Services (IIS) because IIS manages the SMTP service for Exchange. Other vulnerabilities will involve Microsoft Outlook Web Access (OWA), again because of the involvement of IIS managing the HTTP connectivity to the Exchange server. At a minimum, you should be aware of any vulnerabilities that exist for Exchange Server 2003 and, when the patches are released, test and install them.

Generally speaking, the e-mail administrator can expect the following kinds of attacks:

- **Buffer overflows** Buffer overflows send a larger quantity of data to the server than is anticipated. Depending on how the overflow is executed, it could cause the server to stop working or it might run malicious code from the attacker.
- **Data processing errors** These are not common currently, but the concept is that a small program is sent directly to the server and the server runs it. More common today is sending these programs to a network though e-mail as attachments. Depending on their function and purpose, these programs can be viruses, Trojans, or worms (discussed at length later in this chapter).
- **HTML viruses** These do not require user intervention to run unattended scripts.
- **Custom programs written to run against port 25 (SMTP)** The more common types of programs that attack port 25 include e-mail flooding programs or programs that contain their own SMTP engine that will use the port for their own malicious purposes.

Here are some broad actions you can take to guard against the attacks just described, plus others:

- **Physical access to the server** Lock the doors, and use some type of biotech authentication.
- **Viruses, Trojans, and worms** Use antivirus software and regularly scan your servers and workstations.
- **Loss of data** Perform regular backups.
- **Unauthorized use of user accounts** Conduct user training on information security policies and require complex passwords.
- **Denial of service attack** Harden the TCP/IP stack and the router.
- **Platform vulnerabilities** Install all software patches and engage in service that offers minimization. Microsoft has released excellent free

software for updating its patches on your servers. This software is called Software Update Services (SUS).

More Info A discussion of SUS is outside the scope of this chapter, but you can learn more about SUS on Microsoft's Web site at *www.microsoft.com/windows2000/windowsupdate/sus/default.asp*.

The rest of this chapter is intended to help you secure Exchange Server 2003 against these types of attacks. However, before we dive in, let's briefly discuss physical security of your Exchange server.

Physical Security

Physical security is a topic not often mentioned in many security books, particularly in books only about Exchange, but it is a topic worth mentioning. Servers can be left on desks running in a corner cubicle or in an unlocked server room. It is always best practice to store your servers in a secure location using door locks and, in some instances, motion detectors and/or other physical security measures.

When you limit physical access to a server, you limit who can log on locally to the server, who can use the floppy disk drive to introduce a new virus or malicious program on your network, and who can retrieve information directly from the server. Limiting physical access is one of the easiest and most elementary methods of securing your server against internal attacks that exist.

We understand that most administrators reading this book already have these physical security measures in place and we applaud you. For those who haven't physically secured your servers, please do so at your earliest opportunity. Limiting physical access to a server can go a long way toward protecting your information from would-be attackers.

Administrative Security

An *Administrative Group* (AG) is a container that holds other objects for the purpose of securing those objects under a common security context for administrative tasks. Administrative Groups can contain servers, routing groups, policies, and public folder hierarchies.

One of the best ways to secure your Exchange servers is to use the Administrative Groups permissions structure to limit who can make configuration changes on one or more Exchange Server 2003s. Exchange has a tight integration with Microsoft Windows Server 2003 Active Directory. Therefore, the user and/or group accounts in Active Directory can be used to secure the Administrative Groups in Exchange 2003, strictly limiting the individuals who can make configuration changes to objects (including servers) in those administrative groups.

If in your environment more than one set of Exchange servers needs to be managed by more than one team of people, the value in using Administrative Groups will become clear. In this scenario, you can use two Administrative Groups to administer each set of Exchange servers by delegating permissions for each group to each set of administrators. You set this up in the Exchange System Manager (ESM), but you delegate permissions to the Active Directory accounts. Doing this means that only the authorized Administrator for a particular set of servers can modify configuration values on those servers. Regardless of the administrative model you use—centralized, decentralized, or hybrid—you can create Administrative Groups to handle your model and secure your servers.

To create an Administrative Group, open the ESM and navigate to the Administrative Groups object. Right-click the object, point to New, then select Administrative Group (Figure 24-3).

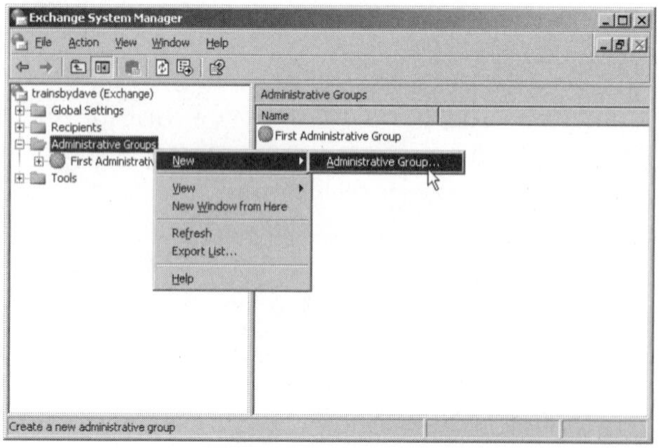

Figure 24-3. *Creating a new Administrative Group in the Exchange System Manager.*

The Properties dialog box will appear for the new AG. The only configuration value you can give the group is the group's name. Enter the name and click OK. You'll see the group appear in the ESM.

After the AG is created, you can rename the group if you desire. In our example, we have two AGs: the default group we renamed to East Administrative Group and the new group we named West Administrative Group (Figure 24-4).

Suppose you want to secure these two AGs with different groups from Active Directory. You want both groups of administrators to be able to manage the objects in their own AG but only view the configuration values for objects in the other AG. To set this up, create two Active Directory security groups. In our example, we'll call the first one ExchangeEast and the other ExchangeWest. After you create these groups, use the Exchange Administration Delegation Wizard to apply Exchange View Only permissions to the Organization object for both groups. You assign permissions in this way because, as you know, the objects in Exchange have a tight integration with the security model in Active Directory and Windows Server 2003, and permissions inheritance is part of this security model. When you apply the Exchange View Only permissions to the Organization object of these groups, all the objects beneath the Organization object, including the AGs, inherit this permission. You apply the permissions to the Organization object because the Exchange Administration Delegation Wizard is available only on the Organization and AG objects in the ESM. If you right-click on any other object, you will not see this wizard available.

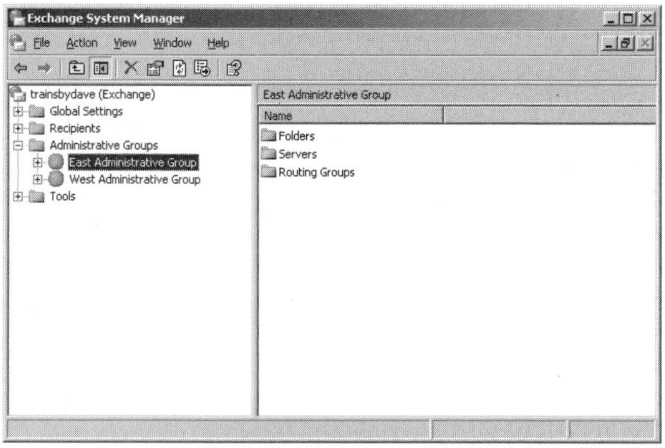

Figure 24-4. *Two Administrative Groups named East and West in the Exchange System Manager.*

To open the Wizard, right-click on the Organization object and select Delegate Control. Click Next to pass the Welcome screen. On the Users Or Groups page, click the Add button and select the two Active Directory security groups you've created. In our example, we select the ExchangeWest and ExchangeEast security groups (Figure 24-5).

When you add a group using the wizard, the default security role is Exchange View Only Administrator. You can change this role by highlighting each group, and then clicking the Edit button. You will be presented with three options:

- **Exchange View Only Administrator** This role allows you to view configurations on the objects, but you are unable to make any changes to those configurations.

- **Exchange Administrator** This role allows you to administrate the object fully with the exception of changing the Administrator role permissions on the object.
- **Exchange Full Administrator** This role allows you to administer the object fully, including the ability to change Administrator role permission assignments.

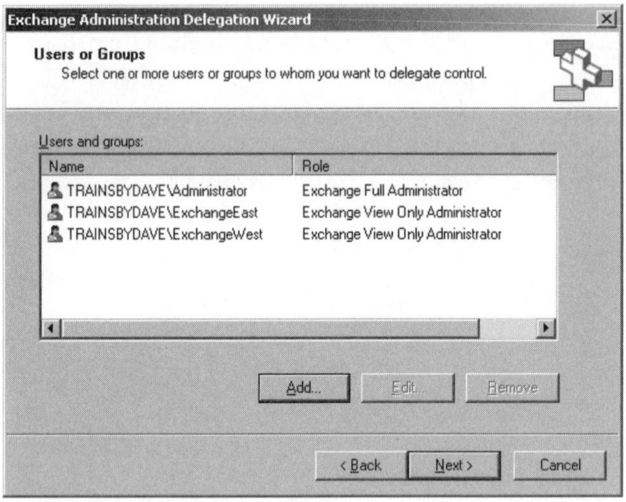

Figure 24-5. *Selecting the ExchangeWest and ExchangeEast security groups in the Exchange Administration Delegation Wizard.*

You can change the default role assignment, but for our example, we'll use the default Exchange View Only Administrator setting because we want this setting to be inherited by the AGs so that each group has the ability to view the configuration values in the other AG's objects.

Your next step is to run the delegation wizard on each individual AG and give Exchange Administrator permissions as follows:

- ExchangeEast assigned to the East Administrative Group
- ExchangeWest assigned to the West Administrative Group

Once you have finished doing this, in the properties of each AG, you'll see that the group responsible for administrating that AG will have Exchange Administrative permissions, but the other group will have the ability to view the configuration values on the AG that they are not permitted to administrate. Figure 24-6 shows the East Administrative Group's permissions assignments; the ExchangeWest has Exchange View Only Administrator permissions and the ExchangeEast has Exchange Administrator permissions.

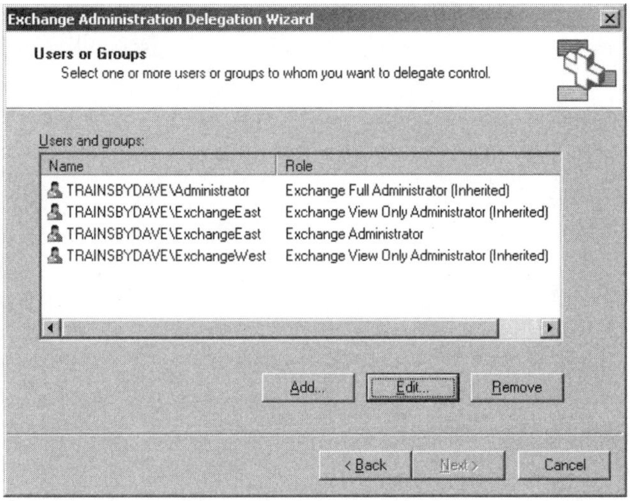

Figure 24-6. *Viewing the East Administrative Group's permissions.*

You must consider two issues with this scenario. First, for a security group to have all the abilities of administration provided by the Exchange Administrator role, that group must also be a member of the Local Administrator's security group. Second, you can't change inherited permissions on an object. This is why the ExchangeEast group appears twice in the permissions assignments: once for the inherited permissions from the organization object, and a second time for the explicit permissions assignment on the AG itself.

Also note that the combination of permissions allows for the most liberal of the permissions to apply. Hence, in this scenario, since the same group (Exchange East) has both Exchange View Only Administrator and Exchange Administrator permissions, the administration permissions will apply.

A second way to limit administrative access to your Exchange servers is to limit who can log on locally to the Exchange servers. You can set this limit by using a Group Policy in Windows Server 2003 and assigning that policy to an Organizational Unit (OU) that hosts all Exchange server accounts in Active Directory (Figure 24-7). You can make this permission assignment by creating (or linking to) a group policy that configures the following policy: Windows Settings/Security Settings/Local Policies/User Rights Assignements/Allow log on locally.

A third way to secure access to the Exchange server is to limit who has the ESM installed on their desktops. By default, when you install only the ESM, Active Directory Users and Computers is also installed. Deploying these two snap-ins on your administrator's desktops creates additional vectors to your Exchange servers. In some environments, this will be acceptable, but in others, it will not.

Be sure that you know where all your ESM snap-ins are installed and remove those snap-ins when the administrator leaves your company or is assigned a different role.

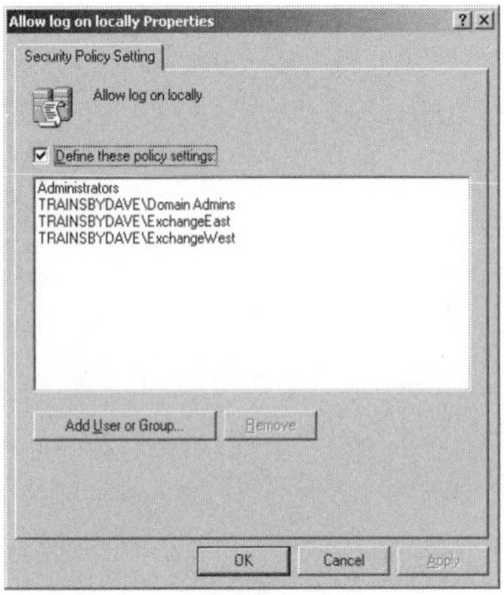

Figure 24-7. *Allowing the log on locally policy setting, adding the ExchangeEast and ExchangeWest security groups.*

A fourth approach to limiting administrator access to your Exchange servers is to require some type of smart card or biotechnology for logon to the servers. Entering a thumbprint, taking a retina scan, or swiping a card will help ensure that only the real Exchange administrators are logging on to your Exchange servers.

SMTP Security

By default, an SMTP server attempts to make a TCP port 25 connection to your Exchange server via an anonymous connection. Anonymous does not mean that a user account set up in your Active Directory proxies the connection request, as is the case with the IIS Anonymous user account, IUSR_<*machinename*>. In the SMTP world, anonymous means that no user name or password is required for the remote SMTP service to make a port 25 connection. Hence, any SMTP Server on the Internet can make, by default, a port 25 connection to your Exchange Server.

To make SMTP more secure, you could require either Basic or Integrated Windows Authentication (IWA) before the SMTP Virtual Server (VS) could accept an inbound connection. But this configuration is unworkable on the Internet because you can't predict who will be connecting to your Exchange server in the future and thus can't assume that the user has an appropriate user name and password to make a connection. Moreover, not many messaging administrators are interested in implementing such a security measure at their end. So even though an anonymous connection to port 25 on your Exchange server represents a vulnerability, it is one that must be managed using a different approach than removing anonymous connections.

How do we protect against these kinds of attacks? By starting with the use of two firewalls. A dual firewall topology allows you to protect your internal Exchange servers while also filtering incoming e-mail against potential attacks. The area between the two firewalls is called the *perimeter network* (also known as DMZ or demilitarized zone). The philosophy is to put up a line of defense against potential attacks. Hence, we're willing to sacrifice our Exchange servers in the perimeter network, but not willing to sacrifice our Exchange servers on the internal network. Because the Exchange servers in the perimeter network do not host any important information—no mailboxes or public folders—they can be both sacrificed during an attack and easily rebuilt. And because they act only as relay servers, we can use them to sanitize incoming e-mail over port 25.

Take a look at Figure 24-8. You see that in the perimeter network are three servers. The external firewall has port 25 open. Mail is first routed to the Content Scanning (CS) server before moving on the Anti-Virus scanning server (AV). You should take note of two points. First, all your external MX records will point to the CS server. Hence, any inbound SMTP traffic will necessarily be routed to your CS server. Second, we conduct content scanning first because of the rate at which new viruses can spread vs. the rate at which our AV definitions are updated. Think back to some of the major viruses in the last few years, which were able to spread worldwide very quickly, usually in a matter of hours. It is almost impossible for any AV company to get the virus, study it, write a definition for it, and then push out the new definition for that virus before it spreads worldwide. You can tell a CS server, however, to quarantine or delete any message that contains certain types of attachments and, in effect, block most viruses based on their type of content rather than on a comparison to a virus definition file.

Even though the CS server will block a number of e-mails, it is still best to run the e-mail through an AV scanning server. Once scanned, the e-mail is sent to the Certificates and Encryption (CE) server.

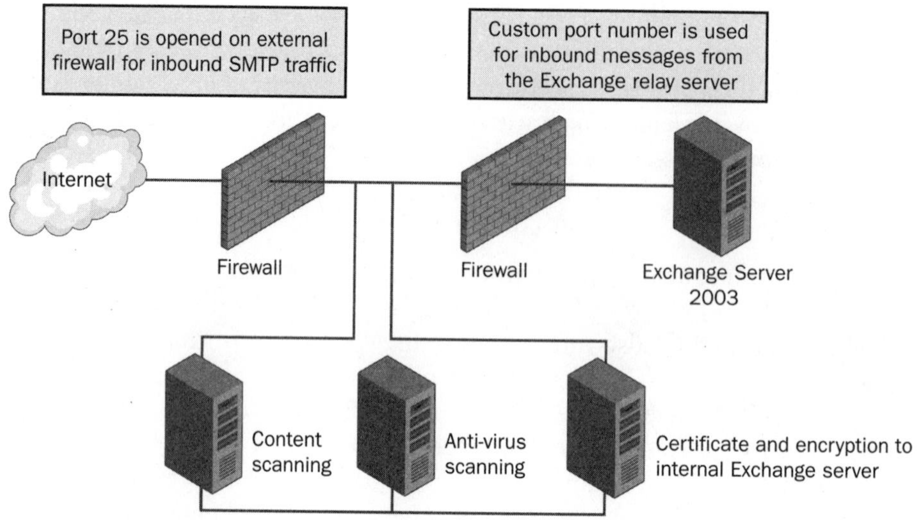

Figure 24-8. *Three Exchange servers in the perimeter network.*

> **Note** You should be aware of two issues regarding the AV server. First, many products offered by the major AV servers perform content scanning at the same time as the virus scanning, on the same VS, using the same software. We have no problem with this method of scanning e-mail. But we wanted to distinguish between content scanning and antivirus scanning to highlight the need to perform both types of scanning in the perimeter network. Second, we understand that not everyone can afford to purchase three individual servers and Exchange licenses for their perimeter network. Again, these ideas are presented to highlight the concepts we're discussing. All three of these functions (content scanning, AV scanning, and message encryption) can be performed using three different virtual servers on a single Exchange box or even using another SMTP platform that is less expensive on less expensive hardware.

The third server through which e-mail is transferred is an Exchange relay server. This server re-sends the encrypted and signed e-mail to the internal Exchange 2003 Server. The internal Exchange 2003 Server should be configured to accept inbound e-mail only from the third Exchange 2003 Server in the perimeter network. Because port 25 is not open on the internal firewall, the two Exchange servers communicate using a different port number. The internal Exchange server should also be running its own AV/CS software, preferably from a vendor that is different from the one the servers are using in the perimeter network. The whole point of implementing this model is to ensure that port 25 traffic is as well protected as possible.

Between the third Exchange 2003 server in the perimeter network and the internal Exchange server, you need to set up certificates and encryption as well as modify the ways that the virtual servers communicate. On the Exchange perimeter network server, you modify the SMTP VS as follows:

- On the Outbound Security tab, select Integrated Windows Authentication, enter a user account created in Active Directory specifically for this purpose, and select TLS Encryption (Figure 24-9). (TLS stands for Transport Layer Security.)

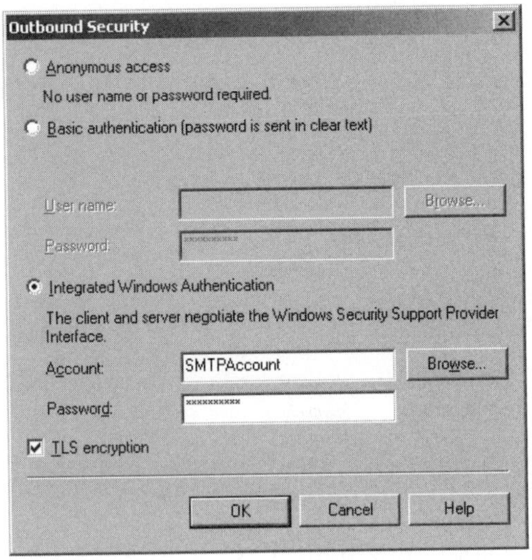

Figure 24-9. *Configuring outbound security for the VS on the CE Exchange Server in the perimeter network.*

- On the Outbound Connections tab, configure an outbound TCP port number that is difficult to guess (Figure 24-10). You need to open this port on your internal firewall for inbound traffic.

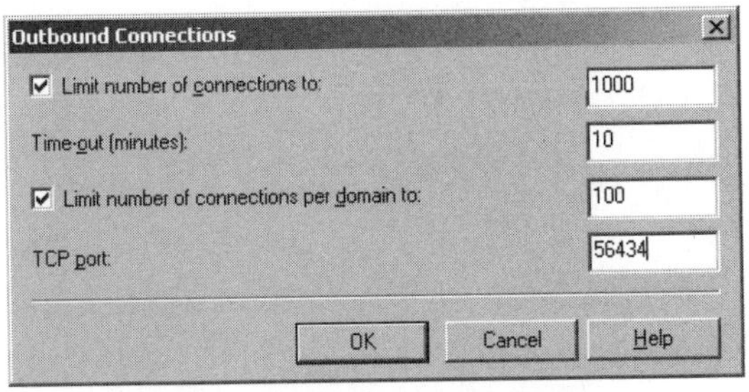

Figure 24-10. *Configuring a unique port number for outbound SMTP traffic on the CE Exchange Server in the perimeter network.*

- On the Advanced Delivery tab, configure the Internet Protocol (IP) address for the internal Exchange Server so that it is the smart host for this VS. When you do this, all e-mail will be forwarded to the internal server (Figure 24-11).

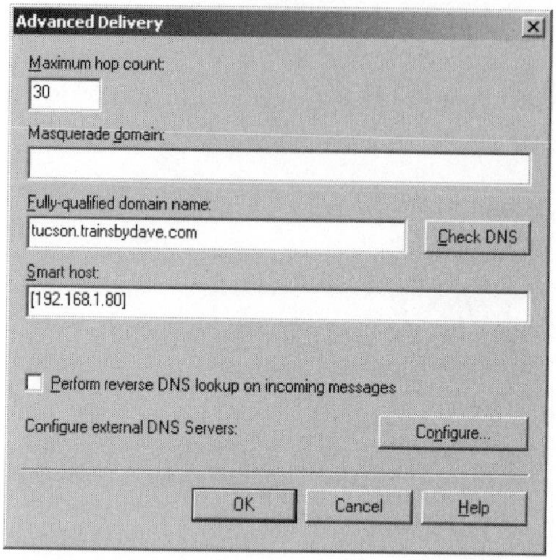

Figure 24-11. *Configuring the internal Exchange server to be the smart host for the CE Exchange Server in the perimeter network.*

On the VS of the internal Exchange Server, you need to create a second VS for inbound traffic and modify the inbound VS as follows:

- On the Authentication page, configure both Basic and IWA, and require TLS. On the Users tab, specify that only the user account configured on the outbound VS of the CE Exchange server in the perimeter network is able to submit e-mail to this inbound VS (Figure 24-12).

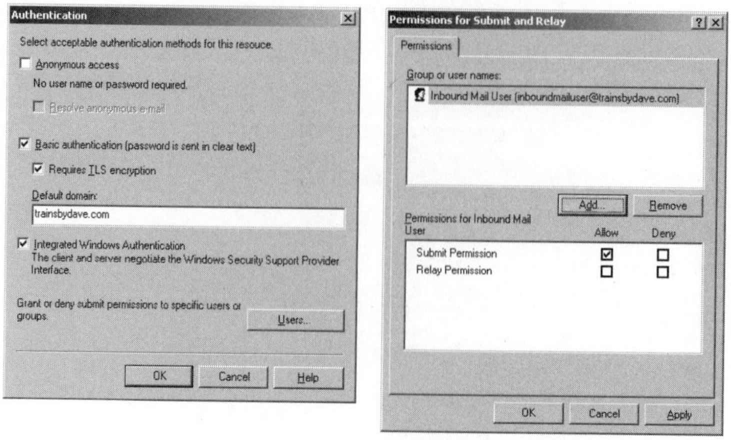

Figure 24-12. *Configuring inbound authentication on the inbound VS of the internal Exchange server.*

- On the Connection page, specify the IP address of the CE Exchange server in the perimeter network as the only server that is allowed to access the inbound VS (Figure 24-13).

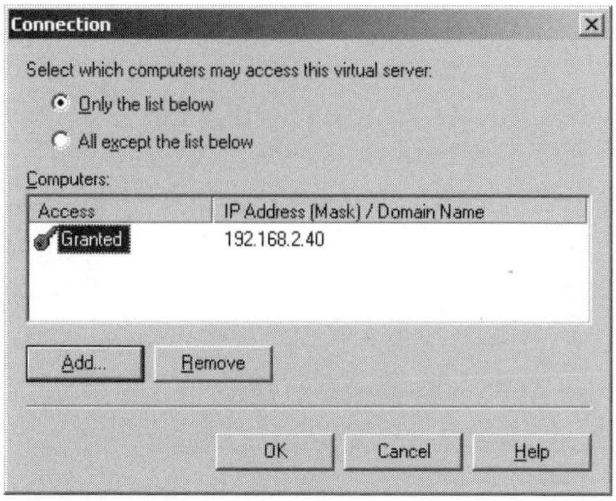

Figure 24-13. *Configuring inbound IP address acceptance on the inbound VS of the internal Exchange server.*

- Use an internal certification authority (CA) to create certificates for both Exchange servers to use for the TLS portion of the message transmission.

No system is foolproof, but this dual firewall topology has several advantages. First, by passing incoming e-mail through a good content scanning tool, you filter for code types that virus scanners don't.

Second, by passing your e-mail through a virus scanner, you're doing your best to ensure that all known viruses are cleaned out. Not passing your e-mail through an updated antivirus scanner after running it through a content scanner is unwise because older viruses might not be caught by the content scanner.

Third, by passing your e-mail through another Exchange 2003 server that will encrypt it and digitally sign it before sending it to the internal Exchange 2000 Server, you receive several types of protection. The IP address of the internal Exchange 2003 server does not need to be published in the public DNS records. This means that an attacker attempting to Telnet into your server will never be able to reach it directly. Also, if you configure the internal Exchange 2003 server to accept e-mail only from the encrypting Exchange server over a port number above 1024, any attempts to make port 25 connections to the internal Exchange server from any other IP address will fail. Finally, to impersonate the third Exchange server in your perimeter network, the attacker must spoof the IP address, grab the certificate, and crack the password of the user account configured between the two servers.

You could spoof the IP address easily enough, except that the internal Exchange 2000 Server is also looking for a digital certificate (whose trusted certification authority is an internal Windows 2000 Certificate Server) before it will accept the connection. Consequently, you not only need to spoof the IP address—you also need a valid certificate from the internal certificate server to make such a connection. Obtaining such a certificate is difficult when the personnel are well trained in network security. Social engineering is the route to take here if you want to get a certificate from the internal certification authority. But even if the hacker could obtain a certificate and spoof the IP address, the hacker would need to find out the user name of the shared account and then crack the password. Although not impossible, these hurtles might create enough headaches to deter the hacker.

If a hacker decides to bring down your perimeter Exchange servers, you've really lost nothing of value other than your time in getting the servers functioning again. Your company might lose some money due to the inability to communicate via e-mail, but it hasn't lost any current data. This is an important point. The server that hosts your data is the one most protected. And the ones most exposed do not host important data. If those servers are lost, at least all the business-critical data is saved on the internal Exchange 2000 Server. For many companies, this is an acceptable level of risk to assume.

As we've explained throughout this chapter, no answer is perfect, and this security scenario does have a few major holes, such as doing nothing to protect against messages sent to the Exchange server via Outlook Web Access. Port 25 is well protected but port 80 access to your Exchange server is wide open. If you want to learn how to secure OWA, refer to Chapter 19, "Supporting Outlook Web Access."

The second major hole in this model is one that cannot be plugged: messages are continuing to flow through all three servers to your internal Exchange server. As long as I can get a packet to your internal Exchange server, I can potentially do harm to it. So remember that 80 percent rule we discussed in the introduction to the chapter: you can make your data only about 80 percent secure. But don't let that discourage you from implementing our strategies.

Computer Viruses

In this section, we expand on computer viruses in general and discuss some implications for viruses on Exchange Server 2003.

What Is a Virus?

A *virus* is a piece of code that attaches itself to other programs or files. When these files run, the code is invoked and begins replicating itself. The replication occurs over the network. Viruses can now exploit the vulnerabilities of nearly every platform.

Some viruses reside in memory after the original program is shut down. When other programs are executed, the virus attaches itself to these new programs until the computer is shut down or turned off. Some viruses have a "dormant" phase and will appear only at certain times or when certain actions are performed.

There are many types of viruses. Some overwrite existing code or data. Others include the ability to recognize whether an executable file is already infected. *Self-recognition* is required if the virus is to avoid multiple infections of a single executable, which can cause excessive growth in size of infected executables and corresponding excessive storage space, contributing to the detection of the virus.

Resident viruses install themselves as part of the operating system upon execution of an infected host program. The virus will remain resident until the system is shut down. Once installed in memory, a resident virus is available to infect all suitable hosts that are accessed.

A *stealth virus* is a resident virus that attempts to evade detection by concealing its presence in infected files. For example, a stealth virus might remove the virus code from an executable when it is read (rather than executed) so that an antivirus software package will see only the non-compromised form of the executable.

Computer viruses spread mainly by the use of e-mail and usually appear in e-mail attachments. If the virus can find its way into the messaging stream, it will use the client capability to send and receive e-mail to replicate itself quickly and do its damage in as fast a way as possible.

As essential aspect of protecting your messaging system against viruses is user education. Users should learn to be guarded about which attachments they are allowed to open. Your information security policies should also outline the types of e-mails and attachments that users are allowed to open. For example, users should be forbidden to open attachments in two instances: when they were not expecting the attachments, and when the attachments arrive from unrecognizable aliases.

Trojans

A *Trojan* (also known as a Trojan Horse) is a malicious program embedded inside a normal, safe-looking program. The difference between a virus and a Trojan is that the Trojan is embedded and the virus is attached to the file or executable.

When the normal program is run, the malicious code is run as well and can cause damage or steal critical information. An example of a Trojan is a word processing program that, when executed, allows the user to compose a document while, in the background, malicious code is running that deletes files or destroys other programs.

Trojans generally are spread through e-mail or *worms*, which are programs that run by themselves. The damage that Trojans can cause is similar to that of a virus: from nominal to critical. Trojans are particularly frightening because in most cases, users are unaware of the damage the Trojan is causing. The malicious work is being masked by the Trojan effect of the program.

Worms

As just mentioned, worms are programs that run by themselves. They do not embed or attach themselves to other programs nor do they need to do this to replicate. They can travel from computer to computer across network connections and are self-replicating. Worms might have portions of themselves running on many different computers, or the entire program might run on a single computer. Typically, worms do not change other programs, although they might carry other code that does.

The first network worms were intended to perform useful network management functions by taking advantage of operating system properties. Malicious worms exploit system vulnerabilities for their own purposes. Release of a worm usually results in brief outbreaks, shutting down entire networks.

The damage that worms can cause, like Trojans and viruses, ranges from the nominal to the critical. The type and extent of damage must be assessed individually for each worm. However, worms can install viruses and Trojans that then run their own code.

An attack that combines a worm, Trojan and/or virus can be a very difficult attack to survive without significant damage. The impact of viruses, Trojans, and worms on your messaging system and network should not be underestimated. Because they use e-mail to exploit system vulnerabilities, installing antivirus software is simply not enough. You must also ensure that known vulnerabilities in all your operating systems are patched. Don't focus only on your servers. Every device should be updated with the most recent patches from each vendor as soon as possible. Most environments will want to test these patches before installing them. But after they have been tested, install them.

Junk E-Mail

Junk e-mail is a huge issue. One client with whom this author recently worked installed its first e-mail filtering software and found that it had 46 percent fewer inbound e-mails.

Exchange 2003 has new capabilities to work with Black Listing companies to delete e-mail that is coming from hosts that are known or suspected of being junk e-mail senders. This area of discussion is called recipient and sender filtering. In Exchange 2003, you can block unwanted e-mail based on IP addresses, sender and recipient e-mail addresses, or e-mail domains. You can also filter e-mail that is sent to users who are not in Active Directory or that the sender does not have permissions to send e-mail to. Filtering is discussed at length in Chapter 20, "Supporting Internet Protocols and SMTP."

Summary

In this chapter, we discussed how hackers think, how to secure incoming SMTP e-mail, and how to secure Administrator access to your Exchange server. We discussed the differences between a virus, a Trojan, and a worm, and outlined a method of securing inbound SMTP traffic. We also referenced two other areas in this book that discuss sender filtering and securing OWA. In the next chapter, we'll discuss how to secure e-mail messages using encryption and certificates.

Chapter 25

Securing Exchange Server 2003 Messages

In the previous two chapters, we discussed how to secure Microsoft Exchange Server 2003 and what to consider when developing a comprehensive information security policy for your e-mail users. This chapter focuses on securing messages. Exchange Server 2003 is tightly integrated with Microsoft Windows Server 2003, and you'll learn how Windows Server 2003 supports a comprehensive Public Key Infrastructure (PKI) to ensure that the messaging component for Exchange Server 2003 is secure. Microsoft Certificate Services and the PKI are the two foundations upon which you will design, deploy, and maintain your public-key security needs.

Windows Server 2003 Security Protocols

Windows Server 2003 provides security via the following security protocols:

- **Kerberos version 5** The default protocol for authentication and logon.
- **NTLM (Windows Challenge/Response)** Provided for backward compatibility with Microsoft Windows NT 4 and earlier, including Windows 3.11.
- **Digital certificates** Used with a PKI deployment; especially useful for authenticating parties outside your organization. The use of digital certificates is becoming more frequent as companies attempt to secure their communications more fully.
- **SSL/TLS (Secure Sockets Layer/Transport Layer Security)** Appropriate for connection-oriented security, such as access to Web-based resources on the Internet.

In this chapter, we'll examine the use of digital certificates and public and private keys to secure messages in Exchange Server 2003. Let's begin by looking at the public-key infrastructure in Windows Server 2003.

Understanding the Public-Key Infrastructure in Windows Server 2003

A PKI deployment involves several basic components. A solid understanding of how these components work is essential to setting up good, basic network security. You can think of the PKI as a collection of resources that work together to provide a secure messaging authentication system. The major components of the Windows Server 2003 PKI are as follows:

- Certificate Services
- Digital certificates
- Policies to manage the certificates
- Microsoft CryptoAPI and cryptographic service providers (CSPs)
- Certificate stores for storing certificates

Encryption and Keys

Basic security starts with *encryption*, which is the process of scrambling data before sending it over a medium. A mathematical function called a *key* is applied to the data, changing it into an unreadable form. Hence, plain text becomes encrypted, or *cipher*, text. Encrypted data is much more difficult for an interceptor to read than plain text data. Encryption technology uses two types of keys: symmetric keys and asymmetric keys.

Symmetric keys, also known as shared keys, are identical: both the sender and the recipient use the same key to encrypt and decrypt the data. *Asymmetric keys* are not identical: one key is used to encrypt the data and a different key is used to decrypt it. With asymmetric keys, one key is known as the *public* key and the other is known as the *private* key. Exchange Server 2003 uses this type of encryption technology.

The public key is often made public by being published in some central place, such as a public folder or the Active Directory directory service. The private key must be secured so that no one but the owner of that key has access to it. A pair of public and private asymmetric keys is generally referred to in cryptography as a *key pair*.

With key pairs, either key can encrypt or decrypt the data, but the corresponding key is required to perform the opposite function, whether that is encrypting or decrypting. If the key that decrypts the data is not available, the encrypted data remains encrypted and is, essentially, useless unless the key can be found and employed. Although in theory either key can perform either function (for example, a private key can be used to encrypt and the public key used to decrypt), Windows Server 2003 and Exchange Server 2003 implement this technology by having the public key perform the encryption while the private key is used for decryption.

In Exchange Server 2003, someone having our public key is not a concern, because that individual can only encrypt data with it. However, the private key must be kept secure, because the private key decrypts the data. The best way to keep a private key secure is to never send it over a medium where a would-be hacker could capture it and use it.

The use of one key to encrypt (the public key) and a different key to decrypt (the private key) forms the foundation of Certificate Services. Table 25-1 summarizes the key types and when they are used.

Table 25-1. Private and public key usage

Action	Encryption/Decryption	Electronic Signatures
Sending a message	Recipient's public key is used to encrypt message contents.	Sender's private signing key is used to apply the signature.
Reading a message	Recipient's private key is used to decrypt the message contents.	Sender's public signing key is used to interpret the applied signature.

Encryption Schemes

Encryption allows a message to be sent via an insecure channel, such as the Internet, safely. The entire message, including attachments, is encrypted. The *strength* of an encryption describes how difficult the encryption is to break, or decrypt. The length of the key determines the encryption strength. Here are some numbers to consider:

8-bit key = 2^8 *keys = 256 keys*

56-bit key= 2^{56} *keys= 72,057,594,037,927,936 keys*

128-bit key= 2^{128} *keys=* 3.4×10^{38} *keys*

Attempting to break a 128-bit encryption and trying one trillion keys per second would take 10,819,926,705,615,920,821 years. Needless to say, 128-bit encryption is very strong. Table 25-2 lists some common encryption schemes.

Table 25-2. Common encryption algorithms

Encryption Type	Description
CAST	A 64-bit symmetric block cipher (which encrypts one *block*, or set length, of data at a time, rather than one byte) developed by Carlisle Adams and Stafford Tavares. It is similar to DES and supports key strengths of 40 bits and 128 bits.
DES	Data Encryption Standard. Developed by IBM for the government for use by the National Institute of Standards and Technology (NIST). This standard uses 56-bit keys with a 64-bit symmetric block cipher. It is the most commonly used encryption algorithm.
3DES	Triple DES; encrypts the data structure three separate times.
DH	The Diffie-Hellman approach for passing symmetric keys.
KEA	Key Exchange Algorithm. An improved version of Diffie-Hellman.
MD2	Message Digest. An algorithm that creates a 128-bit hash value. It was developed by Ron Rivest of RSA (Rivest, Shamir, and Adleman).
MD4	Another RSA algorithm that creates a 128-bit hash value.
MD5	A better version of MD4.
RC2	Rivest's Cipher, a 64-bit symmetric block cipher.
RC4	An RSA stream cipher (which encrypts one byte or bit at a time) that can use variable-length keys. Microsoft's implementation of RC4 uses either a 40-bit or 128-bit key.
RSA	A commonly used public/private key encryption scheme developed at RSA.
SHA	Secure Hash Algorithm, developed at NIST. It produces a 160-bit hash value and is similar to MD5, but more secure and thus slower.

Certificate Services in Windows Server 2003

Public and private keys are not enough to guard your sensitive data. For instance, someone can obtain your public key (by definition it is available to anyone) and then impersonate a server with which you're communicating. An impersonator can easily do this if he or she is in your organization. In this scenario, you might believe that you're communicating with Server1 when in fact you're communicating with a different server. Certificate Services is designed to protect against this type of attack.

Windows Server 2003 certificates form the core of the Windows Server 2003 public-key infrastructure. You can install Windows Server 2003 Certificate Services to create a *certificate authority* (CA) that issues and manages digital certificates. Active Directory can maintain information that a CA needs, such as user account names, group memberships, and certificate templates, as well as information about each CA installed in the domain. Active Directory also maintains certificate mappings to user accounts for authenticating clients and controlling access to network resources.

Digital Certificates and the X.509 Standard

Digital certificates verify a user's identity and are issued by the CA (discussed later in the section "Certificate Authority"). We can trust digital certificates because we trust the source of the certificate, the CA. In addition to issuing the certificate itself, the CA by default creates the public key/private key pair, which is the basis of security in any digital certificate.

Digital certificates generally follow the X.509 standard, which means that they meet the standard criteria for electronic certificates outlined in it. Typically, an X.509 certificate incorporates the following fields:

- Version number
- Serial number of the certificate
- Signature algorithm ID
- Name of the person to whom the certificate was issued
- Expiration date of the certificate
- Subject user name
- Subject public-key information
- Issuer unique ID
- Subject unique ID
- Extensions
- Digital signature of the authority that issued the certificate

SSL/TLS also conforms to the X.509 standard. In Windows Server 2003, external users' digital certificates can be mapped to one or more Windows Server 2003 user accounts for permissions to network resources. Windows Server 2003 then uses the Subject field (the subject user name in the list of fields just given) to identify the user associated with the certificate. In this way, Windows Server 2003 and Certificate Services can map an external user to a user account stored in Active Directory.

The X.509 Standard

The X.509 standard describes two levels of authentication: *simple authentication*, using a password as the only verification of a claimed identity; and *strong authentication*, using credentials generated by cryptographic technologies. The standard recommends that only strong authentication be used as a basis for providing secure services.

The strong authentication method specified in the X.509 standard is based upon public-key technologies. The one huge advantage of this standard, and the reason why it is so popular today, is that user certificates can be held within Active Directory as attributes and can be communicated within the directory systems like any other attribute of a user account.

Although the X.509 standard does not require the use of a particular algorithm to produce the certificates, it notes that for two users to communicate, they must use the same algorithms during authentication.

Certificate Authority

As mentioned earlier, a certificate authority issues certificates and enables parties to trust each other. The CA's private key is used to sign the certificate, and the certificate is needed to verify the signatures. Because certificates originate from a verified authority, the receiving party can explicitly trust them. For example, a client application can import a certificate to be trusted by a user who is reading data from the application.

Clients and CAs can maintain a list of explicitly trusted certificates. Certificates can also be placed on a certificate revocation list (CRL), which lists certificates that are explicitly distrusted. In addition, they can be set to expire after a predetermined amount of time.

Certificate Services Architecture in Windows Server 2003

Figure 25-1 illustrates the components of Windows Server 2003 Certificate Services. These components work together, in cooperation with CryptoAPI and the cryptographic service providers, to perform all the tasks necessary to generate, store, and apply certificates in the enterprise. You can manipulate these objects and modules in the Certification Authority snap-in. (For information about how to install this snap-in, see the section "Installing and Configuring Certificate Services" later in this chapter.)

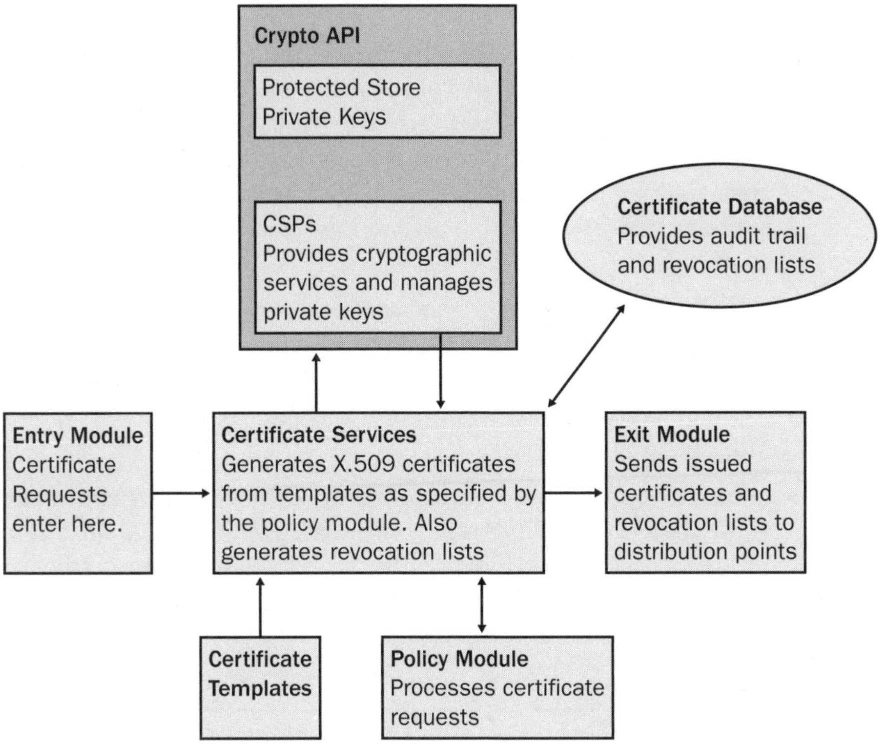

Figure 25-1. *Components of Certificate Services.*

Entry Module

Certificate requests—such as those a user submits via the Web enrollment support page—enter the Entry module of Certificate Services, either through remote procedure calls (RPCs) or HTTP. The requests are placed in a pending queue until they are approved or rejected by the Policy module.

Policy Module

The Policy module determines whether a certificate request should be approved, denied, or left pending for an administrator to review. Once the certificate is approved, the Policy module can verify information in the request against various sources, such as Active Directory or an external database. Additional attributes or extensions can be inserted into the Policy module if a customized client application requires them. For example, a signing limit can be inserted into certificates and used by an online purchasing form to determine whether the user can sign for the amount requested.

Certificate Templates

Certificate templates define the attributes for certificate types. You can configure enterprise CAs to issue specific types of certificates to authorized users and computers. When the CA issues a certificate, a certificate template is used to specify its attributes, such as the authorized uses for the certificate, the cryptographic algorithms that are to be used with it, the public-key length, and its lifetime. Certificate templates are stored in Active Directory. Table 25-3 lists the standard certificate types.

Online certificate templates are used to issue certificates to requestors that have Windows Server 2003 accounts and that support obtaining certificates directly from an enterprise CA. Offline templates are used to issue certificates to requestors that don't have Windows Server 2003 accounts or that don't support obtaining a certificate from an enterprise CA.

When a CA issues an online certificate, it obtains information about the requestor from the requestor's Windows Server 2003 account for inclusion in the certificate. When it issues an offline certificate, it includes in the certificate the information that the requestor entered as part of the request into a Web form, such as a user name, an e-mail address, and a department.

Table 25-3. Certificate types

Certificate Type	Description
Administrator	Used for authenticating clients and for Encrypting File System (EFS), secure e-mail, certificate trust list (CTL) signing, and code signing.
Authenticated Session	Used for authenticating clients.
Basic EFS	Used for EFS (Encrypting File System) operations.
CEP Encryption	Used to enroll Cisco Systems, Inc. routers for Internet Protocol Security (IPSec) authentication certificates from a Windows Server 2003 CA.
Code Signing	Used for code signing operations.
Computer	Used for authenticating clients and servers.
Domain Controller	Used for authenticating domain controllers. When an enterprise CA is installed, this certificate type is installed automatically on domain controllers to support the public-key operations that are required when domain controllers are supporting Certificate Services.
EFS Recovery Agent	Used for EFS encrypted-data recovery operations.
Enrollment Agent	Used for authenticating administrators who request certificates on behalf of smart-card users.
Enrollment Agent (Computer)	Used for authenticating services that request certificates on behalf of other computers.

Table 25-3. Certificate types

Certificate Type	Description
Exchange Enrollment Agent (offline request)	Used for authenticating Microsoft Exchange Server administrators who request certificates on behalf of secure e-mail users.
Exchange Signature Only (offline request)	Used by Exchange Server for client authentication and secure e-mail (used for signing only).
Exchange User (offline request)	Used by Exchange Server for client authentication and secure e-mail (used for both signing and confidentiality of e-mail).
IPSec	Used for IPSec authentication.
IPSec (offline request)	Used for IPSec authentication.
Root Certification Authority	Used for root CA installation operations. (This certificate template cannot be issued from a CA and is used only when installing root CAs.)
Router (offline request)	Used for authentication of routers.
Smart Card Logon	Used for client authentication and logging on with a smart card.
Smart Card User	Used for client authentication, secure e-mail, and logging on with a smart card.
Subordinate Certification Authority (offline request)	Used to issue certificates for subordinate CAs.
Trust List Signing	Used to sign CTLs.
User	Used for client authentication, EFS, and secure e-mail (used for both signing and confidentiality of e-mail).
User Signature Only	Used for client authentication and secure e-mail (used for signing only).
Web Server (offline request)	Used for Web server authentication.

Certificate Database

The certificate database records all certificate transactions, such as certificate requests. It records whether requests were granted or denied, and it also holds information about the certificate, such as its serial number and expiration date. Revoked certificates are flagged and tracked in this database as well. You'll use the Certification Authority snap-in to manage the audit trail.

Exit Modules

Exit modules send the certificate to the location specified in the request. Acceptable destinations include LDAP directory services, file systems, and URLs. You can create customized exit modules so that new certificates are sent in e-mail messages or to a public folder on the network. There can be many or few exit modules, depending on your needs. Modules can be written in the Component

Object Model (COM) interface to allow any entity or directory to be notified when a certificate is issued. In fact, you could write an exit module to notify a database of a new certificate, for billing purposes.

Managing the Public-Key Infrastructure

Now that you understand the Windows Server 2003 public-key infrastructure and are familiar with how Certificate Services works, you need to learn how to install and manage the Certification Authority snap-in. You can use this Microsoft Management Console snap-in to manage one or more CAs. For more information about how to create a customized snap-in, see Chapter 8, "Managing Exchange Server 2003."

Installing and Configuring Certificate Services

If you do not include Certificate Services as an optional component during the installation of Windows Server 2003, you can install it at any time by selecting the Certificate Services component in Add/Remove Programs (Figure 25-2). Immediately upon selecting Certificate Services, you're presented with a message box indicating that once Certificate Services is installed, you can't rename this server or move it from the domain.

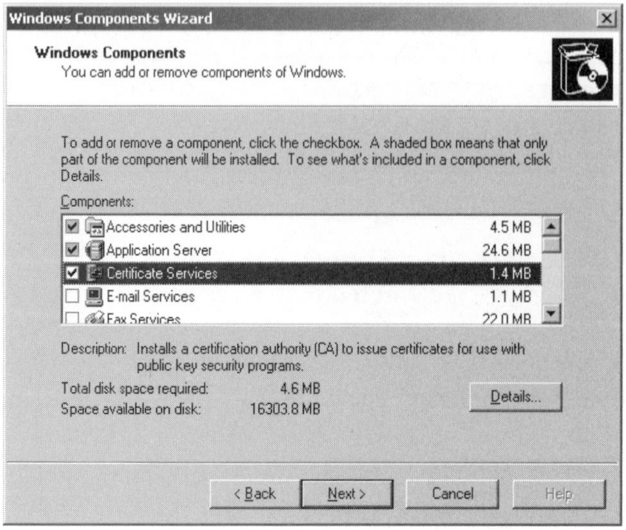

Figure 25-2. *Selecting Certificate Services in Add/Remove Programs.*

On the CA Type selection page (Figure 25-3), you're given the chance to choose the type of CA server you want to install. The default is an enterprise root CA. Select the appropriate type for your installation.

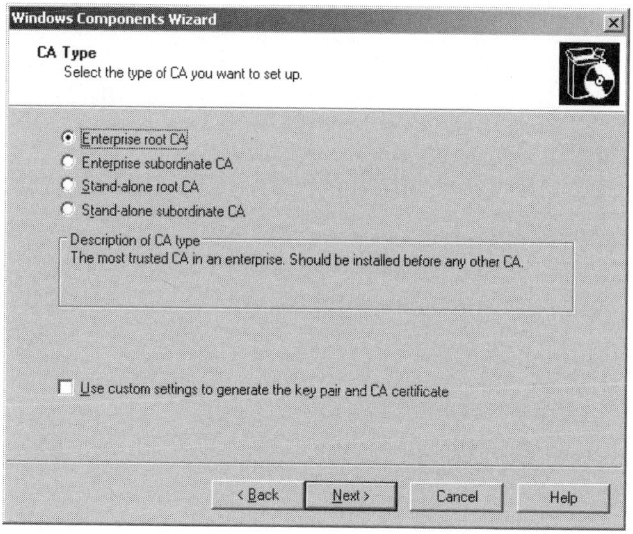

Figure 25-3. *CA Type selection page.*

If you want to configure advanced options for the public and private keys, select the Use Custom Settings To Generate The Key Pair And CA Certificate check box and then click Next. The page shown in Figure 25-4 appears. Table 25-4 describes the choices you're given in this screen.

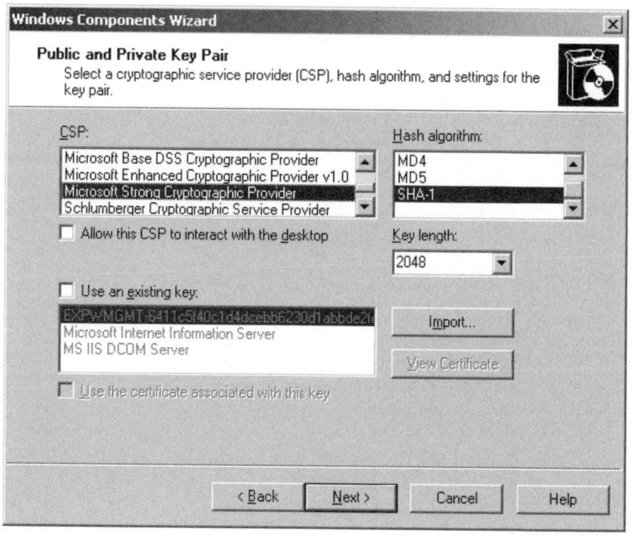

Figure 25-4. *Setting advanced options for public and private key pairs.*

Note Installing an enterprise CA requires Active Directory services, so the CA computer must already be joined to the Windows Server 2003 domain.

Table 25-4. Advanced options for public and private key pairs

Option	Description
CSP	Select the Cryptographic Service Provider (CSP) to be used to generate the public key and private key set for the CA certificate. The default CSP is the Microsoft Strong Cryptographic Provider.
Hash Algorithms	The default is SHA-1, which provides the strongest cryptographic security.
Allow This CSP To Interact With The Desktop	Be sure to select this check box. Unless you do so, system services will not interact with the desktop of the user who is currently logged on. If you're logging on using a smart card or some other hardware device, you need to allow the CSP to interact with the desktop to allow the user to log on.
Key Length	The default key length is 2048 bits for the Strong Cryptographic Provider and 1024 bits for the Basic Cryptographic Provider. The minimum key length is 512 bits, and the maximum is 4096 bits. Generally, the longer the key, the longer the safe lifetime of the private key.
Use Existing Keys	Allows you to choose an existing private key from the list. The existing private key is used for the CA. You might need to use this option to restore a failed CA.
Use The Certificate Associated With This Key	Enables the selection of the certificate that is associated with the existing private key that is used for the CA. You might need to use this option to restore a failed CA.
Import	Gives you the ability to import a private key that is not in the Use Existing Keys list. For example, you might import a private key from an archive for a failed CA.
View Certificate	Displays the certificate associated with the private key in the Use Existing Keys list.

Enter the CA identifying information, as illustrated in Figure 25-5, and then click Next.

You'll see a quick screen indicating that the key pair is being generated. It will appear for fewer than 2 seconds in most cases. After the key is generated, Setup needs to know where to put the database. Enter the appropriate path. As Figure 25-6 shows, you can also select the Store Configuration Information In A Shared Folder check box. This option creates a folder that makes information about CAs available to users. It is useful only if you are installing a standalone CA and do not have Active Directory.

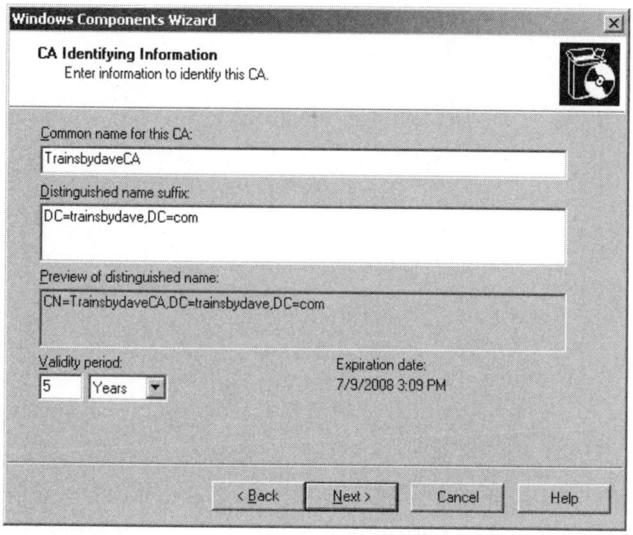

Figure 25-5. *Entering CA identifying information.*

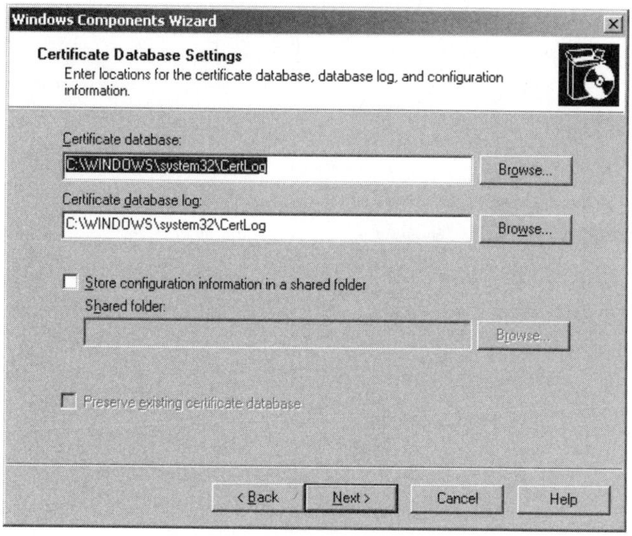

Figure 25-6. *Specifying data storage locations.*

When you click Next, you see a message box indicating that Microsoft Internet Information Services (IIS) services must be stopped. Just click OK, and the wizard will configure the components. When it is done, you are finished installing Certificate Services. A shortcut to the Certification Authority snap-in appears in the Administrative Tools menu. Figure 25-7 illustrates the basic Certification Authority snap-in.

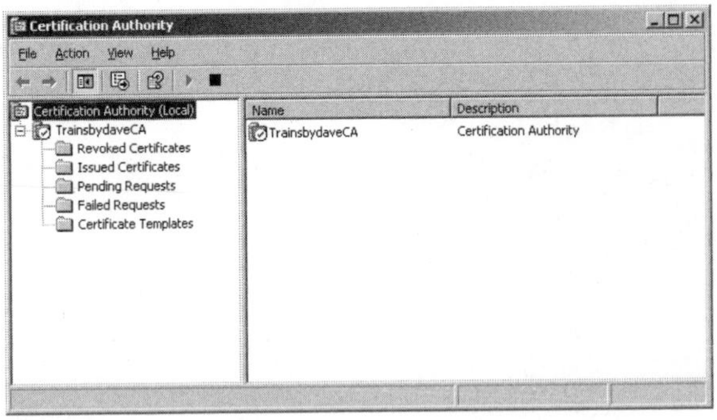

Figure 25-7. *Certification Authority snap-in.*

Installing Web Enrollment Support

By default, when Windows Server 2003 Certificate Services is installed, the same server will also have installed Web enrollment support (Figure 25-8). You can also choose to install the Web enrollment form on another Windows Server 2003–based computer. You might do so if the traffic volume for Certificate Services is high and you need to spread the enrollment traffic load over more than one server.

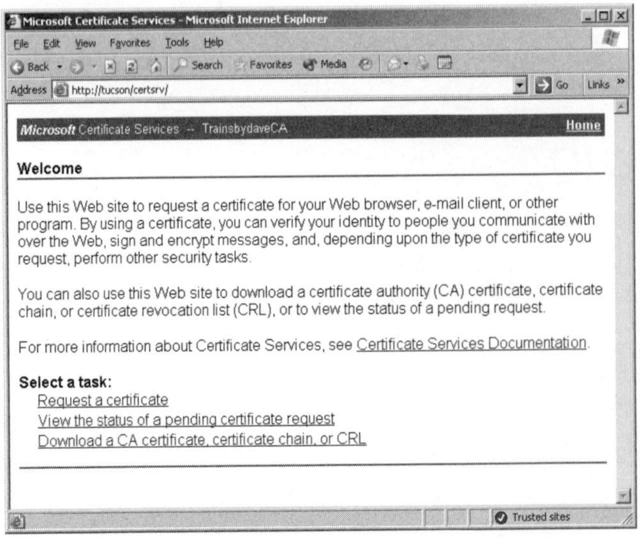

Figure 25-8. *Web enrollment home page.*

The default location for the Web enrollment pages is <drive:>\%*windir*% *System32\Certsrv*, where <drive:> is the letter of the disk drive on which the pages are installed. To install the Web enrollment pages on a server other than the one housing Certificate Services, start the Add/Remove Programs tool in Control Panel and select Certificate Services, as though you were installing it. Then click Details and clear the Certificate Services check box (Figure 25-9). Verify that the Certificate Services Web Enrollment Support check box is selected, and then click OK. Follow the wizard to completion.

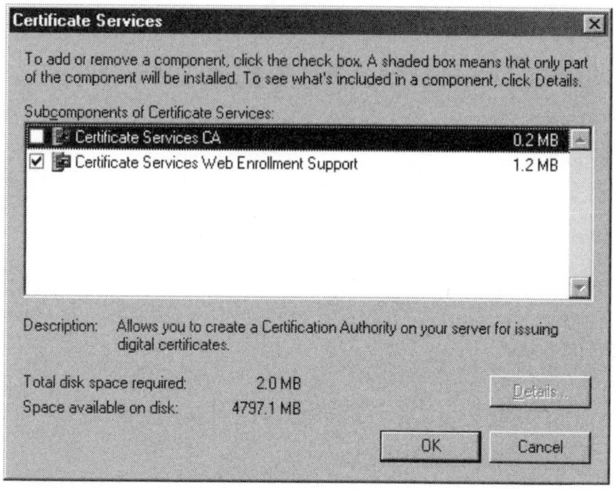

Figure 25-9. *Installing Web enrollment support on a separate server.*

Using the Web Enrollment Pages

Users can access the Web enrollment pages via the default URL *http://*server-name*/certsrv*. On the welcome screen, you have several options. Clicking the Download A CA Certificate, Certificate Chain, Or CRL option retrieves the CA's certificate or the most current CRL. Click Next to display a screen allowing you to perform a couple of different tasks, including establish a trust for the CA certificate chain, which involves installing the certification chain for the CA's certificate in the certificate store of the local computer (Figure 25-10). Selecting this option will be most useful when you need to trust a subordinate CA but do not have the certificate of the root CA in your local certificate store.

More often, you will use this Web site to obtain a new user certificate. To begin the process, click the Request A Certificate link. On the next page that appears (Figure 25-11), you can either request a user certificate or submit an advanced certificate request. For information about the advanced options, see the next section, "Making an Advanced Request."

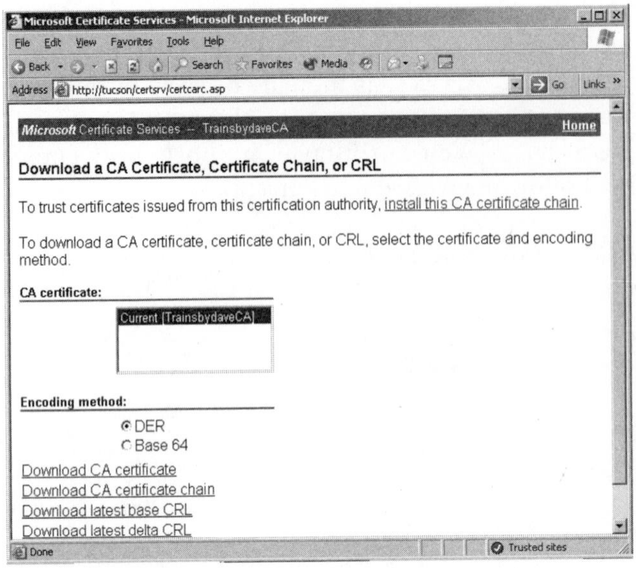

Figure 25-10. *Retrieving the CA's certificate.*

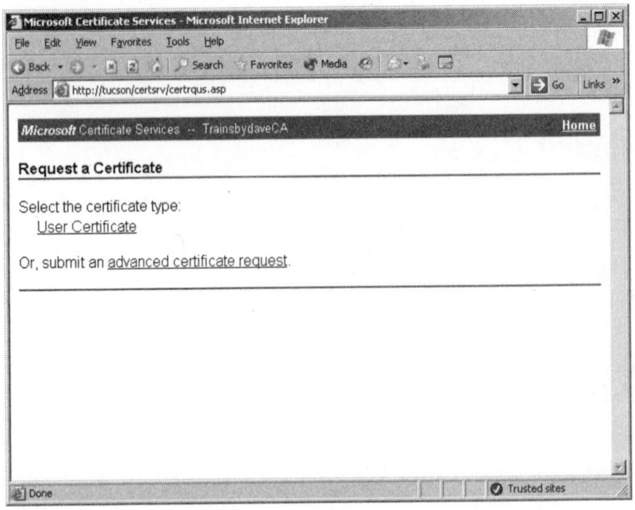

Figure 25-11. *Requesting a new certificate.*

To request a new basic user certificate, click the User Certificate link. The User Certificate - Identifying Information page appears (Figure 25-12). Here you are informed that no more information is needed for the CA to generate a certificate. Clicking the Submit button initiates the certificate generation process. Clicking the More Options link allows you to specify the cryptographic service provider and the request format for the certificate. In most circumstances, you will want to click the Submit button; the More Options area is only for advanced users.

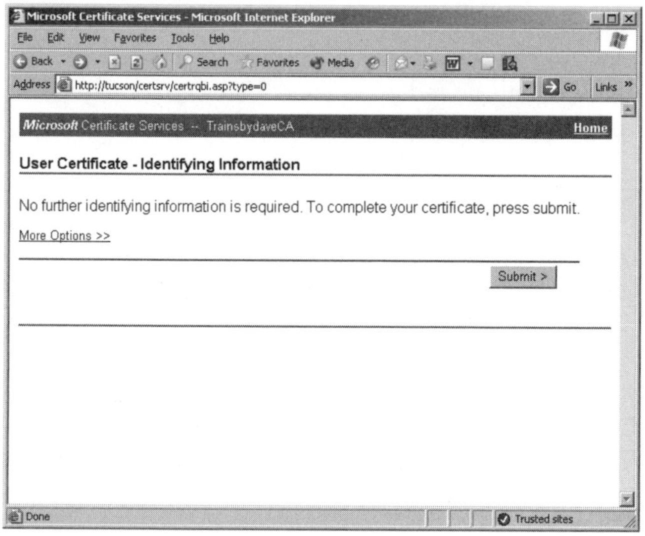

Figure 25-12. *Message indicating system is ready to submit a certificate request.*

After you click Submit, the certificate is generated. Click Yes or OK when the two message boxes appear to finish the submission request. The next support page gives you the opportunity to install the certificate (Figure 25-13).

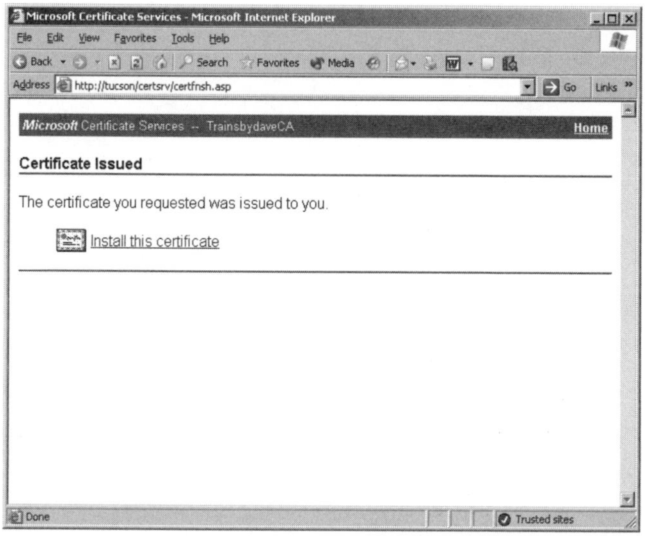

Figure 25-13. *Message indicating system is ready to install the certificate.*

Clicking the Install This Certificate link installs the certificate on the local computer. The certificate is available only to the user for whom the certificate was generated. If other users log on to the computer, they will not be able to use this certificate. The final enrollment page then appears, indicating that the certificate has been installed properly. To verify that the certificate has been created, open the Certification Authority snap-in and open the Issued Certificates folder. The user's certificate is displayed in the details pane (Figure 25-14).

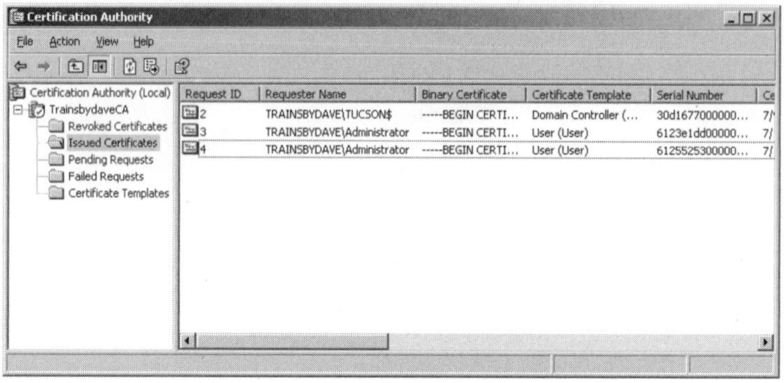

Figure 25-14. *Verifying that a user certificate has been created.*

You can also verify that the user certificate has been installed by opening the Microsoft Outlook 2003 client, choosing Options from the Tools menu, and then clicking on the Security tab (Figure 25-15). In the Encrypted area, click the Settings button to reveal the Change Security Settings screen (Figure 25-16).

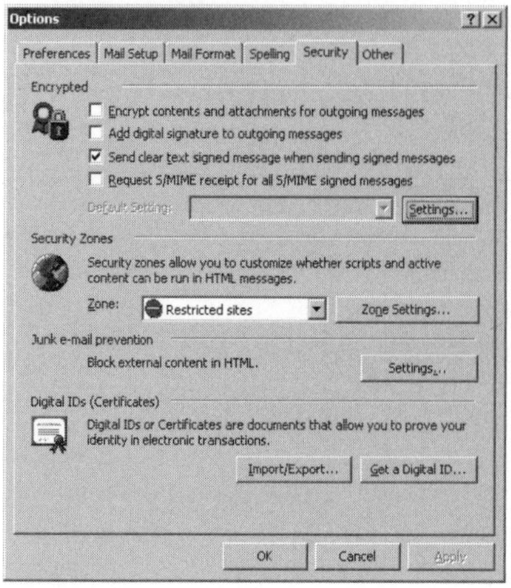

Figure 25-15. *Verifying that a user certificate has been installed.*

Figure 25-16. *Change Security Settings screen.*

Click the Choose button for both the signing and encryption certificate to show that the certificate is installed in Outlook. Select OK in the Select Certificate window to assign the certificate that was just created to the Outlook client (Figure 25-17). Figure 25-18 illustrates how the certificates appear in the Security tab after being selected. The hash algorithm and encryption algorithm can be changed, but not the certificate itself.

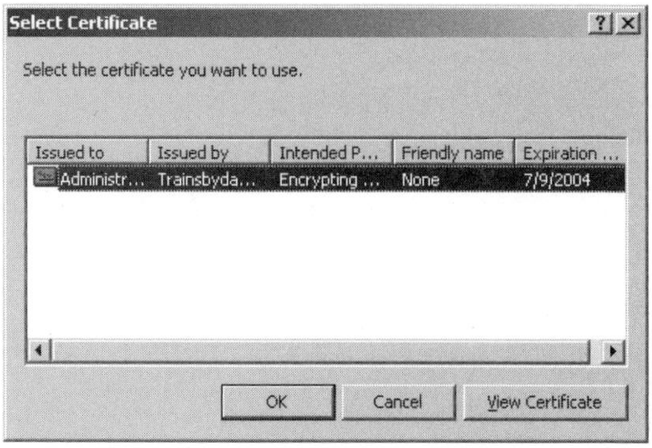

Figure 25-17. *Selecting the Users Certificate for assignment in the Outlook client.*

Figure 25-18. *The Users Certificate assigned to the Outlook client for both encryption and signing.*

If different certificates are installed, you can specify a particular certificate by clicking the Choose button and making a selection (Figure 25-19). Although the items in the list look like multiple copies of the same certificate, they are not. Each item is a unique certificate.

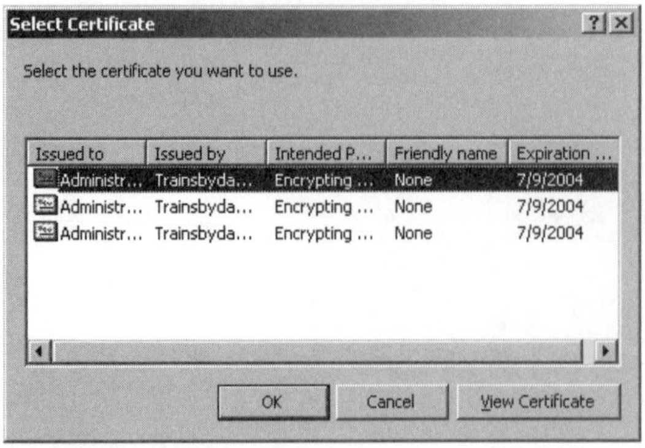

Figure 25-19. *Choosing a certificate for personal use.*

Making an Advanced Request

The Advanced Request option allows you to specify additional options while making a certificate request. Figure 25-20 shows the three types of requests available. The first choice, Create And Submit A Request To This CA, walks you through an advanced form. You can use this advanced form to request any certificate types supported by the enterprise CA. You'll also use this form to configure the key, format, and hash options for the certificate request. Generally, only administrators use this form because it is likely to be too complicated for the average user.

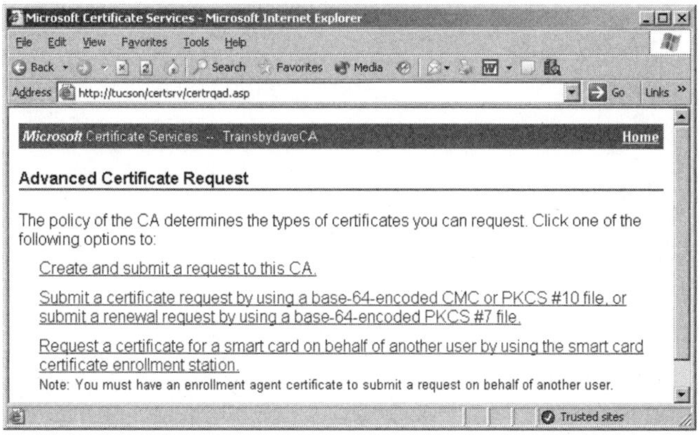

Figure 25-20. *The three options available for an advanced certificate request.*

The second choice, Submit A Certificate Request Using A Base-64-Encoded CMC Or PKCS #10 File, Or Submit A Renewal Request By Using A Base-64-Encoded PKCS #7 File, allows you to submit a certificate request using a file rather than a form. The file must already exist in base 64, using either the #10 or #7 PKCS encoding format. You will need to select which type of certificate is being requested in the Certificate Template section as well.

The last choice, Request A Certificate For A Smart Card On Behalf Of Another User Using The Smart Card Enrollment Station, allows an administrator to create a certificate for a smart-card user that can then be installed onto the physical card.

Viewing Information About Certificates

You can view specific information about certificates by navigating to the Issued Certificates folder in the Certificate Authority and then opening an individual certificate. To open a certificate, right-click it and then choose Open. Figure 25-21 shows the General tab of the property sheet for a user certificate. This tab lists the purpose of the certificate, the issuer, to whom the certificate is issued, and the dates the certificate is valid. If you compare the information for a user certificate with the information for a domain controller certificate (Figure 25-22), you'll notice that the purposes are very different. Remember that the purpose of a certificate is derived from its template.

Figure 25-21. *General tab of the property sheet for a user certificate.*

Figure 25-22. *General tab of the property sheet for a domain controller certificate.*

The Issuer Statement button is grayed out in Figures 25-21 and 25-22 because in this case, the issuing CA does not provide a statement. If the issuing CA for a given certificate does provide a statement, you can click this button to read additional information about the certificate from the issuing CA's Web site.

The Details tab shows the information contained in the certificate. When you select an item in the Field column, the contents of that field are revealed in the Value column. Figure 25-23 shows the Public Key field selected. The Value column indicates that it is a 1024-bit key.

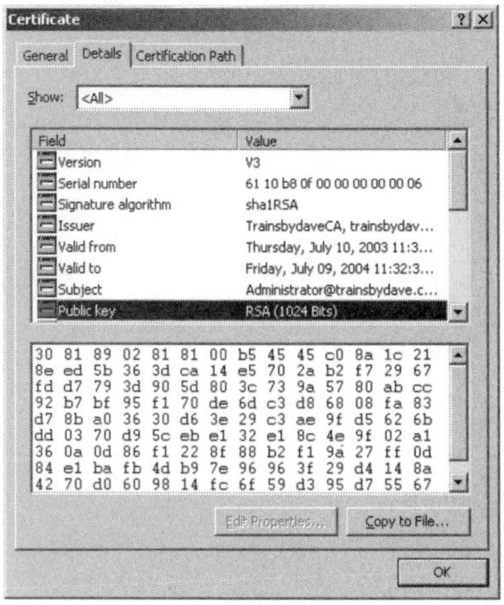

Figure 25-23. *Details tab of a certificate's property sheet.*

The Certification Path tab (Figure 25-24) shows the trust status of the certificate. If there is a problem with either the certificate or the path, a warning will appear in this tab with information explaining the problem.

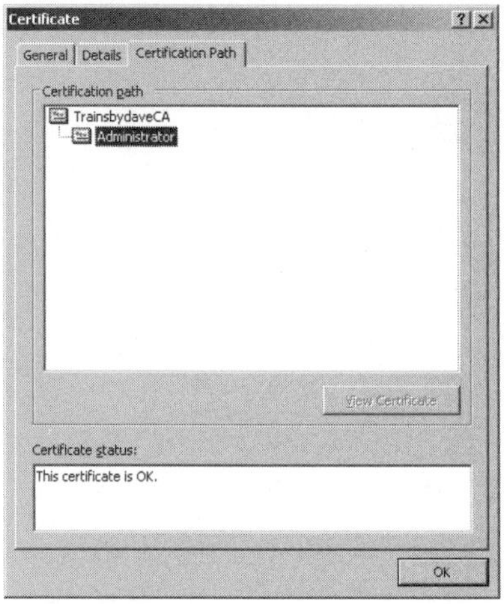

Figure 25-24. *Certification Path tab of a certificate's property sheet.*

On the client side, you can use Outlook 2003 to edit certain certificate properties. With the certificate open, click the Edit Properties button at the bottom of the Certificate's properties Details tab to see the sheet shown in Figure 25-25. Here you can change the friendly name and description for the certificate. You can also restrict the purposes for which the certificate can be used. By default, all purposes are enabled, but you can manually disable certain purposes or disable all purposes, which would make the certificate invalid.

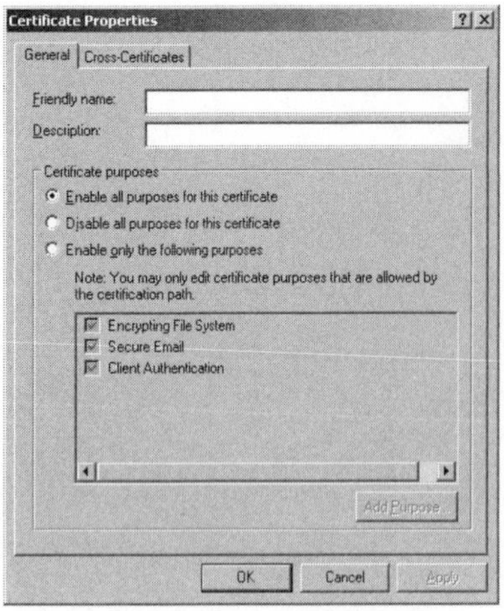

Figure 25-25. *Editing certificate properties in Outlook 2003.*

The Cross-Certificates tab (Figure 25-26) allows you to specify cross-certificates for this certificate. *Cross-certificates* are special certificates that are used to establish complete or qualified one-way trusts between otherwise unrelated CAs. If your organization has multiple, distributed IT departments, you might not be able to establish a single, trusted root. In this situation, you can implement a network hierarchy trust model in which all CAs are self-signed and trust relationships between CAs are based on cross-certificates.

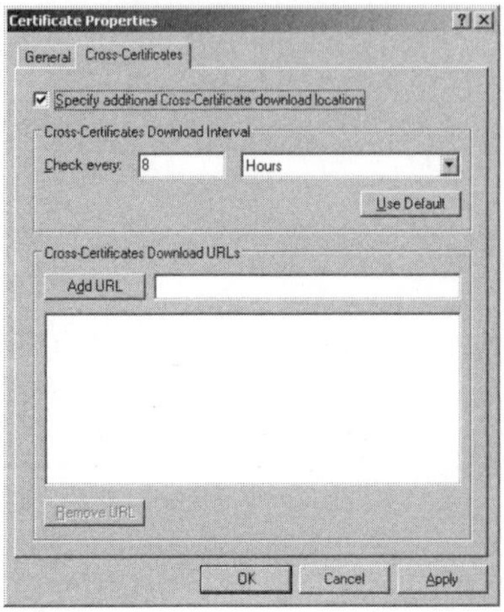

Figure 25-26. *Cross-Certificates tab in the certificate properties.*

Securing Messaging in Outlook 2003

From the client perspective, one question that must be answered is how the Outlook 2003 client knows which certificates to trust. The answer is found in the properties of Microsoft Internet Explorer. When Internet Explorer is installed, a large number of root certificates are embedded in the installation. Outlook uses the Internet Explorer cryptographic service provider to read these certificates and then determine whether the CA is trusted. To see which CAs are trusted, in Internet Explorer, choose Internet Options from the Tools menu, and then display the Content tab and click the Certificates button. Figure 25-27 shows a partial list of the default trusted root certificate authorities that ship with Outlook 2003 and Internet Explorer 6.

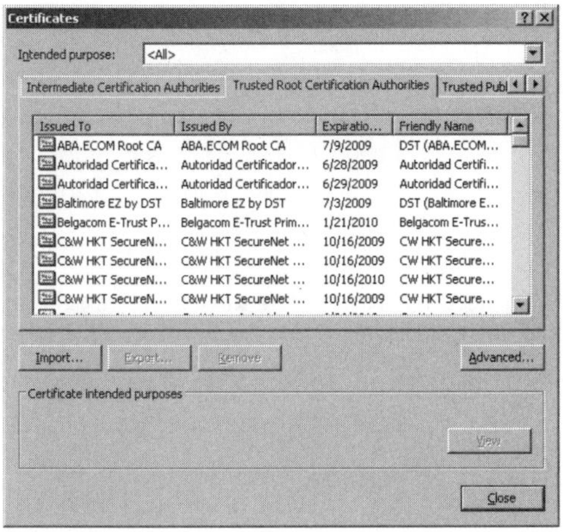

Figure 25-27. *Partial list of trusted root certificate authorities in Internet Explorer.*

Note A cryptographic service provider is the actual code that has the algorithms for encrypting data and creating signatures.

Both root CAs and individual users can be added or removed at this location. Let's assume, for example, that we want to remove a root CA's certificate from the list of trusted root CAs. In the Certificates dialog box, we would display the Trusted Root Certification Authorities tab, highlight the root CA to be removed, and then click Remove. A message box would then appear confirming this action.

Initially Trusting a Certificate

If your company implements its own CA or if you need to trust specific CAs that are not embedded by default in IE, you can import their certificates by clicking the Import button.

You need to think carefully about whether to initially trust a certificate. For instance, if the certificate is included on an installation CD-ROM from Microsoft, you can be sure it's trustworthy. However, if you've downloaded software from the Internet, someone might have slipped in a certificate that you don't want to trust. To prevent this, Microsoft uses Authenticode certificates for its software. With these certificates, if any bits have changed, you are notified during installation that the signature is invalid and that you shouldn't install the software.

You can also verify certificates independently by contacting the root CA directly to see whether the certificate's serial number is valid. Some CAs include serial numbers on their Web sites, or you can contact the system administrator of a corporate CA.

Encryption and Outlook 2003

When both the sender and receiver are using Outlook 2003 along with certificates, their messages are encrypted end to end, meaning that the Outlook 2003 client encrypts them when it sends them and they are not decrypted until opened by the recipient. Encrypted messages in the store remain encrypted. Hence, if someone is able to obtain access to a mailbox on an Exchange Server 2003, the messages are still unreadable because that person does not have the private key to decrypt the message. Only the intended recipient holding the correct private key can decrypt the message.

Here is how Outlook 2003 provides message privacy. First, the sender composes and addresses the message. Outlook then locates the recipient in Active Directory by doing an address book lookup. If the sender has chosen to encrypt outbound messages, Outlook retrieves the recipient's certificate. To see the encryption options, choose Options from the Tools menu in Outlook 2003, and display the Security tab (Figure 25-28).

Outlook extracts the recipient's public key from his or her certificate and generates a one-time *lockbox*, encrypting all the data with a one-time, symmetric key and placing it inside this box. The lockbox, along with its contents, is encrypted with the recipient's public key and then sent to the recipient. When the recipient opens the message, the recipient's client decrypts the lockbox, using the recipient's private key, extracts the symmetric key, and decrypts the message with the symmetric key. Then the recipient can read the message.

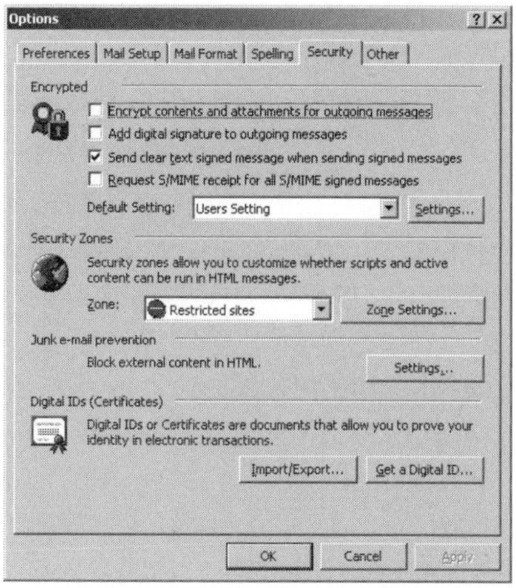

Figure 25-28. *The Security tab, showing options to encrypt outbound messages.*

Digital Signatures and Outlook 2003

Digital signatures are as legally binding as a signature on paper. Digital signatures provide origin authentication, since only the sender holds the private key used to generate the signature. The signature also provides data integrity because the signature is a protected hash of the message, meaning that the document is hashed and then encrypted with the signer's private encryption key and, after verification, it is decrypted with the signer's public key. If even one bit changes during message transmission, the hash will not be the same at the receiving end, and the message will be considered invalid. A given signature is generated for only a single message and will never be used again. Digital signatures work because embedded into each signature is an indicator that explains what hash functions the sender used. The recipient can use the same function and compute the same hash when the message is received. If the hashes match, the signature is considered valid. If the message is encrypted, it must be decrypted before the algorithm can be run to compare the hashes.

S/MIME and Outlook 2003

Secure/Multipurpose Internet Mail Extensions, or S/MIME, was designed by an RSA-led vendor consortium in 1995. Version 3 is in Internet Draft process at the time of this writing. S/MIME allows recipients using non-Microsoft software to see and understand encrypted, secure messages sent from Outlook 2003 users.

More Info For more information about S/MIME, visit the RSA Web site at *http://www.rsasecurity.com*.

When a message is signed, the content of the message is converted to a MIME format. The message headers and body use the algorithm from the user's private key to produce a Message Integrity Check (MIC). The result is the digital signature. The message is then sent with a copy of the sender's public key embedded in the message.

When the message is read, the MIC is generated at the recipient's end and the results are compared to the sender's digital signature. If they match, the signature is considered valid.

When it comes to encryption, the recipient's public key is used to encrypt the data. To send an encrypted message, the sender must be able to retrieve the recipient's public key. The recipient can then decrypt the message using his or her private key. By default, the Outlook client looks to either Active Directory or the recipient's own personal certificate store for the recipient's public key.

For all of this to work, there must be a common CA trusted between the sender and recipient. *Trust verification*, which is the act of determining whether a given public certificate comes from a trusted source, is performed by the Outlook client (and Outlook Express) on the desktop.

Configuring Outlook 2003 for Secure Messaging

Certificate Services is integrated with Active Directory, and you can specify whether you want the certificates to be published in a file system in addition to Active Directory. To configure this setting, open the property sheet for the CA in the Certification Authority snap-in, display the Exit Module tab, and click the Properties button (Figure 25-29).

The advantage of publishing a certificate in Active Directory is that the certificate becomes an attribute of the user's account, as shown in Figure 25-30. Before a user sends an encrypted message to another user, the client can look up the recipient's account in Active Directory to see whether that recipient has a certificate. If one exists, the message is sent as described previously. In addition, the client periodically (every 24 hours) picks up certificate trust and revocation lists that are published by Certificate Services and applies them as needed. In the absence of a hierarchical CA structure, the client can build a linear trust network of different CAs.

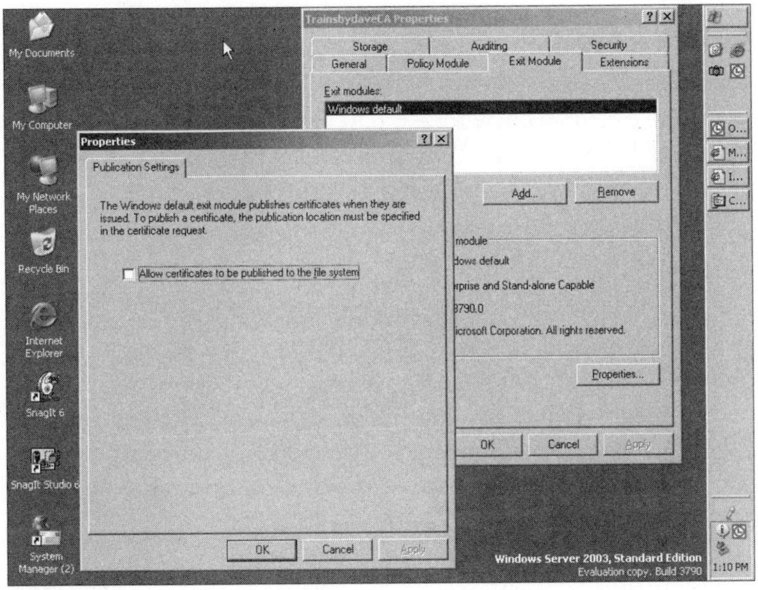

Figure 25-29. *Allowing certificates to be published to the file system option.*

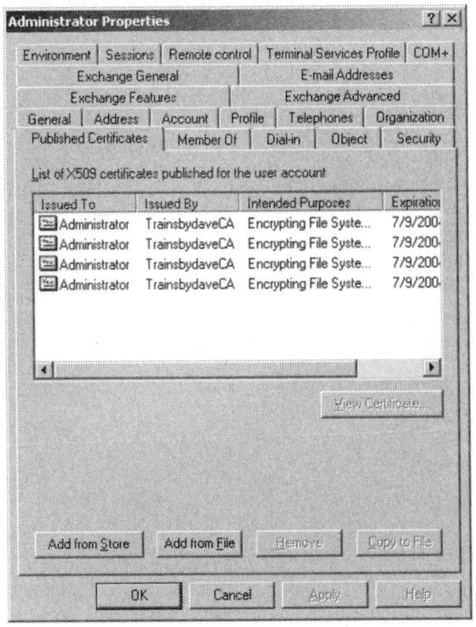

Figure 25-30. *Published Certificates tab of a user's property sheet.*

In the Outlook client, use the Tools/Options/Security tab (refer to Figure 25-27) to select whether you want e-mail to be sent signed, encrypted, or both.

Installing Exchange Certificate Templates

In Microsoft Exchange 2000 Server, you had to manually add the certificate templates of Enrollment Agent (Computer), Exchange User, and Exchange Signature Only certificates before installing Key Management Server (KMS). In Exchange Server 2003, KMS is no longer used and the Users certificate that is installed by default has the following functions:

- Encrypting File System
- Secure E-Mail (both signature and encryption)
- Client Authentication

Because the "generic" users certificate now has these functions bundled into a single certificate, you'll find that the default installation of Certificate Services in Windows Server 2003 should meet most of your needs as far as your users are concerned.

However, at some point you might need to install additional certificate templates to issue certificates for other needs. You can easily accomplish this in the CA snap-in. To add another certificate template to those already there by default, right-click the Certificate Template folder in the Certification Authority snap-in, point to New, and select Certificate Template To Issue. The dialog box shown in Figure 25-31 appears. In this dialog box, you can choose, by default, from the following templates:

- Authenticated Session
- CEP Encryption
- Code Signing
- Enrollment Agent
- Exchange Enrollment Agent (offline request)
- Enrollment Agent (Computer)
- Exchange Signature Only
- Exchange User
- IPSec
- IPSec (offline)
- Router (offline)
- Smartcard Logon
- Smartcard User

- Trust List Signing
- User Signature Only

These are default certificate templates installed with Certificate Services:

- EFS Recovery Agent
- Basic EFS
- Domain Controller
- Web Server
- Computer
- User
- Subordinate Certification Authority
- Administrator

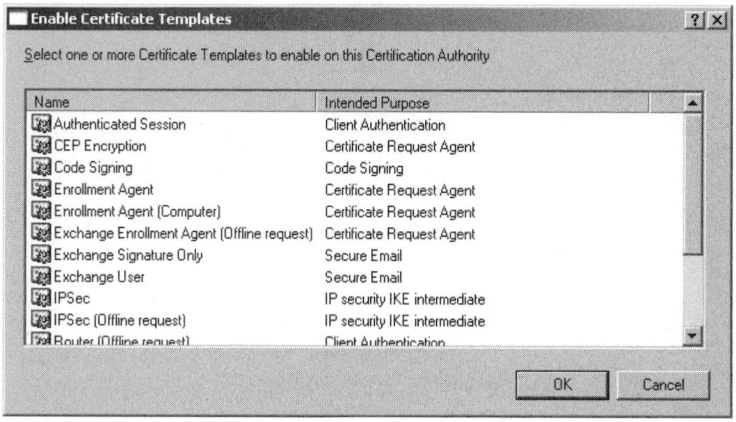

Figure 25-31. *Choosing a certificate template.*

Working with the Local Certificate Store

You can work with the certificates that are installed on a computer or for a user account. If you want to work with certificates that are installed on a computer, create a new Microsoft Management Console (MMC) and add the Certificates snap-in. Select the Computer Account option in the Certificates Snap-in selection box. Then select your own local computer or a remote computer. In a single MMC, you could create multiple snap-ins that manage all the certificates on all your servers and/or workstations in your environment. In large environments, this would be unworkable, but in some environments, this might be preferable.

In Figure 25-32, the MMC has both the local computer and the current user Certificates snap-in installed. Notice that under the Certificates - Current User snap-in, you have access to certificates for the following:

- User
- Trusted root certification authorities
- Enterprise trusts
- Intermediate certification authorities
- User's AD object
- Trusted publishers
- Untrusted certificates
- Third-party root certification authorities
- Trusted people

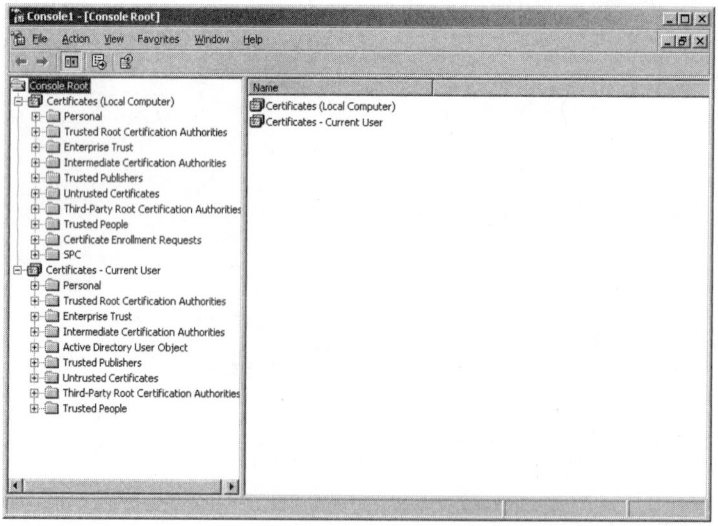

Figure 25-32. *An MMC that has both the local computer and the current user Certificates snap-in installed.*

Under each of these folders is a certificate folder. If you right-click on that certificate folder, you have import, request, or find abilities that are appropriate for each certificate type. For example, you could request a new certificate for the user under the Personal/Certificates folder by right-clicking on that folder, pointing to New, and selecting Request New Certificate. But under the Trusted Root Certificate Authorities, when you right-click on the Certificates folder, you can Import a certificate but not request a new certificate. Hence, the context menus that are presented when you right-click each folder indicate the type of activities in which you can engage.

There are export, import, and certificate request wizards in this snap-in too. These wizards are designed to help you manage the certificates better and more efficiently. Also, a Find feature (right-click the Certificates object or any top-level folder) will help you find a certificate based on an attribute of that certificate.

If you right-click on the Certificates folder under the Personal folder, you can request a new certificate and launch the request wizard. In three short screens, you'll be able to create a new certificate for the user represented by the snap-in. In some ways, this is easier than using the Web enrollment forms, though in large organizations, the Web enrollment forms can greatly reduce administrative effort by having the users create and install their own certificates.

Using this snap-in, you can cut and paste certificates using the context menus. Another feature of this console is the autoenrollment feature. Using this feature, requested certificates can be automatically enrolled so that a certificate-by-certificate manual process is avoided.

The way to ensure that a particular certificate is automatically enrolled when the user requests the certificate is to open the Certificate Template snap-in. You will need to add this snap-in to an existing console or to a new console. After you add the Certificate Template to a console, right-click the Users certificate (it could be any certificate, but the Users certificate will be the one that is most often configured for auto-enrollment) and select to duplicate the template.

Give the template a new name on the General tab (Figure 25-33), configure the validity periods, and then on the Request Handling tab, select the Enroll Subject Without Requiring Any User Input option.

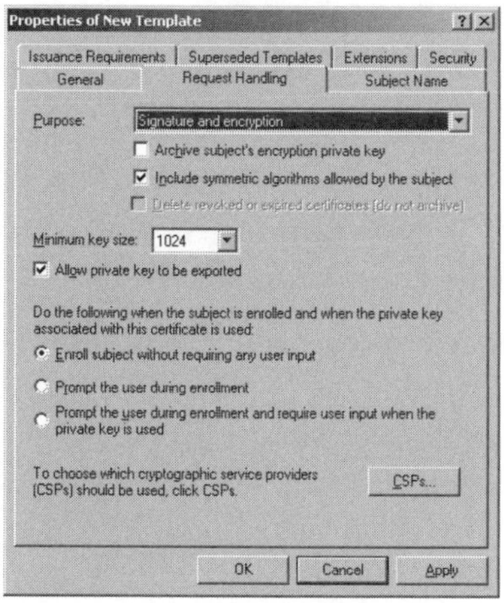

Figure 25-33. *Configuring a user certificate template to autoenroll a user when the certificate request is issued.*

You need to be sure that the Autoenroll permission is applied to the Domain Users security group on the Security tab and that the Publish Certificate In Active Directory check box is selected on the General tab (which it is by default). Then add this certificate to the CA snap-in and allow your users to use that certificate for autoenrollment.

What you should know is that the default group policy in Active Directory 2003 is to enable autoenrollment (Figure 25-34). Hence, in most cases, autoenrollment will happen, whether you are using the Web enrollment forms or the Certificates snap-in functionality.

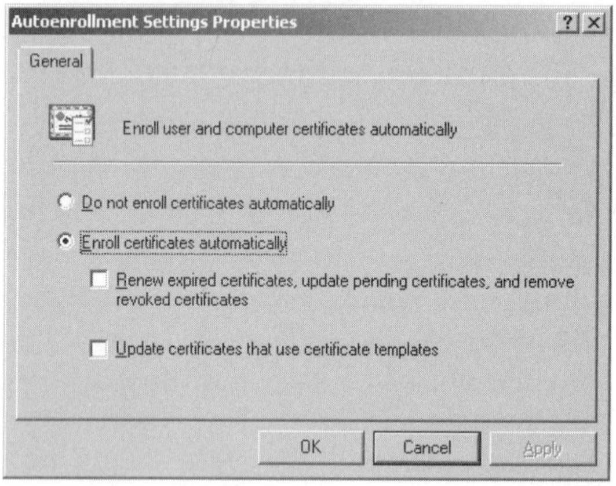

Figure 25-34. *Group Policy Object on the domain object showing the default setting in Active Directory when Windows Server 2003 is installed.*

Understanding How Exchange Server 2003 Integrates with Windows Server 2003 Security

This section focuses on how Exchange Server 2003 uses the Windows Server 2003 security features. The Windows Server 2003 security features can be divided into two broad areas: core operating system features and additional features.

The core operating system features form the basis of a secure implementation of Windows Server 2003. Those features include the following:

- **Active Directory services** Unifies Exchange Server 2003 and Windows Server 2003 objects into one directory
- **Kerberos authentication** Performs authentication for access to domain and local services

- **Access control model** Gives granular control over Active Directory entries and Exchange objects
- **Microsoft Certificate Services** Can be used by other applications to provide security across different layers

Additional applications that enhance the features of the core operating system include the following:

- **IP Security** Used for network, remote access, and virtual private networks
- **Encrypting File System** Provides additional security for mobile users
- **Security Configuration Analyzer** Ensures adherence to security policies

Active Directory

Active Directory in Windows Server 2003 replaces the Security Accounts Manager (SAM) in Windows NT Server 4 as the security database. However, like an object in the SAM, each Active Directory object is given a 96-digit, pseudorandom security identifier (SID) that is globally unique.

Not all objects in Active Directory are assigned a security identifier (SID). For instance, a security group has an SID, but a distribution group does not. Likewise, mail-enabled users have SIDs, but mail-enabled contacts do not. Only those objects that have SIDs can be added to the access control list (ACL) of a resource. If an object does not have an SID, it cannot be placed in the ACL. Therefore, non-SID objects cannot access resources guarded by an ACL.

Kerberos Authentication

Kerberos treats Exchange Server 2003 like a service. When a client needs to contact an Exchange server, the client first requests an Exchange service ticket from the key distribution center (KDC). The ticket is then used for authentication to the Exchange server.

The Exchange services also use Kerberos to make a service account log on to a domain controller through the local system account. This account uses computer credentials that change every seven days. The user name of the Exchange Server 2003 is added to the Exchange Servers group, which is added to the ACL for the core objects.

More Info It is beyond the scope of this book to cover Kerberos authentication in detail. To learn more about Kerberos authentication, what a ticket is, and how this protocol works, consult the "Microsoft Windows 2000 Server Distributed Systems Guide" in the *Microsoft Windows 2000 Server Resource Kit* (Microsoft Press).

Access Control Model

The access control model in Exchange Server 2003 follows that of Windows Server 2003, giving us greater granularity of control for Exchange Server 2003 objects than for Exchange Server 5.5 objects. For instance, you can grant or deny access by container, by item, and at the property level. In addition, Exchange Server 2003 objects are based on the Windows Server 2003 NTFS file system and Active Directory objects. By way of illustration, if a user has access to only five out of the 10 items in a public folder, the user will see only those five items. Moreover, when a user who does not have access rights to certain attributes performs a search, the user has only the results that he or she can see.

Note As you migrate public folders from Exchange 5.5 Server, the distribution lists become distribution groups, which do not have SIDs. As a result, you might need to implement new security settings. In addition, public folders created in Exchange Server 2003 have a Windows Server 2003 ACL. If the folder is to be replicated to the Exchange Server 5.5 system, be sure to test the folder for access control functions, since the ACLs in Windows NT Server 4 and Windows Server 2003 are different.

IP Security

Although KMS provides security on the application layer, IP Security provides security on the IP transport layer; hence, IPSec provides a higher level of security than KMS. In a highly secure environment, IPSec can be used to encrypt information from client to server and from server to server. IPSec works in tandem with Layer 2 Tunneling Protocol (L2TP).

With all these different security features available, you'll need to consider which type of security you would like to implement. Table 25-5 summarizes some of the encryption and authentication methods commonly used today.

Table 25-5. Common encryption and authentication methods

Services	Method Used	Keys
IPSec	Encryption	DES 128-bit
	Authentication	MD5 128-bit
	Integrity	SHA 160-bit
		Kerberos
KMS	Encryption	DES, 3DES 128-bit
	Digital signature	RSA 512-bit
EFS	Encryption	DESX 128-bit

Cross-Forest Authentication

Because Exchange Server 2003 does not allow spoofing or forging of identities, Microsoft has given us a way to perform Cross-Forest Authentication to meet the needs of several scenarios.

One scenario occurs when a company spans two forests and cross-forest e-mail collaboration is needed. Because Exchange is scoped to the forest boundaries, it is a bit silly to set up two sets of contacts in two forests so that everyone in the company can e-mail each other internally and have their e-mail addresses resolve to their display names.

To enable cross-forest authentication, you must create connectors in each forest that uses an authenticated account from the other forest. Once the connectors are set up, e-mail is sent to one forest from the other forest by an authenticated user so that the e-mail addresses will resolve to the display names.

To configure cross-forest authentication, follow these steps:

1. Create an account in each forest that has Send As permissions in the target forest. Add this account to the properties of each Exchange server that will accept incoming e-mail from the other forest.
2. Create an SMTP Connector in the source forest that requires using authentication to send e-mail, and configure the connector to use the account in the target forest for all outgoing e-mail. On the SMTP Connector, ensure that you've configured the address space to include the specific target domain with a cost of "1". Do not include an address space of "*" or any domain name. This will ensure that the SMTP Connector is used only when e-mail is sent between these domains.
3. Do the reverse going the other way between the two forests.

Now, when e-mail is sent between domains, the display names will resolve to the Global Address List names, which is often easier for your users to understand than the external SMTP addresses.

Summary

This chapter provided an overview of approaches to securing messages in Exchange Server 2003. As security technologies become increasingly important and common, you will find that many companies are hiring teams of people who focus only on security. In this chapter, you learned how to install and use Certificate Services and Key Management Service, as well as how to perform some of the more common administrative tasks associated with each service. In the next chapter, we turn our attention away from security to learn how to connect Exchange Server 2003 to other messaging systems.

Part VIII
Maintenance

Chapter 26

Monitoring Exchange Server 2003

One key to running a successful network is keeping a close eye on its operation, especially if you are running a complex system such as a Microsoft Exchange Server 2003. By keeping close watch over your organization and its components, you can spot potential problems before they occur and can quickly respond to the problems that do occur. Monitoring also allows you to identify trends in network use that signal opportunities for optimization and future planning.

This chapter covers many of the tools that you can use to monitor Exchange Server 2003. Some of these tools, such as Event Viewer and System Monitor, are provided by Microsoft Windows Server 2003. Other tools, such as server and link monitors, are part of Exchange Server 2003 itself.

Using Event Viewer

As you might know, Windows Server 2003 records many events in its own event logs. You can view the logs of both local and remote servers by using the Event Viewer utility, which you can find in the Administrative Tools folder on the Programs menu. Windows maintains three distinct logs:

- **Application** The application log is a record of events generated by applications. All Exchange Server 2003 services write their status information to this log. If you enable diagnostics logging for any Exchange components, that information is also recorded in the application log. This log is the most valuable one for monitoring the general health of an Exchange server. Figure 26-1 shows an entry made in the application log following a directory access error.
- **Security** The security log is a record of events based on the auditing settings specified in the local policy of a machine or by group policy that applies to the machine.

- **System** The system log is a record of events that concern components of the system itself, including such events as device driver and network failures.

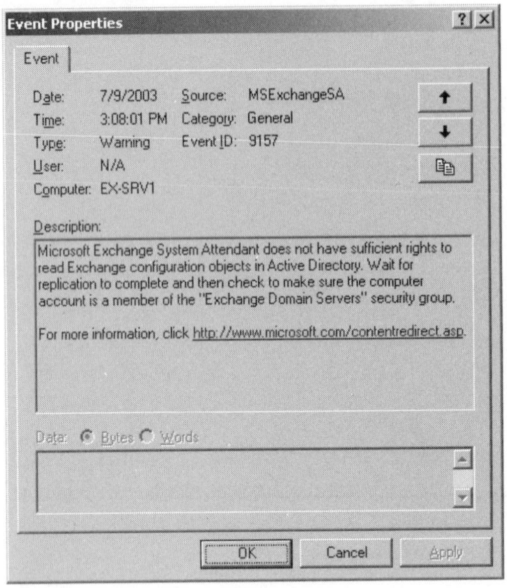

Figure 26-1. *Reviewing an application event created by Exchange Server 2003.*

Note You might also see additional event logs in Event Viewer based upon the services installed on your server. For example, a server running Domain Name System (DNS) will show a DNS Service log. Domain controllers will also show a File Replication Service and Directory Service log.

If you have a particular log file that you want to save, you have at your disposal three formats in which to save it. You can save it as a binary event log file with the .EVT extension, as a text file with the .TXT extension, or as a comma-delimited text file with the .CSV extension. Binary files with the .EVT extension can be read only with Event Viewer; the two text files can be read with your favorite ASCII editor/viewer.

You will encounter five types of events in the three logs, and a unique icon identifies each event type so that you can easily distinguish between the information entries and the error entries. Table 26-1 shows these icons and describes each of them. Normally, you will encounter only the first three icons in the table in relation to Exchange Server. The classification of events is controlled by the applications and system and cannot be configured by the administrators.

Table 26-1. Event types displayed in Event Viewer

Icon	Event	Description
	Error	A significant problem has occurred, such as an Exchange Server service that may not have started properly.
	Warning	An event has occurred that is not currently detrimental to the system but might indicate a possible future problem.
	Information	A successful operation has occurred. For example, an Exchange Server service starting successfully might trigger this type of event.
	Audit success	An audited security access attempt—for example, a successful logon to the system—was successful.
	Audit failure	An audited security access attempt—for example, a failed access to an audited file or directory—was not successful.

Using Diagnostics Logging

All Exchange Server 2003 services log certain critical events to the Windows Server 2003 application log. For some services, however, you can configure additional levels of diagnostics logging. Diagnostics logging is one of the most useful tools for troubleshooting problems in Exchange Server 2003.

You can modify the levels of diagnostics logging for all services on a particular Exchange server by using the Diagnostics Logging tab of the server's property sheet in the Exchange System snap-in, as shown in Figure 26-2. On the left side of this tab, you'll find a hierarchical view of all of the services on the server for which you can enable advanced diagnostics logging. On the right side, you'll find a list of categories that can be logged for the selected service.

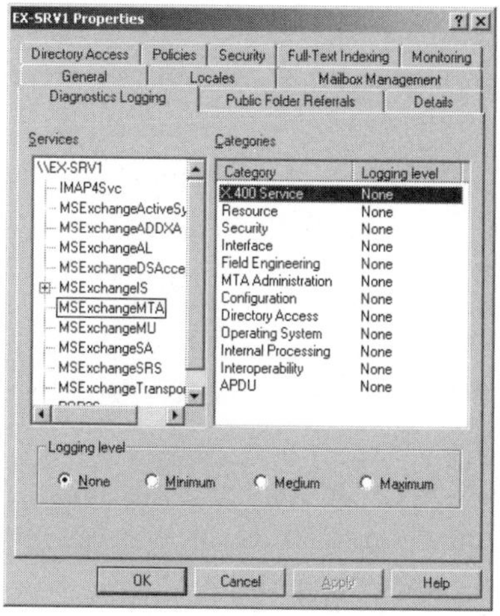

Figure 26-2. *Viewing diagnostics logging categories.*

Real World Size of the Event Viewer Application Log

Diagnostics logging of Exchange Server 2003 components generates many entries in the Event Viewer application log, especially if you have the diagnostics logging level set to Maximum. You should use diagnostics logging only when you are troubleshooting potential problems in specific components, and you should disable it when you are finished. By default, the application log file is set to a maximum size of 512 KB. We generally recommend setting this size to at least 1 MB for general use and even larger when using diagnostics logging. By default, each log file overwrites events older than seven days.

You can configure the default settings for size and overwriting by changing the Maximum Log Size and Event Log Wrapping options on the property sheet for the log. To see this property sheet, in Event Viewer, right-click the log in question and click Properties. The options are in the Log Size area of the General tab. The Maximum Log Size option can be adjusted in 64-KB increments.

You can choose from among three Event Log Wrapping options. They are Overwrite Events As Needed, Overwrite Events Older Than X Days, and Do Not Overwrite Events. (If you select the last option you must clear the log manually.) Make sure that you have set the wrapping option correctly for what you are trying to accomplish. For example, if you have it set to Overwrite Events As Needed, you could lose critical information that might have helped you solve the problem you had when you turned diagnostics on in the first place.

All the major services are represented on this property sheet, including the following:

- **IMAP4Svc** Provides Internet Message Access Protocol (IMAP4) services to clients. If this service is stopped, clients are unable to connect to this computer using the IMAP4 protocol.
- **MSExchangeActiveSyncNotify** Use diagnostics logging on this service to troubleshoot problems with the synchronization between wireless clients and Exchange Server using ActiveSync.
- **MSExchangeADDXA (Microsoft Exchange Active Directory Directory Synchronization Agent)** Use diagnostics logging on this service to troubleshoot problems with directory synchronization with Active Directory.

- **MSExchangeAL (Microsoft Exchange Address List)** Use diagnostics logging on this service to troubleshoot problems with creation and synchronization of address lists.
- **MSExchangeDSAccess (Microsoft Exchange Directory Services Access)** Use diagnostics logging on this service to troubleshoot problems with Active Directory access and interaction.
- **MSExchangeIS (Microsoft Exchange Information Store Service)** You do not actually enable logging for the Information Store service as a whole. The MSExchangeIS item expands, allowing you to enable diagnostics logging individually for the public folder store and the mailbox store and for the various Internet protocols, as shown in Figure 26-3. Use diagnostics logging on this service to monitor background tasks that occur in Exchange, such as information store maintenance.

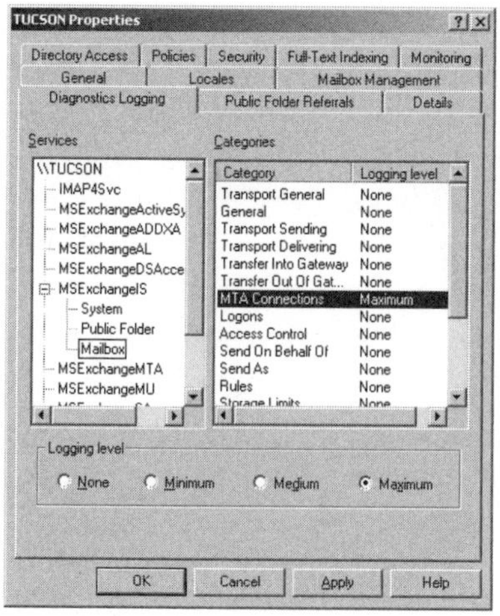

Figure 26-3. *Enabling diagnostics logging for components of the information store.*

- **MSExchangeMTA (Microsoft Exchange Message Transfer Agent)** Use diagnostics logging on this service to troubleshoot problems with message delivery and gateway connectivity.
- **MSExchangeSA (Microsoft Exchange System Attendant)** Provides monitoring, maintenance, and Active Directory lookup services, for example, monitoring of services and connectors, defragmenting the Exchange store, and forwarding Active Directory lookups to a Global Catalog server. If this service is stopped, monitoring, maintenance, and lookup services are unavailable. If this service is disabled, any services that explicitly depend on it will fail to start.

- **POP3Svc Provides Post Office Protocol version 3 (POP3) Services to clients.** If this service is stopped, clients are unable to connect to this computer using the POP3 protocol.

You can enable four distinct levels of logging. All events that occur in Exchange Server 2003 are given an event level of 0, 1, 3, or 5. The logging level you set will determine which levels of events are logged. Those levels are:

- **None** Only events with a logging level of 0 are logged. These events include application and system failures.
- **Minimum** All events with a logging level of 1 or lower are logged.
- **Medium** All events with a logging level of 3 or lower are logged.
- **Maximum** All events with a logging level of 5 or lower are logged. All events concerning a particular service are logged.

Real World Using High Levels of Diagnostics Logging

Although diagnostics logging can be a very useful tool in some circumstances, at other times it can be more of a hindrance than a help. Enabling high levels of diagnostics logging, such as Medium or Maximum, can fill up your event log quickly, often hiding important level 0 events in a flood of trivial events. In addition, many events are logged that might seem like errors but actually are not. These events include the routine errors and timeouts that occur in normal Exchange Server 2003 operation.

Finally, many events will be logged that are really not documented anywhere in the product literature. Exchange developers often use these undocumented events to perform diagnostics.

Our recommendation is to leave diagnostics logging set to None for general purposes. If you need to troubleshoot malfunctions of particular services, try setting the diagnostics logging level to Low or Medium for brief periods.

Using Exchange Monitors

Exchange Server 2003 provides server monitors and connection status indicators that help you watch over your organization by checking the status of servers and connectors. *Server monitors* check the status of designated services as well as the usage of various resources on a particular Exchange server. *Connection status indicators* check the status of a connector between two servers. You configure monitoring of both types of objects using the Exchange System.

To view the available monitors, navigate to the Tools container, expand the Monitoring and Status folder, and select the Status container. The available monitors are displayed in the contents pane, as shown in Figure 26-4. The objects shown are those monitored by the server to which you are currently connected. To view the monitored objects on a different server, right-click the Status container and choose Connect To from the shortcut menu. This displays a list of servers from which you can choose.

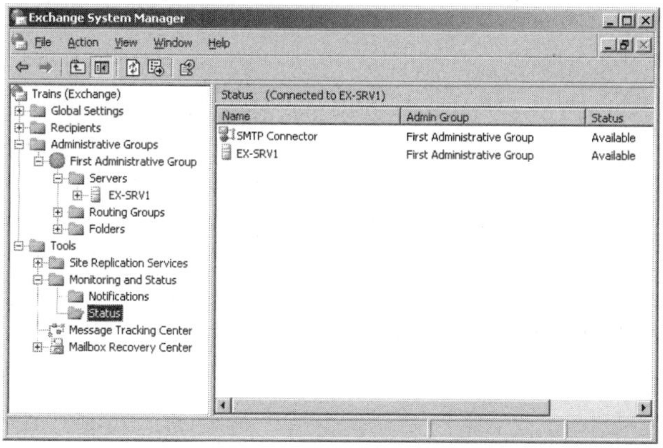

Figure 26-4. *Viewing the existing monitors on a server.*

In addition to specifying what you want to monitor, you also need to configure how you will be notified of any problems with your servers or connectors. This is covered later in the chapter, in the section "Using Notifications."

Using Server Monitors

A server monitor checks designated resources and Windows services on a server to detect critical situations. This type of monitor is created automatically when you install Exchange Server 2003. Server monitors allow you to monitor the status of six important resources:

- Windows services
- SMTP queues
- X.400 queues
- CPU utilization
- Free disk space
- Available virtual memory

To configure the resources to be monitored, right-click the server monitor you want to modify in the Status container and choose Properties.

Note In Microsoft Exchange Server 5.5, you must create a monitor manually for each server, and the Exchange Administrator utility must be running for the monitor to work. In Exchange Server 2003 (and in Exchange 2000 Server), server monitors are created automatically, and they run all the time, regardless of whether you keep Exchange System running.

Windows Services

By default, a server monitor checks various Windows services that affect the performance of Exchange Server 2003. There is a preconfigured set of such services, which will appear as a default set in the server object's properties in the Status folder (Figure 26-5). You can view or edit the services being monitored by selecting the default set of resources and clicking the Detail button. The services shown in Figure 26-6 all have some impact on Exchange Server 2000.

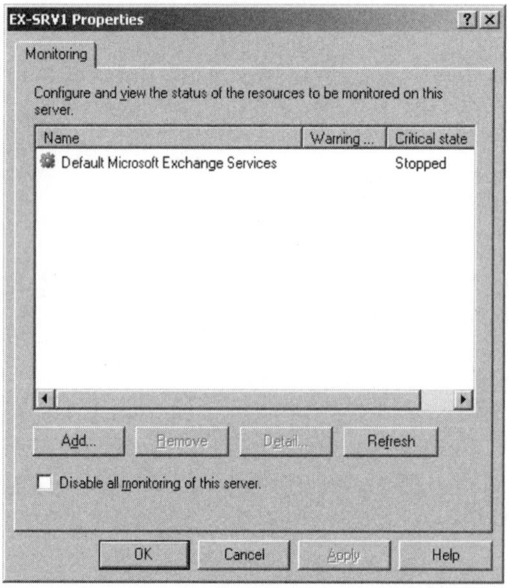

Figure 26-5. *Viewing the resources being monitored.*

You might want to add additional services such as an antivirus service or a backup agent so that you are monitoring not only Exchange Server 2003 but also those services related to the overall functionality of the Exchange organization. You can either add these services to the existing list or create a separate set of Windows services to monitor. To create a separate set, click the Add button on the server's property sheet (refer back to Figure 26-5). The Add Resource dialog box appears, listing the six resources you can monitor (Figure 26-7). Select Windows 2000 Service and click OK. The Services dialog box opens (Figure 26-8). Give the group of services a descriptive name, and add the services you want to monitor by clicking the Add button and selecting them from the resulting list.

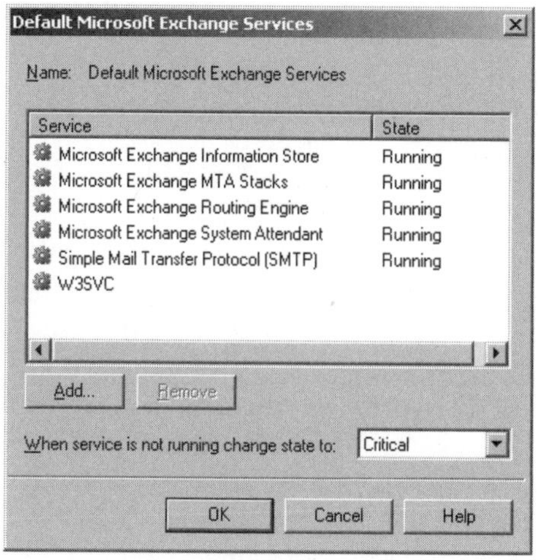

Figure 26-6. *Viewing the Exchange-related services that are monitored by default.*

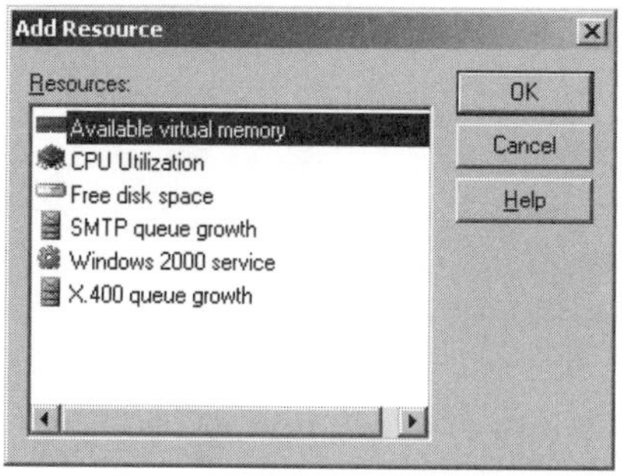

Figure 26-7. *Viewing the resources you can monitor.*

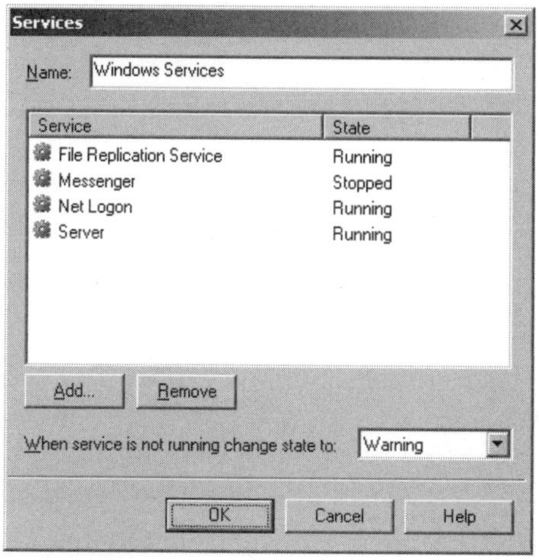

Figure 26-8. *Adding services to be monitored.*

Note The Add Resource dialog box you see when configuring a server monitor shows Windows 2000 Service regardless of whether you are monitoring a server running Windows 2000 Server or Windows Server 2003.

For each group of resources you want to monitor, you need to specify the state the monitor will be in should those resources fail. You have two choices: Warning or Critical. The state you choose determines what notifications are made should the resource cross a certain threshold. (See the section "Using Notifications" later in the chapter.)

Tip At first, you might want to add other Windows services to be monitored along with the default group of services. However, best practice is to separate additional Windows services that are to be monitored by creating a new group for them. The state that a monitor triggers will determine which group a particular service belongs in. If any of the services being monitored in a group fail, one group of monitored services can trigger a Warning state, whereas the other can trigger a Critical state.

SMTP and X.400 Queue Growth

The server monitor can monitor both the SMTP and X.400 queues for continuous queue growth. With this type of monitoring, the server monitor is looking not for a certain number of entries in each queue but rather for continual growth of the length of the queue over time. When you add monitoring for either type of queue from the server's property sheet, you see the appropriate Queue Thresholds dialog box (Figure 26-9), where you specify the number of minutes of continual queue growth that will cause the server to enter a Warning or Critical state.

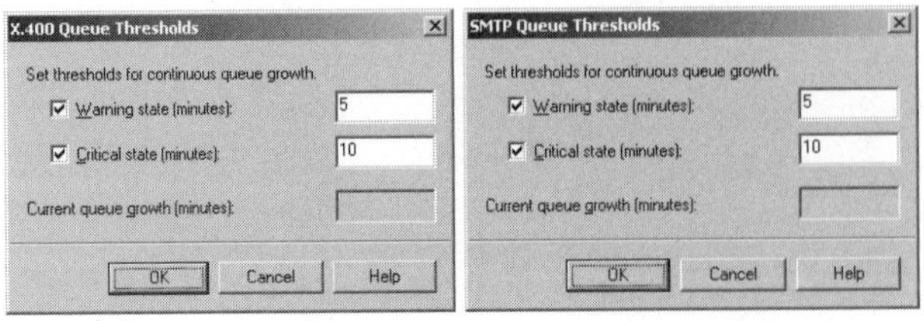

Figure 26-9. *Setting X.400 and SMTP queue thresholds.*

CPU Utilization

A CPU running at a high utilization percentage can indicate either that too many services are running on one server or that the server does not have enough processing power. For this reason, it is a good idea to monitor the server's CPU utilization. You can specify how long the CPU should run above a certain utilization percentage before the server's state changes to Warning or Critical, as well as set the threshold utilization percentages, as shown in Figure 26-10.

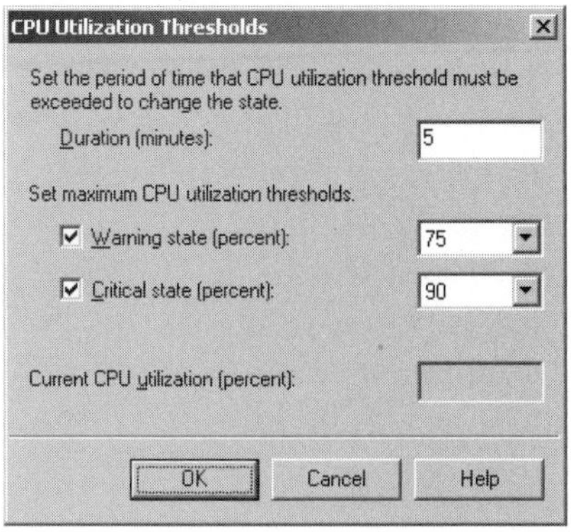

Figure 26-10. *Setting CPU utilization thresholds.*

Note The CPU utilization monitoring capability in Exchange Server 2003 is a great enhancement over the CPU monitoring in Microsoft Windows NT 4 and Exchange Server 5.5, in which you have to use Performance Monitor when you want to monitor server CPU utilization. Even then, you can check only for each instance in which the server exceeds the specified CPU utilization and react either the first time or *every* time. It is when CPU utilization remains high over a period of time that you truly have a problem. The CPU monitoring in Exchange Server 2003 gives a more realistic picture of your server's performance.

Free Disk Space

Exchange Server 2003 can suffer adverse effects if it runs out of disk space. That is why it is important to monitor your server's free disk space and be notified when you need to take action by freeing up disk space or replacing drives with larger ones. Disk space is monitored on a per drive basis. You can specify which drive to monitor and the levels of free disk space below which the server will enter a Warning or Critical state (Figure 26-11).

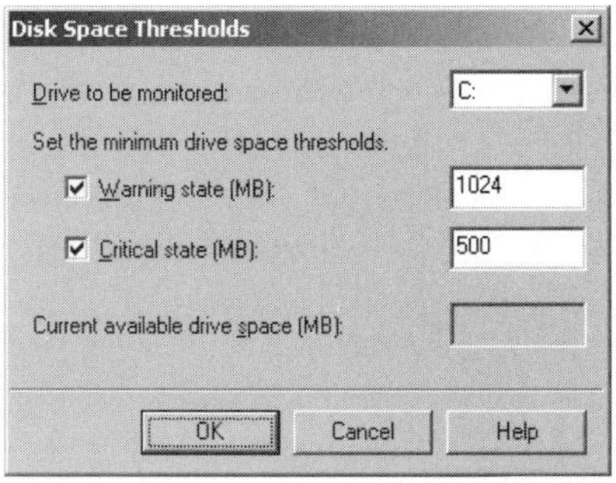

Figure 26-11. *Setting disk space thresholds.*

Available Virtual Memory

Because Windows uses a virtual memory model (one in which the server's memory consists of the physical memory and a page file on disk working together to provide memory services to other system processes), it is important to get an idea of how much memory is available, whether in RAM or on disk. As with CPU utilization, you need to know not only whether the server dips below a certain usage threshold for memory, but whether it remains below that threshold over a period of time. You can specify how long the server's available virtual memory should remain below the specified thresholds before the server's state changes to Warning or Critical (Figure 26-12).

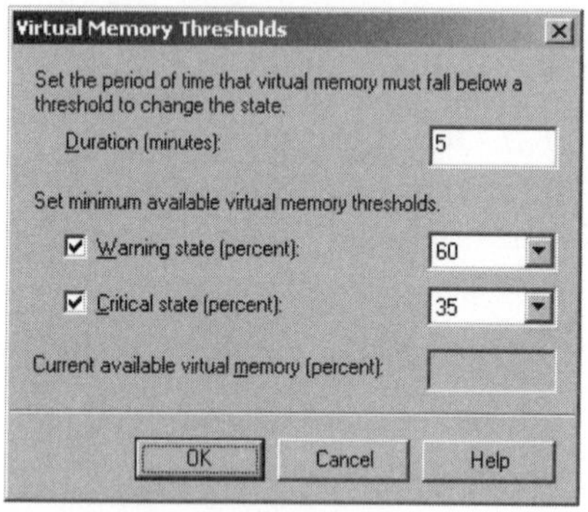

Figure 26-12. *Setting virtual memory thresholds.*

Using Link Monitors

A link monitor is automatically created for each connector present on a server. Like server monitors, link monitors are displayed in the Status container in the Exchange System snap-in (refer back to Figure 26-4). The status of each link monitor is listed as either available or unavailable. Unlike server monitors, there is really nothing you need to configure for a link monitor.

When a link monitor indicates that a connector is unavailable, you can troubleshoot the connector using the Queue Viewer, which is an embedded utility found in the Protocol container in the Exchange System snap-in. For instance, to troubleshoot an SMTP queue problem, you would look at the queues that were created under the SMTP virtual server for the server in question. You might also want to use Exchange Server's message tracking feature, which is described later in the section "Tracking Messages," to see where messages are getting stuck.

Using Notifications

If a server crashes in the middle of the forest and there is nobody to hear, does it make a sound? Monitoring a server is useless if no one is notified when problems occur. Thus, to complete the loop, you need to configure how you want to be notified of specific problems. Exchange Server 2003 gives you the ability to send notifications using e-mail, a script of commands when the monitor enters a given state, or both of these methods. To add a notification, navigate to the Notifications container under Monitoring And Status. Right-click Notifications, point to New, and choose either E-Mail Notification or Script Notification.

Setting Up an E-Mail Notification

If you choose to be notified by e-mail, Exchange Server 2003 provides you with a default detailed e-mail message that lists the current status of all six types of resources that can be monitored. All you have to do to set up e-mail notification is provide information about the resources in question and indicate which state will trigger the e-mail notification (Warning or Critical).

In the property sheet that appears when you choose New E-Mail Notification (Figure 26-13), use the Monitoring Server option to specify which server will perform the monitoring function. Choosing a value for the Servers And Connectors To Monitor option is the most critical step: be careful not to have a server configured to monitor a specific resource with no notifications set up to act upon that monitor. Table 26-2 lists the values for this option and the monitoring scope of each value.

Note We do not recommend that you use an Exchange server to monitor itself. If a Warning or Critical state occurs on a self-monitoring Exchange server, the server might not be able to send e-mail to an administrator. Therefore, you should plan on setting up cross-monitoring of your Exchange servers.

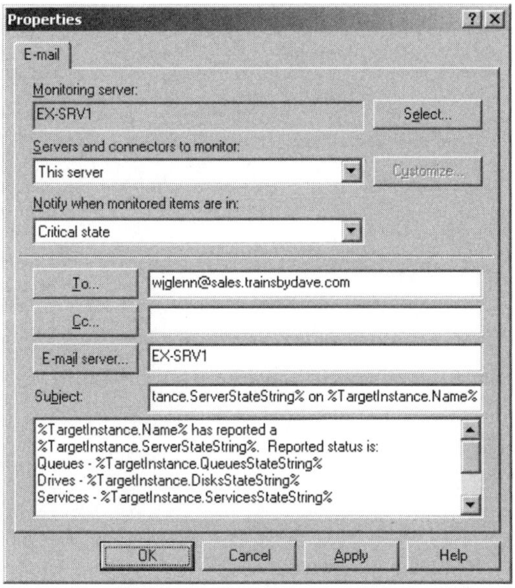

Figure 26-13. *Property sheet for a new e-mail notification.*

Table 26-2. Choices on the Servers And Connectors To Monitor list

Value	Monitoring Scope
This Server	Monitors a specific server for Critical or Warning states.
All Servers	Monitors all Exchange servers for Critical or Warning states.
Any Server In The Routing Group	Monitors any server in the routing group for Critical or Warning states.
All Connectors	Monitors all connectors in the Exchange organization for Critical or Warning states.
Any Connector In The Routing Group	Monitors all connectors in a specific Exchange routing group for Critical or Warning states.
Custom List Of Servers	Allows you to create a customized list of servers to be monitored for Critical or Warning states. After you select this option, click Customize to add servers to the list.
Custom List Of Connectors	Allows you to create a customized list of connectors to be monitored for Critical or Warning states. After you select this option, click Customize to add connectors to the list.

The next step is to establish the recipients of the notification message, using the To and Cc fields (refer back to Figure 26-13). To provide the name of the e-mail server that will deliver the message, either enter the fully qualified domain name (FQDN) of the SMTP server or click the E-Mail Server button to retrieve a list of available Exchange servers.

If you choose to enter the FQDN of an SMTP server, the SMTP server you specify must allow the Exchange server to send e-mail using anonymous relay. Otherwise, e-mail notifications will not be delivered. A well-administered e-mail system will most likely not allow relaying anonymously, so you will need to carefully select the SMTP server that will deliver the notification.

Notice that the subject and message fields in Figure 26-13 are already filled in to provide a default message that informs the recipient of the nature of the notification. You can, of course, modify these fields to meet your own needs, using plain text and Windows Management Instrumentation placeholders.

Note You can use e-mail to provide both immediate notification as well as a historical record of a problem. You can provide immediate notification by sending a message to an alphanumeric pager or cellular phone via a mail-enabled contact while maintaining a historical record by sending a notification to a public folder.

Setting Up a Script Notification

A script notification differs from an e-mail notification in that it runs an executable file rather than sending an e-mail. This type of notification gives you the flexibility to start a variety of processes, limited only by your need, your imagination, and the existence of the needed executable. For example, if a monitor found that the SMTP queue was growing significantly, perhaps indicating that a VB Script–based e-mail virus was running rampant through your system, you could use a script notification to issue a NET STOP command to shut down all Exchange services on your server by stopping the System Attendant service on which they all depend (Figure 26-14).

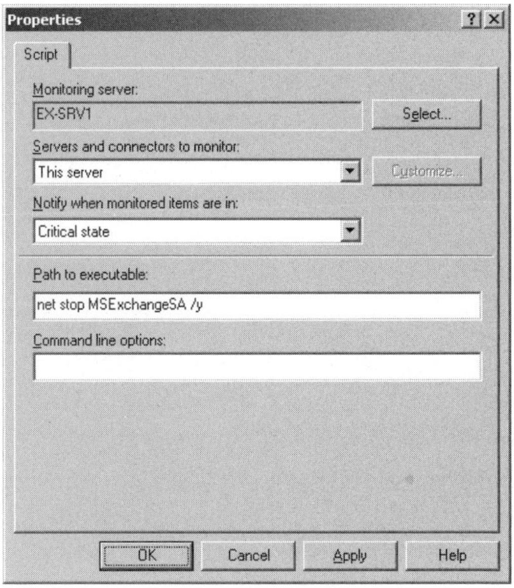

Figure 26-14. *Property sheet for a new script notification.*

Don't forget that you can use a combination of e-mail and script notifications for the same monitored resources. For instance, in the example just given, in addition to having a script notification that shuts down Exchange Server 2003, you could have an e-mail notification that sends an e-mail to your alphanumeric pager using an SMTP server not running Exchange Server 2003.

You will most likely have to experiment a bit with the resources you want to monitor and the notifications in order to establish the correct thresholds, the servers and connectors to be monitored, and the recipients who should be notified.

Tracking Messages

Message tracking is enabled at the server level, using the property sheet for the server container. Once message tracking is enabled, Exchange Server keeps a log of all messages transferred to and from the server. Log files are maintained by the System Attendant service on each server. When message tracking is enabled, you can track individual messages by using the Message Tracking Center (MTC), a component of the Exchange System snap-in.

Enabling Message Tracking for a Server

Before you can use message tracking for a server, you must enable it. Right-click a server in System Manager and choose Properties. On the General tab of the property sheet, select the Enable message tracking option. Exchange informs you that to track messages, you must first grant read access to the share at *\\servername\\servername.log* for any users that need to perform message tracking. You can also use options on the General tab to automatically remove log files after a certain number of days (which helps keep them small) and change the location of the log file itself.

Once message tracking is enabled for a server, all messages transported by that server are noted in the message tracking log. You'll use the Message Tracking Center to search the log.

Using the Message Tracking Center

You launch the MTC by first navigating to and selecting the Message Tracking Center container in the Exchange System snap-in, as shown in Figure 26-15. You can search for messages by the message ID, sender, server, recipients, or message dates (or a combination of any of these). Note, however, that you must specify the server on which you want to search.

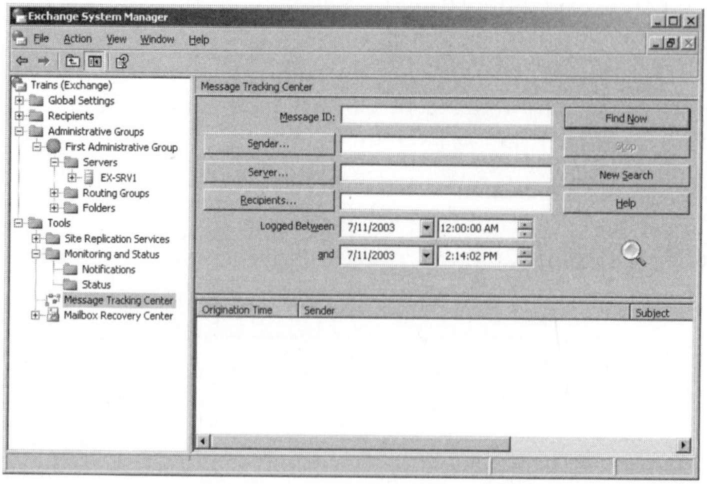

Figure 26-15. *Navigating to the Message Tracking Center container.*

Tip Every message transferred in an Exchange organization has a unique ID that includes the name of the originating Exchange server, the date, and a long series of digits. Choosing this option is best when you want to track one specific message, such as a test message that you create. You can find the ID for any message by viewing the properties of a copy of the message in a mail client.

Fill in the information or click any of the buttons to the left of the fields to browse for objects like users or servers. After you enter your criteria, click Find Now to perform the search. Figure 26-16 shows all messages that were sent to Jim Hance.

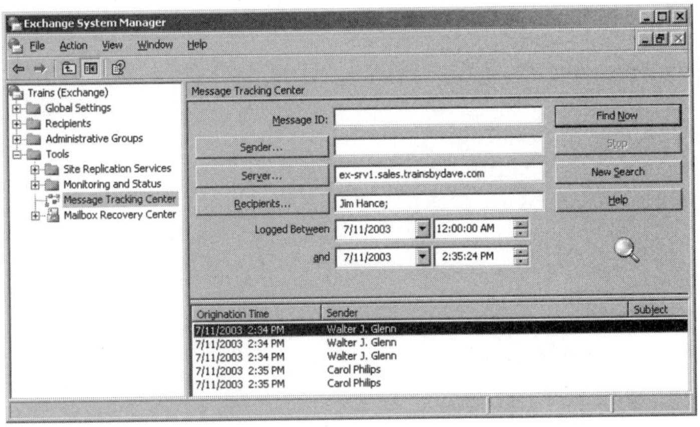

Figure 26-16. *Message Tracking Center dialog box, showing all messages to Jim Hance.*

Once the messages that meet your criteria are displayed, you can open the history of any message by just clicking it. A sample Message History dialog box is shown in Figure 26-17. As you can see, this dialog box displays basic information and a history of the message.

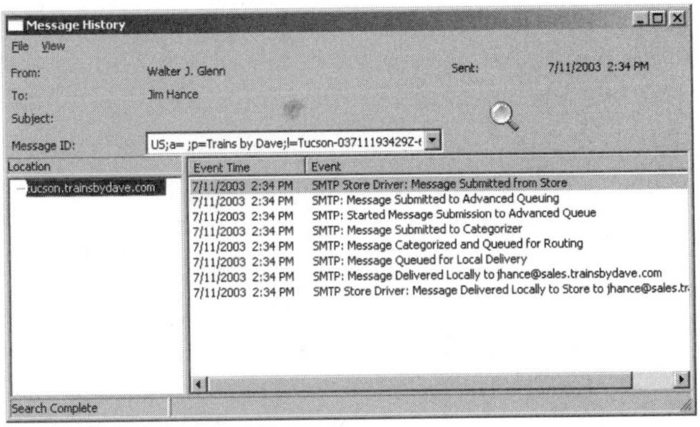

Figure 26-17. *Viewing the history of a message.*

Using System Monitor

System Monitor is a tool that is included with Windows and is available in the Administrative Tools folder. System Monitor graphically charts the performance of hundreds of individual system parameters on a computer running Microsoft Windows Server 2003. When Exchange Server 2003 is installed on a Windows server, you can chart several Exchange-specific counters as well. Chapter 29, "Tuning Exchange Server 2003 Performance," describes in detail how to use System Monitor.

Using SNMP and the MADMAN MIB

Simple Network Management Protocol (SNMP) is a standard, nonsecure communication protocol used to collect information from devices on a TCP/IP network. SNMP was developed within the Internet community to monitor activity on network devices such as routers and bridges. Since then, acceptance of and support for SNMP have grown. Many devices, including computers running Windows, can now be monitored with SNMP.

How SNMP Works

SNMP has a small command set and maintains a centralized database of management information. An SNMP system has three parts:

- **SNMP Agent** The SNMP Agent is the device on a network that is being monitored. This device is typically a computer that has the SNMP Agent software installed. Windows Server 2003 includes SNMP Agent software in the form of the Microsoft SNMP Service. (You install SNMP Service by using Add/Remove Windows Components in the Add/Remove Programs Control Panel tool.)
- **SNMP Management System** The SNMP Management System is the component that does the actual monitoring in an SNMP environment. Windows does not provide an SNMP Management System. Third-party SNMP Management Systems include Hewlett-Packard's OpenView and IBM's NetView.
- **Management Information Base** The Management Information Base (MIB) is a centralized database of all the values that can be monitored for all of the devices in an SNMP system. Different MIBs are provided for monitoring different types of devices and systems. Windows Server 2003 comes with four MIBs: Internet MIB II, LAN Manager MIB II, DHCP MIB, and WINS MIB. These four MIBs allow the remote monitoring and management of most components of Windows.

Exchange Server 2003 and the MADMAN MIB

Exchange Server 2003 includes a special MIB that you can use to enable an SNMP Management System that manages many Exchange Server 2003 functions. This MIB is based on a standardized MIB named the Mail and Directory Management (MADMAN) MIB, which is detailed in RFC 1566. Microsoft's implementation of the MADMAN MIB meets all the specifications of the standard and adds a few touches of its own. The Exchange MADMAN MIB works by converting the System Monitor counters for the MTA and IMS objects to MIBs, using utilities provided with the *Microsoft Windows Server 2003 Resource Kit* Tools, available at *http://www.microsoft.com/downloads/details.aspx?familyid=9d467a69-57ff-4ae7-96ee-b18c4790cffd&displaylang=en;* or link to the tools from *http://www.microsoft.com/windowsserver2003/downloads/default.mspx.*

> **More Info** Despite its name, Simple Network Management Protocol is not so simple to use. This chapter offers only a glimpse of it so that you will know that it is available. If you are interested in deploying SNMP in your Exchange organization, consult the *Microsoft Windows 2000 Server Resource Kit* (Microsoft Press).

Summary

This chapter described how to monitor your network, which is crucial in spotting problems before they grow too large. It also covered many of the tools used to monitor Exchange Server 2003, including Event Viewer, diagnostics logging, and the various types of monitors that are available. The next chapter turns to another aspect of maintenance: approaches to backing up and restoring Exchange servers.

Chapter 27

Disaster Recovery of an Exchange Server 2003 Database

This chapter focuses on the backup and recovery of your Microsoft Exchange Server 2003 databases. You will learn how to perform a recovery of an Exchange Server 2003 database and become familiar with the differences between recovery in Microsoft Exchange 5.5 and recovery in Exchange Server 2003. You will also learn about a new feature in Windows Server 2003 named Volume Shadow Copy and how it integrates with Exchange Server 2003.

Backup and Restore Strategy

It goes without saying that you must have a good backup strategy before you can have a good recovery strategy. Implementing a solid plan and maintaining database consistency can improve the integrity of any Exchange Server 2003 database.

Your backup strategy determines your restore strategy. These operations cannot be planned separately. When you create a backup strategy, you should also consider how you would like to restore your databases. For example, ensure you have enough hard disk space to restore both the database and the log files. If you generate 2000 log files in a single week, you've got 10 GB of information to (potentially) restore. Add to that your database sizes, and you'll begin to see why you need to plan your restore strategy along with your backup strategy.

You can't perform a restore without knowing that your backups are working. You should be verifying your backup jobs every day to ensure you can perform successful restores. Failure to verify backups is a common mistake because it is easy to assume that backup tapes are swapped and that data is backed up properly. Make it part of your daily routine to review all backup logs and to follow up on any errors or inconsistencies.

Understanding the Extensible Storage Engine (ESE) and the Web Storage System (WSS) that is built on the ESE engine are also important to understand before planning your backup and restore strategy. In Chapter 2, "Understanding

Exchange Server Storage Architecture," we outlined how this database works. In this chapter, we dive a bit deeper into parts of ESE that are relevant to the recovery on an ESE database, so be sure you are familiar with the concepts in Chapter 2.

Database GUID

Each ESE database has a globally unique identifier (GUID) that is assigned to the database and stored in Active Directory. This is important to understand, because if the GUIDs do not match at any point, the databases will not mount.

Mailbox GUID

Not only does each database have its own GUID, but each mailbox in the database has a unique GUID too. The mailbox GUID becomes an attribute of the user account in Active Directory to which the mailbox is assigned.

This is why you can disconnect and reconnect mailboxes between different user accounts. This also means that even though you can delete a user from Active Directory, the mailbox still exists in the database if you've configured a Deleted Mailbox Retention time. The default value is 30 days, meaning that when you delete a mail-enabled user account, the mailbox persists in the database for an additional 30 days after the user account is deleted.

Log File Signature

Each transaction log set has a unique signature that is written to the header of each transaction log in the set. If, for some reason, you delete all the log files in your transaction log set, when you restart the server, the ESE creates a new series of log files, starting with a generation number of one. Because log files can have the same name, the ESE stamps the header in each file series with a unique signature so that it can distinguish between different series of log files.

Circular Logging

Except on Exchange Server 2003 servers where recovery of information is *not* important, circular logging is a bad idea. *Circular logging* is intended to reduce storage requirements for the transaction logs after the transactions in the logs are committed to the databases. Fortunately, circular logging is disabled by default.

Checksum

The *checksum* (also called a message hash) is a string of 4-byte bits that is calculated and then added to each page in the database to verify the integrity of each page. The checksum itself doesn't guarantee data integrity; instead, the recalculation of the checksum when the page is read into RAM ensures that the data being read from the database is identical to the data that was written to the database.

In terms of the overall page construction, the first 82 bytes of the database page contain the header information, which contains flags for the type of page as well as information about what kind of data the page contains. When a page is loaded into RAM, the checksum is calculated and the page number is verified. If the checksum doesn't match the one that was written to the page when the page was written to the database, we can be sure that the page is damaged or corrupted. ESE will return an error, the database is stopped, and an event is logged informing you of the damage.

Note that ESE does not cause the damage to the page—it merely reports the damage to you. In nearly all instances, corruption to the database is the result of a hardware device or a device driver malfunctioning. ESE cannot cause page-level corruptions. These corruptions occur when the data is written to the disk and are caused by your hardware or device drivers. This is why it is imperative that you ensure all your firmware and device drivers are using the latest patches and updates. Microsoft Product Support Services (PSS) will work with your hardware manufacturer to resolve any problems that might exist between your hardware and your Exchange Server 2003 database.

Single Database Backup

In Exchange Server 2003, you can use the backup tool included with Windows Server 2003 to back up a single database. If you select an individual database for backup, the backup software will back up the .edb and .stm files for that database along with the needed transaction log files in the storage group. Best practice would be to back up the entire set of transaction logs when backing up an individual database.

You'll also need Backup Operator permissions on the backup computer. Windows Server 2003 backup uses the permissions of the current logon to do the backup. Third-party backup utilities can function like Windows Server 2003 services, which use permissions from the service startup parameters. These are typically the permissions set in the LocalSystem account.

Domain and Configuration Partitions

When it comes to a full server recovery, you must understand that your Exchange Server 2003 configuration information, such as your Administrative Group or Routing Group configurations, is held in the configuration partition of Active Directory. Objects that are mail-enabled are in the domain partition, and if those objects have mailboxes, the mailboxes are stored in the Exchange databases.

Hence, remembering to back up your Active Directory System State data as well as your Exchange databases is critical. Both sets of information are required to perform a full system restoration.

You'll also need to back up the Microsoft Internet Information Services (IIS) metabase. The *metabase* is a structure for storing IIS configuration settings, some of which pertain directly to your Exchange deployment, such as Microsoft Outlook Web Access and Microsoft Outlook Mobile Access synchronization. Failure to back up the IIS metabase will result in the need to rebuild or reinstall portions of Exchange Server 2003. You can view the metabase using utilities such as MetaEdit and Mdutil.

Don't confuse the IIS metabase with the metabase update service in Exchange Server 2003. The metabase update service reads data from Active Directory and writes it into the local IIS metabase. When this service is notified by Active Directory that changes have occurred in the directory, the service gathers these changes and then updates the metabase automatically.

Backing up all the files on a local hard drive is common. However, the file system backup method is not the best method of backing up the IIS metabase because the metabase maintains dependencies on other components that are not saved using a straight file system backup. Also, the backup file might be undergoing modifications at the time of backup. The best method of backup is to perform a system state backup, which backs up the metabase.

Types of Backups

You can perform five basic types of backups with the Windows Server 2003 Backup utility (and with most other backup utilities). The key difference among these backup types is how each one handles the archive bit that is found in every Windows Server 2003 file. When a file is created or modified, the archive bit is set to *on*, as shown by the A in the Attributes column in Figure 27-1. After some types of backups run, the archive bit is set to *off*, which indicates that the file has been backed up. If, prior to the backup, a file's attribute has been set to archive manually by an administrator, that file will be backed up with the others.

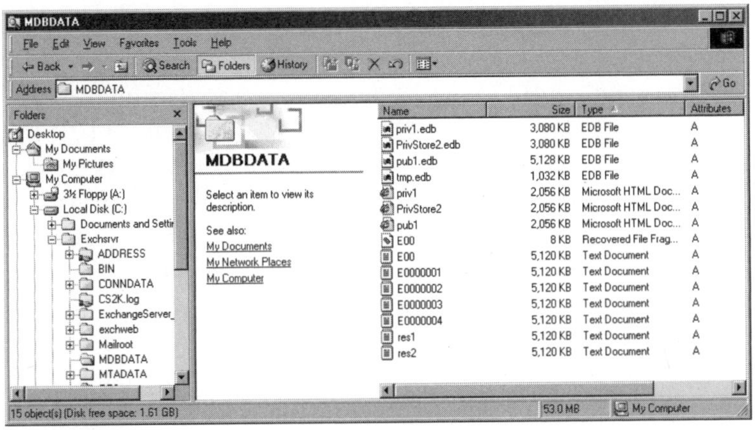

Figure 27-1. *Contents of the Mdbdata folder, showing the archive bit set to* on.

The five types of backups are as follows:

- **Normal** During a normal backup, all selected files are backed up, regardless of how their archive bit is set. After the backup, the archive bit is set to *off* for all files, indicating that those files have been backed up.
- **Copy** During a copy backup, all selected files are backed up, regardless of how their archive bit is set. After the backup, the archive bit is not changed in any file.
- **Incremental** During an incremental backup, all files for which the archive bit is on are backed up. After the backup, the archive bit is set to *off* for all files that were backed up.
- **Differential** During a differential backup, all files for which the archive bit is on are backed up. After the backup, the archive bit is not changed in any file.
- **Daily** During a daily backup, all files that changed on the day of the backup, which are identified by the modified date of the file and not the archive bit, are backed up, and the archive bit is not changed in any file.

> **Note** In this chapter, we will refer to a *full backup*, which is simply a normal backup with all Exchange-related items selected.

When you initially create a backup job, you manually select the files to be backed up. In most backup software programs, including the Microsoft Windows 2000 Backup utility, these jobs can be saved and reused. In some cases, not all selected files are actually backed up. Normal and copy backups back up all selected files, but in the case of an incremental, differential, or daily backup, the selected files must also meet the selection criteria of the backup type, as just listed.

All five types of backups apply to Exchange 2000 data, although only three are commonly used: normal, differential, and incremental. Daily and copy backups normally apply only to file-level (Microsoft Word documents or Microsoft Excel spreadsheets) backups. Of course, none of this applies to an *offline backup*, which is the backup of databases while the store.exe process is stopped. Offline backups are a good way to get a current "snap-shot" of the database while it is in a consistent state. However, the problem with performing an offline backup is that you have to bring all the stores down, something most environments are loath to do. Besides, with the advent of the Volume Shadow Copy (VSC), which we discuss later in this chapter, you'll see that performing an offline backup is not the best choice in most scenarios.

The following list describes what happens with regard to Exchange 2000 Server during each type of (online) backup:

- **Normal** The selected Exchange stores are backed up, and the transaction logs for those stores are purged.
- **Copy** The selected Exchange stores are backed up, but the transaction logs are not flushed.
- **Daily** With respect to Exchange, a daily backup performs the same backup as a copy backup.
- **Differential** Only the transaction logs for the selected stores are backed up. Because differential backups are supposed to back up all changes to the stores since the last normal backup, the transaction logs are not flushed so that they can be backed up again during the next differential or normal backup.
- **Incremental** Only the transaction logs for the selected stores are backed up. Because incremental backups are supposed to back up only the changes to the stores since the last normal or incremental backup, the transaction logs are flushed.

Backup Strategies

Given the five types of backups covered in the preceding section, most administrators use one of three strategies for backing up a server. These strategies all start with a full backup of the Exchange server, performed on a regular basis—for example, every Sunday. One strategy then continues with full backups daily, another involves performing an incremental backup on all other days of the week, and the last calls for performing a differential backup on all other days of the week.

- **Full daily backup** Every day of the week, complete a full backup of your Exchange server. If you follow any other backup strategy, you run the risk of having to revert to a backup that is several days or weeks old. An example of a failure would be when your weekly full backup failed in a normal plus daily incremental backup strategy. You would then have to restore all of the previous week's backups. Money spent on large-capacity backup systems (such as DLTs) is money well spent.
- **Normal plus daily incremental backup** On Sunday of each week, perform a full backup of all files on the Exchange server that you decide need to be backed up. On Monday, perform an incremental backup that backs up all files that have changed since the full backup. On Tuesday, perform another incremental backup that backs up all files that have changed since the last incremental backup on Monday. At the end of the week, you have performed a full backup and six incremental backups. To restore these backups, you would first restore the full backup and then restore each incremental backup, in order.
- **Normal plus daily differential backup** On Sunday of each week, perform a full backup of all files. On Monday, perform a differential backup that backs up all files that have changed since the full backup. On Tuesday, perform another differential backup that backs up all files that have changed since the last full backup, which occurred on Sunday. Each consecutive differential backup backs up all files that have changed since the last full backup. To restore these backups, you would first restore the full backup and then restore only the most recent differential backup.

In all strategies, plan to use your transaction logs to your advantage. Every backup strategy must incorporate the role that transaction logs play in recovering data up to the point of the disaster. Remember, your transaction logs represent what will happen to your database in the future. Often they hold committed transactions that have yet to be written to the database. (Consult Chapter 2 for a good discussion of the transaction log architecture.)

When a disaster strikes your Exchange server, the information generated in your Exchange organization since the last backup can be recovered from the transaction logs. For instance, if your server finished a full backup last night at 11:30 P.M., and then at 4:30 P.M. today the disk containing one of your Exchange stores experienced a failure, you would recover today's information from your transaction logs. This ability to recover assumes you have your transaction logs on a different physical disk from the store that experienced the failure. If the logs were on the same disk as the store, you would be able to recover only up to 11:30 last night, when the backup took place. Let's continue this scenario under the premise that the logs are on a separate disk and the disk with the store experiences a failure. To recover, you do a full restore of last night's backup from tape. Then when you start the store.exe process, store.exe attempts to replay all the transactions in the transaction logs back into the databases. When it is finished playing these transactions back into the database, the service will start and your databases will have been restored to the point in time when your disaster occurred.

When the store.exe process is started under normal (nonrecovery) conditions, such as during a proper shutdown and restart of the Exchange server, all transaction logs will be replayed unless the checkpoint file is available. Essentially, that file tells the store process which portions of the transaction logs have already been written to the databases and which have not. If the checkpoint file is available, only those portions of the transaction logs that were not previously written to the database will be replayed to the database if the transactions in the logs are more recent than the transactions in the database.

We're hopeful you'll see why it is important to make sure that your transaction logs are sitting on a different spindle from your databases, preferably one that has some type of disk fault tolerance, such as mirroring or disk striping with parity. If you lose your databases, you can recover by using the combination of tape backup and transaction logs. If you lose your transaction logs but not your databases, perform a clean shutdown of the store.exe process and your database will be up to date because all the committed transactions in memory will be written to disk. You can better understand now why it is very important to guard your transaction logs.

The Backup Process

You begin the backup process by starting the backup application. The backup application makes calls to the Web Storage System with the type of backup desired, and then the backup procedure begins. WSS informs the ESE that it is entering a backup mode, and then a patch file (.PAT) is generated for each database in the backup (assuming this is a full backup). During an online, full backup, the database is open for business and transactions can still be entered into the databases. If a transaction causes a split operation across the backup boundary (the location in the .edb file that designates what has and has not been backed up), the affected page before the boundary is recorded in the .PAT file. A separate .PAT file is used for each database that is backed up, such as Priv1.pat, Pub1.pat, or Srs.pat. These files are seen only during the backup and restore processes. During differential or incremental backups, a patch file is not created.

When the ESE enters a backup mode, a new log file opens. For example, if Edb.log is the current open log file, Edb.log is closed and is renamed to the latest generation and a new Edb.log is opened. This indicates the point when the ESE can truncate the logs, after the backup is complete.

Also, when the backup begins, backup requests that ESE read the database and sequence the pages. After sequencing, the pages are grouped into 64 KB chunks (16 pages) and then loaded into RAM. ESE then verifies the checksum on each individual page to ensure data integrity. If any page has a calculated checksum that does not match the checksum that was recorded in the page when the page was written to disk, backup stops the process of backing up the database and records an error message in the event logs. Backup does this to prevent the storage of damaged data. The very nice thing about all this is that when you get a successful full, online backup of your Exchange databases using the Exchange agent from your software vendor, you can be certain that the database on your tape has complete integrity, because every page was read into RAM, its checksum calculated, then copied to tape.

Once the backup has successfully completed and all the pages are read, backup copies the logs and patch files to the backup set. The log files are then truncated or deleted at the point when the new generation started at the beginning of the backup. The backup set closes, the ESE enters normal mode, and the backup is complete.

In an incremental or differential backup, only the log files are affected. Operations that involve patch files, checksums, or reading pages sequentially are not executed.

To recap, here are the steps of the backup process:

1. The backup starts, a synchronization point is fixed, and an empty patch file is created.
2. Edb.log is renamed to the next log number regardless of whether it is full, and a new Edb.log is created.
3. The backup for the current storage group begins.
4. A .PAT file is created for each database that is being backed up in the storage group, and the database header is written into the .PAT file.
5. During backup, split operations across the backup boundary are written into the .PAT file.
6. During backup, Windows Server 2003 Backup copies 64 KB of data at a time. Additional transactions are created and saved as normal. Each page's checksum is calculated and compared to the checksum recorded for that page in the page. The checksums are compared to ensure data integrity on each page.

7. Logs used during the backup process (those from the checkpoint forward) and the patch files are copied to tape.
8. The old logs on the disk are deleted.
9. The old patch files on the disk are deleted.
10. Backup finishes.

What we have been describing so far is the online backup process. There is another type of backup called the offline backup. Offline backups differ from online backups in that the database is stopped before the backup process starts, allowing you to save a copy of a consistent database file. Offline backups are always full backups because the database shuts down. An offline backup is always the less preferable choice, because you must dismount the database before performing it.

Restore Process Overview

Before you begin the restore process, the database or storage group must be dismounted and made inaccessible to users. You can do this by using the Exchange System Manager (ESM).

When a restore operation begins, the store informs the ESE that a restore process is starting and ESE enters restore mode. The backup agent copies the database from the tape directly to the database target path. Remember that the database is a file pair of the .EDB and .STM files. The associated log and patch files are copied to the server in a temporary location specified by you so that they aren't saved to the same location as current files in the production environment. If you happen to select the production path as your temporary path, you can overwrite log files and cause a logical corruption of the current production database. So, ensure that your temporary path is not your production path.

After the log and patch files are restored to the temporary location, a new restore storage group starts specifically for the purpose of restoring the database. The database is then copied from tape to the temporary location (and into the restore storage group). Then the patch file data and the log files from the tape backup are copied into the database by the restore database engine.

This means that each transaction in each log file is treated as follows. Each transaction's data and time stamp is read along with the page number in the database that the transaction references. Then the date and time stamp on the page in the database is read and compared to the date and time stamp of the transaction in the transaction log. If the transaction in the log has a more recent date and time stamp than the one on the page in the database, the transaction from the transaction log is written to the database. If the opposite is true—that is, the date and time stamp on the page in the database is more recent than the one on the transaction in the transaction log—ESE skips that transaction and moves to the next transaction to replay it into the database.

Hence, ESE processes the current logs, bringing you back to the point at which your database became corrupted (assuming you have all the transaction logs available from the last full, online, successful backup to the point of the disaster). After this is complete, ESE performs some cleanup by deleting log and patch files from the temporary location and deleting the restore storage instance. Then the storage group is mounted into the production environment and your database is mounted too.

Restoring the Binary Files

Because the Exchange Server 2003 configuration information is held in the Configuration partition of Active Directory, you can recover an Exchange server more simply than in Exchange 5.5. If the Exchange Server 2003 server to which you are restoring files is a member server in a domain, be sure that Active Directory is running. Run Exchange System Manager and verify that a valid server object still exists for the Exchange Server 2003 server in Active Directory. If Active Directory does not exist, restore Active Directory prior to restoring Exchange Server 2003.

If the Exchange server you want to restore is also the domain controller, begin by restoring Active Directory on that computer. You can restore Exchange Server 2003 only after Active Directory is successfully restored. The security ID on the restored server must match the security ID of the original server. If the security IDs do not match, you cannot access Web Storage System until you restore only Web Storage System and then manually rebuild the Windows Server 2003 accounts.

Considerations of Different Restore Scenarios

Sometimes, you don't need to restore an entire server or even an entire database. In this section, we'll discuss the considerations of different restore scenarios. Specifically, we'll look at the following:

- Restoring online backups
- Restoring offline backups
- Restoring a single mailbox
- Restoring a single database
- Restoring a database to a different server
- Restoring log files

Restoring Online Backups

Restoring an online backup of your databases is the preferred method of restoring a database because the transaction log entries can be replayed into the database during the restore process. Online backups will use the patch file along with the transaction logs to restore the database. When possible, this is the preferred method of restoring an Exchange Server 2003 database.

Restoring Offline Backups

If you need to replace hardware on your Exchange Server 2003 server, you might want to consider performing an offline backup and restore. Remember that database services are stopped during an offline backup, so those users whose mailboxes are homed in that storage group will not have e-mail services until the database is restarted.

You might also want to use an offline backup of your databases if, during an online backup, the backup process fails because you receive a -1018, -1022 or some other page-level corruption error. Doing an offline backup of the database allows you to take a snapshot of the database before you work on correcting the problem. The logic here is that if your work further corrupts the database, you can always fall back on the offline copy and try your efforts again.

One major problem with an offline backup is that the pages are not checked for integrity during the backup phase, as they are in an online backup operation. Also, the ability to replay transactions back into the database during the restore operation is not available to you. Essentially, restoring an offline backup restores you to the point where the store.exe process was stopped.

The process of restoring an offline backup is rather simple: copy the database to the correct location on your server and start the store services. Be sure you have the correct transaction log set that went with the database before starting mounting the database.

Restoring a Single Mailbox

If you need to recover a single mailbox that has passed the mailbox retention time period, you need to either use third-party software or restore the entire database to a recovery server. Because both of these operations can take a tremendous amount of time, we recommend setting your mailbox retention times to a number that exceeds nearly every mailbox restore scenario that you've experienced. To do this, open the ESM and navigate to the mailbox store on which you want to set the retention time. Open the store's properties and click on the Limits tab (Figure 27-2). On the Limits tab, set the retention times for Keep Deleted Items For (Days) and Keep Deleted Mailboxes For (Days).

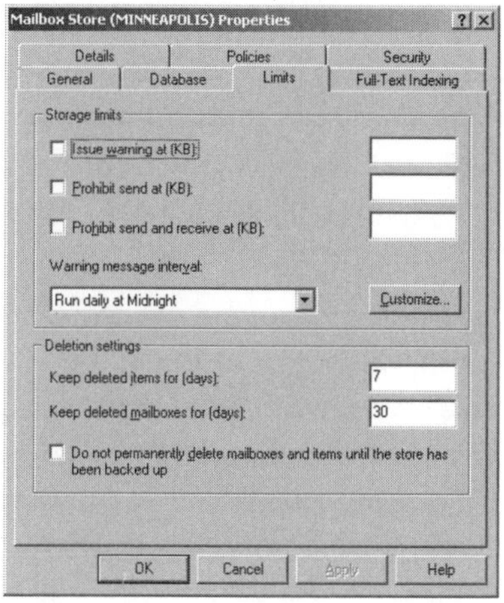

Figure 27-2. *Setting the deleted mailbox retention time in the store properties.*

Because mailboxes are merely an attribute of the user account, reconnecting a mailbox to a new account is easy. This is why, if you need to delete a user account, you retain the mailbox associated with that account for a considerable amount of time. Let it expire via the deleted mailbox retention time only after you know that you don't need that mailbox anymore.

When a mailbox is deleted, it is marked with a red X in the System Manager interface. You can reconnect the mailbox to a new user account by right-clicking the mailbox and using the Reconnect feature.

Restoring a Single Database

If you need to restore a single database, dismount it using the Exchange System Manager and then restore the individual database. Notice that you don't need to stop the store.exe process—it continues to run. Instead, you'll just dismount the database over which you'll need to restore and then restore the copy from your tape backup. The restore process creates a special restore storage group, and the database and transaction log files from the backup are restored in that storage group. After recovery, the consistent database is mounted into its original storage group by ESE.

Note The format of transaction log files is revised in Exchange Server 2003. When you upgrade from Exchange 5.5 to Exchange Server 2003, the existing transaction log files are removed and a new log series is created. Because of the log format change, you cannot restore an Exchange 5.5 database to an Exchange Server 2003 server.

Restoring Databases to a Different Server

You can restore your databases to a different Exchange Server 2003 server other than the one from which it was backed up. Use this method as a last resort to restore individual items or databases. The secondary server must meet the hardware requirements to run Exchange: it must not be connected to the network and it must have enough disk space to restore the entire backup.

To restore a database to a different server, the database display name and the storage group display name must be the same. In addition, the organization name and administrative group name for the server to which you want to restore must match the server from which the database was backed up. You'll also need to configure the current databases to allow them to be overwritten so that the new databases with the new signatures can overwrite them during the restore process.

This method restores only the ESE databases, so do not use it when you need to recover an entire server. After you copy or move your databases to a different server, you need to reconfigure permissions on the mailboxes before your users will be able to use them.

If you have a large number of mailboxes that need to be connected to their corresponding Active Directory accounts, you can use MBCONN (which is mbconn.exe, or the Mailbox Reconnect Tool, located in the \Support\utils\i386 directory on the Exchange Server CD). This tool is especially helpful when you have just replaced or added a new Exchange server to your Exchange organization. If you are familiar with the Exchange 5.5 DS/IS Consistency Adjuster, you'll understand the concepts behind the Mbconn tool. It essentially performs the same functions as the DS/IS Consistency Adjuster.

Single Mailbox

Most third-party backup applications will back up individual mailboxes with backup selection granularity down to the item level (for example, you can back up a single calendar entry or a single message). If you are not using mailbox-level backups, or you are using the Windows Backup utility, the deleted mailbox retention period has expired, and you need to restore a single mailbox, you must use an offline server and restore the mailbox there. In most cases, you won't need to do this because of the mailbox retention features, Dumpster and ExMerge. But let's go over the steps in the event that you do.

First, ensure that the offline server is in a different Windows Server 2003 forest from your production servers. Second, the storage group that hosts the restored database must have the same display name as the original production server. Third, the database you want to restore must have the same display name as the original production server. The database name must be unique on the backup server in all storage groups. For example, if the database name is Priv.edb, there can only be one instance of a Priv.edb database on the secondary server. The organization name and the administrative group name must be the same.

To recover the mailbox, reconnect the mailbox to *a dummy* user account, and use Exmerge to create a .PST (personal store file) of the mailbox. Then import that information into the regular mailbox.

Recovery Scenarios

This section describes recovery requirements and steps in the following scenarios:

- Recovering Exchange Server 2003
- Recovering an Exchange Server 2003 member server
- Requirements for Recovering Exchange Server 2003

There are five common requirements for recovering all Exchange Server 2003 servers:

- Windows Server 2003 and Exchange Server 2003 installation CDs. You'll also need access to service packs and Hotfixes.
- Full backups of the system drives.
- Recent Windows Server 2003 system state backup.
- Online backups of the Exchange databases. Offline backups will not help you in most scenarios.
- A server object in Active Directory for the Exchange server you want to restore.

Recovering an Exchange Server 2003 Member Server

To perform a full recovery of an Exchange Server 2003 Member Server, follow these steps:

1. Reinstall the Windows Server 2003 Operating System. Make sure the logical drives are configured the same as the original server and use also the same name of the original server. Finally, install the same components that were installed on the original server.
2. Do not join the server to the domain. Leave the server in the workgroup. You will join the server to the domain by restoring the system state data.

3. Restore the full drive backups to the server.
4. Restore the System State data of the server. Following the restore of your system state, the event log might show that some Exchange Server 2003 services have failed (if the Exchange binaries were included in the full drive backups). If these services are not installed yet, when you restore the system state, Windows Server 2003 accepts that these services are installed on your server. These services will start after you install Exchange Server 2003 in disaster recovery mode.
5. Install Exchange Server 2003 in Disaster Recovery Mode. This means running setup.exe with the *disasterrecovery* switch. This tells setup to not install the default Exchange installation set, but instead to look in Active Directory for an instance of the server that is already running.
6. Restore the Exchange databases.
7. If your Exchange server was running the Site Replication Service, first open Computer Management and under the Services and Application, click Services. Then select Exchange Site Replication Service from the list of services, and open its properties. Set the startup of the service to automatic and start the service. Note that this step must be performed before allowing the other Exchange services to start after running setup using the *disasterrecovery* switch. Restore the Site Replication Service (SRS) database to the Exchange 2003 Server.

Best Practices

To successfully back up or restore an operation, you must follow some best practices:

- Ensure that the raw storage capacity of your tape exceeds the compressed storage capacity of your database by a comfortable safety margin. If it does not, plan for tape changes when doing backups.
- Routinely clean the tape drives according to manufacturer specifications.
- Do not overuse tapes. Discard them after they reach the maximum number of cycles specified by the manufacturer.
- Store the tapes in a safe and accessible location.
- Check your backup logs every day to ensure the Exchange backups were successful from the previous night.

- Perform a trial backup and restore on a monthly basis to ensure your hardware is working and to keep your restore skills up to snuff.
- Document your backup and restore procedures.

Shadow Copies and Exchange Server 2003

One of the exciting new features in Windows Server 2003 is the Volume Shadow Copy (VSC) service. This service can be used to significantly reduce the amount of time that it takes to back up and restore Exchange Server 2003 databases. The VSC service works with backup applications and hardware to provide a shadow copy–based backup of your Exchange Server 2003 databases.

Essentially, the VSC will ask Exchange Server 2003 to pause—very quickly—to flush the memory structures to the databases, to pause new transactions, and to finish current transactions. Once this is accomplished, a (very) fast hardware copy of the databases is made to a neutral location on the server.

After the copy action is completed, the production databases are released for continued use while the shadow copy version is used for backup to tape. By default, after the backup of the shadow databases is completed, the shadow copy is deleted.

Future versions of this feature might include the scheduling of additional shadow copies periodically during the day, which you can then leave on disk when you require them for restore operations. This feature reduces the data that can be lost when you roll back to earlier database instances and can significantly increase the speed at which databases are recovered.

Summary

In this chapter, we covered a lot of ground pertaining to backup and restore operations. We've outlined how to perform restores of your Exchange databases, the general steps to follow to recover an entire server, and a brief overview of how the VSC feature in Windows Server 2003 can be used to keep your restore times to a minimum. If your databases become corrupted or something goes awry, be sure to use the techniques presented in this chapter to recover your databases and restore your Exchange information.

Chapter 28

Troubleshooting Exchange Server 2003

Nothing is perfect—not your car, your house, or even Exchange Server 2003. It's no wonder, then, that stores selling car parts and building supplies are successful. Even a stable system like Microsoft Exchange Server 2003 can break down once in a while. Troubleshooting Exchange Server 2003 is a skill that you will develop as you solve real problems on your network. One chapter cannot prepare you for all the possibilities you could face as an Exchange administrator. However, this chapter introduces some of the troubleshooting tools that are available in Exchange Server 2003 and discusses some places to find more information and help with specific types of Exchange problems.

Using Troubleshooting Tools

When you troubleshoot a system as complex as Exchange Server 2003, your most valuable tool is your understanding of the system itself. This understanding includes knowledge of how Exchange Server 2003 works in general and how your organization is set up in particular. Ideally, this book has given you a good understanding of Exchange Server 2003 and, if you took the advice in Chapter 5, "Assessing Needs," you have completely documented your network. With this knowledge in hand, you are ready to find and repair whatever might go wrong in your organization. This section introduces some of the tools you will use in the process.

Inbox Repair Tool

Not all problems in an Exchange organization occur on an Exchange server. Many users keep personal folders and offline folders on their client computers. A set of personal folders is stored as a single file with the extension .PST, as shown in Figure 28-1. Multiple sets of personal folders can be stored on a single client. A set of offline folders is stored as a single file with the extension .OST.

Like any other type of file, personal and offline folder files can become corrupt. Fortunately, Microsoft Outlook provides the Inbox Repair Tool, which helps you repair corrupt personal and offline folder files.

Figure 28-1. *Personal folders stored in a .PST file.*

The Inbox Repair Tool (Scanpst.exe) is installed during a typical installation of Microsoft Outlook, but no shortcut is created on the Start menu. You can find the file Scanpst.exe in the \Program Files\Common Files\System\MSMapi\1033 directory for Outlook 2003. Note that these are default paths that can be changed during client installation. When you launch the Inbox Repair Tool, a dialog box appears in which you can enter the path and filename of the corrupt file and then click Start (Figure 28-2).

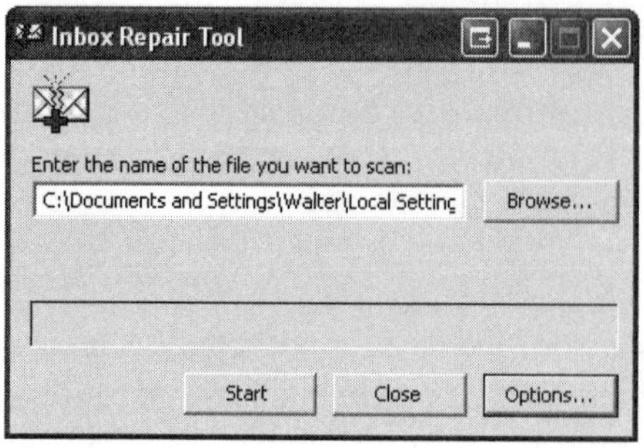

Figure 28-2. *The Inbox Repair Tool.*

Once you start the scanning process, the Inbox Repair Tool examines the entire contents of the specified file and then shows you what it has found, as shown in Figure 28-3. The Inbox Repair Tool does give you a chance to back up the file before you perform repairs on it, and you should always use this option. The Inbox Repair Tool usually moves messages that it cannot repair to a special Lost and Found folder, but it often discards messages that it cannot repair. Without a backup, these messages are permanently lost. When the Inbox Repair Tool finishes running, launch Outlook to access this Lost And Found folder. You should create a new set of personal folders and move any recovered items to these new folders. Often, however, the Inbox Repair Tool will simply fix problems you are having in Outlook and should always be given a chance.

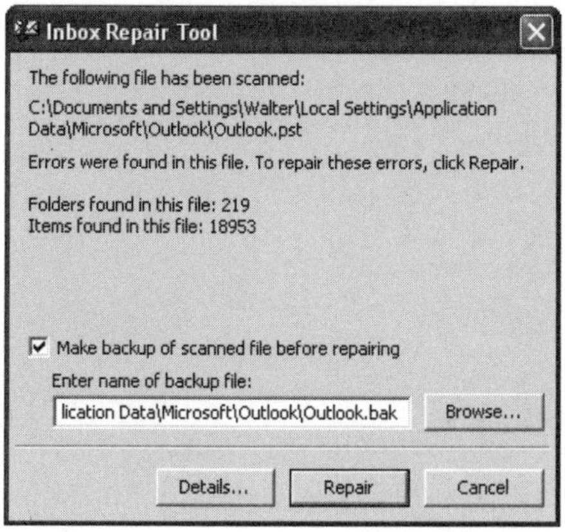

Figure 28-3. *The Inbox Repair Tool scanning a .PST file.*

RPing Utility

Many of the connections among computers in an Exchange organization rely on remote procedure calls (RPCs). As you know, an RPC calls a protocol that allows a program on one computer to execute a program on another computer. Exchange servers in a routing group rely on RPCs to communicate with one another. Exchange clients connect to Exchange servers by using RPCs. Likewise, the Exchange System snap-in connects to remote Exchange servers via RPCs. Often, connectivity problems in an Exchange organization are the result of bad RPC connectivity.

You can use the RPing utility to confirm the RPC connectivity between two systems as well as to make sure that Exchange services are responding to requests from clients and other servers. RPing has two components: a server component (rpings.exe) and a client component (rpingc.exe). You can find both of these components in the Windows Server 2003 Resource Kit tools directory following installation of the Resource Kit tools, which are available at *http://www.microsoft.com/downloads/details.aspx?familyid=9d467a69-57ff-4ae7-96ee-b18c4790cffd&displaylang=en.*

RPing Server

The server component of RPing is a file named rpings.exe, which you must start on the server before using the client component. To run the server component, type **rpings.exe** at the command prompt. This command runs the server component using all available protocol sequences, as shown in Figure 28-4. A *protocol sequence* is a routine that allows the return of a ping for a given networking protocol, such as TCP/IP or IPX/SPX. You can also restrict the server component to any single protocol sequence by using the following switches:

- *-p ipx/spx*
- *-p namedpipes*
- *-p netbios*
- *-p tcpip*
- *-p vines*

To exit the RPing server, type the string **@q** at the RPC server command prompt.

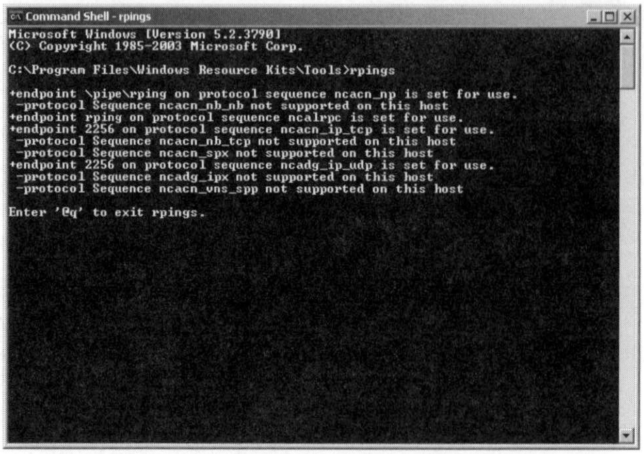

Figure 28-4. *RPing running on an Exchange server.*

RPing Client

After you launch the RPing server on the Exchange server, you use the RPing client, shown in Figure 28-5, on another computer to test RPC connectivity to that server.

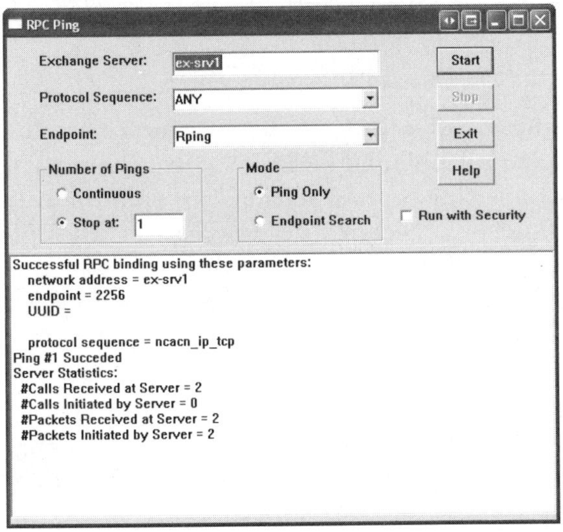

Figure 28-5. *Checking RCP connectivity with Rpingc.exe.*

The options are straightforward, and the information you provide is rather simple:

- **Exchange Server** Specifies the NetBIOS name or IP address (if TCP/IP is used on the network) of the server running the RPing server.
- **Protocol Sequence** Specifies the RPC mechanism that will be used in the test. Options include Any (all protocol sequences are tested), Named Pipes, IPX/SPX, TCP/IP, NetBIOS, and VINES. Set the protocol sequence to correspond to the protocol sequence setting on the RPC server.
- **Endpoint** Specifies protocol-specific ports that the RPC client uses to communicate with the server. Choose Rping to collect information about RPing client-to-server communication itself. Choose Store to simulate communications with the Information Store service on the Exchange server, and choose Admin to simulate communications with the Exchange server.

- **Number Of Pings** Specifies whether to ping the server continuously or a certain number of times. This option is available only if you choose Ping Only mode.11.
- **Mode** Specifies the mode. Ping Only means that the ping is returned directly by the RPC Ping server. Endpoint Search returns Pings from detected endpoints.
- **Run With Security** Verifies authenticated RPCs.

If the RPing from the client is successful with a particular protocol, you'll want to move that protocol to first in the binding order so that the client system doesn't have any problems connecting to the Exchange server. If the RPC Ping is not successful over any protocols, check for a corrupted RPC.DLL file on the client. There are nine RPC.DLL files used to support RPC for Windows clients. All these files are included in the Windows Server 2003 operating system, just as they are for Microsoft Windows 95 and Microsoft Windows 98. For MS-DOS and 16-bit Windows clients, the RPC.DLL files used for RPC are included with Exchange Client. If replacing these .DLL files does not fix the problem, trace the packets between the client system and the Exchange server. A packet analyzer such as Network Monitor, a Windows utility, can be handy in this situation.

More Info For information about using Network Monitor to analyze remote procedure calls on a TCP/IP network, see Microsoft Knowledge Base article Q159298, "Analyzing Exchange RPC Traffic Over TCP/IP."

Note The *Microsoft Windows Server 2003 Resource Kit* Tools, available for download at *http://www.microsoft.com/downloads/details.aspx?familyid=9d467a69-57ff-4ae7-96ee-b18c4790cffd&displaylang=en*, also supplies a utility named RPCPing, which is a simpler command-line tool that tests RPC connectivity for a computer. Open the command prompt, navigate to the Resource Kit tools directory, and type **rpcping /?** for a list of options to use with this command.

Eseutil.exe Offline Tool

The public folder store and the mailbox store on an Exchange server begin as empty database files. As messages accumulate, these databases grow. Unfortunately, they do not shrink when messages are deleted. Instead, the emptied space is simply marked as available for use during routine garbage collection performed by the Information Store service. When new messages are stored in the databases, they are written in any available free space before the database enlarges to hold them. This method of using free space can result in single items actually being broken up and stored in several physical places within the database—a process known as *fragmentation.*

During their scheduled maintenance cycles, the Information Store service defragments the databases. It also checks for database inconsistencies every time the server is shut down or started. Because of this routine maintenance, fragmentation itself is not much of a problem on an Exchange server. However, online defragmentation routines do nothing about the size of the databases themselves. To compact the databases, you must turn to an offline utility. Exchange Server 2003 provides an offline defragmentation tool named Eseutil.exe, which you can use to perform database defragmentation while the Information Store service is stopped.

> **Caution** Eseutil.exe is not meant to be used as a regular tool for maintenance of your Exchange servers. You should use it only when you are in contact with Microsoft Technical Support.

You can launch this tool by typing **eseutil.exe** at the command prompt from the program files\exchsrvr\bin directory. The eseutil.exe command allows you to perform eight distinct functions:

- **Defragmentation (/d)** Defragments the database by moving the used pages in the database into contiguous blocks in a new database. Unused pages are discarded, which is the only way to recover empty space inside the database for other uses. By default, eseutil.exe writes the contents of the database file to a temporary file, tempdfrg.edb. When this process is complete, the temporary database becomes the new database and replaces the original database.

Although you can place this temporary file on another server across the network, this activity is not recommended because it will saturate your bandwidth and could take hours to complete. Once this new database is created, a new signature is written to the database. As a result, previous transaction logs can no longer be played into the database nor can transactions created after the defragmentation be played into the old database. Therefore, after completing the defragmentation, you should perform a full online backup.

- **Recovery** (/r) Performs a soft recovery, bringing all databases into a consistent state. This function is carried out automatically before a defragmentation begins.
- **Integrity** (/g) Checks the integrity of a database. The main purpose of this switch is to provide feedback to the development team for debugging purposes. This is a read-only command and does not make any changes to the database. It will check the database index, build a second index in a temporary database (integ.edb), and compare the two.
- **File Dump** (/m) Displays information about the database files, log files, and checkpoint files of a particular log file.
- **Repair** (/p) Examines the structure of the database and attempts to restore broken links. This process is slow and uncertain and should be used only as a last resort. If the repair finds a physical corruption, which will be seen as a -1018, -1019, or -1022 error in Event Viewer, the injured page is removed, resulting in a loss of data for that page. After the repair is completed, you are instructed to delete all your current transaction logs. This step is necessary because the page numbers in the database will not correspond to the page numbers referenced in the transaction log files. Running a repair also rewrites the database signature.
- **Restore** (/c) Used to bring a store into a consistent state. This function is performed automatically before a defragmentation.
- **Checksum** (/k) Calculates a checksum value and compares it to the data page's checksum value. This function is performed automatically during the repair process.
- **Copy File** (/y) Makes a copy of the checkpoint file.

Other Useful Utilities

You can use many other tools to troubleshoot Exchange Server 2003—too many to cover in detail in this book. Table 28-1 lists some of these tools and briefly describes their purpose as well as where to find them.

Table 28-1. Some utilities for troubleshooting Exchange Server 2003

Filename	Purpose	Location
Dnsdiag.exe	Verifies DNS connectivity for a computer	Support folder on the Exchange Server 2003 CD-ROM. Also available as one of the Windows Support Tools on the Windows Server 2003 CD-ROM.
Err.exe	Converts store, MAPI, and database error codes to error message strings	Support folder on the Exchange Server 2003 CD-ROM.
Filever.exe	Displays versions of .EXE and .DLL files	Support folder on the Exchange Server 2003 CD-ROM.
Isinteg.exe	Checks the integrity of the information stores	\Exchsrvr\Bin in your Exchange installation.
Mdbvu32.exe	Displays information about information stores and .PST and .OST files	Support folder on the Exchange Server 2003 CD-ROM.

Finding Help

As an administrator, you sometimes have problems that you cannot solve by yourself. In these circumstances, knowing where to go for help can save your day. Many sources of information about Exchange Server 2003 are available.

Product Documentation

The product documentation for Exchange Server 2003 is actually quite good. (Many administrators have never even looked at the product documentation, primarily because they have grown accustomed to shoddy documentation in other products.) This documentation is available from the Help menu of Exchange System Manager.

Microsoft TechNet

Each month, Microsoft publishes a collection of information and tools called TechNet. TechNet is a CD-ROM subscription that delivers current information about the evaluation, deployment, and support of all Microsoft products. It consists of nearly 300,000 pages of information, including the full text of all Microsoft resource kits and the entire Microsoft Knowledge Base. Each month, subscribers also receive other CD-ROMs that include useful items, such as all published service packs for all Microsoft products; server and client utilities; and Microsoft Seminar Online.

TechNet is now also published in an extended version, TechNet Plus, that includes Microsoft software currently in beta testing. Much of the content of TechNet, as well as ordering information for the CD-ROM subscription, is available online at *http://www.microsoft.com/technet*. Further support mechanisms include contacting the local Microsoft office or using Microsoft Support through *http://support.microsoft.com*.

Internet Newsgroups

Newsgroups offer the chance to interact with other administrators and to get opinions and ideas about your specific problems. Many newsgroups are available on the Internet. Microsoft maintains a public Usenet server that hosts hundreds of newsgroups on many Microsoft products. The address of this server is *msnews.microsoft.com*. You can also view them on the Web at *http://www.microsoft.com/exchange/community/newsgroups/default.asp*.

Following are a few of the Exchange-specific newsgroups available on this server:

- *microsoft.public.exchange.admin*
- *microsoft.public.exchange.clients*
- *microsoft.public.exchange.clustering*
- *microsoft.public.exchange.connectivity*
- *microsoft.public.exchange.design*
- *microsoft.public.exchange.development*
- *microsoft.public.exchange.misc*
- *microsoft.public.exchange.setup*

Hundreds of people, including Microsoft personnel and Exchange most valuable professionals (MVPs), read and post to these newsgroups daily. These newsgroups are also replicated by many other Usenet servers and might be available through your own Internet service provider's news server.

Summary

This chapter discussed some tools you can use to troubleshoot problems with Exchange Server 2003, including the Inbox Repair tool and the RPC Ping utility. It also described other sources of troubleshooting information, such as TechNet and the Microsoft Knowledge Base. The next chapter completes our discussion of maintaining Exchange Server 2003, with a look at ways to tune your servers for enhanced performance.

Chapter 29

Tuning Exchange Server 2003 Performance

The Performance snap-in is a valuable tool included with Microsoft Windows Server 2003 and is available in the Administrative Tools folder on the Programs menu. It graphically charts the performance of hundreds of individual system parameters on a computer running the Windows operating system. When you install Microsoft Exchange Server 2003 on a computer running Windows Server 2003, several Exchange-specific counters are installed for you to track with the Performance snap-in. This chapter provides an overview of how to use the Performance snap-in to better understand your Exchange system.

Understanding How the Performance Snap-in Works

Although a full discussion of the Performance snap-in is beyond the scope of this chapter, this section covers some of its basic concepts and briefly describes how the Performance snap-in works. Because the bulk of your performance-tuning activities will involve the Windows operating system, our discussion will focus on monitoring Windows Server 2003.

Performance Monitoring Concepts

Before beginning our discussion, we first need to briefly cover some basic concepts and terms. One thing you'll notice right off the bat is that we are using the terms "performance monitoring" and "Performance snap-in." *Performance monitoring* is the activity of gathering measurements and data from individual counters that show how a server is performing its activities. *Performance snap-in* is the snap-in utility in Microsoft Management Console (MMC) that is used to gather this data.

Note In some previous versions of Windows, the Performance snap-in was named System Monitor—a much less confusing name. You'll still see it referred to as System Monitor in some documentation, but for this chapter, we are sticking with its official name, Performance.

More specifically, performance monitoring looks at how the Windows operating system and installed applications use the resources of the system. The four main subsystems that are monitored are the disks, memory, processors, and network components. Later in this chapter, we will look at each of these components and highlight some important counters and measurements for them. In connection with performance monitoring, we need to discuss four concepts: throughput, queue, bottleneck, and response time.

Throughput

Throughput is a measurement of the amount of work done in a given unit of time. Most often, we think of throughput as the amount of data that can be transmitted from one point to another in a given time period. However, the concept of throughput is also applied to data movement within a computer. Throughput can either decrease or increase. When it increases, the load, which represents the amount of data that the system is attempting to transmit, can increase to the point that no more additional data can be transmitted. This is called the *peak* level. If the load begins to decrease, which means that less and less data needs to be transmitted, the throughput will also fall.

When data is being sent from one point to another, or in any end-to-end system, the throughput depends on how each component along the path performs. The slowest point in the overall data path sets the throughput for the entire path. If the slowest point is too slow (which is defined differently in each situation), and a queue begins to develop, that point is referred to as a *bottleneck*, a concept we'll discuss in more detail in just a moment. Often the resource that shows the highest use is the bottleneck, and a bottleneck is often the result of an overconsumption of that resource.

Generally, we do not define a heavily used resource in data transmission as a bottleneck unless a queue is also developing for the resource. For instance, if a router is being heavily used but shows little or no queue length, it is not thought of as a bottleneck. On the other hand, if that router develops a long queue (which is defined differently in each situation for each router), it could be said to be a bottleneck.

Queue

A *queue* is a place where a request for a service sits until it can be processed. For instance, when a file needs to be written to a disk, the request to write that file is first placed in the queue for the disk. The driver for the disk then reads the information out of the queue and writes that information to the disk. Long queues are rarely considered a good thing.

Queues develop under various circumstances. When requests for a service arrive at a rate faster than the resource's throughput, or if certain requests take a long time to fulfill, queues can develop. When a queue becomes long, the work is not being handled efficiently. Windows Server 2003 reports queue development on disks, processors, server work queues, and server message block (SMB) calls of the server service.

Response Time

Response time is the amount of time required to perform a unit of work from start to finish. Generally speaking, response time increases as stress on the resource increases. It can be measured by dividing the queue length for a given resource by the resource throughput. By using the trace log feature in Windows, you can track a unit of work from start to finish to determine its response time.

Bottleneck

As we mentioned earlier, a *bottleneck* represents overconsumption of a resource. You will experience this as a slow response time, but you should think of it as overconsumption. Finding bottlenecks is a key goal in performance tuning because eliminating bottlenecks makes your system run more efficiently. Moreover, if you can predict when a bottleneck will occur, you can do much to proactively solve a problem before it affects your users. Factors that contribute to bottlenecks are the number of requests for the services of a resource, the frequency with which those requests occur, and the duration of each request.

Collecting Data with the Performance Snap-in

Before you can properly tune an Exchange server, you must first collect data that shows how the server is presently running. Data collection involves three distinct elements: objects, counters, and instances. An *object* is any resource, application, or service that can be monitored and measured. You will select various objects for which you want to collect data.

Each object has multiple *counters* that measure various aspects of the object. Examples include the number of packets that a network card has sent or received in a given time period or the amount of time the processor has spent processing kernel-mode threads. The counters are where the data is actually measured and collected.

Finally, a counter might have multiple *instances*. The most common use of multiple instances is to monitor multiple processors on a server or multiple network cards. For example, if a server has two processors, you can either measure the amount of time each processor is spending processing nonidle threads or you can measure the two processors as one unit, and look at the average. Instances allow greater granularity in measuring performance. It is important to note that not all object types support multiple instances.

Each counter is assigned a *counter type*, which determines how the counter data is calculated, averaged, and displayed. In general, counters can be categorized according to their *generic type*, as outlined in Table 29-1. The Performance snap-in supports more than 30 counter types. However, many of these types are not implemented in Windows Server 2003 and so are not listed in the table.

Table 29-1. Generic counter types

Counter Type	Description
Average	Measures a value over time and displays the average of the last two measurements.
Difference	Subtracts the last measurement from the previous measurement and displays the difference, if the result is a positive number. If the result is negative, the display is zero.
Instantaneous	Displays the most recent measurement.
Percentage	Displays the result as a percentage.
Rate	Samples an increasing count of events over time and divides the cache in count values by the change in time to display a rate of activity.

More Info For more information about each counter type—its name, its description, and how the formulas are calculated—consult your system documentation.

Viewing Collected Data

When you first open the Performance snap-in, you see a blank screen called a *chart view*, which displays selected counters in real time as a graph (Figure 29-1). To see data displayed in the chart, you have to add some counters. Choose Add from the toolbar to open the Add Counters dialog box (Figure 29-2).

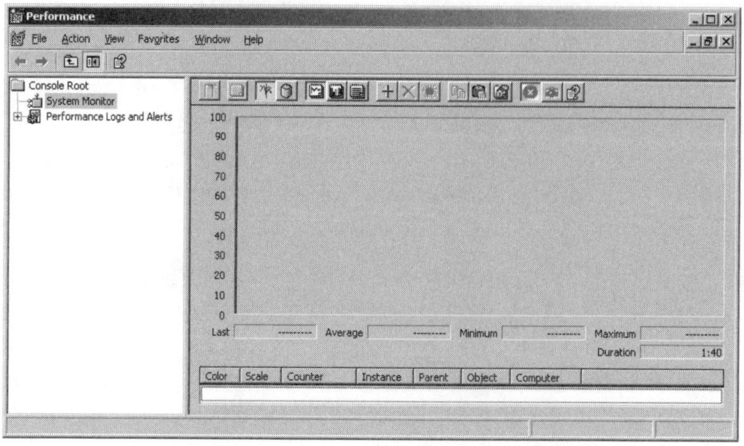

Figure 29-1. *The Performance snap-in chart view.*

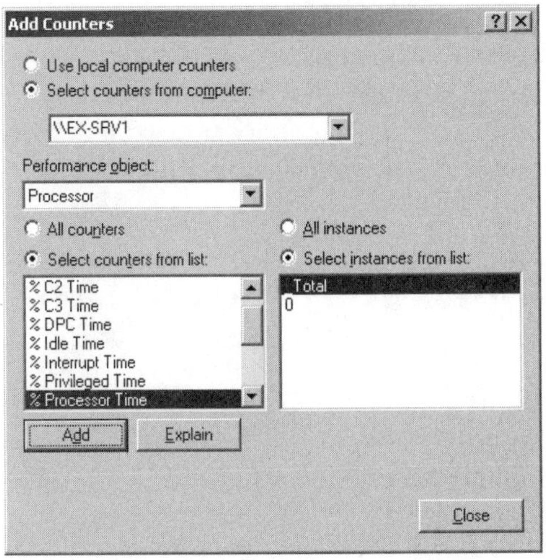

Figure 29-2. *Add Counters dialog box.*

By default, the computer that you monitor is the computer on which you launched the Performance snap-in, but you can monitor remote computers as well. In fact, you can select different counters from multiple computers at the same time. You might do so, for instance, to monitor how a distributed application is running. You can also choose to monitor the same counter on multiple computers for comparative purposes. For instance, in Figure 29-3, we've chosen to monitor the same counter on four servers—Indianapolis, Minneapolis, Tucson, and Folsom—while installing Microsoft Office 2003 on Folsom from the source files on Indianapolis. The two graph lines showing higher levels of processor activity represent the Indianapolis and Folsom servers.

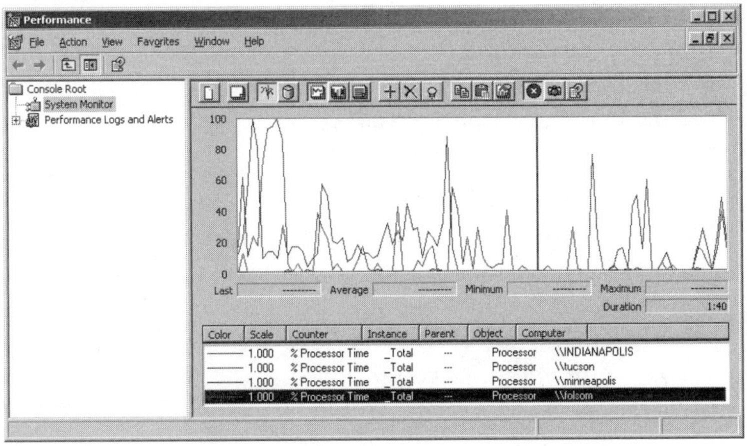

Figure 29-3. *Monitoring the same counter on four servers.*

As you can see in the figure, you can also view digital values for the selected counter by selecting a counter from the list at the bottom and reading the values just under the graph. You can attain the last, average, minimum, and maximum values for each counter selected. In this case, the Folsom server's processor activity was averaging a bit over 14 percent for a period of 1 minute and 40 seconds.

Evaluating the Four Main Subsystems in Windows

Earlier we mentioned the four subsystems that you should always monitor: memory, processor, disk, and network. In this section, we'll briefly discuss each element and offer some advice on tuning these parts of Windows to optimize their work with Exchange Server 2003.

One point that applies to all four of these areas is this: current data is not that helpful unless you have a baseline against which to compare it. This argues in favor of setting up regular monitoring schedules for *all* your servers and then regularly compiling that data to form a baseline of how your servers operate at off-peak, normal, and peak periods of usage. As an example, if one server is averaging 53 pages per minute, that number won't mean much unless you know the period of time that the average represents and whether it depicts abnormal behavior or is an expected result. The only way to understand this comparative information is to conduct regular monitoring of the server.

Evaluating Memory Usage

Use the counters in Table 29-2 to set up a baseline for your system's memory. When you're monitoring these counters, you will see occasional spikes that you can exclude from your baseline because these short-term values will not be representative of your servers. However, do not ignore these spikes if they are occurring with increasing frequency. This increase could indicate that a resource is becoming too heavily utilized.

Recall from Chapter 2, "Understanding Exchange Server Storage Architecture," that the Extensible Storage Engine (ESE) automatically checks the system's performance and allocates to itself all available memory that it anticipates it will need. This allocation means that when you monitor the Memory\Available Bytes counter, the counter might hover around 4000 KB, even if there isn't much activity on the server. In addition, you'll find that the Store.exe process allocates a large amount of memory to itself. This action is by design and does not represent a memory leak or a memory bottleneck.

Table 29-2. Essential memory counters

Counter Name	Description
Memory\Pages/Sec	Shows the rate at which pages are read from or written to the disk to resolve hard page faults. This counter is a primary indicator of the type of page faults that can significantly slow down your system. It is the sum of Memory\Pages Input/Sec and Memory\Page Faults/Sec. Microsoft recommends keeping this value below 20.
Memory\Available Bytes	Shows the amount of physical memory, in bytes, available to processes running on the computers. Microsoft recommends keeping this value above 4000 KB.
Paging File(_Total)\ % Usage	Shows the amount of the paging file in use during the sample interval, as a percentage. A high value indicates that you might need to increase the size of your Pagefile.sys file or add more RAM. Microsoft recommends keeping this value below 75 percent.

The DSAccess cache automatically allocates 4 MB to itself (set in the registry) for holding Lightweight Directory Access Protocol (LDAP) lookup results from the Global Catalog server. Its size can be monitored with the MSExchange-DSAccess Caches\Total Memory Size counter.

To see memory allocations on a per-process basis, use the Memsnap tool, which is part of the Support Tools on your Windows Server 2003 CD-ROM. The Memsnap tool records system memory usage to a log file for later review. It gives just a snapshot of your memory usage, not an ongoing logging of how each process is using memory. Figure 29-4 illustrates what the log file looks like.

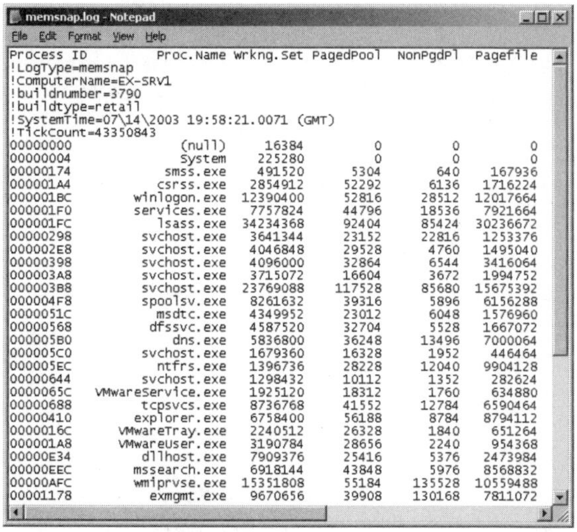


```
Process ID          Proc.Name Wrkng.Set PagedPool  NonPgdPl  Pagefile
!LogType=memsnap
!ComputerName=EX-SRV1
!buildnumber=3790
!buildtype=retail
!SystemTime=07\14\2003 19:58:21.0071 (GMT)
!TickCount=43350843
00000000             (null)     16384         0         0         0
00000004             System    225280         0         0         0
00000174           smss.exe    491520      5304       640    167936
000001A4          csrss.exe   2854912     52292      6136   1716224
000001BC       winlogon.exe  12390400     52816     28512  12017664
000001F0       services.exe   7757824     44796     18536   7921664
000001FC          lsass.exe  34234368     92404     85424  30236672
00000298        svchost.exe   3641344     23152     22816   1253376
000002E8        svchost.exe   4046848     29528      4760   1495040
00000398        svchost.exe   4096000     32864      6544   3416064
000003A8        svchost.exe   3715072     16604      3672   1994752
000003B8        svchost.exe  23769088    117528     85680  15675392
000004F8       spoolsv.exe    8261632     39316      5896   6156288
0000051C         msdtc.exe    4349952     23012      6048   1576960
00000568        dfssvc.exe    4587520     32704      5528   1667072
000005B0           dns.exe    5836800     36248     13496   7000064
000005C0        svchost.exe   1679360     16328      1952    446464
000005EC         ntfrs.exe    1396736     28228     12040   9904128
00000644        svchost.exe   1298432     10112      1352    282624
0000065C VMwareService.exe    1925120     18312      1760    634880
00000688       tcpsvcs.exe    8736768     41552     12784   6590464
00000410      explorer.exe    6758400     56188      8784   8794112
0000016C    VMwareTray.exe    2240512     26328      1840    651264
000001A8    VMwareUser.exe    3190784     28656      2240    954368
00000E34       dllhost.exe    7909376     25416      5376   2473984
00000EEC      mssearch.exe    6918144     43848      5976   8568832
00000AFC      wmiprvse.exe   15351808     55184    135528  10559488
00001178        exmgmt.exe    9670656     39908    130168   7811072
```

Figure 29-4. *Memsnap log file.*

Evaluating Processor Usage

Use the counters listed in Table 29-3 to set up a baseline for your processor usage. The processor always has a thread to process. Most often, the system supplies an idle thread for the processor to process while it is waiting to process an active thread. The Processor\% Processor Time counter does not factor in the idle thread when calculating its value.

Table 29-3. Essential processor counters

Counter Name	Description
Processor\% Processor Time	Shows the percentage of elapsed time that all the threads of this process used to execute instructions. An *instruction* is the basic unit of execution in a computer; a *thread* is the object that executes instructions; and a *process* is the object created when a program is run. Microsoft recommends keeping this value to 80 or below (sustained).
System\Processor Queue Length	Shows the number of threads in the processor queue. There is a single queue for processor time, even on computers with multiple processors. This counter shows ready threads only, not threads that are currently running. Microsoft recommends keeping this value to 2 or less.

The most common causes of processor bottlenecks are insufficient memory and excessive numbers of interrupts from disk or network I/O components. During periods of low activity, the only source of processor interrupts might be the processor's timer ticks. Timer ticks increment the processor's timer. These interrupts occur every 10 to 15 milliseconds, or about 70 to 100 times per second. Use the Processor(_Total)\Interrupts/Sec counter to measure this value. The normal range is in the thousands of interrupts per second for a Windows server and can vary from processor to processor. Installing a new application might cause a dramatic rise in this value.

If you want to improve processor response time or throughput, you can schedule processor-intensive applications to run at a time when system stress is usually low. Use the Scheduled Tasks tool in Control Panel to do this. You can also upgrade to a faster processor with a larger L2 cache. This upgrade will always increase your system's performance, and you can use multiple processors instead of a single processor to balance the processing load.

Evaluating Disk Usage

Windows Server 2003 includes counters that monitor the activity of the physical disk and logical volumes. The *PhysicalDisk* object provides counters that report physical-disk activity, whereas the *LogicalDisk* object provides counters that report statistics for logical disks and storage volumes. By default, the Windows operating system activates only the *PhysicalDisk* performance counters. To activate the *LogicalDisk* counters, go to the command prompt and type **diskperf –yv**. The counters will be activated when you reboot your server.

Table 29-4 lists the counters for evaluating disk performance. They are the same for both the *LogicalDisk* and *PhysicalDisk* objects. We've chosen to use the *PhysicalDisk* object in the table.

Table 29-4. Essential disk counters

Counter Name	Description
PhysicalDisk\Avg. Disk Sec/Transfer	Indicates how fast data is being moved, in seconds. A high value might mean that the system is retrying requests due to lengthy queuing or, less commonly, a disk failure. There are no benchmark recommendations from Microsoft. Watch for significant variances from baseline data.
PhysicalDisk\Avg. Disk Queue Length	Shows the number of requests that are queued and waiting for the disk to process. Microsoft recommends that this value be 2 or less.
PhysicalDisk\Disk Bytes/Sec	Indicates the rate at which bytes are transferred. It is the primary measurement of disk throughput.
PhysicalDisk\Disk Transfers/Sec	Shows the number of completed read and write operations per second. This counter measures disk utilization and is expressed as a percentage. Values over 50 percent might indicate that the disk is becoming a bottleneck.

Diagnosing a disk as a bottleneck is a tricky process that requires both time and experience. We give some helpful tips here, but for a more full discussion of this topic, please see the works cited earlier in this chapter.

What you want to see so that you can diagnose a disk as a bottleneck in your system is either a sustained rate of disk activity that is well above your baseline or an increasing rate of disk activity that represents a dramatic departure from your baseline statistics. In addition, you'll want to see persistent disk queues that are either steadily increasing or that are significantly above your baseline statistics, coupled with *the absence of a significant amount of paging* (less than 20 pages per second). If these factors combine in any other way than those described here, it is unlikely that your disk is a bottleneck. For example, if your system doesn't have enough RAM to accommodate its load, you will find that paging occurs more frequently, creating unnecessary disk activity. If you monitor only the *PhysicalDisk* object, you might see this activity as evidence that your disk is a bottleneck. Therefore, you must also monitor memory counters to determine the real source of this type of problem.

If you do determine that your disk is too slow, consider following one or more of these strategies:

- Rule out a memory shortage, for the reasons just discussed.
- Defragment the disk, using Disk Defragmenter. For information about using Disk Defragmenter, see the online help for Windows Server 2003.
- Consider implementing a stripe set to process I/O requests concurrently over multiple disks. If you need data integrity, implement a stripe set with parity.
- Place multiple drives on different I/O buses.
- Limit the use of file compression or encryption.
- Be sure you're using the best and fastest controller, disk, and I/O bus that you can afford.

Evaluating Network Usage

Windows Server 2003 provides two utilities for monitoring network performance: the Performance snap-in and Network Monitor. We will not discuss Network Monitor here. For more information on Network Monitor, see your system documentation and the resource kit books.

You should monitor other resources, such as disk, memory, and processor objects, along with network objects to obtain an overall perspective on the network objects' results. In addition, you can select which layer of the Open Systems Interconnection (OSI) model you want to monitor. Table 29-5 summarizes each counter and its corresponding OSI layer.

More Info For more information about the OSI model, see Appendix A in the *TCP/IP Core Networking Guide*, part of the *Microsoft Windows 2000 Server Resource Kit* (Microsoft Press).

Table 29-5. Essential network counters and their OSI layer

Counter Name	Description	OSI Layer
Network Interface\ Output Queue Length	Indicates the length of the output packet queue. A queue length of 1 or 2 is often satisfactory. Longer queues indicate that the adapter is waiting for the network and thus cannot keep pace with the server.	Physical
Network Interface\ Packets Outbound Discarded	A high value indicates that the network segment is saturated. An increasing value means that the network buffers cannot keep pace with the outbound flow of packets.	Physical

Table 29-5. Essential network counters and their OSI layer

Counter Name	Description	OSI Layer
Network Interface\Bytes Total/Sec	A high value indicates a large number of successful transmissions.	Physical
Network Segment\Broadcast Frames Received/Sec	You'll need to develop a baseline for this counter and then compare subsequent measurements against it. Since every computer processes every broadcast, frequent broadcasts mean lower overall performance.	Physical
Network Segment\% Network Utilization	Reflects the percentage of network bandwidth used for the local network segment. A lower value is preferred. For an unswitched Ethernet network, a value under 30 percent is best. Collisions will become a problem at 40 percent.	Physical
IP\Datagrams/Sec	Shows the rate at which datagrams are received from or sent to each interface.	Network
TCP\Segments Received/Sec	Shows the rate at which segments are received, including those received in error. This count includes segments received on currently established connections. A low value means that you have too much broadcast traffic.	Transport
TCP\Segments Retransmitted/Sec	Gives the rate at which segments containing one or more previously transmitted bytes are retransmitted. A high value might indicate either a saturated network or a hardware problem.	Transport
Redirector\Network Errors/Sec	Measures serious network errors that indicate the Redirector and one or more servers are having serious communication problems.	Application
Server\Pool Paged Failures	Indicates the number of times that allocations from the paged pool have failed. If this number is high, either the amount of RAM is too little or the pagefile is too small or both. If this number is consistently increasing, increase the physical RAM and the size of the pagefile.	Application

The *Network Interface* object is installed when you install TCP/IP. The *Network Segment* object is installed when you install Network Monitor. To monitor the TCP/IP protocol, use the *TCP/IP*, *UDP*, and *ICMP* objects. (You no longer need to install SNMP to get the IP counters as you did with Microsoft Windows NT.) Use the *NBT Connection* object to track session-layer packets between computers. You can also use this object to monitor routed servers that use NETBIOS name resolution.

Application-layer objects include the *Browser*, *Redirector*, *Server*, and *Server Work Queue* on computers running Windows Server 2003. These objects will help you understand how your file and print services are performing, using the server message block (SMB) protocol.

Using the Performance Snap-in to Tune Exchange Server 2003

It would take an entire book to discuss in depth all the extra counters installed with Exchange Server 2003 and how they can be combined to give you a particular type of report. Instead, we will focus here on the more important counters and offer a few suggestions for using them. We will cover the SMTP, Content Indexing, and Microsoft Outlook Web Access (OWA) counters. If some of the discussion of the SMTP protocols is unfamiliar to you, refer to Chapter 20, "Supporting Internet Protocols and SMTP," where this protocol is discussed in depth.

SMTP System Monitor Counters

The SMTP server receives messages, categorizes them, places them in queues created for the intended destination, and then delivers them to that destination. Messages can be received from port 25, from the Message Transfer Agent (MTA), or from a local store submission. Table 29-6 lists the counters that are most important with the SMTP service. The main object we are looking at here is the *SMTP Server* object. Some counters originate in different objects; these are noted in the Counter column.

Table 29-6. Counters for monitoring SMTP

Stage	Counter	Meaning
Messages received from port 25	Messages Received Total	Total number of messages received.
	Inbound Connections Current	Number of simultaneous inbound connections over port 25.
	Pickup Directory Messages Retrieved/Sec	Rate at which messages are being retrieved from the mail pickup directory. An unusually high number could indicate the use of a large distribution list with many mail-enabled contacts.
Messages received from the Exchange Store	MSExchange Transport Store Driver: Store/MSExchangeMTA Submits	Total number of messages received from the Store/MTA and submitted to the Transport Core.
Messages submitted for processing	Total messages submitted	Total number of messages submitted to queuing for delivery.

Table 29-6. Counters for monitoring SMTP

Stage	Counter	Meaning
Messages categorized	Categorizer Queue Length	Number of messages that are currently being categorized or waiting to be categorized. An increasing number could indicate a problem with an event sink. A value of 0 could indicate that the SMTP service is stopped.
	Categorizations Completed Successfully	Total number of messages successfully categorized.
Categorized messages placed in destination queue	Remote Queue Length	Number of messages going to other servers that are waiting to be sent. An increasing number in this queue could indicate a problem with the physical connection to the Internet or between two Exchange 2003 servers. If one queue in particular has a steadily increasing number, you may want to see if the remote SMTP server is available.
Categorized messages placed in destination queue	Remote Retry Queue Length	Number of messages going to other servers that could not be sent in a former attempt and that will be retried later. A high number here indicates either a physical connection problem or that the remote SMTP server is unavailable.
	Local Queue Length	Number of messages going to local recipients, to the MTA, or to other gateways.
	MSExchangeIS Transport Driver: Current Messages to MSExchangeMTA	Number of messages going to the MTA or to other gateways only. This value is included in the Local Queue Length counter.
	Local Retry Queue Length	Number of messages going to local recipients, to the MTA, or to other gateways that could not be delivered in a former attempt and that will be retried later.
	Badmailed Messages	Number of messages that are malformed, such as having a nonexistent destination domain. These messages are delivered to the Badmail directory. A high number here could indicate that some addresses for mail-enabled contacts were entered incorrectly.

Content Indexing System Monitor Counters

Content Indexing (CI) in Exchange Server 2003 consists of two basic phases. First is the initial crawl, which can take from hours to days and needs to be done only once. Until this initial crawl is completed, the index cannot be used for searching. Second is the incremental crawl, which is done numerous times after the initial crawl and is used to keep the index up-to-date. An incremental crawl usually completes in less than an hour. Table 29-7 lists the most important counters and the circumstances under which those counters are significant. The object we are most concerned with is the *Microsoft Gatherer Projects* object. Table 29-8 shows counters for the *Microsoft Search Indexer Catalogs* object, which can provide important information about indexes.

Table 29-7. Content Indexing counters for the *Microsoft Gatherer Projects* object

Stage	Counter	Meaning
Crawl in progress	Crawl in Progress flag	1 if a crawl is in progress, 0 if not.
	Current Crawl Is Incremental	1 if the current crawl is an incremental crawl, 0 if not.
	Document Additions	Number of documents being added to the index since the last crawl.
	URLs in History	Total number of URLs (documents) that CI has detected. This value will climb during the crawl and, once it levels off, will represent the total number of documents to be indexed.
	Waiting Documents	Total number of URLs (documents) that CI has detected that have not yet been indexed. The difference in rate between this counter and the URLs in History counter is essential in determining how long a crawl might take.

Table 29-8. Content Indexing counters for the *Microsoft Search Indexer Catalogs* object

Stage	Counter	Meaning
Index complete	Index Size	Size of the index.
Number of Documents	Number of documents	Number of documents in the catalog. This value corresponds to the number shown in the Exchange System snap-in.
Merge in progress	Merge Progress	Percentage of completeness for merges. Whereas shadow merges can happen quickly, master merges can take up to an hour.

Finally, Table 29-9 lists two of the most frequently used counters for obtaining information about the number and extent of queries against your indexes. The counters in this table are for the *Microsoft Search Catalogs* object.

Table 29-9. Content Indexing counters for the *Microsoft Search Catalogs* object

Stage	Counter	Meaning
Ongoing	Queries	Total number of queries that have been run against a catalog.
	Results	Total number of results from queries. Note that one query can return thousands of results, so expect this number to be significantly higher than the Queries value.

Outlook Web Access

Outlook Web Access allows users to access their mailboxes over the Internet through a browser, such as Microsoft Internet Explorer or Netscape Navigator. Due to differences in code paths between IE4-level (Internet Explorer 4 and Netscape Navigator) and IE 5.x-level browsers, performance counters in the *MSExchange Web Mail* object exist in three forms: non-IE5, IE5 and later, and _Total (which sums the former two counters). Table 29-10 shows the counters for monitoring Web Mail.

Table 29-10. Counters for monitoring Web Mail

Stage	Counter	Meaning
User connects over port 80	Web Service: Maximum Connections	Total number of OWA connections initiated since the Web Service (W3Svc) was last started.
	Web Service: Current	Number of OWA Connections users that are currently connected.
Messages sent over OWA	Message Sends (Total)	Total number of message sends. After OWA submits a message, the message is handled by SMTP, and the applicable SMTP counters are affected.
OWA requests flow to and from the store	Epoxy: Client Out Que Len: DAV	Number of requests in the queue from the client to the server.
	Epoxy: Store Out Que Len: DAV	Number of responses in the queue from the server to the client.
	Epoxy: Blocks Allocated: DAV	A secondary indication of outstanding OWA requests. High numbers in these three Epoxy counters might indicate the need for an additional OWA server.
Client disconnects	Web Service: Current Connections	Current number of connections to the Web service. OWA has no logout process. Regardless of whether the user closes out the browser session when finished, the OWA user context will time out after 60 minutes of inactivity and that user's cached authentication will expire, causing this counter to decrement.

Summary

Monitoring your network is crucial in spotting problems before they grow too large. This chapter described the counters that are important in measuring the four primary subsystems of your Windows system: the disks, memory, network, and processor. It also examined the more important counters for the SMTP, Content Indexing, and OWA activities. We want to emphasize that regular monitoring of your Exchange servers will help you detect when something is about to go wrong and can give you some warning so that you can fix a problem before it occurs. Use the information in this chapter to devise a regular monitoring strategy for your system.

Part IX
Appendixes

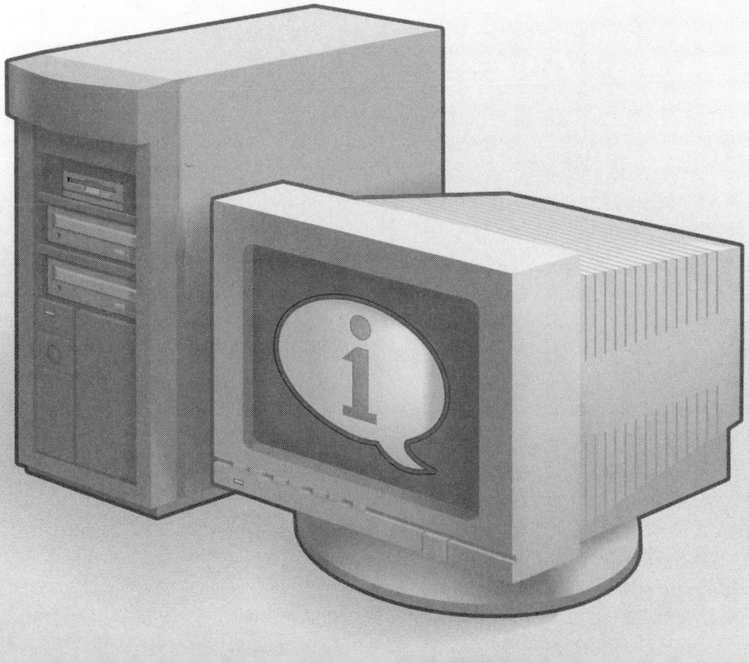

Appendix A

Default Directory Structure for Exchange Server 2003

The following table lists the names of the major Microsoft Exchange directories and subdirectories created during installation, along with their contents. The path for each directory is shown relative to the default root Exchange folder, \Program Files\Exchsrvr.

Table A-1. Default directory structure for Exchange Server 2003

Directory	Contents
\address	Subdirectories used for e-mail address proxy generators.
\address\ccmail\i386	Lotus cc:Mail address proxy generator.
\address\gwise\i386	Novell GroupWise address proxy generator.
\address\ms\i386	Not used in Microsoft Exchange Server 2003. Was used in Microsoft Exchange 2000 Server for the MS Mail address proxy generator.
\address\notes\i386	Lotus Notes address proxy generator.
\address\smtp\i386	SMTP address proxy generator.
\address\x400\i386	X.400 address proxy generator.
\bin	Exchange executables and core services.
\conndata	Temporary storage used by various connectors.
\ExchangeServer_*servername*	Miscellaneous files for support of individual Exchange servers.
\exchweb	Components for Microsoft Outlook Web Access.
\mailroot	Working directories for message transfer.
\mdbdata	Information store database files (Priv.edb, Priv.stm, Pub.edb, Pub.stm).
\mtadata	Message Transfer Agent database files.
\mtadata\mtacheck.out	Results of running the Mtacheck utility.
\OMA	Components for Outlook Mobile Access.
\Res	DLLs for Event Viewer and System Monitor.
\Schema	XML files supporting the Exchange extension of the Active Directory Schema.
server_name.log	Log files for message tracking.
\srsdata	Support files for the Site Replication Service, used for providing Exchange Server 5.5 support.

Appendix B
Delivery Status Notification Codes

Even in the best-conceived and best-managed Microsoft Exchange environments, you are bound to have messages that just can't make it through the system. When a message experiences a fatal error and cannot be delivered, Microsoft Exchange Server 2003 returns a non-delivery report (NDR) to the sender and optionally to an administrator.

As you'll recall, non-delivery reports are system messages that report the delivery status of a message to the sender. (The structure of NDRs is defined in Request for Comments [RFC] 1893.) They are a subclass of a general message information structure referred to as *delivery status notifications* (DSNs). An NDR provides a three-digit delivery status notification code, such as 4.4.1, that identifies the failure more precisely. Each digit of the code provides information about the failure. The first digit indicates one of three different situations:

- **2.x.x** Successful transfer
- **4.x.x** Persistent transient failure
- **5.x.x** Permanent failure

Table B-1 lists the second and third digit codes and their meanings. For example, the code 4.4.1 indicates a persistent transient failure because the host being sent the message did not answer.

Table B-1. Standard delivery status notification codes

Code	Description
x.1.0	Other address status
x.1.1	Bad destination mailbox address
x.1.2	Bad destination system address
x.1.3	Bad destination mailbox address syntax
x.1.4	Destination mailbox address ambiguous
x.1.5	Destination mailbox address valid
x.1.6	Mailbox has moved
x.1.7	Bad sender's mailbox address syntax

Table B-1. Standard delivery status notification codes

Code	Description
x.1.8	Bad sender's system address
x.2.0	Other or undefined mailbox status
x.2.1	Mailbox disabled, not accepting messages
x.2.2	Mailbox full
x.2.3	Message length exceeds administrative limit
x.2.4	Mailing list expansion problem
x.3.0	Other or undefined mail system status
x.3.1	Mail system full
x.3.2	System not accepting network messages
x.3.3	System not capable of selected features
x.3.4	Message too big for system
x.4.0	Other or undefined network or routing status
x.4.1	No answer from host
x.4.2	Bad connection
x.4.3	Routing server failure
x.4.4	Unable to route
x.4.5	Network congestion
x.4.6	Routing loop detected
x.4.7	Delivery time expired
x.5.0	Other or undefined protocol status
x.5.1	Invalid command
x.5.2	Syntax error
x.5.3	Too many recipients
x.5.4	Invalid command arguments
x.5.5	Wrong protocol version
x.6.0	Other or undefined media error
x.6.1	Media not supported
x.6.2	Conversion required and prohibited
x.6.3	Conversion required but not supported
x.6.4	Conversion with loss performed
x.6.5	Conversion failed
x.7.0	Other or undefined security status
x.7.1	Delivery not authorized, message refused
x.7.2	Mailing list expansion prohibited
x.7.3	Security conversion required but not possible
x.7.4	Security features not supported

Table B-1. Standard delivery status notification codes

Code	Description
x.7.5	Cryptographic failure
x.7.6	Cryptographic algorithm not supported
x.7.7	Message integrity failure

Appendix C

Log File Locations

The following table lists the default storage locations of the major log files in Microsoft Exchange Server 2003 and where in the System Manager (or other) interface you can configure them.

Table C-1. Exchange Server 2003 log file locations

Log	Default Location	Where to Configure
Setup Progress Log	C:\ Exchange Server Setup Progress.log	n/a
Diagnostic Logging	Windows Event Viewer Application Log	Diagnostics Logging tab of server property sheet
Message Tracking	C:\Program Files\Exchsrvr *server*.log	General tab of server property sheet
Transaction Logs	C:\Program Files\Exchsrvr \mdbdata	General tab of Storage Group property sheet
NNTP Virtual Server Log	C:\WINDOWS\System32 \LogFiles\NntpSvc# *inyymmdd*.log	General tab of NNTP Virtual Server property sheet
HTTP Virtual Server	C:\WINDOWS\System32 \LogFiles\HttpSvc# *inyymmdd*.log	Internet Services Manager
SMTP Virtual Server Log	C:\WINDOWS\System32 \LogFiles\SmtpSvc# *exyymmdd*.log	General tab of SMTP Virtual Server property sheet
Active Directory Account Cleanup Wizard	\Program Files\Exchsrvr \Bin\adclean.log	Use /L switch with adclean.exe command-line tool
MTA Tracking Log	C:\Program Files\Exchsrvr \metadata	n/a

Glossary

A

access control entry (ACE) An object such as a user or group that is present on an access control list.

access control list (ACL) A list of security permissions applied to an object. An ACL for an item normally includes membership (ACEs) and the actions that each member can perform on the item.

ACE *See access control entry (ACE).*

ACL *See access control list (ACL).*

Active Directory The Microsoft Windows directory service, which replaced the Security Accounts Manager in Microsoft Windows NT 4. Active Directory consists of a forest, one or more domains, organizational units, containers, and objects. Various classes of objects can be represented within Active Directory, including users, groups, computers, printers, and applications.

Active Directory Connector (ADC) A service that runs on a Windows domain controller and allows you to synchronize directory information between Microsoft Exchange Server 5.5 and Active Directory. Unlike Site Replication Service, which replicates information between an Exchange 5.x organization and the configuration naming partition in Active Directory, the ADC replicates information between the Exchange 5.x directory and the domain partition in Active Directory.

Active Directory Services Interface (ADSI) A set of interfaces that allows you to access Active Directory services programmatically.

ADC *See Active Directory Connector (ADC).*

address list A collection of recipient objects that can receive messages through Exchange Server.

address space The part of an e-mail address that designates the system that will receive the message. Typically, the address space is the entire address except the recipient and any delimiter. For example, in the address joe@microsoft.com, @microsoft.com is the address space.

administrative group A collection of Exchange servers that can be administered as a single unit. An administrative group can include policies, routing groups, public folder trees, monitors, servers, conferencing services, and chat networks. When security settings (permissions) are applied to an administrative group, all child objects in the tree inherit the same permissions as the administration group node.

American Standard Code for Information Interchange (ASCII) A code for representing English characters as numbers, with each letter assigned a number from 0 through 127.

ASCII *See American Standard Code for Information Interchange (ASCII).*

attribute The individual properties that make up an object.

authentication The process of verifying a user's identity before authorizing the user to access a resource.

automatic document property promotion A feature that allows for advanced searches on any document property, such as author, size, or department. When Exchange stores a document in a supported file type, the document's properties are automatically parsed and promoted to the information store. Hence, the properties become a part of the document's record in the database. Searches can then be performed on these properties.

B

back-end server A server that holds at least one database that front-end servers can connect to when relaying requests from clients.

ban A control that allows you to forbid messages or connections from a user, a group, a computer, an address, a domain name, or another construct.

BHS *See bridgehead server (BHS).*

bridgehead server (BHS) A server that acts as a message transfer point between Exchange routing groups. This term also refers to a computer that is hosting a directory replication connector.

C

CA *See certificate authority (CA).*

certificate Public key that has been digitally signed by a trusted authority (the certificate authority) and that is used to ensure that public keys have not been tampered with.

certificate authority (CA) An entity that verifies the validity of public keys that have been created for users in the organization through the issuance of certificates. The CA also issues, revokes, and renews certificates.

certificate revocation list (CRL) and certificate trust list (CTL) Lists published by Certificate Services that name certificates whose authenticity cannot be trusted (revocation list) or can be trusted (trust list).

checkpoint file A file used to keep track of transactions that are committed to an Exchange database from a transaction log. Using checkpoint files ensures that transactions cannot be committed more than once.

circular logging A logging technique that involves maintaining only previous log files with uncommitted changes on the server. Fully committed transaction logs are removed to save space.

ConfigCA A special connection agreement implemented as part of the

Active Directory Connector that replicates configuration naming partition data from Exchange 5.x sites to administrative groups in Active Directory and vice versa. ConfigCAs work in conjunction with Site Replication Service.

configuration naming partition A partition of Active Directory that stores information regarding how an Exchange system is organized. Because this information is replicated to all domain controllers in the forest, the Exchange configuration is also replicated throughout the forest. The configuration information includes the Exchange topology (such as routing group information), connectors, protocols, and service settings. *See also domain naming partition* and *schema naming partition*.

connection agreement The configuration of information to replicate using the Active Directory Connector. Configuration information includes the servers that participate in the replication, the object classes (mailbox, custom recipient, distribution list and user, contact, and group) to replicate, the containers and organizational units to use for object placement, and the activity time schedule.

contact A nonsecurity principal that represents a user outside of the organization. A contact generally has an e-mail address, facilitating messaging between the local organization and the remote object. A contact is similar to a custom recipient in Exchange Server 5.5.

CRL *See certificate revocation list (CRL).*

CTL *See certificate trust list (CTL).*

D

DAV *See Distributed Authoring and Versioning (DAV).*

Deployment Tools A set of documentation that guides you through the Exchange Server 2003 installation process and provides checklists to help you ensure successful installation.

digest authentication A form of authentication in Microsoft Internet Information Services (IIS) in which the password is sent as a hashed value that works through proxies and firewalls. This method works with all HTTP 1.1–compliant browsers, but the password is unencrypted in the Microsoft Windows 2003 domain controller.

dismount *See mount.*

distinguished name A name assigned to every object in Active Directory that identifies where the object resides in the overall object hierarchy.

Distributed Authoring and Versioning (DAV) An extension to HTTP 1.1 that allows for the manipulation (reading and writing) of objects and attributes on a Web server. Also known as WebDAV. Exchange natively supports WebDAV. Although not specifically designed for the purpose, DAV allows for the control of data using a filing system–like protocol. DAV commands include PROPFIND and PROPPATCH.

DNS *See Domain Name System (DNS).*

domain The core unit in Active Directory. A domain is made up of a collection of computers that share a common directory database.

domain controller A server running Windows 2000 Server or Windows Server 2003 that has Active Directory installed. Each domain controller is able to authenticate users for its own domain. It holds a complete replica of the domain naming partition for the domain to which it belongs and a complete replica of the configuration and schema naming partitions for the forest.

Domain Name System (DNS) A widely used standards-based protocol that allows clients and servers to resolve names into IP addresses and vice versa. Windows Server 2003 extends this concept even further by supplying a dynamic DNS (DDNS) service that enables clients and servers to automatically register themselves in the database without needing administrators to manually define records.

domain naming partition A partition of Active Directory that stores all domain objects for Exchange Server 2003 and replicates the objects to every domain controller in the domain. Recipient objects, including users, contacts, and groups, are stored in this partition. *See also configuration naming partition* and *schema naming partition*.

domain tree A collection of domains that have a contiguous namespace, such as microsoft.com, dog.microsoft.com, and cat.microsoft.com. Domains within the forest that do not have the same hierarchical domain name are located in a different domain tree. When different domain trees exist in a forest, the domain tree is referred to as a disjointed namespace.

DSAccess The Exchange component that provides directory lookup services for components such as SMTP and MTA. Client requests use the DSProxy service for directory access.

DSProxy The Exchange component that can proxy (and refer) MAPI directory service requests from Microsoft Outlook clients to Active Directory for address book lookup and name resolution.

E

electronic security policy A statement of the methods and actions that are required to implement an information security policy.

epoxy layer *See Exchange Interprocess Communication layer (EXIPC).*

ESE *See Extensible Storage Engine (ESE).*

event sink A piece of code that is activated by a defined trigger, such as the reception of a new message. The code is normally written in any COM-compatible programming language, such as Microsoft Visual Basic, Microsoft VBScript, JavaScript, C, or C++. Exchange Server 2003 supports transport, protocol, and store event sinks. Event sinks on the store can be synchronous (meaning that the code executes as the event is triggered) or asynchronous (meaning that the code executes sometime after the event).

EVS *See Exchange virtual server (EVS).*

Exchange Interprocess Communication layer (EXIPC) A queuing layer, formerly known as the epoxy layer, that allows the IIS and Store processes (Inetinfo.exe and Store.exe) to shuttle data back and forth very quickly. This layer is required to achieve the best possible performance between the protocols and database services on an Exchange server. Conventional applications require the processor to switch contexts when transferring data between two processes. Exchange Server 5.5 incorporates protocols such as NNTP, POP3, and IMAP directly into the Store.exe process, so data transfer is very efficient. The Exchange architecture separates the protocols from the database for ease of management and to support future architectures.

Exchange virtual server (EVS) When using clustered servers, you allocate different resources (such as storage groups) to an EVS. If a node fails, you can move an EVS from the failed node to one of the remaining nodes.

EXIPC *See Exchange Interprocess Communication layer (EXIPC).*

Extensible Storage Engine (ESE) A transaction logging system that ensures data integrity and consistency in the event of a system crash or media failure. Other databases, such as the Active Directory database, also use ESE.

F

failover or failback The process of moving a resource from one server in a cluster to another. Failover happens when a problem occurs on the active server and services must be transferred to the passive server. Failback is the process of restoring resources to the active server after they have been temporarily relocated on a passive server.

filter rules LDAP rules created using recipient policies. Filter rules allow you to specify what kind of e-mail address is generated for each recipient object.

firewall A system designed to prevent unauthorized access to or from a private network. A firewall can be made up of hardware, software, or a combination of both. Firewalls can work by blocking certain types of packets or certain applications.

forest A collection of domains and domain trees. The implicit name of the forest is the name of the first domain installed. All domain controllers within a forest share the same configuration and schema naming partitions. To join an existing forest, you will use the Dcpromo utility. The first domain within the forest cannot be removed.

front end/back end An Exchange configuration in which clients access a bank of protocol servers (the front end) for collaboration information, and these in turn communicate with the data stores on separate servers (the back end) to retrieve the physical data. A front-end/back-end configuration allows for a scalable single point of contact for all Exchange-related data.

functional level The mode in which an Active Directory domain or forest is operating. A domain can exist in a number of functional levels, each of which is determined by the versions of Windows Server running in the domain or forest. In Windows 2000 mixed mode (in which Windows NT, 2000, and 2003 servers can run), the domain has limitations (such as 40,000 objects) imposed by the Windows NT 4 domain model. However, Windows 2000 domain controllers and Windows NT 4 backup domain controllers can coexist within the domain without problems. Switching to Windows 2000 native mode (which allows Windows 2000 and 2003 servers only) allows the directory to scale up to millions of objects. The Windows Server 2003 level provides the full functionality of Windows Server 2003, but requires that all servers run Windows Server 2003.

G

Global Address List The list of all Exchange Server recipients in the entire Exchange organization. Exchange uses address lists to hold and organize the names of the recipients associated with the system.

Global Catalog server A server that holds a complete replica of the configuration and schema naming contexts for an Active Directory forest, a complete replica of the domain naming context in which the server is installed, and a partial replica of all other domains in the forest. The Global Catalog knows about every object in the forest and has representations for them in its directory; however, it might not know about all attributes (such as job title and physical address) for objects in other domains.

globally unique identifier (GUID) An attribute consisting of a 128-bit number that is guaranteed to be unique, used by applications that need to refer to an object by an identifier that remains constant. A GUID is assigned to an object when it is created, and it will never change, even if the object is moved between containers in the same domain.

group An object defined in Active Directory that contains other objects such as users, contacts, and possibly other groups. A group can be either a distribution group or a security group, and its scope can be local, domain, or universal. Distribution groups are similar to distribution lists in Exchange Server 5.5.

GUID *See globally unique identifier (GUID).*

H

heartbeat A group of packets that are sent over a private IP network between nodes to detect the health of the other nodes, as well as the health of the applications and services they manage within the cluster.

hosted organization A collection of Exchange services including but not limited to virtual servers (that is, instances of IMAP4, SMTP, POP3, NNTP, HTTP, or RVP), storage space, and real-time collaboration facilities that exist to serve the needs of a single company. Internet service providers normally use a hosted organization to host multiple companies on the same physical computer. However, a hosted organization is not limited to a single Exchange server.

I

IFS *See Installable File System (IFS).*

IIS *See Internet Information Service (IIS).*

IMAP4 *See Internet Message Access Protocol 4 (IMAP4).*

InetOrgPerson An object—similar to a user object—that is used to migrate users from other LDAP directory services to Active Directory.

information security policy A statement of acceptable behavior or actions regarding the information that is stored on a company's computer.

Installable File System (IFS) A file system that allows users to place any kind of document in the native content file (the streaming file) and then access it from almost any client, regardless of whether that client is a browser, a MAPI client, or simply Microsoft Windows Explorer.

Integrated Windows Authentication A form of IIS authentication in which the password is sent as an encrypted value to the highest security level. This form of authentication does not work through firewalls and proxies.

Internet Information Services (IIS) Microsoft's Web server software for Windows Server 2003. IIS 5 ships with Windows Server 2003 and is installed by default during a typical Windows installation.

Internet Message Access Protocol 4 (IMAP4) A standards-based protocol for accessing mailbox information. IMAP4 is considered to be more advanced than POP3 because it supports basic online capabilities and access to folders other than the Inbox.

K

key pair, asymmetric A pair of encryption keys that are not identical: one key is used to encrypt the data and a different key is used to decrypt it. With asymmetric keys, one key is known as the public key and the other is known as the private key. Exchange 2000 Server uses this type of encryption technology.

key pair, symmetric Identical encryption keys. Both the sender and the recipient use the same key to encrypt and decrypt the data. Also known as shared keys.

L

LDAP *See Lightweight Directory Access Protocol (LDAP).*

Lightweight Directory Access Protocol (LDAP) A standards-based protocol that can be used to interact with conformant directory services. LDAP version 2 allows users and applications to read the contents of a directory database, whereas LDAP version 3 (defined under RFC 2251) allows them to both read from and write to a directory database.

link state algorithm (LSA) The algorithm used to exchange routing status information between Exchange servers.

LSA *See link state algorithm (LSA).*

M

mail-based replication A mechanism to replicate directory information through a messaging transport. This term applies to Exchange 5.x intersite directory replication as well as to Active Directory replication through SMTP.

mailbox recovery center A feature of System Manager that lets you recover multiple disconnected mailboxes (i.e., mailboxes no longer associated with a user) simultaneously.

mail exchanger (MX) record A record in a DNS database that indicates a host responsible for receiving e-mail messages.

MAPI *See Messaging Application Programming Interface (MAPI).*

Masquerade Domain option An option that allows you to indicate a different domain name to be placed in both the Mail From and From fields of all outgoing SMTP messages.

MCU *See multipoint control unit (MCU).*

message tracking A feature of an Exchange server that, along with the subject logging feature, provides a sophisticated way to track messages throughout the Exchange organization, primarily for troubleshooting purposes.

Message Transfer Agent (MTA) The component in all versions of Exchange Server that transfers messages between servers, using the X.400 protocol.

Messaging Application Programming Interface (MAPI) The application programming interface (API) used by Microsoft messaging applications such as Outlook to access collaboration data. MAPI, or more specifically, MAPI RPC, is also used as the transport protocol between Outlook clients and Exchange servers.

metabase A store that contains metadata such as that used by IIS to obtain its configuration data. The metabase can be viewed through utilities such as Metaedit.

metabase update service A component in Exchange that reads data from Active Directory and transposes it into the local IIS metabase. The metabase update service allows the administrator to make remote configuration changes to virtual servers without having a permanent connection to each system.

metadata Data about data. In relation to Exchange, this term can be used in the context of Active Directory and can also be used to describe the structure within the store or the MTA.

MIME *See Multipurpose Internet Mail Extensions (MIME).*

mount To place an individual store in a storage group online. Stores can also be taken offline, or dismounted. You might dismount a store for maintenance, for example.

MTA *See Message Transfer Agent (MTA).*

multipoint control unit (MCU) A reference to the T.120 protocol, which allows clients to connect to data conferencing sessions. MCUs can communicate with each other to transfer conferencing information.

Multipurpose Internet Mail Extensions (MIME) A standard that allows multiple files of various content types to be encapsulated into one message. RFCs 2045 through 2049 currently define MIME and are considered to be one single standard.

MX record *See mail exchanger (MX) record.*

N

Name Service Provider Interface (NSPI) Part of the DSProxy process that can accept Outlook client directory requests and pass them to an address book provider.

namespace A logical collection of resources that can be managed as a single unit. Within Active Directory, a domain defines a namespace.

naming partition A self-contained section of a directory hierarchy that has its own properties, such as replication configuration and permissions structure. Active Directory includes the domain, configuration, and schema naming partitions.

native content file *See rich text file.*

native mode A one-time, irreversible selection for Exchange 2003 in which the Exchange platform is configured to operate without accounting for any previous versions of Exchange in the organization. Once selected, earlier versions of Exchange will not be compatible with Exchange 2003 Server.

NDR *See non-delivery report (NDR).*

network load balancing (NLB) The process of balancing client calls between multiple front-end servers. This activity takes place at the MAC and network layers.

Network News Transfer Protocol (NNTP) A standards-based protocol that includes simple command verbs to transfer Usenet messages between clients and servers as well as between servers. NNTP uses TCP/IP port 119.

NLB *See network load balancing (NLB).*

NNTP *See Network News Transfer Protocol (NNTP).*

non-delivery report (NDR) A report generated when a message is not deliverable for some reason in Exchange Server. The NDR is returned to the message sender and sometimes to an administrator or automated monitor as well.

NSPI *See Name Service Provider Interface (NSPI).*

O

object An entity that is described by a distinct, named set of attributes. In Active Directory, all network resources are represented as objects that can be centrally administered.

OLE DB An API that allows low-level programming languages such as C and C++ to access dissimilar data stores through a common query language. OLE DB is seen as the replacement for open database connectivity (ODBC). Data stores such as those in Exchange and SQL Server allow for OLE DB access, which makes application development easier and faster.

OMA *See Outlook Mobile Access (OMA).*

organizational unit (OU) An Active Directory container object that is used to organize other objects within a domain. An OU can contain user accounts, printers, groups, computers, and other OUs.

OU *See organizational unit (OU).*

Outlook Mobile Access (OMA) Provides users with mobile devices such as Pocket PCs and Smartphones real-time access to Exchange data. Outlook Mobile Access allows access only while connected.

Outlook Web Access (OWA) The Web browser interface to Exchange Server mailbox and public folder data. The OWA client in Exchange Server 5.x uses Active Server Pages to render collaboration data into HTML, whereas the OWA client in Exchange 2000 uses native access to the store.

OWA *See Outlook Web Access (OWA).*

P

PKI *See public-key infrastructure (PKI).*

policy A set of configuration parameters that applies to one or more Exchange objects in the same class. For example, you can create a policy that affects certain settings on some or all of your Exchange servers. If you want to change these settings, all you need to do is modify the policy and it will be applied to the appropriate server's organization.

POP3 *See Post Office Protocol 3 (POP3).*

Post Office Protocol 3 (POP3) A standards-based protocol for simple access to Inbox data. All versions of Exchange server except version 4 support POP3. POP3 uses TCP/IP port 110 for client-to-server access.

property promotion *See automatic document property promotion.*

public folder A folder on an Exchange server that is part of a public store made available to multiple users. A public folder can hold messages, documents, and just about any other type of file.

public folder tree A collection of public folders created under the same hierarchical namespace. Versions of Exchange Server prior to Exchange 2000 Server used only a single tree called All Public Folders. You can define multiple trees in Exchange Server 2003. Each tree is a unit of hierarchy replication and can be replicated to one or more public stores. A public store can host only one tree. MAPI clients such as Outlook can access only a single tree, called All Public Folders, whereas other clients such as a Web browser or any NNTP client can access any tree that is defined.

public-key infrastructure (PKI) A collection of resources that work together to provide a secure network authentication system. The major components of a public key infrastructure are certificates and certificate authorities, policies, and cryptographic service providers.

Q

Queue Viewer A tool built into the Exchange System snap-in that allows you to view any message queue. When messages are sent from an Exchange server, they are placed in a message queue, where they wait until it is their turn to go out over the appropriate connector.

query-based distribution lists A list of recipients that functions like a regular distribution list, except that its membership changes based on queries.

R

Recipient Update service Part of the Exchange System Attendant, this service is responsible for keeping address lists up-to-date and creating proxy addresses for users.

remote procedure calls (RPC) A reliable synchronous protocol that allows a program on one computer to execute a program on another computer. Outlook clients use MAPI RPCs for accessing mailboxes and public folders.

resource In real-time collaboration, a user object in Active Directory that represents a facility. Resources are stored in the System\Exchange organizational unit in Active Directory.

request for comments (RFC) RFCs are a series of notes about the Internet. Anyone can submit an RFC and, if an RFC gains enough support, the RFC might become an Internet standard. Each RFC is designated by an RFC number. Once published, an RFC never changes. Modifications to an original RFC are assigned a new RFC number.

RGC *See Routing Group Connector (RGC).*

rich text file One of the two files that make up an Exchange database. The rich text file (ending in .RTF) holds e-mail messages and MAPI content, and the native content file or streaming file (ending in .STM) holds all non-MAPI information. The term is also used to describe a file formatted according to a formatting standard defined by Microsoft. RTF files are actually ASCII files with special commands embedded in them to indicate formatting.

routing group A collection of Exchange servers that can transfer messaging data to one another in a single hop without going through a bridgehead server. In general, Exchange servers within a single routing group are connected by high-bandwidth links. Connectivity among servers in a routing group is based entirely on SMTP.

Routing Group Connector (RGC) A connector in Exchange Server 2003 that connects routing groups to one another. A Routing Group Connector is unidirectional and can have separate configuration properties (such as allowable message types over the connection). Routing Group Connectors use the concept of local and remote bridgeheads to dictate which servers in the routing groups can communicate over the link. The underlying message transport for a Routing Group Connector is either SMTP or RPC, and it uses link state information to route messages efficiently.

routing service A component in Exchange that builds link state information.

RPC *See remote procedure call (RPC).*

S

SCC *See Site Consistency Checker (SCC).*

schema The metadata (data about data) that describes how objects are used within a given structure. In relation to Exchange Server, this term can be used in the context of Active Directory, but it can also be used to describe the structure within the store or the MTA.

schema naming partition A partition of Active Directory that contains all object types and their attributes that can be created in Active Directory. This information is replicated to all domain controllers in the forest. During the first installation of Exchange Server 2003 in the forest, the Active Directory schema is extended to include new object classes and attributes that are specific to Exchange Server 2003. *See also configuration naming partition* and *domain naming partition*.

security policy *See information security policy* and *electronic security policy*.

security principal An Active Directory object, such as a user or group, that defines a security context. A non-security principal is an object represented in Active Directory that cannot access resources within the enterprise.

shared-everything architecture An architecture that gives any physical server in the cluster access to all the data and application code at any given time and can offer these services to the client as needed. It is also known as active/active architecture.

shared-nothing architecture An architecture that makes one of the physical nodes responsible for running an application while the other servers, or nodes, wait on the sidelines for the first physical server to fail so that they can leap into action and take over the application. Only one server works at any given time for an application. It is also known as active/passive architecture.

Simple Message Transfer Protocol (SMTP) A widely used standards-based protocol that allows for the transfer of messages between different messaging servers. SMTP is defined under RFC 821 and uses simple command verbs to facilitate message transport over TCP/IP port 25.

single-instance storage (SIS) A storage technique in which messages sent to multiple recipients are stored only once as long as all the recipients are located in the same database. SIS is not maintained when a mailbox is moved to a different database, even if that mailbox still resides in the same storage group. Moreover, SIS does not span multiple databases in a single storage group.

sink *See event sink*.

SIS *See single-instance storage (SIS)*.

site In Active Directory, a collection of IP subnets. All computers in the same site have high-speed connectivity—LAN speeds—with one another. Unlike an Exchange site, an Active Directory site does not include a unit of namespace; for example, multiple sites can exist within a single domain, and conversely, a single site can span multiple domains.

Site Consistency Checker (SCC) An updated version of the Knowledge Consistency Checker from Exchange Server 5.5. SCC runs inside the Site Replication Service. It ensures that knowledge consistency is maintained for sites and administrative groups when interoperating between Exchange Server 5.5 and Exchange Server 2003.

Site Replication Service (SRS) The service responsible for replicating Exchange 5.x site and configuration information to the configuration naming partition of Active Directory when an Exchange server belongs to an existing Exchange 5.5 site.

SMTP *See Simple Message Transfer Protocol (SMTP)*.

SRS *See Site Replication Service (SRS)*.

storage group A collection of Exchange databases on an Exchange server that share the same ESE instance and transaction log. Individual databases within a storage group can be mounted and dismounted.

store The generic name given to the storage subsystem on an Exchange server. This term is used interchangeably to describe the Store.exe process and Exchange databases.

sysop Short for system operator. An individual who manages an online service, such as a bulletin board or chat room.

System Attendant One of the core Exchange services. System Attendant performs miscellaneous functions (usually related to directory information), such as generating address lists, offline address books, and directory lookup facilities.

system policies General sets of rules created to apply to servers, mailbox stores, and public stores. Once a policy is created, changing the policy changes the rules for all members of that policy.

T

TCP port In the TCP/IP protocol, a TCP port identifies a logical connection that an application can use to transport data. For example, TCP port 80 is normally used to send HTTP messages.

transaction logs The primary storage area for new transactions made to ESE databases. Data is written to these logs sequentially as transactions occur. Regular database maintenance routines then commit changes in the logs to the actual databases.

Trojan A malicious program that embeds itself inside a normal, safe-looking program. Whereas viruses need to attach themselves to replicate, Trojans embed themselves entirely within another program. When the host program is run, the Trojan runs as well.

U

UPN *See user principal name (UPN).*

user In Active Directory, a security principal (a user who can log on to the domain). A user might have an e-mail address and/or an Exchange mailbox, making the object mail-enabled and/or mailbox-enabled, respectively.

user ban An action that prevents an individual user from accessing a specific chat community. If a banned user attempts to access a community, he or she is refused. The user can be restricted by nickname, user name, or both.

user principal name (UPN) A name that is generated for each object, in the form username@domainname. A UPN allows the underlying domain structure and complexity to be hidden from users. For example, although many domains can exist within a forest, users would seamlessly log on as if they were in the same domain.

V

virtual root A shortcut pointer to a physical storage location. Virtual roots are normally defined to allow users and applications to connect with a short "friendly" path instead of navigating a complex hierarchy. IIS uses the concept of virtual roots to expose resources provided by a Web server.

virtual server An instance of any service type normally implemented in IIS. For example, a virtual server can be an instance of FTP, IMAP, Instant Messaging, HTTP, NNTP, POP3, or SMTP. An Exchange server can host multiple virtual servers of the same type on each computer. Each virtual server can have its own configuration properties, such as bound IP addresses, port number, and authentication type.

virus A piece of code that attaches itself to other programs or files to replicate itself. When the host code is run, the virus runs as well.

W

WebDAV *See Distributed Authoring and Versioning (DAV)*.

wireless synchronization access The ability of Exchange Server 2003 to provide access using ActiveSync so that users of PocketPC and SmartPhone devices can synchronize information directly with Exchange Server.

worm A malicious program that is self-contained and self-replicating. Worms travel across the Internet or network using normal transport protocols. Worms can either run based on a triggering event or run as soon as they have copied themselves to the next computer.

X

X.400 A messaging standard that can be used by many messaging systems. X.400 uses a strict addressing method that reflects a hierarchical environment. An X.400 address reflects the recipient's position in a messaging hierarchy.

X.400 Connector A connector that can be used to connect an Exchange system to a foreign X.400 system or to connect two Exchange routing groups over unstable or low-bandwidth (typically less than 16 Kbps) connections.

X.500 A standard that defines how directories should be structured. X.500 directories are hierarchical, with different levels for each category of information. Both Active Directory and LDAP are loosely based on the X.500 standard.

X.509 A standard that defines digital certificates.

Index

Numbers

A

B

D

E

G

H

I

J-K

L

M

N

O

P

Q

R

S

T

U

V

W

X

Z

Walter J. Glenn is a veteran of more than 17 years in the computer industry. He is a Microsoft Certified Systems Engineer (MCSE) and a Microsoft Certified Trainer (MCT), and he currently splits his time between consulting for small- to medium-sized companies and writing on computer-related topics. Walter's publications include *Microsoft Exchange 2000 Server Administrator's Companion*, *Microsoft Exchange Server 5.5 Administrator's Companion*, and *MCSE: Exchange 2000 Server Administration Study Guide*.

Bill English is an author, a trainer, and a consultant specializing in SharePoint and Microsoft Exchange technologies. Bill is a regular speaker at national conferences and routinely conducts public, private, and corporate training on SharePoint Portal Server and Exchange 2000 Server and Exchange Server 2003. Bill's publications include *Microsoft Exchange 2000 Server Administrator's Companion*, and *The Exchange 2000 Server Administration Readiness Review for Exam 70-224.* Bill has earned the MCSE, MCSA, MCT, and GSEC credentials. In addition, Bill has been awarded the prestigious Most Valuable Professional (MVP) award by Microsoft. Bill lives with his wife and two children in Nowthen, Minnesota. You can reach Bill at benglish@networknowledge.com or visit his Web sites at *http://www.networknowledge.com* and *http://www.sharepointsummit.com*.

Microsoft Press

In-depth technical information and tools for Microsoft Windows Server 2003

Microsoft® Windows Server™ 2003 Deployment Kit: A Microsoft Resource Kit
ISBN 0-7356-1486-5

Plan and deploy a Windows Server 2003 operating system environment with expertise from the team that develops and supports the technology—the Microsoft Windows® team. This multivolume kit delivers in-depth technical information and best practices to automate and customize your installation, configure servers and desktops, design and deploy network services, design and deploy directory and security services, implement Group Policy, create pilot and test plans, and more. You also get more than 125 timesaving tools, deployment job aids, Windows Server 2003 evaluation software, and the entire Windows Server 2003 Help on the CD-ROMs. It's everything you need to help ensure a smooth deployment—while minimizing maintenance and support costs.

Internet Information Services (IIS) 6.0 Resource Kit
ISBN 0-7356-1420-2

Deploy and support IIS 6.0, which is included with Windows Server 2003, with expertise direct from the Microsoft IIS product team. This official Resource Kit packs 1200+ pages of in-depth deployment, operations, and technical information, including step-by-step instructions for common administrative tasks. Get critical details and guidance on security enhancements, the n[illegible] IIS 6.0 architecture, migration strategies, performance tuning, logging, and troubleshooting—alo[illegible] with timesaving tools, IIS 6.0 product documentation, and a searchable eBook on CD. You get all the resources you need to help maximize the security, reliability, manageability, and performance of your Web server—while reducing system administration costs.

To learn more about the full line of Microsoft Press® products for IT professionals, please visit:

microsoft.com/mspress/IT

Microsoft Press products are available worldwide wherever quality computer books are sold. For more information, contact your book or computer retailer, software reseller, or local Micros[illegible] Sales Office, or visit our Web site at **microsoft.com/mspress.** To locate your nearest source for Microsoft Press products, or to order directly, call 1-800-MSPRESS in the United States. (In Canada, call 1-800-268-2222.)

Proof of Purchase

Use this page as proof of purchase if participating in a promotion or rebate offer on this title. Proof of purchase must be used in conjunction with other proof(s) of payment such as your dated sales receipt—see offer details.

Microsoft® Exchange Server 2003 Administrator's Companion

0-7356-1979-4

CUSTOMER NAME

Microsoft Press, PO Box 97017, Redmond, WA 98073-9830

System Requirements

The compact disc that accompanies the *Microsoft Exchange Server 2003 Administrator's Companion* is a 120-day trial software version of Exchange 2003 Enterprise Edition.

Caution If you plan to upgrade from Exchange 2000 Server to Exchange Server 2003, you must install Exchange 2000 Service Pack 3 (SP3) before installing Exchange 2003.

Actual requirements can vary based on your system configuration and the features you choose to install.

Exchange 2003 Standard Edition System Requirements

Component	Requirement	Recommendation
Processor	Intel Pentium or compatible 133-MHz or higher processor	Intel Pentium or compatible 550-MHz processor
Operating system*	Windows 2000 Server or Windows 2000 Advanced Server with SP3 or later; Windows Server 2003, Standard Edition or Windows Server 2003, Enterprise Edition	Windows Server 2003
Memory	256 MB of RAM	512 MB of RAM or more
Available hard-disk space	500 MB on the hard disk where you install Exchange 2003; 200 MB on the system drive	500 MB on the hard disk where you install Exchange 2003; 200 MB on the system drive
Drive	CD drive	CD drive
Display	VGA or higher resolution monitor	VGA or higher resolution monitor
Input device	Microsoft Mouse or compatible input device	Microsoft Mouse or compatible input device

Exchange 2003 Standard Edition System Requirements

Component	Requirement	Recommendation
File format	Disk partitions must be formatted for the NTFS file system, not the FAT file system. This requirement applies to: System partition Partition storing Exchange binaries Partitions containing transaction log files Partitions containing database files Partitions containing other Exchange files	Disk partitions must be formatted for the NTFS file system, not the FAT file system. This requirement applies to: System partition Partition storing Exchange binaries Partitions containing transaction log files Partitions containing database files Partitions containing other Exchange files

* Servers running Exchange that are using the /3GB feature, which maximizes the performance of computers with over 1 gigabyte (GB) of physical memory, can operate only on Windows 2000 Advanced Server, Windows 2000 Datacenter Server, or any edition of Windows Server 2003.

Additional Software Required to Use Specific Features in Exchange 2003 Enterprise Edition

- Exchange 2000 Management Pack for Microsoft Operations Manager for automated system monitoring
- Windows XP with Service Pack 1a (SP1a) or later and Windows Server 2003 for HTTP access from Microsoft Office Outlook 2003

Note You must install the latest updates for Windows XP, Windows Server 2003, and Outlook 2003.

- For support for eight-node clusters, you need Windows Server 2003, Enterprise Edition or Windows Server 2003, Datacenter Edition.

Caution You can upgrade from the Exchange 2003 trial software to the released version of Exchange 2003 by performing an in-place upgrade. While you can upgrade from the trial software version of Exchange 2003 Standard Edition to the released version of Exchange 2003 Enterprise Edition, you cannot downgrade from the trial software version of Exchange 2003 Enterprise Edition to the released version of Exchange 2003 Standard Edition. As a workaround, you must install the trial software version of Exchange 2003 Enterprise Edition before installing the released version of Exchange 2003 Standard Edition.